# Jury Selection in Civil and Criminal Trials

# Volume I

## About the Author

Ann Fagan Ginger is a practicing attorney in Berkeley, California. She lectures widely and has been a Visiting Professor of Law at University of California—Hastings College, University of San Francisco, University of Santa Clara, New College of California, and University of Puget Sound. Her books include *California Criminal Law Practice* volumes I and II (Editor-in-Chief, California Continuing Education of the Bar 1964, 1969, and 1976), *The Relevant Lawyers* (Simon and Schuster 1972), *The Law, the Supreme Court, and the People's Rights* (Barron's 1977), *Human Rights Docket 1979* (Meiklejohn Institute 1979), and *Issues for the Eighties* (Just Books 1981). Her articles include "Police Misconduct Litigation," 15 *Am Jur Trials* 555 (1968) (with Louis A. Bell), "Due Process in Practice," 25 *Hastings LJ* 897 (1974), and "Litigation as a Form of Political Action," 9 *Wayne L Rev* 458 (1963). She is president of Meiklejohn Civil Liberties Institute (Box 673, Berkeley, California 94701), a unique national research center on criminal, civil, public interest, and constitutional litigation, which is used by attorneys, scholars, students, legal workers, and concerned organizations.

# Jury Selection in Civil and Criminal Trials

## Volume I

*Ann Fagan Ginger, LL.M.*

**Library of Congress Cataloging in Publication Data**

Ginger, Ann Fagan.
Jury selection in civil and criminal trials.

Bibliography: p.
Includes index.
1. Jury selection—United States. I. Title.
KF8979.G56 1984 347.73'752 84-7200
ISBN 0-915544-14-8 (v.1) 347.307752
ISBN 0-915544-15-6 (v.2)

Published by Lawpress Corporation, P.O. Drawer 69, Tiburon, California 94920

Acknowledgment is gratefully made to: *Call the Final Witness* by Melvyn Bernard Zerman, copyright ©1977 by Melvyn Bernard Zerman, reprinted by permission of Harper & Row, Publishers, Inc.; *Trial* magazine and Louis Katz for permission to reprint from "The Twelve Man Jury," ©1969; the *California State Bar Journal* and Paul Ligda for permission to reprint from "Viva La Jury," ©1975; the *American Criminal Law Review* and David Kairys for permission to reprint from "Juror Selection: The Law, a Mathematical Method of Analysis and a Case Study," ©1972; Emty Press and Mary Timothy for permission to reprint from *Jury Woman*, ©1974; and Amitai Etzioni for permission to reprint "Scientific Jury Stacking Puts Judicial System on Trial," which appeared in the *Boston Globe*, June 23, 1974; *National Lawyers Guild Practitioner* for permission to reprint excerpts from several articles.

Printed in the United States of America.

*This work is dedicated*

*to all of the clients*

*who decide to trust their fates*

*to juries of their peers*

*and*

*to all of their lawyers*

*who continue the democratic traditions*

*of trial by jury,*

*with*

*special thanks to all my*

*friends and relations*

*in both categories*

*who enriched my life*

*and put up with my eversharp*

*during its long incubation.*

# *Contents*

Preface ix

**PART I. Trying Cases to Juries in the United States**

1. The Judicial System Is Based on Jury Trials 3
2. Jury Trials Are Based on Jury Selection Methods 61
3. Basic Cases and Source Materials 99

**PART II. Getting Started**

4. Analyzing the Facts and Forum 137
5. Conducting Surveys and Constructing Juror Profiles 199

**PART III. Seeking a Jury of Peers**

6. Challenging the Jury Lists 233
7. Motions for Change of Venue or Dismissal 323

**PART IV. Preparing for Voir Dire**

8. Establishing Jury Selection Procedures 395
9. Basic Questions 501
10. Questions in Civil Cases 629
11. Questions in Criminal Cases 693

# Preface

The second edition of a book provides a good opportunity to add new ideas and materials, to throw out paragraphs and citations that did not prove helpful or have been overruled, and finally to think about where the field is going and how to advance those tendencies that seem most fruitful. The first edition of this book appeared in 1975 and was limited to jury selection in criminal trials, although some examples from civil suits had to be included even then, to point up possibilities in criminal cases. The 1977 and 1980 supplements gave me a chance to add, subtract, and refine, based on many letters and comments from people who had used the book, and on other sources.

Jury selection in civil suits is given a prominent place in this edition because so many civil suits are now tried to juries or are settled before a jury trial. There is no sharp line between how a lawyer approaches jury selection in civil and criminal cases; many tactics useful in one type of case can be used to advantage in the other.

This two-volume work is organized according to my present understanding of law practice. Ideally, a lawyer learns from a client the facts in a case—or some of the facts; looks up the law—or some of the law; and then starts working out a strategy for winning. While carrying out the strategy in specific court appearances and pleadings, investigating the facts, searching for more law, and planning the tactics of the litigation, the lawyer may make numerous changes in strategy. These changes lead to further work on the facts, the law, and the tactics.

The Western European and South American lawyers whom I have

met seem to concentrate much sooner than we do on theory, not only in politics, but also in law practice. They do not consider themselves pragmatists; they are theoreticians, and proud of it.

It is clear, however, that the many successful practicing lawyers I have met in this country are also theoreticians. The best of them—that is, the most consistently successful ones—learn not only from their own mistakes, but also from the experiences of their colleagues. And they all seem to have one thing in common: a recognition that they begin to get hold of a case when they work out a theory of the case or make a checklist of its dominant features.

Since this book is being written to be used and read, and since there are more practicing lawyers than legal scholars and jurisprudentialists, I have put discussions of practice before discussions of theory. Since jury selection cuts near the heart of our democratic judicial system, however, I have not stinted on theory. Whenever possible, I have tried to include both factors in the same section. Without theory, practice will often prove unsuccessful. But theories spun in isolation or in law libraries may prove faulty in the courtroom if they are based solely on law review articles discussing reported appellate written opinions. The guts of jury selection is what happens in trial courts, and few cases are appealed on jury selection issues.

The theory of jury selection, therefore, must come from sources other than reported appellate opinions and law review articles analyzing such opinions. It must come from interviews with practicing lawyers, transcripts of jury selection in well-tried cases, and off-the-cuff talks with practitioners about the specific events before and during voir dire in hard-fought jury trials. Sound theory in this field depends on specific examples in specific trials from which valid generalizations or theories can ultimately be developed.

It is a pleasure to thank each person who added a thought, a voir dire question, a model form or brief, notes for a closing argument, or other useful items for these volumes. It is a long list. The notes on Sources throughout the work dutifully record specific contributions. Each case described in chapter 3 (and as many as possible of those described elsewhere) gives the names of all counsel and paralegals. I also owe a great debt to the many court clerks, law librarians, and law clerks who answered endless queries promptly and efficiently.

Many people were particularly helpful in both broad and specific ways on both editions of this work, including especially: John S. Ackerman; Professor Anthony Amsterdam; the Appellate Public Defender's Office of San Francisco; Judge Sidney Aronowitz; Ruth Astle; Judge Spurgeon Avakian; Charles Barr; Stephen Bedrick; Professors Robert

Blauner, Edward Bronson, and Robert Buckhout; Priscilla Camp; Judge Kenneth Lee Chotiner; Steven A. Chase; Dr. Richard Christie; Professor Morton Cohen; Hon. George W. Crockett, Jr.; Mark Cross; Hugh M. Davis, Jr.; Ronald DeNardis; Charles Duncan; John Egnal, Lionel Epstein; George C. Eskin; Edmundo Espinosa; Bernard Fischman; Laurent Frantz; Alvin Friedman; Charles Garry, Thomas Ginger; Michael Goldstein; Michael D. Gooch; Ernest Goodman; Richard Goodman; William Goodman; Dr. Craig Haney; Robert F. Hanley; Connye H. Harper; Paul Harris; Lois Heaney; Victoria Heldman; James Herndon; James Jenner; Marion R. Jenkins; Jamie Kalven; Judge Theodore S. Kasler; Dr. Harry M. Katz; Don C. Keenan; Michael Kennedy; Theodore Koskoff; Nicholas Kozay, Jr.; Edward Lascher; Gerald Lefcourt; Gerald Levie; David Light; Harry Lore; Joan Lovell; Susie MacPherson; Richard Medalie; William Sebastian Moore; Ginnie Muir; Manuel Nestle; Robert A. Obringer; Fred Okrand; Richard Parker; Judge George Phillips (deceased); Allyn Ravits; Joseph Rhine; Dean Robb; Dennis Roberts; Michael E. Rose; Judge Alvin Rubin; Gerri Russell; Daniel Russo; Richard F. Schaden; Elizabeth Schneider; Dr. Jay Schulman; Judge Sherman W. Smith, Richard Soble; Fred Solowey; Robert Treuhaft; James A. Tuck; Professor Jon Van Dyke; Doris Brin Walker; Judge Miriam G. Waltzer; Dennis Weaver; Michael Weiss; David Weitzman; Warren Wilson; G. Keith Wisot; Professor Hans Zeisel, and John Kenneth Zwerling.

A series of wonderful law clerks, law students, lawyers, editors, and proofreaders have worked on each edition and supplement of these volumes. Daniel P. Bates read through the 1500 pages of transcript of the voir dire in the first *Huey Newton* trial to come up with the choice examples excerpted in *Minimizing Racism in Jury Trials* (precursor to these volumes and now out of print). Zipporah Collins set the tone as chief editor on the first edition of this work, assisted by copyeditor Loralee Windsor, developmental editor Ann Lawson, and law clerk Adele Hendrickson. Colleen Rohan did the skillful manuscript typing; Elizabeth Sklut, Linda Rageh, and Mariam Kagan, the proofreading. Carolyn Mohr and Lori Nord did fine work on the 1980 supplement, as development editor and law clerk. Lawyer Valerie Sopher worked hard on this second edition. Law students Jane Goodman, Suzi Albertson, Seth Chazin, and Pat Szumowski did the endless (and creative) checking; Another Point turned messy manuscript into clean type; and Alice Klein did the taxing proofreading. Loralee Windsor was the editor of this second, much expanded edition, full of last-minute inserts and deletions. Both her sense of style and her sense of humor proved essential to the long task. Jerry Fischtrom is the proverbial, but seldom found, good publisher, with concern both for the author and the reader.

I ask all readers to send in materials for the annual supplements, including suggestions for new sections and subjects and amendments of the present text.

*Ann Fagan Ginger*

Berkeley, California
April 9, 1984

# PART I

# Trying Cases to Juries in the United States

## Chapter 1

# *The Judicial System Is Based on Jury Trials*

**I. The People Expect Jury Trials §1.1**

**II. Jury Trials Fulfill Basic Functions §1.2**

**III. The Constitutions Guarantee Juries**
A. United States Constitution
  1. Federal Grand Juries §1.3
  2. Federal Trial Juries
    a. Civil §1.4
    b. Criminal §1.5
  3. State Trial Juries §1.6
B. State Constitutions
  1. Grand Juries §1.7
  2. Trial Juries
    a. Civil §1.8
    b. Criminal §1.9

**IV. The Constitutions Set Jury Standards**
A. Jury Trials Available
  1. In Civil Cases §1.11
    a. Form: Memo on Factual Determinations Not Appealable §1.12
    b. Litigation Not Too Complex §1.13

2. In Criminal Cases §1.14
3. Selection Methods §1.15
B. Twelve-Person Trial Juries
1. Federal Criminal Juries §1.21
2. Federal Civil Juries
a. Sample Memo: To Ensure Community Standards §1.22
b. Sample Memo: Smaller Juries Reach Different Verdicts §1.23
3. State Criminal Juries §1.24
4. State Civil Juries §1.25
C. Unanimous Verdicts §1.31
D. Trials in the Vicinage §1.32
E. Speedy and Public Trials §1.33
F. Right to Counsel §1.34
G. Other Standards §1.35
H. Recent Developments §1.36

**V. Many Controversies Require Jury Trials**
A. The United States Custom of Litigating Public Issues §1.41
B. Public Issues Currently in Litigation §1.42
C. Judges as Decision-Makers on Public Law Issues
1. The Judges §1.43
2. The Judged §1.44
D. Citizens as Decision-Makers
1. On Grand Juries
a. Sample Brief: Role §1.45
b. Sample Brief: Representative Character §1.46
2. On Trial Juries §1.47
E. New Developments §1.49

**VI. Practical Advantages of Jury Trials**
A. To the People as a Whole §1.51
B. To Litigants §1.52
C. To Lawyers §1.53
D. To Judges §1.54
E. To Jurors §1.55
F. To Democratic Government §1.56

## I. THE PEOPLE EXPECT JURY TRIALS §1.1

When people in the United States think about a trial, they think of a trial by a jury of 12 men and women from the local community who must come to a unanimous verdict. They assume the trial will be held in public, with the plaintiff and defendant and their attorneys in full view of the jurors. From newspapers and television accounts, the public expects lawyers for both sides to quiz prospective jurors briefly before challenging some and removing them from the jury. They also assume that the lawyers will engage in some heated exchanges with witnesses and with the judge. They assume the jury will hear from the parties and witnesses for both sides, that the judge will tell them what the law is, and that they will then decide the case.

When people go to lawyers to handle their cases, they assume they will end up in a courtroom where a jury of peers will decide their fate, jurors who look, think, and feel pretty much the way they do. They expect to be able to explain to their fellow citizens why they acted as they did and to gain an understanding and sympathy for actions that were deliberate or negligent, and even for actions that were strange, drunken, or bizarre. Litigants expect their lawyers to be able to appeal to the common humanity, as well as, or instead of, the common sense of jurors, in a way they could not appeal to a judge sitting alone.

People assume their right to trial by jury is guaranteed in the United States Constitution, and will be available in both state and federal courts. Even clients whose causes seem hopeless, with the facts clearly against them, often combine total distrust of the judicial system with a naive faith that they can win before a jury of people like themselves.

People called for jury duty make many similar assumptions. Many look forward to serving on a jury at least once in their lives, if they can afford the time off work. Once in the jury box, they try to stay there and answer questions on voir dire with the certainty that they are the kind of people who can be fair and impartial in any case. Jurors who listen to evidence and then, for some reason, are not permitted to decide the case, are always surprised and often angry that the case was settled or dismissed for some reason before jury deliberations.

While the United States Constitution does not spell out any of the elements required to satisfy the jury trial requirement, the average citizens' definition of a jury trial has been largely correct for most of our history. Some state constitutions do spell out some of these provisions. See §§1.8-1.9.

Strong attacks have been launched against requiring each of these elements in civil and criminal trials (see chapter 23). The major groups studying the operation of federal and state juries are judicial conferences, organizations and research corporations seeking to economize on trial court costs, and bar association committees. For accurate, up-to-date information on the status of proposals for basic changes to limit jury trials, see *Reports* of the National Center for State Courts, 300 Newport Avenue, Williamsburg, VA 23185; *The Third Branch*, published by the Administrative Office of the U.S. Courts and the Federal Judicial Center; and publications of the American Trial Lawyers Association, 1050 31st Street N.W., Washington, D.C. 20007, and California Attorneys for Criminal Justice in Los Angeles.

In opposing the use of summary procedures even in complex antitrust litigation, the United States Supreme Court explained that: "It is only when the witnesses are present and subject to cross-examination that their credibility and the weight to be given their testimony can be appraised. Trial by affidavit is no substitute for trial by jury which so long has been the hallmark of 'even-handed justice.' " *Poller v Columbia Broadcasting Sys.* (1962) 368 US 464, 473. The Court explained the fundamental character of jury trials in criminal cases in *Singer v United States* (1965) 380 US 24, among other places.

This book focuses on jury selection, but considers the larger context in which civil and criminal cases come to trial; appeals to the community conscience (chapter 22); and developments in the law through appellate litigation, bar association action, and legislative changes (chapter 23).

## II. JURY TRIALS FULFILL BASIC FUNCTIONS §1.2

The United States Supreme Court has often commented on the functions of juries and of jury service. The purpose of a jury, in both criminal and civil cases, is to assure a fair and equitable resolution of the factual issues. In criminal cases, the purpose of a jury trial is to prevent government oppression. *Williams v Florida* (1970) 399 US 78, 100. Juries come to commonsense judgments because they consist of "a group of laymen representative of a cross-section of the community who have the duty and the opportunity to deliberate...." *Apodaca v Oregon* (1972) 406 US 404, 410–411. The number of jurors must "be large enough to promote group deliberation, free from outside attempts at intimidation, and to provide a fair possibility for obtaining a representative cross-section of the community." *Williams v Florida*, *supra*, at 100.

Jury service is "a privilege of citizenship." *Thiel v Southern Pac. Co.* (1946) 328 US 217, 224. It is "a form of participation in the process of government, a responsibility and a right." *White v Crook* (MD Ala 1966) 251 F Supp 401. "Community participation in the administration of the criminal law, moreover, is not only consistent with our democratic heritage but is also critical to public confidence in the fairness of the criminal justice system." *Taylor v Louisiana* (1975) 419 US 522, 530.

These judicial statements on the basic functions of jury trials are echoed by the general public. This is due, in considerable measure, to Clarence Darrow, who taught these rules to the jurors he selected to decide the fate of his clients and to his lecture audiences across the country. He, and they, and the reporters who covered his cases helped make these rules part of the American heritage.

Darrow was undoubtedly the founder of the modern school of trial practice, firmly rooted in the sanctity of trial by jury. He built on the traditions and customs of such predecessors as Wendell Phillips, a Boston Brahmin turned publican, and the homespun midwesterner turned railroad lawyer, Abraham Lincoln. Darrow was the son of a midwestern farmer who liked to read and debate political, economic, and moral questions. Clarence apparently got little out of the one year he spent at the University of Michigan Law School. At various times during his long career he was lionized, tried and retried for jury tampering, ignored, and applauded by his colleagues, judges, the public, and the press. His methods of trying cases are followed by many successful lawyers who represent criminal defendants and personal injury plaintiffs today.

Darrow developed his approach in cases raising social questions that are still creating lawsuits: What is the line between militant labor organizing and contempt of court, between political action and inciting to riot, between racial prejudice and proof of criminal conduct, between the death penalty and cruel and unusual punishment, between freedom of religion and forbidding the teaching of evolution, between intent to commit a crime and insanity? Even Darrow did not foresee the breadth of issues that would be brought to trial by ingenious lawyers of the late twentieth century on behalf of determined clients from many social classes. See §§1.41–1.42.

The need to have "justice . . . satisfy the appearance of justice," as Justice Felix Frankfurter put it in *Offutt v United States* (1954) 348 US 11, 14, is also well served by the system of jury trials. The practical advantages of jury trials to the people as a whole; to litigants, lawyers, judges, law enforcement agencies, and jurors; and to the functioning of democratic governments, are discussed in §§1.51–1.56.

## III. THE CONSTITUTIONS GUARANTEE JURIES

### A. United States Constitution

#### 1. Federal Grand Juries §1.3

No person shall be held to answer for a capital or other infamous crime unless on a presentment or indictment of a Grand Jury, except in cases arising in the land or naval forces, or in the militia, when in actual service, in time of war or public danger; . . .

Fifth Amendment

#### 2. Federal Trial Juries

##### a. Civil §1.4

No person . . . shall . . . be deprived of life, liberty, or property, without due process of law; . . .

Fifth Amendment

In suits at common law, where the value in controversy shall exceed twenty dollars, the right to trial by jury shall be preserved, and no fact tried by a jury shall be otherwise re-examined in any court of the United States than according to the rules of the common law.

Seventh Amendment

##### b. Criminal §1.5

The trial of all crimes, except in cases of impeachment, shall be by jury, and such trial shall be held in the State where the said crimes shall have been committed; but when not committed within any State the trial shall be at such place or places as the Congress may by law have directed.

Article III, §2, ¶3

No person . . .shall . . .be deprived of life, liberty, or property, without due process of law; . . .

Fifth Amendment

In all criminal prosecutions, the accused shall enjoy the right to a speedy and public trial, by an impartial jury of the State and district wherein the crime shall have been committed, which districts shall have been previously ascertained by law, and to be informed of the nature and cause of the accusation; . . .and to have the assistance of counsel for his defense.

Sixth Amendment

#### 3. State Trial Juries §1.6

. . .nor shall any State deprive any person of life, liberty, or property without due process of law, nor deny to any person within its jurisdiction the equal protection of the laws.

Fourteenth Amendment

## B. State Constitutions

### 1. Grand Juries §1.7

Constitutional provisions for grand juries vary widely. The California Constitution is often more specific than the constitutions of other states, because it is frequently amended by initiative and referendum.

> Felonies shall be prosecuted as provided by law, either by indictment or, after examination and commitment by a magistrate, by information.
>
> California Constitution, Art. 1, §14

> One or more grand juries shall be drawn and summoned at least once a year in each county.
>
> California Constitution, Art. 1, §23

### 2. Trial Juries

#### a. Civil §1.8

Provisions for civil juries vary from state to state. The California Constitution may be more specific than some other state constitutions, since many sections are added and amended by popular referendum:

> Trial by jury is an inviolate right and shall be secured to all, but in a civil cause three-fourths of the jury may render a verdict. . . . In a civil cause a jury may be waived by the consent of the parties expressed as prescribed by statute.
>
> In civil causes the jury shall consist of 12 persons or a lesser number agreed on by the parties in open court. In civil causes in municipal or justice court the Legislature may provide that the jury shall consist of eight persons or a lesser number agreed on by the parties in open court. . . .
>
> California Constitution, Art. 1, §16

#### b. Criminal §1.9

Provisions for criminal trial juries vary from state to state. The California Constitution may be more specific on this subject than some other state constitutions, since many sections are added and amended by popular referendum, but its provisions are of some interest:

> Trial by jury is an inviolate right and shall be secured to all, . . . A jury may be waived in a criminal cause by the consent of both parties expressed in open court by the defendant and the defendant's counsel . . . .
>
> . . .
>
> In criminal actions in which a felony is charged, the jury shall consist of 12 persons. In criminal actions in which a misdemeanor is charged, the jury shall consist of 12 persons or a lesser number agreed on by the parties in open court.
>
> California Constitution, Art. 1, §16

# IV. THE CONSTITUTIONS SET JURY STANDARDS

## A. Jury Trials Available

### 1. In Civil Cases §1.11

The Seventh Amendment guarantee of jury trial of civil suits has been held to apply to a civil suit for lost wages under the 1968 Age Discrimination in Employment Act, 29 USC §621. *Lorillard v Pons* (1977) 434 US 575. *Cf. Atlas Roofing Co. v Occupational Safety Comm'n* (1976) 430 US 442 (no juries in OSHA violation cases).

On the state level, the Missouri Supreme Court held that a tenant does not have the right to a jury trial in an eviction proceeding under the state constitution. *Rice v Lucas* (Mo Sup Ct 1978) 560 SW2d 850.

These random decisions underscore the fact that not every legal issue is now tried by a jury in federal or state courts. Many of the most significant questions in the lives of ordinary people are decided by nonlawyers (in administrative agencies), by arbitrators (in private disputes), and by judges alone (in equity, juvenile, and probate courts, among others). Even the line between civil and criminal cases has never been entirely clear; therefore whether there is a constitutional right to jury trial on some kinds of charges, such as contempt, has remained subject to litigation.

#### a. Form: Memo on Factual Determinations Not Appealable §1.12

One method of limiting civil jury trials, or their significance, is to permit appeal of factual determinations by juries, as is now permitted under the Louisiana civil law system (see *Melancon v McKeithen* (1972) 409 US 943).

Of course, even in common law jurisdictions, a trial court judge can grant a motion for a new trial under certain circumstances, which has the same effect of denigrating the value of a jury verdict and therefore of trial by jury. Appellate lawyer Siegfried Hesse of Oakland, California, launched an effective attack on this practice in *Yarza v California* (Cal S Ct 4 Civ No 14, 164), a civil suit for damages allegedly caused by the defendant's failure to maintain a state highway in a safe condition. After a jury awarded plaintiff $1,575,000 in damages, the trial judge granted defendant judgment notwithstanding the verdict, and granted a new trial. The state court of appeal reversed the first order but affirmed the second. On appeal to the California Supreme Court, petitioners' brief, filed Nov. 1, 1976, contained the following arguments, which may easily be adapted for use in other cases on this point, citing state statutes or common law where this brief cites the California CCP.

This petition is based on the ground that a hearing is necessary to secure the settlement of the following important questions of law:

1. Do the words [*"the. . .jury clearly should have reached a different verdict"*] in [CCP §657] (1) establish any limit on a trial court's power to order a new trial when the jury's verdict is supported by substantial evidence or (2) affect the standard for review of such an order?
2. If so, may an order granting a new trial on the ground of insufficiency of the evidence be affirmed when the trial court's statement of reasons (1) ignores the substantial uncontradicted evidence supporting the verdict on one basis, and (2) merely establishes that the jury rationally could have reached a contrary verdict on a second basis?

. . .

ARGUMENT

I. WHEN A VERDICT IS SUPPORTED BY SUBSTANTIAL UNCONTRADICTED EVIDENCE, THE TRIAL COURT MAY NOT GRANT A NEW TRIAL ON THE GROUND OF INSUFFICIENCY OF THE EVIDENCE WITHOUT DEMONSTRATING THAT SUCH EVIDENCE IS INSUFFICIENT TO SUPPORT THE VERDICT AS A MATTER OF LAW.

A. The [*1965 amendments*] to [*CCP §657*] impose substantive as well as procedural barriers to a trial court's veto of a jury's factual determinations: its statement of reasons must demonstrate that the jury clearly should have reached a different verdict.
[*Argument*]

B. The trial court's reasons for rejecting the verdict based on [*the dangerous condition of the shoulder*] ignored the substantial uncontradicted evidence which supported that verdict, and therefore did not establish a substantial basis for its conclusion that the jury clearly should have reached a different verdict.
[*Argument*]

II. THE APPELLATE COURT MUST EXAMINE THE EVIDENCE SUPPORTING THE JURY'S VERDICT, AND MUST REVERSE AN ORDER GRANTING A NEW TRIAL ON THE GROUND OF INSUFFICIENCY OF THE EVIDENCE UNLESS THE EVIDENCE RELIED ON BY THE TRIAL COURT ESTABLISHES THAT THE JURY CLEARLY SHOULD HAVE REACHED A DIFFERENT VERDICT.

A. When a verdict is based on substantial but conflicting evidence, the trial court may not grant a new trial merely because the jury could rationally have reached a contrary conclusion on the facts.

The [*Court of Appeal*], in affirming the order for new trial, did not examine the substantial evidence relied on by the jury about [*the surface of the road*], and which corroborated that which the trial court rejected. Instead, it examined only the evidence relied on by the trial court and its reasons for rejecting a portion of the evidence relied on by the jury. [*Cite to record*] Such review, in a factual vacuum, does not comply with the requirements of [*CCP* §*657, as amended in1965*]. . . .

See Leedy, "Demise of the Thirteenth Juror," 44 *Cal SBJ* 380 (1969). This reasoning also comports with the spirit of our constitutional allocation of powers between court and jury. *Lind v Schenley Indus., Inc.* (3d Cir 1960) 278 F2d 79, 90 [order granting new trial reversed].[8]

---

[8]" . . . [W]here no undesirable or pernicious element has occurred or been introduced into the trial and the trial judge nonetheless grants a new trial on the ground that the verdict was against the weight of the evidence, the trial judge in negating the jury's verdict has, to some extent at least, substituted his judgment of the facts and the credibility of the witnesses for that of the jury. Such an action effects a denigration of the jury system and to the extent that new trials are granted the judge takes over, if he does not usurp, the prime function of the jury as the trier of the facts. It then becomes the duty of the appellate tribunal to exercise a closer degree of scrutiny and supervision than in the case where a new trial is granted because of some undesirable or pernicious influence obtruding into the trial. Such a close scrutiny is required in order to protect the litigants' right to a jury trial." This reasoning has been followed in a number of federal cases. See, e.g., *Fireman's Fund Ins. Co. v Aalco Wrecking Co.* (8th Cir 1972) 466 F2d 179, 186–87; *Hourston v Harvlan, Inc.* (3d Cir 1972) 457 F2d 1105, 1107; *O'Neil v W. R. Grace & Co.* (5th Cir 1969) 410 F2d 908, 913–15; *Taylor v Washington Terminal Co.* (D.C. Cir 1969) 409 F2d 145, 148 n13; *Continental Airlines, Inc. v Wagner-Morehouse, Inc.* (7th Cir 1969) 401 F2d 23, 30; *Lewin v Metropolitan Life Ins. Co.* (3d Cir 1968) 394 F2d 608, 615; *Duncan v Duncan* (6th Cir 1967) 377 F2d 49, 52–54.

[*Discussion of other points*]

CONCLUSION

When a judgment based on a verdict is attacked on the ground of insufficiency of the evidence, all presumptions are in favor of the wisdom and accuracy of the jury's determinations. When that judgment is vetoed by a trial court, however, the presumptions were reversed [*before 1965*]. So long as these two rules of totally opposite effect are applied by appellate courts, a never-ending cycle of litigation is possible. A trial court may continue to veto verdicts until one jury agrees with its view of the evidence. Such a prospect suggests constitutional considerations lie behind the [*1965 additions to CCP* §*657*]. Compare Comment, "Twice in Jeopardy," 75 *Yale LJ* 262, 278 (1965) ["Without a rule of finality no procession of juries could effectively acquit a defendant, but a single jury could convict. . . ."].

The only possible justification for the continued deference to trial courts (in the face of [§*657*]) would be that trial judges are more expert in making factual determinations. See *Perry v Fowler* (1951) 102 CA2d 808, 811. But this elitist view contradicts our basic constitutional assumption that a larger, more representative group of laymen is better able to evaluate evidence than a single judge who has been long removed from the lives and circumstances of most of our citizens. See, e.g., *Railroad Co. v Stout* (1874) 84 US (17 Wall.) 657, 663–664. And the foremost student of our jury system concluded that the jury is, in fact, "the 'expert' tribunal for the two great distinctive issues posed by the common law: drawing the profile of negligence and handling the individual pricing of damages." Kalven, "The Dignity of the Civil Jury," 50 Va L Rev 1055, 1058 (1964); see also Wyzanski, "A Trial Judge's Freedom and Responsibility," 65 *Harv L Rev* 1281, 1287 (1972).

Juries can, of course, totally ignore the evidence and render a verdict which constitutes a miscarriage of justice. Such verdicts should be set aside as readily as when any of the other grounds listed in [*CCP* §*657*] exist. But recognition of that power does not require trial courts be allowed to set aside any verdict, merely because reasonable men might conclude differently about what happened or who is to be believed. Those are the precise questions juries are supposed to resolve. Trial courts may readily demonstrate the existence of a genuine miscarriage of justice when one occurs. But otherwise they may not properly ignore the fact that "once a verdict has been returned, . . .the effect of the constitutional provision [for jury trial] is to prohibit improper interference with the jury's decision." *Jehl v Southern Pacific Co.* (1967) 66 C2d 821, 829; *Lind v Schenley Indus., Inc.* (3d Cir 1960) 278 F2d 79, 90.

Finally, in these days of mounting trial calendars, the interests of tomorrow's litigant must be also considered. There is a public as well as a private interest in the finality of today's trial. *Jehl v Southern Pacific Co.*, *supra*, at 829, n9; *Fireman's Fund Ins. Co. v Aalco Wrecking Co.* (8th Cir 1972) 466 F2d 179, 188. Unless the jury's verdict was clearly wrong, an order granting a new trial should, in the public interest, be reversed when the verdict is set aside solely because the trial court disagrees with the jury on the resolution of facts.

A fair reading of "the entire record, including reasonable inferences therefrom," establishes that the instant jury rendered a reasonable verdict. Nothing the trial court has stated justifies its veto of that verdict. Returning this case to the trial court for a new trial would constitute a shocking waste of public funds for that second trial. It would constitute an abuse of an already overburdened judicial system which cannot presently keep its mounting calendars current. It would effectively deny petitioners the full benefit of their right to a jury trial.

For these and the foregoing reasons, this Court should grant a hearing, reverse the order granting a new trial, and order the judgment on the verdict reinstated.

The brief, signed by Siegfried Hesse, Tom Eckhardt, and John D. Duddy, was not successful.

### b. Litigation Not Too Complex §1.13

The right to a jury trial is eroded when defense lawyers in civil cases convince trial judges that the issues are too large and complex for juries to comprehend, and therefore due process requirements override jury trial guaranties. See, *e.g., Zenith Radio Corp. v Matsushita Elec. Indus. Co.* (ED Pa 1979) 478 F Supp 889, 942, *rev'd sub nom. In re Japanese Elec. Prods. Antitrust Litigation* (3d Cir 1980) 631 F2d 1069, *summary judgment for defendants* (ED Pa 1981) 513 F Supp 110; "Recent Developments in Antitrust Law," 58 *Wash ULQ* 1055–1064 (1980), and Berndon, "Instructive Interrogatories: Helping the Civil Jury To Understand," 55 *Conn BJ* 179 (1981). But see *MCI v AT&T*, §3.73, and *In re US Financial Securities Litigation* (9th Cir 1979), 609 F2d 411, in which the Court of Appeals ordered jury trial of ten suits alleging federal and state securities law violations, common law fraud, and negligence, deciding that "Time might be better spent in searching for ways to improve rather than erode the jury system." And see Sperlich, "The Case for Preserving Trial by Jury in Complex Civil Litigation," 65 *Judicature* 397 (1982).

Judges known as conservative opponents of judicial activism may be quite active in discouraging the use of jury trials. Cutting down the number and length of jury trials is considered progress by some. Many of the annual Reports on the Judiciary by Chief Justice Warren E. Burger contradicted traditional governmental practice by recommending severe cuts in the use of a branch of the government established by the Constitution in favor of arbitration and other private programs for dispute resolution. Burger specifically favors ending diversity jurisdiction in the federal courts, which accounted for 39 percent of all cases on trial in the federal district courts and 60 percent of all civil jury trials in the year ending June 30, 1982, and cost the federal system $8.8 million in juror expenses and judicial salaries in 1981. He predicts that this change would result in a 25 percent decrease in caseloads of federal district courts and a 17 percent decrease in appellate filings. *1982 Report* p 6. The chief justice does not discuss why lawyers choose to try some cases in federal district courts when they could be tried in state courts. One of the reasons is the difference in the area from which jurors are selected. Another is the difference in the types of state and federal judges.

Proposals to make it easier for juries to deal with complex litigation are discussed in chapter 23; see Note: McLaughlin, "Questions to Witnesses and Notetaking by the Jury as Aids in Understanding Complex Litigation," 18 *New Eng L Rev* 687 (1982–1983). See also tactics used in *United States v Berkowitz*, §§3.56, 4.16.

### 2. In Criminal Cases §1.14

*Brown v Louisiana* (1980) 447 US 320, 330 held:

> The right to jury trial guaranteed by the Sixth and Fourteenth Amendments "is a fundamental right, essential for preventing miscarriages of justice and for assuring that fair trials are provided for all defendants." *Duncan v Louisiana* (1968) 391 US 145, 158. Trial by jury in serious criminal cases has long been regarded as an indispensable protection against the possibility of governmental oppression; the history of the jury's development demonstrates "a long tradition attaching great importance to the concept of relying on a body of one's peers to determine guilt or innocence as a safeguard against arbitrary law enforcement." *Williams v Florida* (1970) 399 US 78, 87. "Given this purpose, the essential feature of a jury obviously lies in the interposition between the accused and his accuser of the commonsense judgment of a group of laymen, and in the community participation and shared responsibility that results from that group's determination of guilt or innocence." *Williams v Florida, supra*, at 100.

In *Duncan v Louisiana* (1968) 391 US 145, the Supreme Court held that a limited jury trial provision of the Louisiana Constitution violated the Fourteenth Amendment guaranty of due process, and ruled that state criminal defendants must be provided jury trials on all charges requiring jury trials at the federal level. This does not conclude the matter, since the line between "minor offenses" (nonjury) and misdemeanors (jury) at the federal level continues in dispute. But *Duncan* does mean that protection of the right to jury trial in state courts depends on continued guaranty of that right at the federal level. Any legislative efforts to enlarge the class of federal "minor offenses," for example, would have federal and state consequences.

Generally, a person charged with criminal contempt is not entitled to a jury trial as long as punishment imposed does not exceed that imposed for petty offenses; however, right to jury trial exists in favor of a person charged with criminal contempt of a court order where the conduct constituting the contempt charge also happens to constitute a federal or state criminal offense. *United States v Pyle* (ED Pa 1981) 518 F Supp 139, citing 18 USC §§401, 402, 3691.

Jury trials were found to be feasible in the United States territory of Samoa, despite a prosecution claim that the strict caste system and the presence of tribal chieftains would make it impossible for jurors to reach independent, individual decisions. Federal Judge William B. Bryant held that the Samoan culture had changed to the extent that the jury system would now be acceptable. *King v United States* (DC DC 1978), described in *SF Chronicle*, Jan. 4, 1978, p. 45.

Protection of jury trials in state courts by the United States Supreme Court is not guaranteed. For example, state pressure on defendants to forego jury trial in exchange for lesser penalties for pleas of guilty was held constitutional in a five-to-three judgment in *Corbitt v New Jersey* (1978) 439 US 212. (Justice Stewart concurred to make six, because it was not clear to him that the state statute penalized a defendant's decision to plead not guilty.) Justice Stevens, joined by Justices Brennan and Marshall, dissented on the ground of the defendant's unqualified constitutional right to require the state to support its accusation with evidence, citing *United States v Jackson* (1968) 390 US 570.

Going in the other direction, the ABA House of Delegates in 1976 approved three standards for criminal cases: (1) there should be a right to jury trial in any criminal case in which the accused can be punished by confinement in jail or prison; (2) in criminal cases in which the accused can be punished by confinement in jail or prison for more than six months, the jury should consist of 12 persons; (3) in criminal cases, the verdict should be unanimous. These are now part of the *ABA Standards for Criminal Justice*. And the California Supreme Court held that a defendant has a right to a jury trial if cited for possession of up to one ounce of marijuana. The offense carries a maximum $100 fine and no possible jail term. *Tracy v Municipal Court* (1978) 150 Cal Rptr 785.

### 3. Selection Methods §1.15

The federal and state constitutions require that representative jurors be selected from representative lists, comprising "a jury of peers" or cross-section jury, depending on court language. These requirements are spelled out in detail in §§2.2–2.4.

The constitutions also require impartial jurors (see §2.6). And the federal jury act forbids exclusion from jury service on the basis of race, color, religion, sex, or national origin. 28 USC §1862.

To achieve these goals, trial lawyers must voir-dire prospective jurors on racial and ethnic prejudice (see §2.8), on other prejudices and prejudgments (see §2.9), and on some other factors (see §2.10).

## B. Twelve-Person Trial Juries

### 1. Federal Criminal Juries §1.21

A federal criminal jury consists of 12 persons. This traditional definition is found in *Patton v United States* (1930) 281 US 276, 288, and is codified in Rule 23, Federal Rules of Criminal Procedure:

> (b) Jury of Less Than Twelve. Juries shall be of 12 but at any time before verdict the parties may stipulate in writing with the approval of the court that the jury shall consist of any number less than 12 or that a valid verdict may be returned by a jury of less than 12 should the court find it necessary to excuse one or more jurors for any just cause after trial commences.

While the major attack on 12-person juries is currently on civil juries (see §§1.22–1.23), proposals are made from time to time by members of Congress to permit six-member federal criminal juries in capital cases.

In *Williams v Florida* (1970) 399 US 78, the United States Supreme Court concluded that the states are not required by the due process clause of the Fourteenth Amendment to provide for a 12-member jury in all criminal cases. The same day, however, the Court also assumed the continuation of the 12-member federal criminal jury. See *Baldwin v New York* (1970) 399 US 66, 72. See also *Bloom v Illinois* (1968) 391 US 194, 213 (Fortas, J, concurring). Compare *Johnson v Louisiana* (1972) 406 US 356, 369–377 (Powell, J, concurring); *Williams v Florida*, *supra*, at 122–129 (Harlan, J, dissenting). Moreover, in *Williams* the Court expressly reserved ruling on the requirements for civil juries under the Seventh Amendment (399 US at 92 n30), although *Williams* was promptly construed as having removed all constitutional barriers to the immediate reduction in size of federal civil juries. Devitt, "The Six Man Jury in Federal Court," 53 FRD 273 (1971).

### 2. Federal Civil Juries

#### a. Sample Memo: To Ensure Community Standards §1.22

*Source:* Unsuccessful amicus curiae brief by Siegfried Hesse for California Trial Lawyers Association in *Colgrove v Battin* (1973) 413 US 149. The Supreme Court upheld the federal district judge who had been sued for requiring a 6-person jury in a civil defamation suit in which one side had demanded a 12-person jury.

**I. THE 12-MEMBER CIVIL JURY WAS ESTABLISHED TO ENSURE THAT COMMUNITY RATHER THAN INDIVIDUAL STANDARDS WILL DETERMINE WHETHER AND WHEN AN INDIVIDUAL WILL**

**SUFFER LOSS OF PROPERTY OR PERSONAL REPUTATION WITHOUT COMPENSATION.**

**A. Civil jury reform should follow rather than precede a careful determination of the role and value of the civil jury in our legal system and of the comparative social cost of available alternatives to resolve the problems which have led to the instant alteration of the workings of the civil jury.**

. . .

There is no value to rehearse again the various arguments pro and con the role of civil juries. See *Cooley v Strickland Transp. Co.* (5th Cir 1972) 459 F2d 779, 782–783, n9, for many of the more recent commentaries. It would be obtuse, however, to ignore the current widespread concern about trial delay and the increasing cost of justice in our society. See, *e.g.*, *Devitt*, *supra* 53 FRD at 276–277. Nor should we be blind to the fact that the ultimate goal of some "reformers" is abolition of juries altogether. *E.g.*, Sarpy, "Civil Juries, Their Decline and Eventual Fall," 11 *Loyola U L Rev* 243, 266 (1962-1963); Kessler, "The Crime Crisis and Proposed Procedural Reform," 5 *Loyola U L Rev* 1, 31–32 (1972) (advocating reduction in jury size as a "stopgap" measure).

Given the current climate of academic opinion, it is appropriate to recall that change is not necessarily synonymous with reform, and that, with respect to Seventh Amendment rights, proposed curtailments "should be scrutinized with the utmost care." *Dimick v Schiedt* (1935) 293 US 474, 486.

The value of the role of the civil jury in our society must, indeed, be assessed apart from any need to reduce the volume of civil litigation concerning the automobile or to eliminate trial delay generally. The true social cost of civil juries cannot, in any event, be determined without also considering the comparative cost of other alternatives. Thus Professor Harry Kalven reports that an additional 1.6 judges would effect the same decrease in delay as would the elimination of all civil juries in New York City; that the same would be true of a reduction of two weeks in each judge's vacation; that split trials would be at least one-half as effective; and that New Jersey jury trials are already as speedy as New York trials would be without juries. Kalven, "The Dignity of the Civil Jury," 50 *Va L Rev* 1055, 1057–1061 (1964). See also Zeisel and Callahan, "Split Trials and Time Saving: A Statistical Analysis," 76 *Harv L Rev* 1606 (1963).

In this connection it must be noted that the primary cost of juries in the federal system is not a function of their size, but of the lack of their effective use. For the fiscal year of 1971, 45.8 percent of the total cost of petit juries resulted from jurors who never served. The dollar cost of this waste was $6,369,000. That there is considerable room for reform is indicated by the fact that the rate of nonuse varied, from district to district, between the extremes of 17.9 percent to 78.7 percent. The estimated savings from the use of six-member juries in all civil cases, in contrast, would have been $1,799,600, or only 15 percent of the total petit jury cost. Division of Procedural Studies and

Statistics, Administrative Office of the United States Courts, *Juror Utilization in the United States Courts* pp. A-2, B-1, D-5 (Aug. 13, 1971).

*COMMENT:* The 1979 study on *Juror Utilization in the United States Courts* showed improvement in the use of jurors in 46 of the 92 federal district courts, resulting in a decrease of jurors called but never used, including those who never even made it into the jury box for questioning, as well as those who were challenged successfully. This group has decreased 3.8 percent, for an overall national average of 24.6 percent. Nonetheless, as a result of new Jury Fee regulations (effective January 1, 1979) and the increasing number of civil trial days, juror expenditures increased in 1979 to a total of $18,863,500 for petit jurors and $6,730,500 (26.3 percent) for grand jurors.

Delay per se, therefore, should not be considered "a sufficient reason for altering the jury apart from consideration of the quality of the jury as an adjudicator." 50 *Va L Rev* at 1061. The jury has been retained despite the fact that "to some extent we sacrifice efficiency, expedition, and low cost." *Bloom v Illinois*, *supra*, at 209 (criminal case).

**B. The size of the common law civil jury was dictated by the need to ensure broad community representation to avoid the injustice which results from the verdicts of smaller bodies.**

The historical record is silent on the precise composition of the jury intended by the Seventh Amendment. It is nevertheless abundantly clear that the civil jury was highly prized by our Founders. Henderson, "The Background of the Seventh Amendment," 80 *Harv L Rev* 289 (1966).

In *Williams*, this Court concluded that the size of the common law jury was "A historical accident, unnecessary to effect the purpose of the jury system and wholly without significance 'except to mystics.' " 399 US at 102. After-the-fact explanations for the precise number of 12 jurors have indeed sometimes been mystical; and it may have been accidental that 12 rather than 10 or 11 or 14 or 15 members were ultimately selected. But there is no basis in history to conclude that it was accidental that the final choice was not four or six or eight, rather than 12. The ultimate choice was calculated to balance the need for broad community representation with the need for a functioning deliberative body. Wells, "The Origin of the Petty Jury," 27 *Law Q Rev* 347, 356–357 (1911). Because of "its intrinsic fairness [, the jury came] . . . to be regarded as the one regular common-law mode of trial, always to be had when no other was fixed." Thayer, "The Jury and Its Development," 5 *Harv L Rev* 249, 259 (1892). Indeed, jury trial became synonymous with "the common law of the land." *Ibid.* n3. There is no mystery in the fact that "what was wanted was a number that was large enough to create a formidable body of opinion in favor of the side that won." Devlin, *Trial by Jury* 8 (1958). Here, as elsewhere, the question was decided by our ancestors on the basis of practical experience. See Holmes, *The Common Law* 1 (1881).

### b. Sample Memo: Smaller Juries Reach Different Verdicts §1.23

*Source:* Unsuccessful amicus curiae brief by Siegfried Hesse for California Trial Lawyers Association in *Colgrove v Battin* (1973) 413 US 149 (see §1.22).

**II. REDUCTION IN THE NUMBER OF JURORS DEFEATS THE PRIMARY FUNCTION OF CIVIL JURIES, EFFECTS SUBSTANTIAL DIFFERENCES IN INDIVIDUAL VERDICTS, AND DENIES LITIGANTS THE SUBSTANCE OF THEIR SEVENTH AMENDMENT RIGHT TO A JURY TRIAL.**

**A. The tasks performed by each juror are subtle, complex, and vulnerable to the exercise of personal bias and eccentricity.**

The underlying premise of any trial is that reasonable men and women may differ in their perceptions of the disputed facts or in their conceptions of the basic issues at stake. Otherwise the parties could settle their differences without the aid of a neutral fact finder, whether it is a judge or jury. Moreover, if everyone evaluated evidence identically, there would be no need for more than a single fact finder; each additional individual's perceptions and conceptions would be cumulative rather than potentially disparate in nature. We know, however, that there is a wide spectrum in individual ability to perceive accurately, recall accurately, and evaluate rationally what has been remembered. Two-thirds of all criminal juries, for example, disagree on the first ballot. Kalven & Zeisel, *The American Jury* 487 (1966). While there is no readily available data for civil juries, a similar rate of disagreement seems likely since jurors, unlike judges, do not perceive a substantial difference in the burden of persuasion in criminal as compared to civil trials. Simon & Mahan, "Quantifying Burdens of Proof: A View from the Bench, the Jury, and the Classroom," 5 *Law & Soc Rev* 319 (1971).

Ultimately, the jury must decide the simple question: What happened? Its task is much like that of the historian. Weinstein, "Some Difficulties in Devising Rules for Determining Truth in Judicial Trials," 66 *Colum L Rev* 223, 229 (1966); see also *In re Fried* (2d Cir 1947) 161 F2d 453, 462 n21. Unlike the historian, however, the jury must decide immediately, and without qualifications. Its verdict is the result of the collective integration of several levels of perception, memory, and deliberation.

What happens in the courtroom, of course, is nothing remotely like the actual events which the jury is asked to reconstruct. The jurors must depend largely on the testimony of witnesses as to their memories of what they perceived in the past. Each juror, in short, must determine to his individual satisfaction: (1) How accurate was each witness' original perception? (2) How accurate is his present memory of that perception, if he is in fact attempting to tell the truth? and (3) How much weight should I give his testimony, given the probable nature of his original perception and his personal motivations when on the stand?

While in the juryroom, the jurors must in turn rely on their own perceptions of what transpired in the courtroom as well as their memories of those perceptions (perhaps days or weeks later). Finally, each juror must make sense of these different levels of perception and memory to participate meaningfully in the jury's deliberative process. At each stage of this complicated process (highly simplified here) each juror necessarily brings to bear his or her personal experiences, biases, and quirks.

The greater the number of jurors, therefore, consistent with a rational, deliberative process, the less influence will these individual threats to a just determination have on the ultimate verdict. "One man cannot differ with his own judgment and any less than twelve men will reduce the probability of differences to be discussed. A fundamental tenet of the jury tradition, then, lies in its assumption that controverted factual issues are best resolved through reasoned discussion and debate." Broeder, "The Functions of the Jury: Facts or Fictions," 21 *U Chi L Rev* 386, 388 (1954).

**B. Reduction in the size of civil juries results in different verdicts in a substantial percentage of cases since the jury becomes less representative of the community and its values; individual verdicts, as a consequence, are subject to greater deviations from community norms.**

No individual 12-member jury can be expected to be fully representative of all competing community values. *Williams v Florida*, *supra*, 399 US at 102. It does not follow from that fact, however, that a six-member jury can represent community values equally well. A six-member criminal jury will convict and acquit different defendants. Zeisel, " . . . And Then There Were None: The Diminution of The Federal Jury," 38 *U Chi L Rev* 710, 721 (1971); Walbert, "The Effect of Jury Size on the Probability of Conviction: An Evaluation of Williams v Florida," 22 *Case-West Res L Rev* 529 (1971).

Similar results follow the reduction in size of civil juries. A 10 percent minority in the community, for example, will be represented (before challenge) on 72 of every 100 twelve-member juries, but on only 47 of every 100 six-member juries. 38 *U Chi L Rev* at 716. Moreover, a six-member jury will reflect a standard deviation from community norms which is 42 percent greater than that of a 12-member jury. *Id.* at 717–718. Stated another way, 6-member juries will inevitably render far more eccentric verdicts than will 12-member juries.

This Court concluded in *Williams* that the reduction of criminal juries from 12 to 6 members should not affect its function to protect an accused from governmental oppression. 399 US at 100–101. In reaching this conclusion, however, it relied only on a "few experiments . . . in the civil area." *Id.* at 101–102.

Of the six sources cited (399 US at 101 n48), two rely essentially on the lack of evidence that 6-member juries will not function as well as 12-member juries. Wiehl, "The Six Man Jury," 4 *Gonzaga L Rev* 35, 39 (1968); Tamm, "The Five-Man Civil Jury: A Proposed Constitutional Amendment," 51 *Geo L J* 120, 129 (1962). These authors merely shifted the constitutional burden of proof to those advocating retention of juries as constituted for centuries. Two other reports concern the same Massachusetts experiment in which the actual choice presented was between a speedy determination by a 6-member jury or a long delayed determination by a 12-member jury. Cronin, "Six-Member Juries in District Courts," 2 *Bost BJ* 27, 29 (1958); see also "Six-Member Juries Tried in Massachusetts District Court," 42 *J Am Jud Soc'y* 136 (1958). This choice, of course, presents quite different issues than are faced here. The fifth source reported on what was apparently a single trial, which is hardly evidence for anything other than the fact that it happened. "New Jersey Experiments with Six-Man Jury," *Bull of ABA Section of Jud Admin*, May 1966, at p.6. The final source is itself evidence that experienced attorneys prefer 12-member juries to 6-member juries, even when their clients are required to pay for them. Phillips, "A Jury of Six in all Cases," 30 *Conn BJ* 354, 355 (1956). In none of these materials is anything reported beyond individual impressions and opinions. They merely illustrate the fact that "in the absence of empirical data [concerning juries], value jugments all too readily creep in to substitute for facts." 21 *U Chi L Rev* at 424.

*Source:* Affidavit filed in *In re Coordinated Pretrial Proceedings in Antibiotic Antitrust Actions* (D Minn 1974) 410 F Supp 659, by Dr. Hans Zeisel.

The need for thorough voir dire examination grows if the jury to be selected is a six-member jury. Notwithstanding repeated holdings and dicta of the United States Supreme Court to the contrary, there *is* a difference between the way 12-member juries and the way 6-member juries decide cases. The verdicts of 6-member juries are less predictable than those of 12-member juries, which is to say that the gamble the litigants take in bringing a case into court is greater if the jury consists of only 6 members.

There are several ways of arriving at this insight. One is by suggesting the thought-experiment of imagining a one-man jury. Intuitively, we would say that the gamble would be too great. If the case is close to the fifty-fifty line, everything will depend on the predisposition of this one juror; if there is more than one juror, these predispositions, whatever they are, will balance one another, and the more jurors there are, the more stable this balance will be. This intuitive reaction would prove to be correct. And the difference between the 6-member and the 12-member jury would be of the same kind, only smaller, because the difference between 12 and 6 is smaller than the difference between 12 and 1.

The second way of conveying this difference is by thinking of the jury as a statistical sample, drawn from the population of potential jurors. We know from our studies that juries which have to award damages will fix these damages somewhere around the average of what the individual jurors believe these damages should be. And statistical sampling theory, as well as experience, teaches us that the averages of 6-member samples will vary more from one another than the averages of 12-member samples. This conclusion is derived from the same facts that increase the sampling error in public opinion polls, if we reduce the size of the sample. (To be exact, the "gamble" or the variability of the verdicts of juries increases by roughly 40 percent if the size of the jury is cut in half.) But saying that the verdicts of 6-member juries are likely to show greater variations, is but to say that in these juries, the jurors with extreme predisposition are more likely to have a greater share than in the 12-member juries. To counteract this situation even more careful voir dire proceedings are indicated.

In its decision in *Colegrove v Battin* (1973) 413 US 149, the Supreme Court rejected the arguments supporting a continuation of 12-person juries, based in part on studies of juries of 6 persons. During the Nixon administration Watergate crisis, Professors Hans Zeisel and Shari Seidman Diamond reacted sharply to this decision with an article analyzing the weaknesses in these studies, "'Convincing Empirical Evidence' on the Six Member Jury," 41 *U Chi L Rev* 281 (1974), concluding at 294–295:

> Moreover, it would be a mistake to regard the size of the federal civil jury as an isolated question. Some district court judges are already trying criminal cases—albeit by stipulation of counsel—before juries of six members. State legislatures across the country are teeming with bills, some already enacted, to reduce civil and criminal juries and to abandon the unanimity requirement. The movement to reduce the size of the federal civil jury must be seen in this context. If the country wants to reconsider the desirability of the civil jury, it should be done in open and direct debate. Perhaps such a debate should begin. But to pare the jury down and allow it to decay from the insufficiencies we impose is shabby treatment for an institution that has served the nation well.
>
> At this point in the development only Congress can save the 12-member jury. There is much talk now about reestablishing the authority of the Congress vis-a-vis the Executive. If the Congress also cares to reestablish its authority vis-a-vis the judiciary, it can undo this unseemly whittling down of the jury by simply reestablishing the 12-member jury for all federal trials.
>
> At a time when much of our justice system is under suspicion and public mistrust has reached the highest officer in the land, the integrity of the jury has survived. This would seem to be an inappropriate moment to punish it, even if money could be saved. Four million dollars might not be the right price for abandoning half of the American jury.

And see Kaye, "And Then There Were Twelve: Statistical Reasoning, the Supreme Court, and the Size of the Jury," 68 *Cal L Rev* 1004 (1980).

*COMMENT:* This preference for 12-person juries is not shared by some plaintiffs' personal injury lawyers who have achieved excellent results with 6-person civil juries. They explain that a major, well-tried personal injury case brings the jurors very close to the plaintiff and plaintiff's lawyers in a low-key setting. This close relationship is much easier when there are only six jurors (and a seventh alternate) for the lawyers to relate to. See discussion in §4.50. However, it should be noted that many of the lawyers favoring this position practice in Michigan, and particularly in Detroit, where even a six-person jury is almost certain to include several members of the ethnic and economic groups in society most likely to find liability and to vote a large verdict for an injured plaintiff. See §3.41. This situation does not exist in a great many other metropolitan areas of the United States, or in many smaller cities and towns. Leaders of the American Trial Lawyers Association and the Inner Circle of Advocates report that civil juries are awarding higher verdicts to plaintiffs with very serious personal injuries, such as paraplegics and quadraplegics, but are not keeping up with inflationary costs in cases of prolonged disabilities that leave some mobility. *NY Times*, Aug. 1, 1979.

### 3. State Criminal Juries §1.24

Any state can set higher standards for its criminal justice system than those required of it by the United States Constitution as interpreted by the United States Supreme Court at any moment. This point was made by the Alabama Supreme Court in continuing to require 12-person civil juries under the state constitution (see §1.25). Such "independent state grounds" for decision on many fundamental issues are being recommended from California to Mississippi. (See, *e.g.*, Justice Stanley Mosk, "The Constitution of California in the Era of the Burger Court and States' Rights," *Los Angeles Daily Journal*, Dec. 19, 1973 (Reprint Section at 26–29); Comment, "Stop and Frisk in Mississippi," 45 *Miss LJ* 763 (1974).)

The United States Supreme Court's decision that fewer than 12 persons on some state criminal court juries are acceptable under the Sixth and Fourteenth Amendments to the Constitution (*Williams v Florida* (1970) 399 US 78) was combined with acceptance of nonunanimous verdicts in some state criminal cases.

However, in 1978 the Supreme Court held in *Ballew v Georgia* (1978) 435 US 223, that state criminal juries must have six members to satisfy the defendant's rights to jury trial guaranteed in the Sixth and Fourteenth Amendments. In *Burch v Louisiana* (1979) 441 US 130, the Court held that six-person state criminal juries must vote unanimously in order to convict, (see §1.31), and in *Brown v Louisiana* (1980) 447 US 323, at 330–331, this ruling was given retroactive effect:

> Although we have held that the constitutional guarantee of trial by jury prescribes neither the precise number that can constitute a jury, *Williams v Florida, supra* (six-person jury does not violate Sixth and Fourteenth Amendments), nor the exact proportion of the jury that must concur in the verdict, *Apodaca v Oregon* (1972) 406 US 404 (10-to-2 vote in state trial does not violate

the Constitution), we have also declared that there do exist size and unanimity limits that cannot be transgressed if the essence of the jury trial right is to be maintained. Thus *Ballew v Georgia* (1978) 435 US 223, held that a reduction in the size of a jury to below six persons in nonpetty criminal cases raises such substantial doubts as to the fairness of the proceeding and the jury's ability to represent the true sense of the community that it deprives the accused of his right to trial by jury. For "much the same reasons," we concluded in *Burch* that "conviction for a nonpetty offense by only five members of a six-person jury presents a similar threat to preservation of the substance of the jury trial guarantee" and hence violates the Sixth Amendment as applied to the states through the Fourteenth. 441 US at 138. Though the line separating the permissible jury practice from the impermissible may not be the brightest, *cf. Burch v Louisiana*, *supra*, at 137; *Ballew v Georgia*, 435 US at 231–232 (opinion of Blackmun, J); 435 US at 245–246 (opinion of Powell, J), a line must be drawn somewhere, and the constitutional inviolability of that border must be scrupulously respected lest the purpose and functioning of the jury be seriously impaired.

In *Brown* (447 US at 331, 332), the Court explained that Justice Blackmun's opinion in *Ballew*:

cataloged the several considerations that led the Court to conclude that the operation of the jury was inhibited to a constitutionally significant degree by reducing its size to five members. Prominent among these concerns was the recognition, supported by a number of empirical studies, that a decline in jury size leads to less accurate factfinding and a greater risk of convicting an innocent person. 435 US at 232–235. In addition, statistical and empirical data established that because of a concomitant decrease in the number of hung juries, a reduction in the size of the jury panel in criminal cases unfairly disadvantages one side—the defense. 435 US at 236. Lastly, the opinion noted that the opportunity for meaningful and appropriate minority representation diminishes with the size of the jury. 435 US at 236–237.

Caveat: In *Ballew*, Chief Justice Burger and Justices Powell and Rehnquist, while concurring in the judgment, did *not* agree that every feature of federal criminal jury trials must be available in state criminal jury trials, and did *not* agree with the reliance on "numerology" derived from statistical studies. 435 US at 246.

In Lempert, "Undiscovering 'Nondiscernible' Differences: Empirical Research and Jury-Size Cases," 73 *Mich L Rev* 643 (1975), Lempert argued that research methods used with conventional-size juries fail to reveal certain attitudes, *e.g.*, racial prejudice and minority perspectives. They will be even less effective with smaller juries, and this may be an important reason for continuing 12-member juries. He concluded that the final outcome of the 6-member versus 12-member jury controversy will turn on whether people value the presence of minority views in a jury room enough to fight for larger juries. Other studies are referred to in *Ballew*, 435 US at 231–232, n10. And see Kaye, "And Then There Were Twelve: Statistical Reasoning, the Supreme Court, and the Size of the Jury," 68 *Cal L Rev* 1004 (1980).

### 4. State Civil Juries §1.25

Some states have kept 12-person juries because their courts have determined that the right to jury trial, which shall remain inviolate, means a jury of 12. In Alabama, the state constitution now in force was passed in 1901 and gives Alabama courts excellent data on the framers' intentions as to jury size. In *Gilbreath v Wallace* (Ala 1974) 292 So 2d 651, the Alabama Supreme Court relied on this history to retain 12-person juries. (In the following quotation, footnotes have been inserted in the text in parentheses.)

> The next question is whether Act No. 1734, which requires the use of a 6-member jury rather than a 12-member jury, violates the substantive constitutional right of trial by jury.
>
> It is appropriate to note at the outset that the answer is controlled by Art 1, §11 of our state Constitution as construed by the decisions of this Court. While the federal Constitution, as interpreted by the United States Supreme Court, establishes minimum standards, the states have the power and are free to provide greater safeguards and to extend this protection through their own organic law—the State Constitutions. Indeed, the Ninth and Tenth Amendments to the United States Constitution envisage this fundamental truth. (Amendment IX: "The enumeration in the Constitution, of certain rights, shall not be construed to deny or disparage others retained by the people." Amendment X: "The powers not delegated to the United States by the Constitution, nor prohibited by it to the states, are reserved to the states respectively, or to the people." See also *Kraas v American Bakeries Co.* (1935) 231 Ala 278, 164 So 565.)
>
> In Alabama the basic principles which apply to constitutional juries in criminal cases also apply in civil cases. The crucial words which control these principles are "shall remain inviolate." To provide that the right of trial by jury shall remain inviolate is to forbid the state through the legislative, judicial, or executive department—one or all—from ever burdening, disturbing, qualifying, or tampering with this right to the prejudice of the people. *Alford v Alabama ex rel. Attorney General* (1910) 54 So 213. Historically, a jury (with minor exceptions, *e.g.*, insanity inquisitions) has consisted of 12 people selected from the community in which the trial is to be held. The basic purpose of the jury is to render an impartial verdict after due deliberation. In the past, 12 (again with minor exceptions not here applicable) has been considered the minimum number constitutionally necessary to satisfy this purpose. In a line of decisions, several predating the present constitution, this Court has held

that the jury contemplated by Section 11 is a common law jury of 12 and a jury that consisted of a lesser number is not constitutional. *Baader v State* (1917) 210 Ala 76, 77 So 370; [other citations omitted].

Therefore, if we were to hold Act No. 1734 constitutional, it would be necessary to overrule existing and well-established precedents on this question. In our deliberation we have not ignored the recent decisions of the United States Supreme Court which held that a 12-member jury is not a mandatory requisite of the right of trial under the United States Constitution. *Williams v Florida* (1970) 399 US 78 (a state criminal trial composed of 6 members); and *Colgrove v Battin* (1973) 413 US 149 (a federal district civil trial composed of 6 members).

In *Williams*, Mr. Justice White, speaking for the majority, expressed the opinion that there was no particular legal significance embodied in the number 12 and that its use developed from little more than a mystical or superstitious fixation with that number (12 apostles, 12 stones, 12 tribes). Having searched the constitutional debates and compared the alternative proposals to the adopted working of the Seventh Amendment, Justice White concluded that the framers did not attach any constitutional significance to the number of jurors. 399 US at 86–106.

As applied to our own Constitution of 1901, the majority opinion in *Williams* does not persuade us that we should abandon our existing case law. It must be remembered that our duty is to speak the will of the people of this state, as that will is embodied in Section 11 of the Alabama Constitution of 1901. In performing this duty, we are not without guidance. The most cursory reading of the official proceedings of the Constitutional Convention of 1901 leads to but one conclusion: To those who framed, amended, debated, and passed this organic article, the number 12 was not merely of mystical significance. It was virtually sacred.

The second most hotly debated issue during the entire term of the convention was the preservation of the right of trial by jury and in what that right consisted. At the time of the convention, 12 was the number in use. Various proposals which would have reduced the number of jurors were placed before the convention. Each such proposal was soundly rejected and the words which preserved the right of trial by jury under all previous constitutions were carried forward into the Constitution of 1901. 1 Official Proceedings 333, Constitutional Convention of 1901, State of Alabama.

We have often held that the reenactment of an ordinance by the people or their representatives, following our construction of the same, amounts to an implicit approval of that construction. In light of the constitutional proceedings outlined above, we believe the application of the foregoing rule of construction is particularly appropriate. It is clear beyond peradventure that the Constitutional Convention considered and rejected that which the legislature has attempted to do in Act No. 1734. Having examined our previous decisions in this light, we are convinced of their continued soundness.

Accordingly, we hold that Act No. 1734, . . . is unconstitutional insofar as it applies to those cases in which the right of trial by jury is preserved inviolate by the constitution. In our considered judgment, if such a radical restructuring of the judicial process is deemed wise or necessary, it must be accomplished by constitutional amendment or enactment.

*COMMENT*: Concerning the preference of some plaintiff's personal injury lawyers for 6-person juries, see §4.50.

As to the constitutionality of state requirements for 12-person juries when the federal Supreme Court permits 6-person state juries, the California Constitution now contains the following language explicitly supporting independent state approaches to such questions:

> SEC. 24. Rights guaranteed by this Constitution are not dependent on those guaranteed by the United States Constitution. This declaration of rights may not be construed to impair or deny others retained by the people.

## C. Unanimous Verdicts §1.31

Unanimous verdicts by 12-person juries are required in federal criminal cases, unless the parties stipulate to fewer than 12 under Rule 23, Federal Rules of Criminal Procedure. See *Johnson v Louisiana* (1972) 406 US 356, 369 (Powell, J, concurring), and §1.21.

Unanimous verdicts are also necessary in trials of nonpetty offenses by six-person state juries, in order to preserve a defendant's constitutional right to a jury trial. The 9-0 opinion in *Burch v Louisiana* (1979) 441 US 130 settled that question, and *Brown v Louisiana* (1980) 447 US 323 made the decision retroactive. Before this decision, two states, Louisiana and Oklahoma, had permitted conviction of nonpetty offenses by nonunanimous six-person juries.

The unanimity requirement led to ultimate release of defendants in several major political-criminal cases discussed in this book, including *Newton* (§3.22) and *Berrigan Brothers*,(§8.31) in which long trials ended in hung juries. See studies in Hastie, Penrod & Pennington, *Inside the Jury* (1983).

The unanimous verdict of a jury of 12 is central to the popular conception of a "jury trial." Civil and criminal juries of 12 people, unanimous verdicts, and attorney participation in voir dire were strongly approved by the participants in the Annual Chief Justice Earl Warren Conference, June 24-25, 1977, held under the sponsorship of the Roscoe Pound-American Trial Lawyers Foundation. See *The American Jury System: Final Report* (1978) for the papers and recommendations by the participants. See Zeisel, "The Verdict of Five out of Six Civil Jurors: Constitutional Problems," 1 *Am Bar Fdation Research J* 141 (1982).

### D. Trials in the Vicinage §1.32

The law on trial in the vicinage has deep roots. In his memorandum decision dismissing indictments against members of the American Indian Movement in *South Dakota v Waubun Nuwi Nini* (Minnehaha County Cir Ct, 2d Cir, May 5, 1975), Circuit Judge Richard Braithwaite quoted the South Dakota Supreme Court in *In re Nelson* (1902) 19 SD 214:

> The jury must not only be impartial. It must also be of the county in which the crime is alleged to have been committed. Until the accused shall have been tried by such a jury, or shall have waived his right by consenting to a change of place of trial, he cannot be lawfully convicted. If such a jury cannot be secured, there will be no tribunal before whom he can be tried and the ends of justice in an individual instance may be defeated. But however regrettable such a result might be, its possibility or even probability cannot be invoked to justify a disregard of so plain a provision of the State Constitution.

See full opinion in *Waubun Nuwi Nini* in §7.66.

For an extensive historical and analytical discussion of the requirement of jury trial in the vicinity of the crime, see Kershen, "Vicinage," 30 *Okla L Rev* 1, 126–154 (1977).

There is no current effort to collect statistics on or examples of cases in which massive pretrial publicity made it impossible to select impartial juries in the jurisdiction where the alleged crime or tort was committed. Nor are statistics available on cases affected by pervasive racial or ethnic prejudices. Some indication of the extent of these problems can be seen from a few examples of judges who dismissed criminal charges against defendants after being unable to select a sufficient number of unbiased jurors through extensive voir dire when defendants did not seek a change of venue. Federal district judge Myron L. Gordon took this step in *United States v Cotton* (ED Wis, No. 68-CR-113, Sept. 9, 1969), the trial of the "Milwaukee 14," a group of Catholic priests and laymen who broke into a Selective Service office in 1968 during the Vietnam War, removed records, and burned them. After their convictions in a highly publicized state court trial, they were brought to trial in the same area in federal court. See §7.65 for a fuller discussion of this issue.

### E. Speedy and Public Trials §1.33

In *Strunk v United States* (1973) 412 US 434, the Supreme Court faced the question of the constitutional guaranty of speedy trial in a case involving a ten-month delay between return of the indictment and the date of arraignment. The Court upheld the judicial determination that the accused had been denied a speedy trial despite three facts: that the defendant was responsible for a large part of the delay, that he neither claimed nor showed that the preparation of his defense was prejudiced by the delay, and that the United States attorney's office was understaffed. The Court then held that dismissal is the only possible remedy for deprivation of the constitutional right to speedy trial; reduction of sentence will not suffice. For further discussion of this remedy for delay, see §7.68.

In 1974, Congress adopted statutory limitations on time between arrest and trial in the Speedy Trial Act, 18 USC §3161–3174.

The definition of a "public trial" was clarified in *Ohio v Lane* (1979) 60 Ohio St 2d 112, when the Ohio Supreme Court affirmed that jury trial in a penitentiary for prisoners charged with escape violates federal and state constitutional guarantees of due process and equal protection, and dilutes the right to public trial to a constitutionally impermissible degree. On presence of the press, see §8.44, chapter 23.

Using such extensive security precautions that the public has been discouraged from attending criminal trials became almost commonplace in the *Angela Davis* case (§3.23). Too frequently now jurors are separated from defendants by physical barriers, in addition to the traditional barriers of race and social class (as discussed in chapter 6). Juror reactions to this practice must be noted and effects on jury verdicts recorded, so that the right to jury trial is not destroyed in fact while being secured in theory. On juror privacy, see §8.44.

## F. Right to Counsel §1.34

The constitutional right to voir dire on racial and ethnic prejudice (see §2.8) requires the effective assistance of counsel guaranteed in the Sixth Amendment. When judges take over the whole voir dire process, they are denying the effective assistance of counsel in this part of trial. Even if judges use all the questions submitted by counsel, they are forbidding counsel to use the voir dire as part of their total presentation of the case to the jury. (See list of purposes of voir dire in §§8.10–8.24). Only when trial judges begin the process of voir dire, conduct the basic questioning in an efficient manner, and then turn it over to competent counsel who carry it on efficiently, do clients benefit from the effective assistance of counsel to which they have a constitutional right.

The methods lawyers can use to help their clients during the voir dire process are discussed throughout this book. If judges respect the right to effective counsel and the lawyers appearing before them have thought through what they want to accomplish on voir dire, the verdicts of the juries chosen are likely to stand up under appellate attack.

Other problems about right to counsel can arise in a hard-fought jury case. Trial lawyers always run the risk of contempt citations by trial judges and disciplinary actions by bar committees. In recent years, the American Bar Association sharply increased its encouragement of disciplinary proceedings and established the ABA Center for Professional Discipline to carry them out. For up-to-date information on both subjects, see reports from the ABA Center and Standing Committee on Professional Discipline, and publications of the National Conference of Black Lawyers and the National Lawyers Guild. Many more citations and proceedings are instituted than are successfully concluded against defense counsel.

In 1982 the Department of Justice, as part of its attack on "organized crime," instituted or broadened a policy of subpoenaing criminal defense lawyers to appear before federal grand juries. The constitutional problems raised by this tactic are being litigated. (See chapter 23.)

## G. Other Standards §1.35

The federal Jury Selection and Service Act of 1968, as amended, provides one of the few statutory protections against discrimination on the basis of economic class in United States law.

> No citizen shall be excluded from service as a grand or petit juror in the district courts of the United States or in the Court of International Trade on account of race, color, religion, sex, national origin, or economic status. 28 USC §1862.

## H. Recent Developments §1.36

It is now possible to keep up with the law on jury selection the same way you keep up with the law in any other field—by reading the relevant advance sheets, subscribing to services on trial advocacy or criminal law, and reading daily newspapers and legal newspapers. The *Index to Legal Periodicals*, *Current Law Index*, and *Legal Resource Index* provide provocative (and sometimes descriptive) titles to law review articles, comments, and notes in this field, indicating what is happening at the cutting edge of the law. It is a good idea occasionally to ask your law librarian for an index to journals on psychology, applied psychology, and the social sciences, to pick up new ideas from these disciplines.

Increasingly, lawyers are learning to use *Lexis* and *Westlaw* in order to find the latest cases and interesting parallels in other fields of law. It is always necessary to Shepardize all citations.

The Annual Supplement to these volumes will use recent developments sections throughout the book to describe new cases, ideas, and articles that are worthy of note, and to warn of cases overruled and of rules and statutes amended or repealed.

## V. MANY CONTROVERSIES REQUIRE JURY TRIALS

### A. The United States Custom of Litigating Public Issues §1.41

Since 1787, the United States has been peopled, in the main, by individuals who emigrated from distant places in search of a better life, and their descendants. This has produced a feisty population, given to brawling in the streets or, in a somewhat more orderly manner, in the courtrooms. This natural tendency has been encouraged by the system of jury trials, which, by definition, require feisty lawyers who can use legal and street language to convince judges and jurors that their clients are right on the law and the facts.

From the turn of the century until the New Deal era, Clarence Darrow and his flamboyant colleagues refined the tactics for representing clients in specific cases by placing the individual controversies in their broader social context. This led to widespread debate on many hot topics of that and this era, including capital punishment; the insanity defense; and the rights of political dissidents, labor, and oppressed minorities.

During the Great Depression, smart young lawyers headed for the new National Labor Relations Board and other agencies where jury trials were not the forum, where strict rules of evidence and the psychology of cross-examination had no place. World War II accentuated this flow of legal talent, and the ability to write an enforceable rent control regulation, or one limiting excess profits, was more highly prized than the ability to pick a winning jury.

After the defeat of the fascist powers, the Cold War ushered in an era in which Senator Joe McCarthy could defeat all rational discussion of social questions (recognition of Red China, what to do about the danger of nuclear war) by labeling the debaters "Reds." In this period, representation of clients before congressional investigating committees often led to defense in administrative hearings against charges of "disloyalty" or to trials for contempt of Congress. Some political activists were tried for their affiliations with the Communist Party under the Smith Act, 18 USC §2385 (e.g., *Dennis v United States* (1951) 341 US

494), while many more were cited for contempt of Congress or for perjury in taking non-Communist oaths as union leaders.

In this period, lawyers representing political clients had a better chance of winning their cases before old-fashioned liberal judges trained in logic and the First Amendment, than before juries selected by the methods then in use. Most communities were deeply frightened by daily headlines about "atomic secrets" being given to "the enemy" and Red takeovers in schools and trade unions. Lawyers accustomed to working in their offices and settling matters on the telephone found themselves in trial courts, but they were unable to deploy the full panoply of rights and procedures available in criminal jury trials.

The civil rights movement arising after *Brown v Board of Education* (1954) 347 US 483, the movement against United States involvement in Vietnam, and the rise of the movements of women, students, environmentalists, prisoners, minorities, and other oppressed groups, eventually brought a change in popular thinking, in media reporting, and finally in some government policies.

The behavior of Richard Nixon as president quickened and deepened this process, with assistance from the Freedom of Information Act, congressional investigations of his behavior, and other forces. When Nixon and his attorney general sought to tail, jail, and destroy leaders and members of the many movements of the 1960s and 1970s, they unwittingly encouraged the practice of litigating major social questions. In case after criminal case, federal and state prosecutors tried and failed to convince jurors of the guilt of Black Panthers, antiwar protesters, leaders of the Southern civil rights movement, Communist Party members, and environmental groups. In case after case, criminal defendants and their lawyers fought back successfully by placing their clients' activities in the context of the social movements of which they were a part, and of which the jurors had some knowledge. See descriptions of key criminal jury trials in chapter 3.

At almost the same time, political defendants and their organizations were filing civil lawsuits against their attackers: seeking damages for police misconduct or seeking injunctions against government officials for actions jeopardizing desegregation, the environment, or other social values. Many of the lawyers for these class-action plaintiffs were supplied by President Lyndon Johnson's famous "war on poverty" law offices, now part of the Legal Services Corporation. Similar issues were being raised by the private bar in suits against large corporations for negligent acts damaging individual plaintiffs. Many personal injury lawyers were winning large verdicts by discussing the social ills underlying their clients' injuries, and some were moving on to sue manufacturers for product liability. See descriptions of key civil jury trials in chapter 3.

The media provided page one stories as juries refused to convict, as juries awarded high damages in suits against big government and big business, and as appellate courts overturned some decisions reached in courts presided over by openly biased judges (like Judge Julius Hoffman in the Chicago Eight trial, see §3.54). Gradually, the custom of litigating public issues, started largely as a defensive measure to defeat criminal convictions, moved into high gear as an affirmative approach to win monetary damages in tort and contract actions.

## B. Public Issues Currently in Litigation §1.42

What responsibility does a manufacturing company have to conduct tests concerning the danger to its employees of working on a particular product? After conducting tests, is it required to warn its workers of potential dangers? What role should the government—particularly the Environmental Protection Agency, the state and federal labor departments, and departments of public health—play in requiring tests and warnings?

These broad questions keep surfacing, not only in Congress and the state legislatures, but in one corner of that other branch of government, the jury trial. For example, dozens of cases have been filed against Dow Chemical Company, Shell Development Company, and the University of California and one of its professors by workers claiming sterility from working on DBCP. Juries in 1983 found that Dow should have given the workers adequate warnings about the substantial dangers, and awarded them their actual damages. But juries had great difficulty in deciding whether Dow acted "with conscious disregard" of their safety, entitling plaintiffs to punitive damages. An Oakland, California jury had no such difficulty awarding $600,000 in punitive damages to three victims of asbestos-related illnesses in August 1983. *Miller, Pitts and Bell v Fibreboard Mfg. Co., SF Chronicle*, Aug. 5, 1983, p.4. Questions bout "conscious disregard" also arise in cases on disposal of toxic wastes, environmental protection, and product liability. Such problems for jurors will continue until the legislative and administrative branches debate these issues and set standards that are in accord with the developing community conscience.

Does society have a responsibility to provide inexpensive daycare centers for children of working parents? Will the government assess blame when a single parent cannot afford child care and instead leaves a child at home alone while she goes to work? What should be the standards for the use of deadly force by a police officer?

These basic, but seemingly unrelated, social questions converged after the death of Patrick Ridge in Santa Ana, California, in April 1983. Again, a jury—this time a grand jury—was asked to decide what the law requires. Should they indict the police officer who shot and killed the five-year-old boy after mistaking his toy gun for a real one? Or should they indict the boy's mother for gross criminal neglect for leaving her son alone when she went to work because she could not afford a baby sitter? The "conscience of the community" led the jurors not to indict anyone in this incident, but the public policy questions surrounding this case will continue to be raised in many criminal and family law cases until society addresses the underlying problems of insufficient standards for law enforcement officers and an insufficient supply of high quality/low-cost daycare for the children of working parents.

Can a school board take effective action to discourage troubled students from committing acts of violence against fellow students? Does a school board have a responsibility to protect its students from attacks on school property? And how can schools, some of which are now patrolled by police officers, be transformed into places where students again feel safe and are able to learn from dedicated teachers?

These fundamental questions, which face many parents and educators today, become questions for jurors when a 13-year-old junior high school student is beaten and raped in the school stairwell by a 16-year-old suspended student. In April 1983 a New York jury hearing just such a case held the board of education negligent and awarded the plaintiff three million dollars in damages. Earlier, the suspended student was convicted of rape and sentenced to three years in a correctional facility. Questions of school board responsibility for students and the appropriate punishment for young rapists will be raised in many more tort and criminal cases until other branches of government act to resurrect the public school system and to make rape a loathsome crime of violence in the public consciousness.

Is there a pattern of police shootings of black men in some large cities today? Are a significant number of police officers afflicted with racism? If so, who shall pay for their violations of law and of the rights of black citizens?

These questions are being answered in an increasing number of damage suits under the 1870 civil rights act (42 USC §1983) by juries hearing testimony on a series of shootings, as well as on the shooting in the particular case. One such case, in Richmond, California, in 1982-1983, led to changes in police procedures after several black police officers testified for the plaintiff. Later a jury awarded three million dollars to the families of the two deceased victims.

What standards should be set for product safety design, and who should set the standards? Once standards are set, by industry or government, and a product is manufactured and sold, does the manufacturer have a continuing duty to consumers to warn of defects discovered later? Is failure to correct the defects and warn consumers a criminal offense? Who should make this judgment?

Pending action by Congress, these questions are being decided by civil and criminal juries, like the Indiana jury that heard the famous Ford Pinto case in 1979, in which the Ford Motor Company was convicted of reckless homicide and fined $30,000 for the fiery deaths of three young women after the gas tank in their 1973 Pinto exploded on rear-end impact. And in 1982 a California jury awarded $10.5 million to a woman who claimed she suffered toxic shock syndrome after using a Johnson & Johnson O.B. tampon. *Lynete West v Johnson & Johnson Prods Inc.*, *SF Chronicle*, Dec. 24, 1983, p.4.

What is sexual harassment on the job? Is it a serious problem? Can it be proved by objective facts, or is it "all in a woman's mind"? Is it really a tort for which damages can be collected?

As in the other examples in this section, juries are answering these questions, often more rapidly and more favorably to women's rights than legislators, administrators, and, presumably, judges sitting alone. For example, Dr. Ramona Tascoe was awarded $225,000 by a San Francisco federal jury in February 1983 to compensate her for actions and comments of the chief of surgery that led her to resign her residency at a local hospital.

Numerous cases are being filed challenging at-will discharges of long-term employees not covered by individual or union contracts. In communities hit heavily by unemployment, jurors react strongly to this problem, although their verdicts cannot be predicted. See §5.15.

Malpractice charges against doctors, lawyers, and other professionals are also mounting. A sample case is that of the parents of two-year-old Andrea Ferris, who sued because she may never walk, talk, or feed herself owing to brain damage caused by a doctor's mistake in waiting too long before performing a Caesarean section. Facing a jury trial, the Pasadena hospital agreed to make monthly payments throughout Andrea's life, beginning at $7,000 per month the first year and increasing each year to a possible total of $119 million if Andrea lives an expected 77 years. *SF Chronicle*, May 19, 1983, p. 9. A jury in Worcester, Massachusetts, awarded one million dollars to an elderly widow who claimed a nursing home invaded her husband's privacy during the family's fight to let him die after years of senility while receiving life-sustaining kidney treatments. An earlier jury had awarded $2.58 million, which was cut to $100,001 by a judge. *Spring v Holyoke Geriatric Authority*, *SF Chronicle*, Aug. 3, 1983, p. 49.

Media coverage of the trials and settlements mentioned here raises the underlying issues with the general public, and individual jurors often continue to discuss and debate their cases with their circles of friends until a community consensus begins to emerge. In time this may lead to proposals for legislation or regulations to set general standards to cover the conduct that led to the civil or criminal cases.

While this method of developing the law is not systematic, direct, or foolproof, it certainly is based on grassroots participation in decision-making, and it is no more cumbersome than developing the law by legislative or administrative action, or by judicial opinion. It relies heavily on the exercise of First Amendment liberties by jurors, commentators, and the media. And it is in the great tradition of Magna Charta and the United States constitutional guaranty of jury trials.

## C. Judges as Decision-Makers on Public Law Issues

### 1. The Judges §1.43

The majority of judges in state and federal courts are not representative of the people who will come before them as defendants in criminal cases or as plaintiffs in civil jury cases. Most judges are white males from upper and upper middle class families. Many of them went to prestigious law schools with others like themselves and learned something about logic and law through the Socratic method and traditional courses taught by traditional law professors out of traditional casebooks. Many judges practiced corporate and business law or worked as district attorneys while building the reputations in their local communities, bar associations, and political parties that led to their judicial appointment. The few women judges generally share the privileged background of their male counterparts. There are, of course, notable exceptions—judges from working class families who went to night school and represented clients from the wrong side of the tracks.

Some members of both groups have broad intellectual interests that serve them well in the multitude of cases that come before them. Some understand and even empathize with some of the human beings they must judge, but few have experienced the powerlessness that is part of the lives of most of the litigants who come before them; judges are accustomed to being in control of their circumstances.

This has affected various judges in various ways. Some have been sufficiently protected from the crude rude world not to fear it when it reaches into their courtooms. They have sufficient humanity and decency and interest in the law to listen fairly to the facts and to rule fairly on the law even when the particular parties coming before them do not present themselves in an attractive light. Other judges use their positions of power to try to protect themselves and their social class from the great unwashed who daily come to court as a result of fights, negligence, ignorance, poverty, and various forms of discrimination.

The judiciary in this country also includes a new group of state and federal judges who do not fit the majority in critical ways. Under President Jimmy Carter and some state governors, notably Jerry Brown of California, many women and blacks have been appointed or elected to the bench from the ranks of the civil rights and women's movements of the 1960s and 1970s. Some public defenders, legal service attorneys, and liberal law professors have been appointed to the bench since their involvement in the war on poverty and the movements against the Vietnam war and for the environment. Although there has been an enormous increase in the percentage of people appointed from these groups, their previous percentage was so small that at best it will take several decades of continuous attention to court appointments before the judiciary will reflect the present population in the law schools, to say nothing of the present population of litigants and the general public.

Litigants and lawyers must of course beware of making assumptions about the types of judicial rulings that will be made by this first generation of judges coming from the seats of the powerless. Some will certainly act as judges exactly like the majority judges they have displaced. Some will certainly act as judges exactly like their colleagues who remain in the ghettoes and barrios and women's groups from which they came. And others will certainly act sometimes one way and sometimes the other.

To all these judges, a jury trial presents both opportunity and difficulty. Giving the decision-making power to otherwise powerless jurors relieves the judge of the responsibility of making difficult decisions based on conflicting facts and making rulings on questions that are currently the subjects of sharp dispute. Some judges welcome this opportunity not to decide what is best for particular litigants and for society as a whole. Others feel affronted that their decision-making power has been taken from them and seek to control the jury verdict by showing the jurors in a hundred ways that the judge is still in control, the lawyers are not to be followed, and the judge's instructions will lay it all out.

Few judges now sitting ever took a law school course in which they learned how to try a case from beginning to end. Few might be expected to have the common touch, the folk wisdom, of the litigants or jurors in their courtrooms. Of those born with these qualities, few have been able to retain them after years on the bench. Few judges, indeed, wear embroidery on their judicial robes, or any other personalized touches that would indicate to a frightened litigant that underneath the robes sits a human being.

One Detroit judge followed a different approach. He decided to adorn his room with works of art that would indicate a strong commitment to equality in this forum. While sitting on the Recorder's Court, Congressman George W. Crockett, Jr., hung a mural by Leroy Foster there. Parties, counsel, and spectators entering this courtroom immediately faced the full figure of Frederick Douglass, young, black, and proud, breaking the heavy manacles that had marked his slavery. Douglass, is the central figure in the four-by-six-foot mural depicting Douglass's meeting with Old John Brown (lately of Osawatomie, Kansas, and soon of Harper's Ferry, Virginia) on March 12, 1859, in Detroit. The mural includes three local figures, black and white, who were instrumental in arranging the meeting. (The courtroom mural is a photographic reproduction of the original commissioned by the International Afro-American Museum of Detroit and presented to the Detroit Public Library Commission.) On the other courtroom walls Crockett placed a photographic portrait of Dr. Martin Luther King, Jr., and prints of Charles White's portrait of Abraham Lincoln, Pablo O'Higgins's sketch of Frederick Douglass, and Mendez's painting of the Statue of Liberty.

In total contrast, until the late 1970s, the federal courtroom in Jackson, Mississippi, contained a large mural depicting happy black folks working in the cotton fields. After innumerable complaints by civil rights lawyers, a large curtain was pulled over the mural when their cases were being tried.

### 2. The Judged §1.44

The men and women of the United States come from many racial, national, religious, and cultural backgrounds. We work at many occupations that make some of us rich and powerful, many poor and powerless, and the majority of us somewhere in between. We have many quite distinct lifestyles and attitudes about birth, sex, marriage, death, taxes, accidents, and contracts. Our moral judgments differ sharply on almost every issue that comes before the civil and criminal courts, and these differences are not based solely on sectional or regional backgrounds.

We move often from one community to another and from one part of the country to another. A significant number of us are quite recent immigrants, and some are considered illegal. Many of us commit crimes against common morality and crimes against statutes passed by legislators we ourselves elected to office. We get into disputes with each other, with corporate entities, and with agencies of government, and we seek the assistance of lawyers to settle these disputes in court.

We are, in short, a multiracial, multinational, multicultural, multifaithed, litigious people who live together under one federal constitution, 50 state constitutions, and many moral codes. Our common heritage cannot be stated succinctly or appealed to quickly. Frequently our sense of fairness and justice must be uncovered; in difficult situations it often does not rise automatically to the surface.

We are subject to quite rapid shifts in attitudes on political, economic, and moral questions. Within the lifetime of each of us living in the United States today, there may be many fundamental changes in occupation, location, social position, and sense of security. Within each community, the cycle in one generation may include development, decay, redevelopment, economic failure, and despair.

In spite of our society's infinite variety, most of the people who come before the criminal courts are from the lowest economic stratum, and many are young people of color. Many civil actions also involve people from these "powerless" categories. All these plaintiffs and defendants seek what they call "justice," which they think means that their side must win. Often their cases raise issues on which society as a whole has not yet formed a majority opinion, and on which neither judges nor juries know the community conscience. (See chapter 22.)

## D. Citizens as Decision-Makers

### 1. On Grand Juries

#### a. Sample Brief: Role §1.45

*Source:* Rosenwein, "Historic Role of Grand Juries: National Lawyers Guild Amicus Brief in *Rabinowitz v United States* (Before the U.S. Court of Appeals, 5th Circuit)," 24 *Lawyers Guild Practitioner* 21 (1965).

The formative period in the history of the grand jury saw that body develop into the accusatory arm of the government. By the fourteenth century, the form of the grand jury and its function of handing down indictments was much as it is today. (See Edwards, *The Grand Jury* 27 (1906).) This function of the grand jury was soon expanded to include its more significant role—defender of the people's liberty.

The history was summarized by Mr. Justice Field, sitting as Circuit Justice, as follows:

> The institution of the grand jury is of very ancient origin in the history of England; it goes back many centuries. For a long period its powers were not clearly defined; and it would seem, from accounts of commentators on the laws of that country, that it was at first a body which not only accused, but which also tried public offenders. However this may have been in its origin, it was, at the time of the settlement of this country, an informing and accusing tribunal only .... And in the struggles which at times arose in England between the powers of the king and the rights of the king and the rights of the subject, it often stood as a barrier against persecution in his name; until, at length, it came to be regarded as an institution by which the subject was rendered secure against oppression from unfounded prosecution of the crown.

(Charge to Grand Jury, 30 Fed Cas 992, 993, No. 18,255.)

The independence of the grand jury was established by *Colledge's Case* (1681) 8 St Tr 550, and the *Earl of Shaftesbury's Case* (1681) 3 How St Tr 759. In each case, the accused was charged with treason, but the grand jury found a bill "ignoramus" (the jury knows nothing of the charge). When the jurors in *Colledge's* case were asked why they had refused to indict, the answer was that they had acted "according to their consciences and that they would stand by it."(Kuh, "The Grand Jury 'Presentment': Foul Blow or Fair Play?" 55 *Colum L Rev* 1103, 1108 (1955).)

The true significance of these early cases can best be understood when it is realized that the grand jurors' political sympathies were with the accused, not with the king. In this sentiment they had the agreement of many people. (For an extensive discussion of the early history of the grand jury, see Edwards, *The Grand Jury* 1-44 (1906). See also, Kennedy & Briggs, *Grand Jury System* 10 (1955); 55 *Colum L Rev* 1103, 1108.) The action of the jury had a dual character: it was a demonstration of independence from the government and a reflection of popular support for the accused. The king's solution to the action of the juries was the obvious: pick a new jury and get the desired indictment. This was done in the case of Stephen Colledge, who was eventually executed. (55 *Colum L Rev* 1103, 1108; Edwards, *The Grand Jury* 30.) But the grand jury had, by then, taken its place as protector of the people.

In Colonial America the grand jury was noted as an instrument of the people. The most celebrated example of the democratic role of the early American grand jury is in the case of *John Peter Zenger*. Zenger, editor and publisher of the *Weekly Journal*, a New York paper, used his paper to express antiroyalist sentiment. In 1735 a grand jury twice refused to indict him for libel. (Edwards, *The Grand Jury* 32.) Again, the grand jury acted as an instrument of the people: as a barrier against oppression. Its primary concern at the time of the *Zenger* trial was to insure liberty and freedom of the press for the people.

By the end of the Colonial period in American history, the grand jury had established itself as an indispensable arm of democratic government. Juries "enforced or refused to enforce laws as they saw fit and stood guard against indiscriminate prosecution by royal officials." (Younger, *The People's Panel* 26 (1963).) The colonists were so firmly convinced that the grand jury was "a necessary and fundamental safeguard of individual rights against governmental oppression" (Case note: "The Propriety of Holding a Grand Jury in Contempt of Court," 17 *U Miami L Rev* 110, 112 (1962)) that they overtly manifested such belief in the Fifth and Sixth Amendments of the United States Constitution.

The importance of the grand jury as an instrument of democracy did not end with the revolution. Grand juries supervised law enforcement activities of sheriffs and constables, and watched the activities of public officials. "At the time of the Alien and Sedition trials Judge Harry Innes advised a Frankfort, Kentucky, grand jury that its proper place was 'as a strong barrier between the supreme power of the government and the citizens,' rather than as an instrument of the state. . . . Innes told the grand jurors that their duty was to shield the innocent from 'unjust persecutions.' " (Younger, *The People's Panel*, 54–55.)

From the early post-Revolutionary days to the present, grand juries have been thought of as a means of protecting citizens from injustice. Again, in the words of Justice Field:

> In this country, from the popular character of our institutions, there has seldom been any contest between the government and the citizen, which required the existence of the grand jury as a protection against oppressive action of the government. Yet the institution was adopted in this country . . . from considerations similar to those which gave it its chief value in England, and is designed as a means, not only of bringing to trial persons accused of public offenses upon just grounds, but also as a means of protecting the citizen against unfounded accusation, whether it come from government or be prompted by partisan passion or private enmity . . . .
>
> . . . [T]here is a double duty cast upon [the] jurors of this district; one a duty to the government, or more properly speaking, to society, to see that parties against whom there is a just ground to charge the commission of a crime, shall be held to answer the charge; and on the other hand, a duty to the citizen to see that he is not subjected to prosecution upon accusations having no better foundation than public clamor or private malice.

(30 Fed Cas at 993. See also *Beck v Washington* (1962) 369 US 541, 582 [dissenting opinon]; *Hale v Henkel* (1906) 201 US 43, 59.)

In *Rabinowitz v United States* the white student defendant successfully challenged the racial composition of the federal grand jury (5th Cir 1966) 366 F2d 34.

### b. Sample Brief: Representative Character §1.46

*Source:* Rosenwein, "Historic Role of Grand Juries: National Lawyers Guild Amicus Brief in *Rabinowitz v United States* (Before the U.S.

Court of Appeals, 5th Circuit)," 24 *Lawyers Guild Practitioner* 21, 25 (1965).

Two significant characteristics of the grand jury have made it possible for that institution to function "as a safeguard against arbitrary or oppressive action." *United States v Wells* (1908) 163 F 313, 324. Secrecy is the first of these.... The other feature of importance is the grand jury's representative character. The earliest American grand juries were elected, usually by the town meeting. They reflected the revolutionary tenor of the colonists, and were in the lead in opposing the imperial government. (Younger, *The People's Panel* 27 (1963).)

The broad, popular character of the grand jury of the frontier is described by Younger (*The People's Panel* 74–75) as follows:

> Jurymen were indistinguishable from other persons gathered at the county seat to trade and enjoy themselves. The only thing that set them apart from their neighbors was the summons they had received from the sheriff, telling them to appear for grand jury duty at the approaching session of the court. In most western territories and states the clerk of the court chose the grand jurors by lot from the list of eligible persons... All qualified electors were eligible for jury duty in most western areas. In only a few states was land ownership a prerequisite. However, as in the Colonial period, the requirements were not high. Preemption claimants and those who had made their first payment on government land were regarded as landowners.

The relationship of the composition of the grand jury to its function was recognized by Chief Justice Shaw, Supreme Judicial Court of Massachusetts:

> Coming from the various parts of the county, first designated by their townsmen, as persons well fitted by their capacity, integrity, and personal worth of character, to discharge the important functions of jurors, and then for each particular service, designated by lot, without regard to sect or party, rank or condition, the Grand Jury may justly be regarded as a fair representation of the county, participating in all the interests and feelings of the people, and well acquainted with their condition and circumstances. They bring with them all the local knowledge and information, which are requisite to enable them to perform their important duties with efficiency, impartiality, and success.

(Charge to Grand Jury, 8 *AM Jurist* 216 (1832).)

The modern grand jury is thought to be as much a representative of the people as it was in the past:

"A grand jury is a short-lived, representative, nonpolitical body of citizens functioning without hope of personal aggrandizement. It comes from the citizens at large and soon disappears into its anonymity .... "
(Weinstein and Shaw, "Grand Jury Reports—A Safeguard of Democracy," 1962 *Wash U LQ* 191.)

The historical position of the jury, in this case the grand jury, has been recognized by the Supreme Court. Thus, it has been said: "It is a part of the established tradition in the use of juries as instruments of public justice that the jury be a body truly representative of the community." *Smith v Texas* (1940) 311 US 128, 130. To the same effect is *Thiel v Southern Pac. Co.* (1946) 328 US 217, 220.

Unless a grand jury has been selected in a manner which permits it to carry out its historic function—people's representative and guardian against oppression—it is respectfully submitted it has been improperly selected.

The challenge to the racial composition of the federal grand jury was won by the white student defendant in *Rabinowitz v United States* (5th Cir 1966) 366 F2d 34.

For a discussion of modern grand juries and their critics, see chapter 23.

## 2. On Trial Juries §1.47

*Source:* Tocqueville, section on trial by jury in part I of *Democracy in America* 127 (Heffner ed., Mentor ed., 1956).

Since my subject has led me to speak of the administration of justice in the United States, I will not pass over it without adverting to the institution of the jury. Trial by jury may be considered in two separate points of view; as a judicial, and as a political institution . . . .

My present purpose is to consider the jury as a political institution . . . . It would be a very narrow view to look upon the jury as a mere judicial institution; for, however great its influence may be upon the decisions of the courts, it is still greater on the destinies of society at large. The jury is, above all, a political institution, and it must be regarded in this light in order to be duly appreciated. By the jury, I mean a certain number of citizens chosen by lot, and invested with a temporary right of judging. Trial by jury, as applied to the repression of crime, appears to me an eminently republican element in the government, for the following reasons:

The institution of the jury may be aristocratic or democratic, according to the class from which the jurors are taken; but it always preserves its republican character, in that it places the real direction of society in the hands of the governed, or of a portion of the governed, and not in that of the government. Force is never more than a transient element of success, and after force, comes the notion of right. A government which should be able to reach its enemies only upon a field of battle would soon be destroyed. The true sanction of political laws is to be found in penal legislation; and if that sanction be wanting, the law will sooner or later lose its cogency. He who punishes the criminal is therefore the real master of society.

Now, the institution of the jury raises the people itself, or at least a class of citizens, to the bench of judges. The institution of the jury consequently invests the people, or that class of citizens, with the direction of society .... The jury cannot fail to exercise a powerful influence upon the national character .... The jury ... serves to communicate the spirit of the judges to the minds of all the citizens; and this spirit, with the habits which attend it, is the soundest preparation for free institutions. It imbues all classes with a respect for the thing judged, and with the notion of right. If these two elements be removed, the love of independence becomes a mere destructive passion. It teaches men to practice equity; every man learns to judge his neighbor as he would himself be judged. And this is especially true to the jury in civil causes; for, whilst the number of persons who have reason to apprehend a criminal prosecution is small, every one is liable to have a lawsuit. The jury teaches every man not to recoil before the responsibility of his own actions, and impresses him with that manly confidence without which no political virtue can exist. It invests each citizen with a kind of magistracy; it makes them all feel the duties which they are bound to discharge towards society, and the part which they take in its government. By obliging men to turn their attention to other affairs than their own, it rubs off that private selfishness which is the rust of society.

The jury contributes powerfully to form the judgment and to increase the natural intelligence of a people; and thus, in my opinion, is its greatest advantage. It may be regarded as a gratuitous public school, ever open, in which every juror learns his rights, enters into daily communication with the most learned and enlightened members of the upper classes, and becomes practically acquainted with the laws, which are brought within the reach of his capacity by the efforts of the bar, the advice of the judge, and even by the passions of the parties. I think that the practical intelligence and political good sense of the Americans are mainly attributable to the long use which they have made of the jury in civil causes ....

The jury, then, which seems to restrict the rights of the judiciary, does in reality consolidate its power; and in no country are the judges so powerful as where the people share their privileges. It is especially by means of the jury in civil causes, that the American magistrates imbue even the lower classes of society with the spirit of their profession. Thus the jury, which is the most energetic means of making the people rule, is also the most efficacious means of teaching it how to rule well.

### E. New Developments §1.49

See §1.36.

## VI. PRACTICAL ADVANTAGES OF JURY TRIALS

### A. To the People as a Whole §1.51

It may be that the proudest boast of our society is its jury system—its willingness to let 12 people from the community judge both sides in civil and criminal trials. Since trials are held really to determine the ethical standards the society is prepared to enforce at a given moment in a given place, jury trials give jurors tremendous power. A series of acquittals in hard-fought felony trials indicates that the prosecutors are out of step with the people. Large plaintiffs' verdicts in personal injury cases indicate that insurance companies missed the people's mood. Jury verdicts are probably more accurate than Gallup polls in showing attitudes toward the judicial system as presently administered.

A well-tried jury case is one in which the citizens on the jury have had time to adjust to their new jobs as decision makers, and the other participants have had time to reveal themselves to the jurors so that something akin to the truth emerges. In a well-tried case, the jurors are permitted to fulfill their function to decide the case based on the law as given to them by the judge and the facts as they perceive them after hearing direct and cross-examination of witnesses and arguments by counsel, using that particular quality for which the jurors were selected—their reflection of the conscience of the community.

This ideal is, of course, elusive. How often it is achieved depends on a great many factors and actors. But it is a significant goal in a society in which, on occasion, fewer than half the people entitled to vote in popular elections bother to do so, and in which even fewer people participate in other forms of political action unless society is in crisis.

Richard A. Villalobos made the same point, particularly as to members of minority groups, in "Grand Jury Discrimination and the Mexican American," 5 *Loyola U L Rev* 87, 121 (1972):

> Selection as a grand or petit juror presents the sole opportunity for the average citizen to actively participate in the administration of government. Jury service is a fundamental prerogative of citizenship. The opportunity to participate in government through service as a grand or petit juror has been found to be one of profound psychological importance to minority persons. Studies have shown that minority groups are more likely to feel they belong to the community and society if they are available or called as jurors. Such involvement has a profound impact on their attitude toward law and the system of justice in this country. However, since minorities are continuously excluded or greatly underrepresented, their confidence and trust in government deteriorates, while, as "legal outcasts," their sense of inferiority and alienation grows.

Lawrence Speiser, while director of the National Capital Area American Civil Liberties Union, testified to the "persuasive evidence that jury service is a powerful means of education in the democratic process, even for those previously apathetic about their civil responsibilities," before the Subcommittee on Improvements in Judicial Machinery of the Senate Committee on the Judiciary, 90th Congress, 1st Session, p. 334 (1967).

Stated from a different viewpoint: citizen participation in deciding the fate of a person charged with commission of a crime makes it easier for the defendant's family and friends to accept the verdict. The defendant could accept a guilty verdict, sentence, and fine more easily if the jurors were people like himself. When the crime had a victim, the victim and the victim's family could accept a verdict of not guilty or guilty of a lesser offense more readily when meted out by people like themselves than when issued by someone from a different stratum of society. The parallel point applies to civil cases.

In both criminal and civil cases, justice must satisfy the appearance of justice. This places a grave responsibility on the courts in highly publicized trials to ensure that "no one be punished for a crime without a [trial] free of prejudice, passion [or] excitement . . . "(*Sheppard v Maxwell* (1966) 384 US 333, 350). Courts can meet this responsibility only through scrupulous regard for fairness in proceedings that have a significant political or public interest component. Justice Frankfurter succinctly articulated the controlling principle: "[J]ustice must satisfy the appearance of justice." *Offutt v United States* (1954) 348 US 11, 14. The difficulty of maintaining both the reality of fairness and the appearance of fairness is at its greatest in a political or public-interest trial. See, *e.g.*, *Illinois v Allen* (1970) 397 US 337, 352–356 (Douglas, J.). But precisely because government may well be defending itself and its most basic values, it is essential that the proceedings satisfy the "tremendous psychological need for the appearance of justice which a fair trial creates in the public mind." Arnold, "The Criminal Trial as a Symbol of Public Morality," in *Criminal Justice in Our Time* 137, 140 (Howard ed 1965). Unless this standard is met, political cases become not symbols of the best the system has to offer, but symbols of the worst—arduous and capricious justice, political justice. Compare, *e.g.*, *Massachusetts v Sacco* (1926) 255 Mass 369, 151 NE 839; (1927) 259 Mass 128, 156 NE 57; (1927) 261 Mass 12, 158 NE 167; Frankfurter, *The Case of Sacco and Vanzetti* (1927).

The necessity that justice satisfy the appearance of justice is especially great when the plaintiffs or defendants have exercised leadership roles in their communities. Special caution is necessary in order to combat the findings of numerous commissions that have investigated the image of the courts in minority communities. In the 1960s, the Kerner Commission found that "The belief is pervasive among ghetto residents that lower courts in our urban communities dispense 'assembly-line' justice" and that "the apparatus of justice in some areas has itself become a focus for distrust and hostility." *US National Advisory Commission on Civil Disorders Report*, 183 (1968). In California, the San Francisco Committee on Crime found that: "Many residents of minority communities . . . distrust the criminal justice system as a manifestation of a white-dominated power structure having little interest in protecting minority rights or interest." *Report on the San Francisco Public Defender's Office* 14 (Oct. 22, 1970). The United States Commission on Civil Rights did an exhaustive study of the experience of Mexican-Americans with the administration of justice in California and other states and found that: "Mexican Americans are distrustful of the courts and believe them to be insensitive to Mexican American background and culture." *Mexican Americans and the Administration of Justice in the Southwest* 62 (March 1970).

These negative attitudes about the judicial system can change when jurors in highly publicized cases carry out their civic duty in a responsible fashion. For example, nine white Alabama jurors voted with three black jurors to convict a 73-year-old former Ku Klux Klansman of murder in the dynamite explosion that killed four young black girls at a black Birmingham church in 1963. The possibility of blacks sitting on the jury played a role in bringing the case to trial 14 years after the event. (The defense had used peremptory challenges against as many blacks as possible; the prosecution had used peremptories against whites older than 50.) *NY Times*, Nov. 19, 1977, at 1; *Chambliss v Alabama* (Ala Ct of Crim App) 373 So 2d 1185. Two years later, 22 white grand jurors voted with 1 black juror to indict a white village police officer on charges of second degree manslaughter in the fatal shooting of an 18-year-old black youth. The NAACP had marched outside the Westchester County, New York, courthouse because members did not believe that a jury with only one black would bring such an indictment. *NY Times*, Aug. 29, 1979.

## B. To Litigants §1.52

*California v Savio* is a classic example of the mistake in trying significant social questions before a judge alone. The case arose out of the Free Speech Movement (FSM) at the University of California at Berkeley in 1964. The local police made almost 800 misdemeanor arrests during efforts by students to put tables at the entrance to the university in order to collect money and support for the emerging movement for civil rights among southern black students, and for other social and political causes.

The suggested trial alternatives all seemed, to the defense, to be bad:

1. One massive jury trial of 765 defendants
2. A series of 80 jury trials of approximately ten defendants each
3. A nonjury trial of all defendants
4. A series of nonjury trials of ten defendants each

The second alternative had been followed during the same period in the San Francisco sit-in cases arising out of efforts to get blacks hired in hotels and auto sales rooms. 474 defendants were tried, with attendant difficulties in finding defense counsel, etc. (well-described by Marvin Stender in *The Relevant Lawyers* 313 (Ginger, ed. 1972)). The results are analyzed in "San Francisco Sit-In Trials," 24 *Lawyers Guild Practitioner* 10 (1956).

The FSM defense finally moved for a representative jury trial of a smaller number of defendants (perhaps 150), with the fate of the remaining defendants to be the same as those tried. The judge and prosecutor set a price on this alternative: it had to be a nonjury trial. The defense reluctantly agreed because the trial judge had certain unusual qualities: he had been a defense lawyer, not a prosecutor; his record in the community and on the bench indicated he was not prejudiced against students or young people; and he had no known conservative affiliations. In addition, the defendants had little money for fees and could not find enough lawyers to handle 80 jury trials.

The result, however, was disasterous. Nine experienced defense lawyers conducted an orderly trial, after which the judge convicted all defendants on one or two misdemeanor counts, meted out jail sentences arbitrarily among the defendants, and did not write an opinion containing rulings on points of law that the defense could use in preparing an appeal. Despite a many-faceted defense presented in a massive appellate brief (445 pages), the district court of appeal affirmed in a one paragraph opinion. The California Supreme Court refused to hear the appeal, as did the United States Supreme Court (*cert. denied* (1967) 388 US 460). (Copies of the unusual brief are available from Meiklejohn Civil Liberties Institute, Box 673, Berkeley, California 94701.)

This outcome led masses of students and their friends to conclude that freedom of speech will not be protected in courts, and that judicial proceedings are rigged or absurd. These opinions were soon spread throughout the country among students and other exercisers of First Amendment rights.

The jury trial of Dan White in 1979, also in the San Francisco area, taught counsel the same lesson as *Savio*, in reverse. White, former San Francisco police officer and member of the Board of Supervisors, was charged with the first degree murders of liberal Mayor George Moscone and gay Supervisor Harvey Milk. The defense attorney did not seek a change of venue from San Francisco. The voir dire by both sides was brief and superficial. The jury voted unanimously that White was not guilty of murder and was guilty of voluntary manslaughter. This verdict touched off massive demonstrations in San Francisco by people charging that White was really guilty of first degree murder and that the district attorney had not prosecuted the case vigorously. See, *e.g.*, *SF Chronicle*, May 26, 1979, at 1. White's release on parole in January 1984 was assured when the U.S. Attorney for northern California rejected petitions to prosecute White under the federal Civil Rights Act. For an interesting study on this subject, see Baldwin and McConville, "Doubtful Convictions by Jury," *Crim L Rev* 230 (Apr 1979) (5% of British convictions studied were doubtful verdicts, in the eyes of the police, prosecutors, and judges, as well as defendants).

### C. To Lawyers §1.53

In addition to the political and philosophical advantages of trial by a jury of peers, or at least from a cross-section of the community, there are certain practical advantages in trying a case to a jury instead of to a judge. The major tactical advantage is the leeway it gives the judge to make improper and prejudicial rulings on motions and to give erroneous instructions.

Perhaps the major types of reversible error connected with jury selection are the following, listed in more-or-less chronological order:

1. Improper methods of selecting grand jurors (see chapter 6).
2. Denial of change of venue due to community prejudice (see chapter 7).
3. Improper methods of selecting petit jurors (see chapter 6).
4. Improper limitations on voir dire of prospective jurors (see chapter 8).
5. Refusal to dismiss when impossible to empanel unprejudiced jurors (see chapter 7).
6. Failure to grant mistrial due to events during trial that would prejudice jurors (such as media circus condemned in *Sheppard v Maxwell* (1966) 384 US 333).
7. Prejudicial statements by judge in presence of jury (see dismissal of *United States v Powell and Schuman* (ND Cal 1958) (unreported), described in Doris Walker, "The Class Role of US Courts," *Lawyers Guild Practitioner* 41, 45 (1974)).
8. Failure to give proper instructions to jury (*Yates v United States* (1957) 354 US 298; *California v Newton* (Dist Ct App 1970) 8 Cal App 3d 359).

In a criminal case, the prosecution is more likely to present "spectacular" witnesses telling "bizarre" stories when seeking to convince a jury rather than a judge. (See, e.g., angry reversal by the United States Supreme Court in *Mesarosh v United States* (1956) 352 US 1.)

Numerous other types of reversible errors occur in dealing with jurors, e.g., decisions not to sequester jurors, prejudicial comments by court personnel during sequestration, improper instructions during deliberations pressuring jurors to reach a verdict, and improper treatment by counsel in the presence of the jury. (These do not relate to jury selection and, therefore, are outside the scope of this book.)

All these advantages may flow to a bumbling trial novice, as well as to a veteran, since these are mistakes made by trial judges, often without any help from counsel.

Jury trials are full of opportunities for each participant to rise to the occasion, or to falter. As a result, they are intriguing to many lawyers, terrifying to others. There are no secrets in a long jury trial. The jurors get to know the most intimate details about every person in the courtroom who is on public view. A lawyer cannot hide attitudes on a wide range of subjects, nor can a judge. The parties are also subjected to microscopic inspection by 12 curious people, and so are the witnesses. In a short trial, these viewing sessions are truncated and the truth—the secrets—may never come out. On the other hand, a determined judge, or determined lawyers, can, even in a short trial, cut through the forms and trappings of fair procedure to lay bare the heart of the controversy. To win frequently requires this kind of open heart surgery.

Whenever a lawyer decides to try a case to a jury, the lawyer is submitting to the will of people who are not like the lawyer, that is, they are not trained in law school. This means that the jurors are not trained in the Socratic method, they are not taught to think in logical terms from certain premises, they are not all experts, but they believe in their ability to come to decisions on the basis of what they call their "common sense" or "instincts." A lawyer who tries a case to a jury did not learn how to do this in the traditional law school class and has had no law school training in psychology or acting. Whatever the lawyer knows about trying a case to a jury was learned by trial and error, after graduation from school.

Too often this results in the blind lawyer seeking to lead the blind jurors. This exasperates the trial judge, who wishes to stop the charade and take over voir dire. The trial of a case before a jury does involve a unique blend of legal theory and practice. It requires playing to the gallery while making a sophisticated record to use on appeal in the event of a negative verdict. It combines oral and written skills, legal technicalities and social policy, statutory interpretation and use of the rules of evidence, plus common sense, folk wisdom, and appeals to the community conscience.

In recent decades many middle-class, white male lawyers have come to the view that jury trials are essential to the legal system in a democracy and are the only hope of achieving a modicum of justice in individual cases. Their sons and daughters are sometimes arrested as juveniles or young adults for a variety of acts currently labeled crimes; their business clients are arrested on criminal charges ranging from vehicular offenses to illegal campaign contributions; their social consciences lead them to work on cases involving prisoners' rights or revolts in ghetto areas in the major cities; one of their best clients has a personal injury case. Each spring new law graduates join them in the lists.

Frequently they face proposals to limit jury trials in their bar associations. In California, the issue of drastically changing the nature and extent of jury trials has been debated in the integrated state bar association (to which every lawyer must belong). In the early 1970s, an ad hoc Select Committee on Trial Court Delay, funded in large part by the Law Enforcement Assistance Administration (LEAA), was appointed by the chief justice and the governor. It consisted of a criminal court judge, a probation officer, a chief of police; none of the members was a criminal defense lawyer. It produced a series of reports including seven suggestions to eliminate, restrict, or change the nature of criminal jury trials:

1. Six-member juries should be used in all criminal cases except where the offense charged would be punishable by death or a maximum sentence of life imprisonment.
2. A five-sixths majority should be able to convict in all except capital cases.
3. Voir dire of prospective jurors by counsel should be restricted.
4. The number of peremptory challenges should be reduced.
5. Moving traffic violations of a nonserious nature should be reclassified as infractions, thereby eliminating the right to jury trial.
6. Videotaped depositions should be allowed of some witnesses. (Such depositions have been allowed under Rule 30(b)(4) of the Federal Rules of Civil Procedure. *Carson v Burlington Northern, Inc.* (D Neb 1971) 52 FRD 492).
7. Counsel in major felony trials should be required to be certified.

The San Francisco Bay Area Chapter of the National Lawyers Guild introduced a resolution opposing the first four changes at the Conference of Delegates of the California State Bar, an annual meeting where proposed statutory changes are debated by 500 delegates and alternates from all accredited state bar associations. The Guild argued:

> The Constitution of California preserves the right to jury trial as it existed at common law in 1850. These proposals would make a fundamental change in

our organic law without evidence of any necessity for it. The Select Committee proposes that we emasculate constitutional and statutory safeguards against unjust conviction not because the present system is inadequate, but because convictions are not obtained with speed satisfactory to the Committee. No fundamental change in criminal trial procedure should be based upon such a consideration.

National Lawyers Guild statement on Resolution 1-14, Sept. 25, 1972. The delegates overwhelmingly approved the Guild resolution.

"Attempts to restrict, erode or dilute the Constitutionally-guaranteed right to a jury trial should be vigorously rebuffed. The American jury system provides sufficient uniformity and predictability in its verdicts, and, at the same time, gives sufficient expression to the wish of the American people for individualized justice." These were the primary findings of the lawyers, judges, professors, and interdisciplinary students of the jury system participating in the Annual Chief Justice Earl Warren Conference sponsored by the Roscoe Pound-American Trial Lawyers Foundation, June 24-25, 1977.

Lower verdicts for black plaintiffs in civil cases were the rule when all-white juries were impaneled, according to Charles Carter, attorney for the NAACP, speaking at the conference. "I don't want to see juries abolished just when we are getting juries changed to include blacks and other minorities. It is almost an insult for a black lawyer to try a personal injury case for a black plaintiff if everyone knows the verdict will be less because the plaintiff is black." See *The American Jury System: A Final Report* 17 (1978) available from the Trial Lawyers Foundation, 1050 31st Street, N.W., Washington, D.C. 20007.

Governors, presidents, legislators, and judges who are basically opposed to jury trials sometimes begin by arguing that government budget cuts, as well as efficiency, necessitate a cut in jury size, and in jury use.

Supporters of jury trials reply in many ways, usually citing the history and effectiveness of juries in deciding disputes to the satisfaction of the general public.

As the United States moves toward the 21st century, there are broad opportunities for selection of fair-minded jurors in many types of criminal and civil cases. Many citizens have been shaken in their assumption that the government always obeys its own laws. They wonder whether the United States conducts its foreign policy properly (in Vietnam, Chile, South Africa, the Caribbean, the Middle East, and elsewhere); some question whether reliance on nuclear weapons and cold war are valid premises of foreign policy. Citizens have learned the major lesson of Watergate: a healthy skepticism toward government pronouncements and actions. On the domestic level, the civil rights movement and the black power and other struggles of the 1970s and 1980s have succeeded in that most people are willing to vote for black candidates for office—a long step forward from refusal even to admit blacks to voter registration or jury lists in the 1950s. The general public has discovered the positive contributions to society of young men with long hair and of young women in slacks. This has also confused old images of who in the coming generation should be trusted.

These characteristics make for good, independent-minded jurors, to whom a case must be well-proved.

People in power often have temendous doubts about what "the public" actually would think of them if it knew them up close. Many have a profound fear of the public, caused by or combined with contempt. To such people a jury represents "the great unwashed": perhaps a Mr. Dooley will get on the jury; at worst Huck Finn's father; at best, the Widow Douglas. This view is quite sound. These days the jury in any major city must include the nephew of a W.E.B. DuBois, the niece of a Rosa Parks, or the cousins of a Cesar Chavez, a William Winpisinger, a Russell Means, and a Bella Abzug. Participants in jury trials must ask: How will such jurors react to the facts and the law in this case?

A criminal jury judges not only the defendant and defense counsel but also, of necessity, the prosecution—evaluating the prosecuting attorney, government witnesses, the prosecutor's ideology, style, and views of justice, as part of its deliberations about the accused. The jurors must surely ask themselves: "Why did the district attorney bring this case to trial?" A civil jury considers the attorneys for insurance carriers as well as plaintiff's counsel, and asks, "Why didn't they settle this case without trial?"

These jurors, and these questions, help keep the jury system functioning effectively, for lawyers, litigants, and society as a whole.

## D. To Judges §1.54

During his term on the United States Supreme Court, Justice William O. Douglas concluded (*We, the Judges* 389 (1956)):

> A jury reflects the attitudes and mores of the community from which it is drawn. It lives only for the day and does justice according to its limits. The group of 12, who are drawn to hear a case, makes a decision and melts away. It is not present the next day to be criticzed. It is the one governmental agency that has no ambition. It is as human as the people who make it up. It is sometimes the victim of passion. But it also takes the sharp edges off the law and uses conscience to ameliorate a hardship. Since it is of and from the community, it gives the law an acceptance which verdicts of judges cannot do.

After the long and dramatic trial of Angela Davis (see §3.23), the jury deliberated and acquitted the defendant. Trial judge Richard Arnason made a short speech to the jurors, concluding with a quotation from G.K. Chesterton (*Tremendous Trifles* 86 (1920)):

> Our civilization has decided, and very justly decided, that determining the guilt or innocence of men is a thing too important to be trusted to trained men. It wishes for light upon that awful matter, it asks men who know no more law than I know, but who can feel the things that I felt in the jury box. When it wants a library catalogued, or the solar system discovered, or any trifle of that kind, it uses up its specialists. But when it wishes anything done which is really serious, it collects twelve of the ordinary men standing round. The same thing was done, if I remember right, by the Founder of Christianity.

This understanding of the significance of jury trials is obviously shared by many though not all state and federal judges.

## E. To Jurors §1.55

A middle-aged, middle-class, white, suburban woman—on the surface the kind of juror to be challenged for cause or peremptorily in the typical criminal case—was so deeply affected by her service as jury foreperson in a felony trial that she broadcast her own charge to the triers of fact:

"It is our implementation of justice that is on trial now and it is we who are the jurors: those who have served in the jury boxes and in the jails, those yet to be called and yet to be accused, those who never expect to become involved. Deliberation is needed. We must bring in a verdict."

She declares her own conclusion:

"Power to the jury!"

Mary Timothy, wife of a lawyer, parent of a son and two daughters seeking to find their way in the last half of the twentieth century, grew from a conscientious citizen prepared to do her civic duty into the foreperson of the *Angela Davis* jury and ardent advocate of the jury system in the United States. Her book, *Jury Woman*, is excellent reading the night before trying a front-page case. (Available from Volcano Press, 330 Ellis Street, San Francisco, CA 94102.)

The success of juries has been lauded by other jurors whose lives were so affected, and changed, by their jury service that they were impelled to describe their experiences in books and interviews.

Melvyn Bernard Zerman, a juror who deliberated with his fellows for ten hours to reach a not guilty verdict in a murder case, summed up his impressions in *Call the Final Witness* 162–163 (1977):

> Beyond unpredictability is the capacity to rise to a challenge. Serving on the jury was exactly that to each of us; we all recognized that more was being demanded of us—in the way of wisdom, if nothing else—than had often—perhaps ever—been demanded of us before. Some of us were almost embarrassed to be in the position we were. Some of us, when the deliberations grew fierce, were afraid. As we had been warned repeatedly during the *voir dire*, this was not Perry Mason stuff. Anyone who might have waited for the real murderer of Edward Fendt to be suddenly and dramatically exposed would have waited in vain. But we were too serious, too dedicated, even to entertain such thoughts. There was never a time during the deliberations when we lost sight of the reality that confronted us. And for me there was never a time when I doubted that all of us—the holdouts included—were trying to deal with that reality as responsibly as our intelligence and our human understanding allowed.
>
> To paraphrase Bernard Shaw's Eliza Doolittle, the difference between an ordinary man and a juror is not how he behaves, but how he's regarded. This, it seems to me, is the key to the success of the jury system in criminal trials. If a person, whatever his background, knows that much is expected of him—no less than helping to determine the course of someone else's life—in all probability that person will strive with all his capabilty to be wise and just and compassionate, to stretch himself beyond his foibles and his prejudices. One thing you can be sure of: he will not forget that the stakes are high.

A juror who spent almost two years in the *San Quentin Six* trial (see §2.21) said, a year after the trial ended:

> It was the hardest thing I ever had to do. . . . I think about it all the time.

He and his fellow jurors acquitted three defendants outright and voted only 6 guilty verdicts out of a possible 46. He said:

> . . . It has definitely changed my life, my way of thinking about law and justice—and especially about prisons. . . . There are . . . so many ways in which the black-and-white of law does not seem to fit the reality of life. Prison life in particular.

*SF Chronicle*, Aug. 13, 1977, at 4.

After *San Francisco Chronicle* reporter Maitland Zane described his experiences as a juror in a "typical" misdemeanor case, the staff concluded editorially that "the sometimes maligned system really works." Zane found the panel varied, attentive, and serious. They "approached their task of passing judgment with seriousness and dedication." The *Chronicle* applauded: "That there are flaws in the jury system is undeniable; but on the whole it fits into the definition of democracy as a form of government: It is the worst system of government possible, but what else is better?" *SF Chronicle*, Nov. 22, 1977.

I have never met a person who had served on a jury who didn't want to talk about it. Jury duty is a major event in the life of any citizen. It is an unforgettable experience, whether it ends in frustration (as when the case is taken from the jury before a verdict), in victory (when the particular juror's viewpoint prevails), or in defeat (when the juror's viewpoint is rejected and a loathsome compromise is finally reached).

A 1976 study of 3000 jurors in 18 court systems found that 90 percent had a favorable reaction to jury duty. Tom Munsterman maintains that "Jury duty is like motherhood." Munsterman is executive director of the Center for Jury Studies, a private, nonprofit research organization in McLean, Virginia. He found that "People are for it. If we don't get an 80 percent favorable response in any particular court, that court is in deep trouble." See Pabst and Munsterman, "The Value of Jury Duty: Serving Is Believing," 61 *Judicature* 38–42 (1977).

A New York City executive/juror told *Time* magazine:

> It is a major responsibility to reach a verdict, and every jury I have served on has taken the responsibility very seriously. Twelve strangers meet by chance in this strange process, learn to work together, reason together, and finally reach a conclusion that may be crucial in the lives of others. When you achieve this, you feel you have really accomplished something. It brings out the best in most people.

*Time*, Sept. 28, 1981.

The juror is under tremendous pressures that have seldom been mentioned by judges and commentators. They were described very clearly by Ralph Davis and Barbara Lyles in discussing their jury duty in Los Angeles County in 1973 at a Citizens Conference on Racism and the Law, sponsored by the Greater Watts Justice Center, American Civil Liberties Union, National Lawyers Guild, Langston Law Club, and National Conference of Black Lawyers. See Davis and Lyles, "Black Jurors," 30 *Lawyers Guild Practitioner* 111 (1974). These two outspoken jurors stated that while they were aware of the race of the defendant in each case, this was not the decisive factor in determining guilt or innocence. At the same time, being black made them privy to knowledge about various areas in the community that was not available to the average white juror. For example, the second case on which Mr. Davis sat involved a young black man charged with grand theft of an auto.

> It seemed like the only reason that they arrested the defendant was that someone in the gas station across the street looking out into the light in the dark could identify the run-of-the-mill black man from 90 to 100 feet away. They arrested him in the area of York Boulevard. I was raised . . . in Los Angeles, so it is nothing new to me. If you are black and you're on York Boulevard at 4 o'clock in the morning they are going to pick you up. They will pick *me* up

on York Boulevard walking at 4:00 in the morning. This was the only thing that they seemed to have against the man, so we acquitted him.

Ms. Lyles said that at first she considered jury duty as a way to avoid going to work while being paid some money. But as she sat in the jury box and watched the voir dire in several cases, she changed her mind: "I didn't have too many problems dealing with the courts and the D.A. or the defense attorney. My problem was dealing with the people in deliberation. Because I must have really shocked them. They expected less out of me than what I gave them." She concluded:

> All I have to say is that being there on jury duty and serving, I have met different people from all walks of life and enjoyed it very much, and I think that it is something that everyone should get involved in, and when you receive that piece of paper, that questionnaire, return it. If at any time you do get a summons, and you can't serve at that time, you can always get another date. Call and make some arrangements—don't just shove it off. A lot of people do a lot of complaining and nobody wants to do anything about it, and I think it is your duty to complain about things you do care about, but don't sit back at home and say, "I don't want to be bothered." When you go down and serve the jury duty, you are only one in who knows how many people, but you have done your part regardless of which way the case goes.
>
> Be confident in yourself that you have made the right decision and don't get swayed by all the little tricks and names and little things they hook you up into, and all the little personal conflicts that people always say aren't present, but that's impossible. When people are involved there has to be personal conflicts, especially when there are 12 jurors. And with me being a minority juror that was automatically a conflict, right there.

See further comments in §8.22.

Juror satisfaction with jury service is directly related to the ability actually to serve, that is, to decide cases. Studies show that "jurors who sit on one or more trials leave jury duty highly satisfied and impressed with the justice system. Satisfaction is higher when a juror has heard two trials rather than one. Conversely, jurors who never sit on a trial tend to leave jury duty either without strong feelings, or resentful about their service." Graham and Pope, "Jury Mangement Systems," 45 *Missouri L Rev* 277 (1980). For a discussion of ways to improve the use of jurors, and to meet other major objections to jury service (*e.g.*, loss of privacy, low pay), see chapter 23.

## F. To Democratic Government §1.56

Everyone knows that a jury is locked up during its deliberations so that no lobbyist can reach it, no special interest can offer money or power or fame for voting one way or another. More than that. It is common knowledge that in "big" cases the jury is sequestered from the very beginning, so that it will be untouched by current pressures, leaving the jurors to make their decisions based on their own past experiences and beliefs and on what they see and hear in the courtroom. And it is known that jury tampering is a crime and one that is seldom practiced.

In fact, the jury is the closest thing to democratic governance we have invented to meet the needs of decision-making in our pluralistic society. Juries sit while members of the House and Senate in Washington are under constant pressure by lobbyists who promise money and power if legislators will vote with them on a particular issue. Juries sit while the president and his cabinet are bombarded with offers of support or electoral defeat if they will make certain administrative and political decisions. The same pressures are at play on officials in the state and local governments, as juries deliberate in sequestered settings.

Paul Ligda, a California lawyer, summed up the other important features of trials by jury in "Viva La Jury," 49 *Cal SBJ* 453 (1974):

> The possibility of a jury trial exerts a stabilizing influence upon all who may eventually come before it. The policeman's arrest and investigation are guided by the prospective jury's perception of his actions. In reviewing the results of that investigation and deciding whether and what to charge, the prosecutor necessarily considers how a jury will accept the defendant's version of the facts. In each instance, the mere potentiality of examination before twelve unbiased citizens acts as a brake against arbitrary or outlandish behavior. The restraint which the jury imposes against governmental overreaching is a foundation stone of our constitutional system. (As Thomas Jefferson said in his First Inaugural Address: "Equal and exact justice to all men, of whatever state or persuasion . . . freedom of the person under the protection of the *habeas corpus*, and trial by juries impartially selected. These principles form the bright constellation which has gone before us, and guided our steps through an age of revolution and reformation. . . . ")
>
> . . .
>
> The jury trial also remains one of the best opportunities for the legal system to display its sincere, unbiased, and unhurried search for the truth. For many, service on a jury is their sole exposure to the courts. During the trial, they form lasting impressions of our judicial system. Often, jury duty is exciting, and the juror's observations will be passed on to his relatives, friends, and neighbors. The diffusion of those observations and impressions leads to popular trust in government. Elimination or restriction of jury trials may well have the unfortunate and unintended effect of seriously undermining this public confidence.

# Chapter 2

# *Jury Trials Are Based on Jury Selection Methods*


**I. Three Stages in Jury Selection §2.1**

**II. Constitutional Requirements**

A. Representative Jurors from Representative Lists
  1. Jury of Peers §2.2
  2. Cross-section Jury §2.3
  3. Representative Lists §2.4

B. Impartial Jurors §2.6

C. Juror Voir Dire and Challenges §2.7
  1. On Racial and Ethnic Prejudice §2.8
  2. On Other Prejudices and Prejudgments §2.9
  3. On Other Factors §2.10

**III. Methods of Compiling Jury Lists**

A. Federal Grand and Petit Juries
  1. Under 1968 Act §2.11
  2. Arbitrary Methods of Selection §2.12
  3. Stale Lists §2.13
  4. Checklist: Inherent Sources of Error §2.14
  5. Recent Developments §2.15

B. State Grand Juries
1. Judicial Selection System §2.21
2. Jury Commission System §2.22
3. Judge Selection and Interview System §2.23
4. Recent Developments §2.24
C. State Petit Juries
1. Often Different from Grand Jury Systems §2.25
2. Typical System—New York §2.26
3. Typical System—Pennsylvania §2.27
4. Other Systems §2.28
5. Recent Developments §2.29

**IV. Typical Disqualifications and Excuses**
A. Disqualifications and Exemptions §2.30
1. Federal Act and Sample District Court Plan §2.31
2. Typical State Statutes §2.32
3. Women's Exemptions Unconstitutional §2.33
4. Felony Exemptions Improperly Used §2.34
5. Intelligence Tests Used Invalidly and Discriminatorily §2.35
6. Other Disqualifications and Exemptions §2.36
7. Recent Developments §2.37
B. Individual Excuses
1. Federal Act and Sample District Court Plan §2.41
2. Common State Practices §2.42
3. Other Examples §2.43
4. Recent Developments §2.44
C. Typical Results of Disqualification and Excuse §2.46

## I. THREE STAGES IN JURY SELECTION §2.1

"There are three stages in the jury selection process at which the ideal of a representative cross-section can be seriously compromised," according to the California Supreme Court. "The first is the initial compilation of the 'role of eligible juror candidates' . . . or master list from which, by various steps, the venires are drawn. . . . Obviously if that list is not representative of a cross-section of the community, the process is constitutionally defective *ab initio*. The issue has been extensively litigated and has received the close attention of legal commentators.

" . . . Secondly, a number of prospective jurors thus selected are disqualified or excused by judges or various court personnel on grounds of competency, . . . suitability . . . , undue hardship . . . , or . . . occupation. . . . "

Thirdly, peremptory challenges can be used to excuse all or most members of certain groups who make up a significant part of the community. *California v Wheeler* (1978) 148 Cal Rptr 890, 900.

This chapter describes the constitutional requirements at all three stages (§§2.2–2.10); the present methods used to compile jury lists at the federal (§2.11) and state levels (§§2.21–2.28) and some weaknesses in these methods (§§2.12–2.14); and the present rules used to disqualify, exempt, and excuse jurors (§§2.31–2.32, 2.41–2.42) and some weaknesses in the enforcement of these rules (§§2.33–2.35, and 2.46).

Later chapters discuss peremptory and cause challenges, and how they can sometimes be used to redress imbalances created in the first two stages of the jury selection process.

## II. CONSTITUTIONAL REQUIREMENTS

### A. Representative Jurors from Representative Lists

#### 1. Jury of Peers §2.2

Many people in this country talk about their right to be tried by "a jury of peers." This phrase comes from the Magna Charta of 1215, wrung from King John of England by feudal barons, each one demanding the right to a "judgment of his peers." By this they meant a trial by a jury of 12 men according to the course of the common law. The word "peers" means equals: "those who are a man's equal in rank and station," according to Black's Law Dictionary (1968).

The phrase is used today in litigation on jury issues. See Supreme Court cases *Mobile v Bolden* (1980) 446 US 55 n24, and *Duncan v Louisiana* (1968) 391 US 145 at 156. Other courts also use the phrase, e.g., in *United States v Criden* (ED Pa 1980) 501 F Supp 854; *Ply v Arkansas* (Ark Sup Ct 1980) 606 SW2d 556 (dissent); *Utah v Mills* (Utah Sup Ct 1982) 641 P2d 119; and *Drenning v Wisconsin* (Wis Ct of App Dist VI 1980) 295 NW2d 225.

There is extensive sociological data indicating that peers of a criminal defendant or a personal injury plaintiff will vote differently from non-peers, probably because they understand much more about the defendant's or plaintiff's feelings, attitudes, and way of life than do jurors from other social strata. See G. Bermant and J. Shepard, "The Voir Dire Examination, Juror Challenges, and Adversary Advocacy," in *The Trial Process,* ed. B. Sales, pp. 69–114 (New York: Plenum, 1981); J. Monahan and E. Loftus, "The Psychology of Law," 33 *Ann Rev Psych* 441 (1982).

In a period of economic depression, in which the gulf between rich and poor, between employed and unemployed, becomes a deep chasm that is seldom breached, the issue of trial by a jury of peers becomes even more important than in a period of economic normalcy. The federal Jury Selection and Service Act of 1968, as amended, provides: "No citizen shall be excluded from service as a grand or petit juror in the district courts of the United States or in the Court of International Trade on account of race, color, religion, sex, national origin, or economic status." 28 USC §1862.

However, the right to a trial by a jury of peers has been held not to mean, for example, that an indigent woman raising her children with payments from Aid to Families with Dependent Children has a right to be tried by a jury comprised of 12 indigent women raising children on AFDC. Nor does it mean she has a right to have even one such woman sit on her jury. Our courts have held there is no right to be tried by a jury of equals. There is only a right not to have equals or peers *excluded* from jury lists from which the trial jurors are selected. As the Supreme Court explained in *City of Mobile, Ala v Bolden* (1980) 446 US 55, 77 n24:

> . . . But "[f]airness in selection has never been held to require proportional representation of races upon a jury," *Akins v Texas*, 325 US 398, 403; nor has the defendant any "right to demand that members of his race be included," *Alexander v Louisiana*, 405 US 625, 628. The absence from a jury of persons belonging to racial or other cognizable groups offends the Constitution only "if it results from purposeful discrimination." *Castaneda v Partida* (1977) 430 US 482, at 493. See *Alexander v Louisiana*, *supra*; see also *Washington v Davis* (1976) 426 US 229, at 239–240. Thus, the fact that there is a constitutional right to a system of jury selection that is not purposefully exclusionary does not entail a right to a jury of any particular racial composition. . . .

Courts in most jurisdictions still permit parties to use peremptory challenges against every true peer of a plaintiff or defendant, e.g., in most jurisdictions prosecutors can still use peremptories against every black person called to jury duty in a case involving a black defendant, but this is not true in California. See chapter 20.

## 2. Cross-section Jury §2.3

*Source: Grigsby v Mabry* (DC Ark 1980) 483 F Supp 1372, at 1377.

In *Taylor v Louisiana* (1974), 419 US 522, 530, the Supreme Court explained: . . .

> We accept the fair cross-section requirement as fundamental to the jury trial guaranteed by the Sixth Amendment and are convinced that the requirement has [a] solid foundation. . . . This prophylactic vehicle is not provided if the jury pool is made up of only special segments of the populace or if large, distinctive groups are excluded from the pool.

The *Taylor* Court, in considering the exclusion of women from jury service, strongly implied that the defendant need not show specific prejudice from any exclusion of a distinct group, for such an exclusion "deprived him of the *kind* of factfinder to which he was constitutionally entitled." (Emphasis supplied). *Taylor*, *supra*, at 526.

. . .

In *Taylor* the Court reviewed prior cases discussing whether the presence of a fair cross-section on the lists from which petit juries are drawn is essential to the fulfillment of the Sixth Amendment guarantee of an impartial jury in a criminal trial:

> . . . [T]he Court has unambiguously declared that the American concept of the jury trial contemplates a jury drawn from a fair cross-section of the community. A unanimous Court stated in *Smith v Texas* (1940) 311 US 128, 130, that "[i]t is part of the established tradition in the use of juries as instruments of public justice that the jury be a body truly representative of the community." To exclude racial groups from jury service was said to be "at war with our basic concepts of a democratic society and a representative government." A state jury system that resulted in systematic exclusion of Negroes as jurors was therefore held to violate the Equal Protection Clause of the Fourteenth Amendment. *Glasser v United States* (1942) US 60, 85–86, in the context of a federal criminal case and the Sixth Amendment's jury trial requirement, stated that "[o]ur notions of what a proper jury is have developed in harmony with our basic concepts of a democratic system and a representative government," and repeated the Court's understanding that the jury "be a body truly representative of the community . . . and not the organ of any special group or class."

> . . .
>
> Some years later in *Carter v Jury Comm'n* (1970) 396 US 320, 330, the Court observed that the exclusion of Negroes from jury service because of their race "contravenes the very idea of a jury—'a body truly representative of the community' " (Quoting from *Smith v Texas, supra*).

In *Peters v Kiff* (1972) 407 US 493, 502–504 (opinion of Marshall, J., joined by Douglas and Stewart, JJ.), it was stated:

> These principles compel the conclusion that a State cannot, consistent with due process, subject a defendant to indictment or trial by a jury that has been selected in an arbitrary and discriminatory manner, in violation of the Constitution and laws of the United States. Illegal and unconstitutional jury selection procedures cast doubt on the integrity of the whole judicial process. They create the appearance of bias in the decision of individual cases, and they increase the risk of actual bias as well.
>
> . . .
>
> But the exclusion from jury service of a substantial and identifiable class of citizens has a potential impact that is too subtle and too pervasive to admit of confinement to particular issues or particular cases. . . .

The Eighth Circuit Court of Appeals has made it clear that the most important consideration in deciding whether there is indeed an identifiable group is whether the group holds a distinct attitude unrepresented by others on the jury. In the context of a challenge to the exclusion of 18 to 20-year-olds from jury service immediately after the ratification of the Twenty-sixth Amendment, Judge Matthes stated:

> The true basis of a challenge to the master list in this case must rest on the allegation that the compilation of the list excluded an identifiable community group, to wit: persons aged eighteen to twenty. Of course, "[n]either the jury roll nor the venire need to be a perfect mirror of the community or accurately reflect the proportionate strength of every identifiable group." *Swain v Alabama* (1965) 380 US 202, 208. However, since a jury is designed to "express the conscience of the community," *Witherspoon v Illinois* (1968) 391 US 510, 519, "[t]he American tradition of trial by jury . . . necessarily contemplates an impartial jury drawn from a cross-section of the communty." *Thiel v Southern Pac. Co.* (1946) 328 US 217, 220. Thus, juries must be indiscriminately selected "without systematic and intentional exclusion of any . . . substantial portion of the community . . . that cannot be . . . excluded in whole or in part without doing violence to the democratic nature of the jury system." 328 US at 220, 223, 985. This command flows from the requisites of both Due Process, *Peters v Kiff* (1972) 407 US 493 (plurality opinion of Marshall, J.), and the Sixth Amendment, *Williams v Florida* (1970) 399 US 78, 100. *United States v Olson* (8th Cir 1973) 473 F2d 686, 688.

### 3. Representative Lists §2.4

The goal of representative or cross-section juries can only be achieved if jurors are selected from a list that represents a cross-section of the vicinage or community where the trial is to be held. Social science research has now made clear that many lists previously thought to be fair and representative do not actually have these characteristics. Lists of registered voters tend to be weighted toward older white people from higher economic and educational brackets with longer residence in the community. Lists of people with driver's licenses or telephone service tend to reflect the community more closely. Increasingly, more than one list is being used in order to obtain the cross-section required. See discussion in chapter 6.

In a society as mobile as ours, the proportion of registered voters may fluctuate considerably, depending on economic and other issues facing voters. For example, the percentage of black voters increased in the 1983 mayoralty election in Chicago and in the 1982 California gubernatorial election when black candidates were running. There was a 3 percent national increase in eligible voters casting ballots in the 1982 elections, ending a 10 percent decline that started in 1962. Some working class and minority Democrats finally voted again in 1982, after sitting out the 1978 and 1980 elections. *Nation*, Jan. 1, 1983, p. 12. An increase in the number and types of people who register to vote, as well as in the number actually casting ballots, must eventually affect the lists used in jury selection.

In *Brown v Culpepper* (5th Cir 1977) 559 F 2d 274, the court of appeals recognized the importance of challenging unrepresentative lists by reversing the denial of attorneys' fees in such a case. Plaintiffs had sued jury commissioners, a trial court judge, and a court clerk to prohibit them from using certain lists that unfairly limited the number of blacks and women on juries. After their successful suit, counsel sought attorneys' fees, and their success suggests the progress on representative lists in recent years.

## B. Impartial Jurors §2.6

Parties to a lawsuit are entitled to be judged by judges and jurors who have no personal interest in the outcome of the case, nothing to gain or lose from the verdict. Parties are entitled to write on a clean slate, to present their versions of the facts and law to jurors who have heard nothing about the case or who, having heard a little, have come to no conclusions and are prepared to withhold judgment until they have heard both sides. In addition, parties are entitled to a neutral jury.

"A neutral jury is one drawn from a pool which reasonably mirrors the diversity of experience and relevant viewpoints of those persons in the community who can fairly and impartially try the case." *Hovey v Superior Court* (1980) 168 Cal Rptr 128. "The concept of a neutral jury is intimately related to the constitutional doctrine regarding a representative cross-section of the community . . . ," the California Supreme Court explained in a footnote to its famous opinion in *Hovey*, 168 Cal Rptr at 137, n45. "The overriding constitutional principle" in *Taylor v Louisiana* (1975) 419 US 522, *Duren v Missouri* (1979) 439 US 357, and *Witherspoon v Illinois* (1968) 391 US 510, "is that a jury must be drawn from a pool that fairly represents the community." See discussion in §11.71.

Two types of people are sometimes excluded from jury service—members of cognizable classes and single individuals. In *Hovey* the Court said that if those excluded are members of

> traditional minorities such as blacks, persons of Mexican descent, and women—then the court will apply the *Taylor-Duren* analysis, which effectively presumes that the exclusion resulted in a nonneutral jury. If no cognizable class is involved, then the individual challenging the exclusion bears a burden of demonstrating—by empirical proof or otherwise—that the resulting jury is probably not neutral and that this nonneutrality operates to his detriment,

which was the issue on voir dire questions in capital punishment cases like *Witherspoon*.

Parties facing a hostile community from which an impartial jury cannot be selected can seek delay of trial, extensive voir dire, change of venue, or even dismissal. See chapters 7 and 8.

## C. Juror Voir Dire and Challenges §2.7

The United States Supreme Court has made it clear that "the denial or impairment of the right" to exercise one's challenges to prospective jurors "is reversible error without a showing of prejudice." *Swain v Alabama* (1964) 380 US 202, 219. The questions to be asked on voir dire are within the discretion of the trial court, but this discretion is "subject to the essential demands of fairness." *Aldridge v United States* (1931) 283 US 308, 313. A voir dire question requested by a party should be asked if an anticipated response would afford the basis for a challenge. *United States v Blount* (6th Cir 1973) 479 F2d 650. In-depth questioning into areas relevant to the case is required in order to enable parties to exercise their peremptory challenge rights in an intelligent and informed manner. *United States v Bear Runner* (8th Cir 1974) 502 F2d 908, 910–912.

These rules provide the starting point for lawyers preparing for jury voir dire. Recent decisions in many state and federal jurisdictions demonstrate a commitment to meaningful voir dire. See, e.g., *United States v Cassel* (8th Cir 1982) 668 F2d 969, 971; *United States v Corey* (5th Cir 1980) 625 F2d 704, 706; *Louisiana v Claiborne* (La S Ct 1981) 397 So2d 486, 487.

### 1. On Racial and Ethnic Prejudice §2.8

Selecting 12 (or 6) names at random from a fairly drawn jury list does not by itself ensure a cross-section jury for a particular case. Voir dire of each juror is necessary to achieve this constitutional goal.

One of the purposes of voir dire is to remove from the jury those who are not impartial (see chapter 13), and those who will make judgments based on their own biases and preconceptions, rather than on the basis of the evidence presented and their understanding of the law given by the judge in the instructions, filtered through the jurors' perceptions of the community conscience (see chapter 22). Biases, prejudices, preconceptions, and other weaknesses are revealed during a strong voir dire of each juror by attorneys for both sides, as well as by the judge. The wise use of challenges for cause and peremptory challenges will remove people who cannot overcome their weaknesses and will alert the remaining jurors to their responsibility to rise above their customary thinking in order to judge fairly the case before them. See chapters 5–19.

> [T]he Constitution requires questioning prospective jurors about racial or ethnic bias . . . when racial issues are inextricably bound up with the conduct of the trial and there are substantial indications of the likelihood of racial or ethnic prejudice affecting the jurors in the particular case. See *Ristaino v Ross* (1976) 424 US 589; *Ham v South Carolina* (1973) 409 US 524.

This is the language of the Supreme Court in *Rosales-Lopez v United States* (1981) 451 US 182, agreeing that a trial judge must not deny a defendant's request for voir dire on such prejudices when "the circumstances of the case indicate a 'reasonable possibility' that such prejudice might influence the jury."

The California Supreme Court and some other state and federal judges have gone beyond this position. Noting the danger to impartial, cross-section juries from the use of peremptory challenges to remove all blacks or members of other races from juries, the highest California court forbade this practice in *Wheeler v California* (1978) 148 Cal Rptr 890; see chapter 20.

## 2. On Other Prejudices and Prejudgments §2.9

Extensive voir dire based on careful analysis of the elements in a case has uncovered massive prejudgments in some highly publicized cases, sometimes accompanied by significant racial or ethnic prejudice. See, e.g., the description of this problem in the Chicago Eight conspiracy trial arising out of the hard-fought 1968 Democratic Party national convention, in *Dellinger v United States* (7th Cir 1972) 472 F2d 340, see §3.54.

In highly unusual cases, counsel may decide that prejudgments cannot be remedied by the traditional methods of delay or change of venue, and, after extensive voir dire, conclude that it is necessary to file a motion to dismiss the charges in a criminal case due to community prejudice so strong it cannot be overcome. This situation arose in a 1969 case in Milwaukee in which a group of Catholic priests and laymen were charged with removing records from a Selective Service office and burning them. After denying their motion initially, the trial judge questioned 142 prospective jurors, almost all of them individually. Judge Myron L. Gordon, in a bench opinion, described some of his reasons for later granting the unusual motion:

> Many jurors prefaced their admissions of prejudice against these defendants by starting to say: "I'm a good American," or "I was in the service, and I have sons in the service," or words to that effect, which impressed me as meaning that an attitude has been extant in this community that what these defendants have done is in contravention to those attitudes, that is, those concepts of good Americanism and love of Country and the use of the antithesis device persuades me that there would be community reaction against the defendants.
>
> I was also struck by the fact that some jurors would remove the cloak by taking a deep breath and burst out with a statement like: "I am going to be very honest with you," and they would proceed to acknowledge prejudice. I have fear that others in this community, particularly the members who were interrogated, would not remove the cloak which surrounded their views. Roughly, four out of five jurors who were questioned have been removed for apparent bias.

*United States v Cotton* (ED Wis, No. 68–CR–113, Sept. 9, 1969), as reported in 28 *Lawyers Guild Practitioner* 101 (1969), and discussed in chapter 7.

### 3. On Other Factors §2.10

This section is being reserved for discussion of new subjects on which voir dire questions are required. See §2.15.

## III. METHODS OF COMPILING JURY LISTS

## A. Federal Grand and Petit Juries

### 1. Under 1968 Act §2.11

The federal method of jury selection is based on the Jury Selection and Service Act of 1968, 28 USC §§1821, 1862–1869, 1871, 1875, and amendments. Elimination of the "key man" system throughout the federal courts was the primary focus of the act. HR Rep No. 1076, 90th Cong, 2d Sess, at 4 n1 (1968). The act does not forbid the use of sources other than voter registration lists but is quite specific in its requirements. It leaves relatively little room for variation compared with state selection systems, but it does allow a jury commission or a clerk to manage the selection process (18 USC §1863(b)(1)), and it does allow the chief judge or another judge to determine who is qualified, on his own initiative or on the recommendation of the clerk or jury commission (18 USC §1865(a)).

A lawyer concerned about a representative jury should become familiar with all provisions of the act and should also obtain a copy of and study the plan drawn up in the federal district in which the particular case is pending.

### 2. Arbitrary Methods of Selection §2.12

Before enforcement of the 1968 Jury Selection and Service Act got underway, there were many examples of gross unfairness, often based on unspoken and unconstitutional biases, as in the *Spock* case.

*Source:* Brief of defendant-appellant Benjamin Spock, *United States v Spock* (1st Cir 1969) 416 F2d 165, conviction reversed on other grounds.

The Clerk of the [Federal District] Court [in Massachusetts] testified that in selecting a petit jury venire he drew 100 names from a jury box containing 300 names. This box contained the names of persons who had qualified as jurors following their completion of questionnaires sent to them by the Clerk. In selecting the names of persons to whom he mailed the questionnaires, the Clerk consulted street or police lists of the various cities containing the names of the residents of these cities.

He described his method of selecting names from a street list:

Q. . . . Would you take any page and indicate to the Court how you

> have done that? A. . . . I put my finger on the place and on a name on the page and then I make a mark next to it with a pen.
>
> Q. Do you do that by not looking at the page? A. I have to look at it enough to know where it is in relation to my finger.
>
> Q. Yes. A. I do not intend to look *carefully* at the name . . . .
>
> Q. I assume that at some point you have to look at the name in order to send out the questionnaire? A. Correct.

He thus did not use any systematic method, such as taking every third, fourth or ninth name on the list which would have assured nondiscrimination.

Although he stated his intention to send out questionnaires to men and women alike, many more questionnaires were mailed to men than to women, despite the fact that there are more women than men over the age of 21 in the district [according to census figures]. For example, . . . during the years 1965-1967, . . . questionnaires were mailed to 832 men and 286 women . . . .

Since fewer questionnaires were mailed to women, it is only natural that women would be grossly underrepresented on any of the petit jury venires which were selected. The panel of 100 selected in this case contains the names of only 9 women. This list, the Clerk testified, was representative of the jury lists which were normally obtained by the selection process described above.

*COMMENT:* The clerk testified reluctantly that he assumed more women than men would be disqualified or excused from jury service, so in effect he was simply saving time by sending questionnaires to a smaller number of women. For current law, see §2.33.

### 3. Stale Lists §2.13

Even after enforcement of the 1968 Jury Selection and Service Act, problems continue with the use of old lists.

In *United States v Ross* (9th Cir 1972) 468 F2d 1213, *cert. denied* (1973) 410 US 989, the American Civil Liberties Union lost its challenge to the use of "stale" voter lists. The Ninth Circuit held that it was not unreasonable to refill the wheels only every four years, as provided in 28 USC §1863(b)(4), since the most current lists available are used in the refilling process. A little earlier, the Ninth Circuit had held that more constant updating of the wheel would create an "administrative monstrosity." *United States v Duncan* (9th Cir 1972) 456 F2d 1401. As a result, new voters will always remain underrepresented during the second, third, and fourth years of the use of federal wheels, which are refilled every four years.

However, new state statutes are requiring annual preparation of master lists of prospective jurors. See, e.g., *Pa Stat Ann*, title 42, §4521 (Purdon).

## 4. Checklist: Inherent Sources of Error §2.14

*Source:* Affidavit of Hans Zeisel in support of defendants' unsuccessful motion for an order: (a) permitting inspection of jury questionnaires; (b) directing a hearing on the question of the validity of the selection of jurors; and (c) dismissing the indictment, dated Aug. 2, 1971, *United States v Deardorff* (SD NY 1971) 343 F Supp 1033 (federal bribery case).

Hans Zeisel, being first duly sworn, deposes and says:

1. I am Professor of Law and Sociology at the University of Chicago Law School. I am co-author with Professor Harry Kalven, Jr. of *The American Jury* and have studied at various occasions the process of selecting petit and grand jurors.

2. Professor Alan M. Dershowitz of the Harvard Law School informed me that he had been retained as counsel by the defendants in the case of the United States of America against J. Howard Deardorff, Irving Kahn, Robert McKee, Kenneth Tompkins and Teleprompter Corporation. He furthermore informed me that there is prima facie evidence that the grand jury that indicted these defendants is not representative of the population from which such juries must be drawn, hence there is prima facie evidence that this grand jury has been improperly selected.

3. Professor Dershowitz asked me whether I would care to undertake a study of these discrepancies and to determine whether they were the result of unavoidable random deviations, which occasionally occur, or whether they were the result of systematic bias, caused by improper selection procedures. I replied that I would be willing to undertake such a study, and asked that, as a first step, I be given an overview of the rules that guide the selection of grand juries in the U.S. District Court for the Southern District of New York.

*COMMENT:* Every study of a jury selection system must be based on a close study of the rules for jury selection developed in the particular jurisdiction. The rules are available from the court clerk for the federal district court.

4. Thereupon, I received the copy of an affidavit, dated March 15, 1971, by Michael D. Schmitz, Esq., a member of the firm of Shea, Gallop, Climenko & Gould, who are counsel for some of the defendants, together with copies of a number of documents pertaining to the above-mentioned selection procedures.

Based on that affidavit and the enclosed documents, I have summarized below the rules governing the selection process, and added at each stage notes indented into the text, as to how errors in the execution of the selection rules or improper exercise of discretion could have biased the selection process and thereby voided the very purpose of Public Law 90–274, the Jury Selection and Service Act of 1968 [28 USC §§1861–1875].

**Lists Used**

5. The frame for the selection of all petit and grand jurors comprises the most recent voter lists of the 11 counties that form the district over which the court has jurisdiction. The first stage of the selection entails selecting every $n^{th}$ name from these lists, "n" being roughly the ratio of the total number of names on these voter lists over the number of names to be selected.

*COMMENT:* For example, in relation to *Deardorff*, 143,104 names were selected at random from the voter registration lists in June 1969, and jury questionnaires were sent to those drawn from this number.

An increasing number of state jurisdictions are going beyond voter registration lists for sources of names, as is permitted, but not required, in 28 USC §1863 (b)(2), in the federal system. See §2.27.

*Questions:*

i) Has, in fact, every $n^{th}$ name been selected, or were discretions exerted "around" the $n^{th}$ name, so that one could choose one of a handful of names around that point? If so, what bias guided this discretion?

ii) Since every individual voter list is likely to represent a particular section of the community (often delineated by the predominant race or income of that area), it is essential that *every* selection of a series of $n^{th}$ names exhausts *all* the lists of the 11 counties. Any violation of this rule would bias the selection.

6. Next, the so selected names (approximately 4000) are placed in card form into the master jury wheel. From it, according to the needs of the court, the required number of names are drawn in random fashion. [28 USC §1864(a)]

*Question:*

i) Drawing a random sample from 4000 cards is a difficult physical problem; the draft lottery, with less than one-tenth of that number, had difficulties. Was this a true random selection?

7. Questionnaires are being mailed to all the drawn names with the request that they be filled out and returned. If they are not properly returned, the person "may be summoned" to appear in person. [28 USC §1864(a), (b)]

*Question:*

i) One may assume that every selected person is mailed a questionnaire. But enforcement or the nonenforcement of the return is a major potential source of bias. Since availability of a questionnaire is the condition for service, anybody selected who manages *not* to return the questionnaire is lost to the system; and if some strata of the population manage such escape more frequently than other strata, bias [is more likely to] result.

*COMMENT:* In the *Attica Brothers* case (see §3.26), the defense team learned from the deputy jury commissioner of Erie County, New York, a black woman, that the post office frequently did not bother to forward mail delivered in the black neighborhoods. Since there is a higher mobility rate in these neighborhoods than in wealthier neighborhoods, fewer questionnaires were completed and returned. The defense convinced the Erie County jury commissioner to send more questionnaires to neighborhoods with lower return rates so that the ultimate proportions in the jury wheel would remain as representative as the original list from which the names were selected.

**Names Eliminated**

**8. From the list of those individuals who have returned the questionnaire, three categories of names are eliminated:**

a. **Those** *incompetent* to serve.

b. Those *exempt* from service.

c. Those *excused* upon request because jury service would impose on them "undue hardship or extreme inconvenience." [28 USC §1865]

The names that pass all three hurdles are put into the Qualified Jury Wheel.

The causes for (a) and (b) are exhaustively enumerated in the [United States District Court] rules, and originally also the causes for (c) were listed under 8 exhaustive headings. But the rules were amended, so that now "shall be excused upon individual request" also "persons as to whom the Chief Justice finds for reasons other than the foregoing that jury service would constitute undue hardship or extreme inconvenience."

*Question:*

i) Since the precise cause for elimination under (a), (b) or (c) must be noted by the Clerk next to each eliminated name on the list, one should be able to ascertain easily whether the rules have been complied with under (a) and (b). The more serious problem arises from the broad discretionary power to excuse for hardship under (c). What were the reasons for which excuses were granted "other than" the specifically named ones in the original list of 8 such reasons? How many such excuses were granted? How did they affect the representativeness of the remaining names? Also perhaps: To what extent did the Chief Judge, in fact, make these excuses or merely approve the decisions of the Clerk?

9. Finally, there is an emergency provision for selecting jurors through the U.S. Marshal in case the supply from the normal selection process runs out. It is not likely that this procedure is often invoked, but if it is invoked, it offers its own opportunities for bias. [28 USC §1866(f)]

10. Names drawn randomly from the Qualified Jury Wheel are then summoned for service.

*Question:*

i) Is nonresponse to such a summons a negligible factor or does it significantly contribute toward biasing the selection process? Who is in fact allowed to avoid service by simply disregarding the summons? That is: How effective is the enforcement policy?

**Grand Jury Procedures**

11. So far we have discussed the procedures that pertain jointly to both petit and grand jurors. We now come to the specific selection of grand jurors. The basic rule for selecting them is: "The persons whose names appear on each

fifth card drawn from the Qualified Jury Wheel shall be assigned to the Grand Jury pool" (p. 15 of the Selection Plan).

*Question:*

i) It should be easy enough to ascertain whether the rule has been followed strictly, or whether some selecting of grand jurors has taken place that is not provided for in the rules.

12. The amended rules add an alternative procedure: "Provided, however, that whenever the Chief Judge finds that names are needed for only one of the pools [petit or grand] he may direct that all names selected be assigned to that pool."

*Question:*

i) This discretionary power can seriously bias the selection process, because it abandons the "every 5th" rule. In theory, *any* successive run of names can thereby be assigned to the grand jury, and if the assignment is made for a group of quite atypical composition, a major source of bias may be introduced.

13. Finally, if I read the Selection Plan correctly, there is the possibility of a temporary excuse of a juror for hardship, with the understanding that he will serve at some later time.

*Question:*

i) If grand jurors are excused in this fashion, and the excused jurors serve in fact later less frequently, or not at all, or only as petit jurors, bias may result at that last step of the selection process.

**Grand and Petit Jurors**

14. Whether or not there is a *systematic imbalance* between grand jurors and petit jurors, or grand jurors and the pool of eligible jurors, or whether the observed imbalance was accidental, can be ascertained by comparing the demographic characteristics of these three groups.

*COMMENT:* One method of making the comparison is described in §6.26.

If a systematic imbalance exists, it would seem imperative to allow an inquiry designed to find out at exactly which stage or stages these imbalances have been created. Both these inquiries can be conducted without violating the confidential information supplied by the individual potential jurors. Both outlined inquiries are of purely statistical nature, for which individual names are completely irrelevant.

I declare under penalty of perjury that the foregoing is true and correct.

Executed August 2, 1971, at San Diego, California.

[Signed] Hans Zeisel, Declarant

## 5. Recent Developments §2.15

It is now possible to keep up with the law on jury selection the same way you keep up with the law in any other field—by reading the relevant advance sheets, subscribing to services on trial advocacy or criminal law, and reading daily newspapers and legal newspapers. The *Index to Legal Periodicals*, *Current Law Index*, and *Legal Resource Index* provide provocative (and sometimes descriptive) titles to law review articles, comments, and notes in this field, indicating what is happening at the cutting edge of the law. It is a good idea occasionally to ask your law librarian for an index to journals on psychology, applied psychology, and the social sciences, to pick up new ideas from these disciplines.

Increasingly, lawyers are learning to use *Lexis* and *Westlaw* in order to find the latest cases and interesting parallels in other fields of law. It is always necessary to Shepardize all citations.

The Annual Supplement to these volumes will use recent developments sections throughout the book to describe new cases, ideas, and articles that are worthy of note, and to warn of cases overruled and of rules and statutes amended or repealed.

## B. State Grand Juries

### 1. Judicial Selection System §2.21

Many county grand juries in the several states are still selected by the system attacked in 1974 in California, which admittedly results in jurors who are white, well-to-do, and often cronies of the judges. The California example is therefore instructive on this problem.

The California Penal Code provides for two alternative methods of selecting grand jurors. One, outlined in Penal Code §903.3, calls for selection from a list to be provided by the jury commissioner, pursuant to rules adopted by a majority of judges of the superior court. Two, described in §§895–902, requires the court to compile the list itself, subject only to a few standards for juror competence and geographic distribution. Even where the jury commissioner compiles a list, the judges are free to ignore it (§903.4). These general statutes, which go back 102 years to the original Code of Civil Procedure, vest unlimited discretion in superior court judges to find, by whatever means they desire, people "of ordinary intelligence, of sound judgment, and of fair character" (§893(2)) and to swear them in as grand jurors. Judge Vernon Stoll, examining the Marin County system he found to be constitutionally infirm, in *California v Bingham* (Marin County Super Ct, No. 4094, Jan. 17, 1974), expressed doubt "that it is a practical possibility to select a Grand Jury complying with the constitutional requirements through the means provided" in the older statutes, although "[i]t may be accomplished by following the procedures outlined" in the provisions establishing the jury commissioner alternative. Opinion, page 4.

In *California v Bingham*, also known as the *San Quentin Six Case*, defendants Hugo Pinell, Louis Talamantez, John Spain, Fleeta Drumgo, David Johnson, Willie Tate, and Stephen Bingham were charged with the murder of three white guards and two white prisoners who died along with Soledad Brother George Jackson on August 21, 1971. The indictment alleged that the six prisoners conspired with Berkeley attorney Stephen Bingham to escape from the San Quentin Adjustment Center. Bingham disappeared after the incident, and has never been apprehended.

The defendants filed a motion to dismiss the indictment on the ground that identifiable groups in the community were excluded from the grand jury that issued the indictment. Forms based on this motion are in chapter 3. Judge Vernon Stoll granted the motion on January 17, 1974. Stoll held that the selection procedure underrepresented blacks, Latin-Americans, blue-collar working-class people, and young people. Spain, Drumgo, Johnson, and Tate are black; Talamantez and Pinell are Chicano/Latino.

Before 1971, the judges themselves had made all nominations to the grand jury. Prompted by a letter from the Marin Council for Civil Affairs (MCCA), the court selected the 1971 grand jury that would indict the San Quentin Six using some nominees from MCCA-recommended organizations. That year the superior court judges drew the names of 19 grand jurors from 30 nominees. These people had been selected by the five judges, on a consensus basis, from 105 original nominees. These included 78 people whose names were submitted by organizations contacted by the court, 24 nominees of the judges themselves, and 3 volunteers. The list was heavy with representatives of homeowner and business groups.

A judge recounted the deliberations that reduced 105 nominees to 30 finalists:

> We came to [the presiding judge's] chambers and we sat around his desk and, as I recall, we all had the same material and I think I volunteered to keep the score so that we would be able to see how many people were being considered for various areas, various sexes, various occupations, age brackets, et cetera. . . . We maybe had half a dozen categories where we tried to put them in, and we had maybe four or five in the age bracket and we had, I think, four in the geographical brackets and there were other brackets when we were trying to keep track, so we didn't get too many ladies, too many men, or vice versa, so we would find out how they were going just for our general information.

An impartial judge appointed by the California Judicial Council made a finding of fact that this judge was biased and prejudical against San Quentin inmates. The judge himself testified that, based on his experience with "a great many black friends," he believed "that the majority of black people were not motivated very well. It isn't the same thing as lazy." He also noted that "blacks have done a very great deal of protesting, engaging in violence in some cases, to get changes and they have brought about changes." In evaluating nominees according to their economic classes, the judge believed "that those that are wealthy are more establishment and, frankly, believe in law enforcement more than the poor community who would like not only to change the law, but ignore it in some cases. Nevertheless, I think that the grand jury should be balanced, as should a petit jury."

Another of the five judges recalled they were looking for grand jurors who had the time and competence, judging from their occupations and education, to handle any civil or criminal issue that came before them. He suspected this produced a list of nominees in which 95 percent were property owners. Yet he thought the list to be a "conglomeration of everything" with the additional concession that the nominees were probably older than a cross-section of Marin. When asked how it might be possible for a qualified but impoverished prospective grand juror to ignore feeding and clothing himself or herself and a family in order to serve on the grand jury, a third judge answered that "all things are possible for men and women of great determination."

Another judge testified that he had absolutely no opinion whether the value system differed between young and old, poor and rich, the poorly educated and college graduates, or single and married persons. He also professed not to have "the slightest idea" of the background of the typical San Quentin convict, and admitted it did not cross his mind that their membership in identifiable groups should be considered in selection of the grand jury. When told of another judge's admiration for the "small percentage of the population that does most of its work, most of its thinking, most of its organization," he said he respected the common person no more or less than he respected "horses or cows or chickens."

In an earlier challenge to the judicial method of selecting grand jurors in Marin County, in the *Angela Davis* case (see §3.23), a judge had testified that he excluded "Communists" from consideration because "Communists are advocates of hatred, violence and murder. . . . They could hardly be considered good citizens when they spew hatred and violence and murder all over." Points and Authorities in Support of Restricted Motion for Change of Venue, filed Sept. 20, 1971, described in §7.25.

After Superior Court Judge Vernon Stoll granted the defendant's motion to quash the indictment in *California v Pinell*, the appellate court reversed ((Dist Ct App 1974) 117 Cal Rptr 913), stating "There is neither evidence nor suggestion of purposeful discrimination by any of the five superior court judges who were the selectors of the panel.... The trial court... held the selectors to an excessively rigorous standard when it looked only to the result, rather than the manner, of the selection." The California Supreme Court affirmed the reversal, and the United States Supreme Court denied certiorari (442 US 1007).

On the method of making a successful challenge to a grand or petit jury, see chapter 6.

In southern California, in response to the general increase in consciousness that most juries are unrepresentative, and perhaps also in response to specific court challenges, Los Angeles County superior court judges in 1975, for the first time, sought volunteers for county grand jury service. The more than 900 citizens, aged 18 to 80, who volunteered represented a large assortment of occupations, various ethnic groups, and all areas of the county. Presiding Judge Wenke screened the letters for those whose writers seemed best qualified. Then judges who had not yet made nominations talked to writers of letters, and in 59 cases chose to nominate volunteers for grand jury duty, in addition to 195 chosen by traditional methods. As a result, the nominations included more young people and members of ethnic minorities than ever before. A Judge's Committee of Grand Jurors investigated all nominees and also received and considered objections against any of the nominees. Thereafter, a meeting of all the judges of the superior court was held to consider the committee's report and to approve the names that constituted the grand jury list. From the list 40 names were drawn by chance, and a detailed investigation made of the 40. A second drawing was held to secure the names of the 23 men and women who formed the next year's grand jury. The presiding judge designated one juror to serve as the foreperson.

In 1980, the California legislature amended the Code of Civil Procedure §204.7 to require, as far as practical, the use of multiple source lists without significant added cost, deleting the role of the jury commissioner in preparing the list of eligible jury candidates.

### 2. Jury Commission System §2.22

*Source:* Opinion of the United States Supreme Court, *Alexander v Louisiana* (1972) 405 US 625, 627, 628.

According to 1960 U.S. census figures admitted into evidence below, Lafayette Parish contained 44,986 persons over 21 years of age and therefore presumptively eligible for grand jury service; of this total, 9,473 persons (21.06%) were Negro. At the hearing on petitioner's motions to quash the indictment, the evidence revealed that the Lafayette Parish jury commission consisted of five members, all of whom were white, who had been appointed by the court. The commission compiled a list of names from various sources (telephone directory, city directory, voter registration rolls, lists prepared by the school board, and by the jury commissioners themselves) and sent questionnaires to the persons on this list to determine those qualified for grand jury service. The questionnaire included a space to indicate the race of the recipient. Through this process, 7,374 questionnaires were returned, 1,015 of which (13.76%) were from Negroes (189 questionnaires had no racial designation), and the jury commissioners attached to each questionnaire an information card designating, among other things, the race of the person, and a white slip indicating simply the name and address of the person. The commissioners then culled out about 5,000 questionnaires, ostensibly on the ground that these persons were not qualified for grand jury service or were exempted under state law. The remaining 2,000 sets of papers were placed on a table, and the papers of 400 persons were selected, purportedly at random, and placed in a box from which the grand jury panels of 20 for Lafayette Parish were drawn. Twenty-seven of the persons thus selected were Negro (6.75%). On petitioner's grand jury venire, one of the 20 persons drawn was Negro (5%) but none of the 12 persons on the grand jury that indicted him, drawn from this 20, was Negro.

*COMMENT:* See LSA CCrP Art. 409.5D and Art. 416.1A for 1981 and 1982 amendments to jury selection methods, and later amendments.

### 3. Judge Selection and Interview System §2.23

The system long used in Philadelphia is still in use in some jurisdictions, although it was successfully challenged there and has been replaced by a new statewide statutory system.

The process in Philadelphia had three stages. First, each year the entire voter registration list (containing about 1,000,000 names) was divided into voting wards and submitted to the various judges of the state trial court. These lists included each person's name, address, ward, and occupation. The judges were instructed to select a specific number of individuals from each ward (determined by each ward's proportion of the total), but no standards or guidelines for selection were provided. These selections were made by judges, law clerks, tip-staffs, secretaries, and a sheriff. During the second stage questionnaires were sent to those initially chosen, approximately 60,000 persons. The returned questionnaires were reviewed and screened by the clerk and four masters of the Jury Selection Commission. Finally, the remaining individuals, approximately 38,000, were personally interviewed and again screened by the clerk and the masters, ending up with approximately 16,000 names in the juror pool.

A critique of the system found that the selectors attempted to select people with "better" jobs who were not "too busy" to serve. Unemployed persons were totally excluded by some and at least disfavored by the rest. Most of them favored housewives and excluded physicians and clergy. See Kairys, "Juror Selection: The Law, a Mathematical Method of Analysis, and a Case Study," 10 *Am Crim L Rev* 771, 798 (1972), describing the system successfully challenged in *Pennsylvania v Locke* (Philadelphia County Ct of CP, No. MC-70-09-1190, 1191, 70-10-919, 70-12-2416, Oct. 27, 1970).

The Pennsylvania statute adopted in 1980 abolishes this system. See Pa Stat Ann, title 42, §§2121–2124; 4501–4532; 4541–4584 (Purdon).

### 4. Recent Developments §2.24

See §2.15.

## C. State Petit Juries

### 1. Often Different from Grand Jury Systems §2.25

Trial jury selection methods at the state level often differ from grand jury selection methods, although the federal adoption of a unitary system and numerous successful jury challenges have encouraged the trend toward unitary selection methods at the state level as well. Challenges to trial jury lists and procedures are more frequent than challenges to grand jury lists and procedures because indictments by grand juries are increasingly uncommon, being used in only 4 percent of criminal charges in Los Angeles County, for example, in the past decade.

Professor Jon Van Dyke considers some common problems in composition in *Jury Selection Procedures: Our Uncertain Commitment to Representative Panels* (1977). Starting from the premise that the jury is the most democratic of our institutions, Van Dyke notes its inadequacies and suggests reforms to realize his premise, including use of the jury wheel, excuses, and challenges. He rejects juries of fewer than 12 and less-than-unanimous verdicts. Extensive demographic studies, broken down by federal district and by state jurisdictions, show the percentage representation of blue-collar workers, those with low incomes, and people of various levels of education, races, ages, and sexes.

Tables show the rates of conviction by crime category and the discriminatory effects of the excusing process.

Many lawyers may feel that they do not have the resources to challenge both the grand and petit jury selection processes in a single case, and they may decide to limit their attack to the trial jury list. The community from which trial jurors will be drawn will be more likely to recall the charges of unfairness, prejudice, racism, etc., raised in a trial jury challenge than in a grand jury challenge because the latter is made long before the trial jury is chosen.

See chapter 6 for problems common to both kinds of challenges.

### 2. Typical System—New York §2.26

Major attacks were launched on the system of compiling jury lists in New York, including the *Attica Brothers'* successful attack on underrepresentation of women and students before 1974, described in §3.26 and in Levine and Schweber-Koren, "Jury Selection in Erie County: Changing a Sexist System," 11 *Law & Soc'y* 43 (Fall 1976). The attack was not successful as to occupational groups, young people, and the poor, but the result was a series of amendments to the state jury selection statutes greatly increasing the likelihood of representative, cross-section juries. N.Y. Jud. Law, Art. 16, §506 (Mc Kinney).

**§506. Source of names**

The commissioner of jurors shall cause the names of prospective jurors to be selected at random from the voter registration lists, and from such other available lists of the residents of the county as the chief administrator of the courts shall specify, such as lists of utility subscribers, licensed operators of motor vehicles, registered owners of motor vehicles, state and local taxpayers, and persons who have volunteered to serve as jurors by filing with the commissioner their names and places of residence.

Section 507 provides for random selection, by mechanical or other means. Section 508 gives the jury commissioner discretion to decide how many grand and petit jurors are required, and gives the appellate divisions discretion to decide their length of service. Section 509 permits the commissioner to mail a juror qualification questionnaire to each prospective juror and permits personal interviews when necessary to determine qualification. For disqualifications, see §2.32.

### 3. Typical System—Pennsylvania §2.27

The General Assembly of Pennsylvania, responding to attacks on its jury system in litigation and law reviews (see §2.23), in 1980 made many amendments to its Judiciary and Judicial Procedure statutes. Its declaration of policy is explicit and broad (42 Pa. Cons. Stat §4501):

> (1) All persons entitled to a jury trial in a civil action or criminal proceeding shall have the right to jurors selected at random from a representative cross-section of the eligible population of the county.
> (2) All qualified citizens shall have the opportunity to be considered for service as jurors in the courts of this Commonwealth and shall have an obligation to serve as jurors when summoned for that purpose.
> (3) A citizen shall not be excluded from service as a juror on the basis of race, color, religion, sex, national origin, or economic status.

Responding to charges of using stale lists in the past, the 1980 act requires the jury selection commission to prepare a master list "at least annually" (42 Pa. Cons. Stat §4521(a)) from all county voter registration lists, which may, but is not required to be, supplemented by:

> (1) Persons listed in telephone, city, municipal directories and similar directories.
> (2) Persons who pay taxes or are assessed for taxes imposed by any political subdivisions . . . .
> (3) Persons in the county participating in any State, county or local program authorized by law and, to the extent such names are available, persons participating in any Federal program authorized by law . . . .
> (4) Persons who are on school census lists.
> (5) Any other person whose name does not appear in the master list of prospective jurors and who meets the qualifications for jurors set forth in this chapter and who makes application to the commission to be listed on the master list of prospective jurors.

45 Pa. Cons. Stat §4521(a).

The act spells out in detail the method and timing of all challenges to jury selection procedures (45 Pa. Cons. Stat §4526; see chapter 6).

Inexplicably, the General Assembly did not bring juror compensation into the inflation era of the 1980s, setting $9 a day and 17¢ a mile (Pa. Cons. Stat §4561(a)) as compensation for jury duty.

### 4. Other Systems §2.28

This section is being reserved for discussion of new systems of compiling lists for state petit juries. See §2.15.

### 5. Recent Developments §2.29

See §2.15.

# IV. TYPICAL DISQUALIFICATIONS AND EXCUSES

## A. Disqualifications and Exemptions §2.30

The modern trend is to eliminate exemptions and to provide for individual excusals based on hardship.

### 1. Federal Act and Sample District Court Plan §2.31

Federal law, 28 USC §1865(b), lists five automatic exemptions from jury service. It states:

[T]he chief judge of the district court . . . shall deem any person qualified to serve on grand and petit juries in the district court unless he—

(1) is not a citizen of the United States eighteen years old who has resided for a period of one year within the judicial district;

(2) is unable to read, write, and understand the English language with a degree of proficiency sufficient to fill out satisfactorily the juror qualification form;

(3) is unable to speak the English language;

(4) is incapable, by reason of mental or physical infirmity, to render satisfactory jury service; or

(5) has a charge pending against him for the commission of, or has been convicted in a State or Federal court of record of, a crime punishable by imprisonment for more than one year and his civil rights have not been restored.

The plan of the United States District Court for the Central District of California for the random selection of grand and petit jurors, for example, provides additional exemptions from jury service:

12. *Exemption from Jury Service*

The District Court hereby finds that exemption of the following groups of persons or occupational classes is in the public interest and would not be inconsistent with the Act, and accordingly members of such groups are exempt from jury service:

a. Members in active service in the armed forces of the United States.

b. Members of the fire or police departments of any state, district, territory, possession or subdivision thereof.

c. Pulic officers in the executive, legislative, or judicial branches of the government of the United States, or any state, district, territory, or possession or subdivision thereof, who are actively engaged in the performance of official duties. Public officer shall mean a person who is either elected to public office or who is directly appointed by a person elected to public office.

Copies of federal district court plans can be obtained from the clerk for each court.

## 2. Typical State Statutes §2.32

Under the 1980 Pennsylvania revised jury act, the following are qualified for jury service (42 Pa. Cons. Stat §4502):

§4502. Qualification of jurors.

Every citizen of this Commonwealth who is of the required minimum age for voting for State or local officials and who resides in the county shall be qualified to serve as a juror therein unless such citizen:

(1) is unable to read, write, speak and understand the English language;

(2) is incapable, by reason of mental or physical infirmity, to render efficient jury service; or

(3) has been convicted of a crime punishable by imprisonment for more than one year and has not been granted a pardon or amnesty therefor.

§4503. Exemptions from jury duty.

(a) General rule—No person shall be exempt or excused from jury duty except the following:

(1) Persons in active service of the armed forces of the United States or of the Commonwealth of Pennsylvania.

(2) Persons who have served within three years next preceding on any jury except a person who served as a juror for fewer than three days in any one year in which case the exemption period shall be one year.

Under New York Jud. Law, Art. 16, §510 (Mc Kinney), a juror must also:

2. Be less than seventy-six and not less than eighteen years of age.

. . .

5. Be intelligent, of good character, able to read and write the English language with a degree of proficiency sufficient to fill out satisfactorily the juror qualification questionnaire, and be able to speak the English language in an understandable manner.

## 3. Women's Exemptions Unconstitutional §2.33

The United States Supreme Court explicitly stated the law and the reasons for rejecting statutory exemptions for women in *Taylor v Louisiana* (1975) 419 US 522, 534, 535:

The States are free to grant exemptions from jury service to individuals in case of special hardship or incapacity and to those engaged in particular occupations the uninterrupted performance of which is critical to the community's welfare. *Rawlings v Georgia* (1906) 201 US 638. It would not appear that such exemptions would pose substantial threats that the remaining pool of jurors would not be representative of the community. A system excluding all women, however, is a wholly different matter. It is untenable to suggest these days that it would be a special hardship for each and every woman to perform jury service or that society cannot spare *any* women from their present duties.

The Court provided statistics compiled by the Department of Labor in support of this negative conclusion, including the percentages of women in the following classifications in the work force: all women between 18 and 64 years of age; women with children under the age of 18; mothers who were widowed, divorced, or separated; and mothers whose husbands were present in the household. See United States Department of Labor, *Marital and Family Characteristics of the Labor Force*, table F (Mar. 1974).

The Court spelled out the responsibility of jury commissioners to consider each prospective woman juror's situation individually:

[I]t may be burdensome to sort out those who should not be exempted from those who should serve. But that task is performed in the case of men, and the administrative convenience in dealing with women as a class is insufficient justification for diluting the quality of community judgment represented by the jury in criminal trials.

Previously the *Attica Brothers* defense had reminded the trial judge of the provision in §13 of the New York Civil Rights Law:

any person charged with any duty in the selection or summoning of jurors who shall exclude or *fail to summon* any citizen [on account of race, creed, color, national origin, or *sex*] shall . . . be deemed guilty of a misdemeanor. [Emphasis added.]

See also §2.3.

### 4. Felony Exemptions Improperly Used §2.34

In the *Attica Brothers* case (see §3.26), the investigators noticed that numbers of jurors had been illegally disqualified because of arrest, rather than conviction. They conducted a more complete study of all those disqualified from jury duty for crimes during 1972, which showed a pattern that would result in underrepresentation of blacks and young people. The computer printouts from the police department often contained no record of conviction, but people were disqualified anyway. This was particularly true for black people (race is marked on the printout). For example, one black man acquitted of murder in 1942 was disqualified from jury duty in 1972 for his "crime." See §6.64 for a discussion of how the use of misdemeanor arrests to disqualify jurors results in the exclusion of youths from jury service.

## 5. Intelligence Tests Used Invalidly and Discriminatorily §2.35

Many jury selection systems have devised their own methods of testing prospective jurors for being "intelligent," "clear thinking," and "able to comprehend the English language."

In *California v Craig* (Alameda County Super Ct, No. 41750, Apr. 18, 1968) Judge Spurgeon Avakian described and ruled on the "clear thinking" test given to prospective jurors in an often cited, though unreported opinion.

> The statutory qualification for jury service, insofar as the validity of the written test is concerned, is that jurors be "of ordinary intelligence" and "possessed of sufficient knowledge of the English language." California Code of Civil Procedure §198. No definition of those terms is set forth in the statute, but the decisional law requires nondiscriminatory selection from a broad base of the community and forbids a so-called "blue ribbon" approach. *Thiel v Southern Pac. Co.* (1946) 328 US 217. The use of written tests in applying this standard is neither uniform nor unusual in this state.
>
> In Alameda County, the test currently in use was adopted by the Court in 1956, after having been prepared by a psychologist for this particular use. It consists of 25 multiple choice questions. To pass, the juror must have at least 21 correct answers (84%) in ten minutes. . . .
>
> [F]or purposes of this case, a special analysis was made by the Jury Commissioner [of the scores of prospective jurors] of two areas designated by Defendant's attorney. One area consists of 24 contiguous precincts in West Oakland with a total voter registration of 10,862. The other consists of 27 contiguous precincts in the Montclair section of Oakland with a total voter registration of 11,070.
>
> The residents of the West Oakland area are predominantly black and of low economic income. The residents of Montclair are predominantly white and of middle or higher economic income.

| | *West Oakland Area* | *Montclair Area* |
|---|---|---|
| Number of Registered Voters | 10,862 | 11,070 |
| Number drawn from Voter Registers | 133 | 145 |
| Nonresponses, deaths, moved, etc. | 39 | 23 |
| Number processed | 94 | 122 |
| Excused without test | 40 (42.5%) | 53 (43.3%) |
| Took written test | 54 | 69 |
| Failed test* | 44 (81.5%) | 10 (14.5%) |
| Passed test | 10 | 59 |
| Excused after passing test | 1 | 7 |

| | *West Oakland Area* | *Montclair Area* |
|---|---|---|
| Qualified | 9 | 52 |
| Service deferred | 1 | 2 |
| Certified to current panel | 8 | 50 |

*For the two areas combined, 123 took the test and 54 persons, or 44%, failed it.

It should be noted that in the categories in which conscious or even subconscious bias could operate—namely, the excuses by the interviewers without administering the test—a substantially equal percentage was excused from each area . . . .

We come, then, to the test, a copy of which is attached hereto. Why do 14.5% of the Montclair registered voters fail it, and why is the failure rate 81.5% in West Oakland?

A consideration of the test raises a number of questions:

(1) To what extent does it measure moral and social attitudes and level of education rather than mental capacity?

(2) Does it contain cultural, educational or environmental biases which are not present equally in high and low income groups and in different racial groupings?

(3) Is it sufficiently comprehensive to test intelligence?

(4) Is the pass-fail cutting point placed so high as to eliminate substantial numbers of people who do possess "ordinary intelligence"?

Ten questions in the test (Nos. 2, 5, 6, 7, 14, 15, 18, 19, 22, 24) appear to relate primarily to vocabulary or word recognition. Nine are answered as much or more on the basis of personal temperament and attitude or social, political or moral philosophy as on the basis of intelligence (Nos. 4, 8, 9, 10, 11, 14, 20, 23, 25). One (no. 19) calls for knowledge of the law (and, incidentally, has a legally incorrect statement listed on the score sheet as the correct answer).

Only a few questions call primarily for the application of responding processes to situations described so as to neutralize cultural or educational differences.

The risk of built-in bias in favor of what is commonly referred to as middle class mores and vocabulary is obvious in such a situation. The startling difference in the pass-fail rate in the two areas previously mentioned, as well as the high over-all failure rate, strongly suggests that the test separates people on some basis other than "ordinary intelligence." One can well imagine how different the results might have been if half of the vocabulary questions were related to "soul" food, people and music and other terms commonly spoken in West Oakland but almost unheard and unread in Montclair.

It should be noted that the test is not a standardized test and has not been validated by comparison with standard intelligence tests administered to any sampling of the same groups of people; and, obviously, evaluating the comparative performance as jurors of those who passed and those who failed is a practical impossibility.

A psychologist with long experience in constructing and evaluating tests for different purposes testified that the test in question has the appearance of being an intelligence test but contains some items which reflect the cultural bias of the author. He also testified that at least fifty items would be needed in a well-constructed intelligence test to take into account the subcultures of a heterogenous population.

Furthermore, he expressed the opinion that ten minutes is too short a time to allow for this test, that it is not good test procedure to withhold the time limit from those taking the test, and that irrespective of time, 84% is too high a cutting point for a passing grade.

He also expressed the opinion that the test has a tendency to exclude people from the ghettoes because of "inadvertent discrimination"—that is, unintended discrimination resulting from cultural factors.

In terms of the results, he also expressed the opinion that the failure rate in both of the comparison areas was much too high and indicated that a substantial number of people who possessed "ordinary intelligence" were being eliminated in both areas.

The realities of our society emphasize the importance of jury panels drawn from a representative cross-section of the community. We have significant cultural differences almost unknown in our country thirty years ago. Litigants and witnesses come into Court from all walks of life in a highly varied community. Unless jury panels represent the same walks of life and the same pattern of cultural differences, they will be less likely to understand fully the implications of the testimony they hear and the situations they must evaluate, and less likely to bring into their deliberations the background of experience and wisdom required for a just result. Similarly, the narrower the cultural spectrum of our jury panels, the less confidence the under-represented groups will have in the courts as temples of justice.

The general term, "ordinary intelligence," must be interpreted and applied in this context. The Court cannot conclude that 81.5% *of the registered voters* in a large section of Oakland are below the level of "ordinary intelligence."

Accordingly, the challenge to the panel must be sustained.

The following questions from the Alameda County jurors' test are among those commented on by Judge Avakian in his opinion:

*Directions:* Please answer the following questions by putting a circle around the number in front of the *best possible* answer. *Work rapidly.* If you do not know the answer, guess, and go on to the next question.

**4. Why is a man superior to a productive machine?**

1. A man has a sense of humor.
2. A man can think.
3. A machine requires repairs.

**6. Which of the following is a trait of character?**

1. Generosity

2. Health
3. Personality

**8. Why was Civil Service established?**
1. As a sound political move.
2. To provide qualified workers for government jobs.
3. To increase the number of government bureaus.

**9. If you were asked what you thought of a person whom you didn't know, you should say:**
1. I will go and get acquainted.
2. I think he is all right.
3. I don't know him and can't say.

**10. The government of the United States is sound, because:**
1. It follows the will of the majority.
2. It does not allow representative government.
3. It permits the development of dictators.

**11. The most desirable quality of a juror is:**
1. Ambition.
2. Kindly attitude.
3. Logical thinking.

**14. A man's influence in a community should depend upon his:**
1. Wealth.
2. Character.
3. Ambition.

**19. What is the difference between "falsehood" and "perjury"?**
1. No difference. They are the same.
2. Perjury is a falsehood under oath.
3. Falsehood refers to a misdemeanor; perjury refers to a felony.

**20. You should not give money to beggars on the street, because:**
1. It makes it hard for the beggars to get work.
2. It encourages living off of others.
3. It takes away the work of organized charities.

**23. If a person asks you for something you do not have, you should:**
1. Tell him to mind his own business.
2. Say you don't have it.
3. Walk away.

When a California state prisoner challenged this Alameda County intelligence test collaterally in a federal petition for a habeas corpus writ, the Ninth Circuit cited Judge Avakian's unreported opinion in *Craig* (*Carmical v Craven* (9th Cir 1971) 457 F2d 582) and reached the same conclusion (see also §6.22). For a different opinion on a different county intelligence test for jurors, see *California v Powell* (Dist Ct App 1974) 115 Cal Rptr 109. See also §2.46.

### 6. Other Disqualifications and Exemptions §2.36

A deaf person who could read sign language, John G. O'Brien, was sworn in as a juror in a Washington state criminal case (marijuana selling) in Seattle after he answered no to the question: "Do you think there would be a problem in hearing all of the evidence presented to you?" *SF Chronicle*, May 16, 1979. A deaf person, Charles Peck, who had to provide (and pay) his own interpreter, was sworn in as a trial juror in a state criminal case (prostitution-solicitation) tried in Oakland, California, after both sides agreed to allow the interpreter to accompany the 12 jurors into the jury room during deliberations (but not to express his own opinion on the case). *SF Chronicle*, Oct. 25, 1979.

### 7. Recent Developments §2.37

See §2.15.

## B. Individual Excuses

### 1. Federal Act and Sample District Court Plan §2.41

Federal law provides in 28 USC §1866(c) for the excuse of individual jurors as follows:

> [A]ny person summoned for jury service may be (1) excused by the court, upon a showing of undue hardship or extreme inconvenience, for such period as the court deems necessary, at the conclusion of which such person shall be summoned again for jury service under subsections (b) and (c) of this section, or (2) excluded by the court on the ground that such person may be unable to render impartial jury service or that his service as a juror would be likely to disrupt the proceedings, or (3) excluded upon peremptory challenge as provided by law, or (4) excluded pursuant to the procedure specified by law upon a challenge by any party for good cause shown, or (5) excluded upon determination by the court that his service as a juror would be likely to threaten the secrecy of the proceedings, or otherwise adversely affect the integrity of jury deliberations. No person shall be excluded under clause (5) of this subsection unless the judge, in open court, determines that such is warranted and that exclusion of the person will not be inconsistent with sections 1861 and 1862 of this title . . . .

The jury selection plan used by the United States District Court for the Central District of California, for example, lists specific groups whose members may individually request excuse:

> 11. *Groups Whose Members May Individually Request Excuse*
> The District Court hereby finds that jury service by members of the following

occupational classes or groups of persons would entail undue hardship or extreme inconvenience to the members thereof, and the excuse or deferment of such members will not be inconsistent with the Act, and shall be granted upon individual request:

a. Persons over 70 years of age.
b. Actively engaged members of the clergy.
c. Persons who are not otherwise employed and who have legal custody of a child or children under the age of 14 years.
d. Actively practicing attorneys, physicians, dentists, and registered nurses.
e. Any person who has served as a grand or petit juror prior to his current call in a state or federal court within the past two years.
f. School teachers in public, parochial or private school actively teaching.
g. Students enrolled full time in a public, parochial or private school.
h. A sole proprietor of a business.
i. The Court may also excuse a person summoned for jury service upon showing of undue hardship or extreme inconvenience for such period as is deemed necessary.

## 2. Common State Practices §2.42

*Source:* Unreported opinion of Justice Gilbert King, Erie County, New York, Supreme Court, June 27, 1974, *New York v Attica Brothers* (see §3.26).

The former Deputy Commissioner of Jurors testified that it was her general policy to exempt those who indicated on their questionnaires that they were "students" and that she did so without a request from them on the theory that interference with their studies would be a hardship. There is no authority in the Judiciary Law or Appellate Division Rules for exclusion of "students" as a class. However well-intentioned the Deputy Commissioner may have been in attempting to prevent or accommodate anticipated hardships, her actions did result in the systematic and intentional exclusion of students from the jury lists. Complete exclusion of a class regardless of motivation and regardless of whether there is actual hardship involved is impermissible.

*COMMENT:* The challenge to the jury was successful on this point. Later, the New York legislature amended the law to broaden the sources of jurors and to tighten up procedures, which should eliminate such unfair exclusions. See §§2.26, 2.32.

## 3. Other Examples §2.43

This section is being reserved for discussion of new approaches to individual excusals. See §2.15.

### 4. Recent Developments §2.44

See §2.15.

## C. Typical Results of Disqualification and Excuse §2.46

In *California v Craig* (Alameda County Super Ct, No. 41750, Apr. 18, 1968) Judge Spurgeon Avakian summarized the results of disqualification and excuse:

With respect to the number who were processed but either excused or found not qualified, the total of 3,420 is made up of the following groupings:

| | |
|---|---|
| Poor health | 704 |
| Occupational exemption | 542 |
| Women with small children | 454 |
| Lack of understanding of English | 112 |
| Prior jury service | 244 |
| Poor hearing | 125 |
| Business and personal hardship | 161 |
| Travel | 17 |
| Conviction of high crime | 68 |
| Lack of transportation | 34 |
| Mental instability | 19 |
| Failed written test | 940 |
| | 3,420 |

For a discussion of the invalidity of the written test in Alameda County, see §2.35.

A study of possible biases in the jury selection process in the Eastern Division of the federal district court in Massachusetts found a "Middle American" bias on qualified jury wheels and derivative venires.

Stated negatively, we have found that blacks, women, urbanites, the young and the elderly, the poorly and the highly educated, all have less than a fair chance of making venire lists. Various subgroups, like young blacks, were even more sharply underrepresented. These findings, and others, are based on a comparison of venire-list data on 1150 qualified jurors with target proportions estimated from a census-based, normative juror selection model formed to satisfy much of the language of the court's 1970 Plan, but designed to approximate better its constitutional objectives.

An empirical analysis of various stages of the juror selection process has been made to examine the causes of these biases. Both the excuse process (which differentially removes women and the highly educated) and total reliance on voter registration lists (which are biased against blacks and the young) were found to be responsible.

Alker, Hosticka, & Mitchell, "Jury Selection as a Biased Social Process," 11 *Law & Soc'y Rev* 9 (1976). See Note, "Underrepresentation of Economic Groups on Federal Juries," 57 *Boston UL Rev* 198 (1977).

A juror's view of the excuse and selection process provides a useful summary and perspective. Mary Timothy describes her experience as a juror in the *Angela Davis* case (see §3.23) in *Jury Woman* 18 (1974) (available from Volcano Press, 330 Ellis Street, San Francisco, California 94102 for $4.95).

> That first day had been a pretty fair introduction to what was to be the hardest part of being a juror in this long involved trial—the waiting.
>
> Every morning for two weeks I drove to San Jose. The sense of anticipation and excitement I originally felt faded during those two weeks. All of the procedures became routine, even the daily indignity of being searched. I learned to carry nothing metal in my pockets and wear no jewelry. I had my keys and coins in my hand as I hit the door, dropping them into the basins along with purse and books—all in one motion.
>
> I climbed the stairs, stopped at the vending machine for a cup of coffee, went directly to "my" chair, greeted my neighbors and waited for roll call.
>
> Once roll had been taken, those of us remaining in the assembly room were ignored by everyone—except for brief intervals when the T.V. came on and we could watch the questioning of someone in the jury box—or when another name was plucked from the squirrel cage.
>
> It was called the "trial of the century" and we had been selected from the hundreds of thousands of residents in the county. We had come to the courthouse full of excitement and ready for our moment of glory. And now we were stuck in a hall on uncomfortable folding chairs . . . and ignored. There was no glory. There was no excitement. There was nothing but complete and utter boredom.
>
> The lottery of the drawing for the next juror became terribly important. As the cage whirled, the suspense was intense—the announcement of the name was followed by low moans of disappointment—then words of encouragement for the holder of the lucky number.
>
> One young woman, after reporting in the morning, left to take care of personal business right after roll call. Her name was the next one called. When she couldn't be located, the judge issued a warrant for her arrest!
>
> That incident impressed us all.
>
> We had been told no excuses would be considered until we were actually in the jury box and could be questioned by the judge and attorneys. Even medical excuses would not be accepted unless they were supported by a letter from a doctor.
>
> As the days passed and it became obvious that there might be a very long wait before many of the veniremen were called down, the restrictions were eased. First the students heard a rumor that they could be excused if they brought a letter from the head of their department. It was the last week before finals for the winter quarter. If the trial went on for six to eight months, they

would lose a year's work if they served on the jury. While the time lost was important, a break in attendance at college would result in loss of financial aid for many of them, which was even more important.

There was no official notice given, but the rumor spread, and the next morning most of the young people lined up at the front desk with letters in their hands. They were soon on their way back to school.

As the initial excitement gave way to the inevitable boredom, people found all sorts of compelling reasons why it would be impossible for them to serve. Medical excuses were coming in more and more frequently as time dragged on and the chairs got harder. All the aches and pains that had been ignored the first day now were discussed freely; the disabilities people had considered too minor to mention on the cards they filled out for the Jury Commissioner now assumed major importance. The flu bug hit and its victims joined the others checking with their doctors.

It would be perfectly quiet as we sat waiting. Suddenly someone would stand up, walk to the front of the room and confer with the woman at the desk. After a few sentences, the person would come back and sit tensely waiting until the next break—then head for the telephone. That might be the last we would see of the reluctant jury panel member.

The next to leave were the workers. Those whose income depended on day-to-day employment were allowed to present evidence to show that remaining on the panel would cause them undue hardship. The self-employed and those who worked for small concerns would have suffered great financial loss if the trial lasted for many months.

Over forty people disappeared without ever being called down to court. The group remaining was far more homogeneous than the original 116. The students had gone, the workers, the poor, the old and the weak. Those left were largely middle-aged, middle-class people employed by the large industries of the area—industries large enough to absorb the financial loss of an employee's long absence.

Not all large companies, however, had a policy of continuing salary for employees while they served on juries. The Southern Pacific Railroad informed an employee of thirty years that he would be paid for two weeks, but no longer. And yet a local department store allowed a salesperson hired just two weeks before the trial to serve without loss of salary. There was no set pattern but it seemed to me that workers belonging to strong unions, such as the Retail Clerks Union, were guaranteed no loss of job, salary or seniority.

Economics had a great deal to do with the composition of the jury.

With this early exodus, most of the minorities also disappeared. The two black members had gone. One was selected in the first drawing and was down sitting in the jury box. The other, a well-dressed woman with children in school, was excused when one of them got the flu. I had the feeling that she didn't want to be identified with the case—and was glad to have a legitimate excuse to leave.

Thirty more people were released after their preliminary questioning in these first two weeks . . . . I found out later that the individual private questioning dealt with the personal problems of the prospective jurors, their health or financial difficulties which might interfere with their ability to serve through a long and difficult trial.

Can lawyers conduct effective voir dire questioning to ameliorate the loss of representatives of many cognizable classes due to the factors discussed by Mary Timothy? This is the challenge addressed throughout this book.

# Chapter 3

# *Basic Cases and Source Materials*

**I. Need for New Jury Materials**
A. Traditional Materials Inadequate §3.1
B. Law School Trial Practice Courses §3.2
C. Continuing Legal Education §3.3

**II. New Source Materials Now Available**
A. Legal Work Product
1. Case Analyses, Voir Dire Questions §3.11
2. Pleadings, Memos, Briefs §3.12
3. Transcripts and Bench Opinions §3.13
4. A Practical Suggestion for Law Office Libraries §3.14
B. Official Forms §3.16
C. Interdisciplinary Materials §3.17
D. Recent Developments §3.18

**III. Specific Case Materials Used**
A. Types of Cases and Materials Selected §3.21
B. Significant Cases Described
1. State Criminal Cases
a. *California v Newton* (*Huey Newton* Case) §3.22
b. *California v Angela Davis* §3.23
c. *California v Burt* (*Venceremos* Case) §3.24
d. *New York v Shakur* (*Panther 21* Case) §3.25
e. *New York v Attica Brothers* §3.26
f. *Michigan v DeSaussure* (*Detroit 15* Case) §3.27

g. *Taylor v Louisiana* §3.28
h. *California v Block* §3.29
i. *Ristaino v Ross* §3.30
j. *Michigan v Hartwell* §3.31
k. Recent Cases §3.32

2. State Civil Cases
   a. *Brewster v Martin Marietta* §3.41
   b. *Stroud v General Motors* §3.42
   c. Recent Cases §3.43
3. Federal Criminal Cases
   a. *United States v McNeil* §3.51
   b. *United States v Russo* (*Pentagon Papers* Case) §3.52
   c. *United States v Briggs* (*Gainesville Eight* Case) §3.53
   d. *United States v Dellinger* (*Chicago Eight* Case) §3.54
   e. *United States v Anderson* (*Camden 28* Case) §3.55
   f. *United States v Berkowitz* §3.56
   g. *Rosales-Lopez v United States* §3.57
   h. Recent Cases §3.58
4. Federal Civil Cases
   a. *Hampton v Hanrahan* §3.71
   b. *Krause v Rhodes* §3.72
   c. *MCI v AT&T* §3.73
   d. Recent Cases §3.74
5. Courts Martial
   a. *Tangela Gaskins Administrative Discharge* Case §3.91
   b. Recent Cases §3.92

# I. NEED FOR NEW JURY MATERIALS

## A. Traditional Materials Inadequate §3.1

The legal materials presently available come from three basic sources: (1) scholars, law professors, or legal philosophers; (2) commercial publishers; and (3) bar associations.

Traditional law professors write articles, hornbooks, and restatements on specific phases of their fields of interest, relying mainly on United States Supreme Court opinions, law review articles, and books by other law professors, occasionally turning to intermediate appellate court opinions, statutes, or adminstrative regulations. Those who believe in the importance of the clinical approach and who are interdisciplinary in their views cite studies by professors in other fields. There are few references in scholarly writing to transcripts of hearings, memos in support of motions made before or during trial, appellate briefs, amicus briefs, debates or resolutions of bar associations, articles by practitioners, colloquies between bench and bar, or eloquent closing arguments to juries.

Legal scholars tend to denigrate authors to how-to-do-it manuals. They do not know the analytical effort required to make a mountain of pleadings, motions, and memos into a series of forms that can be used with confidence in numerous cases when used with a short, accurate description of the steps required to achieve a certain goal.

Practitioners using legal writings by professors are often frustrated by having to read more pages than they have time to digest, to learn more than they want to know, in order to write a very short summary of the law to satisfy an overnight demand by a trial judge. It is often difficult to find the one relevant book, because it has not been published.

The commercial law publishers are beset or benefited by a series of practical realities. Lawyers live in fear of malpractice and therefore buy sets of volumes to which they will never refer in order to be sure that, if they need to know something late Thursday night when the library is closed, they can at least get an encyclopedic paragraph into their heads. Few authors of commercial law encyclopedias and digests are known to the general bar, and their standards of excellence are largely determined by their own intellectual curiosity and the number of pages they are expected to produce in a given number of hours. Their training and natural tendency is to turn to the same sources used by the scholars—appellate reports.

The practicing lawyer never litigates cases in which the law is crystal clear. Everyone realizes that the cases that are litigated are based on hard facts that tend to make bad law. But few realize that the forms constantly copied from form books are taken from pleadings in cases that would never have been litigated if the papers had been properly drafted in the first place! While this is, of course, an overstatement, it does pose the problem the practitioner faces when searching for a simple, clear form that will hold up against an adverse motion.

## B. Law School Trial Practice Courses §3.2

After many false starts, and with considerable hesitancy on the part of some substantive law professors, clinical courses are now being well conducted in many law schools in the United States. Practitioners are leaving their offices and court trials one day or evening a week to impart some of their bread-and-butter skills to anxious students, who realize that they probably will not find jobs in large law firms where they could receive first-rate instruction on trial techniques in civil and criminal cases.

Increasingly, full-time clinical law professors are getting tenure-track positions. At best, however, case exercises lack the bite of reality faced by the practicing lawyer when there is no money and no time to do the job right, and yet the client's case must be well-presented so that the client will win and thus be able to pay a fee for the work. Many law schools have developed apprenticeship programs, externships, and internships that permit (or require) students to spend many hours working in courtrooms with trial judges, in appellate courts on preparation of briefs, and in private and public law offices.

As the number of law graduates has increased sharply in recent years, with no comparable increase in law jobs, new lawyers have found it necessary to develop their own postgraduate training programs. They seek to learn what they need to know without doing so at the expense of their first few clients.

All the professors, students, and postgraduates mentioned are searching for materials to study that will get them started on the right track in their oral and written work in the trial courts.

## C. Continuing Legal Education §3.3

Bar associations have increasingly sought to provide postgraduate courses and mini-courses to the members in their areas. Through conferences, seminars, cassette tapes, and manuals, continuing education programs have tried to meet the needs of busy practitioners who are engaged in what they call general practice—a euphemism for the endless effort to assist clients and earn a living by putting fingers in several dikes simultaneously.

The American Trial Lawyers Association; similar state associations; the California Attorneys for Criminal Justice; the National Lawyers Guild; the National Conference of Black Lawyers; women lawyers associations; criminal justice committees and subcommittees of local, state, and national bar associations; and many other ethnic and regional bar groups are now holding seminars and work sessions in which skillful lawyers describe how they win jury cases. Some of the material in this book is derived from such sources. However, the rough-and-ready information provided in some such bar association materials is not edited sufficiently to add the necessary qualifications, update the citations, and keep in mind the law from other jurisdictions.

Many practicing lawyers denigrate their own clinical work. When asked to speak or write for bar associations, they tend to drop their advocacy style and turn to law review articles and hornbooks for guidance, rather than setting forth the practical wisdom they have gleaned from everyday experience. Or they may merely describe a colloquy with a trial judge that makes a good story at a bar meeting. They fail to make the unique contribution of describing how they conducted the careful research that went into an appellate brief or argument in a recent case.

## II. NEW SOURCE MATERIALS NOW AVAILABLE

### A. Legal Work Product

#### 1. Case Analyses, Voir Dire Questions §3.11

Plaintiffs' personal injury lawyers and criminal defense lawyers often work in relatively small offices, so that the excellent paperwork they do is not shared widely with associates or partners, as has been done traditionally in large commercial firms. Winning lawyers nonetheless do all the paperwork necessary to convince a judge and/or jury, and this includes not only formulating lists of questions to ask on voir dire, for example, but also writing out a careful analysis of the strong and weak points in each case, and notes to be used in opening and closing statements to the jury.

Chapter 4 contains a number of examples of the trial notes used by trial lawyers in analyzing their cases—the facts, the clients, and the forum. Chapter 5 discusses the methods by which lawyers prepare a model juror profile. These materials should be helpful to lawyers searching for ways to improve their own analyses of their cases even before filing pretrial motions.

The major civil and criminal cases used as sources for the materials in these volumes are described in §§3.22–3.92. Many other cases are discussed once or twice, and are described at the point at which materials from their files are used.

## 2. Pleadings, Memos, Briefs §3.12

A criminal defense lawyer who wants to obtain a change of venue for a client needs a model motion for a change of venue, a memorandum of points and authorities in support of that motion, model affidavits in support, and the approach used to obtain a community survey showing that a change of venue is required. A civil lawyer who wants to conduct an extensive, individual voir dire also needs a model motion and memo.

The deadlines for pretrial motions are becoming increasingly shorter as the indiscriminate demand for speed in trials moves through state and federal legislative bodies. See, *e.g.*, the federal Speedy Trial Act of 1974, 18 USC §§3161–3174, and the discussion in chapters 1, 6, and 7 on the delay sometimes required in order to achieve a modicum of justice. The lawyer needs to know quickly the wording of the documents that must be typed between now and Monday morning, the kind of specialist needed, and the questionnaire to be formulated by the established deadline.

The Meiklejohn Civil Liberties Institute in Berkeley, California, has pioneered in the distribution of legal work product in constitutional law fields, particularly materials on jury selection, due process in criminal cases, international human rights, and economic rights. The Institute library has acquired the complete materials in several major cases, including the University of California Free Speech Movement case, *Savio v California*, *cert. denied* (1967) 388 US 460 (see §1.52); the *Angela Davis* case, (see §3.23); the *Pentagon Papers* case (see §3.52); and *DeFunis v Odegaard & the Univ. of Washington* (1974) 416 US 312, precursor to *Bakke v Regents of the Univ. of California* (1978) 438 US 265. Two books published by the institute, *The Angela Davis Case Collection* (1974) and *The Pentagon Papers Case Collection* (1975), catalog and describe the materials. All papers in both cases are now available on microfilm from Oceana Publications, Dobbs Ferry, New York, which also published the record and all amicus briefs in *DeFunis* (Ginger, ed., 3 vols., 1974). Meiklejohn Institute has also collected important documents in thousands of other cases arising since 1955. Photocopies of pleadings, transcript pages, briefs, and other materials are available on order. Some other associations of civil and criminal trial lawyers have also established brief banks for their members.

Most of the materials in this book were compiled from the Meiklejohn collection. While an effort was made to include primarily material from successful cases, some unsuccessful motions and challenges are also used as models here. Where this has been done, the statement that the pleading was unsuccessful is included. The filing date appears in the source notes; the lawyer must be careful to Shepardize, Lexisize, or Westlawize all material in the pleadings.

### 3. Transcripts and Bench Opinions §3.13

Inexperienced trial lawyers tend to worry about how to examine or cross-examine an expert witness, which may be necessary on a pretrial motion for a change of venue, for extensive voir dire, or for other purposes. Perusal of the transcript of an experienced lawyer examining or cross-examining an expert in such a situation will often reassure the novice. Examples of such transcripts, edited for brevity and content organization, are given in §§8.81, 8.83, 8.87.

A significant source of law is off-the-bench decisions and opinions by trial judges in cases that are never appealed. There is no reason to drop these opinions from legal literature and precedent merely because they were made orally by trial court judges in writing rather than by appellate judges. Often such opinions are well reasoned and deserve inclusion in the *Federal Supplement*. See, *e.g.*, the decision by federal Judge Gordon dismissing charges against the antiwar protesters in *United States v Cotton* (reprinted in §7.65).

This book contains transcripts of off-the-bench opinions in several significant cases on several important motions. The author hopes that use of trial court opinions will increase, and that opinions from county courts that set forth the law clearly will be circulated among the practicing bar by means of photocopies. Such was the fate of a bench decision by Judge Avakian in *California v Craig* (Alameda County Super Ct, No. 41750, Apr. 18, 1968), holding unconstitutional the "intelligence test" for jurors. §2.35. This unreported opinion was cited repeatedly and successfully by California lawyers who learned of it, and the principle was ultimately affirmed by the Ninth Circuit Court of Appeals in *Carmical v Craven* (9th Cir 1971) 457 F2d 582, *cert. denied* (1972) 409 US 929.

### 4. A Practical Suggestion for Law Office Libraries §3.14

As litigation increases, the need intensifies for written and oral material to upgrade the practice of law. A significant improvement could occur in the quality of law practice if lawyers and law office staffs learned that well-writen motions, affidavits, memos of points and authorities, briefs, and other documents should not remain hidden in individual case files at the conclusion of successful cases. The present system (or lack of system) usually consigns these materials to oblivion, to be borrowed and copied only occasionally when a lawyer remembers the name of the case, recalls the materials in the case file, and is able to retrieve them from deep in dead storage. Seldom will lawyers outside a particular office know that such work product exists.

If a legal secretary, law clerk, student running a law office library, or law librarian would simply black out the names of the parties and photocopy a set of good basic materials on a subject like change of venue, they could be placed in a general file for use by everyone in the office. It would be helpful to have a card file showing the subject matter of the pleading or brief, and in what case file it can be found. This kind of cross-referencing is heartily recommended by the author. It does not take long, and over the years it saves a great deal of time.

Some lawyers have developed brief banks on common issues. Unfortunately, these are generally limited to briefs, excluding papers that are not bound and are not the same size as an appellate brief. Thus a good motion or memorandum of points and authorities does not get preserved in a library area for retrieval by means of subject cards.

Criminal defense lawyers should note that state attorneys general and the United States Department of Justice have developed good, efficient brief banks for statewide or national use by prosecutors. In addition, United States attorneys have developed computerized magnetic cards for the rapid preparation of jury instructions and other frequently used forms. (See Ginger, "A Data Bank of Constitutional Rights?" 1 *Hastings Const'l LQ* 133 (1974).)

As many law offices move to computers and data-processing equipment, it should be even easier to store well-written pleadings, motions, voir dire questions, and affidavits, as well as memos and briefs, for use as models in later litigation. Perhaps the computer will be the magic device that erases the distinction between "briefs—to be stored in the library" and "pleadings—to be relegated to the dead files."

## B. Official Forms §3.16

In the search for methods of saving the time of the bench, official forms have come into use that also save the time of the bar. Many are included in this book.

Both federal and state jurisdictions are increasing the number and types of official forms that must be used for the filing of certain types of pleadings. Before embarking on the drafting of a motion or other form, it is wise to check with the appropriate court clerk to discover whether an official form has been prepared for the purpose.

## C. Interdisciplinary Materials §3.17

A number of sociologists and psychologists who have participated in jury selection and other aspects of jury trials have written articles on their experiences for scholarly journals. Lawyers can benefit from the study of materials by professionals from other disciplines, even though they may be upset at some unlawyerlike inaccuracies that creep into sociological descriptions of jury selection, for example; undoubtedly sociologists are equally upset when lawyers spout tidbits of sociological insight, out of context, in speeches to bar association meetings.

The contributions of Dr. Hans Zeisel, Dr. Jay Schulman, Professor Jeffery Paige, Dr. Richard Christie, Dr. Craig Haney, and others have benefited particular plaintiffs and defendants and now are available to the broader legal community. (See Index for section references.)

Professors Zeisel and (the late) Harry Kalven led the study of the American jury system undertaken at the University of Chicago Law School under a Ford Foundation grant. Their underlying purpose was simply to "find out how in fact the jury is performing." At the time, Chief Justice Earl Warren said their study, *The American Jury* (1966), was "the most ambitious empirical study of jury behavior that has been attempted."

Drawing from reports of 3,576 jury trials from numerous courts in the United States in the 1950s, the authors offered a general theory of jury decision-making emanating from rigorous scientific research undertaken in a strictly legal field. Guided by the debatable belief that lawyers were not and could not be good social scientists, the authors saw their task as bringing together into a working relationship the "research skills and fresh perspectives of the one to the socially significant problems of the other." From this scholarly idealism, however, emerged an historical account of the controversy over the jury system, and comparative studies of other jury systems.

The authors used various methods such as comparing hypothetical decisions of the judges with the real verdicts of the juries, and developing basic questionnaires. Integrating traditional social science research with innovative methods, they concluded (1) that jurors in criminal cases do understand the evidence; (2) that they reach sound conclusions; and (3) that when their conclusions differ from those the judge would have reached, it is usually because the jury was serving some of the very purposes for which it was created.

For other important jury studies growing out of the project, and later studies, see indexes to legal and sociological periodicals. For an analysis of the reasons for the inadequacy of many studies, see Lermack, "No Right Number? Social Science Research and the Jury-Size Cases," 54 *NYU L Rev* 951 (1979).

### D. Recent Developments §3.18

It is now possible to keep up with the law on jury selection the same way you keep up with the law in any other field—by reading the relevant advance sheets, subscribing to services on trial advocacy or criminal law, and reading daily newspapers and legal newspapers. The *Index to Legal Periodicals*, *Current Law Index*, and *Legal Resource Index* provide provocative (and sometimes descriptive) titles to law review articles, comments, and notes in this field, indicating what is happening at the cutting edge of the law. It is a good idea occasionally to ask your law librarian for an index to journals on psychology, applied psychology, and the social sciences, to pick up new ideas from these disciplines.

Increasingly, lawyers are learning to use *Lexis* and *Westlaw* in order to find the latest cases and interesting parallels in other fields of law. It is always necessary to Shepardize all citations.

The Annual Supplement to these volumes will use recent developments sections throughout the book to describe new cases, ideas, and articles that are worthy of note, and to warn of cases overruled and of rules and statutes amended or repealed.

## III. SPECIFIC CASE MATERIALS USED

### A. Types of Cases and Materials Selected §3.21

This book is a patchwork quilt of materials used successfully (and sometimes unsuccessfully) in recent grand jury and trial jury cases. It is pieced together in more or less chronological order of steps in the process of jury selection. The author set each piece in an editorial framework to try to make it as useful as possible in as many jurisdictions as possible.

The three tests used for including material in the book were: what could be used most widely in state and federal courts throughout the country, what materials would be least accessible even to a conscientious lawyer, and what unsettled issues require immediate attention.

The author intended to make it possible for a single practitioner or a single public defender in an isolated area to mount a successful challenge to an improperly compiled grand or petit jury list without spending more time or money than is available. The book should also make it possible for a lawyer quickly to provide a trial judge with a good list of voir dire questions that the judge can accept because they have been accepted elsewhere. (Precedent here is proof of use in another jurisdiction, rather than appellate opinions reversing convictions because trial judges refused to permit such use.)

The book presents new examples of old concepts based on old constitutional principles that have recently received new impetus and life from their successful use by skillful practitioners. It emphasizes use of what is new and innovative and calls for rejection of precedents if they are founded in what the Supreme Court calls "the unfortunate facts" of racism, caste prejudice, sexism, and other undemocratic ideologies (see §6.51).

Whenever possible, small pieces have been included from larger works and examples have been taken from many cases to indicate the variety of state and federal cases in which these techniques have proved successful. The text might have been smoother if fewer cases had been used, but it has greater value because lawyers can show trial and appellate judges that the practice being suggested has been accepted by numerous courts at various levels throughout the country.

No national book can state "the law" correctly, because it varies so much from state to state and from state courts to federal courts. Readers are advised to insert in their copies of these books the citations to state and local rules. The author will happily include such citations in supplements as they are received. This book relies heavily on California citations, due to the number of showcase trials in California. In case titles, *People* has been changed to the name of the state, as in *New York v Attica Brothers*. National citations are given when possible. For accurate and current citations to all cases, check the Table of Cases. For example, when the text shows "petition pending," check the Annual Supplements to the Table of Cases for "cert. granted" or citation to a decision issued after the volume was published. Citations, even in reported opinions, have been changed to conform to the style of this book.

The cases mentioned most often throughout the book are described in some detail in §§3.22–3.92 so the reader can understand the facts and legal issues raised in pretrial proceedings. Only points relevant to jury selection are described fully. These cases generated few reported (appellate) opinions; accordingly, full citations are given to pleadings and to unreported bench opinions. Without such reportage, sound and successful work by trial counsel can be lost to the profession, since only-partially-accurate lay reports may be found in newspaper libraries.

Sometimes the successful new use of an old technique results in its demise. This happened to the practice of voir-diring grand jurors in New York State. Creative and conscientious research by defense lawyers in the *Black Panther 21* case (see §3.25) unearthed New York Code of Criminal Procedure §§230, 232, and 234, permitting lawyers for the defense to question grand jurors in the same kind of voir dire permitted in most trial courts. Counsel in that case exercised this right, and the picture of the grand jurors obtained by the voir dire showed how far they strayed from the "fair cross-section" standard that is constitutionally required (see §2.3). After this use of the statutes in the *Panther 21* case (which ended in acquittal), the New York legislature repealed the sections permitting voir dire of grand jurors.

## B. Significant Cases Described

### 1. State Criminal Cases

#### a. *California v Newton* (*Huey Newton* Case) §3.22

Huey Newton was arrested October 28, 1967, at 5:00 a.m., when he and a companion were stopped in their car by two white Oakland police officers. Within a few minutes, Officer John Frey had been shot and killed, and Newton and Officer Herbert Heanes had been wounded. Newton, cofounder and minister of defense for the Black Panther Party for Self Defense, was charged with the murder of Frey, assault with a deadly weapon on Heanes, kidnapping, and conviction of a prior felonious assault.

The trial was held in Alameda County Superior Court, with Judge Monroe Friedman presiding. The defense presented motions challenging the grand and petit jury selection procedures, which were denied. Defense attorney Charles Garry conducted a lengthy voir dire examination (see chapters 15 and 17 for excerpts from the voir dire), and a jury of one black man and 11 whites was chosen. Most of the voir dire questions used are listed in chapters 9 and 11.

The defense argued that Newton had been shot in the abdomen and was in a state of unconsciousness when Frey was shot. Jury instructions on the defense of unconsciousness and of diminished capacity were requested; the latter was given, but the former was not given. The jury found Newton guilty of voluntary manslaughter, acquitted him on the assault, and found the charge of conviction of a prior felonious assault to be true. *California v Newton* (Alameda County Super Ct, No. 41266, Sept. 8, 1968).

On appeal, the conviction was reversed. *California v Newton* (Dist Ct App 1970) 87 Cal Rptr 394. The court found error on evidentiary problems and on jury instructions not given. Other claims of error relating to grand jury procedure and jury selection were held to be without merit. The California Supreme Court denied the government's petition for a hearing.

In 1971 the case was retried, and a hung jury resulted. The case was tried for the third time, later that year, and another hung jury resulted. The case was then dismissed.

Charles Garry and the late Fay Stender of San Francisco handled Newton's defense, with assistance from Alexander Hoffman, Edward Keating, and Carlton Innis, and sociologist Robert Blauner of Berkeley. Blauner's view of the trial can be found in chapter 18.

### b. *California v Angela Davis* §3.23

Angela Davis was indicted as a result of an August 7, 1970, Marin County courthouse incident, in which Jonathan Jackson led an escape attempt involving three San Quentin prison inmates. Two of the inmates, the presiding judge, and Jackson were killed in the attempt; one of the inmates, Ruchell Magee, and the assistant district attorney were injured. The guns used in the incident were registered to Angela Davis, and a warrant for her arrest was issued. Davis was arrested in New York City. Her attorneys fought extradition, but on December 22, 1970, she was returned to California to face charges of murder, kidnapping, and conspiracy, along with codefendant Ruchell Magee.

Extensive publicity appeared in the news media concerning the courthouse incident, Ms. Davis's flight from California, and her subsequent arrest. She was already well known in the state as a member of the Communist Party as a result of her fight to stay on the faculty at the University of California, Los Angeles.

Pretrial proceedings began in Marin County Superior Court (case no. 3744). The trials of Davis and Magee were severed, and on November 2, 1971, the judge granted Davis's motion for change of venue, and the trial was moved to Santa Clara County. Forms requesting change of venue based on those filed in *Davis* are found in chapter 7. A subsequent motion to change venue to San Francisco was denied.

A defense motion to permit Ms. Davis to act as her own co-counsel was granted, and she participated in the voir dire of prospective jurors (see chapter 17) and made the opening statement in her own behalf. The voir dire lasted 12 days, and the defense relied heavily on information received from volunteer defense investigators, as described in chapter 13, and the opinions of black psychologists who assisted the attorneys. Voir dire questions used appear in chapter 11.

The prosecution presented 104 witnesses, and alleged that the August 7, 1970, incident had been part of a conspiracy to free the Soledad Brothers, claiming that Angela Davis was passionately in love with George Jackson, one of these men. The defense presented 12 witnesses in 2½ days. Four months after the trial began and 597 days after her arrest, Angela Davis was acquitted by the jury. *California v Davis* (Santa Clara County Super Ct, No. 52613, June 4, 1972).

Attorneys Leo Branton, Margaret Burnham, Howard Moore, Jr., and Doris Brin Walker represented Ms. Davis during the trial. Sheldon Otis, Michael Tigar, Dennis Roberts, and Alan Brotsky, and representatives from the National Conference of Black Lawyers, the American Civil Liberties Union, and the National Lawyers Guild assisted in preparation of numerous pretrial motions. Four Michigan attorneys from the National Lawyers Guild, Tom Meyer, Ken Mogill, Dean Robb, and Jeff Tate, helped set up the defense jury selection system for the Santa Clara trial.

For a further description of the case, a list of all documents filed in court, and description of significant pleadings and trial court proceedings, see Ginger, *Angela Davis Case Collection: Annotated Procedural Guide and Index* (1974) (Meiklejohn Civil Liberties Institute, Box 673, Berkeley, California 97401). The complete case collection (20,000 pages) is available on microfilm from Oceana Publications, Dobbs Ferry, New York 10522. For a description of the case written by the foreperson of the jury, see Timothy, *Jury Women* (1974). (Available from Volcano Press, 330 Ellis Street, San Francisco, CA 94102.) See also descriptions by the defendant, Davis, *An Autobiography* (1974); by a leader of the defense team, Aptheker, *The Morning Breaks* (1975); and by a journalist, Major, *Justice in the Round* (1973).

### c. *California v Burt (Venceremos* Case) §3.24

On July 18, 1973, Benton Douglas Burt and Andrea Holman Burt were found guilty by a San Bernardino jury of second degree murder, assault, and rescue in a case arising out of a prison escape attempt. On October 6, 1972, Chino prison inmate Ronald Wayne Beaty, then a member of Venceremos, a revolutionary group, had escaped from a state car in an ambush. One guard was killed and another wounded in the escape. Beaty was recaptured on December 11. Before his escape, Beaty had been serving a life sentence with no possibility of parole; after his recapture, he was reportedly offered parole in seven years in exchange for testifying against the Burts and other members of Venceremos.

The Burts, having heard they were wanted in connection with the escape, turned themselves in on October 23 and were charged with the crimes.

Both Andrea and Doug Burt had been involved in prisoners' rights work. He was a former prison inmate who had served a ten-year sentence for receiving five dollars' worth of stolen property. As a jailhouse lawyer and prison activist, he had been under close surveillance by prison authorities, and had come to know Ronald Beaty. Andrea Holman Burt was also active in prisoners' rights work and joined Venceremos in 1971. That same year she traveled to Cuba as part of a work brigade to cut sugar cane and study the Cuban legal system.

The trial was held in San Bernardino County. Massive pretrial publicity surrounded the case. Defense attorney Charles Garry conducted the voir dire (for excerpts, see chapter 17). The prosecutor, Joseph Canty, used peremptory challenges against all poor people, working people, members of minority groups, and people under 30. The resulting jury had a median age of 58 and was all white. The prosecution relied heavily on the testimony of Beaty and continuously discussed the Burts' history as activists; the (white) race of witnesses was contrasted with the (black) race of the convicts they visited. The testimony of other eyewitnesses was inconclusive. The Burts were convicted. *California v Burt* (San Bernardino County Super Ct, No. CR-28514, July 18, 1973). Appeal was denied in the district court of appeal. Attorneys on the appeal were Charles Garry, Benjamin Dreyfus, and Michael Goldstein of San Francisco; and Thomas J. Nolan, Jr., of Menlo Park, California.

### d. *New York v Shakur* (*Panther 21* Case) §3.25

Twenty-one members of the Black Panther Party were arrested in April 1969, in New York City, under a 30-count indictment charging them with conspiracy to commit murder and arson by bombing police precincts, department stores, and a railroad siding.

The defense petitioned the court for permission to conduct a voir dire of the grand jury after the indictments had been returned against all defendants. This was allowed under New York Code of Criminal Procedure §§230, 232, 233, 234 (these sections have since been repealed). (For examples of questions asked during the voir dire of the grand jurors, see chapter 9.)

The trial began in September 1970 in New York County Supreme Court (Case No. 1848–69), with Judge John M. Murtagh presiding.

Jury selection required six weeks; the final jury consisted of four black men, one Puerto Rican man, one black woman, and six white men. The trial lasted for eight months. Much of the evidence presented by the prosecution was based on the testimony of police informants and undercover agents.

On May 13, 1971, two years after the initial arrests, the jury deliberated for 90 minutes, and then returned a verdict of "not guilty" on all counts. The jurors discussed the case with reporters and lawyers later, and mentioned the lack of real evidence, discrepancies on cross-examination, and the bias of the judge as important factors in their decision-making.

Some of the defendants represented themselves during the trial. Attorneys handling the case were Gerald Lefcourt, Carol Lefcourt, William Crain, Sanford Katz, Robert Bloom, and Charles McKinney.

For one view, see Zimroth, *Preservations of Justice: The Prosecution and Acquittal of the Panther 21* (1974).

### e. *New York v Attica Brothers* §3.26

On September 9, 1971, prisoners at Attica State Prison rebelled and took 50 prison guards hostage. The prisoners presented state officials with a list of demands, foremost among them a demand for amnesty from any prosecutions arising from the uprising. Unsuccessful negotiations between state officials and prisoners were conducted through a group of neutrals. Governor Nelson Rockefeller rejected requests by both prisoners and neutrals that he personally come to the prison. On the morning of September 13, state troopers and corrections officers moved in and retook the prison. As a result of that action 39 persons were killed; in all 43 persons died during the uprising (32 inmates and 11 hostages).

The Wyoming County grand jury handed down indictments against 61 of the Attica Brothers for over 1,400 counts of criminal actions; at least 40 separate trials were projected. No state officials were indicted. Venue was changed to Erie County, and extensive pretrial motions were argued.

A massive challenge to the trial jury selection process was submitted. Judge Gilbert King found that students and women were underrepresented and dismissed almost the entire jury pool. *New York v Attica Brothers* (Erie County Sup Ct 1974) 359 NYS2d 699, quoted in §§6.12, 6.56, 6.62. See Bonora, "Attica Jury Challenge: II," *Conspiracy*, Sept. 1974, p.16.

Of the 61 prisoners charged, 5 or 6 pleaded guilty to lesser charges and were not tried; they received concurrent sentences. One charge of sodomy was dismissed for lack of corroboration after the prosecution presented its case. Only three trials went to verdict: one charge of murder was reduced to assault, the defendant was convicted and later pardoned; another murder charge resulted in conviction, and the defendant's sentence was later commuted; one defendant, Shango Kakawana, was acquitted on charges of common law murder and unlawful imprisonment of another prisoner.

On February 26, 1976, the state unconditionally dismissed all but one of the remaining charges against the prisoners. (One charge remains against a fugitive ex-prisoner for the death of another prisoner.)

For an account of the events leading up to the dismissals, see an article by pretrial defense counsel Don Jelinek, "Attica Then, Attica Now," 223 *Nation* 581 (1976). Also see Ernest Goodman's and Shango Kakawana's account of a pro se defendant acquitted of murder charges, "Attica and the Constitutional Pro Se Defendant," printed in 44 *Detroit Lawyer* 7 (1976) and 34 *Lawyers Guild Practitioner* 42 (1977). See generally the report of the McKay Commission, *Attica: The Official Report of the New York State Special Commission on Attica* (1972); Wicker, *A Time to Die* (1975); Badillo and Haynes, *A Bill of No Rights: Attica and the American Prison System* (1972).

Eighty-five attorneys assisted with the defense; the following were listed on pretrial motions cited in this book: Ramsey Clark, Paul Chevigny, Jesse Berman, David Blackstone, Martin R. Stolar, Haywood Burns, William Kunstler, Joseph R. Mack, Jim Carroll, and Emily Goodman of New York; Richard Rosche, Salvatore Martoche, Richard Lippes, Leonard J. Klaif, Norman Effman, Edward I. Koren, Herman Schwartz, Stan Collesano, Vincent E. Doyle, Jr., Thomas Labin, Sean Hill, and Paul Birzon of Buffalo; Elizabeth A. Gaynes of Syracuse, New York; Kenneth Mogill, William Goodman, George Bedrosian, Richard Soble, Richard Skutt, and Neal Bush of Detroit; Dennis Schlenker of Albany, New York; Donald L. Jelinek of Berkeley; Joe Moorehead of San Francisco; Dennis Cunningham, Michael Deutsch, and Walter Williams of Chicago; Robert Handelman and Tony Walsh of Cleveland, Ohio; Morten Cohen of West Hartford, Connecticut; Alan Colman and Marvin Miller of Alexandria, Virginia; James L. Kemp of Rochester, New York; Jim Donnelly and Lewis S. Gurwitz of Cambridge, Massachusetts; and Big Black, pro se, Richard Clark, pro se, Roger Champen, pro se, and Shango Bahati Kakawana, pro se.

Many additional lawyers and legal workers participated in the trials.

### f. *Michigan v DeSaussure (Detroit 15* Case) §3.27

On October 25, 1970, 15 black persons were arrested following a siege by Detroit police of their house in Detroit. The 15 were members of the National Committee to Combat Fascism, which was affiliated with the Black Panther Party. They had moved into the house ten days earlier. The neighborhood was composed largely of poor blacks, Chicanos, and whites.

The Black Panthers had been harassed by Detroit police during the previous year. Many had been arrested and rearrested, and their centers had been surrounded several times, but major incidents had been avoided. The Detroit 15, as they came to be called, consisted of eight young women and seven young men aged 17 to 22. They had instituted breakfast programs for the community children and were in the process of organizing the community for other activities when the arrests took place.

The siege began at about 6:00 p.m. Several hundred police surrounded the area with riot equipment and a tank. During the night, one black policeman was killed by a single high-powered rifle shot; two other black policemen were slightly injured; one police car was stoned, and several others were burned. At about 1:00 a.m., 12 people came out of the house, escorted by community leaders to assure that there would be no massacre. The three who remained inside refused to come out until an hour later when the house had been gassed and numerous shots fired.

During the next few days, the house was searched, and ammunition, four rifles and shotguns, dynamite, and other explosives were found. Hundreds of books, pamphlets, leaflets, and documents were also seized. All the seized items were introduced at the trial to support the conspiracy charge.

Under Michigan practice, because of the seriousness of the charges in the five indictments and because of the number of defendants (12), the prosecutor was entitled to exercise 480 peremptory challenges, and the defense 560. Before the jury was selected, the prosecution had exercised 27 and the defense 53 peremptory challenges. The voir dire lasted five days. Examples of voir dire questions used in the case are listed in chapter 9.

The defendants were tried on a number of charges. After the prosecution case, the defense moved for a directed verdict. The judge granted the motion as to the charges of assault with intent to commit murder and great bodily harm less than murder, and malicious destruction of property. The defense then rested its case.

All the defendants were acquitted on the charges of murder and conspiracy to commit murder. Three of the defendants were found guilty of aggravated assault. The Michigan Court of Appeals reversed in a per curiam unreported opinion, on a search and seizure issue (No. 71–12876).

Defense counsel were Ernest Goodman, Elliott Hall, Neil Bush, and Jeff Taft of Detroit, and Tom Meyer, of Pt. Richmond, California.

### g. *Taylor v Louisiana* §3.28

Billy J. Taylor was tried, convicted, and sentenced to death for aggravated kidnapping in a state court after an unsuccessful attempt to quash the petit jury venire. The conviction was affirmed by the Louisiana Supreme Court (1973) 282 So 2d 491.

The defendant, a male, appealed, charging unconstitutionality of the state statute requiring women (but not men) to file a declaration of willingness to serve on a jury. The parties stipulated that 53 percent of the persons eligible for trial jury service in the parishes (counties) were female, but no more than 10 percent of those on the jury wheel were women. No women were on the 175-person venire drawn for the criminal term beginning with Taylor's trial.

In finding that the Louisiana system of exempting women operated to exclude them from juries, the Supreme Court summarized the laws requiring a venire to be drawn from a fair cross-section of the community, citing both federal and state cases. *Taylor v Louisiana* (1975) 419 US 522. See discussions in §§2.33, 6.56.

Defense counsel was William McM. King, of Covington, Louisiana.

### h. *California v Block* §3.29

On March 31, 1979, 13 people climbed and sat on a fence at Rancho Seco Nuclear Power Plant in Sacramento County, California, in opposition to U.S. production, use, and sale of nuclear weapons and construction and operation of nuclear power plants. Eleven people were charged with trespassing and resisting arrest.

During voir dire, defense counsel tried to elicit juror attitudes toward weapons without disclosing the intended defense of necessity. See voir dire questions in §§9.133–9.134. Counsel raised the defense of necessity (see §11.57); proposed jury instructions based on this defense, and, in closing argument, appealed to the jurors as the conscience of the community (see chapter 22).

After a seven-week trial, the Sacramento County jury acquitted one defendant, found one guilty, and was deadlocked on nine. *California v Block* (Sacramento County Justice Ct, Cr Nos 3235–3245, 1979). The case was set for rehearing and subsequently removed to Sacramento Municipal Court, where the judge stated he would grant the defense of necessity, if urged. The district attorney dismissed the case.

Oakland attorneys Leonard Post and Alan Ramo and Sacramento attorneys Ann Noel and Jim Thomson handled the case.

### i. *Ristaino v Ross* §3.30

James Ross, a black man, was convicted in a Massachusetts state court along with two other black men, on charges of armed robbery, assault and battery with a dangerous weapon, and assault and battery with intent to murder. The victim was a white university security guard. The voir dire was conducted by the trial judge, who is required by statute to inquire generally into prejudice. Each defendant requested that the jurors be questioned about racial prejudice. The judge asked the defense counsel if there was anything peculiar about the case that should be included in the record. The defense attorney replied, "No, just the fact that the victim is white, and the defendants are black." The judge declined to ask any questions regarding racial prejudice, and the defendants were convicted.

Ross filed a petition for a writ of habeas corpus, which was granted by the federal district court, and affirmed by the First Circuit Court of Appeals. The United States Supreme Court, in *Ristaino v Ross* (1976) 424 US 589, held that examination of prospective jurors about racial prejudice is not constitutionally required in such a case because

> the circumstances thus did not suggest a significant likelihood that racial prejudice might infect Ross' trial. This was made clear to the trial judge when Ross was unable to support his motion concerning *voir dire* by pointing to racial factors such as existed in *Ham* or others of comparable significance. In these circumstances, the trial judge acted within the Constitution in determining that the demands of due process could be satisfied by his more generalized but thorough inquiry into the impartiality of the veniremen.

Facing an indignant dissent by Justice Marshall, joined by Justice Brennan, the Court footnoted (424 US at 597 n9):

> Although we hold that *voir dire* questioning directed to racial prejudice was not constitutionally required, the wiser course generally is to propound appropriate questions designed to identify racial prejudice if requested by the defendant. Under our supervisory power we would have required as much of a federal court faced with the circumstances here. See *Aldridge v United States* (1931) 283 US 308 . . . . The States also are free to allow or require questions

not demanded by the Constitution. In fact, the Supreme Judicial Court of Massachusetts has suggested guidelines to Massachusetts trial courts for questioning about racial prejudice on *voir dire*. *Commonwealth v Lumley* (1975) 327 NE2d 683; *Commonwealth v Ross* (1973) 296 NE2d 810, 816.

The Court stressed the significant facts in *Ham v South Carolina* (1973) 409 US 524, that brought a different result: Ham was a prominent civil rights activist and his civil rights activities played an important role in his defense.

Michael G. West, of Cambridge, Massachusetts, handled Ross' appeal.

The subsequent decision in *Rosales-Lopez v United States* (1981) 451 US 182, relied on the principles of this case. See §3.57.

### j. *Michigan v Hartwell* §3.31

Judy Kay Hartwell was charged with second-degree murder for the fatal stabbing of her husband. According to trial testimony, Freddie Hartwell had a long history of violence and abuse toward his wife, particularly when he was drunk. On different occasions he had held a loaded gun to her chin and cocked the trigger, struck her with a sledge hammer when she was pregnant, and shot a gun in the living room where his small son was sitting.

On the day of his death, Hartwell had been drinking steadily for several hours. He returned home drunk and abusive. Judy Hartwell feared that her husband was about to forcibly perform anal sexual intercourse upon her or to tie her to the bed and whip her—both of which she found painful, humiliating, and contrary to her religious beliefs. Ms. Hartwell grabbed a knife to protect herself, and as she tried to run from the room, he lunged at her. She panicked and stabbed him.

Michigan's new Sexual Assault Act (Michigan Compiled Laws §750.520j) contains many progressive provisions, including a prohibition against cross-examination of rape victims about their prior sexual experiences to discredit their testimony. However, the archaic provision that a man cannot be convicted of raping his wife remains.

Voir dire was conducted by both the judge and the attorneys; questions from the case appear in §§11.51 and 11.53.

At trial, Ms. Hartwell argued that she killed in self-defense. Judge Victor J. Baum instructed the jury that a married woman has a legal right forcibly to resist unwanted sexual advances by her husband. Excerpts from his charge to the jury appear in §11.53.

After a week-long trial, Ms. Hartwell was acquitted. *Michigan v*

*Hartwell* (Wayne County Cir Ct, No. 75–091–591 FM, Mar. 16, 1976).

Detroit attorney Mark Weiss handled the case, with assistance from legal worker Marjory Cohen.

#### k. Recent Cases §3.32

This section is being reserved for discussion of recent state criminal cases. See §3.18.

### 2. State Civil Cases

#### a. *Brewster v Martin Marietta* §3.41

In September, 1975, after seven years with the company, a 55-year-old woman was fired from her job with Martin Marietta Aluminum Sales, Inc., a large national corporation. Joy Brewster had established a good work performance record and had worked her way up from secretary to a sales management position, becoming the first woman in the United States to sell industrial aluminum. After giving Mrs. Brewster numerous sales awards, management decided to fire her. Instead of being informed of this decision she was placed on probation, an unprecedented practice with the company, and was terminated five months later.

In 1976, plaintiff filed suit in Wayne County Circuit Court against Martin Marietta on grounds of sex discrimination; an amended complaint added breach of contract, and wrongful discharge. Counsel for plaintiff successfully moved the court for voir dire by counsel rather than judge. The trial on issues of liability and damages was held in Detroit, Michigan, a large metropolitan area where enormous effort has been made over the past 30 years to develop jurors who will be sympathetic to plaintiffs' attorneys and where there is an active and effective personal injury bar.

The four-man, two-woman jury found that the employer's reasons for terminating plaintiff (insubordination and poor job performance) were pretextual. They found instead that she was unfairly treated. The jury awarded $1,270,000: $770,000 for back pay, lost wages, and compensation for unequal pay and $500,000 for mental distress. Counsel had argued for $1.3 million if the jury believed plaintiff could never get another job. During the three-week trial, an unusually close rapport developed among the jurors themselves, and between the jurors and the plaintiff. A couple of weeks after the verdict, the foreman, carrying out an agreement among the jurors, called the plaintiff to find out how she was doing.

(See §§9.11, 9.51, 10.36, 10.91 for voir dire questions; §4.50 for discussion of attorney's approach to the jury; and chapter 12 for standard juror questionnaire.) *Brewster v Martin Marietta Aluminum Sales, Inc.* (Wayne County Circuit Court, No. 76-613-111-NO/78-832-041-CZ, October 1, 1982). Victoria C. Heldman and Richard F. Schaden, Detroit attorneys, represented plaintiff.

### b. *Stroud v General Motors* §3.42

Plaintiff's wife, the mother of three young children, was killed when a car ran a stop sign and crashed into her car. The first car was driven by one of General Motors' corporate employees. In January 1974 counsel for decedent's husband and her children filed a wrongful death action against General Motors in Cadillac, Michigan (Wexford County Circuit Court).

On the morning of the trial, defendant admitted liability, leaving only the issue of damages, namely, the value of the loss of life of a woman, who, at the time of her death, was not working for pay outside the home although she had worked in the past. Plaintiffs claimed $667,281 in damages for the death of Mrs. Stroud; $560,700 for general damages and $106,581 in special damages, which included bills for funeral, ambulance, automobile, and towing. They sought additional damages for the injury to the children caused by the death of thier mother.

Plaintiff's strategy was to try to take control of the courtroom from the outset. Counsel conducted an intensive, extensive, and individualized voir dire. (For examples, see chapter 16.) The case was tried to a six-person jury in a small Michigan town where many prospective jurors knew one or more attorneys for each side. Two jurors had been excused before in a case tried by plaintiff's attorney and another had sat on a similar case tried by the same attorney. Plaintiff's counsel asked each juror to fill out a standard questionnaire before voir dire. (See chapter 12.)

After trial, the jury awarded plaintiff a verdict of $450,000, solely for the death of Mrs. Stroud. General Motors then settled the whole case for $675,000 and did not appeal.

Plaintiffs' counsel were Dean Robb and Thomas Phillips of Traverse City, Michigan; Edward Ten Houten of Cadillac; and John Daugherty of Beulah.

### c. Recent Cases §3.43

This section is being reserved for discussion of new state civil cases. See §3.18.

## 3. Federal Criminal Cases

### a. *United States v McNeil* §3.51

In 1968, Leonard McNeil, a young black man, was sent a draft notice. He did not appear for induction. He went to Canada and later returned to California where he joined with other antiwar activists. He spent much of his time organizing for the Soledad Brothers Defense Committee, and appeared publicly on behalf of both causes.

He was arrested at his home on December 5, 1972, by ten FBI agents for refusing induction. The federal charge carried a five-year sentence and/or $10,000 fine. An additional charge of failing to notify the draft board of his mailing address was later added.

Defense attorneys filed a motion for extensive individual voir dire of prospective jurors, by counsel as well as the judge, and presented the testimony of expert witnesses at a hearing. Judge Oliver J. Carter denied the motion (ND Cal 1973) 357 F Supp 342, but permitted more extensive voir dire than is customary in federal court (see material in chapter 8; voir dire questions in chapter 9). After jury selection, Judge Carter dismissed the charges on legal grounds, on April 25, 1973.

Defense attorneys were Paul Harris of San Francisco and Ann Fagan Ginger of Berkeley.

### b. *United States v Russo* (*Pentagon Papers* Case) §3.52

Daniel Ellsberg and Anthony Joseph Russo, Jr., were indicted on December 29, 1971, for violations of 18 USC §§371, 641, and 793: conspiracy; stealing, concealing, and receiving stolen government property; receiving, communicating, and retaining national defense documents.

While an employee at Rand Corporation, Daniel Ellsberg allegedly removed copies of a secret government study on United States involvement in Vietnam, the so-called Pentagon Papers. He and Tony Russo were alleged to have copied these materials and made them available to members of Congress and the press.

The trial was held in the United States District Court, Central District of California, far from the home base of most of the attorneys and witnesses. The defense filed numerous pretrial motions, including unsuccessful challenges to the grand and trial juries (for excerpts, see chapter 6). For examples of voir dire questions submitted in this case, see chapter 9. The trial lasted six months, and was seen by many as a trial of the war in Vietnam. Senate hearings about the Watergate affair began near the end of the trial, and the burglary of the office of Ellsberg's psychiatrist by White House "plumbers" was revealed. This, along with previous instances of government misconduct, caused Judge William Matthew Byrne, Jr., to grant defense motions to dismiss the case. *United States v Russo* (CD Cal, No. 9373-WMB-CD, May 11, 1973).

The complete collection of material filed in this case, plus the trial transcript (over 35,000 pages) is available at the Meiklejohn Civil Liberties Institute and on microfilm from Oceana Publications, Dobbs Ferry, New York. For a catalog of all documents filed, with annotations of the more important items and of significant testimony, see Ginger, *Pentagon Papers Case Collection: Annotated Procedural Guide and Index* (1975) (available from Meiklejohn Institute, Box 673, Berkeley, California 94701). See also Kenneth Salter, *The Pentagon Papers Trial* (1975), a case book on the theft charges, and Schrag, *Test of Loyalty* (1974).

Attorneys for defendants Ellsberg and Russo were Leonard B. Boudin and Charles Goodell of New York City; Charles Nesson of Harvard University Law School; Leonard Weinglass and H. Peter Young of Los Angeles; and Dolores Donovan of San Francisco.

### c. *United States v Briggs (Gainesville Eight* Case) §3.53

On July 7 and 8, 1972, just before the Democratic National Convention in Miami Beach, 23 leaders of the Vietnam Veterans Against the War (VVAW) were subpoenaed to appear before a federal grand jury in Tallahassee, Florida. The VVAW had previously obtained permits for peaceful demonstrations in Miami that week. On July 13 four VVAW members were held in contempt for refusing to answer questions before the grand jury (the contempt convictions were reversed by the Fifth Circuit). The same day the rest of the grand jury witnesses were released from the subpoenas, without being asked anything but their names. That evening, the grand jury indicted six members of the VVAW (several months later they added indictments against one other veteran and John Briggs, a VVAW supporter).

Seven of the defendants were charged with conspiracy to disrupt the 1972 Republican National Convention by violent means. Scott Camil was also charged with teaching and demonstrating the use of an incendiary device and with possession of an unregistered destructive device. The eighth defendant, Stan Michelson, was charged with being an accessory after the fact and with concealment of a felony.

Defense motions challenging the composition of the jury pool were denied and unsuccessfully appealed. *United States v Briggs* (ND Fla 1973) 366 F Supp 1356.

Numerous pretrial motions were filed. For examples of voir dire questions submitted, see chapter 9. Sociologist Jay Schulman, psychologist Richard Christie, and others devised the demographic rating system for prospective jurors described in chapter 5.

The trial began in July 1973, in Gainesville, Florida. The government relied on the testimony of undercover agents and informers (one FBI agent was a best friend of one of the defendants); three of the informers had held high posts in VVAW. At the end of the government's case, the defense put on only one technical witness and rested. The jury, which had been sequestered for most of the trial, took only four hours to acquit all the defendants on all charges.

Defense attorneys were Doris Peterson, Morton Stavis, Nancy Stearns, Jim Reif, and Rhonda Copelon of the Center for Constitutional Rights, New York; Cameron Cunningham, now of San Francisco; Brady Coleman of Austin, Texas; and Larry Turner of Gainesville.

Copies of all significant defense pretrial pleadings and briefs (approximately 1000 pages) are available from Meiklejohn Civil Liberties Institute, Box 673, Berkeley, California 94701.

### d. *United States v Dellinger (Chicago Eight* Case) §3.54

The prosecution of the Chicago Eight resulted from the demonstrations at the Democratic National Convention in Chicago in August 1968. United States Attorney General Ramsey Clark conducted an investigation and concluded that no federal prosecutions would lie against any persons who had sought to demonstrate opposition to the policies of the national government at that convention.

On March 20, 1969, a federal grand jury indicted eight persons under 18 USC §§2101–2102 for allegedly crossing state lines with the intent to incite a riot at the convention, and under 18 USC §371 for allegedly conspiring to incite such a riot. The trial was held before the late Judge Julius Hoffman in the Eastern District of Illinois. There were numerous confrontations between the judge and the attorneys and defendants, and one defendant, Bobby Seale, was forced to appear in court shackled and gagged. (The action against Seale ended in a mistrial, and this defendant was dropped from this case.) All defendants were acquitted of the conspiracy charges, and two of the defendants were acquitted of the substantive charge. *United States v Dellinger* (ED Ill, No. 69 CR 180, Feb. 18, 1970).

The remaining defendants appealed their conviction and a multitude of contempt charges made during the trial. The Seventh Circuit Court of Appeals held that the Anti-Riot Act is not unconstitutionally vague or overbroad; but that, where a prosecution arose out of protest demonstrations during the convention, involved conflicts with the police, and generated extensive pretrial publicity, it was error to fail to make at least some minimal inquiry on voir dire into the attitude of prospective jurors regarding involvement in the Vietnam war, youth culture, relationships with law enforcement officers, and exposure to pretrial publicity; that general inquiry as to whether there was any reason the veniremen could not be fair and impartial was insufficient; and that the demeanor of the judge and the prosecutors also provided grounds for reversal. *United States v Dellinger* (7th Cir 1972) 472 F2d 340, *cert. denied* (1973) 410 US 970. Excerpts on voir dire procedure are found in chapter 8.

Attorneys in the district court were William Kunstler of New York City; Leonard Weinglass of Los Angeles; and Charles Garry of San Francisco. Attorneys handling the appeal, along with the above, were Morton Stavis, James Reif, and Arthur Kinoy of the Center for Constitutional Rights, New York City; Anthony Amsterdam, now of New York University Law School; David Bogen of the University of Maryland Law School; William Brackett of Chicago; Alan Dershowitz and Charles Nesson of Harvard Law School; Herbert O. Reid, Sr., of Howard University Law School; William Rossmoore of Newark; Michael Tigar of Washington, D.C.; and James Moran, Thomas Sullivan, and John Tucker of Chicago.

### e. *United States v Anderson* (*Camden 28* Case) §3.55

Twenty-eight defendants were charged with entering the draft board in Camden, New Jersey, and destroying draft files. The defendants had previously abandoned a plan to enter the draft board due to lack of resources and technical skill. An acquaintance of one of the defendants, who later admitted being an agent provocateur, encouraged the defendants to continue with their plans and provided money, supplies, diagrams, and all necessary equipment for the raid on the draft board. The FBI was aware of the plan in advance, watched the defendants' "dry run," and waited until they had spent three hours destroying records before making any arrests.

Most of the defendants were members of the Roman Catholic antiwar movement and did not deny the activities. They based their defense on acts of government overreaching, and reminded the jurors of their power to acquit if they felt the defendants' act was justified. The defense used the help of sociologists to select the jury and prepare a demographic rating system, as described in chapter 5. For the defendants' proposed jury instructions and opening statement on jury nullification, see chapter 22. All defendants were acquitted by the jury. *United States v Anderson* (D NJ, No. 602-71, May 19, 1973).

Attorneys in the case were David Kairys of Philadelphia; Carl Broege of Newark; and Martin Stolar of New York City.

### f. *United States v Berkowitz* §3.56

Defendants were three prominent public figures: a high state official, a well-known public relations and political consultant, and a well-known artist, indicted for mail fraud and conspiracy to defraud the United States. Their federal prosecution received extensive media attention prior to the first indictment that continued throughout the trial. Two features of the case made it newsworthy: one defendant and several witnesses were officials in a state government agency with which local citizens had a great deal of contact, and the case involved the alleged misuse of government funds.

Defense attorneys were concerned that jurors might be influenced by their attitudes toward government officials in general, toward "big government" and "excessive costs," and toward Jews, since all the defendants and four of their five attorneys were Jewish. Since two of the defendants, and four of their attorneys, were from the Detroit area, while the trial was held in Grand Rapids, defense counsel were also concerned about jurors' preconceptions about people who live and work in Detroit.

For these reasons, defense counsel proposed, and the trial judge accepted, a method of conducting voir dire to ensure an adequate screening of potential jurors on the sensitive areas, see §8.43. The attorneys conducted the voir dire, questioning jurors individually outside the presence of other jurors regarding pretrial publicity, attitudes toward government, spending of tax funds, and anti-Semitism.

After a five-week trial in which the defense presented no witnesses, the 12-person jury acquitted the three defendants of all charges. *United States v Berkowitz* (WD Mich, SDiv No. 679-61 CR, June 12, 1980). Defense attorneys were Ernest Goodman, William H. Goodman, Kenneth M. Mogill, and Neal Bush of Detroit and John D. Pirich, of Lansing.

### g. *Rosales-Lopez v United States* §3.57

Rosales-Lopez, who was of Mexican descent, was tried and convicted in federal district court, Southern District of California, for his participation in a plan by which three Mexican aliens were illegally brought into the country, i.e., for consipiracy to conceal and concealment of the aliens and for aiding and abetting their illegal transportation. Prior to trial the judge denied defense counsel's motion to conduct voir dire personally, but the judge did ask about half the questions submitted by defendant's counsel. The judge refused to ask the one submitted question directed toward possible prejudice against Mexicans, although he did ask a question about attitudes toward aliens.

The Ninth Circuit affirmed the conviction, 617 F2d 1349. The US Supreme Court granted certiorari and found no reversible error in the voir dire, holding that federal trial courts must make an inquiry into racial prejudice when requested by a defendant accused of a violent crime *and* when defendant and victim were members of different racial or ethnic groups. 451 US 182 (1981). There were no "special circumstances" as defined in *Ristaino v Ross* (1976) 424 US 589, and as found in *Ham v South Carolina* (1973) 409 US 524, requiring a *constitutionally* mandated inquiry in that case.

The race-related voir dire questions could still have been asked, said the Court, if the circumstances of the case indicated that there was a "reasonable possibility" that racial or ethnic prejudice might have influenced the jury. The Supreme Court found no reasonable possibility in this case for two reasons:

1. The trial judge reasonably determined that a juror's prejudice toward *aliens* might affect his or her impartiality, and a juror asked a question about aliens would have understood it to include Mexican aliens.
2. The racial or ethnic differences between the defendant and a key government witness (Anglo) did not amount to a "reasonable possibility" here, where the witness' testimony was substantially corroborated by other witnesses, including witnesses of Mexican descent.

In his dissent, Justice Stevens, joined by Justices Brennan and Marshall, agreed that although the alien question made the voir dire in this case adequate, it was inadequate as a matter of law because it wholly ignored the risk that potential jurors might be prejudiced simply because defendant was of Mexican descent:

> Before any citizen may be permitted to sit in judgment on his peers, some inquiry into his potential bias is essential. Such bias can arise from two principal sources: a special reaction to the facts of the particular case, or a special prejudice against the individual defendant that is unrelated to the particular case. Much as we wish it were otherwise, we should acknowledge the fact that there are many potential jurors who harbor strong prejudices against all members of certain racial, religious, or ethnic groups for no reason other than hostility to the group as a whole. Even when there are no "special circumstances" connected with an alleged criminal transaction indicating an unusual risk of racial or other group bias, a member of the Nazi Party should not be allowed to sit in judgment of a Jewish defendant.

451 US 182, at 196, 197.

John J. Cleary of San Diego represented the petitioner on appeal.

### h. Recent Cases §3.58

This section is being reserved for discussion of new federal criminal cases. See §3.18.

## 4. Federal Civil Cases

### a. *Hampton v Hanrahan* §3.71

On December 4, 1969, Fred Hampton, Illinois Black Panther Party deputy chairman, and Mark Clark, another party leader, were killed in a predawn police raid staged under the direction of Cook County state's attorney Hanrahan, his office, and the FBI. Four other Black Panther Party members and two police officers were wounded in the raid when 100 shots were fired into Hampton's Chicago apartment where the party members were sleeping. Police, who entered the apartment without any warning or warrant to search for illegal weapons, were armed with submachine guns, shotguns, military carbines, and revolvers.

In June 1970 the seven survivors of the raid and the mothers of Hampton and Clark filed a federal civil rights action seeking $47.7 million against the City of Chicago, Cook County, Hanrahan, and 27 other government officials. (See *Hampton v Hanrahan* (ND Ill 1972) 339 F Supp 695.)

In December 1974, plaintiffs joined the FBI as a defendant after it was revealed that an FBI informant provided a floor plan of Hampton's apartment to the Chicago police department. Plaintiffs later moved to join United States Attorney General Mitchell and other top officials knowledgable about the FBI's counterintelligence program (COIN-

TELPRO). The extent of the FBI's involvement was concealed by government attorneys, and the judge denied discovery on COINTELPRO, a program directed against militant black leaders and organizations in the Chicago area with the express purpose to "expose, disrupt, misdirect, discredit, and otherwise neutralize" these leaders and organizations.

On the first day of jury selection, Judge Perry announced to the venire of 400 people that the case was about a "gun battle," a description that supported defendants' theory of the case. A public opinion poll conducted by the National Fair Jury Project in 1975 revealed that seven years of pretrial publicity had left a profound prejudice among the jury pool against the Black Panther Party: 96.4 percent remembered the raid, 67 percent had formed an opinion about who was wrong, and 67 percent of this group had decided against plaintiffs. Nevertheless, the judge refused to allow attorney voir dire. He conducted a tightly controlled voir dire including questions referring to blacks as "colored people." Of the 400 on the special venire, only 23 were black, although 17 percent of the registered voters in Chicago were black. A six-person jury with an average age of 50 was chosen: five white, one black, and four white alternates.

During the 18-month trial, plaintiffs alleged that Judge Perry denigrated plaintiffs' evidence in front of the jury, labeling plaintiffs' questioning as "unimportant," "insulting," and "ridiculous," while at the same time volunteering protective comments for the defense and eliciting information and self-serving opinions. The judge, on his own, informed the jurors of inadmissible evidence prejudicial to plaintiffs and demanded and threatened plaintiffs' counsel, often in front of the jury. On two occasions the judge held plaintiffs' counsel in contempt and had ex parte contact in his chambers with one juror who later became foreperson. Plaintiffs tried twice to recuse Judge Perry, who ruled for defendants throughout the proceedings, but these efforts were not successful, 499 F Supp 64 (1980). At the end of the trial, the judge's long and complex instructions to the jury misstated the law and prejudiced plaintiffs' case by omitting several of plaintiffs' claims.

Judge Perry directed verdicts in favor of 21 of the defendants and entered costs for $100,000 against plaintiffs before sending the case to the jury. The jury heard the publicity around the dismissal and thought the trial was over. The panel deadlocked on the question of liability of the remaining seven defendants who had admitted firing the weapons into the apartment. The judge declared a hung jury and directed verdicts for the seven defendants.

On appeal, the court of appeals held the federal government had obstructed the judicial process by withholding important information, and reinstated the case against 24 defendants. *Hampton v Hanrahan* (7th Cir 1979) 600 F2d 600.

In October 1982 the parties agreed to a $1.85 million settlement, one of the largest in a federal civil rights suit. The settlement was paid in equal shares by the federal government, the City of Chicago, and Cook County, although none of the government agencies involved admitted liability.

Plaintiffs' attorneys were: G. Flint Taylor, Jeffrey Haas, Dennis Cunningham, David Thomas, Michael E. Deutsch, and Stephen Seliger of Chicago; Herbert O. Reid of Washington, D.C.; and James Meyerson of New York.

### b. *Krause v Rhodes* §3.72

In early May 1970 students on the Kent State University campus protested the United States invasion of Cambodia. At that time, students were demonstrating on campuses all over the country, including Jackson State University in Mississippi, where two students were killed. A series of disturbances led local and state officials to call the Ohio National Guard for assistance in suppressing the demonstrations on the Kent State campus. On May 4, 1970, during a peaceful lunchtime assembly on campus, unprovoked Ohio National Guard troops opened fire for 13 seconds killing four persons and leaving 9 wounded.

Later that year, the nine wounded students and personal representatives of the estates of the four deceased students filed individual lawsuits in the federal district court for the Northern District of Ohio on grounds of deprivation of civil rights under the Fourteenth Amendment of the United States Constitution and 42 USC §1983, and pendant state claims for negligence, assault, and wrongful death. They sued National Guard officers and personnel, the president of Kent State University, and the governor of Ohio, James Rhodes.

In June 1971 the district court dismissed three of the complaints on grounds of sovereign and official immunity. The court of appeals affirmed the dismissals (*Krause v Rhodes* (6th Cir 1972) 471 F2d 430), but the Supreme Court unanimously reversed the court of appeals and remanded for trial (*Scheuer v Rhodes* (1974) 416 US 232).

On remand, all 13 cases were consolidated for trial before a jury only on the issue of liability. The parties stipulated that a verdict of 9 of the 12 jurors would be sufficient. Nine jurors found for defendants and plaintiffs appealed.

Two days before jury deliberations, the trial judge informed counsel that a juror had been assaulted and threatened by a person interested in the outcome of the litigation. The judge told the jury of the threat and that it should be taken seriously, but refused to question the threatened juror or any other jurors to determine the impact of the threat. The court of appeals reversed the verdict on grounds of jury tampering (*Krause v Rhodes* (6th Cir 1977) 570 F2d 563) and remanded for a new trial. The Supreme Court denied certiorari (*Rhodes v Krause* (1978) 435 US 924).

In January 1979 an out-of-court settlement was reached for $675,000 and a statement of apology signed by Governor Rhodes and 27 National Guardsmen.

ACLU attorneys who litigated the case for plaintiffs were: Steven A. Sindell and Nelson G. Karl of Cleveland; Michael E. Geltner, Leonard J. Schwartz, Clyde Ellis, Stanley K. Laughlin, Jr., Niki Z. Schwartz, Michael S. Harshman, Louis A. Jacobs, and Robert P. App of Columbus; Sanford Jay Rosen of San Francisco; and Melvin L. Wulf and Joel M. Gora of New York. Other attorneys who represented plaintiffs were: Nicholas B. Waranoff and Amitai Schwartz of San Francisco; David Engdahl of Denver; Walter S. Haffner of Cleveland; Ann Saynetz and Robert S. Baker, of counsel.

### c. *MCI v AT&T* §3.73

An antitrust suit brought by MCI, a leading competitor of AT&T (Bell Telephone Company), resulted in the jury awarding a verdict for the plaintiffs. The judge, following the law for treble damages in an antitrust case, awarded MCI treble damages totalling $1.8 billion.

Plaintiff's team of six attorneys had opted for a jury trial in spite of concerns that a jury would have difficulty comprehending the amount of the damage claim (900 million dollars before trebling). The attorneys were also worried about the prejudicial effect of AT&T's television campaign promoting the Bell telephone system.

In preparation for jury selection, plaintiff's attorneys employed a firm to research the pool from which jurors would be selected. They selected a political polling firm whose accuracy could be verified against election results. The goal was to define a profile of jurors most likely to favor one side or the other based on their demographic characteristics. Plaintiff's attorneys were particularly interested in what kind of people responded most strongly to arguments by plaintiff and the defense and what their attitudes were regarding the important issues in the case, i.e., the importance of competition against the alleged benefits of a regulated monopoly in telecommunications.

The attorneys designed the questionnaire that the pollsters used, along with professional sampling techniques, on a representative sample of the registered voters of counties within the Northern District of Illinois. The poll revealed that a profile favoring plaintiff would be intelligent, self-made jurors who strongly favored competition and the free enterprise system. See chapter 5.

Plaintiff's attorneys further employed the survey in preparing the case by rehearsing opening statements for both sides in front of three mock jury panels. Each panel contained some members who had responded favorably to the questionnaire for plaintiff, some for defendants, as well as some who were neutral. The attorneys watched the jury deliberations behind a one-way mirror and discovered the weaknesses in their arguments; they also discovered that people were not brainwashed by Ma Bell's ad campaign.

Trial began on February 4, 1980, before Judge Grady of the United States District Court, Northern District of Illinois. The actual jury selected failed to match the perfect profile MCI lawyers wanted. However, there was not a single juror seated who matched the profile most opposed to MCI's position.

The federal district judge departed from his usual voir dire procedure. First he listened to statements by jurors claiming they could not sit on the case for a variety of personal/job-related reasons, and excused 20 people, leaving 52 in the pool. He asked each remaining person to stand up and tell something about himself or herself to the judge and jury: What you do, what your spouse does, what kinds of things you like to do in your spare time, your children, their ages, and so forth. People got up one by one and gave magnificently revealing autobiographical sketches. The order in which they gave the data was itself very revealing. As they finished, the judge quite gently asked for supplementary information when appropriate. Then he permitted the lawyers to ask additional questions. Prior to exercising peremptory challenges, counsel followed the judge's suggestion and agreed to excuse 12 who did not seem able to understand the complexities of an antitrust suit.

The judge permitted the jurors to take notes and plaintiff's attorneys provided them with notebooks. Counsel were allowed to supply jurors with important copies of exhibits received into evidence for their notebooks. Each side prepared cross-indexes to the subject matter of the exhibits and glossaries of terms, which the jurors took with them into deliberations, along with the judge's instructions on the law.

Lead counsel for the team representing MCI was Robert F. Hanley of Denver, Colorado.

### d. Recent Cases §3.74

This section is being reserved for discussion of new federal civil cases. See §3.18.

## 5. Courts-Martial

### a. *Tangela Gaskins Administrative Discharge* Case §3.91

From August 4 through 7, 1980, court-martial proceedings were held on board the USS Norton Sound at Long Beach, California. Petty Officer Tangela Gaskins was accused of homosexual conduct and faced discharge from the Navy under 32 CFR §730.15, Secretary of the Navy Instruction 1900.9C, dated 20 January 1978, and Bureau of Naval Personnel Manual Articles 3420180–81, 3420184–85, and 3420187.

Although the Navy used a standard questionnaire form for court-martial proceedings, it was not made available to Ms. Gaskins' civil counsel because the naval officers did not believe much of the information asked in the form was relevant to the proceedings. Nonetheless, counsel was allowed to voir-dire the senior members and two other members of the administrative discharge board on their experience as board members and their attitudes toward homosexuality. (See §§9.75–9.77, 9.90, 9.102, 9.117, 9.121–9.125, 10.97, and 10.99.)

The voir dire was conducted by a criminal defense attorney who used tactics similar to those used in a criminal trial: each question was tied to evidence that could be used against the client. This voir dire could not have been conducted without the precedents from the political/criminal trials of the late 1960s and early 1970s. The attorney knew probing questioning had been used recently in cases where racism and sexism, not homophobia, were in issue. The case came before the administrative board members in a climate in which they could expect to be questioned in depth.

After four lengthy days of hearing, the board was out only 20 minutes and found no credible evidence that Ms. Gaskins engaged in homosexual acts and recommended that she be retained. *Administrative Discharge Board in the Case of DK3 Tangela (NMN) Gaskins, USN*, 142-52-8284.

Ms. Gaskins was represented by civilian counsel, Kenneth L. Chotiner and Susan McGrievy of Los Angeles and Lieutenant Donel L. Davidson, JAGC, United States Naval Reserve. Mr. Chotiner, who conducted the voir dire, is now a judge of the Los Angeles Municipal Court.

### b. Recent Cases §3.92

**PART II**

# Getting Started

# Chapter 4

# *Analyzing the Facts and Forum*


**I. Need to Develop Theory of Case**

A. Walk in the Client's Shoes §4.1

B. Determine Theme and Subthemes §4.2

C. Start Thinking Immediately about Jury Selection §4.3

**II. Examples of Civil Case Analysis**

A. Personal Injury Cases

1. Young Railroad Worker Suing for Emotional Injury
   a. Sample: Attorney's Balance Sheet §4.4
   b. Sample: Points to Explore During Voir Dire §4.5
   c. Sample: Desirable and Undesirable Jurors §4.6
2. Chinese-American Parents Suing for Son's Death
   a. Cross-cultural Problems Raised §4.7
   b. Plaintiffs' Solution §4.8
3. Widower and Young Children Suing for Death of Wife and Mother
   a. Theme §4.9
   b. Narrative Summary §4.10
4. Bizarre Psychological Damages to Polish-American Worker §4.11
5. Other Personal Injury Cases §4.12

B. Other Civil Cases §4.13

**III. Examples of Criminal Case Analysis**

A. Federal

1. White Collar Crime
   a. Sample: Attorney's Balance Sheet §4.15

b. Sample: Theme and Defense Strategy §4.16
2. Other Federal Crimes §4.17
B. State
1. Possession of Concealed Firearms §4.19
2. Striker Charged with Assault §4.20
3. Prosecution of a Rape Case §4.21
C. State or Federal
1. Woman Charged with Conspiracy §4.22
2. Battered Woman Defense
a. Sample: Narrative Summary §4.23
b. Theme §4.24
c. Analysis of Juror Reactions to Defendants §4.25
d. Desirable and Undesirable Jurors §4.26
D. Other Criminal Cases §4.27

**IV. Examples of Common Problems**
A. Cases in Which Key Witnesses Will Be Women
1. Women as Hostile Witnesses §4.30
2. Women as Expert Witnesses §4.31
B. Other Issues §4.32

**V. Analyzing Reaction to Lawyers**
A. Cases Handled by Women Lawyers
1. What Jurors May Expect §4.35
a. "Aggressive" Approach §4.36
b. "Uncertain" Approach §4.37
2. Precedents for Women Lawyers §4.38
3. Emerging Problems §4.39
B. Cases Handled by Out-of-State Lawyers §4.40
C. Other Problems §4.41

**VI. Factors to Analyze in Planning Trial Strategy**
A. From Practice to Theory §4.45
B. Checklist of Factors that Determine Jury Verdicts §4.46
C. Recent Developments §4.47

**VII. Factors to Consider in Selecting Forum**
A. Civil and Criminal Litigants Often Have Choice §4.50
B. Factors to Consider in Making Choice §4.51
C. List of Jury Selection Factors in Federal Courts: Criminal & Civil Trials §4.52
D. Fifty State List of Jury Selection Factors: Criminal Trials §4.53
E. Fifty State List of Jury Selection Factors: Civil Trials §4.54
F. Recent Developments §4.55

# I. NEED TO DEVELOP THEORY OF CASE

## A. Walk in the Client's Shoes §4.1

Every case has a major theme that brings all the threads of the case together. If the jury can understand and accept the theme, you should be able to win the case. Developing the theme is a high priority during pretrial.

In order to find the theme, and to separate it from various subthemes, you need to become immersed in the case. One good way to get started is to go to the scene of the tort, crime, or incident. The purpose is to see, smell, hear, feel, and taste the surroundings in order to approximate the sensations of the participants and to figure out how best to present these feelings to the jurors through testimony. In the process, you try to walk in the shoes of the client and other participants—the victim, opposing party, and key witnesses.

California trial lawyer Susan B. Jordan took a physical walk through the scene of a murder in order to better represent her client:

> One time when I worked in Chicago I represented a member of a gang who had shot somebody in a rival gang. It was a murder case, and I was given a guided tour by the sympathetic gang into the unsympathetic gang's territory. And I want to tell you that it was terrifying. The level of tension and the emotional and psychological feeling of being in a wrong gang's territory were something. We were under minimal protection, you know, there were no police, there was no big group; I never had an experience like that before. It was a war zone, and we were taken there to see the scene of the crime so that we could better understand, and it was an experience that I have never forgotten. And you know, even after that experience, along with my previous experience working with black people in all kinds of situations, unless my client had explained the culture and the environment to me, I wouldn't have understood well enough to handle the case effectively. Nobody could understand, unless it is explained.

"Overcoming Cultural Bias in Jurors: An Interview with Susan B. Jordan," 3 *Trial Diplomacy J* 12, 14 (Spring 1980).

Dean A. Robb, a Michigan trial lawyer, found himself trying to walk in the shoes of his client's deceased wife when he represented the Stroud family (see §3.42), who were suing for damages for the death of their wife and mother. Probably Robb, like most men and many professional women, had given little thought to the "career" of a housewife. This case required him to analyze the "job" of a housewife and mother in familiar terms—that is, in terms of a regular, paying job with wages, hours, job description, title, supervisory tasks, etc.—so that he could discuss the value of the housewife's work with the jury in a way they could follow and accept. His analysis led to his selection of the theme for the case, see §4.9, and to his narrative statement, see §4.10.

## B. Determine Theme and Subthemes §4.2

When it is time to prepare for voir dire in a case, you should be thoroughly familiar with the client, witnesses, and demonstrative evidence. You should also be as familiar as possible with the opposing party, opponent's witnesses, opposing counsel, and their demonstrative evidence. You should know the facts inside out and have a good feel for the case. You may know who the judge will be.

Determine the theme at this point; give it a name, and repeat it throughout the trial. The name should be short enough to fit in a parenthetical description of the case that a reporter might write. Develop a theme that goes *with* the current, *with* the conscience of the community from which the jurors come, so that it is easily acceptable to a majority of jurors.

Write a one- or two-page narrative summarizing the facts as you might present them in your opening statement to the jury. Incorporate your main theme and your subthemes. For examples, see §§4.10, 4.25, and chapter 21. Try this statement out on your family, friends, and friendly strangers—any nonlawyers who could be jurors. The more you practice telling this story to others, the better you will be when you present it to the jury. The more people who hear the story, the more reactions you will get, giving you more things to watch for during voir dire.

Keep asking your listeners and yourself: What central idea will stick in the minds of the judge and jurors?

In a handbook on sexual harassment, a steelworker recalled that when women were first hired in her mill, men had a habit of howling at them like dogs, so she brought a bag of dog biscuits to work and tossed one to the men every time they howled. "Stopping Sexual Harassment" by Elissa Clarke (Labor Education & Research Project, P.O. Box 20001, Detroit, MI 48220). This is an unforgettable portrait of a model plaintiff in a discrimination case, a central image that could win her case. See §§10.92–10.94.

The theme came through very effectively in the case of Christine Craft, former TV anchor who said she was demoted because her station valued her appearance more than her ability. A federal jury awarded her $500,000 in damages for fraud by the station for telling her she was being hired for journalistic ability, then bombarding her with makeup and wardrobe hints. The jury also returned an advisory verdict for Craft on her claim of sex discrimination. Craft said she was told she was too old (at 38), unattractive, and not sufficiently deferential to men. This theme may live longer than her victory, which was first reduced and then reversed on appeal, leading to a second jury trial in 1984.

After establishing the theme of your case, list the critical elements. Analyze the strong and weak points of your side and your opponent's side as dispassionately as you possibly can. The examples of balance sheets later in this chapter have been modeled after financial statements, in order to encourage counsel to look at their cases dispassionately and to plan their strategy and tactics accordingly. See §§4.4, 4.15.

Then list points to explore during voir dire to capitalize on the assets in your case and minimize the liabilities. See §4.5.

In order to select the best forum, when you have a choice in the matter, consider the factors discussed in §4.51. Check the rules concerning jury selection in your jurisdiction, in the comprehensive lists in §§4.52–4.54.

## C. Start Thinking Immediately about Jury Selection §4.3

*Source:* Dean A. Robb, Michigan trial lawyer.

Jury selection really starts when the lawyer first gets the case. It is necessary to start thinking immediately what sort of jurors would be best for the particular client.

For example, when a woman was injured, do you want predominantly men on the jury, if you can get them? And whom do you want to keep off the jury, by challenges for cause or peremptorily? Sometimes you can get people to take themselves off a jury, for example, by making it sound as if the trial is bound to be a long one. You may know that a particular juror is too much of a tightwad to stay on the jury for more than a day or two, because juror's pay is so low. Even if such a person would like to stay on the jury just to defeat you or your client, you may be able to get the person to show prejudice enough for a cause challenge, or encourage a plea of financial hardship.

The sooner you start thinking about what kind of jurors you want, the better. When you know what you want you can begin to think how you can get them and keep them on the jury. In a smaller community you can have a lot more control over this aspect of trial because it is easier to investigate prospective jurors. It is easy, for example, to find out what they have been doing about local issues that have some bearing on your case. But even in a large community, you may be able to get this information, perhaps by checking prospective jurors' voter registration forms to see what initiative petitions they have signed (see chapter 13).

Mores in many United States communities change quite rapidly, so it is essential not to assume that a certain neighborhood will produce the same kind of juror it would have ten years ago, assuming that any neighborhood is ever truly homogeneous. In Oakland, California, a group of people were asked why they gave up being hippies. Six said something had changed in their lives: marriage, becoming parents, needing a job, giving up drugs. But two said they had only changed their outward appearance but had kept the same philosophy: "I look establishment, but my general outlook on life hasn't changed." *SF Chronicle*, Sept. 4, 1982, p. 15.

There are no absolute rules. A plaintiff in a personal injury case usually does not want an engineer on the jury, or an accountant, or the kind of person who works with figures and will want too precise a proof of everything. But in a particular case, if your strongest proof will be made by expert witnesses from these fields, then you should try to get engineers and accountants on the jury.

## III. EXAMPLES OF CIVIL CASE ANALYSIS

### A. Personal Injury Cases

#### 1. Young Railroad Worker Suing for Emotional Injury

*Source:* Attorney Dean Robb of Michigan.

##### a. Sample: Attorney's Balance Sheet §4.4

| *Assets* | *Liabilities* |
|---|---|
| **1. Plaintiff: age; attractiveness to jury; general identification** | |
| 31 years old; very attractive; credible. | Plaintiff superficially does not appear injured.<br>Has tendency to break down easily.<br>Plaintiff and wife lived together at time of injury, married later.<br>Wife's attractiveness could create problems with some (women) jurors.<br>Overall impression might be that plaintiff and wife do not need a big verdict. |

| *Assets* | *Liabilities* |
|---|---|
| **2. Defendant: individual or corporate; visibility in community** | |
| Corporate, government-subsidized railroad. | Defendant railroad company's financial troubles mean taxpayers will pay verdict. |
| **3. Attorneys: attractiveness to jurors** | |
| Plaintiff's: perfect!<br>Defendant's: disabled; jurors will be uncomfortable if short trial. | Plaintiff's: none!<br>Defendant's: counsel's crutches show his disability more serious than plaintiff's.<br>Hard-working; thorough; very competitive; bright.<br>Jurors will like him in long trial. |
| **4. Judge: court atmosphere** | |
| Excellent: quiet, deliberate, patient, extremely fair. Creates perfect courtroom atmosphere. | None. |
| **5. Liability: how it will seem to jurors** | |
| Nearly faultless; runaway loaded freight cars ran into plaintiff's stopped engine. | Some difficulty in presenting railroading facts to jurors. |
| **6. Type of injury: obvious or hidden** | |
| Initially obvious, unexpected, yet saw it happen; a frightening experience. | Appeared to be minor injury; no immediate hospitalization; posttraumatic stress syndrome; changing physical symptoms; depression. "Pain real? Real pain." |
| **7. Out-of-pocket loss by plaintiff: past, future** | |
| Excellent as to clear loss of earnings; railroad stops all support with jury verdict. | Would jury believe plaintiff was permanently and partially disabled? Probably not. Medical paid by railroad until day of trial. |
| **8. Witnesses for plaintiff re:** | |
| **A. Liability: fact witnesses** | |
| Brakeman risked his life to avoid crash.<br>Car inspector: pro-railroad, but fair. | |

| *Assets* | *Liabilities* |
|---|---|
| **B. Liability: expert witnesses** | |
| Use railroad brakemen on safe operation. | |
| **C. Damages: expert witnesses** | |
| Treating doctor: devoted to his patient; general credibility excellent; prepared. | Young, inexperienced; too technical; doesn't look like Dr. Kildare! |
| Treating psychiatrist: fair on direct examination, with color videotape taken two months before trial. | Poor to terrible on cross; scared of trial, lawyers; doesn't think conceptually; answers too quickly; makes lots of mistakes on facts that should be known. |
| Consulting psychiatrist: excellent; thoroughly prepared; highly regarded in community. | Too far ahead of this particular jury(?); could be intimidating; could frighten them. |
| **D. Damages: lay witnesses** | |
| Good to excellent on before-and-after changes in plaintiff; very credible; impressive. | Hard for anyone to understand depression, anxiety, and fear in someone else. |
| **9. Demonstrative evidence: models; drawings; photos; projections** | |
| Good pictures of the setting; overhead projection transparencies of 83 doctor visits, 116 visits for physiotherapy. | No pictures of the damaged equipment; no good way to demonstrate injury other than words and images. |

### b. Sample: Points to Explore during Voir Dire §4.5

Before trying to describe features of the most desirable jurors for your side on this particular case, list the case-specific subjects that need to be explored with jurors during voir dire. In the young railroad worker's case, the following require some discussion:

1. Everyone is different and may have different reactions to similar occurrences. For example:
   - A devastating injury to one might be minor to another, and a wrongdoer is not entitled to pick the strongest victim.
   - A young man might have difficulty accepting a permanent injury that will haunt him the rest of his (long) life [unspoken]: an older person might be able to accept it with more equanimity.

2. Disability can result from pain alone, and pain is personal and individual.

- Mental pain is as real as physical pain, because the body is an integral whole, not a series of medical specialties.
- Negative physical findings of an objective nature do not mean there is no disability.

3. Everyone has feelings about psychiatrists, psychologists, and the field of mental health.

- What are the jurors' feelings?
- Psychiatrists are, first of all, doctors.

4. Plaintiff was a railroad worker who made good money, perhaps more than the earnings of some of the jurors.

5. It is extremely difficult to believe that anyone who looks as well as plaintiff could be seriously and permanently injured.

- Plaintiff could have a catastrophic injury even though he was not hospitalized immediately.
- After plaintiff returned to work, he could not continue, although the cause of his problem was not immediately clear.

#### c. Sample: Desirable and Undesirable Jurors §4.6

*Desirable Jurors*

On liability

Intelligent, worldly, well-read, open-minded, and tolerant

Middle to upper-middle class people

Middle-aged people

Even mix of men and women

On Damages

Businesspeople and professionals or their spouses

*Undesirable Jurors*

Blue-collar workers, who might not respond as easily to *emotional* injury as they would to *physical* disability

Rural people

Younger jurors

### 2. Chinese-American Parents Suing for Son's Death

#### a. Cross-cultural Problems Raised §4.7

Parents in Michigan sued for damages for the death of their son, a 23-year-old premedical student. The unique problems in this case surfaced immediately: the parents were Chinese nationals who could barely speak English. They looked on death somewhat differently from most people raised today in the United States, and they felt the loss of a son was a greater loss than the loss of a daughter would be.

The defendants were at an immediate advantage because they could rely on selecting a jury from a panel including no Chinese-Americans and no Asians from other countries. Plaintiffs could not complain because this would still be a fair cross-section Michigan jury, although it would not contain anyone who would truly understand the nature of the loss to plaintiffs insofar as it differed from the loss to typical American parents.

### b. Plaintiffs' Solution §4.8

Counsel hired a Chinese-American anthropologist from San Francisco to analyze these questions in order to present expert testimony on the nature of damages. But in the end, plaintiffs did not use him as a witness. They decided it would be impossible for a Michigan jury to give this Chinese family more for the loss of their son than they would give to a typical U.S. family for the loss of a son or daughter.

This left the issue of presenting plaintiffs to the jury in the best possible light, even though their English was halting. Counsel decided to deal very lightly with the couple's differences, but to let the parents tell the story themselves, in their own way. This turned out to be an excellent approach. The parents were very effective witnesses, and plaintiffs won an acceptable award.

## 3. Widower and Young Children Suing for Death of Wife and Mother

### a. Theme §4.9

In a personal injury case for damages for the death of a young woman, *Stroud v General Motors* (see §3.42), plaintiffs' counsel represented the husband of the deceased, and the minor children. The deceased had been a homemaker, and therefore had no loss of wages to use as a method of evaluating damages for the loss of her life, as would be true of a man who was the manager of a corporation, for example, whose annual salary would provide the actuarial basis from which a forensic economist could set a dollar amount that might be considered a monetary replacement for the loss to his family.

Plaintiff's counsel worked out a theme including several elements: 1. Being a wife and mother means keeping a family together, which has great value. 2. This value can be approximated, although a housewife is not paid any wages and her value is not figured in monetary terms during her life. 3. The deceased was an excellent homemaker to her husband and children. 4. They have not found any substitute, and probably will not find one soon, if ever.

### b. Narrative Summary §4.10

Dean A. Robb, of Michigan, attorney in the *Stroud* case, see §3.42, obviously worked hard on the narrative statement in this case. In his opening statement to the jury, in chapter 21, Robb introduced his theme early, and touched on it frequently, as the following excerpts indicate:

Ladies and gentlemen of the jury:

Mary Ann was born April 30, 1940, the youngest of eight children, in Dearborn, Michigan. She graduated from Dearborn High School in 1959. The testimony will be that she was a very lovable child but a very quiet child. She baby-sat a lot; she helped her mother who ran a candy store. Maybe some of you have been in big families and you know something about being a child in a big family, but anyway, I think that you'll find we're calling one of her sisters by deposition . . .

. . . I'm not going to tell you much about [her marriage] because I want you to hear it from the witnesses, but you'll find, I'm sure, that she was a happy mother, a careful housewife, a very loving mother and I like to think of her as I heard about her during the last year, as sort of the core of that family . . . . She ran the house in a manner that made Ken want to come home; she helped plan the life of the family. You'll find that they visited friends and relatives together; they always took the kids along. She really held the family together. . . . And that what has been lost here—it's just been lost—this mother, wife, leader, emotional taker-carer of—that's not the right word but a person who just held this unit together.

. . . And we're going to put some figures on some of this in replacement value because the law wants us to . . . put part of this loss in terms of money. The cook, the dishwasher, the dietician—we don't call ourselves that exactly, but as you think about it—a part-time baker, a part-time waitress, sometimes a nurse, sometimes a baby-sitter, a governess in the sense of teaching and leading the children, a chamber-maid, a purchasing agent, if you will, in terms of shopping, watching the family dollar, doing the laundry, being the home economist, sometimes being the handy-man or handy-woman, sometimes being the hostess, sometimes being the general housekeeper, sometimes being the secretary; practically always being the "where do you find this or that?" [person]. And I think the testimony will be that, particularly after they moved . . . and went into this business, that she assisted the family unit by doing driving, helping with taking care of the house, helping teach the children recreational things and so forth. In giving you these kinds of things, we'll put some value on some of them, replacement value.

. . . [T]he proofs will be that [Mr. Stroud has] not been able to even emotionally consider remarriage, and as hard as he's trying, he doesn't think and others don't think that he's even quite as good as a father as he was before. And that's the kind of loss that these witnesses are going to describe.

As to the kids, I'm going to let the witnesses speak to you about them because I don't want to get this on an emotional level, . . .

COMMENT: As women sue to recover for more and more types of past discrimination, problems of evaluating non-monetary services multiply. The California Supreme Court in 1984 faced the question whether a doctor owed his divorced wife some of his earnings from the medical degree he received while she was the family's primary provider. If the Court ruled for Janet Sullivan, it also had to decide the dollar value of her unrecompensed services. *Sullivan v Sullivan* (1984).

Today, Legal Economic Evaluations, Inc. of Palo Alto, California, and similar consulting firms throughout the country, can provide appraisals for wrongful death and other losses based on the kinds of data available to counsel in *Stroud*. A few examples of their evaluations indicate the continuing importance of demographic factors:

Occupation: Housewife
Age at death: 26
Salary at death: $0
Background: White female, husband working, four children, life expectancy of 52.1 more years and 42.79 more years of work.
Loss: $172,585*

Occupation: High school student
Age at death: 18
Salary at death: $0
Background: White male, not married, life expectancy of 53.5 more years and 43.2 years of work
Loss: $236,754**

Occupation: Police officer
Age at death: 38
Salary at death $17,400
Background: White male, spouse not working, five children, life expectancy of 33.6 more years and 23.2 more years of work
Loss: $320,720

Occupation: Computer operator
Age at death: 34
Salary at death: $22,000

Background: White male, wife not working, no children, life expectancy of 38.2 more years and 27.6 more years of work
Loss: $550,000

Occupation: Pilot
Age at death: 36
Salary at death: $43,000
Background: Black male, spouse not working, three children, life expectancy of 34.5 more years and 26.1 more years of work
Loss: $1,010,200

Occupation: Graphic artist
Age at death: 38
Salary at death: $90,000
Background: White male, spouse not working, three children, life expectancy of 35.4 more years and 25.0 more years of work
Loss: $1,922,760

---

*Assumes the value of housework at $12,000 a year, based on Dept. of Agriculture figures
**It was assumed he would have been paid a salary of $25,740 upon graduation from college

*Source: San Francisco Sunday Examiner & Chronicle*, Aug. 7, 1983, p. A3.

On the dollar value of a college degree, in making appraisals of lifetime income, the Census Bureau, in March 1983, issued its first update on expected earnings in nearly a decade. For the first time it calculated separately the lifetime earnings of women. A Bureau study found that

> men with four years of college can expect lifetime earnings of from $1.19 million to $2.75 million, in 1981 dollars, compared with earnings of from $860,000 to $1.87 million for men with only high school diplomas.
>
> Lifetime earnings for women with four years of college should be $520,000 to $1.12 million, and for women with only high school diplomas the range is from $380,000 to $800,000.

*SF Chronicle*, Mar. 14, 1983, p. 5.

### 4. Bizarre Psychological Damages to Polish-American Worker §4.11

*Source:* Victoria Heldman, Detroit trial lawyer.

Difficult problems arise when a physical injury results in a bizarre psychological reaction that jurors will not be able to accept without a great deal of help from plaintiff's witnesses. For example, a worker lost his arm in a machine, and sued the manufacturer of the machine for damages. One of his damages was a sharply diminished self-esteem. He went from being a Polish guy with attitudes on the racial superiority of whites to actually being an oppressed black person, culturally and physically. His lawyers had difficulty watching his transformation, and wondered how they could voir dire in this case.

They developed questions on racism, how jurors felt about a white man putting on a black man's countenance because he had lost his self-esteem? How would the jurors feel about an injured white man who began living with a black woman? The issues were so numerous and so sensitive that it was a nightmare, particularly in a place like Wayne County, Michigan, with a majority of blacks living in the city of Detroit and a majority of whites living in the surrounding county.

After preparing a list of voir dire questions, in which they did not feel confident, plaintiff's counsel settled the case before trial.

#### 5. Other Personal Injury Cases §4.12

This section is being reserved for additional kinds of cases to be presented in supplements to this volume.

### B. Other Civil Cases §4.13

This section is being reserved for examples of analysis of nonpersonal injury cases, to be presented in supplements to this volume.

## III. EXAMPLES OF CRIMINAL CASE ANALYSIS

### A. Federal

#### 1. White Collar Crime

*Source:* Ernest Goodman, Detroit trial lawyer.

##### a. Sample: Attorney's Balance Sheet §4.15

Three Detroit Jewish public figures, on of them a high state official, were indicted for mail fraud and conspiracy to defraud the United States. They were to be tried in Grand Rapids, a community across the state from Detroit, having only a small Jewish population, and much less urban than Detroit. The prosecution of the defendants was based on their failure to obey numerous, lengthy regulations. For details, see *United States v Berkowitz,* §3.56.

| *Assets* | *Liabilities* |
|---|---|
| **1. Defendants: ages; attractiveness to jury; general identification** | |
| Defendants and defendants' wives friendly, ordinary looking. | Out-of-towners from Detroit.<br>Majority Jewish in an area where anti-Semitism may be considerable.<br>Majority government employees. |
| . . . | |
| **4. Judge** | |
| Told counsel he always emphasized duty to acquit if district attorney did not prove case beyond reasonable doubt. | |
| **5. Charges** | |
| Technical violations of innumerable regulations. | Difficult for jurors to get interested in, or understand regulations. |

### b. Sample: Theme and Defense Strategy §4.16

Theme

No ordinary person could possibly know, understand, and comply with all the complicated regulations the *Berkowitz* defendants faced.

Defendants' Strategy

1. To meet expected aloofness, if not antagonism, of jurors toward defendants and their counsel, there should be an air of friendliness between defendants and their counsel and everyone in the courtroom, to create an atmosphere touching the jurors. Defendants' spouses, who plan to attend every day, should be identifiable as spouses by the jurors. Members of the defense team should make a point of talking to law clerks, bailiff, court reporter, and so on.
2. To cause the jurors to ask themselves: "How could anyone possibly comply with so many regulations?" the defense should not stipulate to anything. This would force the prosecution to introduce massive numbers of exhibits (1,100), and to read them into the record before the jury, including several regulations as long as 50 pages each.
3. To help the prosecution witnesses testifying as experts on the meaning of the regulations to come across as favorable to the defense

case, defense counsel should modulate cross-examination and make it possible for opposing witnesses to support some part of the defense case.
4. To avoid putting on a defense at the close of the government case.
5. To make their case through cross-examination of not hostile prosecution witnesses, relying on, and repeating, the trial judge's instructions to jurors during trial that they have a duty to acquit if the prosecution does not prove the case beyond a reasonable doubt.

This strategy was successful.

### 2. Other Federal Crimes §4.17

This section is being reserved for additional examples of case analysis to be presented in supplements to this volume.

## B. State

### 1. Possession of Concealed Firearms §4.19

*Source:* Dennis Weaver, a San Francisco trial lawyer.

The defendant was a 55-year-old disabled seaman charged with possession of a loaded concealed firearm. The facts were that he was mugged in his apartment house elevator by two men with guns. He rushed upstairs to his landlord's apartment, asked a friend to call the police, and said he was going to get his gun. When the police arrived, they went for the defendant.

When the client described the facts, he mentioned that he had a cat, and the two muggers had said they were going to kill his cat. Deciding that cat lovers were likely to support his client's defense of his pet, counsel asked prospective jurors about their pets. One juror went on and on about her cat. The DA used a peremptory to remove her. The defense continued to ask briefly about pets. The defense also asked jurors whether they could be fair in judging a person less fortunate than themselves.

These strategies were effective; the jury acquitted in 20 minutes.

### 2. Striker Charged with Assault §4.20

*Source:* Dean Robb of Michigan.

A striker was charged with throwing a rock at someone who was in the struck plant. The victim was not even a scab, just an innocent bystander. A police officer had seen the defendant throw the rock. Defense counsel saw that it would be very difficult to win an acquittal.

Analyzing the witnesses as the jury would encounter them, defense counsel could not help noticing that his client was really ugly—he looked as if he had just come out of prison, whereas the officer who arrested him was unusually handsome—he looked as if he had just come off a movie lot. Both would take the stand. Counsel selected jurors with these facts in mind.

He decided the theme of this case was that this was an unfair fight between a good-looking cop, in his blue uniform, and an ugly client. To make this point to the jury, the gray-haired lawyer stood near his client during his opening statement to the jury, giving the impression that "We're a little bit mournful. We've got a few years on us; we're not as good looking as this cop." What he said was, "This case is *The People of the State of Michigan versus Caspar Grubb*—that's an unfair fight right off the bat, isn't it? And look at my client—he looks like he just got out of ten years in the pen." When he said that, the defendant smiled right at the jury. "His smile was as big as a picture," recalled his lawyer. "I never will forget that as long as I live. And the jurors accepted him."

The lawyer had not told the client he was going to do this. It was done spontaneously in the process of humanizing the client to the jury.

Counsel had assumed the case was a sure loser unless the cop overstepped, which he did. "I made it an unfair fight, and of course the cop, thinking it was unfair, ended up making it unfair. But the minute the defendant smiled, him being so ugly, the jury immediately began pulling for Ol' Ugly instead of for Good-looking Cop. I worked on how I could balance the credibility in that case."

### 3. Prosecution of a Rape Case §4.21

In analyzing the facts and developing the theme in a rape case, prosecutors and defense counsel must be aware of current attitudes toward this crime in order to provide effective representation.

At a meeting of civil rights lawyers in California in 1976, a defense lawyer told a story about the James brothers robbing a train. Frank James allegedly told the passengers he was going to rob all the men and rape all the women. A timorous man got up the courage to say he would at least fight to the death against the latter, to which, a little old lady objected strenuously. In warm anticipation, she said, "Young man, let them carry out this caper in their own way!"

A defense lawyer who adheres to this philosophy in selecting women jurors in rape cases today is likely to earn a verdict against his client. Women in this era, and men in tune with their feelings, reject the old saw that a raped woman relaxes and enjoys it. Most women, those who read traditional women's magazines as well as active feminists, have heard about the insensitivity of police officers toward women claiming they were raped, and their sympathies may well rest with the victims.

Martin Blinder, psychiatrist and law professor, wrote in 1973 that "women are surprisingly good defense jurors in rape trials." But Blinder's analysis of rape victims (*Psychiatry in the Everyday Practice of Law* 83 (1973)):

> Some people make decidedly better victims than others .... consider the tipsy, mini-skirted woman with a compulsive proclivity for dark streets.[17]

17. If instilled within a woman's unconscious that sex is bad and forbidden she may be able to engage in it only if forced upon her ("I didn't want to, of course, but he pinned me down and rendered me helpless so what could I do?"), preferably in a fashion sufficiently punishing so as to neutralize her guilt ("I may have been naughty but I at least paid the price").

requires reexamination in light of changing attitudes toward rape victims. See voir dire questions in §11.52.

In planning trial strategy, counsel must also take into account statutes and cases limiting the questions that can be asked of the complaining witness about her prior sexual experiences. See, e.g., California Evidence Code §1103(2), which prohibits evidence of the complaining witness's prior sexual conduct to prove her consent; *Michigan v Sturgis* (1971) 191 NW2d 618, which held that the trial court did not abuse its discretion by refusing to permit defense counsel to cross-examine the complainant with respect to her prior sexual activities.

The verdict in *Michigan v Hartwell*, described in §3.31, indicates a new willingness to expand the concept of rape to include a husband-wife relationship and to justify a homicide committed by a wife avoiding forced sexual relations. Equally clearly, members of minority groups continue to fear frame-ups by white women, like that in the famous *Scottsboro* case (*Norris v Alabama* (1937) 302 US 642; see also Patterson, *Scottsboro Boy* (1969)).

## C. State or Federal

### 1. Woman Charged with Conspiracy §4.22

In analyzing the facts in a civil or criminal conspiracy case, it is possible that the defense can make use of both new and traditional attitudes about women. Under traditional views, many wives disapprove of their husbands' actions and do not assist them, but do nothing to stop them, for fear of destroying their marriages or incurring verbal or physical abuse. Thus, a wife's silence may not be taken to prove her assent. If a wife took no action in furtherance of a conspiracy in which her husband engaged, even if there is no evidence that she opposed the conspiracy, a jury may be willing to find her innocent of conspiracy charges.

On the other hand, under modern views it cannnot be assumed that a liberated wife has participated in her husband's acts, whether legal or illegal. In the absence of proof, today it is as reasonable to infer ignorance of an illegal conspiracy as to infer participation on the part of an independent-minded wife.

## 2. Battered Woman Defense

### a. Sample: Narrative Summary §4.23

Yvonne Wanrow, a Native American mother, was charged with killing William Wesler on August 12, 1972. The day before, she learned that he had tried to pull her young son off his bicycle; that he had molested the young daughter of her friend, Ms. Hooper, a few months before; and that he had been a mental patient. Ms. Hooper called the police, who came, said they couldn't arrest Wesler "until Monday morning," and suggested she "wait until he gets in the house" before conking him over the head.

Ms. Wanrow, Ms. Hooper, and another couple stayed up to watch for possible prowlers. Ms. Wanrow, 5'4", had a broken leg and was using a crutch. At 5 a.m., Wesler, 6'2" and intoxicated, entered the house and approached one of the sleeping children. Wanrow testified to being gravely startled by this situation and to having shot Wesler in what amounted to a reflex action. Ms. Hooper then called the police, stating, "There's a guy broke in, and my girlfriend shot him." The defendant also talked with the police operator.

After presentation of the evidence, the jury was instructed on the law, including self-defense, and commenced deliberations. The jury reached its verdict of guilty of second-degree murder and first-degree assault. Defendant appealed.

The Washington State Supreme Court reversed the conviction on two grounds: (1) the trial court improperly instructed the jury in the law of self-defense in relation to the defendant as a woman and as someone reacting to facts learned several hours earlier; (2) local regulations authorize recording emergency calls but make them inadmissible into evidence. *Wanrow v Washington* (1977) 538 P2d 849.

Before retrial, Ms. Wanrow pleaded guilty to manslaughter and was sentenced to five years' probation.

### b. Theme §4.24

A woman 5'4", with a cast on her leg and using a crutch, has a right to defend herself against an assaul by an intoxicated 6'2" man, and may use a weapon if she honestly believes she is in danger of great bodily harm. This was the main theme developed by the defense in the *Wanrow* case, with the subtheme that a woman may honestly have a different belief about her danger than a man would have "in the same circumstances" because a woman has less training and experience in self-defense than a man, so the "circumstances" are never the same.

While the jury rejected this theme, after hearing the trial judge's instruction on self-defense, it became the ground for reversal on appeal in an opinion worth quoting at some length:

> The second paragraph of instruction No. 10 contains an equally erroneous and prejudicial statement of the law. That portion of the instruction reads:
>
> > However, when there is no reasonable ground for the person attacked to believe that *his* person is in imminent danger of death or great bodily harm, and it appears to *him* that only an ordinary battery is all that is intended, and all that *he* has reasonable grounds to fear from *his* assailant, *he* has a right to stand *his* ground and repel such threatened assault, yet *he* has no right to repel a threatened assault with naked hands, by the use of a deadly weapon in a deadly manner, unless *he* believes, *and has reasonable grounds* to believe, that *he* is in imminent danger of death or great bodily harm.
>
> (Italics ours.) In our society women suffer from a conspicuous lack of access to training in and the means of developing those skills necessary to effectively repel a male assailant without resorting to the use of deadly weapons. (See B. Babcock, A. Freedman, E. Norton, and S. Ross, *Sex Discrimination and the Law: Causes and Remedies* 943–1070 (1975); S. Brownmiller, *Against Our Will: Men, Women and Rape* (1975).) Instruction No. 12 does indicate that the "relative size and strength of the persons involved" may be considered; however, it does not make clear that the defendant's actions are to be judged against her own subjective impressions and not those which a detached jury might determine to be objectively reasonable. *State v Miller* (1926) 141 Wash 104, 250 P 645; *State v Tyree* (1927) 143 Wash 313, 255 P 382; *State v Dunning* (1973) 8 Wash App 340, 342, 506 P2d 321. The applicable rule of law is clearly stated in *Miller*, 141 Wash at 105:
>
> > If the appellants, at the time of the alleged assault upon them, as reasonably and ordinarily cautious and prudent men, honestly believed that they were in danger of great bodily harm, they would have the right

> to resort to self defense, and their conduct is to be judged by the condition appearing to them at the time, not by the condition as it might appear to the jury in the light of testimony before it.
>
> The second paragraph of instruction No. 10 not only establishes an objective standard, but through the persistent use of the masculine gender leaves the jury with the impression the objective standard to be applied is that applicable to an altercation between two men. The impression created—that a 5'4" woman with a cast on her leg and using a crutch must, under the law, somehow repel an assault by a 6'2" intoxicated man without employing weapons in her defense, unless the jury finds her determination of the degree of danger to be objectively reasonable—constitutes a separate and distinct misstatement of the law and, in the context of this case, violates the respondent's right to equal protection of the law. The respondent was entitled to have the jury consider her actions in the light of her own perceptions of the situation, including those perceptions which were the product of our nation's "long and unfortunate history of sex discrimination." *Frontiero v Richardson* (1973) 411 US 677, 684, 36 L Ed 2d 583, 93 S Ct 1764. Until such time as the effects of that history are eradicated, care must be taken to assure that our self-defense instructions afford women the right to have their conduct judged in light of the individual physical handicaps which are the product of sex discrimination. To fail to do so is to deny the right of the individual woman involved to trial by the same rules which are applicable to male defendants. See *Lamb v Brown* (10th Cir 1972) 456 F2d 18. See also *Reed v Reed* (1971) 404 US 71, 30 L Ed 2d 225, 92 S Ct 251; *Darrin v Gould* (1975) 85 Wash 2d 859, 540 P2d 882. The portion of the instruction above quoted misstates our law in creating an objective standard of "reasonableness." It then compounds that error by utilizing language suggesting that the respondent's conduct must be measured against that of a reasonable male individual finding himself in the same circumstances.
>
> We conclude that the instruction here in question contains an improper statement of the law on a vital issue in the case, is inconsistent, misleading and prejudicial when read in conjunction with other instructions pertaining to the same issue, and therefore is a proper basis for a finding of reversible error.

The Washington Supreme Court also held the instruction erroneous for limiting jury consideration of self-defense to events "at or immediately before the killing":

> Instruction No. 10, setting forth the law of self-defense, incorrectly limited the jury's consideration of acts and circumstances pertinent to respondent's perception of the alleged threat to her person. An examination of the record of the testimony and of the colloquies which took place with regard to the instructions on self-defense indicate the critical importance of these instructions to the respondent's theory of the case. Based upon the evidence we have already set out, it is obviously crucial that the jury be precisely instructed as to the defense of justification.

In the opening paragraph of instruction No. 10, the jury, in evaluating the gravity of the danger to the respondent, was directed to consider only those acts and circumstances occurring "at or immediately before the killing . . . " (Instruction No. 10 reads: "To justify killing in self-defense, there need be no actual or real danger to the life or person of the party killing, but there must be, or reasonably appear to be, at or immediately before the killing, some overt act, or some circumstances which would reasonably indicate to the party killing that the person slain, is, at the time, endeavoring to kill him or inflict upon him great bodily harm." [The instruction continues with the paragraph quoted above.]) This is not now, and never has been, the law of self-defense in Washington. On the contrary, the justification of self-defense is to be evaluated in light of *all* the facts and circumstances known to the defendant, including those known substantially before the killing.

In *State v Ellis* (1902) 30 Wash 369, 70 P 963, this court reversed a first-degree murder conviction obtained under self-defense instructions quite similar to that in the present case. The defendant sought to show that the deceased had a reputation and habit of carrying and using deadly weapons when engaged in quarrels . . . . Thus, circumstances predating the killing by weeks and months were deemed entirely proper, and in fact essential, to a proper disposition of the claim of self-defense.

Similarly, in *State v Churchill* (1909) 52 Wash 210, 100 P 309, the court upheld self-defense instructions directing the jury to . . . " 'take into consideration *all* the facts and circumstances bearing on the question and surrounding defendant and existing at *or prior to the time of the alleged shooting* . . . ' " (Italics ours.) 52 Wash at 220. This court found these instructions "clear, apt, and comprehensive" and free from error. 52 Wash at 225.

. . . .

The State attempts to minimize this deficiency in instruction No. 10 by invoking the rule that an instruction is "sufficient" if counsel may satisfactorily argue his or her theory of the case. This is a mistaken application of the rule and will cause widespread mischief in civil as well as criminal cases if adopted here. The test of "sufficiency" is just that, and is not a rule to be applied where the instruction is an *erroneous* statement of the law. This distinction is apparent from *Smith v McDaniel* (1959) 53 Wash 2d 604, 335 P2d 582, a negligence case in which the test was first enunciated. . . .

As shown by the discussion above, instruction No. 10 erred in limiting the acts and circumstances which the jury could consider in evaluating the nature of the threat of harm as perceived by respondent. Under the well-established rule, this error is presumed to have been prejudicial. Moreover, far from affirmatively showing that the error was harmless, the record demonstrates the limitation to circumstances "at or immediately before the killing" was of crucial importance in the present case. Respondent's knowledge of the victim's reputation for aggressive acts was gained many hours before the killing and was based upon events which occurred over a period of years. Under the law of this state, the jury should have been allowed to consider this information in making the critical determination of the " 'degree of force which . . . a reasonable person in the same situtation . . . seeing what [s]he sees and knowing what [s]he knows, then would believe to be necessary.' " *State v Dunning* (1973) 8 Wash App 340, 342, 506 P2d 321 . . . .

See voir dire questions on self-defense in §11.51.

### c. Analysis of Juror Reactions to Defendants §4.25

When representing a woman charged with assault or murder who claims that she acted in self-defense, counsel face jurors with quite different attitudes toward the defendant than in cases in which a man defendant makes the same claim. Charting some of these differences may sharpen analysis of what kinds of jurors are desirable and how to conduct voir dire.

| *Jurors* | *Male Defendant* | *Female Defendant* |
|---|---|---|
| Authoritarian personalities | Identify with Prosectution | Identify with Defendant: might be chivalrous or patronizing |
| Women | Might be sympathetic | May feel threatened by a woman who broke the old stereotype and fought back;<br>May feel defendant "waived her rights" by staying with the batterer |

### d. Desirable and Undesirable Jurors §4.26

Desirable Jurors

*Androgynous individuals:* people who do not automatically differentiate between male and female characteristics; people who could ignore stereotypes dictated by traditional sexual expectations that women will submit to being battered without defending themselves.

*Experienced people:* men and women who could consider what is a "fair fight" between a man and a woman, and what is "excessive force" in such a situation, when the woman has not been trained in self-defense and uses a weapon when she finally decides this is "necessary," although a man trained in self-defense might not come to the same conclusion based on the same facts, that is, facing the same adversary. See *Michigan v Hartwell,* §3.31

Undesirable Jurors

Traditionalists with narrow life experiences: might be unable to imagine the predicament that led to defendant's act of self-defense.

See *Washington v Wanrow* (Wash. Sup. Ct. 1977) 538 P2d 849; Eisenberg & Seymour, "Defending Battered Women: A Model Voir Dire," 16 *Trial* 30–33 (Dec. 1980); Ann Jones, "Women Who Kill" (1980) and a review by West in 6 *Women's Rights L Rptr* 310 (1980).

### D. Other Criminal Cases §4.27

This section is being reserved for analysis of additional criminal cases to be presented in supplements to this volume.

## IV. EXAMPLES OF COMMON PROBLEMS

### A. Cases in Which Key Witnesses Will Be Women

#### 1. Women as Hostile Witnesses §4.30

In analyzing the facts in a case, the nature of the hostile witnesses is a major factor. What tactics are in order when a woman will be such a witness? And what is appropriate when it is likely that strong cross-examination may lead the witness to tears? What kinds of jurors will evaluate the woman's testimony objectively, despite its emotional impact? The answer is not easy.

Women jurors may know, better than men, that for a woman witness to burst into tears is not the end of the world. They may also know that a woman's mind frequently goes on working while she weeps, and that the witness will probably stop crying and go on talking if the lawyer gives her a minute or two to compose herself. And women jurors may know that few women can produce tears on call, that many start crying against their will.

Perhaps women tend to hold women to higher standards than men do, and men tend to hold men to higher standards than women do. Experts who have this opinion explain that women know more about what is expected of women than about what is expected of men. Therefore, they are more concerned when women do not meet these standards, and more critical of them for failing. The ame rule applies to men.

If this is so, a woman juror may hold a woman witness to this higher standard. Will a woman juror be alienated by a hard-driving cross-examination of a woman witness? She may not, if she holds the woman witness to a higher standard than the lawyer and believes that the woman witness should not permit herself to dissolve into tears, but should answer the questions, however unpleasant or painful, even if a male witness would break down (into swearing) under similar cross-examination.

When a woman will be a hostile witness, lawyers should probably look for men and women jurors who admire strong-minded women or women who exercise leadership qualities. If the juror's mother was a feminist or openly showed her self-respect and strength, a weeping woman witness will be less threatening to the juror. Male jurors who "like their women feminine" may not understand the psychological interplay that is going on and may be turned off by a rough cross-examination of the poor delicate woman on the stand.

For different reactions of men and women jurors to female and male lawyers cross-examining hostile witnesses, see §4.36.

### 2. Women as Expert Witnesses §4.31

It is still unusual for a woman to appear on the witness stand as an expert, whether as medical doctor, engineer, criminalist, psychiatrist, or in any other learned profession or scientific specialty. As a result, there is little quantitative evidence on the kinds of women experts who will be most convincing to men and women jurors. Nor do we have many clues to what women experts can do to make their testimony more credible and convincing to men and women jurors.

However, certain general rules about expert witnesses apply equally to women and men. Young experts may be suspect unless something in their manner makes clear that they really are entitled to be considered experts and that this has not made them conceited. Also, the expert's credentials should be stated clearly and fully in language the jrors can understand, so that the fact that the witness is an expert is indisputable.

Beyond that, women experts may have difficulty being accepted by both men and women jurors.

This is a period of rapid change in women's expectations about their lives and opportunities (if not in their actual circumstances). Many women may wish they had different roles from those they actually play. A working woman may wish she could stay home with her children all-day or half-time. A full-time mother may be very envious of the woman who has a "real" job in the outside world. An older woman may wish she were 25 now and could get all those good jobs she reads about. A 25-year-old woman may envy the older women who do not get turned down for jobs as she does because she does not have enough experience.

Of course, it is also very true that women of all ages are taking renewed pride in their sex, that they applaud other women of all ages who achieved expertise in any field, particularly in those formerly monopolized by men. But it would be a mistake to assume that this feeling is universal.

A lawyer who intends to present a woman expert witness should try to probe the feelings of women (and men) jurors on this issue to uncover any biases the jurors may have that would lead them to discount or disbelieve the expert's testimony. Some of the questions in §§9.70–9.74 can be adapted to the woman/man expert witness problem.

A young woman expert who is also attractive may have more difficulty being accepted as an expert than one who is less attractive. This may be due to people's envy of those who seem to have been endowed with both beauty and brains out of proportion to the rest of the population. Or this may be a myth.

Whatever the case, an attractive woman expert witness should be thoroughly prepared to present testimony in a professional manner that will foreclose charges of either aloofness or casualness. Since our society has not yet developed a stereotype of the professional woman expert witness's behavior, due to the newness of the role, basic rules for all witnesses are probably the best guides.

On voir dire, counsel may be able to refer to strong professional women characters in recent Hollywood movies, seeking jurors' reactions to Sally Field as "Norma Rae," Diane Keaton as Louise Bryant in "Reds," Jane Fonda in many roles, or Jill Clayburgh as the first woman Supreme Court justice in "First Monday in October." Answers to such questions may be helpful in using peremptory challenges on jurors who probably could not find credible the testimony of a woman expert witness.

### B. Other Issues §4.32

See §4.12.

## V. ANALYZING REACTIONS TO LAWYERS

### A. Cases Handled by Women Lawyers

#### 1. What Jurors May Expect §4.35

In analyzing a case in order to plan trial strategy, the nature of the lawyers must be included. If a woman lawyer will appear for one of the parties, counsel must consider how this fact will affect the trial.

Traditionally, American women have not been expected to raise their arms in anger or to raise their voices in public dispute. Arguing is not considered ladylike and women's debate teams have not flourished. As a result, women lawyers today face numerous problems, major and minor: What should they wear to court to make the best impression? What style should they follow: Should they act like "ladies," "ordinary women," or "professional women"? Are they to be judged by the same standards as others in their field or must they be either better or clearly different?

### a. "Aggressive" Approach §4.36

A woman juror may hold a woman lawyer to a higher standard than she would hold a man. She may be alienated by a hard-driving cross-examination by a woman lawyer of a woman witness, even if she would not be alienated by exactly the same tactics used by a man lawyer. She may think women lawyers should be "better than" men, or should practice their profession in a more genteel or ladylike fashion.

The reverse may be also true: A woman juror may permit a man lawyer more leeway in cross-examining a woman witness than a man juror would permit. She may expect men lawyers to be aggressive, demanding, and persistent in their questioning of witnesses. This may fit well with her notion of a good, professional, male lawyer.

On the other hand, a woman juror who has been "cross-examined" more than once in her life by a browbeating male (husband, boss, police officer) may take a hostile attitude toward a male defense lawyer who seems to behave in this manner.

What will a male juror think of a woman lawyer who is as aggressive as a man lawyer is generally expected to be?

It is probably true that a woman lawyer who has been quite open in manner throughout the case, who has spoken up clearly and forcefully on previous occasions in colloquies with the judge and in arguments with opposing counsel, will be accepted without hostility when she goes after a woman witness. She should be able to complete her cross-examination effectively without alienating men or women jurors if they see that she is not nasty, petty, or vindictive.

When a woman will be a hostile witness, women lawyers should probably look for men and women jurors who admire strong-minded women or women who exercise leadership qualities. Men lawyers should probably select men jurors who understand that a shrinking violet may really belong to the family of Venus's-flytraps.

### b. "Uncertain" Approach §4.37

What do men and women jurors think of women lawyers who have appeared before them? Few surveys have been conducted on this subject to date, but some insights may be gleaned from such a poll by the Minnesota Women Lawyers in 1980. Pollsters questioned 100 jurors who heard 60 jury cases (40 criminal and 20 civil) tried by women lawyers in Hennepin County. The study concluded that sexual stereotypes are still widespread, which may interfere with the ability of women lawyers to represent their clients in jury trials. Many of those polled said they would hire women to represent them only in family or juvenile law cases. A number characterized the women attorneys as appearing inexperienced, unsure of themselves, less convincing than their male opponents.

In fact, traditional, large firms have been slow to permit women to participate in all areas of practice. A 1983 study in San Francisco showed no women partners in more than 60 percent of the law firms with 15 or more lawyers, and they made up less than 3 percent of the total number of partners, according to the Employment Committee of Queen's Bench study.

The full-range of styles of women trial lawyers will only be displayed when the appearance of women trial lawyers is commonplace and their numbers approach 50 percent, as in the population as a whole.

### 2. Precedents for Women Lawyers §4.38

Women lawyers seeking ideas on styles of practice have a rich encyclopedia to turn to, although its existence is not widely known. In this field, as in many others, it is not necessary to rediscover the wheel. We simply have to find accurate reports of the experiences of our ancestors—from the first Women's Rights Convention in Seneca Falls, New York, in 1848, right up to the present.

The hidden history of United States women provides answers to many questions raised by modern women lawyers (as well as to some questions the modern women's movement has not yet asked). It is replete with suggestions on how women can make effective speeches, because everyone interested in making a particular change in society has had to learn how to get and hold a platform before she or he could address a particular issue. Much can be learned and adapted from the experiences of lecturer Margaret Fuller, friend of Emerson and Thoreau, and one of the most articulate fighters for abolition and women's rights (see Margaret Bell's excellent biography, *Margaret Fuller* (1930)). And see biographies of other women abolitionists, from Lucy Stone, the northern Quaker, to the Grimkes, her southern Quaker sisters. Any librarian can find reports of the speeches of Harriet Tubman, Sojourner Truth, and other black women who fought vociferously for the rights of blacks and women from platforms all over the country. Study the work of Sarah Bagley, who organized the women workers in the Lowell cotton mills to cut the workday to ten hours in 1844, and of Elizabeth Gurley Flynn, who organized women in the same Lowell industry almost a century later. All of these women are described in biographies or autobiographies, and some have been written about extensively. See, e.g., Bernard, *Journey Toward Freedom: The Story of Sojourner Truth* (1969); Conrad, *Harriet Tubman* (1942); Flynn, *The Rebel Girl: An Autobiography* (1973); Flexner, *Century of Struggle: The Women's Rights Movement in the United States* (1959); Hahn, *Once Upon a Pedestal* (1974); Tax, *Rivington Street* (1982).

These women participated in many firsts: first woman to address the Massachusetts legislature, first to address a congressional committee, first to try to register to vote, first to organize a lecture series. They described exactly how they felt and how they mastered their feelings and won their audiences. Jane Addams's Hull House, from the 1890s on, trained many inspired advocates, all of whom left biographies or autobiographies full of suggestions for today's women lawyers: Florence Kelley, a lawyer, was the first inspector of factories for Illinois and later secretary of the National Consumers League; Dr. Alice Hamilton was one of the foremost American authorities on industrial disease; Julia Lathrop was first chief of the Children's Bureau; and Grace and Edith Abbott were fighters against the exploitation of children and aliens. See Addams, *Twenty Years at Hull-House* (1938); Addams, *My Friend, Julia Lathrop* (1935); Goldmark, *Impatient Crusader* (1953); Hamilton, *Exploring the Dangerous Trades* (1943).

It might truly be said that the first women lawyers in this country were amazons, strong women, frequently beautiful in spirit, with enormous wit and the determination to use it, either openly or obliquely. See, e.g., brief biographies of Carol King (immigration lawyer in New York City from 1921 to 1952) and Pearl Hart (immigration and juvenile court lawyer in Chicago from 1914 to 1975), in Meiklejohn Institute, *A Calendar of Lawyers, 1977* (Box 673, Berkeley, CA 94701).

These women had to be outstanding to get admitted to college and law school, and to make it through. In the face of their clear superiority, they were sometimes treated almost like equals. They were so few that they posed no threat. They were so competent they might almost be forgiven for entering a man's field. As more women passed the bar, some were not amazons and a few were ordinary women. They found it very tough sledding—they could not get jobs in law offices, paying clients, or equal treatment from bench or bar. Still, more and more persevered.

Women lawyers today face problems in dealing with male professionals who are aware of women's increasing participation in the courtroom, but have never analyzed their stereotyped reactions to women lawyers, and have done nothing to help defeat sexism, for the benefit of women, men, and the judicial system. See, e.g., Blinder, *Psychiatry in the Everyday Practice of Law* 120 (1973):

> It is appropriate to mention here that the female attorney, however competent, labors under an inadvertent handicap when she does trial work. Her voice tones, inevitably and appropriately incisive, strident and critical as she conducts a cross-examination or challenges opposing counsel, often fall upon the ears of the juror, male or female, as a childhood echo of his own mother's angry, critical moods. Without realizing it, the juror cringes inside as the attorney mounts her attack, identifying with the object of the attorney's indignation, effectively neutralizing and possibly reversing her efforts. The aspirations eloquently expressed by the Feminist Movement have thus far done little to alter the validity of this observation.

### 3. Emerging Problems §4.39

See §4.12.

## B. Cases Handled by Out-of-State Lawyers §4.40

As more and more lawyers try cases outside the jurisdictions in which their offices are located, a list of "do's" and "don't's" is developing.

| *Don't* | *Do* |
|---|---|
| 1. Don't arrive on the date of trial ignorant of the recent history of the area, local landmarks, and common subjects of pride and scorn. | 1. Visit the scene of the incident, become familiar with the geography and sight of the trial city, and learn to pronounce street and district names correctly. |
| 2. Don't assume any rule of law or procedure is the same as it is in your home state. | 2. Check every elementary and special rule of substantive and procedural law in the foreign jurisdiction. |
| 3. Don't ignore your local co-counsel. | 3. Plan to rely on local co-counsel throughout the trial, and let the judge and jury see that you do. |
| 4. Don't try to pretend you are at home by wearing different clothes or changing your speech patterns. | 4. Dress as you would in your own courthouse, avoiding stereotypes from your region or the foreign jurisdiction. |
| | 5. Mention your home city during voir dire and indicate your pleasure or interest in trying this case in a strange city. |

### C. Other Problems §4.41

See §4.12

## VI. FACTORS TO ANALYZE IN PLANNING TRIAL STRATEGY

### A. From Practice to Theory §4.45

In this chapter, the examples were presented before the analysis, so that the theory would be drawn from experience.

What factors were the lawyers considering when they developed their strategies? See the balance sheets lawyers developed in §§4.4, 4.15; voir dire questions in §4.5; profiles of desirable and undesirable jurors in §§4.6, 4.26; narrative summaries in §§4.10, 4.23; jurors' expected reactions to clients in §§4.5, 4.7, 4.11, 4.25; jurors' expected reactions to the cross-examination of hostile witnesses, §4.30, to expert witnesses, §4.31, to women lawyers, §§4.35–4.37, to out-of-state lawyers, §4.40.

### B. Checklist of Factors that Determine Jury Verdicts §4.46

I. Background
  A. General conditions in the community
    1. Economic, political, social, historical, regional
    2. Community conscience on issues related to your case
  B. Specific recent occurrences in the community
    1. Local elections, lawsuits, campaigns
    2. Local tragedies (major fire, earthquake), local victories (new stadium)
    3. Actions directly and indirectly related to your case
  C. Time factors
    1. Distance of trial from event leading up to trial
    2. Reminders of the event in the press
    3. Length of trial

II. Nature of the litigation
  A. Major or minor, e.g., capital offense or misdemeanor, major medical damages or minor property damage
  B. Public or private dispute, i.e., public-interest issue or one of individual rights or wrongs
  C. Traditional issue or a new issue, e.g., loss of life in a fire, or loss of emotional stability due to a false diagnosis of AIDS

III. Resources for the case
  A. Family/committee supporting the litigant

- B. Personnel
  1. Counsel
  2. Experts
  3. Amicus curiae
     a. To help with legal research
     b. To appear in person or by brief on unique issues
- C. Financial
  1. From the client
  2. From the community
  3. From organizations, foundations, etc.
- D. Time
  1. Short deadlines between selection of counsel and trial
  2. Ample pretrial period
- E. Media coverage
  1. Approach: helpful, neutral, negative; none
  2. Timing: of the event, pretrial, trial, appeal

IV. Facts
- A. Specific facts in the case
- B. "The unfortunate facts" touching the case
  1. Prejudices aroused by the parties or issues
     a. Racial, nationality
     b. Sexual, sexual preference
     c. Class, occupation
     d. Age
     e. Appearance, regional accents
     f. Political, economic, social factors
  2. Fears aroused by the issues
     a. Publicity if selected for jury duty
     b. Loss of esteem if jurors vote a particular verdict
- C. Demonstrative evidence for both sides
- D. Ease or difficulty of presenting evidence to jurors
  1. Offers of proof accepted?
  2. Judicial notice taken?
  3. Expert witnesses
- E. Opponent's strongest points of fact
  1. Are they admissible?
  2. How to minimize their effect
  3. How to use to your advantage

V. Participants
- A. Parties on both sides
- B. Counsel for each side
  1. Experience

2. Style, characteristics
3. Competence

C. Witnesses for both sides
1. Availability
2. Attractiveness to the jury
3. Credibility to the jury
4. Strength on direct examination and cross-examination

D. Victims

E. Trial judge

F. Jurors
1. Juror pay
2. Length of trial

G. Media

VI. Law

A. Procedural problems created by statutes and court rules

B. Substantive law
1. Winning legal issues
a. Traditional
b. Innovative
c. Problems of admissibility
d. Difficulty of conveying legal issues to the jury
2. Opponent's strongest points of law
a. Are they admissible?
b. How to minimize their effect
c. How to use to your advantage

After carefully listing the factors relevant to your case, you have an opportunity to devise tactics to capitalize on the favorable factors and to minimize the negative effects of unfavorable factors.

## C. Recent Developments §4.47

It is now possible to keep up with new practice tips on case analysis in almost the same way you keep up with the law in any other field—by reading periodicals on trial advocacy and criminal law, and by reading daily newspapers and legal newspapers. It is a good idea occasionally to ask your law librarian for an index to journals on psychology, applied psychology, and the social sciences, to pick up new ideas from these disciplines.

The Annual Supplement to these volumes will use recent developments sections throughout the book to describe new cases, ideas, and articles that are worthy of note, and to warn of innovative ideas that failed, of cases overruled, and of rules and statutes amended or repealed.

## VII. FACTORS TO CONSIDER IN SELECTING FORUM

### A. Civil and Criminal Litigants Often Have Choice §4.50

In any criminal case in which jury trial is possible, the defendants can seek a change of venue if counsel can prove that a fair and impartial jury cannot be impanelled. In any criminal case, the prosecution has considerable leeway in selecting the place of arrest and the charges, in order to determine the forum.

In some state civil and criminal cases, counsel can remove to federal court if counsel can prove that fair trial is impossible in the state court.

In any civil case, plaintiff can select the forum, and usually has more than one convenient jurisdiction from which to choose. In many civil cases, defendant can object to the forum and sometimes can cause a case to be tried in a forum more favorable to defendant.

Before selecting the forum, or accepting the forum selected by the opponent, counsel should methodically consider alternative forums, to decide whether it is worth the effort to seek a change of venue or take whatever other action is necessary to try the case elsewhere.

It should be noted that some state courts are moving toward one-trial juries. Jurors come in and stay a maximum of one week or until they have served once; then they are excused for several years. In the federal courts in the same states, jurors may serve a little longer, so that there may be some experienced jurors in your pool. You need to decide whether this will work for or against you in a particular case.

In a malpractice case in a small community, you may want to get away from a local hospital or doctor whom the jurors may rely on for treatment. You may decide to sue in federal court so that you will get a federal jury drawn from a larger geographical area, so that no jurors are likely to fear that their future medical care could be affected by their vote in your case.

In some states, lawyers can choose between 12-person state juries and 6-person federal juries in civil cases. Lawyers from Michigan and other states with 6-person civil juries, and lawyers who try cases to 6-person federal civil juries, become accustomed to the intimate relationships possible in selecting 6 jurors and 2 alternates. E.g., when the Arizona struck system is used in selecting a 6-person jury plus 2 alternates, with three peremptory challenges per party and two plaintiffs and one defendant, or vice versa, the lawyers face 17 people at a time. This permits the attorneys conducting voir dire to get a feeling about each of the 17 individually. They can take side glances at the 17, observing their behavior without being obvious about it.

Good trial attorneys build a very personal relationship with as many jurors as possible, starting during voir dire. In a short trial, they find it difficult to build such relationships with 14 jurors. Even in a three- or four-week trial, it is not easy to get a sense of the thought processes and reactions of this many individuals. As a result, Victoria Heldman, of Detroit, says she would prefer to take a chance on convincing 5 out of 6 jurors, or even 6 out of 6 (when a unanimous verdict is required), than to try to convince the majority of a jury of 12.

Many trial lawyers, always concerned about the need for 12 jurors in criminal cases, also prefer 12 jurors in civil cases. See §§1.21–1.25.

## B. Factors to Consider in Making Choice §4.51

It is a good idea to list the relevant factors and to compare your chances in each possible jurisdiction.

| | *In Jurisdiction 1* | *In Jurisidiction 2* |
|---|---|---|
| A. Jury factors | | |
| 1. Chances of experienced jurors | | |
| 2. Number of jurors and alternates | | |
| 3. Number of jurors to win | | |
| 4. Customary number of peremptory challenges* | | |
| 5. Likelihood of gaining additional peremptory challenges from trial judge | | |
| 6. Geographical area from which jurors selected | | |

*To find arguments for granting additional peremptory challenges, see "Rule as to Number of Peremptory Challenges," which discusses the validity and construction of statutes and court rules prescribing the number of peremptory challenges in criminal cases according to the nature of the offense or the extent of punishment, in 8 ALR4th 149. And see Annotation: Distribution and Exercise of Peremptory Challenges in Federal Civil Cases under 28 USC §1970, in 50 ALR Fed 350.

| | *In Jurisdiction 1* | *In Jurisidiction 2* |
|---|---|---|
| 7. Trial delay expected | | |
| 8. Pretrial coverage of related issues and of the case itself: amount, character | | |
| 9. Fairness, impartiality, breadth of lists from which jurors will be selected | | |
| 10. Chances of cross-section jury by race, sex, class, nationality, age, geographical area, experience | | |
| 11. Chances of jurors who have shared some experience with your client | | |
| 12. Size and nature of jury verdicts in similar cases | | |
| 13. Community conscience on the issues in your case in the area from which jurors will be selected | | |
| B. Voir dire factors | | |
| 1. Method of conducting voir dire: judge, lawyers, combination | | |
| 2. Custom as to breadth of questioning | | |
| 3. Rules re prohibiting peremptory challenges based solely on the race of the jurors | | |

| | *In Jurisdiction 1* | *In Jurisidiction 2* |
|---|---|---|
| C. Judicial factors | | |
| 1. Which judge is likely to hear your case (in jurisdictions where this can be predicted) | | |
| 2. Probable effect of recent local litigation on issues similar to those in your case | | |
| 3. Probable speed and outcome of appeal, if that becomes necessary | | |
| D. Subjective factors | | |
| 1. Possibilities for friends of the parties to attend trial | | |
| 2. Possibilities for favorable coverage by the media | | |
| 3. Chances of spontaneous help from strangers in the community who hear about the case | | |

## C. List of Jury Selection Factors in Federal Courts: Criminal & Civil Trials §4.52

*CAVEAT:* No short list of statutory provisions can be entirely accurate, even when current. The following brief descriptions of federal law are primarily helpful as a source of citations to code sections and rules in the Federal Rules of Civil Procedure and Federal Rules of Criminal Procedure. **Always check to see whether changes have been made since this material was compiled.**

CRIMINAL

*Number of jurors:* 12 (or any number less than 12 by stipulation with court's approval before verdict) 18 USC Rules of Crim Proc 23(b) (Cum Supp 1983)

*Peremptory challenges* (18 USC Rules of Crim Proc 24(b) (1975))
Capital cases: Prosecution—20; Defense—20
Noncapital felonies: Prosecution—6; Defense—10
Misdemeanors: Prosecution—3; Defense—3
*Method of voir dire:* Court or Counsel (18 USC Rules of Crim Proc 24(a) (1975))
For examples of extensive voir dire, see cases described in §§3.51–3.58.

CIVIL
*Number of jurors:* 12 (or any number less than 12, by stipulation; see §1.22) 28 USC Rules of Civ Proc 48 (1968)
*Peremptory challenges* (28 USC §1870 (1966))
Plaintiff—3; Defendant—3
*Method of voir dire:* Court or Counsel (28 USC Rules of Civ Proc 47(a) (1968))
For examples of extensive voir dire, see cases described in §§3.71–3.73.

MILITARY
See example of *Tangela Gaskins* administrative discharge case in §§3.91, 10.97–10.99, chapter 16.

## D. Fifty State List of Jury Selection Factors: Criminal Trials §4.53

*CAVEAT:* No short list of provisions on jury selection can be accurate, because there are too many slight variations within one state and among the several states. Every effort has been made to make this list both short and accurate, but every permutation (between "noncapital felonies" and "Class A, B, and C crimes," for example) has not been recorded here. Few court opinions are cited, although they may have modified local practice. In some cases, an out-of-state lawyer was not able to find a citation to court rules, state statutes, or other sources accessible at a local library.

For all of these reasons, please use the following primarily as a source of citations you can use to find the latest rules and statutes governing a state other than your own.

ALABAMA (struck system)
*Number of jurors:* 12 (parties can agree on fewer than 12)
Code of Ala §12-16-100(a) (Cum Supp 1982)
*Peremptory challenges* (Code of Ala §12-16-100(a) (Cum Supp 1982))
Capital cases: State—12; Defense—12
Noncapital felonies: State—3; Defense—6
Misdemeanors: State—3; Defense—3

*Method of voir dire:* Counsel (Rules of Ala Sup Ct (1975), *cf.* Rules of Civ Proc 47(a) (1975))

ALASKA
*Number of jurors:* 12
AK Const art 1 §11 (1973)
*Peremptory challenges* (Rule 24, Alaska Rules of Crim Proc)
Felonies: State—6; Defense—10
Misdemeanors: State—3; Defense—3
*Method of voir dire:* Court & Counsel (Alaska Rules of Crim Proc 24) (1968)

ARIZONA
*Number of jurors:* 12 (only if charge carries death penalty or 30 years' imprisonment; otherwise 8 jurors, but not fewer than 6)
Ariz Rev Stat §21-102 (1975); Ariz Const art 2 §23 (Cum Supp 1982)
*Peremptory challenges* (Ariz Rules of Crim Proc 18.4 (1973))
Capital cases: State—10; Defense—10
Noncapital felonies: State—6; Defense—6
Misdemeanors: State—2; Defense—2
*Method of voir dire:* Court (Ariz Rules of Crim Proc 18.5(d) (1973))

ARKANSAS
*Number of jurors:* 12 (in misdemeanor cases, parties can agree to fewer than 12)
Ark Stat Ann §43–1901 (1977)
*Peremptory challenges* (Ark Stat Ann §§43–1921, 43–1922 (Cum Supp 1983))
Capital cases: State—10; Defense—12
Noncapital felonies: State—6; Defense—8
Misdemeanors: State—3; Defense—3
*Method of voir dire:* Court & Counsel (Ark Rules of Crim Proc 32.2 (1977))

CALIFORNIA
*Number of jurors:* 12 (in misdemeanor cases, parties can agree to fewer than 12)
Cal Civ Proc Code §194 (1982)
*Peremptory challenges* (Cal Pen C §§1070, 1070.5 (Cum Supp 1983))
Capital cases: State—26; Defense—26
Noncapital felonies: State—10; Defense—10
Misdemeanors: State—6; Defense—6
*Method of voir dire:* Court & Counsel (Cal Pen C §1078 (Cum Supp 1983))

COLORADO
*Number of jurors:* 12 (parties can agree to fewer than 12)
Col Const art 2 §23 (1980)
*Peremptory challenges* (Col Rev Stat 16-10-104 (Cum Supp 1982))
Capital cases: State—10; Defense—10
Noncapital felonies: State—5; Defense—5
Misdemeanors: State—3; Defense—3
*Method of voir dire:* Court & Counsel (Col Rules of Crim Proc 24(a) (Cum Supp 1982))

CONNECTICUT
*Number of jurors:* 6 (jury of 12 if charge carries death penalty or life imprisonment unless accused consents to jury of 10) (Conn Gen Stat §54–82b(c) (Cum Supp 1982))
*Peremptory challenges* (Conn Gen Stat §54–82g (Cum Supp 1982))
Capital cases: State—25; Defense—25
Noncapital felonies: State—6; Defense—6 (15 each if offense punishable by life imprisonment)
Misdemeanors: State—3; Defense—3
*Method of voir dire:* Counsel (Conn Gen Stat §54–82f (Cum Supp 1982))

DELAWARE
*Number of jurors:* 12 (Del Code Ann 10 §4518 (1975)).
*Peremptory challenges* (Del Sup Ct Crim Rules 24(b) (1975))
Capital cases: State—12; Defense—20
Noncapital felonies: State—6; Defense—6
Misdemeanors: State—6; Defense—6
*Method of voir dire:* Court & Counsel (Del Sup Ct Crim Rules 24 (Cum Supp 1977))

FLORIDA
*Number of jurors:* 12 (6 in all noncapital cases)
FL Rules of Crim Proc 3.210 (1983)
*Peremptory challenges* (FL Stat Ann §913.08 (1973))
Capital cases: State—10; Defense—10
Noncapital felonies: State—6; Defense—6
Misdemeanors: State—3; Defense—3
*Method of voir dire:* Court & Counsel (FL Rules of Crim Proc 3.300(b) (Cum Supp 1983))

GEORGIA
*Number of jurors:* 12
Georgia Const art §1 ¶11(b) (1983)

*Peremptory challenges* (Off Code of GA §15-12-165 (1982))
Capital cases: State—10; Defense—20
Noncapital felonies: State—6; Defense—12
Misdemeanors: State—6; Defense—12
*Method of voir dire:* Court & Counsel (Off Code of GA §15-12-133 (1982))

HAWAII
*Number of jurors:* 12 (parties can agree to fewer than 12)
Hawaii Rev Stat §635–26 (1976)
*Peremptory challenges* (Hawaii Rev Stat §635–30 (1976)
Capital cases: State—12; Defense—12
Noncapital felonies: State—3; Defense—3
Misdemeanors: State—3; Defense—3
*Method of voir dire:* Counsel (Hawaii Rev Stat §635–27 (1976))

IDAHO
*Number of jurors:* 12 (6 in all misdemeanor cases)
Idaho Code §2–105 (1979)
*Peremptory challenges* (Idaho Code §19–2016 (1979))
Capital cases: State—10; Defense—10
Noncapital felonies: State—6; Defense—6
Misdemeanors: State—6; Defense—6
*Method of voir dire:* Court & Counsel (Idaho Code §19–2025 (1979))

ILLINOIS
*Number of jurors:* 12
Ill Stat 38 ¶115–4(b) (Cum Supp 1983)
*Peremptory challenges* (Ill Stat 38 ¶115-4(e) (Cum Supp 1983))
Capital cases: State—20; Defense—20
Noncapital felonies: State—10; Defense—10
Misdemeanors: State—5; Defense—5
*Method of voir dire:* Court & Counsel (Ill Stat 38 ¶115-4(f) (Cum Supp 1983))

INDIANA
*Number of jurors:* 6 (12 if charge is murder or class A, B, or C felony, unless parties agree to fewer)
Ind Stat Ann §35-37-1-1 (Cum Supp 1983)
*Peremptory challenges* (Ind Stat Ann §§35-37-1-4, 35-37-1-3 (Cum Supp 1983))
Capital cases: State—20; Defense—20
Noncapital felonies: State—10; Defense—10
Misdemeanors: State—5; Defense—5

*Method of voir dire:* Court & Counsel (Ind Stat Ann §35-37-1-5 (Cum Supp 1983))

IOWA

*Number of jurors:* 12

Iowa Code Ann §813.2, Rule 17(15) (1979)

*Peremptory challenges* (Iowa Code Ann §813.2, Rule 17(10) (1979))

Capital cases: State—8; Defense—8 (plus each side has a right to strike 2)

Noncapital felonies: State—4; Defense—4 (plus each side has a right to strike 2)

Misdemeanors: State—2; Defense—2 (plus each side has a right to strike 2)

*Method of voir dire:* Court & Counsel (*Iowa v Windsor* (1982) 316 NW2d 684)

KANSAS

*Number of jurors:* 12

Kans Stat Ann §§22–3409, 22–3411a (1981)

*Peremptory challenges* (Kans Stat Ann §22–3412 (1981))

Capital cases: State—12; Defense—12

Noncapital felonies: State—8; Defense—8 (6 for all felonies other than class A or B)

Misdemeanors: State—4; Defense—4

*Method of voir dire:* Court & Counsel (Kans Stat Ann §22–3408(3) (1981))

KENTUCKY

*Number of jurors:* 12 in circuit court, 6 in district court (parties can agree to fewer than 12)

Kent Rev Stat §29A.280 (1980)

*Peremptory challenges* (Kent Rules of Crim Proc 9.40 (1978)

Capital cases: State—5; Defense—8

Noncapital felonies: State—5; Defense—8

Misdemeanors: State—3; Defense—3

*Method of voir dire:* Court & Counsel (Kent Rules of Crim Proc 9.38 (1978)

LOUISIANA

*Number of jurors:* 12 (6 if charge is punishable by confinement at hard labor or confinement without hard labor for more than 6 mo.)

LA Code of Crim Proc art 782 (1981)

*Peremptory challenges* (LA Code of Crim Proc, art 781 (1981)

Capital cases: State—12; Defense—12

Noncapital felonies: State—6; Defense—6
Misdemeanors: State—6; Defense—6
*Method of voir dire:* Counsel (LA Const art 1 §17 (1974))

MAINE
*Number of jurors:* 12 (parties can agree on fewer than 12)
ME Rules of Crim Proc 23(b) (1983).
*Peremptory challenges* (ME Rev Stat Ann Title 15 §1258 (1980), ME Rules of Crim Proc 24(3) (1983))
Capital cases: State—10; Defense—20
Noncapital felonies: State—8; Defense—8
Misdemeanors: State—4; Defense—4
*Method of voir dire:* Counsel (ME Rev Stat Ann Title 15 §1258-A (1980))

MARYLAND
*Number of jurors:* 12 (parties can agree to fewer than 12)
Ann Code of MD, Rules of Proc 751 (Cum Supp 1982)
*Peremptory challenges* (Ann Code of MD, Rules of Proc 753 (Cum Supp 1982))
Capital cases: State—10; Defense—20
Noncapital felonies: State—4; Defense—4
Misdemeanors: State—4; Defense—4
*Method of voir dire:* Court & Counsel (Ann Code of MD, Rules of Proc 752 (Cum Supp 1982))

MASSACHUSETTS
*Number of jurors:* 6
MA Gen Laws Ann 218 §26A (Cum Supp 1983)
*Peremptory challenges* (MA Gen Laws Ann, Rules of Crim Proc 20(c)(1) (1980)
Capital cases: State—12; Defense—12
Noncapital felonies: State—2; Defense—2
Misdemeanors: State—2; Defense—2
*Method of voir dire:* Court & Counsel (MA Gen Laws Ann, Rules of Crim Proc 20(b)(1) (1980)

MICHIGAN
*Number of jurors:* 12
Mich Const, art 1 §14 (1963)
*Peremptory challenges* (Mich Comp Laws Ann §§768.12, 768.13 (1982))
Capital cases: State—15; Defense—20
Noncapital felonies: State—5; Defense—5

Misdemeanors: State—5; Defense—5
*Method of voir dire:* Court & Counsel (*Michigan v Prast* (1982) 319 NW2d 627)

MINNESOTA
*Number of jurors:* 6 (12 if charge is gross misdemeanor or felony, unless defendant consents to 6)
Minn Stat Ann §593.01 (Cum Supp 1983)
*Peremptory challenges* (Minn Stat Ann, Rules of Crim Proc 26.02 subdiv. (6) (1983))
Capital cases: State—9; Defense—15
Noncapital felonies: State—3; Defense—5
Misdemeanors: State—3; Defense—5
*Method of voir dire:* Court & Counsel (Minn Rules of Crim Proc 26.02 subdiv. (4) (1983))

MISSISSIPPI
*Number of jurors:* 12
Miss Const art 3 §31 (1972)
*Peremptory challenges* (Miss Code Ann §99-17-3 (1972))
Capital cases: State—12; Defense—12
Noncapital felonies: State—6; Defense—6
Misdemeanors: State—6; Defense—6
*Method of voir dire:* Counsel (Miss Code Ann §13-5-69 (1972))

MISSOURI (cities greater than 200,000)
*Number of jurors:* 12 (parties can agree to fewer than 12 but not fewer than 6)
Vernon's Ann Mo Stat §543.210 (Cum Supp 1983)
*Peremptory challenges* (Vernon's Ann Mo Stat §546.180 (Cum Supp 1983))
Capital cases: State—9; Defense—9
Noncapital felonies: State—6; Defense—6
Misdemeanors: State—2; Defense—2
*Method of voir dire:* Counsel; Court permitted to participate

MONTANA
*Number of jurors:* 12 (parties can agree to fewer than 12); 6 for all cases brought in Justice & City courts
Mont Code Ann §46-16-301 (1981)
*Peremptory challenges* (Mont Code Ann §46-16-305 (1981))
Capital cases: State—8; Defense—8
Noncapital felonies: State—6; Defense—6 (3 for 6-person jury)
Misdemeanors: State—6; Defense—6 (3 for 6-person jury)

*Method of voir dire:* Counsel & Court (Mont Code Ann §46-16-303(2)(1981))

NEBRASKA
*Number of jurors:* 12
Neb Const art 1 §6 (1979)
*Peremptory challenges* (Rev Stat of Neb §29-2005 (1979))
Capital cases: State—10; Defense—12
Noncapital felonies: State—6; Defense—6
Misdemeanors: State—3; Defense—3
*Method of voir dire:* Court (Rev Stat Ann §29-2006 (1979))

NEVADA
*Number of jurors:* 12 (parties can agree to fewer than 12)
Nev Rev Stat 175.021 (1979)
*Peremptory challenges* (Nev Rev Stat 175.051 (1975))
Capital cases: State—8; Defense—8
Noncapital felonies: State—4; Defense—4
Misdemeanors: State—4; Defense—4
*Method of voir dire:* Court (Nev Rev Stat 175.031 (1979))

NEW HAMPSHIRE
*Number of jurors:* See the State of New Hampshire Ct Rules
(If charge punishable by 1 year or less, then 6 (NH Rev Stat Ann §606:8 (1974))
*Peremptory challenges* (NH Rev Stat Ann §§606:3 (1974), 606:4 (Cum Supp 1981), 606:9 (1974)
Capital cases: State—10 (20 if charge is first-degree murder); Defense—20
Noncapital felonies: State—3; Defense—3 (2 for 6-person jury)
Misdemeanors: State—3; Defense—3 (2 for 6-person jury)
*Method of voir dire:* Court (NH Rev Stat Ann §500-A:12 (Cum Supp 1981))

NEW JERSEY
*Number of jurors:* 12
NJ Stat Ann 2A:74-1 (Cum Supp 1983)
*Peremptory challenges* (NJ Stat Ann 2A:78-7 (1976))
Capital cases: State—12; Defense—20
Noncapital felonies: State—10; Defense—10
Misdemeanors: State—10; Defense—10
*Method of voir dire:* Counsel & Court (NJ Stat Ann 2A:78-4 (1976))

NEW MEXICO
*Number of jurors:* 12

NM Stat Ann §38-5-13 (1978)
*Peremptory challenges* (NM Rules of Crim Proc 39(d)(1) (1980))
Capital cases: State—8; Defense—12
Noncapital felonies: State—3; Defense—5
Misdemeanors: State—3; Defense—5
*Method of voir dire:* Counsel & Court (NM Rules of Crim Proc 39 (1980))

NEW YORK
*Number of jurors:* 12
McK's Cons Laws of NY Ann §270.05 (1982)
*Peremptory challenges* (McK's Cons Laws of NY Ann §270.25 (1982))
Capital cases: State—20; Defense—20
Noncapital felonies: State—15; Defense—15
Misdemeanors: State—10; Defense—10
*Method of voir dire:* Counsel & Court (McK's Cons Laws of NY Ann §270.15 (1982))

NORTH CAROLINA
*Number of jurors:* 12
Gen Stat of NC §15A–1201 (1978)
*Peremptory challenges* (Gen Stat of NC §15A–1217 (1978))
Capital cases: State—14; Defense—14
Noncapital felonies: State—6; Defense—6
Misdemeanors: State—6; Defense—6
*Method of voir dire:* Counsel & Court (Gen Stat of NC §15A–1214 (1978))

NORTH DAKOTA
*Number of jurors:* 12 (6 in all misdemeanor cases)
ND Century Code 29-17-12 (1981)
*Peremptory challenges* (ND Century Code, Rules of Crim Proc 24(b)(1)(1974))
Capital cases: State—15; Defense—15
Noncapital felonies: State—10; Defense—10
Misdemeanors: State—6; Defense—6
*Method of voir dire:* Counsel (ND Century Code, Rules of Crim Proc 24(a) (1974))

OHIO
*Number of jurors:* 12 (8 in misdemeanor cases)
Page's Ohio Rev Code Ann, Rules of Crim Proc 23(B) (1982)
*Peremptory challenges* (Page's Ohio Rev Code Ann §2945.21 (1982))
Capital cases: State—12; Defense—12

Noncapital felonies: State—4; Defense—4
Misdemeanors: State—3; Defense—3
*Method of voir dire:* Court & Counsel (Page's Ohio Rev Code Ann §2945.27 (1982))

OKLAHOMA
*Number of jurors:* 12 (6 in all misdemeanor cases)
Okl Stat Ann 22 §601 (1969)
*Peremptory challenges* (Okl Stat Ann 22 §655 (1982))
Capital cases: State—9; Defense—9
Noncapital felonies: State—5; Defense—5
Misdemeanors: State—3; Defense—3
*Method of voir dire:* Court & Counsel (Okl Ct Rules & Proc, Rules Dist Ct 8 (1982))

OREGON
*Number of jurors:* 12 (only if charge carries death penalty or 30 years imprisonment; otherwise 8, but not fewer than 6)
Ore Rev Stat 136.210 (1981)
*Peremptory challenges* (Ore Rev Stat 136.230 (1981))
Capital cases: State—6; Defense—12
Noncapital felonies: State—3; Defense—6
Misdemeanors: State—3; Defense—6
*Method of voir dire:* Court & Counsel (Ore Rev Stat 136.210 (1981))

PENNSYLVANIA
*Number of jurors:* 12 (parties can agree to fewer than 12 but not fewer than 6)
PA Rules of Crim Proc 1103 (1983)
*Peremptory challenges* (PA Rules of Crim Proc 1126 (1983))
Capital cases: State—20; Defense—20
Noncapital felonies: State—7; Defense—7
Misdemeanors: State—5; Defense—5
*Method of voir dire:* Court & Counsel (PA Rules of Crim Proc 1106(d) (1983))

RHODE ISLAND
*Number of jurors:* 12 (only if charge carries death penalty or 30 years imprisonment; otherwise 8, but not fewer than 6)
Gen Laws of RI, Crim Proc Rule 23(b) (1976))
*Peremptory challenges* (Gen Laws of RI, Crim Proc Rule 24(b) (1976))
Capital cases: State—6; Defense—6
Noncapital felonies: State—3; Defense—3

Misdemeanors: State—3; Defense—3
*Method of voir dire:* Court & Counsel (Gen Laws of RI, Crim Proc Super Ct Rule 24(a) (1976))

SOUTH CAROLINA (struck system)
*Number of jurors:* 6
Code of Laws of SC §14-25-125 (Cum Supp 1982)
*Peremptory challenges* (Code of Laws of SC §14-7-1110 (1976))
Capital cases: State—5; Defense—10
Noncapital felonies: State—5; Defense—5
Misdemeanors: State—5; Defense—5
*Method of voir dire:* Court (Code of Laws of SC §14-7-1020 (1976))

SOUTH DAKOTA
*Number of jurors:* 12 (only if charge carries death penalty or 30 years imprisonment; otherwise 8 but not fewer than 6)
SD Codified Laws 23A-18-2 (1979)
*Peremptory challenges* (SD Codified Laws 23A-20-20 (Cum Supp 1983))
Capital cases: State—20; Defense—20
Noncapital felonies: State—10; Defense—10
Misdemeanors: State—3; Defense—3
*Method of voir dire:* Court & Counsel (SD Codified Laws 23A-20-6 (1979))

TENNESSEE
*Number of jurors:* 12
Tenn Const art 1 §6 (1980)
*Peremptory challenges* (Tenn Code Ann, Rules of Crim Proc 24(d) (1981))
Capital cases: State—8; Defense—15
Noncapital felonies: State—4; Defense—8
Misdemeanors: State—3; Defense—3
*Method of voir dire:* Counsel (Tenn Code Ann 22-3-101 (1980))

TEXAS
*Number of jurors:* 12 (6 in county court)
Vernon's Tex Stat Ann, Code of Crim Proc art 33.01 (1966)
*Peremptory challenges* (Vernon's Tex Stat Ann, Code of Crim Proc art 35.15(a), (c) (1966); art 35.15(b) (1982 Supp))
Capital cases: State—15; Defense—15
Noncapital felonies: State—10; Defense—10
Misdemeanors: State—5; Defense—5

*Method of voir dire:* Court & Counsel (Vernon's Tex Stat Ann, Code of Crim Proc art 35.17 (1982)

UTAH

*Number of jurors:* 12 if capital charge; 8 if noncapital charge; if misdemeanor charge, parties can agree to fewer than 8
Utah Code Ann 78-46-5 (Supp 1981)

*Peremptory challenges* (Utah Code Ann 77-35-18(d) (1982))
Capital cases: State--10; Defense—10
Noncapital felonies: State—4; Defense—4
Misdemeanors: State—3; Defense—3

*Method of voir dire:* Counsel or Court (Utah Code Ann 77-35-18(b) (1982))

VERMONT

*Number of jurors:* 12 (only if charge carries death penalty or 30 years imprisonment; otherwise 8, but not fewer than 6)
VT Stat Ann, Rules of Crim Proc 23(b) (1974)

*Peremptory challenges* (VT Stat Ann T.12 §1941 (1973))
Capital cases: State—6; Defense—6
Noncapital felonies: State—6; Defense—6
Misdemeanors: State—6; Defense—6

*Method of voir dire:* Counsel or Court (VT Stat Ann, Rules of Crim Proc 24(a) (1983))

VIRGINIA

*Number of jurors:* 12 (7 if misdemeanor)
Code of VA §19.2–262 (1983)

*Peremptory challenges* (Code of VA, Rules of Ct 3A:20(c) (1983 Cum Supp))
Capital cases: State—4; Defense—4
Noncapital felonies: State—4; Defense—4
Misdemeanors: State—3; Defense—3

*Method of voir dire:* Court & Counsel (Code of VA, Rules of Ct 3A:20(a) (1983 Cum Supp))

WASHINGTON

*Number of jurors:* 12 (only if charge carries death penalty or 30 years imprisonment; otherwise 8, but not fewer than 6)
Rev Code of Wash Ann 2.36.050 (Cum Supp 1983)

*Peremptory challenges* (Rev Code of Wash Ann 10.49.060 (1980))
Capital cases: State—12; Defense—12
Noncapital felonies: State—6; Defense—6
Misdemeanors: State—3; Defense—3

*Method of voir dire:* Court & Counsel (Rev Code of Wash Ann, Cr R 6.4 (1980))

WEST VIRGINIA
*Number of jurors:* 12 (only if charge carries death penalty or 30 years imprisonment; otherwise 8, but not fewer than 6)
WV Code, R of Crim Proc 23(b) (1982)
*Peremptory challenges* (WV Code, R of Crim Proc 24(b) (1982))
Capital cases: State—2; Defense—6
Noncapital felonies: State—2; Defense—6
Misdemeanors: State—4; Defense—4
*Method of voir dire:* Court & Counsel (WV Code §56-6-12 (1966))

WISCONSIN
*Number of jurors:* 12 (only if charge carries death penalty or 30 years imprisonment; otherwise 8, but not fewer than 6)
Wisc Stat Ann 756.096(3)(a) (1981)
*Peremptory challenges* (Wisc Stat Ann 972.03 (1971))
Capital cases: State—6; Defense—6
Noncapital felonies: State—4; Defense—4
Misdemeanors: State—4; Defense—4
*Method of voir dire:* Court & Counsel (Wisc Stat Ann 805.08(1) (1977))

WYOMING
*Number of jurors:* 12
Wy Stat Ann, Unif Rules for Dist Ct 17 (1983)
*Peremptory challenges* (Wy Stat Ann, Rules of Crim Proc 25 (1983))
Capital cases: State—12; Defense—12
Noncapital felonies: State—8; Defense—8
Misdemeanors: State—4; Defense—4
*Method of voir dire:* Court & Counsel (Wy Stat Ann, Unif Rules for Dist Ct 17 (1983))

## E. Fifty State List of Jury Selection Factors: Civil Trials §4.54

*CAVEAT:* No short list of provisions on jury selection can be accurate, because there are too many slight variations within one state and among the several states. Every effort has been made to make this list both short and accurate, but every permutation (between "circuit" and "district" courts, or based on amount of damages, for example) has not been recorded here. Few court opinions are cited, although they may have modified local practice. In some cases, an out-of-state lawyer was not able to find a citation to court rules, state statutes, or other sources accessible at a local library.

For all of these reasons, please use the following primarily as a source of citations you can use to find the latest rules and statutes governing a state other than your own.

ALABAMA (struck system)
*Number of jurors:* 12 (parties can agree to fewer than 12; rule not applicable in district courts)
Rules of Ala Sup Ct, Rules of Civ Proc 48 (1975)
*Peremptory challenges* (Code of Ala §12-16-140 (1975))
Plaintiff: 6
Defendant: 6
*Method of voir dire:* Counsel or Court (Rules of Ala Sup Ct, Rules of Civ Proc 47(a) (1975))

ALASKA
*Number of jurors:* 12
AK Stat §09.20.090 (1973)
*Peremptory challenges*
Plaintiff: 3
Defendant: 3
*Method of voir dire:* Court & Counsel (AK Rules of Civ Proc 47 (1968))

ARIZONA
*Number of jurors:* 8
Ariz Rev Stat Ann §21-102 (1975)
*Peremptory challenges* (Ariz Rules of Civ Proc 47(e) (1973))
Plaintiff: 4
Defendant: 4
*Method of voir dire:* Court & Counsel (Ariz Rules of Civ Proc 47(b) (1973))

ARKANSAS (struck system)
*Number of jurors:* 12 (parties can agree to fewer than 12)
Ark Rules of Civ Proc 48 (1979)
*Peremptory challenges* (Ark Stat Ann §39-229 (1962))
Plaintiff: 3
Defendant: 3
*Method of voir dire:* Court & Counsel (Ark Rules of Civ Proc 47 (1979))

CALIFORNIA
*Number of jurors:* 12 (parties can agree to fewer than 12; Los Angeles

County experimenting with 8 in civil actions until July 1, 1985)
Cal Civ Proc Code §194 (1982)
*Peremptory challenges* (Cal Civ Proc Code §601 (Cum Supp 1983))
Plaintiff: 6
Defendant: 6
*Method of voir dire:* Court & Counsel (Cal Rules of Court, Rules for Super Ct 228 (1983)

COLORADO
*Number of jurors:* 6 (parties can agree to fewer than 6 but not fewer than 3)
Col Rev Stat §13-70-102 (1974)
*Peremptory challenges* (Col Rules of Civ Proc 47(h) (1973))
Plaintiff: 4
Defendant: 4
*Method of voir dire:* Court & Counsel (Col Rules of Civ Proc 47(a) (Cum Supp 1982))

CONNECTICUT
*Number of jurors:* 6
Const Amend, art 4th (Cum Supp 1982)
*Peremptory challenges* (Conn Gen Stat §51–241 (Cum Supp 1982))
Plaintiff: 3
Defendant: 3
*Method of voir dire:* Counsel (Conn Gen Stat §51–240 (Cum Supp 1982))

DELAWARE
*Number of jurors:* 12
Del Code Ann Title 10 §4518 (1984), Del Sup Ct Civ Rules 38(d) (1975)
*Peremptory challenges* (Del Code Ann Title 10 §4519 (1984))
Plaintiff: 6
Defendant: 6
*Method of voir dire:*

FLORIDA
*Number of jurors:* 6
FL Stat Ann §69.071 (Cum Supp 1982)
*Peremptory challenges* (FL Rules of Civ Proc 1.431(d) (1983))
Plaintiff: 3
Defendant: 3
*Method of voir dire:* Counsel (FL Rules of Civ Proc 1.431(b) (Cum Supp 1983))

GEORGIA (struck system)
*Number of jurors:* 12 (absent a written stipulation to fewer; 6 for

claims of less than $5000)
Off Code of GA §15-12-122b (1982)
*Peremptory challenges* (Off Code of GA §15-12-122b (1982))
Plaintiff: 12 (6 for 6-person jury)
Defendant: 12 (6 for 6-person jury)
*Method of voir dire:* Court & Counsel (Off Code of GA §15-12-133 (1982))

HAWAII
*Number of jurors:* 12 (parties can agree to fewer than 12)
Hawaii Rev Stat §635–26(b) (1976)
*Peremptory challenges* (Hawaii Rev Stat §635–29(b) (1976))
Plaintiff: 3
Defendant: 3
*Method of voir dire:* Counsel (Hawaii Rev Stat §635–27 (1976))

IDAHO
*Number of jurors:* 12 (parties can agree to fewer than 12)
Idaho Code §2–105 (1979)
*Peremptory challenges* (Idaho Rules of Civ Proc 47(j) (1979))
Plaintiff: 4
Defendant: 4
(If county, municipal or quasi-municipal corporation, or governmental unit of county is a party, then each party entitled to 8 peremptories)
*Method of voir dire:* Court & Counsel (Idaho Rules of Civ Proc 47(i)(1975))

ILLINOIS
*Number of jurors:* 6 (as long as damages don't exceed $10,000, unless either party demands 12)
Ill Stat Ann 110 ¶2-1105(b) (1983)
*Peremptory challenges* (Ill Stat Ann 110 ¶2-1106(a) (1983))
Plaintiff: 5
Defendant: 5
*Method of voir dire:* Court & Counsel (Ill Stat 110A ¶234 (Cum Supp 1983))

INDIANA
*Number of jurors:* 6
Ind Stat Ann §34-1-20.5-1 (Cum Supp 1983)
*Peremptory challenges* (Ind Stat Ann §34-1-20.5-4 (Cum Supp 1983))
Plaintiff: 3
Defendant: 3

*Method of voir dire:* Counsel & Court (Ind Stat Ann §34-1-20.5-4 (Cum Supp 1983))

IOWA (struck system)
*Number of jurors:* 8
Iowa Rules of Civ Proc 187(i) (1983)
*Peremptory challenges* (Iowa Rules of Civ Proc 187(g) (1983))
Plaintiff: 4
Defendant: 4
*Method of voir dire:* Court & Counsel (Iowa Rules of Civ Proc 187(b) (1983))

KANSAS
*Number of jurors:* 12 (parties can agree to fewer than 12; 6 if damages claimed are less than $5000)
Kans Stat Ann §§60–248(a), 61–1716 (Cum Supp 1982)
*Peremptory challenges* (Kans Stat Ann §60–247(c) (1976))
Plaintiff: 3
Defendant: 3
*Method of voir dire:* Counsel (Kans Stat Ann §60–247(b) (1976))

KENTUCKY
*Number of jurors:* 6 in district court; 12 in circuit court (parties can agree to fewer than 12)
Kent Rev Stat 29A.280 (1980)
*Peremptory challenges* (Kent Rules of Civ Proc 47.03 (1983))
Plaintiff: 3
Defendant: 3
*Method of voir dire:* Court & Counsel (Kent Rules of Civ Proc 47.01 (1983))

LOUISIANA
*Number of jurors:* 12 (parties can agree to fewer than 12)
LA Code of Civ Proc, art 1761 (1961)
*Peremptory challenges* (LA Code of Civ Proc, art 1764 (1961)
Plaintiff: 6
Defendant: 6
*Method of voir dire:* Court & Counsel (LA Code of Civ Proc, art 1763 (1961))

MAINE
*Number of jurors:* 8 (parties can agree to another number)
ME Rules of Civ Proc 38 (1983)
*Peremptory challenges* (ME Rev Stat Ann §1204 (1980), ME Rules of

Civ Proc 47 (1983))
Plaintiff: 3
Defendant: 3
*Method of voir dire:* Court (Counsel may suggest added questions) (ME Rules of Civ Proc 47(a) (1983))

MARYLAND
*Number of jurors:* 12 (parties can agree to fewer than 12)
Ann Code of MD, Rules of Proc 543 §a3 (1977)
*Peremptory challenges* (Ann Code of MD, Rules of Proc 543 §2a (1977))
Plaintiff: 4
Defendant: 4
*Method of voir dire:* Court & Counsel (Ann Code of MD, Rules of Proc 543 §d (1977))

MASSACHUSETTS
*Number of jurors:* 12 (parties can agree to fewer than 12)
MA Gen Laws Ann, Rules of Civ Proc 48 (1978)
*Peremptory challenges* (MA Gen Laws Ann 234 §29 (Cum Supp 1983))
Plaintiff: 4
Defendant: 4
*Method of voir dire:* Court & Counsel (MA Gen Laws Ann 234 §28 (Cum Supp 1983))

MICHIGAN
*Number of jurors:* 6
Mich Com Laws Ann §600.1352 (1981)
*Peremptory challenges* (Michigan General Court Rules 511.5)
Plaintiff: 3
Defendant: 3
*Method of voir dire:* Court & Counsel (*Michigan v Prast* (1982) 319 NW2d 627)

MINNESOTA
*Number of jurors:* 6
Minn Stat Ann §593.01 (Cum Supp 1983)
*Peremptory challenges* (Minn Stat Ann §546.10 (Cum Supp 1983))
Plaintiff: 2
Defendant: 2
*Method of voir dire:* Counsel (Minn Stat Ann §546.10 (Cum Supp 1983))

MISSISSIPPI
*Number of jurors:* 12
Miss Const art 3 §31 (1972)

*Peremptory challenges* (Miss Code Ann §11-7-145 (1972))
Plaintiff: 4 (and as many more when a party shows cause)
Defendant: 4 (and as many more when a party shows cause)
*Method of voir dire:* Counsel (Miss Code Ann §13-5-69 (1972))

MISSOURI
*Number of jurors:* 12 (cities greater than 200,000)
Vernon's Ann Mo Stat §494.210 (1952)
*Peremptory challenges* (Vernon's Ann Mo Stat §494.200 (1952))
Plaintiff: 3
Defendant: 3
*Method of voir dire:* Counsel; Court permitted to participate

MONTANA
*Number of jurors:* 12 (parties can agree to fewer than 12; 6 if relief prayed for is less than $10,000 and trial judge so decides)
Mont Code Ann §3-15-106 (1981)
*Peremptory challenges* (Mont Code Ann §25-7-224 (1981))
Plaintiff: 4 (2 for 6-person jury)
Defendant: 4 (2 for 6-person jury)
*Method of voir dire:* Court & Counsel (Mont Rules of Civ Proc 47(a) (1981))

NEBRASKA
*Number of jurors:* 12 (but legislature may authorize less than 12 in courts inferior to District Court Neb Const Art 1, §6 (1979))
County & municipal courts: 6 (Rev Stat of Neb §24–536)
*Peremptory challenges*
Plaintiff: no statute—dependent on rules of the court
Defendant: no statute—dependent on rules of the court
*Method of voir dire:* Court (Rev Stat Ann §25–1631.03 (1979))

NEVADA
*Number of jurors:* 8 (parties can agree to fewer than 8 but not fewer than 4)
Nev Rev Stat 16.030 (1979)
*Peremptory challenges* (Nev Rev Stat 16.040(1) (1979))
Plaintiff: 4
Defendant: 4
*Method of voir dire:* Court & Counsel (Nev Rev Stat 16.030(6), 175.031 (1979))

NEW HAMPSHIRE
*Number of jurors:* 12 (NH Const Pt 1, art 20 (1971))

*Peremptory challenges* (NH Rev Stat Ann §519.19 (1974))
Plaintiff: 3
Defendant: 3
*Method of voir dire:* Court (NH Rev Stat Ann §500–A:12 (Cum Supp 1981))

NEW JERSEY
*Number of jurors:* 12
NJ Stat Ann 2A:74-1 (Cum Supp 1983)
*Peremptory challenges* (NJ Stat Ann 2A:78-7 (1976))
Plaintiff: 6
Defendant: 6
*Method of voir dire:* Court & Counsel (NJ Stat Ann 2A:78-4 (1976))

NEW MEXICO
*Number of jurors:* 6 (unless a party demands 12)
NM Stat Ann 38-5-13 (1978); NM Rules of Civ Proc 38 (Cum Supp 1983)
*Peremptory challenges* (NM Stat Ann 38-5-14 (1978))
Plaintiff: 5
Defendant: 5
*Method of voir dire:* Court & Counsel (NM Rules of Civ Proc 47(a) (1980))

NEW YORK
*Number of jurors:* 6
McK's Cons Laws of NY Ann §4104 (Cum Supp 1983)
*Peremptory challenges* (McK's Cons Laws of NY Ann §4109 (Cum Supp 1983))
Plaintiff: 3
Defendant: 3
*Method of voir dire:* Counsel (McK's Cons Laws of NY Ann §4107 (Cum Supp 1983))

NORTH CAROLINA
*Number of jurors:* 12 (or fewer if parties so stipulate, unless jury required by statute as in divorce cases)
Gen Stat of NC §1A-1, Rule 48 (1969)
*Peremptory challenges* (Gen Stat of NC §9-19 (1981))
Plaintiff: 8
Defendant: 8
*Method of voir dire:* Court & Counsel (Gen Stat of NC §9–15 (1981))

NORTH DAKOTA
*Number of jurors:* 6 (unless a party demands 12)

ND Century Code 28-14-03.1 (1981)
*Peremptory challenges* (ND Century Code, Rules of Civ Proc 47(b) (1981))
Plaintiff: 6
Defendant: 6
*Method of voir dire:* Counsel or Court (ND Century Code, Rule of Civ Proc 47(a) (1981))

OHIO
*Number of jurors:* 8 (parties can demand fewer than 8)
Page's Ohio Rev Code Ann, Rules of Civ Proc 38(B) (1982)
*Peremptory challenges* (Page's Ohio Rev Code Ann, Rules of Civ Proc 47(A) (1982))
Plaintiff: 3
Defendant: 3
*Method of voir dire:* Court & Counsel (Page's Ohio Rev Code Ann, Rules of Civ Proc 47(A) (1982))

OKLAHOMA
*Number of jurors:* 12 (6 if case involves less than $2500)
Okl Const art 2 §19
*Peremptory challenges* (Okl Stat Ann §573 (1960))
Plaintiff: 3
Defendant: 3
*Method of voir dire:* Court & Counsel (Okl Ct Rules & Proc, Rules Dist Ct 8 (1982))

OREGON
*Number of jurors:* 6
Ore Rev Stat 54.010 (1981)
*Peremptory challenges* (Ore Rev Stat 54.040 (1981))
Plaintiff: 3
Defendant: 3
*Method of voir dire:* Court & Counsel (Ore Rev Stat, Rules of Civ Proc 57C (1981))

PENNSYLVANIA
*Number of jurors:* Initially 8, not to fall below 6
Philadelphia Civil Rules 220 (1972)
*Peremptory challenges* (PA Rules of Civ Proc 221 (1983))
Plaintiff: 4
Defendant: 4
*Method of voir dire:* Court & Counsel (common law)

RHODE ISLAND
*Number of jurors:* 6
Gen Laws of RI 9-10-11.1 (Cum Supp 1982)
*Peremptory challenges* (Gen Laws of RI 9-10-18 (Cum Supp 1982))
Plaintiff: 1 out of 3 called
Defendant: 1 out of 3 called
*Method of voir dire:* Court & Counsel (Gen Laws of RI 9-10-14 (Cum Supp 1982))

SOUTH CAROLINA (struck system)
*Number of jurors:* 12
Code of Laws of SC §14-7-1050 (1976)
*Peremptory challenges* (Code of Laws of SC §14-7-1050 (1976))
Plaintiff: 4
Defendant: 4
*Method of voir dire:* Court (Code of Laws of SC §14-7-1020 (1976))

SOUTH DAKOTA
*Number of jurors:* 12 (parties may stipulate any lower number or majority verdict)
SD Comp Laws 15-6-48 (1967)
*Peremptory challenges* (SD Comp Laws 15-14-8 (1967))
Plaintiff: 3
Defendant: 3
*Method of voir dire:* Counsel (SD Comp Laws 15-14-15 (1967))

TENNESSEE
*Number of jurors:* 12 (parties may stipulate any number less than provided by law or majority verdict)
Tenn Code Ann, Rules of Civ Proc 48 (1981)
*Peremptory challenges* (Tenn Code Ann 22-3-105 (1980))
Plaintiff: 4
Defendant: 4
*Method of voir dire:* Counsel (Tenn Code Ann 22-3-101 (1980))

TEXAS
*Number of jurors:* 12 in district courts (parties can stipulate to fewer); 6 in county courts
Vernon's Civ Stat of Tex Ann art 2191 (1964)
*Peremptory challenges* (Texas Rules of Ct 233 (1982))
Plaintiff: 6 (3 in county court)
Defendant: 6 (3 in county court)
*Method of voir dire:* Court (*Texas Emp Ins. Ass'n v Loesch* (1971) 538 SW2d 435)

UTAH

*Number of jurors:* 8 (parties can agree to fewer than 8)
Utah Code Ann 78-46-5 (Supp 1981)
*Peremptory challenges* (Utah Code Ann, Rules of Civ Proc 47(e) (1977))
Plaintiff: 3
Defendant: 3
*Method of voir dire:* Court & Counsel (Utah Code Ann, Rules of Civ Proc 47(a) (1977))

VERMONT

*Number of jurors:* 12 (parties may stipulate any lower number or majority verdict)
VT Stat Ann, Rules of Civ Proc 48 (1971)
*Peremptory challenges* (VT Stat Ann T.12 §1941 (1973))
Plaintiff: 6
Defendant: 6
*Method of voir dire:* Counsel or Court (VT Stat Ann, Rules of Civ Proc 47(a) (1971))

VIRGINIA (struck system)

*Number of jurors:* 7 (5 if less than $5000 involved)
Code of VA §8.01-359 (1977)
*Peremptory challenges* (Code of VA §8.01-359 (1977))
Plaintiff: 3
Defendant: 3
*Method of voir dire:* Court & Counsel (Code of VA §8.01–358 (Cum Supp 1983))

WASHINGTON

*Number of jurors:* 12 or fewer in superior court; 6 in limited jurisdiction courts
Rev Code of Wash Ann 2.36.050 (Cum Supp 1983)
*Peremptory challenges* (Rev Code of Wash Ann 4.44.130 (Cum Supp 1983))
Plaintiff: 3
Defendant: 3
*Method of voir dire:* Counsel (Rev Code of Wash Ann 4.44.210 (1962))

WEST VIRGINIA

*Number of jurors:* 12 (parties may stipulate any lower number or majority verdict)
WV Code, Rules of Civ Proc 48 (1982)

*Peremptory challenges* (WV Code §56-6-12 (1966))
Plaintiff: 4
Defendant: 4
*Method of voir dire:* Court & Counsel (WV Code §56-6-12 (1966); Rules of Civ Proc 47(a) (1982))

WISCONSIN
*Number of jurors:* 6 (parties can agree to more than 6 but no more than 12)
Wisc Stat Ann 756.096(3)(b) (1981)
*Peremptory challenges* (Wisc Stat Ann 805.08(3) (Cum Supp 1983))
Plaintiff: 3
Defendant: 3
*Method of voir dire:* Court & Counsel (Wisc Stat Ann 805.08(1) (1977))

WYOMING
*Number of jurors:* 6 (unless a party demands 12)
Wy Stat Ann §1-11-119 (1983)
*Peremptory challenges* (Wy Stat Ann §1-11-202 (1983))
Plaintiff: 3
Defendant: 3
*Method of voir dire:* Court & Counsel (Wy Stat Ann, Unif Rules for Dist Ct 17 (1983))

## F. Recent Developments §4.55

See §4.47

# Chapter 5

# *Conducting Surveys and Constructing Juror Profiles*


**I. Thinking about Jury Selection**
A. Cerebration §5.1
B. Too Much Guesswork §5.2

**II. Building a Case Team**
A. Counsel and Legal Workers §5.5
B. Experts from Other Disciplines §5.6
C. Community-based Volunteers §5.7
D. Building a Network §5.8
E. A Practical Approach §5.9
F. New Developments §5.10

**III. Conducting Initial Community Surveys**
A. Survey Procedures §5.11
B. Examples of Successful Surveys §5.12
C. Form: Initial Questions and Screening §5.13
D. Community Background Surveys §5.14
E. Discovering Current Community Attitudes §5.15
F. New Techniques §5.16

**IV. Conducting Formal Community Surveys**
A. To Support Pretrial Motions
1. Challenging Jury Lists §5.20
2. Seeking Change of Venue §5.21
3. For Other Purposes §5.22
B. Survey Procedures
1. Form: Declaration Describing Typical Survey Procedures §5.25
2. Form: Results of Demographic Survey of Grand Jury Nominees §5.26
3. Form: Affidavits of Experts Supporting Motion for Fair Jury Selection Procedures §5.27

**V. Constructing Model Juror Profiles**
A. Two Methods of Constructing Juror Profiles §5.30
1. Clinical Selection Model §5.31
2. Demographic Selection Model §5.32
B. Sample Juror Profiles
1. Guilt-prone Jurors in Florida §5.35
2. Antitrust-prone Jurors in Illinois §5.36
3. Best and Worst Defense Jurors in Maryland §5.37
4. Other Examples §5.38

# I. THINKING ABOUT JURY SELECTION

## A. Cerebration §5.1

Lawyers seeking to learn the skills of jury selection have traditionally listened and watched experienced trial lawyers in action, either as their assistants or simply as observers in the courtroom. They have listened to speeches or tapes of speeches by experienced trial lawyers or have read transcripts (usually unedited) or articles written hastily for trial lawyers' magazines. Many have simply been thrown into the courtroom to do their best in cases they or their employers considered impossible to win or relatively unimportant so that any mistakes they made would not have serious adverse effects on the clients or counsel.

Since jury selection is, to a considerable degree, an oral art, perhaps these methods have been the best that could have been used to pass along this art to date. Certainly generations of excellent trial lawyers have been developed by these methods, and countless cases have been won.

Unfortunately, during the same period these methods have undoubtedly permitted the conviction of many innocent defendants. Many defendants who may have been guilty have been convicted by juries selected improperly and questioned inadequately, many civil plaintiffs did not win adequate awards, and many lawyers who believe in due process have decided not to participate in trial work because it is too unscientific, too illogical, and therefore too hard on the emotions and the intellect.

In the oral tradition, Theodore Koskoff of Connecticut, an experienced civil and criminal trial lawyer, has shared some of his ideas on jury selection in presentations to the American Trial Lawyers Association. His short overview of jury selection techniques contains the basic spirit of good trial lawyers. It shows respect for the planning function—the time you spend early in a case thinking analytically about the facts as they will probably come out in testimony, about the client and other witnesses and how they will appear to the jurors, and about yourself as the trial lawyer and how you will probably come across to a jury.(See chapter 4.) It shows the experienced trial lawyer's awareness of his or her own past errors, the determination not to repeat them, and the need always to be open to suggestions from other practitioners.

Koskoff also demonstrates some of the characteristics that distinguish a good trial lawyer from a law school graduate who occasionally tries a case. These include a strong interest in other human beings in general, a habit of observing them, and a basic recognition that each human being is different and has a right to be different. These habits are intensified when the lawyer starts sizing up each person who enters the jury box.

Koskoff notes:

> The first step in jury selection is cerebration. What kind of a jury do you want: men or women, bright or dull, young or old, black or white, what occupations, what ethnic composition? Well, that all depends on the kind of case you have. Although studies have been done on what the perfect average juror is like, applied to an individual case, the studies are useless. Each individual case requires a custom-built jury. This is true in both criminal and civil cases.
>
> Let me illustrate what I mean. If you were trying a criminal case, you certainly wouldn't want a juror who would identify with the victim of the crime. If the victim is a forty-five-year-old married woman who is in the real estate business and has two grown children, you obviously would not want a forty-five-year-old married woman who is in the real estate business and has two grown children on your jury. Such a juror, more likely than not, would identify with the victim, not with your client and not with your case. She would be a very bad juror for you in that case. But if you were representing the estate of the victim in a wrongful death case, that same person would probably be a good juror for you.
>
> The complexion of the jury you want varies with the type of case you have. By careful analysis, one can make an essentially unscientific process a little more scientific.

## B. Too Much Guesswork §5.2

While it is possible, as Theodore Koskoff has pointed out in §5.1, to cut down on the guesswork in jury selection, lawyers working alone with traditional legal tools cannot eliminate guessing or advance very far beyond intuition and reliance on individual experience.

They are faced with four basic questions: (1) what kinds of people do they want on the jury; (2) what kinds of people do they want to keep off the jury; (3) can they discover whether a particular prospective juror falls in the good or the bad category; and (4) can they make this discovery without tipping off the opposition?

Lawyers still come from a more or less homogeneous background, while today they face a heterogeneous group of prospective jurors. Although an increasing number of women and men of color are trying cases throughout the country, most trial lawyers are still white, middle-class men. They face jurors selected increasingly from a broader spectrum of society in terms of sex, race, age, and social class. And they face jurors in a period in which social values are in a state of flux, so that a person from a particular group cannot be assumed automatically to have a particular opinion. A white-haired, retired woman bank clerk, for example, may have a favorite grandson serving time for possession of marijuana or for demonstrating opposition to nuclear weapons.

Lawyers no longer know most of the people in the communities in which they try their cases, nor do they have friends or friends of friends who know most of these people. It is unlikely that a lawyer in a large city will see on a jury anyone whom he has ever seen before or whose parents, cousins, or even third cousins, are known to him.

Faced with these new factors, lawyers need assistance. But they are unlikely to develop a scientific method for jury selection on their own. They are not trained in this method. While a few may have studied the scientific method as undergraduates, the legal method is not the scientific method. Lawyers are trained in discovering facts (an approximation of the truth) by means of questions to witnesses (or jurors) asked by two opposing sides, and especially by cross-examination. They are (theoretically) trained in the use of logic, not in the study of individual behavior in a group situation.

Dr. Jay Schulman, a forensic sociologist, has summarized the shortcomings in the customary defense jury selection methods in the typical case as seen from that profession's vantage point. His observations apply equally to plaintiff's lawyers in civil cases. He sees that the prosecution has an initial edge in jury selection through selection of the charges and the forum. Schulman complains that defense attorneys typically give their opponents an even greater edge by resorting to "folk wisdom," such as "A person who reads *Screw* is probably a good defense juror," "Never challenge a black," "High status people who can make analytical distinctions make the best defense jurors," or "Old people make convicting jurors."

The difficulty with folk wisdom of any kind is that it is too general, too global. Not all people who read *Screw* are gays or oppressed people; many blacks are authoritarians; in many parts of the country, people of high educational and occupational attainment are norm-makers and norm-keepers, intricately connected with local power structures; some older people are highly mellow and empathic individuals.

Trial lawyers also tend to rely on the undiagnosed "vibrations" they feel they pick up from prospective jurors, who may present themselves falsely. Many people present themselves in ambiguous or contradictory ways because their selves are organized in ambiguous and contradictory ways.

Mary Timothy, foreperson of the *Angela Davis* jury, discusses this question from a different viewpoint in *Jury Woman* 305 (1974; available from Volcano Press, 330 Ellis St., San Francisco 94102):

> Jurors have a right to not be stereotyped. Not being able to fully explore

the juror's attitudes leads the attorney into the position of having to select the members by use of stereotypes: construction workers are for "law and order"—young people are politically liberal—blacks will never convict another black—women make decisions based on emotions rather than logic.

## II. BUILDING A CASE TEAM

### A. Counsel and Legal Workers §5.5

If counsel and client decide to conduct a community survey to support pretrial motions challenging the jury list, for change of venue, or for other reasons, they will need to build a trial committee or team to perform the multitudinous tasks described in §§5.11–5.14 and 5.32. Such a team may be a local survey research organization, the National Jury Project, or a group of volunteers interested in one of the parties or in the issues raised in the case.

When volunteers are involved, a few people in the committee usually become concerned about the client personally, which is a side benefit. In a criminal case, they arrange to have the defendant provided with appropriate clothing and other necessaries for court appearances. They deal with problems that may arise about the defendant's diet, medication, and other factors in the defendant's life that were instantly disrupted by the arrest and permanently disrupted by the incarceration prior to trial. The lawyer may not find the time to attend to such matters, even though aware of their importance; but aggressive pretrial work generally brings forth others to help in this task. For a graphic description of the effect of pretrial incarceration on the spirit and physical well-being of an articulate defendant, and her need for consultations and conversations on subjects other than her forthcoming trial, see Angela Davis, *An Autobiography* 32-45 (1974).

Sometimes a hung jury is the best that can be hoped for or achieved. Sometimes a criminal jury convicts and there is a lengthy appeal that may result in a reversal and a new trial; sometimes a personal injury case is retried. The criminal defendant or injured plaintiff will need the kind of human relationships and encouragement that a busy trial lawyer may not be able to provide. The team that worked on the jury challenge, together with the client's family and friends, can be encouraged to organize themselves to help the litigant, much as a family and friend group often develops around a patient with a long-term illness. Such a group creates problems as well as solving them, as stories about many famous trials reveal. Nonetheless, it is a living group, and this is preferable to relying solely on the group of the "friends" involved in the incident, some of whom may actually turn out to be witnesses for the other side, or vanish at a critical point.

## B. Experts from Other Disciplines §5.6

The scientific method has been refined considerably since the days when Clarence Darrow tried to use the latest scientific information in determining the best defense in a criminal case. Lawyers today know that there are effective methods of gaining information about prospective jurors by means of a so-called reportorial or investigative approach. See chapter 13 on third-party information networks. Information can also be gained by studying an individual psychologically, that is, through observation by a person trained in the psychological or psychiatric disciplines. Another method of checking on an individual requires use of sociological methods developed to study group behavior in order to place the individual in all the groups to which he or she belongs and to predict his or her response to events in the courtroom based on the customary response to parallel situations by other members of these groups.

Since lawyers are not reporters, private detectives, psychiatrists, psychologists, or sociologists, they have been unable to produce the kinds of scientific results in jury selection that might have been possible through an interdisciplinary approach. Their problem is how to use the legal method of voir dire questioning of a prospective juror to determine that juror's probable response to plaintiff's and defendant's testimony and argument, and to jury instructions issued by the court. In other words, each lawyer is trying to find out from the answers to questions A and B what a juror will probably think when the juror listens to testimony on points 1 to 100, although counsel knows relatively little about points 1 to 50, namely, the other side's case. Facing such a series of hypothetical problems, an attorney obviously needs whatever scientific assistance can be obtained, particularly when opposing counsel has exclusive information on some prospective jurors (see chapter 13).

Good lawyers who try cases that are difficult to win have long known that they must have close relationships with experts in various fields whom they can call on for help in difficult factual situations. There is nothing new about a defense lawyer calling a psychiatrist to testify about the alleged insanity of a criminal defendant. Thus defense lawyer Charles R. Garry, in the first *Huey Newton* trial (see §3.22), came to the notion of calling a psychiatrist, Dr. Bernard Diamond, to testify about the difficulty of selecting jurors who would be free of racial prejudice and prejudgment on the basis of color. At the same time, sociologist Robert Blauner, a professor at the University of California, Berkeley, became interested in the *Newton* case, seeing in this real life situation an exciting opportunity to understand and probe group action among a selected segment of the lay society, namely a trial jury of 12 (with 4 alternates) asked to decide a racially charged issue of guilt or innocence. (See his conclusions in chapter 18).

Today, sociologists, psychologists, psychiatrists, and experienced legal investigators frequently participate in the investigation of potential jurors, voir dire, and jury selection when the trial lawyer is unable to devote sufficient time, energy, and resources to this part of the work. "Jury selection can be a dramatic, fascinating example of applied social psychology," in the opinion of Gary Moran and John Craig Comfort, in "Scientific Juror Selection: Sex As a Moderator of Demographic and Personality Predicators of Impaneled Felony Jury Behavior," 41 *J Personality and Soc Psych* 1052–63 (Nov. 1982).

The roles, techniques, analyses, and effectiveness of social scientists are discussed in chapters 13, 18, and 19.

## C. Community-based Volunteers §5.7

Plaintiffs in police misconduct cases and other damage actions may have deep community roots, or may be relative newcomers. Frequently defendants in major criminal trials face judges and juries from jurisdictions where the defendants have never lived or worked, where they have no friends and no easy access to the community. This occurred in the conspiracy trial of Dr. Benjamin Spock and four others, which was held in Boston where apparently only one of the defendants had recently lived, and in the *Pentagon Papers* case (see §3.52), conducted in Los Angeles, far from the "movement" bases of the two defendants. It also occurred in the case of the Vietnam Veterans Against the War, tried in Gainesville, Florida (the *Gainesville Eight* trial—see §3.53). In each of these instances, the defendants and most of their counsel were outsiders coming into communities during periods in which the prosecution assumed the local community would largely favor it and oppose the defendants.

Even under the best circumstances, it is not easy to rally large numbers of people to assist the plaintiff in a personal injury case or the defense in a criminal case. This difficulty is increased when the trial staff is entirely recruited from outsiders, and the local community leaders who would normally take charge of the trial of a local person are not immediately known to the parties. (On problems of out-of-court counsel in tort cases, see §4.40.)

In addition, several of these headline cases involved defendants who did not personally know each other (as in the *Spock* case), or who were not members of any local or national groups that would immediately come to their assistance. Even when national support groups could be formed quickly, it took considerabe time for some of the defendants to find their local constituencies, so to speak, in the communities where they were to be tried. And, of course, the overwhelming problems in trying a political case are not limited to building a volunteer jury investigation team. There are so many areas requiring staff work that, without widespread community relationships, extensive jury investigation can have only limited success.

Despite the obstacles, volunteers, staff members, and forensic experts (sociologists and psychologists) have achieved near-miracles by following a well-thought-out campaign, including the use of juror profiles (see §§5.35–5.37) and third-party investigative work (see chapter 13).

## D. Building a Network §5.8

In any survey work, it is either necessary to hire experienced people to do the whole job or to build a network of volunteers working under the careful supervision of some experienced people. The number of steps in a network depends on the size of the target population in the judicial district: four links should be sufficient for even the largest metropolitan judicial district. For example, a group of ten friends is assembled; they are asked to locate three friends each, bringing the group of friends to 40 (10 + 30). The 30 new people are also asked to locate three friends each, bringing 90 more people into the network of friends, for a total of 130. The fourth link brings 270 more people into the network of friends for a grand total of 400.

This form of community of friends, when operated boldly, has been able to discover some kind of third-party information on 70 to 80 percent of a venire list. A much smaller number can conduct a useful informal survey whose results will be used in making tactical decisions, or a valid formal survey whose results will be reported to the trial court.

## E. A Practical Approach §5.9

A busy trial lawyer can get a good jury survey organized and the results translated into useful findings in a relatively short time. Jury surveys are not too expensive, complicated, or time-consuming if the lawyer works with legal workers, paralegals, and community people in a principled way. The cost can be kept to a minimum, particularly in a case with important consequences to the community. Computer programmers and data analysts can be found in most communities, and they can suggest ways of precoding to simplify the transfer of information from schedules to data cards when time is at a premium.

If the lawyer starts planning soon enough, a quick, informal, but valid survey can be made to discover community attitudes toward the parties or issues in the case. This information is invaluable in deciding whether and where to sue or defend, whether to ask for a jury trial, and in constucting profiles of model jurors (see §§5.35–5.38). A survey may also help you construct the theme of the case (see §4.2) and plan the opening statement (see §§4.10 and 4.23, and chapter 21).

More time and formality are required when a survey will be used to support pretrial motions challenging jury lists (§5.20), seeking a change of venue (§5.21), or a different voir dire procedure (§5.27). See procedures described in §5.25.

Still more time will be required to conduct an intensive third party investigation of prospective jurors in order to have specific information on the jurors ultimately called to hear the particular case without touching any of the prospective jurors directly (see chapter 13).

### F. New Developments §5.10

It is possible to keep up with new jury selection techniques by subscribing to services on trial advocacy or criminal law, and reading daily newspapers and legal newspapers. It is a good idea occasionally to ask your law librarian for an index to journals on psychology, applied psychology, and the social sciences, to pick up new ideas from these disciplines.

The Annual Supplement to these volumes will use recent developments sections throughout the book to describe new cases, ideas, and articles that are worthy of note and to warn of innovative techniques that failed, of cases overruled, and of rules and statutes amended or repealed.

## III. CONDUCTING INITIAL COMMUNITY SURVEYS

### A. Survey Procedures §5.11

The goal in making an initial community survey is to discover the relationship between demographic characteristics of prospective jurors (age, race, sex, address, occupation, religious and national backgrounds, organizational affiliations, etc.) and their attitudes toward parties and issues in the particular case (parties/witnesses of other races, cultural and lifestyle differences among the parties, standards of negligence (civil), reasonable doubt (criminal), and other rules of law, etc.). This information is very helpful in constructing model profiles of the best and worst jurors for your side. It is also the basis for jury challenges, motions for change of venue, continuances, and extra peremptory challenges to combat community prejudgments of the case or the issues in the case.

The success of any survey depends on the careful selection of an accurate sample, the careful selection of significant factors on which to question the sample, the impartiality of interviewers in asking the questions, care in taking notes of answers, and finally, care in recording and analyzing the results.

The most accurate sample for a survey is drawn from those people who have been called for jury service in the past, provided there have been no subsequent major changes in the nature of the master jury wheel or list. Other things being equal, people who have been called for jury service previously are most likely to resemble the people who will be called for jury service in the future. The next best population from which to get a sample is the list of registered voters for the judicial district. The best sample will be at least 1 percent of the eligible juror population.

If it is impossible to follow this formal approach, it is still possible to conduct a useful survey by having interviewers make telephone calls from a local telephone book, continuing only those calls that yield registered voters in the jurisdiction who are not currently serving on juries. It is *not* possible to conduct a useful survey by having interviewers call their friends and acquaintances, who will not yield a representative sample.

Once the sample has been selected, interviewing can begin. In each interview, an interviewer asks questions to elicit demographic information, reads a summary of the case, and asks questions about the case. When the survey is being conducted to support a motion for a change of venue, for a continuance, for more than the usual number of peremptory challenges, or for similar purposes, the questioning should also include questions on media contact, knowledge of the case, and attitudes toward plaintiff, defendant, and the issues specific to the case. In a criminal case, questions should usually include degree of trust in government, law enforcement, and the legal system, attitudes toward divergent lifestyles, and, in a political case, toward social change.

Survey questions are similar to voir dire questions; see chapters 9–11 for ideas.

A useful survey on a particular case requires a carefully drafted statement of the facts, similar to the attorney's opening statement to the jury. Attention to writing the statement may result in interviewee reactions that will help you revise and improve the statement before using it in trial.

You may want to have interviewers ask very specific questions about the strengths and weaknesses of your case and your opponent's case. In order to get these kinds of responses, the statement of facts must include a strong description of your opponent's case, as well as your own. The value of this approach was demonstrated in *MCI v AT&T*, see §5.12.

At the interview phase, the most important person is the field supervisor, who must allocate interview assignments, monitor the work of the interviewers, and collect the interviews. Telephone interviews conducted by staff people or well-motivated volunteers who have been through a good training session will produce information of high quality. Pay scales are not as critical as motivation in getting quality information.

The rules for conducting successful community survey interviews are similar to the rules for conducting the initial part of the voir dire itself. In both instances, the purpose is to get accurate information about the interviewee. Therefore there are no "wrong" answers, and the exact words the interviewee uses are very important, because they reflect accurately each individual's attitudes and feelings. When interviewees suggest they have additional ideas, it is worthwhile to pursue them because such insights may prove useful in planning voir dire strategy. The interviewer should be careful to record answers accurately.

During voir dire some attorneys move from gathering information to seeking to get jurors to commit themselves to be impartial. In order to accomplish this, they may argue with prospective jurors, almost cross-examine them. (See excerpts from Charles Garry's voir dire in the *Newton* case in chapter 17.)

Interviewers *never* argue with their subjects, no matter how "objectionable" the answers are, because the purpose of the interviews is to try to understand the thought processes of the subjects, not to convince them of anything.

## B. Examples of Successful Surveys §5.12

*Source: MCI v AT&T*, a billion dollar antitrust suit (described in §3.73).

In preparation for trial of this federal district court jury case, plaintiff's counsel wanted a sample survey of registered voters in the jurisdiction to discover:

1. What kinds of people reacted most favorably to plaintiff's strongest arguments
2. Which of plaintiff's arguments these people found most convincing
3. What kinds of people reacted most favorably to defendant's strongest arguments
4. Which of defendant's arguments these people found most convincing
5. The attitudes of everyone interviewed concerning:
   a. The issues in the case
   b. The relative benefits of competition and regulated monopoly in the telecommunications field
   c. A possible award of $900,000,000 to plaintiff
   d. The defendant and the effect of defendant's massive television advertising campaign
6. The attitudes of everyone interviewed toward plaintiff's witnesses, in order to determine:
   a. Which witnesses to call first
   b. How to clarify each witness's testimony

Counsel used the survey information in preparing profiles of desirable and undesirable jurors (see §5.36), which they felt contributed to a great deal toward their winning a jury verdict.

*Source: Maryland v Rap Brown*, a criminal charge against a black activist.

The defense conducted a small "crash" survey in a state criminal case against Rap Brown, who had been a leader of the Student Nonviolent Coordinating Committee in the South during the 1960s. Defense counsel analyzed their client, the charge, the prosecution strategy, and the facts, and prepared questions that would indicate the likelihood that the person interviewed would be able to follow the law on burden of proof and presumption of innocence after listening to the testimony, arguments, and jury instructions, in view of the intense community feeling on the race question and SNCC in the jurisdiction, i.e., Howard County, Maryland, including the new town of Columbia.

The defense counsel only had a weekend to prepare a demographic profile of the kind of juror they should select. They found that six demographic factors told the tale: sex, race, age, occupation, religion, and place of residence. They constructed profiles of "best" and "worst" defense jurors (see §5.37), and won the case.

## C. Form: Initial Questions and Screening §5.13

Some basic information about citizens of a community can be obtained in the process of finding people willing to submit to a longer interview at a later time, by appointment, to go over the specific facts in a case.

Interviewers should introduce themselves; identify themselves accurately, i.e., state whether working for plaintiff's or defendant's counsel; ask respondents to spend a few minutes to help with a study; say that all answers will be completely confidential.

*Note:* Insert record-keeping data, e.g., name of interviewer, respondent, etc., according to the plan of the supervisor. Since each supervisor prefers a different form, none is provided here.

1. Are you registered to vote?

*Note:* If the answer is No, terminate the interview unless you are in a jurisdiction that uses other lists for jury selection, e.g., lists of people with driver's licenses or home telephones, in which event, ask whether respondent would be on such lists.

2. Do you live in [*jurisdiction of trial court*]?

*Note:* If the answer is No, thank respondent and terminate the interview.

3. What is your occupation?

*Note:* If respondent is unemployed, retired, or disabled, ask about prior work.

Type of Work:
Employer:

4. What is your marital status:
Married
Divorced
Separated
Widowed
Never married

*Note:* If respondent answers "married" or mentions "living with" someone, record this and ask the following questions with this in mind.

5. What is your [*spouse's/partner's*] occupation?
   Type of work:
   Employer:
6. Have you ever served on a jury?
7. Are you on call for jury service right now?

*Note:* Terminate the interview if the answer to question 7 is Yes. Any further interrogation might be construed as jury tampering.

If respondent's occupation suggests it is inappropriate to continue the interview, this is a good time to do so. Otherwise, ask a few more broad questions related to the issues in your case, e.g.:

8. Are you strongly in favor, somewhat in favor, somewhat opposed, or strongly opposed to:
   Compensation for emotional injuries?
   Compensation for damages caused by police misconduct?
   Capital punishment? [*But see chapter 11.*]
   [*Other issues*]

*Note:* Close with demographic questions on age, race, religious affiliation; ask whether respondent would be willing to be interviewed at some length on issues in a particular case; if Yes, make arrangements for time and place (preferably respondent's home); and thank respondent for helping in the research.

## D. Community Background Surveys §5.14

In a case to be tried by a lawyer from outside the jurisdiction, or in a hotly-contested case arising from a local incident or problem, counsel may learn a great deal from a community background survey. The survey may be limited to broad issues in the community that touch the issues in the case or may include case-specific questions. Even a small sample of respondents, selected from diverse parts of the community, will provide insights helpful in constructing juror profiles, in drafting voir dire questions, and in deciding trial strategy.

While interviews for such a survey can be conducted by telephone, the respondent should be asked to relax and plan to spend some time on the questions.

Respondents should be asked to give their address and describe their block/neighborhood/community as it is today; to tell whether it is changing, and, if so, how; to list issues that have created controversies in the community recently (over athletic facilities, political campaigns, bus service, police misconduct, etc.); to describe groups active in the area: what they are, what they do, and who participates in them; to list leaders in the area: whom they represent, what they stand for, and how they voted on recent community issues; and similar open-ended questions.

For case-specific questions used in a formal survey, whose results were submitted to the trial judge, see §5.27. The questions in an informal survey are similar; the care in selecting respondents is simply less rigorous.

All interviews need to end with enough demographic questions to permit some generalizations from the specific respondents to others sharing several demographic features: socioeconomic status, area of residence, age, political or group affiliation, etc.

## E. Discovering Current Community Attitudes §5.15

Conducting a survey about a pending case in the community where the trial will be conducted often uncovers attitudes that surprise local lawyers who pride themselves on keeping in touch with their communities. New insights obtained in a survey must be considered in planning trial strategy.

A good example of this approach occurred in Detroit a few years ago. Schaden and Heldman won a verdict against the Ford Motor Company in what was probably the first case charging a defective gas tank. The plaintiffs' theory was that all gas tanks were defective—a difficult theory to prove to the satisfaction of an auto-wise Detroit jury. But they won a $2,000,000 verdict. (In due course the auto companies developed a winning defense to use in such cases.) Later, with five pending cases charging defective transmissions in Ford cars, the lawyers sat through the trial of a similar case handled by excellent tort lawyers. They could not understand the reason for the jury verdict of "no cause." They hired the National Jury Project to conduct a postverdict study of the jurors in that case to uncover the reason for their decision.

In September 1981 the project conducted in-depth interviews and learned that a drastic change had occurred in juror attitudes in Wayne County. The economy had taken its toll. In jury deliberations when the liability was not clear cut, the jurors said, "We are not going to vote against the Ford Motor Company because it is going to hurt them, which will jeopardize our jobs and the whole economy in Detroit."

The lawyers felt that this survey of a very small sample (12 jurors) was significant. Future jurors were likely to have the same opinion. They concluded that this survey was well worth the cost. As a result, they began settling many of their pending automobile cases for 60 to 75 percent of their value, rather than trying them in the Detroit area. Detroit juries would still vote for plaintiffs and for proper damages, including $1,270,000 for a woman charging an unfair discharge from a nontraditional job, described in §3.41. But they would no longer vote liability, let alone large damages, in suits against the auto companies.

It is important for lawyers to remind themselves how often the demographics in a particular community may change. For example, a jury survey conducted in southern Florida before 1965 would be far off the mark today, due to the massive immigration of Latin Americans and Central Americans to that area, which has changed the attitudes of many prospective jurors on a series of questions related to immigration, ethnic groups, etc. The same is true of the Sun Belt, which has received waves of immigrants from Detroit and other northern, union areas, and a significant number of immigrants from Vietnam and other Southeast Asian countries.

Even where there have been few shifts in population, juror attitudes will be much affected by the recent movement for the liberation of women and the economic necessity for housewives to become paid workers outside the home.

The clear message is: Don't assume you know much about the jurors in your community if you have not tried a jury case in the past year or two.

### F. New Techniques §5.16

See §5.10.

## IV. CONDUCTING FORMAL COMMUNITY SURVEYS

### A. To Support Pretrial Motions

#### 1. Challenging Jury Lists §5.20

A lawyer challenging the list used to select grand or petit jurors will want supporting data showing that the selection process discriminates against some cognizable community group or groups. (See chapter 6.) A successful survey will show a statistically significant variance in the percentage of members of a particular group in the community and the percentage on the jury list.

The most accurate and authoritative source of statistical information on groups in a community and on the community as a whole is the United States Census. The main census tracts to use are "General Social and Economic Characteristics" and "General Population Characteristics." Tables cover county units, education of residents, occupations, and income. One table covers age, race, and gender. The occupational categories and lists of occupations for each category are in an appendix.

In a grand jury challenge, the participants must become familiar with the mechanics of selection, including who makes nominations of grand jurors, who has custody of lists of nominees (usually a county jury commissioner), and where grand jury questionnaires and voter registration forms are on file. The latter can be used to double-check information obtained in the survey.

Someone with a basic understanding of sociological methods—how to train interviewers, draw samples, etc.—should be available for consultation. This expert should determine the necessary size of a survey sample of nominees. Usually a statistician is the best expert and may also make a good witness when it is necessary to validate the survey. A survey going back five years is usually needed to show a pattern of discrimination; a single year can be used if the selection process has changed significantly from previous years.

The survey questions should be drafted to elicit responses directly comparable to source data from the US census. In past surveys, the focus has been on race, gender, ethnic background, poverty status, age, and class (as shown by occupation, education, and income). In some communities a challenge could be based on neighborhood resident patterns. It is important to consult with a sociologist to decide how to define certain groups (i.e., how should "youth" be defined? 18-30? 21-30?), income groups (i.e., how should "the poor" be defined? Under $10,000?), and occupation (i.e., are clerical workers blue collar, white collar, or pink collar? What about service workers?)

Interviewers, particularly volunteers, should be thoroughly briefed on the importance of accuracy and objectivity. Volunteers may be recruited by professors teaching undergraduate sociology classes or from groups active in the community. An effort should be made to anticipate interviewees' questions about the purpose of the survey and the nature of the case. The individual whose testimony in court will validate the survey should be designated supervisor and given responsibility for coordinating it.

In several cases telephone surveys alone did not yield an adequate sample of nominees because of unlisted numbers, changes of addresses, etc. The desire for anonymity, which has led to a great many unlisted telephone numbers, will require some analysis and counter-measures. And telephone numbers listed without addresses will require questioning as to addresses that was not necessary some years ago. It may become necessary to mail out a questionnaire and cover letter to uncontacted nominees. The questionnaire and a personal note may also be sent to nominees who were uncooperative over the phone. When time is not a factor but money is, it may be desirable to mail first and call later. However, the response to mailings tends to be relatively poor.

The *Attica Brothers* defense team (see §3.26), between October 1973 and March 1974, conducted a telephone survey of 1,500 persons drawn and summoned for jury duty during 1972. Beth Bonora, Marty Feinriter, and Tom Antenucci recruited and trained over 50 telephone interviewers who not only polled jurors but also traced jurors whose telephone numbers had been changed. The main goal of the survey was to determine the racial composition of the pool, which was not available on jury questionnaires. To insure a good response rate, pollsters began by asking about jury duty in general. People were usually very anxious to discuss their experiences, which often consisted of a frustrating two weeks sitting in the bullpen without even getting to serve on a jury. (See chapter 23.) A second series of attitudinal questions were used to obtain a preliminary profile of Erie County juror attitudes toward the *Attica Brothers* cases. The third series included demographic questions similar to those in the form in §5.13. Keypunchers and a computer expert were able to process the data rapidly.

Once the data are tabulated, the statistician and sociologist can determine which categories to raise in the court challenge. If there are data showing a strong variance between the number of members of a cognizable class (e.g., women or blacks) in the community and among the nominees, and the client has standing as a member of that class, it may be appropriate to drop the remainder of the data. Of course, lawyers must be available to help, particularly after the data have been collected, and in time to prepare the challenge.

Someone with graphic skills can prepare graphs, maps, etc., to be used as courtroom exhibits and for public display. It may also be appropriate to conclude a memo or brief with a discussion of the interrelationships between several cognizable classes (see §§6.34, 6.61).

## 2. Seeking Change of Venue §5.21

In the Soledad Brothers case (described in §7.36), a telephone survey was used to conduct brief interviews about attitudes toward Negroes, prisoners, prison guards, and the killing of the guard at Soledad Prison, with which the defendants were charged. The purpose of the survey was to support a motion for a change of venue on the ground that the jury list in Salinas County could not produce an unbiased jury to try the Soledad Brothers. For this reason the survey was much more extensive than a survey to test community responses to assist in constructing juror profiles, etc. The survey covered an estimated total of 1,363 residents who were eligible as jurors, and the response rate of 59 percent was adequate to generalize with confidence to the total adult resident population of the county.

In addtion a series of interviews was conducted with a "snowball" sample of knowledgeable and responsible prominent citizens in the vicinity. These opinion leaders included members of the Salinas city council, the mayor, proprietors and managers of several large establishments in the area, presidents of several voluntary associations (including the Junior Chamber of Commerce), and reporters from local newspapers. While the sample was small, viewed in terms of the entire population of the county, it was a substantial sample of this special segment of the community. The interviews focused not on the respondents' own views and attitudes about the community but rather on their informed opinions about prevalent attitudes in the community, particularly those germane to the case. They were asked to tell about social and demographic changes in Salinas in recent years, community views on the Soledad Prison facility, prevalent views of prison personnel, prisoners, and ex-convicts, and prevalent community views concerning the particular case, including attitudes toward the accused and toward the victim.

This telephone survey was very successful. It led to the granting of the motion for a change of venue.

The two surviving Soledad Brothers were tried in San Francisco Superior Court in 1972, two years after they were first charged. They were acquitted by an all-white jury on March 27, 1972.

Results of other formal community surveys are presented in chapters discussing motions filed on jury issues. See §§6.1, 6.83, 7.26, 7.38.

### 3. For Other Purposes §5.22

This section is being reserved to discuss additional pretrial motions in annual supplements to this volume.

## B. Survey Procedures

### 1. Form: Declaration Describing Typical Survey Procedures §5.25

*Source:* Adapted from declaration of Jeffery M. Paige, dated Sept. 20, 1971, *California v Davis* (see §3.23).

**Project:** Six-county telephone survey of attitudes toward *Angela Davis* case.

**Principal Investigator:** Jeffery M. Paige, Assistant Professor, Department of Sociology, University of California, Berkeley, and Assistant Research Sociologist, Survey Research Center.

**Purpose:** The study was undertaken at the request of Howard Moore and Sheldon Otis, attorneys for the defendant in *California v Davis*, in order to assess biases of potential jurors in six Bay Area counties. The study was designed to assess general patterns of prejudice toward blacks, Communists, and radicals and specific attitudes about the *Davis* case.

**Population:** The population to be studied consisted of registered voters with listed telephone numbers in the counties of San Francisco, Alameda, Marin, San Mateo, Santa Clara, and Sacramento.

**Sampling:** The sample was drawn in such a way as to assure that every individual in the population had an equal probability of selection. This procedure is essential if valid statistical inferences are to be made about the population from which a sample is drawn. Names were selected by simple random sampling from current voter registration lists in the county clerk's office in each of the six counties.

**Interviewing:** Interviewers were volunteer undergraduate students in the social sciences. Each was required to attend a 2½-hour training session in which the principal investigator outlined procedures for respondent selection and principles of interviewing. Approximately 10 interviewers were assigned to each county for a total of 60 interviewers. The interviewers were closely supervised by six graduate social science students, all of whom had received training in statistics and research methods. The interviewers were given a list of respondent names and telephone numbers and told to interview each person on the list. No substitutions were permitted, and the interviewers were required to make a total of four callbacks if initial calls did not produce an interview. This procedure produced a total of 601 interviews or approximately 100 interviews per county. All interviews were conducted between August 14 and August 21, 1971.

**Error Estimation:** The procedures followed in selecting the sample and in conducting interviews are those customary in scientific work on public opinion. These procedures are necessary in order to permit inferences from a small sample to a much larger population. Nevertheless, the reliability of a sample statistic for any county is determined by the absolute size of the sample. The error involved, in accepting a percentage calculated on a sample as an estimate of the true percentage in the population from which the sample is drawn, declines proportionately to the square root of the size of the sample. Larger samples reduce potential error but, of course, increase costs. The sample size for each of the six counties is approximately 100. A sample of this size means that there is only one chance in twenty that the sample value will differ from the true population value by more than plus or minus 9 percent.

Since the responses to survey questions are to be compared between pairs of counties, it is useful to know the size of a difference that can be considered a true difference in the pattern of responses of the counties' populations. In general a difference of approximately 13 percent or greater between the percentages reported for any two counties can be regarded as statistically meaningful. A difference this great can occur only one time in twenty by chance alone if there is no difference in the true population values for the two counties. Within these limits the results of the survey can be regarded as representing true differences in the interview responses of registered voters in the six counties.

*Note:* For the substantive results of this survey, see §7.38.

## 2. Form: Results of Demographic Survey of Grand Jury Nominees §5.26

*Source:* Kairys, "Juror Selection," 10 *Am Crim L Rev* 771, 804 (1972), describing the form used in a Philadelphia jury challenge. Methods of jury selection have been changed totally in Philadelphia since this study was made, and of course inflation has made the specific income figures useful only in a relative sense. See table, opposite page.

## 3. Form: Affidavits of Experts Supporting Motion for Fair Jury Selection Procedures §5.27

A good example of survey results is the collection of affidavits and exhibits filed in *Hampton v Hanrahan* (ND Ill, E Div, No. 70 C 1384, 1976), a civil suit for damages against Chicago law enforcement officers for the death of Black Panther Party leaders Fred Hampton and Mark Clark; see §3.71. The long jury trial began in 1976.

*Source:* Excerpts from affidavit of Professor Jay Schulman in support of plaintiffs' motion for fair jury selection procedures, filed Nov. 24, 1975, *Hampton v Hanrahan*.

5. With the help of Dr. Kathy McCourt, the Senior Study Director at the National Opinion Research Center in Chicago, a sample of registered voters was drawn from Cook, DuPage, and Lake Counties.

6. A sample of 837 people, with the same qualifications as prospective jurors, was generated from a computer organized program at the National Opinion Research Center.

| | | | | | | | | | | | | | | | | | | | | |
|---|---|---|---|---|---|---|---|---|---|---|---|---|---|---|---|---|---|---|---|---|
| Family Income | 25,000 and Over | | | | | | | | | | | | | | | | | | | |
| | 15,000-24,999 | | X | | | | | | | | | | | X | | | | | | |
| | 10,000-14,999 | | | | | | | | X | | | | | | | | | | | |
| | 9,000-9,999 | | | | | | | | | X | | | | | | | | | | |
| | 8,000-8,999 | | | X | | | | | | | | | | | | | | X | | |
| | 7,000-7,999 | | | | | | | X | | | | | | | | | | | | |
| | 6,000-6,999 | | | | | | | | | | | | | | | | | | | |
| | 5,000-5,999 | | | | | | | | | | | | | | | | | | | |
| | 4,000-4,999 | | | | | | | | | | | | | | | X | | | | |
| | 3,000-3,999 | | | | | | | | | | | | | | | | | | | |
| | 2,000-2,999 | | | | | | | | | | | | | | | | | | | |
| | 1,000-1,999 | | | | | | | | | | | | | | | | | | | |
| | Under 1,000 | | | | | | | | | | | | | | | | | | | |
| Family | Cars | 1 | 2 | 2 | | | | 1 | 2 | 1 | | | | 1 | 0 | 0 | | 1 | | |
| | Kids | 0 | 4 | 2 | | | | 4 | 3 | 0 | | | | 0 | 2 | 1 | | 3 | | |
| | Single | | | | | | | | | X | | | | | | | | | | |
| | Married | X | X | X | | | | X | X | | | | | X | X | X | | X | | |
| Home | Units | 1 | 1 | 1 | | | | 1 | 1 | 1 | | | | 6 | 1 | 2 | | 2 | | |
| | People | 2 | 6 | 2 | | | | 6 | 5 | 3 | | | | 2 | 2 | 2 | | 5 | | |
| | Rooms | 6 | 6 | 6 | | | | 6 | 6 | 6 | | | | 4 | 10 | 3 | | 8 | | |
| | Rent | | | | | | | | | | | | | X | | X | | | | |
| | Own | X | X | X | | | | X | X | X | | | | | X | | | X | | |
| Religion | None | | | | | | | | | | | | | X | | | | | | |
| | Jew | | | | | | | | | | | | | | X | | | | | |
| | Protestant | X | | X | | | | X | | | | | | | | | | | | |
| | Catholic | | X | | | | | | X | X | | | | | | X | | X | | |
| Race | Nonwhite | X | | | | | | X | | | | | | | | X | | | | |
| | White | | X | X | | | | | X | X | | | | X | X | | | X | | |
| January | Poll Grand Juror | 1 | 2 | 3 | 4 | 5 | 6 | 7 | 8 | 9 | 10 | 11 | 12 | 13 | 14 | 15 | 16 | 17 | 18 | . . . |

7. These 837 people were interviewed by telephone over a period of approximately 11 weeks by about 15 volunteers, closely supervised by my associate, Ms. Diane Rapaport. I, in turn, supervised Ms. Rapaport. Telephone interviews are a standard procedure in the public opinion industry and are considered an acceptable means of surveying opinion. Interviews were conducted only with registered voters (who are potential jurors).

8. The survey questionnaire was constructed by myself, together with a group of volunteers familiar with the greater Chicago area and the facts of this case. We had the help of Dr. McCourt, Professor Richard Christie of Columbia University in New York, and Professor Richard Berk of Northwestern University.

9. The coding was done by volunteers, closely supervised by Ms. Rapaport, Dr. McCourt and Professor Berk. The keypunching was done professionally according to quality research standards. The programming and computer work was done by Professor Berk.

10. *Findings:* The answers to the questions below show that potential jurors in the Northern District of Illinois show a large amount of preconceptions about the facts of this case, prejudice against black people and the Plaintiffs involved in this case, and towards supporting and believing law enforcement officials:

10.1 Q. In December of 1969, fourteen police officers assigned to State's Attorney Edward Hanrahan raided a Black Panther apartment looking for illegal weapons. There was gunfire and the raid resulted in the deaths of two Black Panthers, Fred Hampton and Mark Clark. Do you recall this incident?
96.4%—yes
3.6%—no

10.2 Q. How closely did you follow the (above) events at that time?
29%—a lot
38.1%—somewhat
26.4%—a little
5.6%—not at all
[note: 94.4% said they followed the media coverage of the December 4th raid.]

10.3 Q. (referring to above) What is your opinion—do you think the police were wrong, the Panthers were wrong, or are you uncertain?
19.7%—police were wrong
17.6%—Panthers were wrong
26.5%—both were wrong
36.2%—uncertain
[note: 63.8% had an opinion as to who was wrong.]

10.4 Q. Police should not hesitate to use force to maintain order.
66% agreed
33% disagreed
1% had no opinion or refused to answer

10.5 Q. The government should use any means necessary to destroy groups which threaten our present system of government.
49% agreed
50% disagreed
1% had no opinion or refused to answer

10.6 Q. In a court of law would you be more likely to believe the testimony of a police officer or a Black Panther?
46.1%—police officer
5.0%—Black Panther
48.9%—Depends, don't know, or refused to answer

10.7 Q. If it were determined by the courts that the police acted illegally do you think the families of the dead Panthers should be able to collect money for damages?
65%—yes
4%—depends
31%—no

10.8 Q. Black people are more prone to violence than white people.
38% agreed
58% disagreed
4% had no opinion or refused to answer

11. *Discussion:*

11.1 Questions 10.1 and 10.2 show that well over 90% of the potential jurors have already been exposed to the facts of this case, and question 10.3 shows that about ⅔ of them have already formed an opinion as to who was wrong. Because [*plaintiffs*] must show they were not at fault, 44.1% of those polled would on the basis of their present opinion decide against the plaintiffs in this matter. This is over ⅔ of those who presently have an opinion.

11.2 Questions 10.4 and 10.5 show that ½ to ⅔ of potential jurors believe that force such as that used by the state and local Defendants in this case is *generally* proper if a threat is perceived.

11.3 Question 10.6 shows that about ½ of the potential jurors are predisposed to believe police officers, especially as opposed to Black Panthers.

11.4 Question 10.7 shows that about ⅓ of the potential jurors would not award damages to the Hampton and Clark families, even if a court of law found that Mark Clark and Fred Hampton were killed as a result of illegal action.

11.5 Question 10.8 shows that over ⅓ of the potential jurors are probably biased against black people and believe them to be violent.

12. *Conclusions:*

a. Most potential jurors already have opinions about this case.

b. There is substantial, abiding and pervasive prejudice toward black people, the Black Panther Party and the Plaintiffs in this case among the potential jurors in the Northern District of Illinois.

c. There is clear and prejudicial predisposition toward believing law enforcement officials and supporting actions such as those taken by the Defendants in this case in the Northern District of Illinois.
d. Other studies I have done suggest to me that these biases are more abiding, more pervasive, more volatile and more concentrated than the prejudice toward Watergate defendants and anti-war defendants.
e. In my opinion, the Plaintiffs in this case cannot have a fair jury trial on their claims unless they are afforded lawyer-conducted, extensive individual voir dire to effectively screen jurors and to guide their use of peremptory challenges. I further believe that they must be given a sufficient number of peremptory challenges and *at least* as many as the Defendants, so that they can use them when they perceive bias.

*Source:* Concluding paragraph of affidavit of Professor Richard A. Berk in support of plaintiffs' motion for fair jury selection procedures, filed Oct. 24, 1975, *Hampton v Hanrahan*.

8. A sample of 837 prospective jurors was gathered, the data transferred to computer cards and statistical analysis undertaken. I was primarily responsible for the statistical analysis in collaboration with Professor Schulman and Professor Christie. The techniques employed reflect "State of the Art" procedures and computer programs of well known and widely recognized accuracy. There is absolutely no reason to suspect that the findings can in any way be attributed to statistical artifacts in the analysis or that other commonly used approaches would have produced different results. Therefore, the data provide an excellent vehicle for assessing the potential biases of prospective jurors in Cook, Lake, and DuPage Counties.

See also affidavit of Dr. Alice Marie Padawer-Singer in support of motion for change of venue in *United States v Soliah* in §8.82.

## V. CONSTRUCTING MODEL JUROR PROFILES

### A. Two Methods of Constructing Juror Profiles §5.30

The common methodology of several of the social sciences is to develop working behavior models as guides to understanding and predicting human responses. Two models for jury selection have been developed since 1968, when highly publicized jury trials were conducted involving black and anti-war activists: the clinical selection model and the demographic selection model. An attorney can use either method, or can combine the results of both methods in a single case, while also carefully observing individual juror behavior (see chapters 18 and 19).

The basic difference between the clinical selection model and the demographic selection model is in the sources used to construct the list of characteristics that comprise the "good" and "bad" jurors from the trial lawyer's viewpoint.

### 1. Clinical Selection Model §5.31

In the clinical selection model, the psychologist or psychiatrist constructs juror profiles from previous studies of large numbers of people made by psychologists and sociologists over long periods of time and for many purposes (usually not connected with jury selection). See, e.g., Robinson, Rusk, and Head, *Measures of Political Attitudes* (Ann Arbor, University of Michigan Center for Political Studies/Institute for Social Research, 1973); materials available from the Center for Responsive Psychology, Brooklyn College, C.U.N.Y., Brooklyn, N.Y. 11210; Moran and Comfort, "Scientific Jury Selection: Sex as a Moderator of Demographic and Personality Predictors of Impaneled Felony Juror Behavior," 41 *J Personality & Soc Psych* 1052–63 (Nov. 1982).

These studies have isolated the authoritarian personality, for example, and have produced questionnaires that will identify such people with considerable accuracy. The trial lawyer's job is to discover whether an authoritarian personality will be able to judge the parties impartially in the particular case, or whether such a juror should be challenged.

In the clinical model, the expert may not discuss with the lawyer or client the source of the factors used in the jury profile. The expert is treated as an independent expert, that is, as a doctor is treated when asked about medical symptoms, merely giving a diagnosis. No surveys are made of opinions in the community from which the jury will be selected.

However, experience has shown that it is wrong to generalize from a national sample of the United States to judicial districts. Even the smallest judicial district, such as a county, has its own unique social and cultural patterning which must be understood and taken into account in jury selection. It is even wrong to generalize from one judicial district to another. Trial teams found that the social and cultural structure of the Gainesville Division of the Northern District of Florida is markedly different from the Pensacola and Marianna Divisions within the same district. In the Middle District of Pennsylvania, professionals and high status individuals *as a group* were dangerous for the defense; the same group was good for the defense in Howard County, Maryland. Similarly, in the 1970s, women appeared more empathic and less punitive than men in the Northeast, in the Midwest, and in the Far West, but not in the South.

## 2. Demographic Selection Model §5.32

There are six steps in jury selection following this model.

1. Experts establish lists of people in the trial court jurisdiction who constitute a representative cross-section of the population that might be called for jury service. (This may simply be a list of persons who have recently served on juries).
2. The trial lawyer and nonlawyer experts prepare preliminary voir dire questions to test current attitudes in the community on issues related to the case directly and indirectly.
3. A network of people (paid or volunteer) interview the sample list, using the voir dire questions and keeping track of demographic factors in order to construct profiles of "good" and "bad" jurors for the particular party.
4. The trial lawyer and experts from other disciplines prepare juror profiles and a rating system based on the answers.
5. The network gathers third party information on the people called for jury duty (see chapter 13).
6. The lawyer revises the voir dire questions in light of the answers by the community sample.

All the information obtained is correlated in the final rating of each juror before peremptory challenges are made. By using lists of factors, numerical ratings, and several raters, counsel can reduce the guesswork and achieve a more scientific result.

This approach was apparently used first in the antiwar protesters' trial of the *Berrigan Brothers* in Harrisburg (see §8.31). Social scientists conducted a telephone survey and in-depth interviews with 252 people representative of potential jurors. They concluded that the ideal juror would be a female Democrat with no religious preference and a white-collar or skilled blue-collar job. A good defense juror would also sympathize with some elements of defendants' views on the Vietnam war, at least tolerate the idea that citizens have a right to resist government policies nonviolently, and indicate a presumption of defendants' innocence until the government proved their guilt. The jury selected stood 10 to 2 for acquittal when a mistrial was declared.

The same procedure was refined and used, with good results, in the trial of the *Camden 28* antiwar protesters (see §3.55), in the *Gainesville Eight* trial of Vietnam Veterans Against the War (see §3.53), and is now standard procedure in many civil and criminal trials. Some experts now believe that a small, carefully selected model, interviewed at considerable length, will provide as accurate information as a larger model interviewed in less depth.

## B. Sample Juror Profiles

### 1. Guilt-prone Jurors in Florida §5.35

*Source:* Moran and Comfort, in 41 *J Personality & Soc Psych* 1052–63 (Nov. 1982).

Social scientists recently conducted a study of 319 men and women who had served on felony juries that reached verdicts in 1975–1976 in state courts in Miami, Florida. The subjects answered a battery of questions concerning 23 demographic/personality predictors and five juror behavioral criteria. Almost ⅔ had voted to convict; ⅓ had served on juries that acquitted; 3.7 percent had served on hung juries.

Jurors who voted to convict had different characteristics from those who voted to acquit. In addition, guilt-prone men had some different characteristics from guilt-prone women.

| *Guilt-prone Men* | *Guilt-prone Women* |
|---|---|
| Had lower income | Believed in naive correlation between virtue and reward |
| Were more interested in having a family | Were nonanomic: believed their actions could affect society |
| Had more children | Held authoritarian views on legal issues |
| Were conventionally socialized | Were antithetical to constitutional civil liberties |
| Were authoritarian | Had high empathy scores: evaluators of defendants' moral culpability |
| Did not attribute exaggerated virtue to themselves | Had less-recent immigrant ancestors |
| Were more honest | Believed it their responsibility to assist in administration of imminent justice |
| Were fearful of lying in court | Believed in a just world |
| Were modest | Might presume defendants' guilt |

While this study confirms some findings of other modern studies and may be somewhat useful in constructing juror profiles in criminal cases in general, it is not necessary to rely on older studies in distant jurisdictions unrelated to the fact pattern in your own specific case. It is possible to conduct an initial community survey including the facts and special features in your case and to construct specific jury profiles based on the results. See §§5.11–5.14.

## 2. Antitrust-prone Jurors in Illinois §5.36

*Source:* Robert F. Hanley, plaintiff's chief trial counsel in *MCI v AT&T*, a federal antitrust suit between a small new corporation and one of the oldest and largest in the country. See case description in §3.73.

On the basis of the survey and mock jury work done before trial, described in §5.12, plaintiff's counsel constructed the following juror profiles.

*Most Favorable to Plaintiff*

1. Intelligent people.
2. People who could listen, take notes during trial, take into their deliberations important exhibits of both sides, along with the judge's instructions, and use them in reaching a verdict.
3. Self-made people.
4. People who strongly favor competition and the free enterprise system.

*Least Favorable to Plaintiff*

1. People unable to follow complicated facts, charts, and diagrams illustrating financial transactions and relationships.
2. People unable to make a judgment in a case involving a demand for a billion dollars in damages.
3. People convinced of the superiority of the Bell telephone system as presently constituted.
4. Old people.
5. Young people.

## 3. Best and Worst Defense Jurors in Maryland §5.37

*Source:* Dr. Jay Schulman, jury selection expert in *Maryland v Rap Brown*, a criminal charge against a leading black militant of the 1960s.

On the basis of the survey work, described in §5.12, defense counsel constructed juror profiles of "best" and "worst" jurors. While it helps the defense to know that the people who must be avoided are the managers and brokers of local community life, and not blue-collar workers, "rednecks," or even farmers, what the defense needs to know most is *which* young people might be *best*, *which* blue-collar people might be good, which older people might be good, which Methodists might be good, which Presbyterians might be dangerous, which people from Columbia might be dangerous, which blacks might be dangerous, etc. This information is necessary because the other side can also spot the "best" and "worst" jurors for each side, and will use peremptory challenges accordingly. The well-informed lawyer needs a good profile of jurors in the middle range.

*Best Jurors for the Defense*

- People tolerant of dissent generally
- Black people
  - White
  - Women
  - People-oriented professionals
  - Spouses of people-oriented professionals
  - Presbyterians, Episcopalians or Congregationalists
- People aged 25–49
- Residents of new town of Columbia

*Worst Jurors for the Defense*

- People whose values embrace
  - Authority
  - Patriotism
  - Conformity
  - "Government right or wrong"
- White males over 45
- Managers, engineers, government employees, real estate brokers'
- Members of local establishment
- Methodists or Pentecostals
- Residents of rural area or small towns

Development of juror profiles is now recognized as a fact of trial life. For example, in *California v Jimmie Ray Williams* (Cal Sup Ct 1981) 174 CR 317, 29 C3d 392, the court footnoted the example of the New York trial of Watergate defendants Maurice Stans and John Mitchell, in which "the defense was advised to seek a jury of working class persons of Catholic background, neither poor nor rich ($8,000 to $10,000 per year), who read the *New York News*." And see Note, The Constitutional Need for Discovery of Pre-Voir Dire Juror Studies, 49 *SoCal L Rev* 597, 605 (1967).

## 4. Other Examples §5.38

This section is being reserved for additional sample juror profiles, to be presented in annual supplements to this volume.

# PART III

# Seeking a Jury of Peers

Chapter 6

# Challenging the Jury Lists

**I. Why Challenge Jury Composition**

A. Possibilities of Successful Challenge
   1. Victories §6.1
   2. Roots and Significance §6.2
   3. Constitutional Bases §6.3
   4. Statutory Basis §6.4

B. Part of Overall Trial Strategy §6.5

C. Value of Unsuccessful Challenges §6.6

D. Materials Presented
   1. State and Federal Cases Interchangeable §6.7
   2. Grand and Petit Jury Cases Interchangeable §6.8
   3. Scope of Materials §6.9

E. Recent Developments §6.10

**II. Preliminary Work on Statistical Challenge**

A. Timing of Challenge
   1. Federal §6.11
   2. State §6.12

B. Discovery
   1. Form: Preliminary Motion for Inspection of Court Records §6.15
   2. Memo in Support of Motion for Inspection §6.16
   3. Form: Supporting Affidavit §6.17
   4. Sample: Argument on Appeal When Discovery Denied §6.18

C. Recent Developments §6.19

**III. Challenging Jury Selection Methods**
A. Establishing a Prima Facie Case of Exclusion or Underrepresentation §6.21
    1. Not Necessary to Prove Intent §6.22
    2. Comparison of Jury List with Other Lists §6.23
B. Procedures §6.24
C. Form: Motion to Quash Indictment §6.25
D. Form: Motion to Quash Jury Panel §6.26
E. Recent Developments §6.29
F. Memorandum in Support of Challenge §6.31
    1. Facts §6.32
    2. Definitions and Contradictions
        a. Cognizable Classes §6.33
        b. Relationships among Cognizable Classes §6.34
        c. Contradictions Inherent in a Jury Challenge §6.35
    3. Standing to Raise Issue
        a. Form: Majority Group Members Have Standing in Federal Courts §6.41
        b. Form: Majority Group Members Have Standing in State Courts §6.42
        c. Form: Members of a Class Excluded from Jury Duty Have Standing to File Suit §6.43
        d. Recent Developments §6.45
    4. Fair Cross-Section Constitutionally Required
        a. Form: Fifth and Sixth Amendments and Equal Protection Clauses of Fifth and Fourteenth Amendments Require Fair Cross-Section Juries §6.46
        b. Form: Systematic Exclusion of Distinctive Groups Unconstitutional §6.47
        c. Recent Developments §6.49
    5. Distinctive Groups in This Community Underrepresented
        a. Black People §6.51
        b. Blue-Collar Workers §6.52
        c. Poor People §6.53
        d. Young People §6.54
        e. Black, Blue-Collar, Poor Young People §6.55
        f. Women §6.56
        g. Latinos/Chicanos/Mexican-Americans/Hispanics §6.57
        h. Asian-Americans §6.58
        i. Native Americans §6.59
        j. Nonvoters §6.60
        k. All Minority Groups Underrepresented on Voting Lists §6.61
        l. Students §6.62
        m. Short-Term Residents §6.63
        n. Misdemeanor Arrestees and Ex-Felons §6.64

o. Nontheists §6.65
p. Aleutian Natives §6.66
q. Resident Aliens §6.67
r. Other Cognizable Classes §6.68
6. Constitutional and Practical Selection Plan Proposed §6.71
7. Form: Conclusion §6.72
8. Affidavits Attached §6.73
9. Recent Developments §6.79
G. Evidentiary Hearing
1. Forensic Experts Needed §6.81
2. Demonstrative Evidence §6.82
3. Proving Disparity Mathematically §6.83
4. Opinion: Burden of Proof Met §6.84
5. Recent Developments §6.89

# I. WHY CHALLENGE JURY COMPOSITION

## A. Possibilities of Successful Challenge

### 1. Victories §6.1

Counsel in every state and federal case should consider challenging the composition of the jury before trial, in view of the likelihood that the jury list will not produce a cross-section jury and that an attempt to raise the question after trial may be summarily rejected by the Supreme Court, regardless of the factual basis for such a challenge. See *Davis v United States* (1973) 411 US 233, especially dissent of Marshall, J, at 245; *Tollett v Henderson* (1973) 411 US 258, especially dissent of Marshall, J, at 269.

In making this consideration, counsel should note that attorneys' fees were awarded in a suit against "conscientious" jury commissioners who nonetheless admitted that both grand and traverse jury lists for Mitchell County, Georgia, were unconstitutionally composed. *Brown v Culpepper* (5th Cir 1977) 539 F2d 274.

Failure of defense counsel in any criminal case to *consider* the legal and factual bases for a challenge to the grand and/or petit jury should amount to malpractice. While not every such consideration will result in an affirmative decision, failure to consider the matter will surely doom lawyers to try cases based on indictments issued by unrepresentative grand juries before unrepresentative petit juries.

The difficulties in making a challenge to a grand or petit jury list are largely problems of finding time to do the factual and legal work required, which may be solved by use of volunteers (see chapter 13), by having several law offices (including public defenders) combine their efforts, or by having a committee raise money for a paid staff. Materials collected in this chapter, which relate to civil and criminal cases, and to grand and trial juries, should be of assistance in making a realistic determination of the need for such a challenge and its potential for success. (See §6.8 on interchangeability of precedents.)

Two major factors suggest that counsel should decide to mount such challenges.

1. It is unlikely that grand jurors in any particular case carried out their constitutional duty to use their independent judgment in deciding to issue an indictment, or even seriously debated rejection of any specific charge requested by the prosecution (see chapter 23).
2. It is also unlikely that state or federal grand or petit jurors anywhere in the country are consistently representative of a fair cross-

section of the community (see §§6.51–6.68 for examples of exclusions of many cognizable classes; but see §6.71 for a random selection plan).

To a conscientious attorney, the first factor means that the prosecution may not have presented to the grand jury convincing, admissible evidence of the defendant's guilt. Issuance of an indictment does not necessarily indicate that the prosecution possesses such evidence. Therefore, in the interests of the individual defendant and of society as a whole, a lawyer should seek to avoid a full-scale trial even if it would result in an acquittal of all charges.

The second factor has led to a long series of successful jury challenges since adoption of the Fourteenth Amendment equal protection clause. For example, a challenge to the petit jury selection system in a small Nebraska county was successful before trial in *Nebraska v Janis and Buckman* (Sheridan County Dist Ct, Nos. C-1604, 1605, Jan. 4, 1980), discussed in §6.59. A challenge to the method of selecting Philadelphia County, Pennsylvania, grand and petit juries was successful even before conclusion of the challenge raised in *Philadelphia v Locke* (Philadelphia County Ct of CP, No. MC-09-1190, 1191, 70-10-919, 70-12, 2416, Oct. 27, 1970), described in Kairys, "Juror Selection: The Law, a Mathematical Analysis, and a Case Study," 10 *Am Crim L Rev* 771 (1972). By 1980, Pennsylvania had adopted a new statewide system of jury selection, including the use of several lists in addition to voter registration lists, in order to increase the representative character of juries. 42 P Stat Ann, title 42, §§2121–2124; 4501–4532; 4541–4584 (Purdon). The *Locke* challenge was one step leading to this new statute.

In 1973 the trial judge in the *San Quentin Six* case ruled that the Marin County, California, grand jury was improperly selected by the local judges, as described in §2.21. (This ruling was reversed in 1974, *California v Pinell* (Dist Ct App 1974) 117 Cal Rptr 913; *cert. den.* 422 US 1007 (1975).)

To these successful (or temporarily successful) state grand jury challenges can be added successful federal grand jury challenges and successful petit jury challenges at both state and federal levels, since the same standards apply to state and federal juries and to grand and petit juries (see §§6.7–6.8). (Designations by type of jury and jurisdiction are supplied here parenthetically.)

In 1975 the Supreme Court held unconstitutional the exclusion of women from Louisiana juries caused by a state statute requiring women, but not men, to file written declarations of willingness to serve. *Taylor v Louisiana* (1975) 419 US 522. In 1974 the defense team for the *Attica*

*Brothers* case (see §3.26) successfully challenged the underrepresentation of women and students on the jury lists in Erie County, New York (see §§6.56, 6.62) (state petit). Exclusion of prospective members of the jury pool in the Detroit Recorders (criminal) Court was ruled unconstitutional when the reasons for exclusion included wearing silver nail polish, having liquor on one's breath, chewing gum, wearing a miniskirt, being kooky college kids, and being fully bearded. *Michigan v Viera* (Detroit Recorders Ct, No. A-152-598, A-152-697, April 30, 1970, unreported opinion) (state petit).

A challenge to underrepresentation of blacks in the South will fail if the percent of underrepresentation is too small, as in *Tennessee v Jefferson* (Tenn 1975) 529 SW2d 674, where blacks represented 19 percent of those eligible for jury duty, while only 16 percent of those summoned and reporting were blacks. Challenges were also filed unsuccessfully by the defense in the *Angela Davis* case (see §3.23) (state); the *Pentagon Papers* case (see §3.52) (federal); and the *Gainesville Eight* case (see §3.53), *United States v Briggs* (ND Fla 1973) 366 F Supp 1356 (federal). However, a change of venue was granted later in *Davis* (see chapter 7), and extensive voir dire was permitted in the *Davis* and *Pentagon Papers* cases (see examples of questions asked in chapters 9 and 11).

The underlying reasons it is difficult to win a challenge to jury selection methods are spelled out in §6.35.

## 2. Roots and Significance §6.2

A lawyer for an individual client who challenges a grand or petit jury list as being unrepresentative of the community is building on work done in the civil rights movement of the 1950s and 1960s. At the same time, the whole progressive movement benefits from the work of the individual lawyer for an individual client who helps to complete the task begun by the voter registration drives in the South and in black communities in the North and West.

The civil rights movement of the 1950s and the ensuing black power movement of the 1960s raised a continuum of demands, starting with desegregation of public schools and other public facilities, moving into voter registration and the election of blacks to public office, and then going into affirmative action programs in employment and education. One expected outcome of the voter registration drive was that more black names on the election rolls would mean more black names on jury lists and thus more blacks on grand and trial juries.

There are now innumerable examples of trials in which the outcome of the case was almost certainly different because one or more members of minority groups were seated and remained on the trial jury. See, e.g., the study of 37 juries that tried civil rights activists for sitting in at San Francisco hotels and auto showrooms. 24 *Lawyers Guild Practitioner* 10 (1965). With identical facts and the same law in all 37 cases, juries voted differently when at least one black person was part of the deliberations. There are indications that the second side of some grand jury investigations—into the operation of jails and other government agencies—is also altered by the presence of minority group members in the grand jury room.

However, the unwillingness of the government at many levels to address the basic problems of oppressed minority groups, the inability of government to solve these basic problems, and the revelations of government corruption during Watergate (among other reasons) caused members of oppressed groups not to register to vote in the same proportions as whites. As a result, minority group representation on grand and petit juries cannot be assured simply by demanding the use of voter registration lists as the sole source of names for jury lists. See §§6.59, 6.60, 6.71.

The extension of suffrage to new groups has likewise failed to correct jury selection limitations automatically. The Nineteenth Amendment guaranty of women's suffrage (ratified in 1920) only recently bore this part of its intended fruit when the Supreme Court rejected limitations on jury duty by women, *Taylor v Louisiana* (1975) 419 US 522; see §6.56. The Twenty-Fourth Amendment prohibition of poll taxes (ratified in 1964) stopped one form of discrimination against poor people. But few are on voting lists, or even on lists of telephone users, so they will not be selected for jury duty. See §6.53. And many members of the working poor cannot afford jury duty because of the low jury fees or fear of being fired for missing work. The Twenty-Sixth Amendment guaranty of voting rights for 18- to 21-year-old citizens (ratified in 1971) has not yet placed significant numbers of 18-to-21-year-olds on jury lists in some jurisdictions. See §6.54.

The demand that a fair cross-section of the community sit on the jury that will indict or try an individual accused of violating society's rules is thus a political as well as legal demand. This is appropriate, since a successful jury challenge depends on work by many people in the community, as well as the individual lawyer and client (see §§5.7–5.9). Once a fair cross-section is seated in the jury box owing to the use of a proper jury list, it takes determination on the part of the lawyer, the client, the trial judge, and, ultimately, the community (through pressure on the prosecuting attorney's office or large corporate party) to keep minority group members on the jury by putting a stop to the common practice of using peremptory challenges against members of minority groups (see chapter 20).

Challenges to grand jury and petit jury selection practices also serve a significant narrower function. They require lawyers to pore over pieces of the judicial process, checking descriptions of the people in their judicial districts against jury rolls for periods of time, just as lawyers in past generations pored over titles to pieces of real property, checking them against maps and conveyances for periods of time. A jury search, like a title search, requires paper work, patience, and determination. Like a careful title search, it will yield rich rewards for the client, perhaps preventing easements on the jury box by the cronies of judges and jury commissioners, or preventing waste in the judicial system due to reversals for lack of fair cross-section juries (see citations §6.1). It assists the bar and bench in the neverending task of patrolling the judicial system to keep it on its constitutionally appointed path.

### 3. Constitutional Bases §6.3

The constitutional bases for challenging grand and petit jury selection systems are clear. The Fifth Amendment guarantees indictment by grand jury in federal criminal cases. The Sixth Amendment guarantees trial by jury in federal criminal cases. The Seventh Amendment guarantees trial by jury in federal civil cases. See §1.4. The United States Supreme Court has ruled that the Fourteenth Amendment due process clause doe not require grand jury indictments of state criminal defendants (*Hernandez v Texas* (1954) 347 US 475); they may be charged by information. The Fourteenth Amendment equal protection clause does require a state that provides for indictments to select grand jurors fairly, using the same standards established for federal cases under the Fifth Amendment (see §6.7).

The Fourteenth Amendment due process clause requires trial by petit jury; that is, it incorporates the Sixth Amendment federal jury trial guaranty into defendants' protections against state governmental action. The equal protection clause of the Fourteenth Amendment requires that county petit jurors be fairly selected, using the standards established for federal cases under the Sixth and Seventh Amendments. Today, federal guaranties of equal protection come under a Supreme Court interpretation reading an equal protection clause into the Fifth Amendment due process clause (in *Bolling v Sharpe* (1954) 347 US 497), and are written into the 1968 Jury Selection and Service Act, 28 USC §§1861–1874.

The attack on an unrepresentative jury selection system must be against the pool from which the jurors are chosen, rather than against the unrepresentative character of a particular 6- or 12-person jury. See *Swain v Alabama* (1964) 380 US 202, 208; *Thiel v Southern Pac. Co.* (1946) 328 US 217, 220; *Strauder v West Virginia* (1880) 100 US 303, 309. There is no right to challenge an individual jury on the basis that its members are not representative of the community. See, e.g., *Carter v Jury Comm'n* (1970) 396 US 320, 339 (dictum).

## 4. Statutory Basis §6.4

"In a number of state and federal decisions, juror-selection systems have been invalidated because they violate applicable statutes governing selection procedures," David Kairys points out in "Juror Selection: The Law, a Mathematical Method of Analysis, and a Case Study," 10 *Am Crim L Rev* 771, 782 (1972):

> Courts quite uniformly and consistently require strict compliance with statutory mandates concerning both selection procedures and substantive standards for selection. See, *e.g.*, *Ballard v United States* (1946) 329 US 187, 195. The Court, dealing with a federal statute, stated that, "[t]he evil lies in the admitted exclusion of an eligible class or group . . . in disregard of the prescribed standards." See, *e.g.*, *Thiel v Southern Pac. Co.* (1946) 328 US 217, 220; *United States v Zirpolo* (3d Cir 1971) 450 F2d 424 (limitation of proportion of women, "is a departure from the statutory scheme"); *Abbott v Mines* (6th Cir 1969) 411 F2d 353; *Rabinowitz v United States* (5th Cir 1966) 366 F2d 34; *Labat v Bennett* (5th Cir 1966) 365 F2d 698 (en banc), *cert. denied* (1967) 386 US 991 (federal court dealing with state statute; alternate holding); *United States v Hoffa* (SD Fla 1961) 196 F Supp 25; *Allen v Georgia* (1964) 137 SE2d 711; *Walter v Indiana* (1935) 195 NE 268; *Maryland v Vincent* (1900) 91 Md 718; *Clare v Maryland* (1869) 30 Md 163; *Michigan v Viera* (Recorder's Court for the City of Detroit, Nos. A-152-598, A-152-697, Apr. 13, 1970); *Satterfield v Nebraska* (1961) 109 NW2d 415 ("[p]rovisions of statutes relating to the selection of grand and petit jurors are mandatory and must be strictly followed"); *Hammer v Oklahoma* (Okla 1959) 337 P2d 1097; *Jackson v Yockum* (Okla 1952) 244 P2d 1134; *Kell v Brillinger* (1877) 84 Pa 276.
>
> In all these cases, the courts have held, explicitly or implicitly, that noncompliance with the statutory mandates renders the jury illegal and invalidates its actions. As the Supreme Court held in *Ballard v United States* (1946) 329 US 187, 195:
>
>> [R]eversible error does not depend on a showing of prejudice in an individual case. The evil lies in the admitted exclusion of an eligible class or group in the community in disregard of the prescribed standards of jury selection . . . , [the] departure from the statutory scheme . . . . The injury is not limited to the defendant—there is an injury to the jury

system, to the law as an institution, to the community at large, and to the democratic ideal reflected in the processes of our courts.

Jury selection decisions based on violation of statutory law seem to fall into two categories. First, selecting officials may not initiate or use standards for selection, qualification, excuse or exclusion which are not clearly mandated by statute, regardless of whether such standards are sensible or whether the officials have a proper motive, such as excusing people whom service will inconvenience or who would usually request to be excused. See, *e.g.*, *Ballard*, *supra*, at 195; *Zirpolo* (explanation that proportion of women limited because women request to be excused more often, though believed by the court, is insufficient; reversal required "irrespective of purpose"); *Labat* (explanation that exclusion of daily wage earners, though not in statute, was for their convenience and because it is "fruitless" to summon them, held unacceptable); *Rabinowitz* ("the jury commissioners . . . treated the statutory standards as minimum qualifications"); *Walter*. In *Walter*, the Supreme Court of Indiana, in laying down the rationale for the strict compliance rule, said that no jury commissioner has the power to exclude a class of citizens that the legislature has pronounced eligible. To allow the commissioners to introduce their own subjective reasons in determining eligibility would result in the exclusion of not one, but numerous classes from jury service. Exclusion because of sex, political affiliation, religious belief, ancestry, occupation or location of residence in violation of the statutes result in an unlawful jury. 195 NE at 270–271.

Secondly, selecting officials may not violate statutory procedures for selection, particularly procedures relating to how and by whom the selection should be made. *Hammer v Oklahoma* (Okla 1959) 337 P2d 1097 (there a judge had drawn and used a second group of names before exhausting the first group in violation of the state statute; the court reversed the conviction, even in the face of another statute requiring only "substantial compliance" with the statutory mandate). If a particular statute designates a specific individual to make the selections, that duty may not be delegated. Further, if the actual procedure for selection of individuals from the "jury wheel" is specified, that procedure may not be altered.

## B. Part of Overall Trial Strategy §6.5

The effort to convince a trial jury to vote a large award of damages to a civil plaintiff may begin with a challenge to the list from which the jurors will be selected. The effort to convince a trial jury to acquit a defendant may begin with the effort to quash the indictment because it was handed down by a grand jury that did not represent a fair cross-section of the community. These beginnings may lead to an effort to throw out the list from which the trial jurors were selected, for the same reason. There is very little chance of winning a hard fought civil or criminal case unless the judge and jurors come to understand the nature of our judicial system, both the original theory and the way it works today. This also requires some lessons in the nature of our modern urban society, with its large and growing pockets of poverty, inadequate medical care, racism, and despair.

No incisive cross-examination, no surprise witness, no oratorical device in closing argument can bring the judge and jurors to understand how the plaintiff's injury has affected the plaintiff's life or why the criminal defendant acted in a certain way unless the jurors have first been forced to think in a new way about who *they* are, why they think as they do, and why they happen to be sitting in the jury box instead of in the plaintiff's seat or in the defendant's dock. These new insights will not come to 13 adults in a short period of time, although they may seem to hit a particular juror in a flash. For this reason, the trial lawyer must start a campaign to reeducate the judge and jury long before the trial begins. Similarly, before the lawyer can project an accurate image of the client and the community from which the client comes, the lawyer, also, must do some analysis of the forces that led the lawyer to be a lawyer and not an injured plaintiff or a criminal defendant.

In order to win a challenge to the composition of a grand or petit jury, the lawyer will have to ask for (and respect) the services of many nonlawyers: sociologists, statisticians, legal workers, volunteers, investigators, and staff people who work on surveys and check court records. This experience, if understood fully by the lawyer, should prepare him or her to handle the whole case in a different manner than is customary, with more cooperation between the attorney and the client, the client's family and friends, and sometimes a trial or defense committee.

Occasionally a small, unfunded defense team can mount a quick, successful challenge. See, e.g., *Nebraska v Janis and Buckman*, §6.59. Considering the mountain of paper work usually required to conduct a challenge to the jury selection process, a typical question is: Is it worth it when the chances of success are slight? Most trial lawyers experienced in handling major cases will answer yes, because they feel that the chances are not so slight if the challenge is conducted properly (see §6.1), and because they have seen a change in the attitudes of many judges as evidence is produced showing how unrepresentative the jury list really is (see §6.6). This can be true if the challenge itself is not successful.

In calculating the possibilities of winning a jury challenge before a trial judge or appellate bench, it may be well to recall certain remarkable examples of social consciousness in United States history. With only a few free black males able to vote, it was primarily free white male voters who backed the Thirteenth, Fourteenth, and Fifteenth Amendments guaranteeing rights to black former slaves. Males passed the Nineteenth Amendment guaranteeing the vote to women. People able to pay a poll tax passed the Twenty-Fourth Amendment abolishing such a tax for the enfranchisement of indigents. And people over 21 passed the Twenty-Sixth Amendment guaranteeing the vote to those 18 to 20. All these amendments were adopted by state legislatures or conventions. The same kinds of lawyers who sat as legislators or delegates now sit on state and federal benches deciding jury challenges.

Statistically, relatively few defendants are now indicted by grand juries at the state level. (The figure is only 4 percent in Los Angeles, according to Graham and Letwin, "The Preliminary Hearing in Los Angeles: Some Field Findings and Legal-Policy Observations," 18 *UCLA L Rev* 635 (1971).) However, the kind of big case that requires a staff large enough to handle a grand jury challenge is often the kind of case where indictment is used. The *Attica Brothers* jury challenge (see §3.26) is instructive. The defense committee found that neither the jury commissioner, nor the county attorney, nor the prosecutor was particularly anxious to defend a selection system that had existed virtually unchanged for 50 years (and that even included some old juror cards marked "negro" or "col."). But the *Attica Brothers* cases would not be popular ones for making changes unless the community came to understand the unfairness that had existed for years and that affected all litigants, not just the Attica prison defendants.

The Attica defense approached the League of Women Voters, Churchwomen United, and other community groups to discuss the need for jury reform. Occasionally this led to discussion of the prison conditions leading to the *Attica Brothers* cases. Sometimes funds were raised or the media decided to report the jury issue, if not the prison issues. When the motion to strike the Erie County jury pool was filed in April 1974, after months of work, the Attica defense invited several hundred community people to a breakfast briefing to hear the results of the jury study, which showed malfunctioning of the selection system and suggested the ramifications for every person going to trial in Erie County.

On June 27, 1974, the court did eliminate 97 percent of the old jury pools (see trial court opinion, §6.56). Years later, New York State amended its jury selection act to broaden sources of jury lists (see §2.26).

## C. Value of Unsuccessful Challenges §6.6

Even judges who reject jury challenges cannot unlearn what they have learned about the side of the communities they never see: the poor, black, young, blue-collar, transient, nonvoters who are neither criminal defendants nor personal injury plaintiffs but law-abiding citizens with the right to sit in judgment of their peers. Some of the judges' new attitudes rub off on the trial jurors as judges treat counsel and parties with more respect, if not empathy.

The determination of the motion for a change of venue (chapter 7) and the limits the judge will allow on voir dire (chapter 8) are based on the same factors raised in a jury selection challenge. Even if the judge ruled that the challenger did not sustain the burden of proving the jury list was unrepresentative in terms of race, ethnicity, sex, financial class, or background, the judge may have grown more sensitive to the cross-section requirement. This may show itself in the grant of a venue change or in the court's permission for, or assistance in, broader voir dire by counsel of prospective trial jurors drawn from the same list.

Intransigent judges who learn nothing affirmative from a grand or petit jury challenge are not convincing when they instruct a jury on the law, if the lawyers have educated the jurors about their unrepresentative character and they have learned that lesson. (This probably explains the acquittals in the New York *Panther 21* case—see §3.25.)

The media, of course, play a vital role in our judicial process. Reporters who sit through a tedious challenge to five years of jury lists and who skim through thc mountain of exhibits proving the unrepresentative character of those lists will remember these statistics as they describe the rest of the trial. In their reports, the plaintiff or defendant will emerge as both an individual and a representative of a group whose members do not sit in judgment on him or her. The pretrial accounts of the jury challenge have a way of influencing prospective trial jurors, though this is, of course, very indirect and more a matter of changing the general community attitude toward the case.

In sum, a well-publicized jury challenge may educate prospective trial jurors in the event of defeat, and, in the event of victory, may educate prospective jurors chosen under a new, representative plan.

## D. Materials Presented

### 1. State and Federal Cases Interchangeable §6.7

The Fifth Amendment requires grand juries to indict criminal defendants in federal cases. The Sixth Amendment requires petit juries to try criminal defendants in federal cases. The Fourteenth Amendment due process clause has been interpreted to require petit juries to try criminal defendants in state cases. *Duncan v Louisiana* (1968) 391 US

145. The Fourteenth Amendment equal protection clause requires that grand and petit juries be representative of the community in state cases.

In its opinion in *Taylor v Louisiana* (1975) 419 US 522, 526–538, a state case, the Supreme Court cited a series of federal and state cases, including *Ballard v United States* (1946) 329 US 187 and *Smith v Texas* (1940) 311 US 128, in reaching its decision invalidating a state system for selecting (petit) jurors.

In other words, "[o]nce the State chooses to provide grand and petit juries, whether or not constitutionally required to do so, it must hew to federal constitutional criteria in ensuring that the selection of membership is free of racial bias." *Carter v Jury Comm'n of Greene County* (1970) 396 US 320, 330, citing *Ex parte Virginia* (1880) 100 US 339, 346–347; *Virginia v Rives* (1880) US 313, 321. See also *Duncan v Louisiana*, 391 US at 158 n30.

## 2. Grand and Petit Jury Cases Interchangeable §6.8

The United States Supreme Court has so far retained its decision, in *Hurtado v California* (1884) 110 US 516, that indictment by grand jury is not required in order to satisfy due process requirements of the Fourteenth Amendment applicable to the states, while indictment is specifically required in federal cases by the Fifth Amendment, and trial by petit jury is required by the Sixth Amendment and by the due process clause of the Fourteenth Amendment (*Duncan v Louisiana* (1968) 391 US 145).

However, whenever a county grand jury is provided, it must meet the same standard as a petit jury in reasonably reflecting a fair cross-section of the community, which is the federal criterion required by the Sixth Amendment. *Carter v Jury Comm'n Greene County* (1970) 396 US 320. The equal protection clause of the Fourteenth Amendment sets the same standard in state cases. (On the interchangeability of due process and equal protection standards, see Ginger, "Due Process in Practice or Whatever's Fair," 25 *Hastings LJ* 897, 932–934 (1974).)

At the federal level, the 1968 Jury Selection and Service Act requires "grand and petit juries selected at random from a fair cross-section of the community." 28 USC §1861. For example, in *Test v United States* (1975) 420 US 28, the defendant was to be tried by a jury selected from the same master list used in selecting the grand jury that had indicted him.

It should also be noted that precedents based on constitutional challenges to jury selection methods may often be used when the challenge is based on a court's supervisory powers or on a statute (see *Taylor v Louisiana* (1975) 419 US 522, and discussion in §6.41).

### 3. Scope of Materials §6.9

It is not realistic to try to publish every bit of material that might be helpful in challenging jury selection methods, since this problem requires more types of pleadings, exhibits, and declarations than any other in this book, and lawyers are probably less familiar with the procedure than with any other discussed here. It is recommended that any lawyer planning a jury challenge read this chapter as an outline and then write for copies of pleadings, memos, sociological studies, examinations of expert witnesses, and other specific materials needed for a particular case. The chapter contains frequent references to materials collected in the Meiklejohn Civil Liberties Institute (Box 673, Berkeley, California 94701) that can be ordered as needed. The subliminal message is that a lawyer can write acceptable pleadings in this field without resort to form books once the basic structure of a grand jury challenge is understood.

The issue of youth as a cognizable class is hotly contested in a great many jurisdictions. Samples of many attacks on underrepresentation of 18- to 29-year-olds are therefore provided (see §§6.54–6.55). Similar materials must be developed and collected on other disputed cognizable classes, including those discussed in less detail in §§6.59–6.68.

## E. Recent Developments §6.10

It is now possible to keep up with the law on jury selection the same way you keep up with the law in any other field—by reading the relevant advance sheets, subscribing to services on trial advocacy or criminal law, and reading daily newspapers and legal newspapers. The *Index to Legal Periodicals*, *Current Law Index*, and *Legal Resource Index* provide provocative (and sometimes descriptive) titles to law review articles, comments, and notes in this field, indicating what is happening at the cutting edge of the law. It is a good idea occasionally to ask your law librarian for an index to journals on psychology, applied psychology, and the social sciences, to pick up new ideas from these disciplines.

Increasingly, lawyers are learning to use *Lexis* and *Westlaw* in order to find the latest cases and interesting parallels in other fields of law. It is always necessary to Shepardize all citations.

The Annual Supplement to these volumes will use recent developments sections throughout the book to describe new cases, ideas, and articles that are worthy of note, and to warn of cases overruled and of rules and statutes amended or repealed.

## II. PRELIMINARY WORK ON STATISTICAL CHALLENGE

### A. Timing of Challenge

#### 1. Federal §6.11

The Jury Selection and Service Act of 1968 spells out the procedures for challenging federal juries, including when to move. Under 28 USC §1867 the defendant and the attorney general may move to dismiss the indictment or stay the proceedings on the ground of substantial failure to comply with the provisions of §1867. The motion must be made before the voir dire examination begins or within seven days after they discover, or could have discovered by the exercise of diligence, the grounds for the motion.

#### 2. State §6.12

The proper timing of a challenge to the petit jury list may be a problem unless the state rules are clearly spelled out by statute or precedent. E.g., the 1980 Pennsylvania Act on jury selection, applicable throughout the state, does set forth the timing and procedures for challenging the array:

§4526. Challenging compliance with selection procedures.

(a) Challenge to array.—Within ten days after publication of the array a party to a matter on a then published list of cases scheduled for jury trial may petition the court to stay the proceedings in the case where he is a party and to select a new jury array, or for other appropriate relief, on the ground of failure to substantially comply with this subchapter.

(b) Hearing on petition.—At the hearing on the petition filed under subsection (a), the moving party is entitled to present in support of the petition the testimony of the jury commissioners or their clerks, any relevant records and papers not public or otherwise available used by the jury commissioners or their clerks and any other relevant evidence. If the court determines that in selecting persons to fill the array the commissioners have failed to substantially comply with this subchapter, the court shall stay the proceedings-requiring the service of jurors pending the selection of a new array in conformity with this subchapter or may grant other appropriate relief.

(c) Exclusive remedy.—Unless and until suspended or superseded by general rules, the procedures prescribed by this section are the exclusive means by which a person accused of a crime, the Commonwealth or a party in a civil case may challenge an array of jurors on the ground that the array was not selected in conformity with this subchapter.

. . .

(e) Challenge to panel of jurors.—A jury panel for the trial of any case may be challenged only on the grounds that it was not selected at random from the array. Such challenge must be made by a party immediately after the panel of jurors has been selected by the administrative staff of the court and before interrogation of jurors commences.

In the *Attica Brothers* case in New York (see §3.26), Justice King recognized the problem the defendants faced in trying to file their challenge at the proper time. He held that the defendants had proceeded at the only possible time under New York state law.

The procedures for initiating and conducting a challenge to a jury panel, including an evidentiary hearing if indicated, are set forth in Section 270.10 of the Criminal Procedure Law. The defendants conceded that a challenge to a jury panel can only be made at the time of trial and may be made "only by the defendant" who is then about to be tried.

The People contend that this motion is premature since none of the defendants has been brought to trial in Erie County or a panel returned for a term in which they are to be tried. These defendants were indicted in Wyoming County and their cases transferred to Erie County for all further proceedings and for trial by order of the Appellate Division, Fourth Department.

The People further contend that since the challenge is to the jury *pool* and not a jury *panel* there is no authority for this proceeding.

No statutory basis or procedure similar to that set forth in CPL §270.10 exists for a challenge to a jury pool. The cases, however, leave no doubt that a defendant's constitutional and common law right to a trial by jury of his peers and to the equal protection of the laws under the Fourteenth Amendment create, as an essential corollary, the right to assert the failure of those charged with the jury selection process to comply with the Constitutional guarantee and all State statutes, rules and regulations enacted to implement it.

The objections to the timeliness of the motion and to the lack of statutory authority for its initiation must yield to the overriding consideration that a present resolution of this question is necessary for the orderly administration of justice.

The United States Supreme Court held in 1979 that a federal habeas corpus petition can be used to claim racial discrimination in the selection of members of a state grand jury and will support the issuance of a writ setting aside a conviction and ordering the indictment quashed, even if the petit jury was properly selected and the trial was free of constitutional error. *Rose v Mitchell* (1979) 443 US 545.

One factor in favor of making a jury challenge early is that the data collected can be used to prepare juror profiles; see chapter 5.

## B. Discovery

### 1. Form: Preliminary Motion for Inspection of Court Records §6.15

*Source:* Adapted from successful motion for inspection, reproduction, and copying of records and papers in the custody of the jury clerk pursuant to 28 USC §1867(a), (d), and (f), filed Apr. 19, 1972, *United States v Russo* (see §3.52).

| | |
|---|---|
| ______________________, Plaintiff, | MOTION FOR INSPECTION, REPRODUCTION, AND COPYING OF RECORDS AND PAPERS IN THE CUSTODY OF THE JURY CLERK PURSUANT TO 28 USC §1867(a), (d), and (f); AFFIDAVITS; MEMORANDUM OF POINTS AND AUTHORITIES |
| v | |
| ______________________, Defendant. | |

Defendant moves, pursuant to 28 USC §1867(a), (d), and (f), for an order directing the jury clerk to allow defendant, [*his/her*] attorneys, and representatives of [*his/her*] attorneys to inspect, reproduce, and copy the contents of records and papers used by the jury clerk in the selection process for the grand jury that returned the above-entitled indictment and for the prospective petit jury in the instant case.

*COMMENT:* This motion is preparatory to a challenge to both grand and petit juries.

Defendant specifically requests the records necessary for [*him/her*] to conduct a statistical study of the jury selection process at each level of functioning for the [*Central*] District of [*California*].

Defendant's challenge to the jury selection process is contained in the accompanying motion to strike the jury array and to stay the proceedings, which is incorporated by this reference as if fully set forth here. The attached affidavit of [*Leo Breiman*], statistician, also supports this motion and is incorporated by this reference as if fully set forth here.

*COMMENT:* See §6.17 for affidavit.

Defense moves that:

1. Defendant and [*his/her*] representatives be provided with the [*3000*]

juror qualification questionnaires corresponding to the names drawn from the qualified jury wheel in the first draw using questionnaires from the [*1970*] mailing to persons whose names were provided from voter registration lists current as of [*December 1969*];

2. Defendant and [*his/her*] representatives be provided a random sample of [*6000*] of the approximately [*24,300*] juror qualification questionnaires that were received by the jury clerk and were not placed in the qualified jury wheel because the prospective juror was disqualified, exempt, or excused.

Defendant requests that [*he/she*] be provided with not only the above questionnaires, but also any other documents or papers relevant to the determination of the juror status of the persons in the above requested sample. This would include, but is not limited to, letters requesting excusal and orders granting excusal. Defendant requests the right to order the transcripts of jury impanelment (held every [*six*] months) at which prospective jurors contained in the sample were excused.

Defendant further requests that, if, in the judgment of the statistician who will be conducting the study, statistical accuracy requires that certain prospective jurors in the sample be contacted directly to provide information that was not completed on the juror qualification questionnaire (namely, the optional questions on race and occupation), this court grant permission to defendant and [*his/her*] representatives to make such limited contact. If this permission is granted, defendant would not make such contact without prior consultation with the Court and the United States attorney.

Defendant does not request the names of any prospective jurors contained in the requested sample, except as it may be necessary for the purpose outlined in the preceding paragraph.

Defendant further moves this court for an order requiring the jury clerk, and such other assistants as may be necessary, to provide defendant with all information at their disposal concerning the procedures followed in implementing [*General Order No. 55*] of the [*Central*] District of [*California*].

This motion is based on all the attached affidavits, the attached memorandum of points and authorities, the files and records in this case, the accompanying motion to strike the jury array and stay the proceedings, and any oral or documentary evidence that may be presented at a hearing on this motion.

Respectfully submitted,

By____________________
Attorney for Defendant

## 2. Memo in Support of Motion for Inspection §6.16

In light of the unequivocal decision of the United States Supreme Court in *Test v United States* (1975) 420 US 28, there should be no difficulty in obtaining adequate discovery of all jury selection material necessary to mount a successful federal challenge.

In *Test*, the Supreme Court held that the Jury Selection and Service Act of 1968, in 28 USC §1867(f),

> makes clear that a litigant[3] has essentially an *unqualified* right to inspect jury lists.[4] It grants access in order to aid parties in the "preparation" of motions challenging jury selection procedures. Indeed, without inspection, a party almost invariably would be unable to determine whether he has a potentially meritorious jury challenge. Thus, an unqualified right to inspection is required not only by the plain text of the statute, but also by the statute's overall purpose of insuring "grand and petit juries selected at random from a fair cross-section of the community." 28 USC §1861.

3. The statute grants the rights to challenge selection procedures and inspect lists to the United States and the defendant in a criminal case, and to any party in a civil case.
4. The statute does limit inspection to "reasonable times." No issue of timeliness has been raised in this Court.

If difficulties arise in obtaining the kind of information required by a statistical consultant, as described in the affidavit in §6.17, counsel can write to Meiklejohn Civil Liberties Institute, Box 673, Berkeley, California 94701 for copies of memoranda filed in other federal cases.

In 1971 the United States Supreme Court, relying on a complete statistical analysis of the jury selection process that was part of the record, reversed the conviction in *Alexander v Louisiana* (1971) 405 US 625. This analysis was the result of the defendant's inspection of the jury questionnaires and other records, which showed that the final jury array had only 5 percent blacks while the population had 20 percent. For discovery problems at the state court level, see §6.18.

## 3. Form: Supporting Affidavit §6.17

*Source:* Excerpts from affidavit of Leo Breiman, dated Apr. 18, 1972, in support of successful motion for inspection, *United States v Russo* (see §3.52), based on data from the 1970 census. Similar data is collected in each 10-year census.

I, [*Leo Breiman*], being duly sworn, depose and say:

I am a statistical consultant doing work in the [*Los Angeles*] area. I have appended to this affidavit a resume of my professional qualifications.

I have been asked by the defense to gather and analyze data in order to answer the following questions:

(1) Does the list of registered voters in the desiganted area accurately reflect the distribution of the general population of the area?

(2) Does the final jury array accurately reflect the distribution of the general population and/or the voter registration lists of the area?

(3) If the analysis in question 2 reveals significant differences, study and analyze the selection procedure at each level leading to these differences.

The designated area consists of the [*seven-county*] area forming the [*Central*] District of [*California*]. Population distribution is defined as being the proportions of the population that fall into designated groups and strata. In particular I was asked to consider the following characteristics: age, annual income, race (black, Mexican-American), education, sex, occupation, and rural/urban residence.

After a preliminary study, my conclusion was that the above questions could be answered only if the court would direct the jury commissioner to release certain data to me. None of the requested data pertains to presently qualified jurors or to names on the master wheel that still have a chance of being qualified on the next draw. On the other hand, all of the requested data are from the current ([*1970*]) master wheel, so that the conclusions reached will be timely.

### A. Current Evidence Relevant to the Above Questions

The most thorough current study of the voter registration population was carried out by the United States Bureau of the Census in its [*November 1970*] *Current Population Survey*. This survey sampled 50,000 households across the country with a sample of about 120,000 individuals. The nationwide summary is published under the title [*"Voting and Registration in the election of November 1970" (U.S. Bureau of the Census. Current Population Reports; Population Characteristics Series P-20, No. 228, December 1971)*]. This publication compares the distribution of the 21-year-old and over population of the United States to the distribution of the registered voter population with respect to the particular characteristics listed above. Among the stated conclusions are that the following groups were significantly underrepresented in voting participation as compared to their proportion of the over-20 population: persons under 30 years of age; Negroes; the low annual income group; the low years-of-school-completed group; women; certain employment and occupational categories.

The same holds true of the voter registration population. First, we did an analysis of the age characteristics of the over-20 population compared with the registered voter population. This is summarized in the table below:

| *Group* | *Percentage of over-20 population* | *Percentage of registered voters* |
|---|---|---|
| 21-29 | 19.6 | 13.5 |
| 30-64 | 64.5 | 69.3 |
| 65 and over | 15.9 | 17.2 |

If the 18- to 20-year-old population is included (as estimated from US Bureau of the Census, Current Population Report, "Educational Attainment: March 1971," No. 230, Series P-20 (December 1971)) and counted as nonregistered, then more than one out of every four people is under 30 (26.2 percent) but less than one out of every seven registered voters is under 30 (13.5). Indications are from those states where data are available on 18- to 20-year-old voter participation, that the registration is probably significantly less than that in the 21- to 29-year-old group. (US Bureau of the Census, Report No. 230, Series P-20 (December 1971).) Thus, the plausible prediction is that with 18- to 20-year-old registration, the discrepancy between the under-30 and the over-30 age groups in voter registration representation will become larger.

Age is the most significant index affecting degree of voter registration representation in the nationwide figures, but others are also important. In particular, the effects of race, income, and educational level are easily discernible. Combinations of these factors result in even more unbalanced representation. For example, in the over-20 population, the group less than 25 years old making less than $5,000 annually is about one in every 45 people (2.2 percent), but it numbers only about one in every 110 people in the voter registration lists (0.9 percent). The possibility exists that this disproportion is even greater in the [*Central*] District counties since [*California has a larger percentage of young people than does the country as a whole*]. (See US Bureau of the Census, Current Population Reports; Population Characteristics, "Educational Attainment: March 1971," No. 230, Series P-20 (December 1971).)

As to the second question, there is very little information available that compares registered voter distribution with the distribution of qualified jurors.

### B. Usable Data—Sources, Availability, Cost, and Accuracy

I thoroughly investigated possible sources of voter registration characteristics for the [*seven-county*] area. In tracking down possible sources I discussed the matter with the following: [*United States Bureau of the Census, Los Angeles Office and Washington Office; UCLA Survey Research Center; Secretary of State, Sacramento, Electronic Data Processing Division; Registrar of Voters, Los Angeles/etc.*]

There are only two sources from which we can get the required data. The first is the [*November 1970*] survey made by the Bureau of the Census mentioned above. I discussed with the Demographic Survey Division, Bureau of the Census, Washington, D.C., the possibility of getting the data summarized for the [*seven-county*] area in question.

*COMMENT:* The affidavit then explains that this would take too long and be too expensive for reasons that are given in detail. Other alternatives may be described and their inadequacies similarly explained.

### C. The Proposed Analysis Plan

As a result of my preliminary investigation, I concluded that the only feasible method for analyzing both the final jury array and the registered voter populations would be to sample directly (1) the questionnaires corresponding to names on the master wheel drawn from the registered voter population, and (2) the questionnaires filled out by jurors in the final jury array. But a primary consideration in designing the sampling scheme was not to compromise the confidential position of names on the master wheel that were still available for the next draw. My understanding is that of the approximately [*36,800*] names drawn in [*1970*] from the voter registration lists who filled out questionnaires, approximately [*24,300*] were not placed in the qualified jury wheel, leaving [*12,500*]. At [*six*]-month intervals, [*3,000*] of these [*12,500*] names on the qualified jury wheel were sent summonses, of which about [*1,200*] were finally qualified.

I propose that:

[*Insert specific requests made in motion,*
i.e., *paragraphs 1 and 2 in §6.15*]

The point of this sampling scheme is that it produces a sample of [*9000*], preserving the same proportions as the original draw of [*36,000*] completed questionnaires from the master wheel, and at the same time using information involving only individuals who either are no longer qualified in the present [*six*]-month period or were disqualified or excused.

The [*9000*] questionnaires are data randomly sampled from the population of registered voters. The final [*1200*] questionnaires filled out by the jurors who qualified are a random sample from the population of members of the final jury array. The structure of the sample is such that, if necessary, I can analyze the selection procedure at each level. The analysis of the data on these questionnaires will give fairly accurate estimates of the characteristics of the two populations, at a fairly reasonable cost.

*COMMENT:* The affidavit goes on to explain the lack of significance of undelivered questionnaires. But in the *Attica Brothers* case (see §3.26), the defense team learned that the post office frequently did not bother to forward mail delivered in the black neighborhoods. As a result, fewer questionnaires were completed and returned from these areas. The defense convinced the Erie County jury commissioner to send more questionnaires to neighborhoods with lower return rates to counteract the higher mobility in those low-income areas.

A more serious problem is posed by the fact that the last two questions on the questionnaire (involving race and occupation) are optional. My understanding is that these questions are not answered in [*10 to 15 percent*] of the questionnaires. Since those declining to answer may include a large proportion of minority races, ignoring these partially completed questionnaires may cause a serious bias. A sound method for filling in the missing race data is as follows: From the address and/or zip code number, the individual's census tract location can be determined. The first-round census data give the racial distributions for each census tract. For example, if the census tract is 80 percent black and 20 percent white, tally that individual as .8 black and .2 white.

The missing occupation data will be harder to supply. But as the Voter Characteristics Report indicates that occupation is not as significant a determination of registration as the other characteristics listed, we may either ignore it altogether or assign it in two or three broad categories by census tract proportions (assuming that the latter are available).

*COMMENT:* The affidavit next discusses the need to obtain data on the prospective jurors' annual incomes, which are not supplied by the official jury questionnaire. It then discusses the commonly accepted statistical procedure for assessing the accuracy of the proposed estimation method. For other approaches, see Kairys, "Juror Selection," 10 *Am Crim L Rev* 771 (1972); Sperlich and Jaspovice, "Statistical Decision Theory and the Selection of Grand Jurors," 2 *Hastings Const L Q* 75 (1975).

Dated: April 18, 1972

[Signed] Leo Breiman

### 4. Sample: Argument on Appeal When Discovery Denied §6.18

*Source:* Adapted from appellants' opening brief, filed Dec. 1974 in California court of appeal, *California v Burt* (see §3.24).

The defense had an independent right to discover evidence that would have permitted it to challenge the county's petit jury selection procedures for failure to comply with the law.

*COMMENT:* The evidence sought was the names of petit jurors and data concerning them; see §6.15.

The question raised here complements the issue decided in *In re Wells* (1971) 98 Cal Rptr 1, and *Montez v Superior Court* (1970) 88 Cal Rptr 736. In these two cases the defense presented statistical evidence on the characteristics of the grand jury pools but had been prevented from calling the judge-selectors of the nominees to examine them as to their selection methods. The courts deciding those cases held that the failure of the statistical evidence to establish discrimination had not justified denying the defendants access to other evidence about the selection process that could still show the invalidity of the system.

[*Describe similar or analogous facts in instant case,* e.g.]

Here the opposite problem is presented. The judge specifically ruled that the statistical evidence was unnecessary because "the testimony from the jury commissioner accomplishes the same purpose." It did not accomplish the same purpose. Even with all the apparent elements of random selection, members of the commissioner's office could have practiced intentional discrimination at two steps in the process: the screening of the returned questionnaires and the selection of prospective jurors to be summoned from the list of 3000. The second procedure was computerized after the hearing before Judge Campbell and before trial, however. "But the courts have consistently held that statistics speak louder than the jury commissioners" (*Brooks v Beto* (5th Cir 1966) 366 F2d 1, 12). Surely a court cannot conclude the inquiry at the point where the commissioners claim they operate a fair system. Defendants must be permitted to gather the statistics.

Moreover, even if the system operated exactly as the witness stated, there was no basis for withholding the evidence sought. A survey of prospective jurors could well have demonstrated that a process that selected those who registered to vote, returned their jury questionnaires, and were found competent, not exempt, and not excusable failed to produce a jury pool that represented a cross-section of the community. Even the first link in the chain of inferences on which the judge relied, the conclusive presumption that total dependence on the voter registration list was valid, was completely unjustified.

*COMMENT:* For discussion of the inadequacy of voter registration lists only in compiling lists for jury duty, see §6.60.

### C. Recent Developments §6.19

See §6.10.

## III. CHALLENGING JURY SELECTION METHODS

### A. Establishing a Prima Facie Case of Exclusion or Underrepresentation §6.21

The law on establishing a prima facie case was spelled out by the Supreme Court in *Castaneda v Partida* (1977) 430 US 482, 492–494:

> This Court has long recognized that "it is a denial of the equal protection of the laws to try a defendant of a particular race or color under an indictment issued by a grand jury . . . from which all persons of his race or color have, solely because of that race or color, been excluded by the State . . . ."[12] *Hernandez v Texas* (1954) 347 US 475, 477. See *Alexander v Louisiana* (1972) 405 US 625, 628; *Carter v Jury Comm'n* (1970) 396 US 320, 330. See also *Peters v Kiff* (1972) 407 US 493, 497 (plurality opinion); *id.*, at 507 (dissenting opinion). While the earlier cases involved absolute exclusion of an identifiable group, later cases established the principle that substantial under-representation of the group constitutes a constitutional violation as well, if it results from purposeful discrimination. See *Turner v Fouche* (1970) 396 US 346; *Carter v Jury Comm'n, supra*; *Whitus v Georgia* (1967) 385 US 545, 552; *Swain v Alabama* (1965) 380 US 202; *Cassell v Texas* (1950) 339 US 282. Recent cases have established the fact that an official act is not unconstitutional *solely* because it has a racially disproportionate impact. *Washington v Davis* (1976) 426 US 229, 239; see *Arlington Heights v Metropolitan Housing Corp.* (1977) 429 US 252, 264–265. Nevertheless, as the Court recognized in *Arlington Heights*, "[s]ometimes a clear pattern, unexplainable on grounds other than race, emerges from the effect of the state action even when the governing legislation appears

---

12. Cases in this Court holding unconstitutional discriminatory selection procedures in the grand jury context include *Alexander v Louisiana* (1972) 405 US 625; *Arnold v North Carolina* (1964) 376 US 773; *Eubanks v Louisiana* (1958) 356 US 584; *Reece v Georgia* (1955) 350 US 85; *Cassell v Texas* (1950) 339 US 282; *Hill v Texas* (1942) 316 US 400; *Smith v Texas* (1940) 311 US 128; *Pierre v Louisiana* (1939) 306 US 354; *Rogers v Alabama* (1904) 192 US 226; *Carter v Texas* (1900) 177 US 442; and *Bush v Kentucky* (1883) 107 US 110.

neutral on its face." *Id.*, at 266. In *Washington v Davis*, the application of these principles to the jury cases was considered:

> It is also clear from the cases dealing with racial discrimination in the selection of juries that the systematic exclusion of Negroes is itself such an "unequal application of the law . . . as to show intentional discrimination." . . . A prima facie case of discriminatory purpose may be proved as well by the absence of Negroes on a particular jury combined with the failure of the jury commissioners to be informed of eligible Negro jurors in a community . . . . or with racially non-neutral selection procedures . . . . With a prima facie case made out, "the burden of proof shifts to the State to rebut the presumption of unconstitutional action by showing that permissible racially neutral selection criteria and procedures have produced the monochromatic result." *Alexander* [*v Louisiana*, 405 US] at 632.

426 US at 241. See *Arlington Heights*, *supra*, at 266 n13.

Thus, in order to show that an equal protection violation has occurred in the context of grand jury selection, the defendant must show that the procedure employed resulted in substantial under-representation of his race or of the identifiable group to which he belongs. The first step is to establish that the group is one that is a recognizable, distinct class, singled out for different treatment under the laws, as written or as applied. *Hernandez v Texas*, 347 US at 478–479. Next, the degree of under-representation must be proved, by comparing the proportion of the group in the total population to the proportion called to serve as grand jurors, over a significant period of time. *Id.*, at 480. See *Norris v Alabama* (1935) 294 US 587. This method of proof, sometimes called the "rule of exclusion," has been held to be available as a method of proving discrimination in jury selection against a delineated class.[13] *Hernandez v Texas*, 347 US at 480. Finally, as noted above, a selection procedure that is susceptible to abuse or not racially neutral supports the presumption of discrimination raised by the statistical showing. *Washington v Davis*, 426 US at 241; *Alexander v Louisiana*, 405 US at 630. Once the defendant has shown substantial under-representation of his group, he has made out a prima facie case of discriminatory purpose, and the burden then shifts to the State to rebut that case.

What statistics will establish a prima facie case? In *Castaneda*, the Supreme Court discussed this question in the text and in a lengthy footnote, 430 US at 495–496:

---

13. The idea behind the rule of exclusion is not at all complex. If a disparity is sufficiently large, then it is unlikely that it is due solely to chance or accident, and, in the absence of evidence to the contrary, one must conclude that racial or other class-related factors entered into the selection process. See *Arlington Heights v Metropolitan Housing Corp.* (1977) 429 US 252, 266 n13; *Washington v Davis* (1976) 426 US 229, 241; *Eubanks v Louisiana*, 356 US 587; *Smith v Texas*, 311 US at 131. Cf. n17 *infra*.

The disparity proved by the 1970 Census statistics showed that the population of the county was 79.1% Mexican-American, but that, over an 11-year period, only 39% of the persons summoned for grand jury service were Mexican-American. This difference of 40% is greater than that found significant in *Turner v Fouche*, *supra* (60% Negroes in the general population, 37% on the grand jury lists). Since the State presented no evidence showing why the 11-year period was not reliable, we take it as the relevant base for comparison. The mathematical disparties that have been accepted by this Court as adequate for a prima facie have all been within the range presented here. For example, in *Whitus v Georgia*, *supra*, the number of Negroes listed on the tax digest amounted to 27.1% of the population, but only 9.1% of those on the grand jury venire. The disparity was held to be sufficient to make out a prima facie case of discrimination. See *Sims v Georgia* (1967) 389 US 404 (24.4% on tax lists, 4.7% on grand jury lists); *Jones v Georgia* (1967) 389 US 24 (19.4% on tax lists, 5.0% on jury lists). We agree with the District Court and the Court of Appeals that the proof in this case was enough to establish a prima facie case of discrimination against the Mexican-Americans in the Hidalgo County grand jury selection.[17]

---

17. If the jurors were drawn randomly from the general population, then the number of Mexican-Americans in the sample could be modeled by a binomial distribution. See Finkelstein, "The Application of Statistical Decision Theory to the Jury Discrimination Cases," 80 *Harv L Rev* 338, 353–356 (1966). See generally P. Howel, *Introduction to Mathematical Statistics* 58–61, 79–86 (4th ed. 1971); F. Mosteller, R. Rourke, & G. Thomas, *Probability With Statistical Applications* 130–146, 270–291 (2d ed. 1970). Given that 79.1% of the population is Mexican-American, the expected number of Mexican-Americans among the 870 persons summoned to serve as grand jurors over the 11-year period is approximately 688. The observed number is 339. Of course, in any given drawing some fluctuation from the expected number is predicted. The important point, however, is that the statistical model shows that the results of a random drawing are likely to fall in the vicinity of the expected value .... The measure of the predicted fluctuations from the expected value is the standard deviation, defined for the binomial distribution as the square root of the product of the total number in the sample (here 870) times the probability of selecting a Mexican-American (0.791) times the probability of selecting a non-Mexican-American (0.209) .... Thus, in this case the standard deviation is approximately 12. As a general rule for such large samples, if the difference between the expected value and the observed number is greater than two or three standard deviations, then the hypothesis that the jury drawing was random would be suspect to a social scientist. The 11-year data here reflect a difference between the expected and observed number of Mexican-Americans of approximately 29 standard deviations. A detailed calculation reveals that the likelihood that such a substantial departure from the expected value would occur by chance is less than 1 in $10^{140}$.

The data for the 2½-year period during which the state district judge supervised the selection process similarly support the inference that the exclusion of Mexican-Americans did not occur by chance. Of 220 persons called to serve as grand jurors, only 100 were Mexican-Americans. The expected Mexican-American representation is approximately 174 and the standard deviation, as calculated from the binomial model, is approximately 6. The discrepancy between the expected and observed values is more than 12 standard deviations. Again, a detailed calculation shows that the likelihood of drawing not more than 100 Mexican-Americans by chance is negligible, being less than 1 in $10^{25}$.

See discussion of standard deviations at §6.83.

Respondent's brief provides a useful compilation of federal cases not mentioned in the Court opinion.

Prima facie case made:

*Murrah v Arkansas* (8th Cir 1976) 532 F2d 105: 19.7 percent adult black population, but only 5.6 to 7.3 percent on jury roll; *Black v Curb* (5th Cir 1972) 464 F2d 165: 69 percent total black population and 60 percent adult black population, but only 35 percent black representation on jury list; *Colson v Smith* (5th Cir 1971) 438 F2d 1075: 30.7 percent adult black population and 14 percent black taxpayers, but only 1.2 percent blacks on venires and 1.3 percent black representation in the grand jury pool; *Preston v Mandeville* (5th Cir 1970) 428 F2d 1392: 29.3 percent adult black population, but only 15 percent black representation on master jury roll; *Muniz v Beto* (5th Cir 1970) 434 F2d 697: between 15 and 20 percent registered Mexican-American voters, but only 3 percent of grand jurors Mexican-American during ten-year period; *Salary v Wilson* (5th Cir 1969) 415 F2d 467: 55 percent adult black population, but only 12.9 and 7 percent black representation on jury rolls in last two years; *Jones v Smith* (5th Cir 1969) 420 F2d 774: 31.9 percent adult black population and 15.3 percent black taxpayers, but only 4.85 percent black representation on single jury panel drawn from segregated tax digest; *Pullum v Greene* (5th Cir 1968) 396 F2d 251: 55.5 percent total black population, but only 17.9 and 21.7 percent black representation on revised jury lists; *Goins v Allgood* (5th Cir 1968) 391 F2d 692: 32 percent total black population, but only 16 percent blacks on grand juries; *Rabinowitz v United States* (5th Cir 1966) 366 F2d 34 (en banc): 34.5 percent black voters, but only 5.9 percent black representation on jury lists; *Labat v Bennett* (5th Cir 1966) 365 F2d 698 (en banc): 32 percent total black population, but only 3.7 percent black representation on venires; *Scott v Walker* (5th Cir 1966) 358 F2d 561 (en banc): 15 percent registered black voters, but only 3 to 5 blacks among 300 veniremen over previous five-year period, though proof was scarce; *Davis v Davis* (5th Cir 1966) 361 F2d 770 (en banc): 20 percent total black population and 16 percent adult male black population, but only 7.5 percent blacks on jury venires, and jury commissioners failed to seek out qualified blacks; *Vanleeward v Rutledge* (5th Cir 1966) 369 F2d 584: 30 percent adult black population and 14 percent black taxpayers, but only .75 percent blacks on jury lists.

Prima facie case not made:

*Thompson v Sheppard* (5th Cir 1974) 490 F2d 830: 30.2 percent total black population, and 19.2 percent black representation on jury lists drawn at random from county voting list; *Simmons v United States* (5th Cir 1969) 406 F2d 456: 20.48 percent black population, and 15.77 percent black representation in jury wheel; *Hunt v United States* (5th Cir 1968) 400 F2d 306: 35 percent total Mexican-American population, and 17.5 percent Mexican-American representation in jury pool.

On a showing of a prima facie case of discrimination, the burden shifts to the other side to prove the absence of discriminatory intent. Rebuttal evidence may include testimony from the judges responsible for the selection of jurors concerning the method of selection and the qualifications. *United States v Manbeck* (1981) 514 F Supp 141, citing *Duren v Missouri* (1979) 439 US 357, at 368 and *Castaneda v Partida* (1977) 430 US 482, at 498.

### 1. Not Necessary to Prove Intent §6.22

When the opposition admits the challenger's allegations about the results of the jury selection system used in a case, the challenger has a much easier task in establishing a prima facie case of underrepresentation because the issue becomes a purely legal one. For example, in *Carmical v Craven* (9th Cir 1971) 457 F2d 582, 585, the Ninth Circuit found a prima facie case based on the results of the "clear thinking" intelligence test used in Alameda County, California (quoted in §2.35):

> The facts accepted as true for purposes of this appeal established a prima facie case of class exclusion from the jury selection process. In *Whitus v Georgia* (1967) 385 US 545, jurors were selected from tax digests previously maintained on a segregated basis. Blacks constituted 27.1 percent of persons potentially eligible for jury service. Only 9.1 percent of the grand jury venire and 7.8 percent of the petit jury venire were blacks. There was no evidence that any of the 27.1 percent eligible black jurors were disqualified from jury service. There existed a 3-to-1 disparity between blacks eligible for jury service and those on the grand jury venire and a 3.5-to-1 disparity on the petit jury venire. Ten out of 123 persons on both venires, or 8.1 percent, were blacks, a disparity of 3.3-to-1. Here, the test excluded from jury service 81.5 percent of the registered voters from black and low income neighborhoods but only 14.5 percent of the registered voters from predominantly white areas, leaving 18.5 percent of the blacks but 85.5 percent of the whites. The state offered no evidence that any voter disqualified by the test was disqualified for other reasons. The ratio of eligible black and low income persons who would be eligible for jury service if the test excluded the same percentage of them as it did whites to those placed on the master list is 4.6 to 1, a disparity greater than that condemned in *Whitus*.

The court then found that:

> The sole issue on appeal is a narrow question of law: Is proof alone that the "clear thinking" test in fact resulted in large-scale exclusion of identifiable classes of veniremen otherwise eligible for jury service sufficient to make out a prima facie case of constitutionally impermissible jury selection, or, as the state contends, must Carmical also have offered evidence that the "clear thinking" test was intentionally designed to produce that result? 457 F2d at 586.

Following Supreme Court precedents, the Ninth Circuit held:

> When a jury selection system actually results in master jury panels from which identifiable classes are grossly excluded, the subjective intent of those who develop and enforce the system is immaterial. [Citing *Norris v Alabama* (1935) 294 US 587, 598.]
>
> . . . The lack of specific intent to discriminate on the part of Alameda County's jury officials cannot offset the grossly discriminatory effect of their jury selection process. (*Cf. Griggs v Duke Power Co.* (1971) 401 US 424; *Gaston County v United States* (1969) 395 US 285; *Gomillion v Lightfoot* (1960) 364 US 339.)

457 F2d at 587. The court noted that:

> The opinions take into account the historical prevalence of intentional discrimination against Negroes, but the Court has never implied that the absence of that factor destroys a prima facie case. Rather, the Court has charged state officials with an affirmative duty to seek, and include within the jury selection process, all persons qualified under state law.

The "systematic and intentional exclusion" requirement is discussed in Note, "Challenging New York Grand Jury Composition: The Barrier of the 'Systematic and Intentional Exclusion' Requirement," 6 *Fordham Urb LJ* 317–332 (1978).

## 2. Comparision of Jury List with Other Lists §6.23

Over 50 volunteers spent more than 500 hours examining the files and other records of the Erie County, New York, jury commissioner in the *Attica Brothers* case challenge (see §3.26). The figures on certain cognizable classes (e.g., blacks, women, and youth) present in the jury pool were compared with census figures on their presence in the population of the county and with figures on their presence on voter registration lists. The defense presented the following table to the county court:

| | *% of Population* | *% of Registered Voters* | *% of Jury Pool* | *Under-representation* |
|---|---|---|---|---|
| Blacks (age 21-74) | 8.4 | 7.4 | 5.5 | 34% |
| Women (age 21-74) | 53 | 53 | 16 | 68% |
| Young people (age 21-29) | 20 | 17 | 3 | 82% |

Bonora, "Attica Jury Challenge: II," *Conspiracy*, Sept. 1974, p. 16.

In effect, the court ignored these data, holding the defense to the burden of proving intentional and systematic discrimination against cognizable classes, citing *New York v Chestnut* (Ct of App 1970) 26 NY2d 481, 488, and rejecting "youth" as a cognizable class. However, the court did find that the jury commissioners had deliberately discriminated against women and students, two cognizable classes, though without intent to diminish representation of these groups in the jury wheel. (The staff of the jury commission stated repeatedly they had eliminated names of women and students without waiting for them to seek excuses because customarily many women and students requested excuses, so the result would be the same and time would be saved by the staff's "informally granting" excuses before they were sought.)

The defense found no underrepresentation of women through use of the registered voters list, and underrepresentation of only 1 percent among blacks and only 3 percent among young people. This suggested that the use of voter registration lists, at least in Erie County, New York, was not a major cause of underrepresentation on juries. (But see §§6.60 and 6.61.) Clearly, any trial team would have to show very great disparity in order to convince a trial court to order jury commissioners to shift to a different, untried list of citizens that might be more representative than a list of registered voters. This occurred in Pennsylvania, starting with a challenge to a Philadelphia jury list and ending with a new statewide jury statute authorizing the use of several sources for jurors. Pa Stat Ann, title 42, §4521, discussed in §6.1. In England, where there is no requirement of registration in order to vote, jurors are selected from the list of residents, see chapter 23.

## B. Procedures §6.24

The two common ways in which jury challenges are decided are by trial courts on motions to quash grand jury indictments or to strike petit jury lists and by appellate courts when the issue is raised as a point on appeal after verdict. The third way, seldom used, is when citizens sue jury commissioners demanding to have their names placed on jury lists (see §6.43).

When a convicted defendant seeks to have his conviction reversed on appeal due to improper methods of selecting grand or petit jurors, the appellate court usually limits its considerations to whether the selection method used was constitutionally infirm. Little consideration is given to how a proper selection method could be established. Of course, the lawyer must be prepared to make a full case before the trial judge on the motion to quash or to strike, since the record made on this motion is the only one that can be used if the motion is lost, the defendant is convicted after trial, and counsel seeks to raise improper jury selection as a point on appeal.

The procedural steps in a grand jury challenge, following the preliminary work (described in §§6.11–6.18), include filing a motion to quash the indictment (§6.25), filing a memorandum of points and authorities in support of the motion (when required by statute or court rule, and even when not required, in order to acquaint the court with the basis for the motion), filing supporting declarations by experts who will later testify, holding a hearing for the taking of testimony in support of the motion, and, where necessary, taking an appeal from a denial of the motion. Most of these steps are also required in a trial jury challenge.

Counsel should select from the following legal arguments in support of a jury challenge (§§6.32–6.68) only those relevant to the particular case. It is considered good strategy to contest underrepresentation of only those cognizable classes for whom there is crystal clear statistical evidence. The conduct of the evidentiary hearing is described briefly in §§6.81–6.84.

It is only when a trial judge seriously considers finding the present system unconstitutional and quashing the indictment or jury list that consideration is given to how a constitutional system could be established. Clearly, counsel cannot demand that one system be abolished unless a better system can be put in its place (see §6.71).

## C. Form: Motion to Quash Indictment §6.25

*Source:* Adapted from motion to set aside and quash the indictment (under Penal Code §995) due to grand jury irregularities, dated Sept.

15, 1973, *California v Bingham* (see §2.21). This motion was successful in the trial court, reversed on appeal, and the reversal was upheld by the California Supreme Court.

A similar motion can be drafted challenging a petit jury selection system.

Defendant [*Johnny Larry Spain*] by and through [*his*] attorneys, moves:

I. To set aside the indictment returned by the grand jury on [*October 1, 1971*], and to quash that indictment in this action on the grounds that it was not found, endorsed, or prescribed by law, in that:

A. The statutes under which the grand jury was formed are unconstitutional on their face;

B. The statutes under which the grand jury was formed are unconstitutional as applied because:

1. The system impermissibly vested total discretion in the [*judges*] of the [*Marin*] County [*Superior*] Court for the initial selection of nominees, the selection of organizations from which nominees are obtained, and the elimination of "unsuitable" prospective nominees;
2. The system permitted the [*judges*] of the [*Marin*] County [*Superior*] Court to "handpick" selectees in order to achieve the appearance of adequate representation on the grand jury of blacks and other determinable segments of the population;
3. Determinable segments of the [*Marin*] County population including, but not limited to:
   a. People under 30 years of age
   b. People with annual incomes under $10,000

*COMMENT:* This dollar figure should be inflated to cover the average employed person in the community at the time of trial.

   c. People employed in occupations other than technical, managerial, professional, and executive
   d. People with Spanish-American surnames
   e. People without some college education
   f. People who are unmarried
   g. Felons

   were systematically excluded or substanially underrepresented;

*COMMENT:* The following point was raised in the *Angela Davis* case (see §3.23), which also arose in Marin County, California. (The 1974 amendment to article I, §4 has been added.)

4. California Penal Code §911, under which the indicting grand jury was sworn, is unconstitutional on its face and as applied because it violates the First Amendment and the due process and equal protection clauses of the Fourteenth Amendment of the United States Constitution: It systematically excludes nontheists from grand jury service by requiring grand jurors to swear a religious test oath in violation of article 1, §4, and article XX, §3 of the California Constitution.

C. Proceeding against defendant by indictment rather than by information violates [*his*] right to due process and equal protection of the laws;

*COMMENT:* See chapter 23 on the right to preliminary hearing whether charged by indictment or by information in California.

D. The [*California*] constitutional provisions and the statutes giving the district attorney the right to proceed either by indictment or by information are unconstitutional in that they deprive defendant of due process of law in giving the district attorney an unfettered choice of procedures without any standards.

II. To set aside and quash the indictment in that the proceedings of the grand jury that indicted the defendant were irregular because members of the grand jury were biased.

III. For evidentiary hearings to establish any and all of the foregoing, including:

A. The selection process used in picking the [*1971–1972*] grand jury

B. The process used by the district attorney to elect a proceeding by way of indictment

C. The irregularities in the grand jury and its proceedings because of the bias of grand jurors

Pursuant to [*California Penal Code §924.1*], defendant further moves for an order of this Court granting leave to former grand jurors willing to testify about the foregoing.

This motion is based on the attached points and authorities and exhibits, documentary and oral evidence to be adduced at the hearings on the motion, and such additional evidence and authorities as the Court may require.

*COMMENT:* The defense in *California v Bingham* (the *San Quentin Six* case) also sought to have the indictment quashed because "The District Attorney was guilty of prejudicial misconduct" and the grand jury "deliberations and the voting procedures did not comply with due process of law."

## D. Form: Motion to Quash Jury Panel §6.26

*Source:* Adapted from motion to quash the petit jury panel, dated Jan. 6, 1976, *Hampton v Hanrahan* (see §3.71). The style of this motion is clear, understandable, and convincing, presenting four distinct types of underrepresentation that can be proved in many jusidictions. The motion is a good model, although the trial judge denied it. It was filed by Neal Bush of Detroit.

Now come Plaintiffs, by and through their attorneys, and move to quash the jury panel in this case for the following reasons:

1. On [*January 5, 1976*] all members of the jury panel for [*January 1976*] appeared in the [*Courtroom 2525*] of this court.
2. [*Because of the nature of this case, a significantly larger number of potential jurors were called for service.*]
3. Approximately [*400*] jurors appeared. Out of those, no more than [*23*] were [*black*].
4. During the morning of [*January 5, 1976*], a special panel numbering [*150*] was selected from the total panel.
5. Of this special panel, [*15*] persons are [*black*]. Therefore, [*10 percent*] of the potential jurors in this case are [*black*].
6. The [*Eastern*] Division of the District Court for the [*Northern*] District of [*Illinois*] is composed of the counties: [*Cook, DeKalb, DuPage, Grundy, Kane, Kendell, Lake, LaSalle, McHenry, Will*].

*COMMENT:* The first proof of underrepresentation is based on United States Census records.

7. According to the [*1970*] United States Census, [*15 percent*] of the adult population, those eighteen and over, are [*black*].
8. There is a [*33 percent*] disparity between the number of [*blacks*] in the adult population in this court division according to the [*1970*] United States Census, and the number of [*blacks*] in the jury panel in this case.
9. The probability of only [*15*][*black*] persons appearing in a jury panel of [*150*] persons when [*15 percent*] of the total adult population is [*black*] is [*4.3 out of 100*].

*COMMENT:* The second proof of underrepresentation is based on census figures corrected for inaccuracies in counting black people.

10. Further, the United States Census Bureau has determined that [*blacks*] were significantly underrepresented in the census in this [*area of the*]

county, and that, in fact, [*blacks*] account for [*22 percent*] of the adult population in this court division.

11. There is a [*55 percent*] disparity between the actual number of [*blacks*] in the population of this court division and the number of [*blacks*] in the jury panel in this case.

12. The probability of only [*15*][*black*] persons appearing on a jury panel of [*150*] persons when [*22 percent*] of the total adult population of the court division is [*black*] is less than [*1 out of 1000*].

*COMMENT:* The third proof of underrepresentation is based on the jury pool.

13. In this division of the court [*17 percent*] of all jurors who have been qualified for jury service are [*black*]. (See Appendix [*A*])

*COMMENT:* An unimpeachable source should furnish an affidavit (to be presented in Appendix A) concerning the number and percent of black jurors qualified for jury service.

14. There is a [*41 percent*] disparity between the number of [*blacks*] in the pool of those who have qualified for jury service and the number of [*blacks*] in the jury panel in this case.

15. The probability of only [*15*][*black*] persons appearing in a jury panel of [*150*] persons when [*17 percent*] of those who have qualified for jury duty are [*black*] is [*1.2 out of 100*].

*COMMENT:* The fourth proof of underrepresentation is based on the registered voters list.

16. Potential jurors in this division of the court are chosen from voter registration lists.

17. Most of the actual jurors in this division of the court are chosen from [*seven*] counties of the [*ten*] county area. These seven counties from which most jurors are selected are [*List counties*].

18. In the area from which jurors are actually chosen, [*black*] people comprise [*23.6 percent*] of the [*registered voters*].

19. There is a [*57 percent*] disparity between the number of [*blacks*] who are [*registered voters*] in the area from which jurors are actually chosen and the number of [*blacks*] in the jury panel in this case.

20. The probability of only [*15*][*black*] persons appearing in a jury panel of [*150*] persons when [*23.6 percent*] of the [*registered voters*] in the actual area are [*black*] is [*4 out of 10,000*].

21. These disparities demonstrate, and create at the very least a *prima*

*facie* case, that the jury panel selected in this case was not randomly selected from the adult population of the counties that comprise this court division, from those persons qualified for jury service in this court division, or from those registered voters in the actual area from which jurors are selected in this court division, and is biased against [*black*] people.

WHEREFORE Plaintiff request that (1) this Court hold an evidentiary hearing in this matter, and (2) at the conclusion of said hearing, quash the jury panel presently selected in this case.

This motion is based on all the pleadings in this case previously filed, the records of the Court concerning selection of potential jurors in this case, the records and files of the Clerk of the Court, and the accompanying affidavits.

## E. Recent Developments §6.29

See §6.10.

## F. Memorandum in Support of Challenge §6.31

The memorandum of points and authorities filed in support of the motion to quash the indictment or to challenge the petit jury may be based on any of the relevant material in §§6.32–6.68. Some of that material comes from memos to trial courts, some from briefs on appeal after failure of a jury challenge and conviction; other sections are segments of trial court opinions upholding jury challenges on a number of grounds.

To assist the reader in using the material in writing memos and briefs, the customary style used in outlining and typing headings is presented in addition to the section headings used in this book.

### 1. Facts §6.32

**I. STATEMENT OF FACTS**

This opening section of the memo or brief should succinctly state the facts of the case: the substantive charges in the complaint, a chronology of the steps taken by both sides, the procedural posture of the case at this point, a description of the parties, and so forth.

Then counsel should describe the facts concerning the jury challenge: the method of juror selection used (see examples in chapter 2), the procedural steps taken by both sides concerning the challenge (see §§6.11–6.15), and the present posture of the challenge. The legal and factual issues facing the trial or appellate court should be clearly stated.

As in all briefs, time spent in drafting the statement of facts is well spent. Getting the judge familiar with the parties and the facts requires an advocate's skill in selecting those items that are relevant and deleting those that really do not matter, however important they may have seemed at one stage. Unless the judge becomes interested in the challenging party and the legal issue posed by the jury challenge, there is no chance that the judge will take the time to read (or even skim) the stack of pleadings, exhibits, and briefs that pile up in the case. Nor will the judge have the patience to permit the required extensive testimony of experts on the reasons for the unconstitutionality of the present jury selection method. The mind of the judge must be engaged for this exercise to succeed. The first opportunity to accomplish this goal is in the statement of facts. It should not be wasted.

## 2. Definitions and Contradictions

### a. Cognizable Classes §6.33

In 1906, Justice Oliver Wendell Holmes said the question in jury list cases was whether the group alleged to be a distinctive or cognizable class would "act otherwise than those who were drawn would act." *Rawlings v Georgia* (1906) 201 US 638, 640.

In 1946, Justice Douglas provided useful guidelines in *Ballard v United States* (1946) 329 US 187, 193–194, when he answered that at least one new group, women, should be considered a class because they were not fungible with another known class:

> The thought is that the factors which tend to influence the action of women are the same as those which influence the action of men—personality, background, economic status—and not sex. Yet it is not enough to say that women when sitting as jurors neither act nor tend to act as a class. Men likewise do not act as a class. But, if the shoe were on the other foot, who would claim that a jury was truly representative of the community if all men were intentionally and systematically excluded from the panel? The truth is that the two sexes are not fungible; a community made up exclusively of one is different from a community composed of both; the subtle interplay of influence one on the other is among the imponderables. To insulate the courtroom from either may not in a given case make an iota of difference. Yet a flavor, a distinct quality is lost if either sex is excluded. The exclusion of one may indeed make the jury less representative of the community than would be true if an economic or racial group were excluded.

In 1975, the Court (8-1) quoted this approach approvingly in *Taylor v Louisiana* (1975) 419 US 522, 531, 532. Recent opinion polls show distinct differences between women and men on many issues likely to be raised, directly or indirectly in jury trials, from capital punishment to prisons and peace. See discussions in chapters 4 and 5 on women in the courtroom.

### b. Relationships among Cognizable Classes §6.34

The need to define "cognizable classes" creates a contradiction. On the one hand, it is necessary to define a group clearly in order to have it fall into the legal category of a cognizable class. On the other hand, in reality several groups run into each other in their relationship to the legal and economic system and really form one large cognizable class with several subclasses. Specifically, black people are a distinct group, legally recognized as such as a result of the abolition of slavery in the Civil War, the adoption of the Reconstruction Amendments, and decades of heroic work by civil rights clients and lawyers, primarily in the South.

This cognizable class will be underrepresented if jurors are simply selected at random from the voter registration lists. In some areas during some periods, black people do not register to vote in arge numbers because some are short-term residents, and because a higher proportion of blacks than of the population as a whole are young, and young people of all races tend not to register to vote and not to become long-term residents. Some black people have not always seen the electoral process as a meaningful way to change existing conditions (although the election of black and Latino mayors and other officials marks a trend toward heavier participation in electoral politics).

The same combination of characteristics also applies to other ethnic and racial minorities in our population, applies increasingly to age groups (the young and the elderly), and may apply to some life-style groups. Adoption of the Nineteenth Amendment (women's suffrage), Twenty-Fourth Amendment (abolishing poll taxes), and the Twenty-Sixth Amendment (youth suffrage) attest to these groups being cognizable classes that the majority group has ultimately voted to include in the electoral process.

In reading the following sections on specific, cognizable classes, it is essential to keep in mind their interrelationship.

### c. Contradictions Inherent in a Jury Challenge §6.35

It is often true in legal work, as in the world at large, that there are contradictions inherent in a logical approach that must be spelled out explicitly at the outset in order to make theory conform to reality and to affect reality through practice. This is particularly true of a hotly contested issue like the judicial acceptance of the existence of cognizable classes in the community that cannot constitutionally be excluded from or even underrepresented on jury lists.

The first problem in attacking existing jury selection systems is that counsel is seeking to upset the status quo, always a dangerous pastime. (See Judge Wyzanski's difficulties in §6.60.) The second problem is that counsel is challenging decision-making by white, established men of means who have, throughout most of our history, run the grand and petit jury system and peopled it exclusively with their own kind or those clearly beholden to them. The third problem is that this challenge requires reliance on the concept of legal equality of all persons, which was introduced into our system by the men and women who won the American Revolutionary War and was extended by the black and white men and women who won the Civil War and the suffrage amendments. This challenge requires proof that the concept is honored more today in the breach than in the observance. The fourth problem is that counsel is explicitly demanding the inclusion of nonwhite, young and old men and women without means in the decision-making process. The fifth problem is that counsel is insisting not merely on token inclusion of such citizens, but inclusion in proportion to their number in the society as a whole, where they constitute a near majority. The sixth and last problem is that the person asked to make the decision often must begin by acknowledging his own white, male, financially secure, and privileged position.

A jury challenge involves these kinds of contradictions, as well as the difficult task of proposing a new, constitutional system that the court can implement if you are successful. (Occasionally, however, common sense is used, and on those all-too-rare occasions the task is not difficult; see §6.59.)

### 3. Standing to Raise Issue

#### a. Form: Majority Group Members Have Standing in Federal Courts §6.41

*Source:* Adapted from postargument memorandum in support of defendants' unsuccessful motion to quash indictment, filed 1971, *United States v Deardorff* (SD NY 1971) 343 F Supp 1033.

This form can be adapted for use in a challenge to the array or to a trial jury list.

## II. DEFENDANT HAS STANDING TO CHALLENGE GRAND JURY, SINCE DEFENDANT NEED NOT BE A MEMBER OF [*EXCLUDED/ UNDERREPRESENTED*] CLASS

Defendant has discovered no case where a *federal* defendant was denied standing to object to the composition of a *federal* grand jury on the ground that he was not a member of the allegedly excluded or underrepresented class.

In *Thiel v Southern Pac. Co.* (1946) 328 US 217, 225, the Court could not sanction the method by which the jury panel was selected. On that basis it became unnecessary to determine whether the petitioner was in any way prejudiced by the wrongful exclusion or whether he was one of the excluded class. Accord, *Dow v Carnegie-Illinois Steel Corp.* (3d Cir 1955) 224 F2d 414, 422–423, *cert. denied* (1956) 350 US 971; *United States v Zirpolo* (3d Cir 1971) 450 F2d 424. In *United States v Leonetti* (SD NY 1968) 291 F Supp 461, a constitutional challenge was posed by *federal* defendants who were also not members of the allegedly underrepresented classes. In that case the court considered the constitutional challenge on the merits, holding (at 474 n3) that "any federal criminal defendant has standing to challenge the jury systems used or to be used in his case."

Nor have courts distinguished between challenges brought by federal defendants on constitutional grounds and those brought under the supervisory power or the statute. In *United States v Butera* (1st Cir 1970) 420 F2d 564, for example, the defendant challenged the exclusion of the "young and the very old" on constitutional grounds and the issue was decided on constitutional grounds. Yet the court concluded (at 567 n2) that "the fact that defendant Butera was not a member of any of the alleged excluded groups is of no consequence in our case." In numerous other cases as well, constitutional challenges raised by federal defendants who were not members of the allegedly excluded class have been decided on the merits. See, e.g., *United States v Leonetti* (SD NY 1968) 291 F Supp 461; *United States v Kuhn* (5th Cir 1971) 441 F2d 179; *Rabinowitz v United States* (5th Cir 1966) 366 F2d 34.

In any event, the defendants in this case challenge the exclusion and underrepresentation of [*young adults*] not only on constitutional grounds, but also on statutory and supervisory grounds, which concededly do not require membership in the class.

Moreover, these grounds are inexorably intermeshed. The "supervisory power" of the federal courts derives much of its content from constitutional principles. See, e.g., *Dow v Carnegie-Illinois Steel Corp.* (3d Cir 1955) 244 F2d 414, 423. And as Congress recognized when it enacted the Jury

Selection and Service Act of 1968, that act was intended to reflect the policies of the Constitution. Indeed, the chairman of the Judiciary Committee, in successfully urging rejection of the "prejudice" requirement, made it clear that the requirements to sustain a constitutional challenge are the same as the requirements to sustain a challenge under the statute as enacted. He pointed out that a prejudice requirement "would go beyond what has been required to sustain a constitutional challenge." 114 *Cong Rec* 3991 (1968).

In a case—like the instant one—where the challenge is on combined constitutional, statutory, and supervisory grounds, it would be difficult to justify a holding that defendants lacked standing to raise certain arguments against the illegal exclusion and underrepresentation, while they had standing to raise other, intimately connected, arguments.

*COMMENT:* See alternative sections II on standing to be used in state court challenges (§6.42), and on standing to be used when citizens sue as plaintiffs challenging their exclusion from jury lists (§6.43).

### b. Form: Majority Group Members Have Standing in State Courts §6.42

*COMMENT:* This form for Section II should be used in a state court case, instead of that in §6.41.

**II. DEFENDANT HAS STANDING TO CHALLENGE GRAND JURY, SINCE DEFENDANT NEED NOT BE A MEMBER OF [*EXCLUDED/UNDERREPRESENTED*] CLASS**

The rule is clear that members of majority groups have standing in state courts to challenge the exclusion of members of cognizable minority groups. The Supreme Court recently reversed the state conviction of a white criminal defendant who alleged that the systematic exclusion of blacks from the grand and petit juries that indicted and convicted him violated his due process and equal protection rights. *Peters v Kiff* (1972) 407 US 493. More recently, *Taylor v Louisiana* (1975) 419 US 522, also involved a majority-group member, a male, successfully challenging a statute limiting representation of women on a state court venire.

### c. Form: Members of a Class Excluded from Jury Duty Have Standing to File Suit §6.43

In appropriate situations, a class of persons can challenge grand and petit jury selection methods without being defendants in criminal cases.

For example, black citizens of Alabama sued in order to be placed on county jury lists in *Carter v Jury Comm'n of Greene County* (1970) 396 US 320. They were akin to (white) volunteers for jury duty common in many jurisdictions. Their successful suit demonstrated that suits can be brought in federal (or state) courts. (At that time it was possible to challenge the constitutionality of state jury selection statutes in federal court and be heard by federal three-judge courts with a direct appeal to the United States Supreme Court under 28 USC §§2281 and 2284. The statute has been amended to prohibit three-judge courts in such cases.)

The tactic of suing affirmatively to become jurors can occasionally be used by members of any excluded cognizable class or combination of classes seeking to be placed on grand or petit jury lists in anticipation of a particular criminal trial or series of trials.

*Source:* Adapted from defendants' supplemental affidavit in support of unsuccessful motion to dismiss indictment pursuant to 28 USC §1867(a) and to strike the jury array, filed June 13, 1972, *United States v Russo* (see §3.52).

## II. PLAINTIFFS, MEMBERS OF A CLASS EXCLUDED FROM JURY SERVICE, ARE AGGRIEVED PERSONS WITH STANDING TO CHALLENGE GRAND JURY COMPOSITION

Because almost all jury challenges have been in the context of litigants challenging the selection process, the courts have concerned themselves primarily with the question of litigants' interests in a jury that represents a cross-section of the community. However, in the past few years, there has been an upswing in jury challenges by way of affirmative class actions. The most illustrious of these is *Carter v Jury Comm'n of Greene County* (1970) 396 US 320. (See also *Turner v Fouche* (1970) 396 US 346, a companion case.) *Carter* establishes that persons excluded from jury service are aggrieved persons who have an interest in redress; that constitutional claim arises from exclusion; that whatever terminology may be used to describe jury service, its protection is similar to the protection extended to the elective franchise; and that, accordingly, the states as well as the federal government must hew to constitutional criteria in establishing standards for jury service. The Court in *Carter* held (at 329–330):

> Defendants in criminal proceedings do not have the only cognizable legal interest in nondiscriminatory jury selection. People excluded from juries because of their race are as much aggrieved as those indicted and tried by juries chosen under a system of racial exclusion.Surely there is no jurisdictional or procedural bar to an attack

> upon systematic jury discrimination by way of a civil suit such as the one brought here. The federal claim is bottomed on the simple proposition that the State, acting through its agents, has refused to consider the appellants for jury service solely because of their race. Whether jury service be deemed a right, a privilege, or a duty, the State may no more extend it to some of its citizens and deny it to others on racial grounds than it may invidiously discriminate in the offering and withholding of the elective franchise.

It is now indisputable that the right to serve on juries is a right. In *Thiel v Southern Pac. Co.* (1946) 328 US 217, 224, the Court described jury service as "a privilege of citizenship." In *White v Crook* (MD Ala 1966) 251 F Supp 401, the court referred to jury service as "a form of participation in the process of government, a responsibility and a right," and the sponsors of the predecessor to the Jury Selection and Service Act of 1968 referred to jury service as "another civil right—the right to serve as a juror." See *United States v Rabinowitz* (5th Cir 1966) 366 F2d 34, 68.

*COMMENT:* The defense in the *Pentagon Papers* case then proceeded to argue that the standard for determining whether a limitation on jury service is constitutional is whether it is necessary to promote a compelling state interest, citing *Shapiro v Thompson* (1969) 394 US 618, 634, and *Dunn v Blumstein* (1972) 405 US 330. The defense was urging that a one-year residence requirement for jury duty does not meet that standard (see §6.63).

### d. Recent Developments §6.45

See §6.10.

## 4. Fair Cross-Section Constitutionally Required

### a. Form: Fifth and Sixth Amendments and Equal Protection Clauses of Fifth and Fourteenth Amendments Require Fair Cross-Section Juries §6.46

**III. THE [*PROSECUTION/DEFENDANT*] *HAS NOT SATISFIED THE CONSTITUTIONAL REQUIREMENT FOR A FAIR CROSS-SECTION JURY***

*COMMENT:* The word "defendant" is used when citizens excluded from jury duty are suing as plaintiffs against jury commissioners (see §6.43).

*[Federal grand jury alternative]*

### A. The Fifth Amendment Requirement Is Clear

*COMMENT:* Counsel may want to emphasize the relevant sections of the 1968 Jury Selection and Service Act, referred to below.

*[Federal petit jury alternative]*

### A. The Sixth Amendment Requirement Is Clear

*[State grand jury alternative]*

### A. The Fourteenth Amendment Equal Protection Clause and the Fifth Amendment Require a Grand Jury Selected from a Fair Cross-Section of the Community

*COMMENT:* It will be necessary in many such cases to use material on the interchangeability of state and federal precedents (see §6.7) and of grand and petit jury precedents (see §6.8). It must be remembered in state grand jury challenges that a state is not required to provide grand jury indictments under the federal Constitution, but if grand jurors sit, they must be selected under federal constitutional standards (see §6.8).

*[State petit jury alternative]*

### A. The Equal Protection Clause and the Sixth Amendment Require a Trial Jury Selected from a Fair Cross-Section of the Community

*COMMENT:* It may be necessary in many such cases to use material on the interchangeability of state and federal precedents (see §6.7) and of grand and petit jury precedents (see §6.8).

The United States Supreme Court in *Taylor v Louisiana* (1975) 419 US 522, at 526, 527, recently summarized the law on jury selection standards in state and federal courts:

> Both in the course of exercising its supervisory powers over trials in federal courts and in the constitutional context, the Court has unambiguously declared that the American concept of the jury trial contemplates a jury drawn from a fair cross-section of the community. A unanimous Court stated in *Smith v Texas* (1940) 311 US 128, 130, that "[i]t is part of the established tradition in the use of juries as

> instruments of public justice that the jury be a body truly representative of the community." To exclude racial groups from jury service was said to be "at war with our basic concepts of a democratic society and a representative government." A state jury system that resulted in systematic exclusion of Negroes as jurors was therefore held to violate the Equal Protection Clause of the Fourteenth Amendment. *Glasser v United States* (1942) 315 US 60, 85, in the context of a federal criminal case and the Sixth Amendment's jury trial requirement, stated that "our notions of what a proper jury is have developed in harmony with our basic concepts of a democratic system and representative government," and repeated the Court's understanding that the jury "be a body truly representative of the community . . . and not the organ of any special group or class."
>
> . . . Recent federal legislation governing jury selection within the federal court system has a similar thrust . . . . [In the Federal Jury Selection Act of 1968], Congress stated "the policy of the United States that all litigants in Federal courts entitled to trial by jury shall have the right to grand and petit juries selected at random from a fair cross-section of the community in the district or division in which the court convenes." 28 USC §1861.

The Court also restated (419 US at 530, 531) the underlying reasons for the cross-section requirement:

> We accept the fair cross-section requirement as fundamental to the jury trial guaranteed by the Sixth Amendment and are convinced that the requirement has solid foundation. The purpose of a jury is to guard against the exercise of arbitrary power—to make available the commonsense judgment of the community as a hedge against the overzealous or mistaken prosecutor and in preference to the professional or perhaps overconditioned or biased response of a judge. *Duncan v Louisiana*, 391 US at 155–156. This prophylactic vehicle is not provided if the jury pool is made up of only special segments of the populace or if large, distinctive groups are excluded from the pool. Community participation in the administration of the criminal law, moreover, is not only consistent with our democratic heritage but is also critical to public confidence in the fairness of the criminal justice system. Restricting jury service to only special groups or excluding identifiable segments playing major roles in the community cannot be squared with the constitutional concept of jury trial. "Trial by jury presupposes a jury drawn from a pool broadly representative of the community as well as impartial in a specific case . . . . The broad representative character of the jury should be maintained,

partly as assurance of a diffused impartiality and partly because sharing in the administration of justice is a phase of civic responsibility." *Thiel v Southern Pac. Co.* (1946) 328 US 217, 227 (Frankfurter, J, dissenting).

### b. Form: Systematic Exclusion of Distinctive Groups Unconstitutional §6.47

**B. The Systematic Exclusion of Cognizable Classes Is Unconstitutional**

The rule on enforcement of the "fair cross-section" requirement is stated succinctly in *Taylor v Louisiana* (1975) 419 US 522, at 538:

> [T]he jury wheels, pools of names, panels or venires from which juries are drawn must not systematically exclude distinctive groups in the community and thereby fail to be reasonably representative thereof.

This has been the rule for decades.

It is clear that the cross-section requirement stems not only from an equal protection position against racial discrimination, but also from a due process view of the functions of grand and petit juries. In 1972, Justice Marshall, in announcing the Court's judgment in *Peters v Kiff* (1972) 407 US 493, 503–504, said:

> [T]he exclusion from jury service of a substantial and identifiable class of citizens has a potential impact that is too subtle and too pervasive to admit of confinement to particular issues or particular cases.
>
> . . . When any large and identifiable segment of the community is excluded from jury service, the effect is to remove from the jury room qualities of human nature and varieties of human experience, the range of which is unknown and perhaps unknowable. It is not necessary to assume that the excluded group will consistently vote as a class in order to conclude, as we do, that its exclusion deprives the jury of a perspective on human events that may have unsuspected importance in any case that may be presented.

In *Hernandez v Texas* (1954) 347 US 475, 478, the Court also recognized the changing status of racial, national, religious, and other minority groups:

> Throughout our history differences in race and color have defined easily identifiable groups which have at times required the aid of the courts in securing equal treatment under the laws. But community

> prejudices are not static, and from time to time other differences from the community norm may define other groups which need the same protection. Whether such a group exists within a community is a question of fact. When the existence of a distinct class is demonstrated, and it is further shown that the laws, as written or applied, single out that class for different treatment not based on some reasonable classification, the guaranties of the Constitution have been violated.

In *Taylor v Louisiana*, *supra*, 419 US at 537, the Court carried forward this analysis in language applicable to the instant case:

> If it was ever the case that women were unqualified to sit on juries or were so situated that none of them should be required to perform jury service, that time has long since passed. If at one time it could be held that Sixth Amendment juries must be drawn from a fair cross-section of the community but that this requirement permitted the almost total exclusion of women, this is not the case today. *Communities differ at different times and places. What is a fair cross-section at one time or place is not necessarily a fair cross-section at another time or a different place.* Nothing persuasive has been presented to us in this case suggesting that all-male venires in the parishes involved here are fairly representative of the local population otherwise eligible for jury service. [Emphasis added.]

*COMMENT:* Another approach is to rewrite the beginning of the paragraph and to insert the name of the excluded or underrepresented class in brackets after the word "women" in the quotation, e.g., "women [*and Latinos*] were . . . . "

The Fifth Circuit eloquently upheld a class suit by five named blacks and women alleging discrimination in jury composition, in *Foster v Sparks* (5th Cir 1975) 506 F2d 805, 808–810:

> [T]he thrust of plaintiffs' complaint is not that they have been injured because they have been excluded as individuals from the grand or traverse jury lists because of race or sex discrimination. Rather, they contend that blacks as a class and females as a class have been systematically excluded from participation in the government of Quitman County, and that these class exclusions have skewed public actions in the county in a manner unfavorable to blacks and females. Plaintiffs would derive little comfort from personal participation in county government if the selection process were such as to ensure that they could participate only as token blacks and females in unconstitutionally unrepresentative white, male institutions.

> . . .
>
> In conclusion, one hundred years after discrimination in jury selection was made a federal crime, we remand this jury discrimination case to the district court for further proceedings consistent with this opinion. Defendants contend that they have now complied with the mandates of Georgia law and of the United States Constitution. If the district court should decide that the named plaintiffs can maintain this class action, then that court will afford defendants an opportunity to demonstrate that the millenium has arrived in Quitman County. Class actions are potent and effective tools in enforcing statutory and constitutional rights. We must not lightly dull their cutting edge in the sacred name of the jury selection process.

A useful 25-page appendix to the opinion (506 F2d at 811) contains the report of a subcommittee of the Committee on the Operation of the Jury System, by Circuit Judge Walter P. Gewin, which analyzes jury selection decisions by category (age, sex, etc.).

### c. Recent Developments §6.49

See §6.10.

## 5. Distinctive Groups in This Community Underrepresented

### a. Black People §6.51

The Burger Court, like its predecessors, has faced one of the basic facts of life in the United States:

> For we also cannot deny that, 114 years after the close of the War Between the States and nearly 100 years after *Strauder* [*v West Virginia* (1880) 100 US 303], racial and other forms of discrimination still remain a fact of life, in the administration of justice as in our society as a whole. Perhaps today that discrimination takes a form more subtle than before. But it is not less real or pernicious.

*Rose v Mitchell* (1979) 443 US 545, at 558–559.

> It remains an unfortunate fact in our society that violent crimes perpetrated against members of other racial or ethnic groups often raises . . . a possibility [*that racial prejudice will influence a jury*].

*Rosales-Lopez v United States* (1981) 451 US 182, 192.

Exclusion from jury service on grounds of race is clearly prohibited. *Strauder*, *supra*. And Supreme Court justices "are unwilling to make the assumption that the exclusion of Negroes has relevance only for issues involving race." *Peters v Kiff* (1972) 407 US 493, 503 (Marshall, J., in support of plurality judgment).

At the same time, the Supreme Court in 1979 could not find that there had never been a black foreman or forewoman on a grand jury in Tipton County, Tennessee, based on the testimony of three foremen. *Rose v Mitchell, supra*, 443 US at 570. But it did rule that the claim of discrimination in state grand jury selection could be raised on habeas corpus in federal court.

In two hard-fought California cases, state and federal defendants challenged the lack of black representation on grand juries.

The trial court in *California v Pinell* (*San Quentin Six* case, see §2.21) found inadequate representation of the county's black community through the grand jury selection process. The defense never contended that blacks were excluded from the 1971 grand jury. The defense proved that blacks representative of the Marin black community were excluded by the system used. Judge Broderick nominated Mrs. Ruth A. Smith, whom he knew as an associate member of the Marin County Republican Central Committee, a teacher whose annual income was $25,000 or more. The second nominee, Mrs. De Reath Collins, wife of a dentist with an annual income of $20,000 or more, had a background and status radically unlike the black community in Marin County. She, too, was nominated by one of the judges.

The Marin Human Rights Commission statistics with respect to the Marin black community showed that poverty and a lower social caste marked the community as a whole, along with residential segregation into Marin City. Neither nominee resided there. Clearly the 1971 grand jury selection process failed to represent the mass of blacks in the county, and could assure no more than white middle-class values hidden inside black skin, according to respondents' unsuccessful appellate brief.

See also §6.55 on underrepresentation of young black people.

In *United States v Russo* (see §3.52), defendants were unsuccessful in their motions to dismiss the indictment pursuant to 28 USC §1867(a) (grand jury challenge) and to stay the proceedings.

They argued that black people, who constitute 7.3 percent of the district population, were only 3.4 percent of the source list for the *Pentagon Papers* grand jury, according to the figures in the affidavit of Leo Breiman. This constituted a 53-percent underrepresentation.

The fact that black people represent a relatively small percentage of the overall population should not obscure the severity of their underrepresentation. If anything, such underrepresentation should be cause for particular apprehension. This is so for a variety of reasons: the importance of encouraging maximum participation of minority groups in the processes of government; the fact that a disproportionate number of criminal defendants are members of minority groups; and the absolute necessity of having minority viewpoints represented on the juries if the integrity of the judicial process is to have any credence with significant members of our society. As Kalven and Zeisel have pointed out in their landmark work, *The American Jury* 490 (1966), "[i]n roughly one case in ten, the minority [in jury deliberations] eventually succeeds in reversing an initial majority, and these cases may be of special importance."

### b. Blue-Collar Workers §6.52

The Supreme Court held in *Thiel v Southern Pac. Co.* (1946) 328 US 217, that blue-collar workers, called "wage earners," are a cognizable class.

The *Thiel* opinion did not make clear to what extent the Court's action was constitutionally required and to what extent it was a prudent exercise of the Court's supervisory powers in federal cases, but this does not detract from Justice Frank Murphy's demonstration that economic classifications shatter any attempt to select juries representative of the community unless they are faced openly.

There was substantial evidence of lower class (typically blue collar) underrepresentation in the selection of the 1971 Marin grand jury that indicted the defendants in *California v Pinell* (see §2.21). This issue was raised, unsuccessfully, on appeal.

The defense contended that poor people, blue-collar workers, menial clerical workers, and people without a college education, were systematically underrepesented by the 1971 grand jury procedure. Sociologists for both sides confirmed the common belief that these social strata coalesce to produce society's lower class.

Indeed, Judge Wilson agreed that the minimal statutory grand juror's salary acted as an insurmountable barrier to the poor working class, whose survival depends on regular receipt of low wages in occupations that do not permit time off for grand jury activities.

Both sociologists, Dr. Blauner [see chapter 18] and Dr. Scott, agreed that occupation is a fairly reliable index to social class, and that blue-collar workers are those who work as craftsmen, foremen, skilled workers, operatives, semi-skilled workers, laborers, service workers, and farm workers.

Clerical workers differ from blue-collar workers in the sense that their work, while menial, is with symbols rather than hands, which makes them a hybrid classification between the blue-collar and managerial-technical-professional levels. However, in an oversimplified blue-white classification, they would be put in the white-collar group.

Both sociologists testified that blue-collar, unemployed and kindred persons are identifiable, and have class characteristics that differ substantially from middle or upper classes. Dr. Scott, the prosecution witness, considered this class authoritarian and conservative in comparison with middle or upper classes but there can be no doubt working-class people have a point of view different from those in higher strata.

The 1970 census data on occupations of Marin residents were compared with similar material on the 105 grand jury nominees in a defense survey entered into evidence at the hearing. Investigator Ruth Astle compiled the survey, using in part data from the county clerk, the judges, and the nominees themselves. See description of such a survey in chapter 5. She found that 11 of the 105 nominees and 1 of the 30 finalists were known to be blue-collar or clerical; one person's occupation was unknown.

Dr. Peter W. Sperlich, a professor of political science from the University of California at Berkeley, analyzed these figures after testifying to his professional qualifications in the use of statistical probability theory and other statistical methods. He resolved all doubts in favor of the prosecution by assuming that the unknown person was blue collar. From these data he calculated that the likelihood of obtaining the grand jury's lower-class-occupation underrepresentation in an unbiased system would be (a) three chances in ten quadrillion, for the 105 nominees; and (b) five chances in one hundred million for the 30 finalists.

For discussion of methods of calculating and proving nonrandom selection, see Finkelstein, "The Application of Statistical Decision Theory to Jury Discrimination Cases," 80 *Harv L Rev* 338 (1966); Kairys, "Juror Selection: The Law, a Mathematical Method of Analysis, and a Case Study," 10 *Crim L Rev* 771 (1972); Sperlich and Jaspovice, "Statistical Decision Theory and the Selection of Grand Jurors: Testing for Discrimination in a Single Panel," 2 *Hastings Const'l LQ* 75 (1975), and §6.83.

On appeal in *Pinell*, the attorney general argued that of the 30 finalists, 7 possibly fell within the category of lower class (typically blue collar). The defense analyzed these one by one. For example, it acknowledged that Mr. Silva, a bus driver, with an income of $8,400, was rightly working class, but it noted that in a less serious case, the manner in which Mr. Silva had been nominated for the 1971 grand jury would have been the subject of a courthouse joke. It appears that Judge Keating nominated an M.E. Silva, who was a successful dairyman and former Novato mayor, and by pure mistake the bus driver from Mill Valley with the same name received the summons and served on the grand jury. The Mr. Silva who served was working class; the Mr. Silva chosen by the challenged selection process hardly fit that category.

Mrs. Wilson, a housewife, was cited by the attorney general as having an income of $7,000. However, the questionnaire sent to Marin Council for Civic Affairs organizations for nominees revealed that Mrs. Wilson was nominated by the League of Women Voters and had served as a former city councilwoman in Fairfax, a member of the MCCA, and a member of the Association of Bay Area Governments (ABAG). Investigator Astle's survey showed that Mrs. Wilson reported an income of $10,000 to $15,000 per year. She was a college graduate with a bachelor of arts degree. The attorney general's argument that this grand juror represented a lower stratum of society was, the defense said, absurd.

Additional support for considering economic, occupational, or social classes as cognizable classes for purposes of jury challenges can be found in: 28 USC §1862; *Labat v Bennett* (5th Cir 1966) 365 F2d 698, *cert. denied* (1967) 386 US 991; *Witcher v Peyton* (4th Cir 1969) 405 F2d 725; *United States ex rel. Geralds v Deegan* (SD NY 1969) 307 F Supp 56; *Michigan v Viera* (Detroit Recorder's Ct, Nos. A-152-598 and A-152-697, Apr. 13, 1970). However, it is easy to lose a challenge based on underrepresentation of "working class" members; see, e.g., *United States v Manbeck* (D SC 1981) 514 F Supp 141; *New Jersey v Porro* (NJ App Div 1978) 385 A2d 1258, *cert. denied sub nom. Porro v Woodcock* (1977) 434 US 861 (despite statistics showing that blue-collar workers were underrepresented on the jury array by 29 percent and laborers by 30 percent, compared to the county's general population).

Since women have become a major sector of the work force, some sociologists use a new phrase to describe women in menial and dead-end jobs: pink-collar workers. See §2.33 and chapters 4 and 5. Their underrepresentation will also skew a jury away from neutrality and the cross-section requirement.

### c. Poor People §6.53

The federal Jury Selection and Service Act of 1968, as amended, specifically provides that "No citizen shall be excluded from service as a grand or petit juror . . . on account of . . . economic status." 28 USC §1862.

In *Massachusetts v Shelley* (Mass Sup Jud Ct 1980) 409 NE2d 732, at 740, the court agreed that "Poverty might define a class."

Underrepresentation of poor people on a jury panel was successfully challenged in *California v Castro* (San Joaquin County Super Ct, No. 26416, Sept. 16, 1975), handled by attorneys Thomas Meyer, Barbara Rhine, and Peter Haberfeld. The state appealed to the California District Court of Appeal, which reversed on other grounds (Dist Ct App, No. 3 Crim 8469, Apr. 14, 1977), and the state supreme court affirmed the reversal (Sup Ct, Crim No. 20004, Jan. 17, 1979), but ordered the court of appeal opinion not published.

The approach of the trial judge is likely to be followed in the economic recession of the 1980s, as more and more people become poor. The judge first rejected the challenges to the composition of the grand jury based on young people (18–29) and on blue-collar workers as cognizable classes. He then found:

> that there is a distinct class, identifiable or cognizable group of low income persons in the county. The testimony of defendants' sociologist is not only believable, but is buttressed by other evidence. There is evidence of the existence of a Welfare Rights Organization, a Head-Start Program and Community Action Councils within the community. This group constitutes 26.3% of all families in the county. The census data uses $3000 family income as poverty level; table 124 of the census lists the total number of families of income less than 125% of the poverty level as constituting 15.4% of all families within the county. The use of family income of $6000 is described as a threshold level for poverty, allowing for 4 years of inflation since the 1970 census. The judicial nominees in this category, presuming the one unknown in their favor, were 11.5% of total judicial nominees. The Court also finds that the defendants have status to raise the issue of this category, since they fall within the definition of such a group.
>
> The People argue that the category of low income families in constantly changing and does not remain the same as set forth in the 1970 census. The poverty level has risen to $5050 for a family of four in 1975, for Welfare purposes. The only inference that can be drawn from such an increase is that the sociologist was correct in his definition of the category of $6000 family income.

The judge rejected the contention "that it would be an invasion of privacy and embarrassing to the nominees if they were asked their family income. There is no evidence that such an inquiry is embarrassing or that it even has to be made in order to secure nominees of low income; such nominees could be solicited from organizations."

The court relied on *California v Superior Court* (*Dean*) (1971) 38 Cal App 3d 966, 971:

> The decisions requiring the accused to show systematic, purposeful discrimination do not square with others which condemn discrimination stemming

from negligence or inertia. The latter recognize that official compilers of jury lists may drift into discrimination by not taking affirmative action to prevent it. In formulating a panel for a grand jury endowed with the criminal indictment function, officials must adhere to a standard more stringent than mere abstention from intentional discrimination; they have an affirmative duty to develop and pursue procedures aimed at achieving a fair cross-section of the community.

. . .

Has the affirmative duty been met in this case? The answer is no. The judicial selectors are relying upon the random selection to provide a good cross-section of the community. At the same time they are looking for minorities, youth, and women. The selectors equate minorities with low income, but they believe that low income persons will claim exemptions. These beliefs, opinions and theories are inconsistent. It is clear that there was only a cursory examination of the kinds of persons or of the quality of persons selected for the Grand Jury Panel; no real studies nor investigations were made or conducted, and, as a result, the selectors, who professed to be seeking an adequate cross-section of the entire community, ignored low income persons, who constitute a sizable portion of the population, and who are substantially under-represented on the panel.

The judge asked: "Does it really make any difference if the people are required to proceed with a preliminary hearing before a magistrate instead of this Grand Jury?" and he then answered: "an unrepresentative Grand Jury is detrimental to community aspirations and incompatible with the egalitarian aims of the 14th Amendment. If the selectors do not meet the prescriptions of constitutional standards, what can be expected from those who must comply with proscriptions of the law?"

A jury selection method that has the ultimate effect of discriminating against an economic group violates equal protection. A wealth-based classification is as traditionally suspect as a racial classification. *Thiel v Southern Pac. Co.* (1946) 328 US 217.

In *Harper v Virginia State Bd. of Election* (1966) 383 US 663, the Supreme Court decided that even a minimal poll tax of $1.50 was a wealth-based classification and therefore suspect; it was stricken. In a comprehensive opinion, the Court reviewed the cases determining that neither wealth, nor race, nor homesite "affords a permissible basis for distinguishing between qualified voters within the State." 383 US at 667. It held: "To introduce wealth . . . as a measure of a voter's qualification is to introduce a capricious or irrelevant factor. The degree of the discrimination is irrelevant." 383 US at 668. Earlier, in 1964, the Twenty-Fourth Amendment was ratified, outlawing poll taxes in federal elections.

In short, "'a man's mere property status, without more, cannot be used by a state to test, qualify, or limit his rights as a citizen of the

United States.'" *Lubin v Panish* (1974) 415 US 709, 721 (concurring opinion of Justice Douglas, quoting Justice Jackson concurring in *United States v California* (1941) 314 US 160, 184).

In *California v Taylor*, defendants Harold Taylor, John Bowman, and Ray Michael Boudreaux were charged with two counts of assault with a deadly weapon and four counts of assault with a deadly weapon with intent to commit murder. The alleged victims were all members of the Los Angeles police department. All three defendants were black, poor, and at the time of their arrest, in their twenties.

The defendants presented a pretrial motion challenging the Los Angeles Superior Court policy of selecting jurors exclusively from the registered voters list, as it underrepresents the poor, black, and young. The underrepresentation of this combination of cognizable classes led Judge Sherman W. Smith to grant the challenge on October 11, 1974. His order was reversed by the district court of appeal, and the reversal was affirmed by the California Supreme Court. *McCourtney v Superior Court* (Dist Ct App, No. 45230, Nov. 26, 1974), *cert. denied*, 421 US 1011 (1975).

Judge Smith's order was based on the testimony of expert witnesses that a representative jury panel of 100 prospective jurors would have to include 15 poor people, and thus almost every single trial jury would have at least 1 poor person on it. "Even if the one side or the other tried to exclude poor people from the panel mathematically using peremptory challenges, they would have to use 15 peremptory challenges to make sure to get rid of everybody."

Under present procedures in the county there were only 5 poor people per 100 panel members, on the average. As a result, on over half the juries studied, there were no poor people at all. Taking a look at nonretired poor, the underrepresentation was even worse. These were only 3 per 100 on the panel, on the average, rather than a proportional 13, which meant that the chances of nonretired poor people appearing on the final jury "would be very, very small. It would be less than 33 percent." The testimony indicated that low-income blacks and Latinos had less than 1 chance in 20 of appearing on the panel. "The chances that they would turn up on a final jury are practically nil. I think that it works out to be 1 out of 85."

In his unreported memorandum of decision and order, Judge Smith wrote a useful summary of the findings by experts that he found persuasive:

> The testimony of Drs. Breiman, Ben-Levi, Johnson, Grisby and Schwartz lends itself to the following findings. (Quoted statements are taken directly from their testimony.)

1. Families who make less than $5000 per year are considered poor. The poor are a cognizable class and were underrepresented on the panel to the extent of 66⅔ percent.

2. Blacks, Latins, and the young are also cognizable classes and are disproportionately represented on the panel, but not to as large an extent as the poor.

3. A substantial number of Latins, blacks, and the young are among the poor.

4. Underrepresentation of the poor necessarily includes a large proportion of blacks and Latins in addition to the young Anglo-whites.

5. Poor people, who are black or Latin, are virtually excluded.

6. It has been an acceptable fact in the sociology that the poorer you are, the less likely you are to register to vote. "They are just not interested in voting. They have no faith in the political system to advance their interest, and become apathetic to it."

7. The poor itself has a life-style and life experiences that are totally different from the group classified as nonpoor. "Sometimes we go so far as to take these attitudes that the nonpoor have and call them prejudices because that is what they work out to be."

8. The nonpoor see behavior of poor people in such a distorted light that it is very difficult for them to understand what people are doing. "A nonpoor person sitting as a juror listening to testimony from a poor person which relates to their experiences could cause disbelief on the part of the nonpoor person because of the differences in life-style. This is important, because most cases coming before the juries generally involve assessing the credibility of people who represent institutional authority of one thought or another against the credibility of the defendants who are not representatives of authority."

9. The jury panel was substantially whiter, better educated, and more affluent than the citizenry as a whole.

10. Poor people tend to have more contacts with police on an unfriendly basis than the affluent. "Police are unfair, unjust. They overreact. That, if you call them or a family calls them, they are just as likely to bust you as to bust whoever it is that you call them on. They will stop you for no reason whatsoever or they seem to hassle you more than they hassle anybody else, and they are abusive."

11. Poor blacks in addition to blacks in general are a cognizable class.

12. Blacks in American society have undergone a set of experiences that are not similar in many instances to other groups in American society. "The particular type of talk which black people have developed in ghettos—the so-called black English—lends itself to prejudices on the part of a white juror against one who speaks this way simply because it is different. And blacks, particularly poor blacks, who have a higher contact with law enforcement agencies, have a different background in judging who would be the aggressor between the police and the blacks than the white who has less contact." . . .

13. Youths constitute a cognizable class.

14. By studying census tracts in relation to the registration rolls, it is found

that persons on the lowest economical level are proportionately 31 percent underrepresented and persons in the highest economical level are 34 percent overrepresented.

15. The more affluent a census tract, the greater representation of registered voters. "Frankly, it is something which sociologists knew all along, but here we have hard data to show it."

16. The more affluent a census tract, the greater proportion of Anglo-whites on a scale of 1-10. The lowest decile consisted of 55 percent blacks and 28 percent Spanish-speaking persons, and the number 10 decile—the most affluent—consisted of 92 percent Anglo-whites. The first three deciles (groups), which comprised the three lowest economic levels, consisted of 98 percent blacks.

17. The jury panel consisted of 4 percent part-time workers and 2 percent unemployed.

See also *United States v Andrews* (D Mass 1972) 342 F Supp 1261 (concerning "paupers"), *rev'd on procedural grounds* (1st Cir 1972) 462 F2d 914. "Underrepresentation of Economic Groups on Federal Juries," Comment in 57 *BU L Rev* 198–224 (1977).

### d. Young People §6.54

The notion that young people constitute a distinct part of the community is not new. Literature has acknowledged this as a fact for centuries. The following sampling is very small, but from persuasive sources:

"I am young and ye are very old; wherefore I was afraid and durst not show you mine opinion." Job 32:6.

"It is very natural for young men to be vehement, acrimonious and severe." Samuel Johnson, *The Rambler*, No. 121.

"Young men, in the conduct and management of actions, embrace more than they can hold; stir more than they can quiet; fly to the ends without consideration of the means and degrees . . . . Men of age reject too much, consult too long, adventure too little, repent too soon and seldom drive business home to the null period, but content themselves with a mediocrity of success." Francis Bacon, *Of Youth and Age*.

"Youth does not dare to look itself in the mirror of conscience when it is leaning toward injustice; maturity has already seen its image at such a moment—in this lies all the difference between these two periods in life." Balzac, *Pere Goriot*.

"When we are at the end of life, to die means to go away; when we are at the beginning to go away means to die." Victor Hugo, *Les Miserables*.

This sampling was used by the defendants in *United States v Russo* in their unsuccessful motion to strike the jury array and stay the proceedings (see §3.52).

Young people have distinct ideas and experiences. See generally Keniston, *The Uncommitted* (1965). Certainly an important factor that demonstrates that young people are a cognizable group is the fact that large segments of this society harbor hostility toward youth. *Report of the President's Commission on Campus Unrest* (CCH College & Univ Reps, Series No. 277, 1970), p. 8, emphasized this hostility, saying: "A nation's drive to use weapons of war upon its youth is a nation on the edge of chaos. A nation that has lost the allegiance of part of its youth is a nation that has lost part of its future."

Furthermore, to hold that young people do not constitute a population group that is definable and possibly subject to prejudice is surely to overlook the growing recognition that young people in our country have developed their own culture and ideals. Reich, *The Greening of America* (1970); Erikson, *Identity, Youth and Crisis* (1968). Many older people feel threatened by this separate and identifiable community, but most young people, even those who do not consider themselves a part of such a community, accept it without fear.

In *California v Pinell* (see §2.21), respondents' brief in the California Court of Appeal argued that the question whether the young constitute an identifiable group is undecided in the California courts. *United States v Butera* (1st Cir 1970) 420 F2d 564, holds that they are. In *California v Johnson* (Dist Ct App 1974) 113 Cal Rptr 303, 313 n5, guidelines for deciding the issue were set forth: "In order to rely on the exclusion of an age or economic unit from jury service as a challenge to the jury, the defendant should show exclusion of that group will remove from the jury significant qualities, and deprive it of important perspectives. He does not, of course, have to demonstrate actual prejudice."

The *Pinell* brief proceeds to discuss the judges' testimony adduced in the trial court hearing, and indicates a common problem faced in jury challenges—contradictory testimony by experts:

> Each of the Superior Court judges who selected nominees for the 1971 Marin County grand jury conceded that the grand jury *should* reflect a balanced selection of adults of all ages, so that the views of young adults would be duly represented, along with those of their seniors. Judge Gardiner described the views of the older establishment as following the Protestant work ethic and as being law abiding, in contrast to the young antiestablishment views. Although he was reluctant to adopt the term "generation gap," he did describe with percentages the large numbers of Marin young people who either lead or follow a "hippie" way of life.
>
> Notwithstanding the unanimous opinion by the Marin County superior court

judges that the county's young adults have a different point of view from that of their elders, some of the most heated questioning in this hearing was directed to the two sociologists when they testified on the issue.

For the defense, Dr. Robert Blauner, associate professor of sociology, University of California at Berkeley, testified eloquently to dramatic recent history proving that young adults of all strata in society share a tendency to question the established order, to experiment in new, more humanistic, life-styles, and to be concerned about what really happens in society instead of adopting society's hypocrisies. This is particularly true "[i]n the case of . . . the white middle-class who went to the universities and the colleges in the 1960s and accounted for a large part of the protest on the campus, and the whole antiwar movement, because they were more concerned about the question of social injustice than were their parents." Similarly, young blacks led and developed the civil rights and black power movements, and working-class youths have been more rebellious against the monotony of the assembly line, for example, than middle-aged workers.

For the prosecution, Dr. John Scott, associate professor of sociology, University of California at Davis, testified that middle-class young people tend to be financially dependent on their parents, so that, with the exception of age-specific issues (the draft, voting, their right to contract, their "right to commit torts," their right to drink), these young adults share a "community of interest" with "all members of the family." Consequently, the "interests of youth have been more effectively represented by persons of their parent's generation than by the youth themselves."

On the third day of cross-examination, Dr. Scott conceded that, while the *interests* of youth might well be protected by their older colleagues on a grand jury, the *point of view* of youth would not be shared by such older grand jurors. Among other things, young adults commonly tend (1) to be idealistic, (2) to support innovative concepts in organizations, and (3) to possess the attributes of those whose future status has not been established.

Psychologists, sociologists, and psychiatrists of impeccable credentials are often prepared to participate in judicial proceedings to establish that youth are a cognizable class now underrepresented in decision-making, as on juries. Almost any large city or university can supply one or more experts who will file declarations or appear in court, if necessary. It is desirable to obtain a recent statement, as rapid changes in the environment in which young people develop make studies from the 1960s and 1970s outdated.

In 1974, Los Angeles Superior Court Judge Sherman W. Smith filed an unreported memorandum of decision and order in *California v Taylor* (see §6.53), holding that adults 18 to 29 years old are a cognizable class.

Judicial confirmation of youths as a special and distinct class of citizens has come to pass. To determine whether a "distinct" or "cognizable" group exists which is being denied equal protection of the law, Justice Frankfurter [dissenting] outlined the following criteria in *Thiel v Southern Pac. Co.* (1945) 328 US 220, 230:

1. Do these citizens "have a different outlook psychologically and economically?
2. Do these citizens "adopt a different social outlook?"
3. Do these citizens "have a different sense of justice and a different conception of a juror's responsibility?"

As Justice Holmes put it, would the class excluded "act otherwise than those who were drawn would act"? *Rawlings v Georgia* (1906) 201 US 638, 640.

The opinion of the Court in *United States v Butera* (1st Cir 1970) 420 F2d 564, directly meets the criteria set down by Justices Holmes and Frankfurter with a judicial finding that today young people have "a different outlook" and "a different sense of justice" which might lead them to "act otherwise" than older citizens. *Thiel v Southern Pac. Co., supra.*

As the Court said:

> [W]e are satisfied that young adults constitute a cognizable—though admittedly ill-defined—group for purposes of defendant's prima facie case. We cannot allow the requirement of a "distinct" group to be applied so stringently with regard to age grouping that possible discrimination against a large class of persons—in our case those between 21 and 34—will be insulated from attack. Nor can we close our eyes to the contemporary national preoccupation with a "generation gap" which creates the impression that the attitudes of young adults are in some sense distinct from those of older adults. That apparent distinctness is sufficient for us to say that neither class could be excluded from jury pools without some justification.

*United States v Butera*, at 570.

Judge Keith arrived at a similar conclusion in *United States v Sinclair* (ED Mich, No. 44375, 1971) (unreported):

> This Court agrees with defense counsel that "young people" are a cognizable group. Many young people in the United States today have different values, different standards, different attitudes, different lifestyles and different feelings towards our political system and its processes than do their elders. In recognizing this group, the Court does not mean to say that in order to be a member of this class it is necessary that one exemplify all of the above traits or characteristics, or that those 30 years of age and older are automatically excluded from the group; nor does the group include all those 29 years old and under. The group cannot be simply defined; however, such a group or class does exist and the vast majority of those within the group are 29 years and under. See *United States v Butera, supra.*

Judge Smith was convinced on the point by statistics provided by the defense in *Taylor* on the age groups of California defendants and the relationship of income and voter registration to age groups. He summarized the data in *Taylor* as follows:

> The State of California itself recognizes youth as a distinct category in various contexts. As the Bureau of Criminal Statistics 1970 figures reveal, youths account for more than 50 percent of those brought to trial for felonies each year in the State of California. In Los Angeles County those under 25 were brought to trial in 63 percent of felony trials in 1967; 51.5 percent in 1968; 54.6 percent in 1969; and 51.2 percent (nearly 16,000 persons) in 1970. Another 6,124, or nearly 20 percent of felony defendants in Los Angeles County in 1970, were in the 25-29 age group—so that about 70 percent felony defendants are youths. See California Department of Justice, Division of Law Enforcement, Bureau of Criminal Statistics, *Felony Defendant's Disposed of in California Courts* (1970).
>
> When referring to US Bureau of the Census, "Population Characteristics, Voting and Registration in the Election of November 1960," *Current Population Reports*, Series P-20, No. 228 (December 1971), statistics indicate that in defendants Bowman's and Taylor's age (21-24 yrs) and income (under $3000) categories, 67.2 percent, or over two-thirds of their peers, were not registered to vote, and thus were not on the jury rolls. In defendant Boudreaux's age (25-34) and income (under $3000) categories, 57.2 percent were not registered.

Underrepresentation of young people has an additional weakness. It automatically results in underrepresentation of cognizable classes with a higher birthrate than the majority group. For example, in Mississippi in 1970, the median age of white persons was 28.8 years while the median age of black persons was 19.4 years. Therefore, a greater percentage of blacks fall in the underrepresented "youth" category than do whites. See 1970 census figures cited in motion to quash indictment and petit venire in *Wann v Mississippi* (1975) 327 So 2d 264. See Ginger and Powers, "Mississippi Juror Age Requirement—Unfair to the Defendant, Unfair to the Young, and Unfair to the Public—Is It Unconstitutional?" 47 *Miss LJ* 1 (1976), testimony by Dr. Gordon Henderson, professor of political science at Tougaloo College, Mississippi, on the distinctive characteristics of young people available from Meiklejohn Institute, Box 673, Berkeley, California 94701. Dr. Henderson's testimony was used in an unsuccessful challenge to the grand jury indictment in *Mississippi v Tedder* (Hinds County Cir Ct, No. N-1487, July 22, 1975). The issue was not decided in a companion case, *Joyce v Mississippi* (Miss 1976) 327 So 2d 255, 18 *Crim L Rptr* 2412.

The appellate court in *New York v Balian* (App Div 1975) 371 NYS2D 516 held that the trial court should have allowed the defendant to prove at a hearing his allegations that students, persons under 21, and persons under 30 were systematically and deliberately excluded from juries.

In many jurisdictions today facts can be adduced showing that young people are underrepresented on jury lists, both the youngest potential jurors (18–21) and the next group (22–29). See Zeigler, "Young Adults as a Cognizable Group in Jury Selection," 76 *Mich L Rev* 1045–1110 (1978). But see *United States v Blair* (D Md 1980) 493 F Supp 398.

### e. Black, Blue-Collar, Poor Young People §6.55

Many criminal defendants, and some personal injury plaintiffs, are young, black, blue-collar, and poor people. They have a right to challenge a jury devoid of their peers. Counsel may decide to collect statistics to discover the degree of underrepresentation of these combined groups, rather than of a single category.

Gerald Lefcourt followed this approach in describing the grand jury that indicted the *Panther 21* defendants (*New York v Shakur*, see §3.25) in "Voir Dire of New York Grand Jury," 28 *Lawyers Guild Practitioner* 78, 85 (1969):

> The voir dire revealed that of the panel drawn and examined, 23 were male and 4 were female. The average age was 58 and the range was from 49 to 71 years. The average annual income of the prospective jurors was $23,875, with a minimum of $6000, and a maximum of $100,000. The average net worth was $187,792 with 10 prospective jurors admitting to net worth of over $100,000. All of those examined had had previous experience on the grand jury and one woman stated that she had been sitting on grand juries for 40 years. The panel was split about evenly between volunteers and nonvolunteers.
>
> As far as professions were concerned, the following approximate breakdown is indicative:
>
> Managerial—5
> White-collar—10
> Retired—8
> Blue-collar—3
>
> The voir dire illustrates dramatically that the individuals called as grand jurors are almost uniformly white upper-middle class. The record shows that only one of those examined for this particular session of the grand jury was not white and that only three had what could be classified as lower-class occupations. None of these jurors was disqualified from hearing evidence against the 21 Black Panther Party members.

The trial jury in that case included six people of color and six white men. They acquitted all the defendants after an eight-month trial.

### f. Women §6.56

As more women go to work outside the home, they also participate more actively in political campaigns and take stands on social questions. Frequent polls show that women do not take the same positions as men on current issues, many of which are present, in some form, in jury trials.

In a prehearing memorandum in support of the defendants' motion to strike the Erie County jury pool, filed in 1974, in *New York v Attica Brothers* (see §3.26), the defense noted that, while women composed 53 percent of the 21- to 74-year-old population of Erie County in 1974, only 16.8 percent of those in the Erie County jury pool were women. This discrepancy, an underrepresentation of 68 percent, constitutes a prima facie case of unconstitutional discrimination that must be rebutted by the prosecution, the defense contended. The motion to strike was granted on this and other grounds, see below.

In *Taylor v Louisiana* (1975) 419 US 522, 524, the parties stipulated that 53 percent of persons eligible for trial jury service in the relevant parishes (counties) were female, but no more than 10 percent of those on the jury wheel were women. No females were on the venire of 175 persons drawn for jury service beginning April 13, 1972, more than 50 years after ratification of the Nineteenth Amendment guaranteeing women's suffrage.

In 1946, the Supreme Court had noted the federal statutory "design to make a jury a cross-section of the community" and therefore, in the exercise of its supervisory powers over the federal courts, reversed a conviction by a jury from which women had been excluded. *Ballard v United States* (1946) 329 US 187. In 1975 in *Taylor*, the Court reversed the conviction by a county jury from which women had been systematically excluded under provisions of a state constitution and statute. The Court found that the "Louisiana jury selection system does not disqualify women from jury service, but in operation its conceded systematic impact is that only a few women, grossly disproportionate to the number of eligible women in the communtiy, are called for jury service." 419 US at 525.

The Court noted that "Today, women are qualified as jurors in all the States. The jury service statutes and rules of most States do not on their face extend to women the type of exemption presently before the Court, although the exemption provisions of some States do appear to treat men and women differently in certain respects." 419 US at 533, n13. The Court also said (419 US at 537):

> The fair cross-section principle must have much leeway in application. The States remain free to prescribe relevant qualifications for their jurors and to provide reasonable exemptions so long as it may be fairly said that the jury lists or panels are representative of the community. *Carter v Jury Comm'n of Greene County* (1970) 396 US 320, as did *Brown v Allen* (1953) 344 US 443,

> *Rawlings v Georgia* (1906) 201 US 638, and other cases, recognized broad discretion in the States in this respect.

419 US at 537.

The *Taylor* Court based its decision on the existence of differences between women and men: "This conclusion necessarily entails the judgment that women are sufficiently numerous and distinct from men that if they are systematically eliminated from jury panels, the Sixth Amendment's fair cross-section requirement cannot be satisfied." The Court relied, in part, on "controlled studies of the performance of women as jurors," conducted since *Ballard*, that "concluded that women bring to juries their own perspectives and values that influence both jury deliberation and result. See generally Rudolph, "Women on Juries—Voluntary or Compulsory?" 44 *J Am Jud Soc'y* 206 (1961); 55 *J Sociology & Social Research* 442 (1971); 3 *J Applied Social Psych* 267 (1973); 19 *Sociometry* 3 (1956)."

In 1979, the Court held that the Sixth Amendment and the due process clause of the Fourteenth Amendment are violated by a state statute granting women automatic jury service exemptions on request. Such a statute violates the "fair cross-section" requirement by producing jury venires averaging less than 15 percent female. In *Duren v Missouri* (1979) 439 US 357, the Court followed the prima facie test established in *Taylor*. The state did not meet the burden of justifying its infringement of the defendant's constitutional right by showing that the attainment of a "fair cross-section" jury would be incompatible with a significant state interest. Justice White, for the eight-to-one majority, held that the administrative convenience of exempting all women because some have preclusive domestic responsibilities is not a sufficient justification for the disproportionate exclusion of women and the dilution of the quality of the community judgment. (Justice Rehnquist dissented.)

Another invalid practice may be followed in some jurisdictions in the name of efficiency: deliberately picking the names of more men than women, "based on the experience of the Commissioner's Office that women claimed or were granted their statutory exemption in such large numbers that in order to assure panels of jurors large enough to accommodate the continuing needs of the courts it was necessary, as a practical matter, to summon more men than women in the initial selection process."

Judge Gilbert H. King, Erie County, New York, Supreme Court, struck down this practice on June 27, 1974, in *New York v Attica Brothers* (see §3.26):

> Neither the practicality of the system employed nor the sincerity of the Commissioner's intentions and purposes permitted the deliberate exclusion of

women from the initial selection process. The practice was in direct conflict with Section 13 of the Civil Rights Law and 1025.2 of the Appellate Division Fourth Department Rules which expressly forbid disqualification or discrimination from jury service by reason of sex.

The unreported opinion was not appealed. Recently, New York state amended its jury selection act to improve its representative character; see §2.26.

Each jury challenge is easy to lose, including challenges on the basis of discrimination against women. In *United States v Manbeck* (D SC 1981) 514 F Supp 141, defendants made a prima facie showing of race and sex discrimination in selection of forepersons and deputy forepersons, but after the burden shifted, the government proved absence of discriminatory intent.

### g. Latinos/Chicanos/Mexican-Americans/Hispanics §6.57

While few will argue today that Latinos, Hispanics, Mexican-Americans, Spanish-surnamed people, Puerto Ricans, or Chicanos are not a cognizable class for jury selection purposes, the more common argument will be that the particular jurisdiction contains very few from this group and therefore their absence from the jury lists is not significant. This argument is most likely to be made in a case in which none of the parties is from this group. (But see §§6.41–6.42 on standing to raise the issue.)

The Mexican-American Legal Defense and Educational Fund provided a short, accurate history of the Mexican people in the United States, their distinctive characteristics, and the discrimination to which they have been subjected, including their exclusion from jury lists in proper proportions, in its amicus brief, printed in 2 Ginger, *DeFunis versus Odegaard and the University of Washington* 927–935 (Oceana 1974). For additional materials on Latinos as a cognizable class, contact the MALDEF national office in San Francisco, California.

According to MALDEF's amicus brief, the district judge in *Test v United States* "openly conceded that Blacks and Spanish-surnamed persons were underrepresented on the very jury lists he refused to open to scrutiny." The Supreme Court in *Test* held, per curiam, that the Jury Selection and Service Act of 1968 required that the defendant be permitted to inspect the jury lists in attempting to support his challenge to the jury selection procedures, and remanded the case without expressing its views on the merits of the challenge. *Test v United States* (1975) 420 US 28.

The second issue was dealt with in the respondents' brief on appeal, dated June 10, 1974, in *California v Pinell* (see §2.21). In response to the attorney general's argument that Latin Americans were not an identifiable group in Marin County, the brief argued that the judges were simply ignorant of the community whereas the respondents had presented detailed testimony on the common social characteristics of members of the group. "The fact that Latin Americans were shown to be an identifiable group is important to these respondents, however. The judges' complete ignorance of the existence of this segment of the community is stark evidence of their failure to familiarize themselves with the community and to develop an adequate selection system." See *Montoya v Colorado* (Colo 1959) 345 P2d 1062, on people with "Spanish-sounding names" as a cognizable class.

To prove that Puerto Ricans are a cognizable class, counsel can cite voter registration cases, e.g., *Katzenbach v Morgan* (1966) 384 US 641, and *United States ex rel. Lequillou v Davis* (SD VI 1953) 115 F Supp 392.

Once the governing body accepts the fact that Latinos are a cognizable class, the problem is not automatically solved by appointing Latinos as a majority (three out of five) on a jury commission. This may not ensure a constitutionally acceptable list of grand jurors, according to respondent's brief (pp. 42–43) in *Castaneda v Partida* 1977) 430 US 482:

> That Mexican-American commissioners would select Anglos in disproportionate numbers to their own ethnic group is not a phenomenon unique to South Texas, nor does it vitiate the Respondent's prima facie case of discrimination. A very recent opinion of another Court of Appeals shows the same forces at play. *Murrah v Arkansas* (8th Cir 1976) 532 F2d 105. In a jurisdiction where approximately 19.7% of the population was black, the state court chose ten jury commissioners, two of whom were black. Nevertheless, those jury commissioners returned jury venires that were only 5.6% to 7.25% Negro. The Court of Appeals found discrimination on the basis of that record, in spite of the fact that 20% of the commissioners were themselves black. The testimony of those commissioners was particularly illuminating. One of the black commissioners testified that he submitted names of more black persons than white, while the other indicated that she had picked only one or two black persons, and the rest white. Such results graphically demonstrate the subtle interplay of the various forces existing in the selection process.

The Supreme Court agreed, at the conclusion of its opinion (430 US at 499–500):

> In light of our holding that respondent proved a prima facie case of discrimination that was not rebutted by any of the evidence presently in the record, we have only to consider whether the District Court's "governing majority" theory filled the evidentiary gap. In our view, it did not dispel the presumption

of purposeful discrimination in the circumstances of this case. Because of the many facets of human motivation, it would be unwise to presume as a matter of law that human beings of one definable group will not discriminate against other members of their group. Indeed, even the dissent of Mr. Justice Powell does not suggest that such a presumption would be appropriate . . . . The problem is a complex one, about which widely differing views can be held, and, as such, it would be somewhat precipitous to take judicial notice of one view over another on the basis of a record as barren as this.

. . . The only arguably relevant fact in this record on the issue is that three of the five jury commissioners in respondent's case were Mexican-American. Knowing only this, we would be forced to rely on the reasoning that we have rejected—that human beings would not discriminate against their own kind—in order to find that the presumption of purposeful discrimination was rebutted. Without the benefit of this simple behavioral presumption, discriminatory intent can be rebutted only with evidence in the record about the way in which the commissioners operated and their reasons for doing so. It was the State's burden to supply such evidence, once respondent established his prima facie case. The State's failure in this regard leaves unchallenged respondent's proof of purposeful discrimination.

Finally, even if a "governing majority" theory has general applicability in cases of this kind, the inadequacy of the record in this case does not permit such an approach. Among the evidentiary deficiencies are the lack of any indication of how long the Mexican-Americans have enjoyed "governing majority" status, the absence of information about the relative power inherent in the elective offices held by Mexican-Americans, and the uncertain relevance of the general political power to the specific issue in this case. Even for the most recent time period, when presumably the political power of Mexican-Americans was at its greatest, the discrepancy between the number of Mexican-Americans in the total population and the number on the grand jury lists was substantial. Thus, under the facts presented in this case, the "governing majority" theory is not developed fully enough to satisfy the State's burden of rebuttal.

Justice Powell wrote an angry dissent; Chief Justice Burger and Justices Stewart and Rehnquist also dissented.

### h. Asian-Americans §6.58

In appealing the conviction of a San Francisco Chinese-American youth in *Lee v California* (1974) (Dist Ct App, No. 11487, Feb. 7, 1974) *cert. denied* (1974) 419 US 969, defense counsel argued that the trial judge committed reversible error by prohibiting voir dire of prospective jurors on their attitudes toward Asian-Americans. Defense attorneys Benjamin Dreyfus and Charles Garry argued that "the unique California history of prejudice against the Chinese people compels application" of *Ham v South Carolina* (1973) 409 US 524 and *Aldridge v United States* (1931) 283 US 308, to Chinese defendants. Compare *Ristaino v Ross* (1976) 424 US 589.

The (unsuccessful) petition for certiorari in *Lee* contains material that can be used effectively in any argument that Asian-Americans are a cognizable class for purposes of jury selection. A copy of the petition may be obtained from Meiklejohn Civil Liberties Institute, Box 673, Berkeley, California 94701.

Counsel for Japanese-Americans can refer to the unconstitutional (and unnecessary) detention of members of this group during World War II to prove that they are a cognizable class. See *Korematsu v United States* (1944) 323 US 214, upholding such detentions and *Ex parte Endo* (1944) 323 US 283, questioning the legality of such detention. And see the decision granting the petition for writ of error coram nobis in *Korematsu v United States* (ND Cal, No. C83 0277 MHP, Nov. 4, 1983). For voir dire questions on anti-Japanese prejudice, see §10.66. For additional material, contact the Asian Law Caucus of San Francisco, and similar organizations.

### i. Native Americans §6.59

*Nebraska v Buckman* is a classic, current example of the facts of underrepresentation of a cognizable class and the work that resulted in a quick victory on this issue for an under-funded trial team in a small county.

*Sources:* Defense counsel's notes and transcripts of hearing on motion to quash the venire or, in the alternative, to supplement the venire with names of additional Indian persons. *Nebraska v Janis & Buckman* (Sheridan County Dist Ct, Nos. C-1604, 1605, Jan. 5, 1980). James D. Leach and Bruce Ellison of Rapid City, South Dakota 57701, and Randy McLaughlin and William Kunstler of the Center for Constitutional Rights, 853 Broadway, New York, New York 10003, represented the defendants.

#### 1. Proving a Cognizable Class

This was easy because the group alleged was Indians and the state was Nebraska. However, just to make sure, counsel asked most of the witnesses questions like: "Do Indians in Sheridan County tend to stick together and do whites in Sheridan County tend to stick with whites?"

## 2. Proving Underrepresentation

a. *Number of Indians in the jury pool.* Nebraska bases its jury lists on voter registration lists. The defense called two witnesses. Charles Plantz, a local attorney, testified that he had seen most of the jury panels from which juries had been selected in Sheridan County over the past seven years, that this was around 1600 people, that he would have noticed any Indian people on such panels since it was so unusual to see them there, and that he remembered only five or six Indian people on the panels. He also testified that he had received the key number list of 2137 jurors whose names had been selected for possible service over the past five years by the Clerk, that he would recognize the names of any Indian people on the list from his knowledge of the community (based on his lifelong residence and his law practice), and that he recognized 20 such names. He had reviewed the Clerk's list of 987 jurors who had actually appeared in court for service on juries over the past five years, and he recognized four or five Indian people on that list.

David Clegg testified that he had seen four jury panels in Sheridan County over the past two years, that this was 200 to 250 people, and that he had never seen an Indian person on the panels. He also testified that he reviewed the lists of prospective jurors for those panels (300 or more people). In his experience, 90 percent or so of the Indian people in the area have names that are recognizably Indian (either names like "Long Soldier" or names of French origin that are known as "Indian" names, like "Janis"). There were no names he recognized as Indian.

The defense evidence showed 1 percent or fewer Indian people on the jury lists for the county.

b. *Number of Indians in Sheridan County.* Defense expert witness Dewart Walker, from the University of Colorado, gave his expert opinion that Sheridan County contained 5.75 to 6 percent Indian people. This was based on the 1970 census (which showed 4.28 percent Indians); on the testimony of three welfare officers (each of whom testified there were 30 to 50 percent Indian people on his or her welfare rolls); on the testimony of a person from the school department, who testified there were approximately 8 percent Indian children in county schools; and on Walker's extensive experience, which included comparisons of census counts with his own counts of Indian people (although not in Sheridan County).

The defense noted that even without Walker they could have established, by use of the census data, that there were 4.28 percent Indians in the county. This indicated a substantial disparity between the number of Indians in the county and number of Indians on the jury lists.

3. Proving Underrepresentation Results from the System of Jury Selection Used

Walker testified as an expert that Indian people do not register to vote in nearly as great numbers as do white people. Under one reading of *Duren v Missouri* (1979) 439 US 357, this was enough. But the defense went on.

Walker testified that the reason Indian people do not register to vote is a combination of their exclusionby the dominant white society and their resulting self-exclusion. This tied nonregistration to past discrimination against Indian people. So did Walker's testimony that Indian people were not allowed to vote until 1924 and that until the end of World War II there was a conscious policy by the government to keep them on the reservations and out of white society.

The defense argued that, where present effects are the result of past discrimination, the law has to correct the past discrimination (as in the school busing cases). And they pointed out that the federal statute on jury selection explicitly says that voter registration lists can be used alone only if they provide a fair cross-section of the community. The defense introduced as evidence a motion Bob Yellow Bird made about five years before, alleging underrepresentation of Indian people, and argued that this indicated that the county clearly was aware of the problem for that long and had had a chance to correct it.

4. Proposing a Workable Alternative

Walker testified it would be fairly easy to construct a relatively unbiased list from sources other than voter registration lists.

THE COURT: What's your next motion?

MR. LEACH: Your honor, our next motion is to quash the venire, or in the alternative, to supplement the venire with names of additional Indian persons.

THE COURT: Before you proceed on that, . . . you have an absolute right to interrogate the Clerk on this, but I concluded, after reading the case in the Supreme Court that you cited to me and the other cases, that the position that you take has merit, so it has been supplemented.

MR. LEACH: Okay. Could you—

THE COURT: . . . [Y]ou can clear this with the Clerk or put the Clerk on the stand if you feel it's appropriate, but I instructed the Clerk to supplement the list of jurors summoned in the following way: To secure the names and addresses of persons whom the County Department of Public Welfare carried on its rolls as Native Americans in all categories other than that category that dealt with aid to the blind and disabled, taking the position that those people, on the face of it, would be ineligible to serve because of physical disability. The Clerk also secured school census records where they were available and went through the school census records and attempted, based upon just a visual examination of the list, to determine the names of Indians. The Clerk also attempted to determine whether or not the tribal rolls could be used for the purpose of securing additional names, but learned that the addresses on the tribal rolls, according to her informant, . . . just said "resident of the State of Nebraska." They didn't say resident of Rushville or Hay Springs.

Now, the Clerk . . . wound up with— . . .

THE CLERK: Sixty-five I believe.

THE COURT: Sixty-five names. Now, the testimony of the expert was that somewhere between 4 to 6 percent of the population of Sheridan County was made up of Indian—or Native Americans. The Clerk summoned, initially, 91 people to appear for this particular jury session. I instructed the Clerk, at random, to select six additional names from those [65] that she had on her supplemental list and those people were summoned to appear tomorrow . . . . [As to the] driver's license records . . . there's no such thing as a list and it would have required manually going through each driver's license and there just simply wasn't time to do that.

. . .

THE COURT: All right. So that my record's straight, . . . I'll overrule your motion to quash or to supplement . . . the venire for the reason that it's now moot, subject to your right to reopen it sometime today should you wish to do so.

Thereafter, defendant Buckman, charged with murder and subject to capital punishment, pleaded guilty to manslaughter, and similar charges against defendant Janis were dismissed.

For up-to-date information on jury issues, contact the Committee on Native Americans (CONAS), National Lawyers Guild, 853 Broadway, New York, New York 10003, and similar organizations.

### j. Nonvoters §6.60

As voters fail to vote and keep their registrations active, and as prospective new voters fail to register to vote, nonvoters become a larger and larger group in society. This massive abstention from participation in the processes of government creates grave problems for democracy. It also creates grave problems for a judicial system seeking to select juries representative of the community from lists of registered voters.

The 1983 elections of black and Latino officials (including Mayor Harold Washington of Chicago and Mayor Fredrico Pena of Denver), as a result of voter registration campaigns in black and Latino communities, and the presidential candidacy of Jesse Jackson may mark a shift to heavier participation in the electoral process and therefore more representative jury lists.

Problems in using the voter registration list to get representative panels are discussed in Gelfand and Davis, "The Jury List in Connecticut: Is the Voter Registration List Truly Representative?" 52 *Conn BJ* 449–474 (1978), and proposals for supplementing voter lists are offered at 475–502. New state statutes do use supplemental lists, e.g., New York (see NY Jud Law Art 16 §506 (McKinney)) and Pennsylvania (see Pa Stat Ann, title 43 §§2121–2124; 4501–4532; 4541–4584 (Purdon)). However, as the federal court judge noted in *United States v Blair* (D Md, 1980) 493 F Supp 398, 410 n16, as to the federal system, "counsel have been unable to cite any case decided since the 1968 Act in which a federal court has held that the use of voter registration lists was inadequate and that alternative sources should have been employed."

Federal Judge Wyzanski of Boston, whose judicial district utilized voter registration lists alone in composing its jury pool, complained in *United States v Burkett* (D Mass 1972) 342 F Supp 1264, 1265–1266, that this approach challenged "the whole system of justice in America":

> A jury selection system which is fundamentally based upon voters' registration lists in a state in which no one is required to register for voting, and in which it is obvious to anyone who scans the voters' registration lists that the black, those of Oriental origin, those with Spanish surnames, women, young persons, and poor and deprived persons generally tend not to register to vote, in proportions related to their number in the citizenry, . . . is a jury system which raises constitutional problems of serious import.
>
> . . .
>
> Any person familiar in the slightest degree with the grand juries and petit juries in this district is aware that the use of the Massachusetts voting lists . . . and the policy of excusing affluent and educated persons from jury duty have produced juries predominantly white, lower-middle class, and middle-aged . . . . The effect of that apparently purposeful emphasis in prejudicing young defendants, victims of denials of civil rights, persons from nonwhite races, and others needs no elaboration. Here participatory democracy is a sham.

In 1973, Judge Wyzanski disqualified himself from deciding motions challenging federal jury composition, because he rejected the use of voter lists acceptable to other judges on the Massachusetts federal district bench:

> As time passed, I tried to learn whether the voting list plan was operating more fairly than I had expected. I could see no increase in the percentage of

blacks, or young, or college-educated persons. The jury seemed still to be composed predominantly of middle-aged, middle-income, middle-intelligent white persons.

I began to inquire as to reasons. It was obvious that blacks and young persons did not register to vote in the same proportions as middle-aged persons....

Another difficulty which was obvious was that all the persons on the Massachusetts voting lists were not put into a computer and then selected at random.... Without being too precise, it was plain that this method favored the suburbs over the metropolis, and indeed was particularly favorable to smaller towns. Also it favored the short street over the long street, and the persons residing in single dwellings instead of multiple. There was a built-in discrimination against ghettoes and dormitories.

Memorandum of Judge Wyzanski, United States District Court for the District of Massachusetts, Jan. 15, 1973, "Statement of Disqualification from Cases Postponed Because of Motions Relating to Jury Composition," 12 *Crim L Rep* 2403 (1973).

Where underrepresentation comparable to that of nonvoters has been present, the courts have acted to rectify the situation. In *Carter v Jury Comm'n of Greene County* (1970) 396 US 320, an underrepresentation of approximately 51 percent was found to be unacceptable (population 65 percent black; initial list 32 percent black), and a new list had to be prepared. Even more closely parallel, in *Turner v Fouche* (1970) 396 US 346, an underrepresentation of 38 percent was found to be unacceptable (population 60 percent black; initial list 37 percent black.)

The Bureau of the Census can always supply up-to-date figures on the classes of people who vote and who do not vote, based on statistics from the most recent elections, for each geographical area.

### k. All Minority Groups Underrepresented on Voting Lists §6.61

Voting lists have been the traditional source of names for jury lists. Politicians and pollsters have long known that members of oppressed minorities are less likely to register and vote than members of the majority group. One little known reason for this disparity was uncovered in a study conducted by the League of Women Voters Education Fund. It discovered that among the contributions to disenfranchisement of minorities were the procedures employed by voting administrators. According to this study, election officials have never been required to take affirmative steps to encourage people to vote. Furthermore, they have never been required to adopt practices to increase voting convenience. The study noted that 38 percent of all polling places observed were not clearly marked, 58 percent of the surveyed polling places lacked convenient public transportation, and 89 percent of the local voter officials in the communities observed did not publish a voter information guide. Williams, "Voting Barriers: Strategies for Removing Obstacles to the Black Ballot," 2 *Black LJ* 164, 165 (1972).

In the brief amicus curiae of the Mexican-American Legal Defense and Education Fund in *Test v United States* (1975) 420 US 28, the underrepresentation of Latinos was discussed in particular. MALDEF maintained that voter lists frequently fail to reflect a fair cross-section of the community, particularly as to Mexican-Americans. In 1970, the United States Supreme Court noted congressional findings that, while the Voting Rights Act of 1965 had an appreciable impact on the voter registrations of blacks, voter registration of Spanish-Americans had remained very low. *Oregon v Mitchell* (1970) 400 US 112, 132. Justice Black observed (at 132) that: "Congress also had evidence to show that voter registration in areas with large Spanish-American populations was consistently below the state and national averages."

The nationwide expression of this underrepresentation of Spanish-surnamed citizens is manifest in the statistics recently compiled by the Bureau of the Census with regard to the 1972 national election. (Census counts themselves have been found to substantially under-count Mexican-Americans and other minorities. *Confederacion de la Raza Unida v Brown* (ND Cal 1972) 345 F Supp 909.) The bureau found that less than half of all Spanish-surnamed citizens of voting age reported themselves to be registered voters, while little more than a third were reportedly actual voters. US Bureau of the Census, "Voting and Registration in the Election of November 1972," *Current Population Reports, Population Characteristics*, series P-20, No. 253 (1973), pp. 17–18, 22–23.

The most recent census contains similar statistics, although the number and percentage of minority voters vary as candidates and issues vary.

### l. Students §6.62

*Source:* Opinion of Erie County Supreme Court Judge Gilbert H. King, *New York v Attica Brothers* (Sup Ct 1974) 359 NYS2d 699 (see §3.26) jury pool challenge.

The former Deputy Commissioner of Jurors testified that it was her general policy to exempt those who indicated on their questionnaires that they were "students" and that she did so without a request from them on the theory that interference with their studies would be a hardship. There is no authority in

> the Judiciary Law or Appellate Division Rules for exclusion of "students" as a class. However well-intentioned the Deputy Commissioner may have been in attempting to prevent or accommodate anticipated hardships, her actions did result in the systematic and intentional exclusion of students from the jury lists. Complete exclusion of a class regardless of motivation and regardless of whether there is actual hardship involved is impermissible. *Thiel v Southern Pac. Co.* (1946) 328 US 217 (complete exclusion of all daily wage earners). This is not to say that students may not properly have their service postponed for hardship reasons but their student status does not create, or automatically entitle them to, postponement or exemption.
>
> Student exclusion as a class no longer is practiced by the Commissioner's office. The current practice is to add students to the qualified list as they respond to the questionnaires, and to exclude them only if their questionnaires disclose their absence from Erie County or if they offer other satisfactory reasons for hardship consideration. This practice adequately complies with acceptable practices.

The New York trial judge distinguished between this unacceptable practice as to the class of students and other exemptions by the commissioner:

> Other practices challenged by the defendants include exemption of certain occupations such as dairy farmers, operators of one man businesses, and the like and the Commissioner's interpretation and application of Subdivisions 3, 4 and 5 of Section 662 of the Judiciary Law. The exemptions based on interpretation and application of the law were generally determined on an individual basis. They involved a judgment decision by the Commissioner or his Deputy and were a proper exercise of the authority granted by Section 678-a of the Judiciary Law and 1025.6 of the Rules of Supreme Court, Appellate Division, 4th Department. Many of the decisions of the Commissioner were the result of an understandable desire to accommodate not to discriminate and it cannot be said that any of the criteria used by him were so totally lacking in reasonable justification as to constitute an invidious discrimination and render it unconstitutional. See *New York v Chestnut* (Ct App 1970) 26 NY2d 481, 311 NYS2d 853. No metropolitan jury commissioner's office could function effectively and fairly without the right and authority to make value judgments on juror qualifications within the law in individual cases. The Commissioner of Jurors did not abuse or exceed his authority in these matters.

Full-time students are a "large, distinctive, and cognizable group," according to dissenting Judge Halpern in *New Jersey v Porro* (NJ App Div 1978) 385 A2d 1258, 1265; although the systematic and automatic exclusion of 44,000 full-time students was due to the "benign intentions of the jury commissioners," the exclusion should not be tolerated. This view did not prevail, and certiorari was denied *sub nom. Porro v Woodcock* (1977) 434 US 861. However, since January 1, 1977, students have been included on the list of prospective jurors, being excused only on a case by case basis.

### m. Short-Term Residents §6.63

The Jury Selection and Service Act of 1968 requires federal district courts automatically to disqualify from jury service any person who has not "resided for a period of one year within the judicial district." 28 USC §1865(b)(1). Similar restrictions exist in most states.

The American Bar Association Commission on Standards of Judicial Administration disapproves this requirement (*Management of the Jury System* 11 (1975)):

> The prospective juror should be a citizen of the United States and a resident of the jurisdiction, but there should be no requirement as to duration of citizenship or residency. Most states impose a length-of-residence condition on eligibility; but no persuasive reasoning has been uncovered to support such a condition in light of the goals of the juror selection system.

Defense counsel in the *Pentagon Papers* case made persuasive, although unsuccessful, arguments to strike the jury array and stay the proceedings, and later to dismiss the indictment, based in part on the exclusion of short-term residents from the federal jury list. (See *United States v Russo*, §3.52.)

> The absence from a jury of persons who have recently entered into the state removes persons who will have had a wider variety of experience than the average juror. Such a person will have the perspective of having lived in different settings and having come into contact with a wide variety of persons. To exclude such persons is to exclude a highly significant part of the collective experience of a community, and "it is part of the established tradition in the use of juries as instruments of public justice that the jury be a body *truly representative* of the community." (Emphasis added.) *Glasser v United States* (1942) 315 US 60, 85, citing *Smith v Texas* (1940) 311 US 128, 130.
>
> Further, those most affected by residence requirements are young people, blacks, and lower-class cultural minorities. See MacLeod and Wilberding, "State Voting Residency Requirements and Civil Rights," 38 *Geo Wash L Rev* 93 (1969); Lindquist, "An Analysis of Juror Selection Procedure in the United States District Courts," 41 *Temp LQ* 32 (1967). The one-year residence requirement denies to millions of people the opportunity to serve on federal juries. Approximately 3.3 percent of the people in the United States move interstate each year, and another approximately 3.4 percent move intrastate (intercounty) each year. US Bureau of the Census, *Current Population Reports; Population Characteristics*, "Mobility of the Population of the United States, March 1969-March 1970," Series P-20, No. 210 (Jan. 15, 1967), table 1, pp. 7-8. Accordingly, the restriction affects somewhere between 3½ percent and 6 percent of the

population, more than three million people by the most conservative figures. (For instance, in California with four judicial districts, intrastate migration results in substantial disqualification from jury service.)

To defendant's knowledge, the only justification advanced for this requirement is that it "assures some substantial nexus between a juror and the community whose sense of justice the jury as a whole is expected to reflect." 1968 US Code Cong & Ad News (90th Cong, 2d Sess) 1796. Such a justification is simply insufficient to legitimate the sweeping classification involved here.

First, of course, there is the simple fact that part of the community composition is of people who have only recently arrived. Their attitudes and experiences are a part of the collective perspective of the community. This is particularly so in California, which has a very high mobility rate.

Secondly, such a view of community ignores the present historical situation, which is very different from what it was a hundred years ago. The revolution in communications brought [about] by the development of radio and television has engendered a fund of common experience throughout the nation. News programs are shown nationwide, as are special documentaries and general entertainment. The flow of information spreads throughout the country overnight. If "against the backdrop of mid-nineteenth century circumstances, residency requirements were well-conceived, [i]n light of a mid-twentieth century perspective . . . [they] . . . are obsolete." MacLeod and Wilberding, "State Voting Residency Requirements and Civil Rights," 38 *Geo Wash L Rev* 93, 95 (1969).

This case has received and will continue to receive national and international publicity. The issues are of profound significance, raising constitutional questions of the greatest magnitude, as well as questions about the relationship between citizen and nation (not to mention questions about a national foreign policy of almost 20 years' duration). These are not parochial issues concerning one small community. The trial here is one that touches all citizens, whether they have resided in this judicial district for one year or not.

The same is true of most trial situations. Whether the defendant is charged with a violation of the draft laws, crossing interstate lines with intent to incite a riot, or a host of other charges, violations of national law and the concerns they raise are not limited to a single community. And other issues—for example, crime in the streets, law and order, the viability of drug sanctions—are concerns that pervade the nation.

Whatever validity there may once have been to the notion that a jury is composed of persons integrally involved in the community, where juries and accused and accusers had some personal knowledge of each other, it is sorely out of touch with present-day society and its urban sprawls, where a city of 100,000 people is considered small. This situation is reflected in the fact that, if a prospective juror knows the accused or an attorney personally, that is the basis for a virtually uncontested challenge for cause.

For the vicinage requirement in jury trials, see §§1.32, 2.4.

### n. Misdemeanor Arrestees and Ex-Felons §6.64

Judge Ted Rubin of the Denver Juvenile Court found systematic exclusion of certain groups of youth by means of unmonitored administrative practices by the jury commission. In *Colorado, in the Interest of VC, a Child* (Denver Juv Ct, No. C-42225, Jan. 6, 1971), Judge Rubin held, in an unreported opinion and order:

> Thirdly, the arrogation by the Jury Commissioner's Office of who should be disqualified because of "criminal offenses," excluding those with recent and relatively extensive police records of arrest, traffic offenses, and misdemeanors is violative of statute and would act discriminatorily against younger adults in that statistics of crime in our community and nation reflect that much more crime is committed by younger adults than older adults—at least, detected crime—and that these would tend to be more the persons who would have misdemeanor arrests, or even misdemeanor convictions or arrests for any purpose, who are arbitrarily excluded by the Jury Commissioner's Office. Again, this is not a large number, as stated by Mr. Erickson, but adds to the total which pyramids into what I consider to be systematic exclusion.
>
> The court would also need to add to the third point that the Jury Commissioner only checks police records on male prospective jurors and not on females, and this also tends to some skewing, although minor, in who may be chosen for the array.

Ex-felons and resident aliens can be excluded by state statute (California Code of Civil Procedure §199) from California state trial juries without violating the constitutional rights of a defendant who is a felon (charged with a crime against a fellow prisoner), the California Supreme Court held. *Rubio v Superior Court* (1979) 154 Cal Rptr 734.

### o. Nontheists §6.65

Many jurisdictions have statutes making it impossible for nontheists to serve on juries. California Penal Code §911, for example, requires grand jurors to take the following oath: "I will present the truth, the whole truth, and nothing but the truth, according to the best of my skill and understanding *so help me God*." [Emphasis added.] In the *Angela Davis* case (see §3.23) the defense challenged the constitutionality of this provision, alleging that nontheists comprise approximately 32 percent of the population of California and, presumably, a similar proportion of the population in Marin County, where the indictment was brought.

On November 5, 1974, California voters amended article I, §4, of the California Constitution to include the statement: "A person is not incompetent to be a witness or juror because of his or her opinions on religious beliefs."

In the successful challenge to jury selection methods in Philadelphia, the challenger proved underrepresentation of non-Catholics on juries (65.5 percent of population non-Catholic, but only 51.6 percent non-Catholic jurors). Kairys, "Juror Selection: The Law, A Mathematical Method of Analysis, and a Case Study," 10 *Am Crim L Rev* 771, 797 (1972). In the *Camden 28* case (see §3.55), with several clergymen and women as defendants, a challenge to automatic excusal of the clergy was made, unsuccessfully.

On discrimination based on religion or religious belief, see, e.g., *Maryland v Madison* (Ct App 1965) 240 Md 265, 213 A2d 880 ("discrimination because of opinions about religion is one of the classic examples of denial of equal protection of the laws"); *Juarez v Texas* (Ct Crim App 1925) 102 Tex Crim 297, 277 SW 1091; *Wisconsin v Holmstrom* (1969) 43 Wis 465, 168 NW2d 574; see also *Schowgurow v Maryland* (Ct App 1965) 240 Md 121, 213 A2d 475 (a Buddhist challenged a state constitutional provision that jurors would not be deemed incompetent to serve as long as they believed in the existence of God); *cf. Seeger v United States* (1965) 380 US 163. Exclusion of clergy from jury duty is no longer valid; see *Ballard v United States* (1946) 329 US 187, 195 (dicta).

## p. Aleutian Natives §6.66

Excluding Aleutian natives from grand jury duty in Alaska was challenged by Matthew D. Jamin, assistant public defender (PO Box 304, Kodiak, Alaska 99615), in *Alaska v Stepetin* (Alaska Super Ct, No.3-KO-78-502 Cr, 1978). The defense deposed native leaders as well as a lawyer and a professor of justice at the University of Alaska Criminal Justice Center. In 200 pages they provided graphic pictures of rural life and bush justice, leading ineluctably to the conclusion that a court clerk denies constitutional rights to a rural defendant when the clerk decides it is too much trouble to fly people in from remote villages and islands to sit as grand jurors and instead selects local people. A description of these remote villages is given by Angell, "Alaska Village Justice, an Exploratory Study" (Criminal Justice Center, University of Alaska, Anchorage, 1979):

> The average village included in this survey is small and isolated over a hundred miles from a commercial center, connected only by aircraft or wil-

derness travel. The average village is without the conveniences which are considered essential—when gauged by the standards of people in even the poorest areas of other places in the United States.

Not only is the community without any type of sewer system or running water; in all likelihood it does not even have a fire extinguisher, or an organized method for fighting fires. It will have a Health Aide—a person who usually has received training in the rudimentary knowledge of medical problems—and a white teacher for primary school children.

It will have one or more "stores" which stock basic dry and canned goods and sell at high prices. It has one "community" telephone which suffers from frequent periods of down-time. When the telephone is not working, emergency calls can usually be made on a radio provided by either the school or health system. But, obtaining a response is frequently difficult.

The formal governmental structure of the community is a second class city under Alaska law. There will be an elected city council and a mayor who is the chief administrator. Everyone serves without pay.

There is about a seventy-five percent chance it will have at least a part-time person who is considered the police department. There will be no other representative of the "justice" system in the community except in an emergency or for handling of special problems. There is better than a fifty-fifty chance that the community will have a cell which can be used for the temporary detention of dangerous, disorderly, suicidal, or drunk prisoners. The governmental revenues are almost entirely from state and federal grants in aid.

Aircraft usually fly into the village at least weekly, and mechanical transportation is used within the immediate area of the community.

The community has a higher proportion of young dependents than the state as a whole.

The life in the community is preferred by natives who were reared in the environment in spite of any short-comings and problems. The villages are home to those born there. They are familiar and provide a sense of security which accompanies close social relationships. However, the life is not always simple or easy. The consequences of the difficulties may be seen in (1) a high suicide rate, (2) high accident and injury rates, and (3) a lower than usual proportion of the people in the community in the thirty to fifty age category . . . . Juvenile delinquency is likely to be an increasing problem in the villages.

After this showing, the trial court quashed the indictment and the state did not seek to reindict. In a later case, defense counsel did not make a sufficient record to show harm to defendant from improper impaneling of the grand jury, *Nicholson v Alaska* (Alas Ct of App 1982) 656 P2d 1209.

### q. Resident Aliens §6.67

Excluding resident aliens from state jury duty by statute was held constitutional by the California Supreme Court in *Rubio v Superior*

*Court* (1979) 154 Cal Rptr 734. However, this decision is open to attack in light of the US Supreme Court decision permitting resident aliens to practice law in the several states, a much more intense form of participation in governance than sitting on an occasional jury. *In re Application of Griffiths for Admission to the Bar* (1973) 413 US 717.

### r. Other Cognizable Classes §6.68

In our highly mobile society, with pockets of people from a particular group often congregating in one region for a period of time, additional cognizable classes will be identified from time to time. Counsel should seek their inclusion on jury lists as they surface, and certainly when they become fixtures in the community.

On charges of exclusion of deaf and blind citizens as jurors, and problems of proving their competency as jurors, see Note, "Due Process: The Deaf and Blind as Jurors," 17 *New England L Rev* 119 (1981–1982).

## 6. Constitutional and Practical Selection Plan Proposed §6.71

The 1968 Jury Selection and Service Act provides that "The [jury selection] plan *shall* prescribe some other source or sources of names *in addition* to voter lists where ncccssary to foster the policy" of the act. (Emphasis added.) 28 USC §1863(2). To date, the author knows of no other source of names that has been found acceptable to federal courts; see *United States v Blair* (DC Md 1980) 493 F Supp 398, 410 n16.

The Nebraska trial court judge in *Nebraska v Janis and Buckman* followed a direct, simple method of finding additional jurors from available lists—county welfare rolls and school census records. See §6.59.

Attorney David Kairys, in "Juror Selection," 10 *Am Crim L Rev* 771–772, proposed a sophisticated, computerized selection system based on census data rather than voter registration or other lists:

> Census data, which is the most comprehensive available source, is stored in computers, and it would be quite simple to program the computers for a random selection from all persons eighteen years and older. The program can be written to include, automatically, everyone eighteen or over at the time of selection; thus, for example, someone who was sixteen at the time the 1970 Census would be included in the pool after his or her eighteenth birthday in 1972. The Census data could also be supplemented by voter and other lists and a juror registration, which could be open to anyone who moves to a new jurisdiction or who wishes to be in the juror pool but not on census or voter lists.

The courts, faced with an increasing number and variety of juror selection challenges, particularly in political cases, have consistently attempted to formulate constitutional standards without confronting the inherent statistical nature of the problem. If it is claimed that a selection system is unrepresentative, some mathematical formulation must be established in order to distinquish insignificant from unconstitutional deviations from the cross-sectional ideal.

In *Pennsylvania v Locke*, described in Kairys's article in some detail, defense proposed the use of the census list and selection by computer. During the trial, the judges on the Philadelphia court agreed that the defendant had proved unconstitutional underrepresentation of cognizable classes, and agreed to have counsel and the jury commissioner establish a new system. The judges rejected use of the census for the list of names, but computer use was included in the plan. Under the new plan, a predetermined number of people were picked randomly by a computer from the voter registration list. Each was sent a questionnaire. Few were interviewed after filling out the questionnaires. Studies of civil and criminal verdicts using the new plan indicated a significant difference from verdicts obtained from juries selected under the old plan. In 1980, Pennsylvania passed a new statute on jury selection, see §2.23.

## 7. Form: Conclusion §6.72

### CONCLUSION

*COMMENT:* The following form can be edited for use in a memorandum or brief challenging federal or state grand or petit (or both) jury lists. Note that the Fifth Amendment guaranty of federal grand jury indictment does not extend to the states, while the Sixth and Seventh Amendment guaranties of trial by jury do extend to the states through the Fourteenth Amendment due process clause.

The [*defendant/appellant/plaintiffs*] urge[*s*] this court to [*grant the motion to quash the jury panel/motion to quash the indictment/reverse the conviction/etc.*] based on the facts and legal arguments presented above.

After extensive consideration of [*blacks/youth/etc.*] and [*women/short-term residents/etc.*] as cognizable classes, and the presentation of extensive statistical material, we come back to the fundamental question: Who shall sit on our [*state/federal*] [*grand/and/petit*] juries to decide [*what charges shall be brought/guilt or innocence/liability or blamelessness*]?

This raises a subsidiary question: Who shall decide who shall sit on our juries? Shall the decision be made by an individual [*trial judge/jury commissioner/court clerk*] or select group, or shall the decision be made by use of an objective system such as [*an automatic selection of every __th name on the latest census lists/etc.*]?

*COMMENT:* For description of the automatic selection method, see §6.71.

We ask the court to decide this case according to the historic agreements on which our government is based. These compacts were reached after a mighty debate had raged between those who argued, with Alexander Hamilton, that we needed a government of "the ich, the wise, and the good," and those who argued, with Thomas Jefferson, that "all men are created equal," and projected the ideal of equal participation in the governance of their new land.

The resulting agreements are spelled out in the amendments to our Constitution. The Fifth Amendment guarantees indictment by a representative grand jury (in federal cases). The Sixth Amendment guarantees trial by representative jury (applicable to the states through the Fourteenth Amendment). The Fifteenth Amendment guarantees the vote to all blacks and ethnic groups. The Nineteenth Amendment guarantees the vote to all women; the Twenty-Fourth Amendment assures it to all poor people (through abolition of the poll tax); and the Twenty-Sixth accords it to those between 18 and 21 years of age. We have spelled out the violation of those agreements in this jurisdiction by proving underrepresentation of large segments of our community over a period of years.

While the proof has been complex, the solution is, fortunately, quite simple: institution of a new, automatic system as far removed from human prejudice as can be devised. We have demonstrated that the system proposed in our pleadings, briefs, and testimony is preferable to the existing system, and that it is workable.

The court that returns to sound constitutional principles by cutting away an outmoded, unfair system takes a great step toward encouraging citizen participation in all levels of government and in making real the democratic promises on which our country is based.

## 8. Affidavits Attached §6.73

At the end of the motion to quash the indictment or the jury panel and the memorandum in support of the motion, affidavits should be attached and made a part of the pleading setting forth the statistics on which the challenge is based, see §§6.17, 6.53, and the method by which the statistics were collected. If a survey or poll was conducted by telephone, a simple affidavit will suffice.

__________, being duly sworn, deposes and says that:

1. The facts and information at the bottom of page ____ of the attached document, which is a copy of a jury selection questionnaire card with provision for addition of further information, were obtained by me by phoning the person named on the questionnaire __________, on the ____ day of __________, 19____, at __________;

2. I called the residence of said person and spoke to and got the information from a person who identified himself or herself as said person;

3. I immediately recorded the said facts and information; and

4. Said facts and information are true to the best of my knowledge, information, and belief.

______________________________

### 9. Recent Developments §6.79

See §6.10.

## G. Evidentiary Hearing

### 1. Forensic Experts Needed §6.81

An indication of the types of experts needed to convince a judge of underrepresentation is given by the list of those who convinced Los Angeles Superior Court Judge Sherman W. Smith in *California v Taylor* (see §6.53), although his decision was reversed by the district court of appeal. The list included experts then attached to certain organizations: Leo Breiman, a doctor of mathematics, a consultant statistician and formerly on the faculty at UCLA; Bruce Johnson, a doctor of sociology and a member of the faculty at the University of California in San Diego with a specialty in urban social problems, race relations, and political sociology; Eugene Grisby, III, a doctor of sociology and an expert in areas of black history, white-black relations, and urban settings, on the faculty at UCLA; Michael Schwartz, a doctor of sociology, assistant professor of sociology at New York State University, and visiting professor at the University of California in Santa Barbara, with a specialty in race relations, social stratification, political sociology, methodology, and mathematical sociology; and Michael Ben-Levi, assistant professor of sociology at Loyola-Marymount University, with specialized training in research methods, social organization, and sociology of criminal law.

The experts should be prepared to explain the principles used in determining underrepresentation, and to present the statistical evidence. See the kinds of statistics presented in §6.26.

## 2. Demonstrative Evidence §6.82

In order to demonstrate discrimination by race, sex, economic class, geographical area, or on any other basis, experts can prepare a variety of maps, tables, and graphs to present to the court. Since geographical discrimination often masks discrimination based on race and economic status, proof of area underrepresentation is described here.

To show geographical discrimination, a large map can be marked with a dot for the residence of each juror. This may show the dots clustered in the richer, white, and suburban areas and sparse in the poorer, black, and urban areas, where the population is actually denser.

A table can show (1) the number of jurors from each of the voting wards; (2) the number that would have been proportional to the population (expected value); and (3) the percentage of over- or underrepresentation. White, suburban, middle-class wards may be uniformly overrepresented.

A map divided into "ward groups" can be marked to indicate those overrepresented by more than one-third (cross-hatching) and those underrepresented by more than one-third (dotting). (One-third is chosen because it is a statistically significant proportion.)

The mathematical expert can provide a formula for proving disparity (see §6.83) and apply it to compare the geographical distribution of jurors to the distribution of the population in the "census groups." Using a cutoff probability of one out of a thousand, the statistical table will indicate that the difference between the actual juror distribution and a proportional distribution is wholly inconsistent with unbiased selection.

Two exhibits can be introduced showing discrimination based on financial status: (1) a graph comparing annual income levels for the whole population and for the jurors; (2) a table based on the mathematical method calculating the probability of obtaining that distribution of financial status by random selection.

A mathematical method table can also be constructed to determine whether young people (18-21, 21-28) have been discriminated against.

The evidence on geography may also show racial discrimination if predominantly black areas are grossly underrepresented and predominantly white areas are grossly overrepresented.

### 3. Proving Disparity Mathematically §6.83

In *Hampton v Hanrahan* (see §3.71), plaintiffs challenged the petit jury panel and presented four proofs of underrepresentation of black people: (1) as a percent of the total black population in the judicial district, according to the current census; (2) as a percent of that district, according to census figures corrected for undercounting black people; (3) as a percent of the district jury pool; (4) as a percent of black registered voters. Plaintiffs alleged disparities of 33, 55, 41 and 57 percent; and alleged the probabilities of these disparities as 4.3 out of 100, 1 out of 1000, 1.2 out of 100, and 4 out of 10,000.

The mathematical method works quite simply and can be understood without mathematical training.

If a juror pool is representative, it will have approximately the same proportional composition as the whole community. That is, if blacks are 50 percent of the population, the juror pool should be approximately 50 percent black. The pool might be 49 percent or even 45 percent black, as a matter of chance. But if the black proportion of the pool is substantially less than 50 percent, it can be inferred from the disparity that the pool is not representative.

Another way to make the same point is to talk about flipping coins. Judges (and media people who cover trials) can quickly follow this approach: When you flip a coin 100 times, it should come up heads about 50 times. If the coin comes up heads 60 times, we have to begin to wonder if the coin is fair. If all 100 flips are heads, we must conclude that the coin has two heads. And anyone would come to the same conclusion, even without seeing or examining the coin or the flipping process.

If the odds are 1 out of 10, the probability is .10 or 10 percent. If the odds are only 1 out of 1000, the disparity is .001 or one-tenth of 1 percent, and the system that results in such a disparity is clearly unconstitutional. Statisticians regularly use a probability of .05 (5 percent), or odds of 5 out of 100, as a conservative cutoff point in matters of great importance. Lindgren and McElgrath, *Introduction to Probability and Statistics* (1959). Thus, a disparity is considered significant if the odds in favor of its occurring are only 5 out of 100, or, conversely, if we are at least 95 percent sure that the disparity is significant.

Nonetheless, in *Hampton*, the trial judge rejected the jury challenge, although, years later, after extensive trial and appeal, defendants settled the case and received a large award. The motion describes the nature of disparities very clearly (see §6.26).

See Kairys, "Juror Selection," 10 *Am Crim L Rev* 771, 786 (1972); Finkelstein, "The Application of Statistical Decision Theory to Jury Discrimination Cases," 80 *Harv L Rev* 338, 344 n26 (1966); Sperlich and Jaspovice, "Methods for the Analysis of Jury Panel Selections: Testing for Discrimination in a Series of Panels," 6 Hast Const'l L Q 787 (1979).

### 4. Opinion: Burden of Proof Met §6.84

*Source:* Unreported memorandum of decision and order, by Los Angeles Superior Court Judge Sherman W. Smith, filed Oct. 11, 1974, *California v Taylor* (see §6.54), reversed by district court of appeal.

The defendants have met their burden. The evidence shows that the jury panel in question, and presumably other jury panels, dramatically underrepresent the poor to the extent of 66⅔ percent. This is substantial and meaningful. This underrepresentation of the poor makes it legally difficult, if not impossible, to select a jury which would afford them a democratic melting pot.

Furthermore, anyone who has observed the operation of the criminal courts in this county knows that the overwhelming majority of those who are defendants within them are poor, as exemplified in the representation by the Public Defender. To perpetuate a two-third underrepresentation of the poor would not only be unfair but would be a perversion of justice.

*COMMENT:* For discussion of establishing a prima facie case of discrimination, see §6.21.

### 5. Recent Developments §6.89.

See §6.10.

# Chapter 7

# *Motions for Change of Venue or Dismissal*


**I. Change of Venue to Secure Impartial Jury**

A. Background of Right
  1. Federal and State Constitutional Guaranties §7.1
  2. History of Use §7.2
  3. Court to Resolve Doubts in Favor of Change §7.3

B. Tactics behind Use of Motion
  1. Comparison with Other Remedies §7.5
  2. Use of Restricted Motion to Specific County §7.6

C. Motion and Supporting Papers
  1. Form: Motion for Change of Venue §7.11
  2. Points and Authorities in Support of Motion
    a. Form: Court Is Constitutionally Required to Change Venue from County Where Fair and Impartial Trial Cannot Be Had §7.12
    b. Form: County Residents Hold Specific and Strong Prejudices against Defendant Because Events for Which Defendant Is Being Prosecuted Had Direct Effect on Their Lives and Life of County §7.13
      (1) Form: Victim Was Prominent Citizen of County §7.14
      (2) Others Involved Were Prominent in County §7.15
      (3) Form: Defendant Is Outsider against Whom There Is Strong Prejudice §7.16
      (4) Defendant Is Blamed for Security Conditions at Court Building §7.17

(5) Form: Trial Costs Cause Residents to Become Prejudiced against Defendant §7.18
(6) Prejudice Will Not Be Dissipated by Passage of Time Due to Nature of Crime and Size and Nature of Community §7.19
c. Form: Defendant Is Member of Unpopular Class §7.20
d. Recent Developments §7.21
3. Form: Points and Authorities in Support of Restricted Motion
a. Defendant Has Constitutional Right Not to Be Transferred to Second County Where Fair and Impartial Trial May Be Impossible §7.25
b. Results of Public Opinion Survey Must Be Viewed as Conclusive on What Is a Constitutionally Permissible Transfer County §7.26
c. Defendant Has Constitutional Right to Specify County to Which Court May Order Case Transferred §7.27
d. Transfer to Another County Is Contrary to Constitutional Vicinage Requirement §7.28
e. Recent Developments §7.29
4. Form: Points and Authorities on Demand for Evidentiary Hearing §7.31
5. Results of Public Opinion Polls
a. Form: Qualifying Expert §7.36
b. Form: Declaration of Survey Taker §7.37
c. Presentation of Results §7.38
D. Granting of Motion
1. Standards §7.41
2. Order Granting Motion §7.42
3. Motion to Quash Indictment on Basis of Grant §7.43
4. Recent Developments §7.45
E. Alternatives to Change of Venue §7.46
1. Form: Motion for Statewide Jury §7.47
2. Publicity-Free Pretrial
a. Federal Jurisdiction to Decide This Issue §7.48
b. Supreme Court Ruling on Merits §7.49
3. Voir Dire Examination
a. Venue Motion Ruling Must Precede Voir Dire—State §7.51
b. Voir Dire Must Precede Venue Motion Ruling—Federal §7.52
4. Recent Developments §7.59

**II. Dismissal on Jury Grounds**
A. When Dismissal Appropriate §7.61
B. Motion to Dismiss for Inability to Obtain a Fair Trial §7.62

C. Opinions on Granting Motions to Dismiss §7.63
  1. Dismissal for Community Prejudice §7.64
  2. Dismissal for Inability to Select Impartial Jurors §7.65
  3. Dismissal for Denial of Speedy Trial
    a. General Rule §7.66
    b. Due to Stale Jury Lists §7.67
  4. Refusal to Dismiss for Pretrial Publicity §7.68
  5. Recent Developments §7.71

# I. CHANGE OF VENUE TO SECURE IMPARTIAL JURY

## A. Background of Right

### 1. Federal and State Constitutional Guaranties §7.1

Motions of change of venue are often granted to serve the ends of justice in both civil and criminal cases. There is a string of recent decisions in California, for example, granting such motions: *Silva v Superior Court* (1981) 173 Cal Rptr 832; *Moore v Powell* (1977) 138 Cal Rptr 914 (motion granted in trial court, case dismissed later on other grounds); *City of Alameda v Superior Court for Alameda County* (1974) 116 Cal Rptr 806. Restricted motions for change of venue also arise frequently in both civil and criminal cases (see §7.25).

*Source:* Adapted from points and authorities in support of restricted motion for change of venue, filed Sept. 20, 1971, *California v Davis* (Marin County Super Ct, No. 3744) (see §3.23).

A bedrock of American jurisprudence is the right of a criminal defendant who is tried by a jury to have a fair and impartial trial. As applied to the selection of criminal trial jurors, the words "fair and impartial" are not empty adjectives, but rather are saturated with a fundamental and constitutionally derived meaning. The Sixth Amendment to the United States Constitution explicitly guarantees to an accused the right to a "speedy and public trial by an impartial jury,"and the Fourteenth Amendment requires the application of the same right to the states. *Duncan v Louisiana* (1968) 391 US 145.

The California Supreme Court, in *California v Yoakum* (1879) 53 Cal 566, 571, long ago observed the fundamental significance of the constitutional right to a fair and impartial trial:

> The prisoner, whether guilty or not, is unquestionably entitled by the law of the land to have a fair and impartial trial. Unless this result be attained, one of the most important purposes for which Government is organized and Courts of Justice established will have definitely failed.

The Sixth Amendment (and its counterpart in state constitutions) is the criminal defendant's protection against an irrational, inflamed, or vengeance-seeking jury. Ideally, it should shield an accused who is the central figure in a well-publicized, emotion-fraught prosecution from every juror who holds a preconception of his guilt. It should substantiate the black defendant's entitlement to exclude white racists from his trial jury and should guarantee him a non-racially-biased jury. Impartiality in not simply a desirable juror quality but also a constitutional prerequisite for every criminal juror. See, e.g., *Ward v Village of Monroe-*

*ville* (1972) 409 US 57; *Tumey v Ohio* (1927) 273 US 510 (due process right to a disinterested finder of fact).

Within this constitutional framework, the right to change venue is seen as "fundamental to the American scheme of justice," and it is traditionally available "in the context of the criminal processes maintained by the American states." *Duncan v Louisiana* (1968) 391 US 145, 149 n14.

In a number of cases, the United States Supreme Court has recently made it clear that the right to a venue change is essential to the fulfillment of the criminal defendant's Sixth and Fourteenth Amendment right to an impartial jury. In *Groppi v Wisconsin* (1971) 400 US 505, the Court held it to be unconstitutional to deny an accused misdemeanant the right to move for a venue change (where that was the only procedure that would ensure impartiality) while granting that right to an accused felon. *Irvin v Dowd* (1961) 366 US 717, 728, established that a defendant has a due process right to be tried "in an atmosphere undisturbed by so huge a wave of public passion . . . . " *Rideau v Louisiana* (1963) 373 US 723 found a change of venue constitutionally required because of the nature of the pretrial publicity, without finding any need to consider the attitudes revealed by the jurors on the voir dire.

In recent California decisions, *Maine v Superior Court* (Cal 1968) 438 P2d 372 specified that the standard should be "reasonable likelihood" of an unfair trial; *Fain v Superior Court* (Cal 1970) 84 Cal Rptr 135 noted that "doubts should be resolved in favor of granting the motion" for change.

Put concisely, the law is clear that the right to change venue is predicated on the right to a fair and impartial jury trial guaranteed by the Sixth and Fourteenth Amendments and by state constitutions; that, as such, the right is constitutionally derived and enjoys constitutional protection; that the sole constitutionally relevant purpose of the venue change is to make the right to an impartial jury a reality; and that all doubts are to be resolved in favor of granting a request for a change of venue. See §7.3.

## 2. History of Use §7.2

The use of motions for change of venue in relation to the right to a speedy, public trial by an impartial jury of peers in the vicinage where the crime was committed is discussed in useful detail in Kershen, "Vicinage," 30 *Okla L Rev* 1, 126–54 (1977). Professor Kershen argues persuasively that a criminal defendant cannot constitutionally be whipsawed into seeking (and accepting) a jury outside the vicinage when an impartial jury cannot be selected in the vicinage. The defendant has several rights—to a speedy trial, to a public trial, to an impartial jury, and to a local jury. The defendant cannot be forced to choose between winning a motion for change of venue and being tried by prejudiced neighbors. If the community cannot provide a defendant with each of the four rights to which he or she is entitled, no trial can be held. See §7.62. The Supreme Court recognized in *Nebraska Press Ass'n v Stewart* (1976) 427 US 539, 600 n22, that "the smaller the community, the more likely it is that there will be a need for a change of venue in any event when a heinous crime is committed."

The murder of popular black school superintendent, Dr. Marcus Foster, occurred in Oakland, California, a large city in the metropolitan Bay Area, but it was considered such a "heinous crime." Foster was shot and killed on November 6, 1973; the following day, a communication from the Symbionese Liberation Army (SLA) claimed credit for the shooting. Numerous memorial services and eulogies followed Foster's death. Joseph Remiro and Russell Little were arrested January 10, 1974, in Concord, California. The van that they were driving contained SLA literature, and the two were linked to the SLA in the press. On February 4, 1974, Patricia Hearst was kidnapped from her Berkeley apartment by members of the SLA, and extensive publicity about all aspects of the case appeared in the national press.

Attorneys for Remiro and Little filed a motion for change of venue from Alameda County Superior Court; a six-day hearing was held before Judge William J. McGuiness. He denied the motion. *California v Little* (Alameda County Super Ct, No. 57134, June 15, 1974). An appeal was taken to the district court of appeal, and the lower court was overruled. *Little v Superior Court* (Dist Ct App, No. 1 Civil 35209, Aug. 15, 1974). Venue was changed to Sacramento County.

Defendants' further motions for change of venue from Sacramento County were denied. Defendants were convicted of first degree murder in 1975. The California Court of Appeal reversed in part, holding that it was reversible error per se in *Little* to give the "dynamite" jury instruction that minority jurors should reexamine their independent views in light of the majority view. *California v Remiro* and *Little* (1979) 153 Cal Rptr 89, applying *California v Gainer* (1977) 139 Cal Rptr 861.

*Source:* Adapted from petition for writ of mandate and request for stay, dated June 18, 1974, *Russell Little v Superior Court*.

Venue in criminal trials is normally in the county or district in which the crime is alleged to have been committed. However, even at common law, courts were considered traditionally to possess power to transfer a case to another county when a fair trial could not otherwise be obtained. Some states have codified this concept. For example, in 1872 the California legislature enacted Penal Code §1033, which provided: "A criminal action pending in a Superior Court may be removed from the court in which it is pending on application of the defendant on the ground that a fair and impartial trial cannot be had in the county."

The California experience on the use of the motion is significant. Before 1968 and the landmark decision in *Maine v Superior Court* (Cal 1968) 438 P2d 372, trial courts demonstrated an extreme reluctance to grant motions based, for example, on prejudicial pretrial publicity. This reluctance can be explained partially by a desire to avoid delay and additional expense and partially by judges' "inherent refusal to admit that their particular court cannot provide [an] impartial forum." See Faber, "Change of Venue in Criminal Cases: The Defendant's Right to Specify the County of Transfer," 26 *Stan L Rev* 131, 133 (1973). Appellate courts also fostered this reluctance by according trial courts great discretion in deciding change of venue motions and by refusing to reverse convictions following denial of such motions unless the defendant could show that he had in fact been denied a fair trial. 26 *Stan L Rev* at 133. For example, until 1968 the California Supreme Court had reversed convictions for failure to grant a change of venue only 4 times in 66 cases considered on appeal. *Maine v Superior Court* (Cal 1968) 438 P2d 372, 377 n6.

The judicial perspective on the validity of motions for change of venue was revolutionized by *Maine*, which held that a writ of mandate lies to review denial of a motion for change of venue. The Supreme Court noted (438 P2d at 375) that the former procedure, whereby defense counsel could renew a motion for change of venue after the jury had been impaneled, was an inadequate protection of the defendant's right to a fair trial:

> Defense counsel, moreover, is placed in an unnecessarily awkward position: Unless he exhausts all his peremptory challenges, he cannot claim on appeal, in the absence of a specific showing of prejudice, that the jury was not impartial. Yet, convinced that he must go to trial because his motion for a venue change was at first denied and in all likelihood will not ultimately prevail, he may fail to use every peremptory challenge sensing that the jurors he had examined may be comparatively less biased than others who might be seated were his peremptory challenges exhausted. (See *California v Modesto* (Cal 1967) 427 P2d 788, 795.)

Records of the Administrative Director of Courts and the Judicial

Council indicate a drastic improvement in the success rate of defense venue motions after *Maine*. Between December 1970 and March 1973, 24 trials were moved by appellate courts, reversing trial court denials of venue change motions. In the previous 20 months, only 4 trials were moved by appellate courts, in *Fain v Superior Court* (Cal 1970) 84 Cal Rptr 135; *Smith v Superior Court* (Dist Ct App 1969) 80 Cal Rptr 693; *California v Tidwell* (Cal 1970) 89 Cal Rptr 44; and *Lansdown v Superior Court* (Dist Ct App 1970) 89 Cal Rptr 154.

The California venue statute, Penal Code §1033, was amended in 1971 to read:

> In a criminal action pending in the superior court, the court shall order a change of venue:
> (a) On motion of the defendant, to another county when it appears that there is a reasonable likelihood that a fair and impartial trial cannot be had in the county.
> (b) On its own motion or on motion of any party, to an adjoining county when it appears as a result of the exhaustion of all of the jury panels called that it will be impossible to secure a jury to try the cause in the county.

### 3. Court to Resolve Doubts in Favor of Change §7.3

When the defendant brings a motion to change venue prior to trial, all doubts should be resolved in favor of the motion. California authorities supporting this rule are numerous: *Fain v Superior Court* (Cal 1970) 84 Cal Rptr 135, 140; *Maine v Superior Court* (Cal 1968) 438 P2d 372, 380; *Corona v Superior Court* (Dist Ct App 1972) 101 Cal Rptr 411, 413; *Clifton v Superior Court* (1970) 86 Cal Rptr 612, 616.

Indiana allows an automatic change of venue with no showing of cause. Ind. Rules of Procedure, Trial Rule 76. The constitutionality of this rule was upheld in a civil suit, *Piwowar v Washington Lumber & Coal Co.* (Ind Ct of App 1980) 405 NE2d 576.

Orders granting changes of venue have also been issued in a number of cases in other jurisdictions. In *Alabama v Tommy Lee Hines*, County Judge Jack Riley granted the defendant's motion for a second change of venue, although state law bars more than one venue change. Riley ruled that the Alabama statute is superseded by the Sixth Amendment guaranty of trial by an impartial jury and the due process clause of the Fourteenth Amendment. The trial of Hines, a black defendant, for one rape in Cullman County, after the first change of venue, was before an all-white jury in a 99-percent white county. The second and third trials for rape of white women were moved to Birmingham. (All resulted in convictions.)

In *United States v Means* (D ND 1976) 409 F Supp 115, Judge Van Sicke granted a change of venue from Bismarck (in the Southwestern Division) to Fargo (in the Southeastern Division).

State court judges granted changes of venue in *Minnesota v Calwell* (St. Louis County 6th Jud Dist Ct, No. 13521, Jan. 1979), *Georgia v Woods* (Pulaski County Super Ct, Cr No. 32621, 1976), and *New Jersey v Carter* (Passaic County 167–66, July 1976), after some techniques described in this chapter were used.

Trial publicity led to a change of venue for a retrial in *United States v Yeldell*, the trial of a millionaire developer charged with bribing a public official. The defendant was convicted in October 1978 in the federal district court for the District of Columbia. Federal Judge Gerhard A. Gesell granted a mistrial due to irregularities in jury selection that were discovered after conviction, and this ruling was upheld by the United States Court of Appeals, which ordered a new trial. Defense counsel then moved for a change of venue to Philadelphia, due to widespread local publicity, and Judge Gesell granted the motion. *NY Times*, Nov. 22, 1979.

Pretrial publicity led to expert testimony supporting a motion for a change of venue, which the trial judge denied without explanation or opinion, causing the appellate court to vacate the sentence in *Pennsylvania v Stuart Cohen* (Pa Sup Ct 1980) 413 A2d 1066.

## B. Tactics behind Use of Motion

### 1. Comparison with Other Remedies §7.5

In addition to a motion for change of venue, several other remedies and procedures are available to protect a party's right to an impartial jury. Counsel may move for a continuance to allow prejudicial publicity and juror bias to subside. The parties may rely on voir dire to eliminate jurors who cannot judge the case impartially. A motion for dismissal may even be granted if it appears impossible to secure a speedy and fair trial (see §§7.61–7.71). For other pretrial motions, see chapter 8. For other methods of countering massive hostility toward a party, see §7.42.

While a continuance may sometimes serve the same purpose as a change of venue, in some highly charged cases the pervasive atmosphere of prejudice will not dissipate with the passage of time. Nor will a continuance change the general biases of prospective jurors against the party's class or group, if these attitudes are shown to be prevalent among area residents by the results of a public opinion survey (see chapter 5).

Courts have repeatedly held that the opportunity provided by voir dire examination is no substitute for a venue change from a community impregnated with prejudice. In a string of recent decisions, the United States Supreme Court has explicitly recognized that voir dire may be inadequate because it is often impossible to determine, much less defeat, the subtle operation of prejudice in a trial in a particular community. *Irvin v Dowd* (1961) 366 US 717; *Rideau v Louisiana* (1963) 373 US 723; *Sheppard v Maxwell* (1966) 384 US 333. The California Supreme Court made the same observations in *Maine v Superior Court* (Cal 1968) 438 P2d 372. On the ineffectiveness of voir dire, see generally Levitt, "Expediting Voir Dire: An Empirical Study," 44 *So Cal L Rev* 916, n29B (1971).

## 2. Use of Restricted Motion to Specific County §7.6

*Source:* Adapted from points and authorities in support of restricted motion for change of venue, filed Sept. 20, 1971, *California v Davis* (Marin County Super Ct, No. 3744) (see §3.23).

When a party conducts a public opinion survey to support a motion for change of venue (see chapter 5), it may also poll residents of surrounding counties to learn whether one or more is less pervaded by prejudice about the party or the case than the county from which change is sought. If a less-biased county is found, counsel may move specifically that venue be changed to that county. This "restricted" motion is based on several arguments:

(1) If the court finds grounds for changing venue, the case must be transferred to a jurisdiction free of those grounds.

(2) The public opinion survey provides conclusive evidence of the convenient county that is most impartial and thus best qualified constitutionally to decide the case.

(3) A party has the right, under the due process clause of the Fourteenth Amendment, to move for a change to a specific county because the state may neither impair a constitutional right to the empaneling of an impartial jury nor condition the exercise of that right by forbidding a restricted motion for change of venue when the defendant seeks to avoid a change to a new county where an impartial jury could not be empaneled.

For a memorandum of points and authorities on these grounds, see §§7.25–7.27.

## C. Motion and Supporting Papers

### 1. Form: Motion for Change of Venue §7.11

*Source:* Adapted from motion for change of venue to San Francisco, for an evidentiary hearing, and declaration and affidavit in support thereof, filed Sept. 20, 1971, *California v Davis* (Marin County Super Ct, No. 3744) (see §3.23).

Defendant, [*Angela Y. Davis*], moves the Court for an order removing the above-numbered and entitled criminal action now pending against [*her*] in the [*Superior Court for Marin County, State of California*], on the ground that there is a reasonable likelihood, in the absence of such relief, that a fair and impartial trial cannot be had. In support thereof, defendant avers that:

1. [*Marin*] County residents hold specific and strong prejudices against defendant because:

(a) the victims of the alleged crimes and the defendant occupy special places in the community;

[*(b) the scene of the alleged crimes and the site of these proceedings is the county's civic center building, the Hall of Justice itself;*]

[*(c)*] the expenses of this prosecution are substantial and are being borne by [*Marin*] County taxpayers; and

[*(d)*] the crimes of which the defendant is accused are of such a nature [*(kidnapping, murder, conspiracy to kidnap, murder, and accomplish the escape and rescue of certain named state prison inmates, violations of California Penal Code §§209, 187, 4530(a), and 4550, respectively)*] as to create a reasonable likelihood that a fair and impartial trial cannot be had in [*Marin*] County.

2. Strong, general and well-diffused prejudice or bias exists in [*Marin*] County against defendant as a member of an unpopular class. Defendant is a [*black woman and an admitted member of the Communist Party of the United States*]. Further, in connection with all of the above, the influence of the news media, both print and broadcast, and other factors have created a reasonable likelihood that a fair and impartial trial cannot be held in [*Marin*] County.

[*If restricted motion is desired, add*]

3. In conjunction with and as a condition to defendant's motion for change of venue from [*Marin*] County, defendant further moves the Court to remove this criminal action to [*San Francisco City and*] County, which is the only convenient venue where defendant has any likelihood of ob-

taining a fair and impartial trial. The documents and declarations attached to this motion and incorporated in it by reference and the evidentiary matter to be adduced at a hearing on this motion demonstrate that the prevalence of prejudice and bias against defendant and [*her*] class is significantly less in [*San Francisco City and*] County than in other counties in this area.

*COMMENT:* On the use of restricted motions for change to a specific county, see §7.6; for points and authorities in support of such a change, see §§7.25–7.27. This part of the motion was unsuccessful in the *Davis* case. See §7.42.

[*In all cases, continue*]

[*4*]. The grounds of this motion are made to appear more fully in the memorandum and exhibits attached to and incorporated in this motion, namely:

[*(a) Exhibit A, a sheaf of news clippings from the* Independent Journal, *a daily newspaper published and distributed in Marin County, California;*

*(b) Exhibit B, responses of two members of the Marin County grand jury affixed to a jury questionnaire and a letter, respectively, from the defendant, mailed in connection with defendant's motion to dismiss the indictment on the grounds of discrimination in the composition of the grand jury;*

*(c) Exhibit C, declaration of Jeffery M. Paige, who conducted a public opinion survey on defendant's request to determine the existence of opinions and attitudes in six Bay Area counties relative to Communists, black militants, and defendant herself; and*

*(d) Exhibit D, the affidavit of defendant, Angela Y. Davis.*]

[*5*]. Defendant moves the Court for an order allowing an evidentiary hearing to determine whether a reasonable likelihood exists in [*Marin*] County that defendant cannot obtain a fair and impartial trial [*and to determine whether San Francisco City and County is free from like objections*].

[*6*]. The relief sought here is authorized by the fair and impartial trial provisions of the Sixth Amendment to the United States Constitution, as these provisions are made applicable to this state by the due process clause of the Fourteenth Amendment to the United States Constitution, by the [*California*] Constitution, [*art I, §7*] and by [*California Penal Code, §1033*].

*COMMENT:* On the right of a misdemeanor defendant to change of venue for inability to secure fair trial, 34 ALR3d 804; on a prosecutor seeking change of venue, 46 ALR3d 295.

## 2. Points and Authorities in Support of Motion

### a. Form: Court Is Constitutionally Required to Change Venue from County Where Fair and Impartial Trial Cannot Be Had §7.12

*Source:* Adapted from points and authorities in support of restricted motion for change of venue, filed Sept. 20, 1971, *California v Davis* (Marin County Super Ct, No. 3744) (see §3.23).

A variety of reasons appear why [*Angela Y. Davis*] cannot get a fair and impartial trial in [*Marin*] County. There are two principal reasons, each of which would, standing alone, require a change of venue under [*Penal Code §1033*]. First, because the events of [*August 7, 1970*], which precipitated this criminal prosecution, have engendered unique prejudices in the community from which the jury will be selected, [*Marin*] is an improper county in which to try this case. Secondly, because [*Marin*] County residents hold strong biases against the class to which defendant belongs, namely [*politically dissident black militants*], these residents are unfit to serve as jurors in this case.

*COMMENT:* Due process requires change of venue when probability of prejudice is shown; actual prejudice is not required. *Washington v Bonner* (Wash App 1978) 587 P2d 580.

### b. Form: County Residents Hold Specific and Strong Prejudices against Defendant Because Events for Which Defendant Is Being Prosecuted Had Direct Effect on Their Lives and Life of County §7.13

*Source:* Adapted from points and authorities in support of restricted motion for change of venue, filed Sept. 20, 1971, *California v Davis* (Marin County Super Ct, No. 3744) (see §3.23).

In each case where a motion for venue change is made, the court is required to examine the unique features of the crime charged, the defendant, and the community, with a view toward determining whether a fair and impartial trial can be had. *Maine v Superior Court* (Cal 1968) 438 P2d 372, *Fain v Superior Court* (Cal 1970) 84 Cal Rptr 135. If the court finds that there is a "reasonable likelihood" that a fair and impartial trial cannot be held, *Maine* requires that the motion must be granted. In *Frazier v Superior Court* (Cal 1971) 95 Cal Rptr 798, the court, following the decisions in *Maine* and *Fain*, set out factors to be considered by the trial court in making its determination. They are:

(1) The victim of the crime was a "prominent local citizen."

(2) The victim's death was met with "expressions of public sympathy and generosity."

(3) The defendant was not part of the "on-going life of the community."

(4) The "size and nature of the community" was such that prejudice would not dissipate with the passage of time.

(5) The "fiscal impact of the trial" on the county was a source of prejudice and resentment.

(6) The alleged crime, murder, was "shocking" and "sensational."

On the basis of these, as well as the one additional factor that there existed widespread prejudice against defendant as a member of an unpopular class, the California Supreme Court held in *Frazier* that a change of venue was necessary to "ensure that . . . defendant obtains the fair and impartial trial to which he is constitutionally entitled." 95 Cal Rptr at 802, 803.

Application of the above criteria to the present case, in light of the attached declarations, exhibits, and results of a public opinion survey, compels a similar conclusion that this case cannot constitutionally be tried in [*Marin*] County:

[*Describe the jurisdiction, e.g.*]

[*With a total population of 206,038, Marin County ranks 18th in size out of a total of 58 California counties. The overwhelming majority of this population is white, with black residents confined almost entirely to Marin City and San Quentin Prison.* 1970 Census, General Population Characteristics, *p. 35.*

*Marin residents refer to their county as a "bedroom community," by which they mean to say that it is a largely residential, suburban area peopled by private homeowners* (1970 Census, General Housing characteristics, *p. 37*) *who work outside the county. The community is a tightly knit one, and most Marinites have firm roots in the county. See, for example, the testimony of Marin County Superior Court Judges, Reporter's Transcript 8/2/71, 8/3/71: all have lived in the county for more than ten years. Because of the size of the population, county news and gossip travel quickly.*]

[*Marin*] County's routine and life-style were shaken by the events of [*August 7, 1970*]. Indeed, the news of these events spread far outside the county lines—throughout the country and around the world. Communities everywhere reacted to the event, and many—news media, politicians, and others—took the occasion to heap abuse and vent their hostility and confusion on [*black radicals*] in general, whom they blamed for the outburst, and on this defendant in particular. Life for many in this country was different after [*August 7, 1970*].

The critical point to be made here, however, is that no other community has felt the impact of the events of [*August 7*] as has [*Marin*] County. [*Marinites*] resent what they feel to be the "onslaught of catastrophe in their county life," and their resentment is expressed in the form of bitter hostility against this defendant.

*COMMENT:* On change of venue in state civil suit because many inhabitants of local jurisdiction have interests adverse to party, see 10 ALR 4th 1046.

### (1) Form: Victim Was Prominent Citizen of County §7.14

*Source:* Adapted from points and authorities in support of restricted motion for change of venue, filed Sept. 20, 1971, *California v Davis* (Marin County Super Ct, No. 3744) (see §3.23).

The late [*Judge Harold Haley*], killed on [*August 7*], and with whose murder defendant is charged, was a prominent and well-known [*Marin*] County citizen, whose death was met with expressions of public sympathy.

*COMMENT:* The memorandum at this point described Judge Haley's career, his prominence in the county, and the public reaction to his death. It noted that four judges and the district attorney had already declined to act in the case because of their friendship with the deceased.

[*It is inconceivable that 12 Marin lay persons, not accustomed to viewing issues with the impartiality and objectivity so critical to the exercise of judgment in this judicial system, could erase prejudices and biases from their minds when four judges and a district attorney have, by their refusals to act in this case, suggested they might hold such prejudices, or that the public might believe they hold them.*]

In *Frazier v Superior Court* (Cal 1971) 95 Cal Rptr 798, 802, as here, the person the defendant was accused of killing was a prominent long-time local citizen "whose fate drew expressions of public sympathy and generosity."

There, as here, "Testimonials to the deep sense of loss caused by his [*death*] . . . filled the newspapers." 95 Cal Rptr at 799. This circumstance, the *Frazier* court held, paralleled the situation in *Maine v Superior Court* (Cal 1968) 438 P2d 372, and *Fain v Superior Court* (Cal 1970) 84 Cal Rptr 135, where similar community sympathy and support for residents said to have been victimized by an alleged criminal act were counterposed to widespread local hostility toward and prejudice against the defendant. See also *California v McKay* (Cal 1951) 236 P2d 145, 151, where the court found that, because of the official position of the victim in the community in addition to other factors, a "dispassionate investigation of the case cannot be had."

The *Maine* court asserted that it did not "hold it to be an invariable rule that sympathy for a victim demonstrates antipathy to the alleged perpetrators of an offense." But, the court noted, "pervasive civic involvement in the fate of a victim, particularly when the events all transpire in a relatively small community, is a strong indication that the venue should be changed." 438 P2d at 379.

Here, as in *Maine* and *Frazier*, defendant is a stranger to a community "shocked," "frightened," and "filled with vengeance" by the violent death of one of its popular, prominent members. A large segment of the [*Marin*] community harbors intense hatred for [*Angela Davis*].

[*Marin*] County prejudice against defendant is interwoven with and to some degree directly traceable to this community's reaction to the death of the well-known [*Judge Haley*], and this factor, along with others, renders [*Marin*] County an unsuitable locale for the trial of this matter.

### (2) Others Involved Were Prominent in County §7.15

*Source:* Adapted from points and authorities in support of restricted motion for change of venue, filed Sept. 20, 1971, *California v Davis* (Marin County Super Ct, No. 3744) (see §3.23).

When Jonathan Jackson took command of the Marin County courtroom on August 7, 12 Marin residents were seated in the jury box. The district attorney, the courtroom personnel, and deputies from the sheriff's office who later became involved are likewise residents of the county. Indeed, of the percipient witnesses listed by the prosecution, at least 293 live or work in Marin. Of the 103 witnesses presently scheduled to testify against defendant at trial, 44 live or work in Marin. Not only was the judge well known in Marin, but the same can also be said of others—many of whom will testify for the prosecution. An injured district attorney, Gary Thomas, the county sheriff, and Mill Valley Police Chief Terzich, all prosecution witnesses, are public officials with innumerable contacts and acquaintanceships in the county. Similarily, the August 7 jurors, most long-time residents, are known throughout this community. More than 700 civic center employees were in the building at the time of the events, and some may be called by the state as witnesses.

Because of the vast number of Marin residents who are directly or indirectly involved in the events, as compared with the county population, the likelihood is that every prospective juror from a venire drawn in the county will have a familial, business, or social relationship with, or will know someone who knows, one person or more from the "other side" who was close to the events. The community's sympathy extends to the people its residents know. Many blame this defendant, who, before August 7, was not personally known by anyone in this county, for what they consider to be the disruptive effect August 7 has had on their friends' lives and on the life of their county.

*COMMENT:* It is interesting to note that the Court of Appeals for the District of Columbia Circuit found that Watergate culprit Dwight Chapin was not prominent enough to need a change of venue. *United States v Chapin* (DC Cir 1977) 515 F2d 1274, 1287. At most, 22 of 120 prospective jurors had heard of the defendant or the case, and most knew only that a trial would occur.

### (3) Form: Defendant Is Outsider against Whom There Is Strong Prejudice §7.16

*Source:* Adapted from points and authorities in support of restricted motion for change of venue, filed Sept. 20, 1971, *California v Davis* (Marin County Super Ct, No. 3744) (see §3.23).

Defendant is not voluntarily in [*Marin*] County, nor is [*she*] in any real sense part of the "ongoing life of the community." [*She*] is a stranger to this county, an outsider accused of crimes against well-known members of the community. Moreover, [*she*] is a part of an unpopular group in the society, a group believed by [*Marinites*] to hold values, attitudes, and a culture that diametrically oppose theirs. See [*Point* ___] below.

*COMMENT:* The memorandum refers to the point presented in §7.20.

It is clear from *Maine v Superior Court* (Cal 1968) 438 P2d 372, *Fain v Superior Court* (Cal 1970) 84 Cal Rptr 135, and *Frazier v Superior Court* (Cal 1971) 95 Cal Rptr 798, where each court made special mention of the fact that the defendants were "outsiders," that this is an important consideration to be taken into account in determining this motion.

### (4) Defendant Is Blamed for Security Conditions at Court Building §7.17

It is increasingly common for major trials to lead to heavy surveillance of everyone entering a local courthouse. Citizens, including prospective jurors, often resent this development, and it could affect their vote on the verdict.

*Source:* Adapted from points and authorities in support of restricted motion for change of venue, filed Sept. 20, 1971, *California v Davis* (Marin County Super Ct, No. 3744) (see §3.23).

The Marin County Civic Center, designed by Frank Lloyd Wright, opened its doors in December 1969; it is the pride of the community. Since August 7, the center has literally been transformed into an armed camp. The entrances, halls, and courtrooms are secured by armed guards. Suspicion greets every entrant to the building—all are compelled to cross a slightly elevated platform to permit a metal detector to scan their persons; women's purses, briefcases, and parcels are searched, and everyone is frisked. Following the August 7 shootings, a Marin County supervisor proposed that all San Quentin prisoners be tried at a place other than Marin County courtrooms, and only recently, following the well-publicized events at San Quentin on August 21, 1971, he had occasion to renew his request. He explicitly attributed these problems to the trial of Angela Davis and that of Ruchell Magee.

A Marin jury sitting in this case might well occupy the same seats that the August 7 jurors sat in. In any event, a courtroom similar in design and close in proximity would be the scene of this trial if held here. How can a juror sitting in the seat of his August 7 counterpart listen impartially to the evidence in this trial? Even if witnesses consciously try to avoid doing so, there will be gestures to the former courtroom of Judge Haley, and references to "over there" or "just down the corridor" as events are described. Jurors cannot fail to make note of the security in the building as well as changes in courtroom procedure since August 7, 1970. They will see, for example, that the bailiffs and sheriff's deputies assigned to the courtroom and serving as their custodians are now armed. Indeed, in all the annals of jury trials, there are few where a jury would be compelled to feel more personally involved, merely by virtue of their status as jurors in Marin County in the case of Angela Y. Davis.

### (5) Form: Trial Costs Cause Residents to Become Prejudiced against Defendant §7.18

*Source:* Adapted from points and authorities in support of restricted motion for change of venue, filed Sept. 20, 1971, *California v Davis* (Marin County Super Ct, No. 3744) (see §3.23).

The cost of this prosecution, borne by [*Marin*] County taxpayers, is a source of prejudice and hostility directed against defendant. It is estimated that [*Marin*] County will have to pay [*$1.2 million to $2 million*] to finance this trial, which is more than the entire county spent on [*its educational system*] in [*1969-1970*], and more [*than twice all*] the funds allocated for [*recreation and cultural services*] in the county during the same period. [*"Adopted Budget Requirements by Function and Provision for Reserves, Fiscal Year 1969-70,"* 1970 California Fact Book, *p. 45.*] There is speculation that a tax increase of [*29 percent*] may be required, and by [*August 19, 1970*], [*$57,774*] had been spent for increases in the [*sheriff's*] staff and [*$250,000*] for security measures. The community, misdirecting its bitterness about the costs of this trial, holds defendant responsible for the increase in their taxes. Numerous stories in the local press about this issue have fanned community resentment about these costs.

One ingredient relied upon by the court in *Frazier v Superior Court* (Cal 1971) 95 Cal Rptr 798, in reaching its holding that Santa Cruz was an improper trial county was the natural prejudice against the defendant resulting from the high cost of that trial to county homeowners. In describing the financial burden to taxpayers as a source of prejudice, the court (at 801) said:

> Finally, the fiscal impact of the Frazier case—its actual and potential drain on the Santa Cruz County coffers—has since been brought to the public's attention. Thus in reporting on a substantial budget overrun in the sheriff's office and the negative reaction of the county board of supervisors, the newspapers stated that a major portion of the deficit was caused by the expenses of investigating the Ohta murders and the extraordinary security precautions that have surrounded Frazier's custody from the day of his arrest.

[*The court went on to note (at 802) that the local press had compared the situation in* Frazier *with the one in this case with respect to expense*]:

> And in editorializing on the high cost to the public of such trials as those of Sirhan Sirhan, Charles Manson, and Angela Davis, the principal local paper told its readers that "Santa Cruz County may find itself in a similar bind with the upcoming John Linley Frazier trial . . . . "

Here, as in *Maine v Superior Court* (Cal 1968) 438 P2d 372, *Frazier*, and *California v Tidwell* (Cal 1970) 89 Cal Rptr 44, the cost to taxpayers of the state's prosecution has contributed significantly to sustained prejudice against defendant.

*COMMENT:* This problem can also arise even in a misdemeanor case when hundreds of people participate in civil disobedience, are arrested, held for several days, and tried by a jury after lengthy voir dire, because costs of incarceration and trial mount.

### (6) Prejudice Will Not Be Dissipated by Passage of Time Due to Nature of Crime and Size and Nature of Community §7.19

*Source:* Adapted from points and authorities in support of restricted motion for change of venue, filed Sept. 20, 1971, *California v Davis* (Marin County Super Ct, No. 3744) (see §3.23).

In connection with this motion, defendant undertook to conduct a public opinion survey in order to assess biases of potential jurors in six Bay Area counties. The study was designed to assess general patterns of prejudice about blacks, Communists, and radicals and specific attitudes about this case. The affidavit of Professor Jeffery Paige attached to the motion for change of venue describes the method used in conducting the survey, and sets forth the results.

*COMMENT:* On the necessity and procedures for conducting such a survey, see chapter 5. On presentation of the survey results, see §§7.36–7.38.

One question asked of those surveyed was whether they had discussed the August 7 incident with friends or relatives. The results (presented in figure 1 of the survey) show that more than three-fourths of Marin respondents had discussed the incident. This figure contrasts sharply with the results in the other five counties, where an average of roughly one-half of the respondents stated that they had discussed the events. From this Professor Paige drew the obvious conclusion that interest in the shootout in Marin was much greater than in any other county. (Survey, p. 4.)

Although the events of August 7, 1970 jolted many California citizens, Marin residents were particularly shaken by those events. The courthouse shootings and their aftermath have been the subject of heated discussion and debate as well as idle conversation. One finds talk about the incident in local newspapers, churches, restaurants, and other places where people gather, even 13 months after it occurred. Invariably, Angela Davis and her trial become topics of discussion, particularly in this county, where citizens feel doubly "abused," having witnessed the debacle of August 7 in their own civic center, and now being required to bear the costs of the trial of one accused of committing the alleged crimes of that day.

The community's immediate response to the events of August 7—one of "shock," "vengeance," and "hate"—has not been tempered by the passage of a year. If anything, tensions have been exacerbated and prejudice against defendant intensified because of the barrage of hostile local publicity about the pretrial hearings in this matter, the costs to the county of the prosecution, the attendant security, and defendant's incarceration.

It is unlikely that emotions will subside as time passes as long as the monetary costs and the visible changes at the civic center building remain to plague residents. Ms. Davis and the state's case against her will continue to be major topics of local conversation as long as the trial remains in this county, and Ms. Davis will continue to symbolize everything that local residents think is destructive to their way of life. This case is securely "embedded in the public consciousness." *Maine v Superior Court* (Cal 1968) 438 P2d 372, 380.

### c. Form: Defendant Is Member of Unpopular Class §7.20

*Source:* Adapted from points and authorities in support of restricted motion for change of venue, filed Sept. 20, 1971, *California v Davis* (Marin County Super Ct, No. 3744) (see §3.23).

The existence of strong generalized prejudice against defendant as a member of an unpopular class makes [*Marin*] County a constitutionally unsuitable place for [*her*] trial. In addition to all of the reasons described above, a critical factor on which the decision in *Frazier v Superior Court* (Cal 1971) 95 Cal Rptr 798 turned was the presence of pervasive community hostility directed against members of the defendant's sociocultural class. The *Frazier* court held that this antagonism, which was widespread and openly expressed even before the defendant was identified with the crimes committed in that case, was "perhaps more elusive but potentially no less significant" than community hostility specifically directed against the defendant as an individual. 95 Cal Rptr at 802.

In *Frazier*, the defendant, whom the court described as belonging to the class loosely known as "hippies," was accused of the murders of five established community residents. The court dealt at great length with community prejudices against and attitudes toward defendant's class, concluding (95 Cal Rptr at 803):

> We recognize that in some criminal trials there is at least the possibility, regrettably, that the defendant may be judged on his appearance and life style rather than on his proven acts . . . . [S]o long as there is hostility towards the group or subculture with which he is identified, he runs the very real risk of being judged not for what he has done but for what he is, or appears to be.

If there was hostility toward Frazier as a member of the "hippie" class in Santa Cruz, there is indeed animosity existing in [*Marin*] County toward [*politically dissident black militants*], a class with which this defendant is identified.

[*Marin*] County residents, who are overwhelmingly [*white*], have little or no contacts with [*blacks*], and where there *is* contact it is based on [*racist*] attitudes and customs. [*As in almost all suburban communities, the residential segregation that prevails in the county is maintained by discriminatory housing practices. (See, W. Record,* Minority Groups and Intergroup Relations in the San Francisco Bay Area *11 (1963). This study by Wilson Record of the Department of Sociology, Sacramento State College, was published by the Institute of Governmental Studies, University of California, Berkeley. On housing discrimination in the county, the report observed: "Minority families attempting to move into private housing in Marin County have been discouraged by reports of discrimination as well as by discrimination itself.")*] In short, [*Marin*] reflects in every particular—[*racial*] attitudes, life-style, public policies and practices—the [*racial*] polarization characteristic of present-day American life and so aptly described and documented in recent government reports. See, *e.g.*, *National Advisory Commission on Civil Disorders Report* (Kerner Commission Report) (1968).

*COMMENT:* For reports on racial polarization, prejudice, and acts of racism, see reports by the United States Commission on Civil Rights on both local and national incidents prior to 1984, and reports by state and local commissions, e.g., Governor's Task Force on Civil Rights, *Report on Racial, Ethnic and Religious Violence in California 1982*, (DFEH 201).

A purpose of the public opinion survey attached to the motion for change of venue was to determine general attitudes toward the defendant's social and political characteristics in [*Marin and five other Bay Area counties*]. A series of questions designed to establish the patterns of [*racial and political*] bias by county were asked of the respondents before any mention was made of [*Angela Davis*]. To the question, [*"Do you approve of marriage between blacks and whites,"*] about [*one-half*] of [*Marin*] respondents replied in the negative. Only [*29*] percent said they approved, and [*14*] percent said they didn't know how they felt. These results are shown in figure [*2*] of the survey results. This item indicates the prevalence of an attitude of prejudice against [*blacks*], [*especially in areas of close and intimate social relations*]. A majority of [*Marin*] residents think that [*some degree of racial separation exists and should continue to exist. They do not look toward the total integration of blacks into society as a desirable goal*]. Persons who hold such views cannot be expected to put aside their prejudices against [*blacks*] as a class and judge this defendant, a militant advocate of the movement to [*eliminate all vestiges of racism from American society*], with fairness and detachment.

To another question, [*"Do you think Communists should be allowed to teach on our campuses,"*] [*55*] percent responded no, while only [*32*] percent thought [*Communists should be permitted to teach*], and [*12*] percent had no opinion. The results of this question (shown in figure [*4*]), put to interviewees without any specific reference to [*Angela Davis*], firmly established the [*Marin*] community's bias against persons of defendant's [*political persuasion*]. If more than [*half*] of this community's residents think that [*Communists ought to be denied their constitutional right to teach*], how can this defendant, [*whose membership in the Communist Party is a widely known fact (see Survey, p. 3)*], expect to find 12 jurors who will erase their fears and preconceptions about [*her political beliefs*] and reach an objective judgment on [*her*] guilt or innocence of the crimes here charged? In [*Marin*] County, defendant has less than a [*50*]-percent chance of securing jurors not prejudiced against [*her*] because of [*her political affiliations*] even before they walk into the courtroom and hear [*her*] name.

*COMMENT:* The memorandum similarly analyzed the results of other interview questions, to indicate the level of prejudice in the county against the defendant's class and associations. It then concluded:

No matter how transparent and weak the government's case, no matter how incisive and well formulated the jury instructions, no matter how manifest defendant's innocence, the obstacles presented by a [*Marin*] juror's deep-seated, life-long prejudice against [*her race and her political beliefs*] may so impede the juror's ability to exercise dispassionate judgment that he or she may not be able to pronounce this defendant not guilty. [*Angela Davis*], [*a black Communist revolutionary*], and [*her*] ilk are seen as the cause of the turmoil in the country, the discord in the community, and the general disruption of the American way of life. This juror does not want [*her*] stirring up more trouble in the universities and the community; and the juror's desire to see this defendant and [*her*] "kind" silenced once and for all obscures and transcends any abstract notion of "innocence until proved guilty" that jurors are supposed to entertain.

### d. Recent Developments §7.21

It is now possible to keep up with the law on jury selection the same way you keep up with the law in any other field—by reading the relevant advance sheets, subscribing to services on trial advocacy or criminal law, and reading daily newspapers and legal newspapers. The *Index to Legal Periodicals*, *Current Law Index*, and *Legal Resource Index* provide provocative (and sometimes descriptive) titles to law review articles, comments, and notes in this field, indicating what is happening at the cutting edge of the law. It is a good idea occasionally to ask your law librarian for an index to journals on psychology, applied psychology, and the social sciences, to pick up new idea's from these disciplines.

Increasingly, lawyers are learning to use *Lexis* and *Westlaw* in order to find the latest cases and interesting parallels in other fields of law. It is always necessary to Shepardize all citations.

The Annual Supplement to these volumes will use recent developments sections throughout the book to describe new cases, ideas, and articles that are worthy of note, and to warn of cases overruled and of rules and statutes amended or repealed.

### 3. Form: Points and Authorities in Support of Restricted Motion

#### a. Defendant Has Constitutional Right Not to Be Transferred to Second County Where Fair and Impartial Trial May Be Impossible §7.25

*Source:* Adapted from points and authorities in support of restricted motion for change of venue, filed Sept. 20, 1971, *California v Davis* (Marin County Super Ct, No. 3744) (see §§3.23, 7.42).

Defendant has a constitutional right not to be transferred out of [*Marin*] County to a second county where there exists a reasonable likelihood that [*she*] cannot receive a fair and impartial trial. Defendant has demonstrated that [*Marin*] County cannot provide a fair and impartial trial of [*her*] cause. The logical next step this court faces is to transfer this matter to a county where a trial meeting constitutional standards can be had. [*See California Penal Code* §*1035.*] This Court must find a county free from the objections that disqualify [*Marin*] County as a trial site. Those objections, set out in detail in [*Part I*] of this brief, are: (1) [*Marin*] residents hold a generalized bias against defendant because [*she is a member of an unpopular class, namely, politically dissident black militants*]; and (2) [*Marinites*] hold a specific prejudice against defendant because [*she, a stranger to their county, is accused of what they consider to be serious crimes against widely known members of the community*].

If there exists in the proposed transfer county the same generalized bias that is repugnant to defendant's right to a fair and impartial trial in [*Marin*] County, then such a county does not meet the requirement that it be free from the objection that disqualified [*Marin*]. This conclusion is reached by analysis of *Maine v Superior Court* (Cal 1968) 438 P2d 372 and *Frazier v Superior Court* (Cal 1971) 95 Cal Rptr 798. In those cases, the California Supreme Court formulated the standard for grantinig a motion: if there is a "reasonable likelihood that a fair trial cannot be had," the Court said, the venue is improper. The clear import of *Maine* and *Frazier* is that an unsatisfactory county cannot be substituted for a county that is unsatisfactory for the same, different, or additional reasons. A corollary rule to the one explicitly spelled out in those cases is that a transfer county must be found in which a fair trial may be had.

The United States Constitution compels the same result. If defendant has a constitutional right not to be tried in [*Marin*] County because community prejudice against members of [*her*] class is such that [*she*] cannot reasonably expect to get a fair and impartial trial in that county, then [*she*] has a constitutional right not to be tried in a county that is worse than [*Marin*] on that particular score.

We submit that this Court may take judicial notice of the fact that the widespread prejudice against defendant's class that pervades [*Marin*] exists to some extent in every other California community as well. Although we do not argue here that, on this basis alone, the Constitution requires dismissal of the charges, it is our position that the Constitution does require this Court to maximize defendant's chance for a fair and impartial trial by sending this case to the county that, in a wholly relative sense, is most free from the objectionable class bias that disqualifies this county.

By use of the word "impartial," the framers of the Sixth Amendment, and the courts that subsequently interpreted it, did not intend to restrict jury service to only the citizen who holds absolutely no attitudes, biases, or impressions—whether strong or insubstantial—about a particular case or party. Rather, the word is meant to imply relative neutrality. See Levitt, "Expediting Voir Dire: An Empirical Study," 44 *So Cal L Rev* 916 (1971). The concept is a tool by which the court and the two sides in a criminal trial can weed out all potential jurors with biases of sufficient strength to affect their independent consideration and judgment of the evidence presented to them within the framework of the trial.

In *Sheppard v Maxwell* (1966) 384 US 333, the United States Supreme Court held that it was the potential for prejudice, rather than actual bias, that was determinative on a motion for a change. In *Groppi v Wisconsin* (1971) 400 US 505, the Court held that every defendant with a right to a jury trial was entitled to exercise all procedures essential to ensure that the jury provided was in fact impartial. It is a simple and sensible step from *Sheppard* and *Groppi* to defendant's restricted motion in this matter, the object of which is to ensure [*her*] transfer to a place with the *least potential* for prejudice.

California Penal Code §1078 provides: "It shall be the duty of the trial court to examine the prospective jurors *to select a fair and impartial jury*." (Emphasis added.) Thus, both the Constitution and the law of this state place a burden squarely on the shoulders of this Court to take every step necessary to ensure and protect the highest possible level of juror impartiality. We conclude that on this motion the Court is constitutionally required to employ its otherwise unguided discretion to select the county that will provide this defendant with the greatest opportunity to secure fair and impartial jurors.

### b. Results of Public Opinion Survey Must Be Viewed as Conclusive on What Is a Constitutionally Permissible Transfer County §7.26

*Source:* Adapted from points and authorities in support of restricted motion for change of venue, filed Sept. 20, 1971, *California v Davis* (Marin County Super Ct, No. 3744) (see §3.23).

Although the California Penal Code provides this Court with no specific guidelines on the evidentiary matters to be considered on a motion for venue change, the California Supreme Court, in *Maine v Superior Court* (Cal 1968) 438 P2d 372, specifically detailed three methods of proof to be used. Pointing to the *Reardon Report* (American Bar Association Project on Minimum Standards for Criminal Justice, *Standards Relating to Fair Trial and Free Press* (1968)), a comprehensive study of the effect of prejudicial publicity on the right to a fair trial, the Court adopted the following standard proposed by that committee: "This determination [whether there exists a reasonable likelihood that a fair trial cannot be had in a given forum] may be based on such evidence as *qualified public opinion surveys* or opinion testimony offered by individuals, or on the court's own evaluation . . . . " (Emphasis added.) 438 P2d at 377.

*COMMENT:* The ABA Standards are amended on an irregular basis. Be sure to check current standards as they become available in the loose-leaf service, *ABA Standards for Criminal Justice* (Little, Brown, 2d ed. 1982), specifically §8–3.3(c).

Of the three methods of proof proposed by the *Maine* court, defendant contends that a public opinion survey, such as the one conducted in this case, is by far the most, if not the only, accurate and authoritative means of reaching an informed judgment on the issue of the nature and degree of prejudice against defendant's class in possible transfer counties. See Zeisel, "The Uniqueness of Survey Evidence," 45 *Cornell LQ* 322 (1960).

The specific issue dealt with by the *Reardon Report* was the effect of prejudicial pretrial publicity on the right to a fair trial. Although opinion testimony of individuals might be a sufficient means of assessing the prejudicial effects of publicity, such testimony by itself is not the best means of measuring an "elusive" quality like class bias. And it is axiomatic that a survey of many opinions is a more telling barometer of community attitudes in a number of counties than a single judge's own evaluation. Indeed, citing *Rideau v Louisiana* (1963) 373 US 723, the *Reardon Report* specifically points out that a single judge's estimate of the nature and extent of prejudice is a substitute for other methods of proof only on "occasions when the inherently prejudicial nature of the material, coupled with knowledge of its wide dissemination in the community, requires the granting of relief without elaborate soundings of community sentiment." *Reardon Report* 153.

Particularly when the prejudice on which the defendant's motion is based exists to some degree in other counties as well, a public opinion poll is the only scientific method of evaluating relative degrees of prejudice in the potential transfer counties. In the *Reardon Report*, the American Bar Association joined "a number of commentators [who] have urged the use [of public opinion surveys] as furnishing a more scientific basis for a determination of community sentiment—*and for comparison with sentiment in other communities in the jurisdiction*—than any other available device." (Emphasis added.) *Reardon Report* 152. Thus, the report clearly contemplates a comparative survey, such as was conducted here, to inform the court's decision on where to move a case.

To summarize, defendant's argument is: (1) widespread and deep-seated prejudice against defendant as a member of an unpopular class exists throughout the state; (2) some counties are not as tainted by this type of prejudice as others; (3) in [*Marin*] County, the prejudice reaches proportions rendering this an unconstitutional venue for this trial; (4) defendant has a right to be transferred from [*Marin*] to the "convenient" county least infected by this prejudice; (5) a public opinion survey is the best available method of comparing the level of prejudice in given counties; and (6) in the absence of contrary evidence of a higher probative value, this Court is constitutionally required to accept the results of the poll taken about this case and transfer this case to [*San Francisco*], the county where this prejudice against [*politically dissident black militants*] is least pervasive.

### c. Defendant Has Constitutional Right to Specify County to Which Court May Order Case Transferred §7.27

*Source:* Adapted from points and authorities in support of unsuccessful restricted motion for change of venue, filed Sept. 20, 1971, *California v Davis* (Marin County Super Ct, No. 3744) (see §§3.23, 7.42).

Defendant has shown that [*she*] will not be able to receive a fair trial in [*Marin*] County, and that [*she*] is constitutionally and statutorily entitled to a change of venue. Defendant's motion for a change of venue in this case is what we term a "restricted" one, i.e., it is a motion to change venue to a specified county. In this instance, defendant has specified [*San Francisco City and*] County, because that is the only constitutionally permissible county in the vicinity to which this Court may transfer this case.

Restricted motions for change of venue have been considered as a matter of course in civil cases. See, e.g., *Silva v Superior Court* (1981) 173 Cal Rptr 832; *City of Alameda v Superior Court for Alameda County* (1974) 116 Cal Rptr 806; *Scribner v Superior Court* (1971) 97 Cal Rptr 217; *Pearson v Superior Court* (Dist Ct App 1962) 18 Cal Rptr 578; *DeLong v DeLong* (Dist Ct App 1954) 273 P2d 921; *Rios v Lacey Trucking Co.* (Dist Ct App 1954) 268 P2d 160. See also California Code of Civil Procedure §397. Such restricted motions are even more appropriate in criminal cases; in fact, in circumstances such as are presented by this case, they are constitutionally required.

Defendant has established that the due process clause of the Fourteenth Amendment to the United States Constitution guarantees the same right to change venue that is guaranteed by California Penal Code §1033. At the same time, the due process clause prohibits governmental action that would impair or inhibit defendant's free exercise of a constitutional right (such as the right to change venue), unless that governmental action is necessary to some compelling governmental interest. Thus, in *Griffin v California* (1965) 380 US 609, the United States Supreme Court held that prosecution comments to the jury on the defendant's failure to take the stand in his own defense were an unconstitutional impairment of the defendant's right to remain silent under the self-incrimination privilege in the Fifth Amendment. Similarly, in *United States v Jackson* (1968) 390 US 570, the Supreme Court held unconstitutional the Federal Kidnapping Act provision that only the jury could impose the death penalty, since this made the "risk of death" the price for asserting the constitutional right to a jury trial. In *Green v United States* (1957) 355 US 184, the Supreme Court held that a defendant whose conviction of second-degree murder had been reversed on appeal could not be retried for first-degree murder, because this would condition the defendant's exercise of his constitutional right against double jeopardy on his relinquishment of his right to appeal an unjust conviction. In a related holding the California Supreme Court, in *California v Henderson* (Cal 1963) 386 P2d 677, held that a defendant who was convicted of first-degree murder and sentenced to life imprisonment at his first trial could not be sentenced to death on a retrial of the charges, because his "right to appeal from an erroneous judgment is unreasonably impaired when he is required to risk his life to invoke that right." 386 P2d at 686. See also *Fay v Noia* (1963) 372 US 391; *Worcester v Commissioner* (1st Cir 1966) 370 F2d 173.

These cases firmly establish the principle that the state may not impair a defendant's exercise of his constitutional rights and the corollary principle that the state may not condition the exercise of a constitutional right on the relinquishment of another right (whether constitutional or not). These principles constitutionally guarantee defendant's right to move for change of venue specifically to [*San Francisco City and*] County: to deny the right to a restricted motion for change of venue would be unconstitutionally to impair defendant's exercise of the constitutionally guaranteed right to change venue.

If a restricted change of venue motion were not permitted, defendant would be forced to choose between (1) making a "general" motion for a venue change—which would expose [*her*] to the possibility of being transferred to any county in the state—and (2) staying in [*Marin*]. But, while defendant maintains that [*she*] cannot receive a fair trial in Marin County, [*she*] also asserts that there is only one other "convenient" county that would offer a better opportunity for a fair trial. Defendant bases this opinion wholly on the results of the public opinion survey attached to the motion. Possible trial sites other than the five counties included in the survey were ruled out because they are not, in the language of California Penal Code §1035, "for the convenience of all parties." Counties outside [*the Bay Area*] would be inconvenient both to the state and to defendant. Their distance from [*her*] attorneys would render any [*non-Bay-Area*] county inconvenient to defendant. More importantly, given the present state of [*her*] financial affairs, it would be virtually impossible for defendant to finance a move to a distant county at this time.

The interests of the state are not served by a major move either. It would impose a severe financial burden on the taxpayers who must foot the bill for this prosecution to authorize its transfer to a far distant county.

Defendant believes that it will be impossible for [*her*] to receive a fair trial in any county in California because of the [*racist*] nature of California, and United States society. At the same time, however, [*she*] recognizes that, unless the prosecution against [*her*] is dismissed, as it should be, a trial will take place somewhere in California. Defendant is moving to change venue to [*San Francisco City and*] County because it is the only county in which defendant is confident that [*she*] has a chance, albeit slight, of receiving something closer to a fair trial than she can receive in [*Marin*] County. [*Defendant is not unmindful of the problems that are presented by the selection of San Francisco as a place of venue. As the results of the survey show, San Franciscans exhibit a high degree of prejudice against blacks (35 percent think black militants should be banned from college campuses) and against this defendant in particular (40 percent hold an unfavorable opinion of her); however, San Francisco "is considerably less prejudiced than any of the other five counties." Survey, p. 5.*] Because defendant recognizes that, with the exception of [*San Francisco*], [*her*] chances of receiving a fair trial are actually worse in every other county in the area than they are in [*Marin*] County, [*she*] fears placing [*her*] fate in the "grab bag" by making a general motion to change venue from [*Marin*] County.

It is not an answer to defendant's restricted motion to say that [*she*] should attempt to pick a jury in whatever county is selected by this Court and, if it appears unlikely that a fair and impartial jury can be selected in the transfer county, then avail [*herself*] of the right to make a second motion for a change from that county. Although the law places no limit on a defendant's right to seek changes of venue (*Irvin v Dowd* (1961) 366 US 717), realistically, defendant is limited by poverty, which prevents [*her*] from filing repeated motions, and by [*her*] status as an incarcerated person. It is contrary to the interests of justice to force this defendant to file more than one motion, and to attempt to pick a jury in more than one venue, for such a procedure would not only exhaust the energies and money of defendant, but also strain the resources of the judicial system. Voir dire examination, properly conducted, consumes much judicial time; to conduct voir dire in more than one jurisdiction in the same case would place an impossible burden on criminal trial courts.

In one of the Watergate cases, the appellate court held that a defendant may not transfer a case from a metropolitan to a more rural community, far from the scene of the alleged criminal activity. *United States v Chapin* (DC Cir 1977) 515 F2d 1274, 1288. The court held that the jury's verdict of acquittal on a substantial portion of the charges negated defendant's effort to show prejudice. See 50 ALR 3d 760.

### d. Transfer to Another County Is Contrary to Constitutional Vicinage Requirement §7.28

*Source:* Adapted from unsuccessful petition for writ of mandate, filed April 1975, in *Russell Little v Superior Court* (see §7.2).

The transfer of venue to [*Sacramento*] County deprived defendants of their right to be tried in the available judicial district that best approximates, in terms of racial and minority composition, the judicial district in which the crime was committed, contrary to the "vicinage" guaranty of the Sixth and Fourteenth Amendments to the United States Constitution.

In *California v Jones* (1973) 108 Cal Rptr 345, 349, the California Supreme Court recognized the "vicinage" requirement of the United States Constitution and held that "the Sixth and Fourteenth Amendments . . . guarantee a criminal defendant in a state trial the right to be tried by an impartial jury comprising a representative cross-section of, and selected residents of, the judicial district where the crime was committed."

[*Petitioners*] contend that the change of venue should have been made to the available judicial district that best approximates, in terms of racial and minority group composition, the judicial district in which the crime was committed. The transfer to [*Sacramento*] County denied [*them*] a jury as closely similar as possible to one drawn from the original judicial district, as [*they*] had been guaranteed by the California Supreme Court decision that placed this right within those guaranteed by the Sixth and Fourteenth Amendments.

The chart appended to this [*memorandum*], prepared from the [*1970*] Tabulated United States Census, depicts the racial mix of [*California*] counties with population over 250,000. [*Alameda*] County, the county of original venue, has a population that is [*21*] percent nonwhite; [*Los Angeles*] has [*14*] percent nonwhite; [*Monterey*] [*12*] percent. By contrast, [*Sacramento*] is only [*10*] percent nonwhite and [*Santa Clara*] is [*6*] percent. Even though the composition of the [*Los Angeles*] community is substantially less heterogeneous than that of [*Alameda*], of the four available suggested judicial districts [*Los Angeles*] County most closely approximates [*Alameda*], and for that reason [*petitioners*] urged the [*Alameda County Superior*] Court to transfer [*their*] case there. Instead, the court selected [*Sacramento*] County with a nonwhite population less than half that of [*Alameda*] County.

The United States Supreme Court has repeatedly recognized that the government may not condition the assertion of one constitutional right upon the surrender of another unless justified in so doing by a substantial government-held interest. *Simmons v United States* (1968) 390 US 377; *United States v Jackson* (1968) 390 US 570; *Brooks v Tennessee* (1972) 406 US 605. Under this doctrine, the court, when considering such a plan, will weigh (1) the extent to which the exercise of rights, constitutional or not, is burdened; (2) the importance of protection of these rights; and (3) the countervailing public interest behind the challenged procedures, including a determination of whether the state interests could be served by less restrictive alternatives. For example, in *Brady v United States* (1970) 397 US 742, the constitutionality of plea-bargaining was upheld using this analysis. The Court found that, because both parties received substantial benefits from the practice (defendant gains a reduced sentence and is relieved of the burdens of trial; the state gains prompt punishment and conservation of scarce prosecutorial and judicial resources), and because the present system of criminal jurisprudence would collapse without it, plea-bargaining is not invalid as an unconstitutional condition.

*COMMENT:* California lawyers should consider using a different example, in view of Proposition 8, adopted in 1982, which prohibits plea-bargaining. See California Penal Code §1192.7.

In *Brady*, Justice White carefully explained the holding in *United States v Jackson*, *supra*, and distinguished its facts from *Brady*. In *Jackson*, the court struck down the death penalty provision of the federal kidnapping law, which allowed imposition of the death penalty only upon the recommendation of a jury, because it "imposes an impermissible burden upon the exercise of a constitutional right." (390 US at 572.) The inevitable effects would be to chill assertion of the Fifth Amendment right not to plead guilty and to deter the exercise of the Sixth Amendment right to a jury trial. Because the state interest of "limiting the death penalty to cases in which a jury recommends it" could be "achieved without penalizing those defendants who plead not guilty" and elect a jury trial, the death penalty provision "needlessly penalizes the assertion of a constitutional right" (390 US at 583) and was therefore unconstitutional.

The parallel to the instant case is obvious: the [*defendants'*] Sixth Amendment constitutional right to a fair and impartial trial is unnecessarily jeopardized by the denial of transfer to [*Los Angeles*] County, and the state cannot justify this denial solely on grounds of cost or convenience. [*Defendants Remiro and Little*] will suffer loss of their constitutional rights by a denial of transfer of venue to [*Los Angeles*] County.

Further support for this doctrine can be found in *Crampton v Ohio* (1971) 402 US 138 (upholding a unitary trial scheme); *Brooks v Tennessee* (1972) 406 US 605 (invalidating the rule that a defendant who wishes to testify must be the first defense witness); and *Chaffin v Stynchomb* (1973) 412 US 17 (upholding the right of the jury to impose a longer sentence upon retrial after appeal). The condition on a constitutional right was upheld where the state interest was found to be strong and where invalidating it would require a wide-ranging overhaul of the criminal system (as in *Crampton*) and where the chilling effect on the exercise of a constitutional right to appeal was so "speculative" as to be a very slight factor (as in *Chaffin*). The condition was struck down in *Brooks* because it placed the accused in a very real dilemma as to whether to exercise his Fifth Amendment right not to testify and also impaired his Sixth Amendment right to effective assistance of counsel, and the state interest (prevention of the accused's testimony being overly influenced by that of other witnesses) was found to be weak.

The [*trial court*] did mention the factors of convenience and cost; however, [*Oakland*] and [*Los Angeles*] are linked by frequent, quick, and inexpensive air service. Even if transfer to [*Sacramento*] were somewhat less expensive, which has not been substantiated, [*defendants*] would submit that such a difference in cost cannot justify the sacrifice of [*their*] constitutional rights regarding the composition of the jury panel. [*Rule 842 of the California Rules of Court*] requires that the choice be made in the interest of justice, not economy. And, given the potential burden above demonstrated on the exercise of [*petitioners'*] constitutional rights, the interests of justice would best [*have been*] served by transfer to a locale satisfying the vicinage requirement.

Although this argument was unsuccessful in both state and federal courts, the federal judge in the Eastern District of California did certify to the Ninth Circuit Court of Appeals that this was a justiciable issue.

The defense team conducted extensive surveys of the population in support of its motion for change of venue, as well as to challenge the composition of the jury panel, and to aid in the jury selection process, in the highly publicized *Joan Little* case, the black woman prisoner charged with murder of an armed white prison guard. (Courtney Mullin, Ph.D. candidate in psychology at North Carolina State University, organized the surveys, with help from Drs. Jay Schulman and Richard Christie.) Although North Carolina law restricts a change of venue to adjoining counties, the trial judge held that it was within the discretion of the court to move the trial beyond the boundaries described in the statute when necessary to the administration of justice. He transferred the trial from Washington County to Raleigh, 100 miles away in Wake County, a much more cosmopolitan area. Little testified that the guard, armed with an icepick, forced her to perform an act of oral sex. He dropped the icepick; she grabbed it, stabbed him in self-defense, and fled from the jail. After a lengthy trial, the jury acquitted her, on August 15, 1975. See McConahay, "Uses of Social Science in Trials with Political and Racial Overtones: The Trial of Joan Little," 41 *Law & Contemp Prob* 205 (1977).

Numerous law review articles have also discussed the vicinage question. See 23 *Catholic L Rev* 394 (1973); 2 *Fordham Urban LJ* 395 (1974); 25 *Hastings LJ* 547 (1974); 2 *Hofstra L Rev* 415 (1974); 5 *Rutgers Camden LJ* 514 (1974); 20 *Wayne L Rev* 1301 (1974).

### e. Recent Developments §7.29

See §7.21

### 4. Form: Points and Authorities on Demand for Evidentiary Hearing §7.31

*Source:* Adapted from points and authorities in support of restricted motion for change of venue, filed Sept. 20, 1971, *California v Davis* (Marin County Super Ct, No. 3744) (see §3.23).

In *Frazier v Superior Court* (Cal 1971) 95 Cal Rptr 798, a superior court refusal to grant the defendant a change of venue was reversed by the California Supreme Court, which ordered that court to "hold a hearing to determine a place where a fair and impartial trial can be had, and transfer the cause to that place." 95 Cal Rptr at 804.

The declarations and exhibits submitted in support of defendant's motion for a venue change to [*San Francisco*] conclusively established defendant's constitutional right to the relief requested by the motion. However, under *Frazier*, defendant is entitled to an evidentiary hearing to submit further evidence in support of [*her*] claim that [*San Francisco*] is the only county to which this case may be moved.

### 5. Results of Public Opinion Polls

#### a. Form: Qualifying Expert §7.36

*Source:* Adapted from declaration under penalty of perjury, executed June 9, 1970, *Soledad Brothers* case (see §5.21).

I,[*Walter L. Goldfrank*], declare:

During [*the months of May and the early part of June*] I conducted a survey of attitudes in [*Monterey*] County. I am qualified to conduct this survey and competent to analyze its results because of the following qualifications:

I am [*Acting Assistant Professor of Sociology at Merrill College, University of California at Santa Cruz, a position I have held for two years.*] I was trained at [*Harvard College and at the University of Madrid, and I am a candidate for the doctoral degree at Columbia University*]. I have been trained in survey research at [*the Bureau of Applied Social Research, which is connected to Columbia University*]. I have participated in [*four*] major survey research projects, and, as research associate to various professors, I have used survey data in other studies. I have [*two*] publications in the field. I am a member of the American Sociological Association.

*COMMENT:* This paragraph qualified a relatively new expert in his field. For a summary of the qualifications of an expert with innumerable books and positions, see §8.85. For the kinds of qualifications of experts a trial judge found convincing, see §6.81.

### b. Form: Declaration of Survey Taker §7.37

*Source:* Adapted from declaration of Jeffery M. Paige, dated Sept. 20, 1971, *California v Davis* (see §3.23).

I designed the public opinion survey attached to this declaration, supervised its administration, collated the results, and prepared the graphs. I prepared the attached report and believe that the facts stated in it are true and correct and that the report is true and accurate.

I make this declaration under penalty of perjury.
Done this [*20th*] day of [*September, 1971*].

[*Signature of declarant*]

### c. Presentation of Results §7.38

The procedure for conducting a survey is described in chapter 5. One effective method of presenting the results to the trial court is offered here.

*Source:* Adapted from declaration of Jeffery M. Paige, dated Sept. 20, 1971, *California v Davis* (see §3.23).

The survey indicates that knowledge about Angela Davis and the Marin County courthouse shootout is extraordinarily widespread in the Bay Area. Less than 2 percent of Bay Area registered voters reported that they had not heard about the shootout and only 0.5 percent did not recognize Ms. Davis. These levels of recognition can be compared only to interest in major political figures such as presidential candidates. Presidential aspirant George McGovern, for example, despite persistent campaigning, is still recognized by only 60 percent of registered voters in recent national polls.

*COMMENT:* The *Davis* survey was taken more than a year before the 1972 presidential election.

These levels of recognition indicate intense interest in both the case and Ms. Davis throughout the Bay Area.

Knowledge about Ms. Davis's social and political characteristics and about her alleged involvement in the Marin shootout is somewhat less widely diffused than simple recognition but is still remarkably widespread. Thus, 76 percent of the respondents said they believed that Angela Davis was a black militant,

78 percent believed that she was a Communist, and 84 percent knew that she had been a college professor. There is also widespread belief that Ms. Davis was actually involved in the actions with which she is now charged. While 59 percent of all respondents believed that she bought the guns used in the Marin County shootout, only 4 percent believed she had not bought them, and the remaining 37 percent were unsure. Similarly, 75 percent of the respondents believed that Ms. Davis fled California to avoid prosecution. Even though most respondents believe that Ms. Davis actually carried out the actions with which she is charged, they are not prepared to state that she is guilty. Thus, only 46 percent of the respondents would give a definite answer to a question asking simply if Ms. Davis is guilty or not guilty. Interviewer reports indicate that many respondents who believe that Ms. Davis was involved in illegal actions said that her guilt could only be determined by the courts. Of those who were willing to express an opinion, however, 72 percent believe that she is guilty.

Interest in the shootout seems to be evenly distributed across five of the counties. As might be expected, interest in the shootout in Marin is much greater than in any of the other five counties. This fact is clearly demonstrated by the response to a question asking whether the respondent had discussed the case with friends and relatives. While only about half the respondents in most counties had discussed the incident, more than three-quarters of Marin respondents said they had talked about it. The difference between Marin and any of the other five counties can be clearly seen in figure 1, where the white and black bars of the graph indicate the relative proportion of respondents who have and have not discussed the case.

With the notable exception of Marin, information and interest are evenly distributed in the six counties. Potential bias against Ms. Davis, however, is considerably more pronounced in some counties than in others. Bias was assessed by a series of standard survey questions concerned with prejudice against black people, black militants, and Communists and by a specific question about attitudes toward Ms. Davis. These questions reveal a clear pattern of prejudice by county. San Francisco City and County respondents are distinctly less prejudiced than respondents in any other county. Alameda County respondents are almost as tolerant as those in San Francisco but the proportion of prejudiced responses increases in the other counties. In comparison to Marin County, the current site of the court proceedings in the *Davis* case, San Francisco and Alameda counties are in general less prejudiced, while San Mateo, Santa Clara, and Sacramento counties are either equally or more prejudiced. These relationships are apparent in the responses to a number of questions.

Figure 2 presents a graph of the proportion of respondents in each county who approve or disapprove of marriage between blacks and whites. This question has been widely used by both scientific and commercial pollsters as a measure of deeply rooted prejudice against various minorities, including blacks. It is clear from figure 2 that the proportion of respondents approving of interracial marriage is above 50 percent in San Francisco, is slightly less in Alameda, and averages only 30 percent in the other counties. Similarly the percentage of respondents disapproving of interracial marriage is much higher in Marin, San Mateo, Santa Clara, and Sacramento counties than it is in San Francisco and Alameda. A second question concerned with residential segregation revealed a similar pattern of responses by county, with San Francisco again less prejudiced than any of the other counties.

San Franciscans are also least likely to advocate discrimination against black militants in university employment. Figure 3 indicates that the proportion of respondents who said that black militants should not be allowed to teach on university campuses is less than 35 percent in San Francisco, while it averages more than 50 percent in the other five counties. In this case the pattern of responses for Alameda County is closer to the other four counties than it is to San Francisco.

Respondents were asked if their opinion of Angela Davis was favorable, unfavorable, or neither favorable nor unfavorable. As is clear from the patterns of responses by county presented in figure 5, San Francisco City and County has the largest proportion of respondents with neither favorable nor unfavorable attitudes about Ms. Davis. All the other counties except Alameda have an overwhelming number of unfavorable responses, and a small number of neutral responses. Only in San Francisco does the percentage of respondents with attitudes neither favorable nor unfavorable exceed the number with unfavorable attitudes. In Marin, San Mateo, Santa Clara, and Sacramento the proportion of unfavorable responses exceeds the neutral responses by more than two to one. This means that more than two-thirds of the respondents in these counties held an unfavorable opinion of Ms. Davis.

These conclusions refer to the population of registered voters in the respective counties, which, of course, represents the pool of potential jurors. Thus the choice of county for the trial can be expected to affect significantly the degree of bias to be found among the potential jurors.

*COMMENT:* The results were presented in several tables and graphs, samples of which are given on the opposite page.

## D. Granting of Motion

### 1. Standards §7.41

*Source:* Adapted from successful petition for writ of mandate and request for stay dated June 18, 1974, *Russell Little v Superior Court* (see §7.2).

The California Supreme Court held, in *Maine v Superior Court* (Cal 1968) 438 P2d 372, that defendants may use mandamus to review a trial court's denial of a motion for change of venue. The standards to be used by the appellate courts on mandamus are also to be used by trial courts on venue motions. The *Maine* court stated (438 P2d at 377) that *actual prejudice* need not be shown before a motion for change of venue must be granted. Rather,

**Table 3. Attitudes toward Defendant's Social and Political Characteristics in Six Bay Area Counties**

**Should black militants be permitted to teach on university campuses?**

| *County* | *Yes* | *No* | *Don't Know* |
|---|---|---|---|
| San Francisco | 49 | 34 | 17 |
| Alameda | 32 | 49 | 19 |
| Marin | 38 | 45 | 17 |
| San Mateo | 30 | 55 | 15 |
| Santa Clara | 35 | 51 | 14 |
| Sacramento | 34 | 56 | 10 |

**Figure 3. Should black militants be allowed to teach on university campuses?**

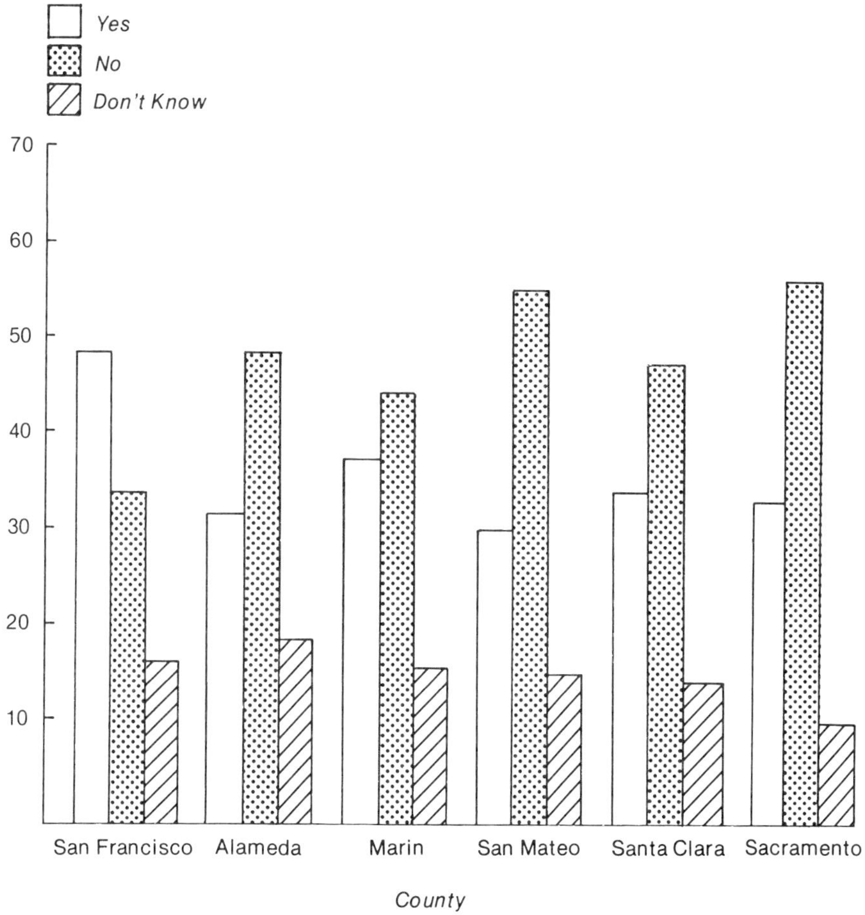

a motion for change of venue or continuance shall be granted whenever it is determined that because of the dissemination of potentially prejudicial material, there is a reasonable likelihood that in the absence of such relief, a fair trial cannot be had. This determination may be based on such evidence as qualified public opinion surveys or opinion testimony offered by individuals, or on the court's own evaluation of the nature, frequency, and timing of the material involved. A showing of actual prejudice shall not be required.

In *Fain v Superior Court* (Cal 1970) 84 Cal Rptr 135, the Supreme Court reasserted its holding in *Maine* that actual prejudice need not be shown, applying this rule to a case where there had been no attempt to have a survey or opinion poll taken. Thus, the court expressly rejected any requirement that a particular method of showing prejudice be used to support a motion for change of venue. See also *Clifton v Superior Court* (Dist Ct App 1970) 86 Cal Rptr 612 (newspaper articles on accused's membership in motorcycle gang known as "Death Riders").

Standards for evaluating the validity of a change of venue due to excessive publicity are elaborated in a series of decisions by California appellate courts ordering venue changes:

*California v Tidwell* (Cal 1970) 89 Cal Rptr 44: murder charge—undue publicity due to district attorney and investigating officers notifying press at every step of investigation.

*Frazier v Superior Court* (Cal 1971) 95 Cal Rptr 798: murdered family—newspaper stories on defendant's threats to family and on public debate re fiscal impact of trial, in small, cohesive community that would remain conscious of crime.

*Lansdown v Superior Court* (Dist Ct App 1970) 89 Cal Rptr 154: willful child abuse and desertion—unfavorable publicity about another missing child of defendant, radio station questioning defense attorney's advice to remain silent on this, added publicity of finding missing child's body, murder charges filed in that case and media implicating defendant in cases of both children.

*Corona v Superior Court* (Dist Ct App 1972) 101 Cal Rptr 411: multiple murders—local, state, and national newspaper and broadcast accounts of discovery of bodies, plus multitude of local color stories, repeatedly detailing defendant's possible connection.

*Smith v Superior Court* (Dist Ct App 1969) 80 Cal Rptr 693: bribery of public officials and perjury—highly industrialized, populous county with massive increasing news coverage; case became a cause célèbre in local politics and led to dispute between mayor and largest county newspaper, causing nationwide publicity, Pulitzer Prize to paper precipitating grand jury investigation of defendant.

*Griffin v Superior Court* (Dist Ct App 1972) 103 Cal Rptr 379: murder trial—extensive publicity during first trial, persistent references to defendant's prior criminal record in news articles, small community affected by barrage of publicity.

The *Lansdown* court expressly rejected the size of the community as being determinative (89 Cal Rptr at 157):

> Real party in interest would distinguish *Maine* (Mendocino County) and *Fain* (Stanislaus County) from this case, upon the ground of population; that is, prejudicial publicity is less likely to be widely heard, read and seen in a metropolitan area than in a rural area and, by corollary, it is more likely to be forgotten in a metropolitan area where sensational crimes are more commonplace than in a rural area.
>
> Population, qua population, is not alone determinative; it is but one factor and it must be shown how size, whether of area or of population, neutralizes or dilutes the impact of adverse publicity.

Three other factors are of considerable importance in weighing the legitimacy of a motion for change of venue: (1) the relative unfamiliarity of the defendant, (2) the relative prominence and popularity of the victim within the community, and (3) the notoriousness of the crime itself. Courts have frequently noted (see *Frazier*, *Tidwell*, *Fain*, *Maine* and *Miller*) that where the defendant is a "stranger" in the county or a person who has "dropped out" from the regular pattern of community life, there is an increased possibility of community prejudice against him. In *Frazier*, a well-known and respected surgeon, his entire family, and his personal secretary were murdered in what was described as an execution-type killing. The court took cognizance of the fact that suspicions within the Santa Cruz community focused on the "hippie element" of which there was a widespread distrust and dislike and with which the defendant in that case was associated. The California Supreme Court issued a peremptory writ of mandate directing the trial court to grant the motion for change of venue, stating (95 Cal Rptr at 803):

> There may not be, as the trial court found, hostility towards this particular defendant as an individual; but so long as there is hostility towards the group or subculture with which he is identified, he runs the very real risk of being judged not for what he has done but for what he is, or what he appears to be . . . . We fashioned in *Maine* the remedy of a pretrial change of venue precisely to obviate such a risk.

In *Frazier*, *Tidwell*, *Fain*, and *Maine*, courts have had occasion to comment on the relative prominence and popularity of the victim as a factor that further increases the probability of prejudice against the defendant. In *Tidwell*, the court emphasized the fact that the victims were well-known ranchers in Lassen County. In *Frazier*, the victims were an outstanding orthopedic surgeon, his immediate family, and his personal secretary. In *Maine*, the homicide victim was the son of the county's district attorney and the assault victim was the daughter of the local sheriff. In each of these cases, the California Supreme Court ruled that the trial court had improperly denied change of venue.

A third consideration in evaluating the legitimacy of change of venue is the notoriousness of the crime itself and the manner of the killing. In *Frazier* (95 Cal Rptr at 804), the court stated:

> No amount of self-restraint or judicial caution, however, could change the facts and circumstances of this case. This was not an ordinary homicide . . . rather we deal here with an alienated member of an unpopular subculture accused of a bizarre and senseless mass murder of prominent citizens of a small community. For the reasons explained in our prior decision on the subject, only a change of venue can ensure that such a defendant obtain [the] fair and impartial trial to which he is constitutionally entitled.

### 2. Order Granting Motion §7.42

*Source:* Order of Judge Richard Arnason granting defendant's motion for change of venue, filed Nov. 2, 1971, *California v Davis* (Marin County Super Ct, No. 3744) (see §3.23).

> Proceeding next with the Venue Motion, the ruling of the Court is as set forth: The California Supreme Court, in the pivotal cases of *Maine, Fain, Tidwell* and *Frazier*, has set forth the proper test to be applied in a hearing on a motion for a change of venue in a criminal case. The test is that a change of venue must be granted when a defendant shows a reasonable likelihood that in the absence of such relief a fair trial cannot be had. The Court finds, upon the record in this case, that there is a reasonable likelihood that Miss Davis cannot obtain a fair trial in Marin County.
>
> The Court further finds that this Court is vested with full and complete jurisdiction to act on the motion for a Change of Venue. The attempted restriction purporting to limit the motion only to the City and County of San Francisco is void and an invalid attempt to restrict the Court's inherent and statutory jurisdiction. Additionally, the record reflects that the defendant has conceded that the Court has full and complete jurisdiction to act on this motion.
>
> The Motion for a Change of Venue is granted . . . . Venue is transferred to the County of Santa Clara. This order shall become fully effective and operative ten days from this date.

Venue was changed, but not to the county specifically requested by the defendant in her restricted motion. Rather, the *Davis* case was tried in a county with a very small black population before a jury including only one member of the largest minority group, Chicanos. To meet this problem, the defense undertook a series of desperate measures. A local committee of volunteers launched an unprecedented personalized investigation of over 3000 prospective jurors (described in chapter 13). Experts from other disciplines were engaged to assist in jury selection (as described in chapter 19). The defendant, acting as her own co-counsel, conducted part of the voir dire (see chapters 15 and 17); her attorneys conducted an extensive voir dire on each area of expected prejudgment (see generally the questions in chapters 9 and 11); and they excoriated the district attorney when he relentlessly pursued one black woman prospective juror and then used a peremptory challenge against her (see chapter 20). The defense also redoubled its efforts to change the public image of Ms. Davis as a dangerous criminal entering the courtroom daily from her cell; counsel renewed their habeas corpus petition for her release on bail, and this effort was successful five days before the trial began. Ms. Davis also made her own opening statement in response to a highly personal attack by the district attorney. On these tactics, see Aptheker, Introduction to Ginger, *Angela Davis Case Collection*, xii-xxix (Meiklejohn Civil Liberties Institute 1974). For an account of the effect of these tactics on jury deliberations leading to acquittal on all charges, see Timothy, *Jury Woman* (1974).

### 3. Motion to Quash Indictment on Basis of Grant §7.43

In the *Attica Brothers* cases (see §3.26), a change of venue was granted by the New York Appellate Division, under New York Criminal Procedure Law §230.20, on a finding that it would be impossible to select unbiased and unprejudiced trial jurors in Wyoming County. Since the prejudiced petit jurors came from the same list as the grand jurors who found the indictment, the defense then moved that the underlying indictment be quashed: unbiased grand juors could not have come from a list that would not yield unbiased petit jurors. The motion noted:

> If a fair jury could not be found in Wyoming County, it must be acknowledged by this Court that the grand jury was not fair. The activities of the grand jury demonstrate this fact. While 60 prisoners were indicted, not one prison officer, not one state guard was indicted. The McKay Commission, the independent body established to investigate Attica, found evidence of criminal activity on the part of "law enforcement officials" .... Only a biased and prejudiced grand jury could fail to indict on this evidence.

The motion was denied. However, a similar motion should undoubtedly be filed whenever grand and petit jurors are selected from the same list and a venue change motion is granted due to the impossibility of selecting unbiased petit jurors.

### 4. Recent Developments §7.45

See §7.21.

## E. Alternatives to Change of Venue §7.46

Many courts consider granting a change of venue motion so serious that they prefer to consider what they deem less drastic alternatives, such as gagging the press to ensure bias-free local jurors (see §§7.48–7.49), or conducting extensive jury voir dire to eliminate local jurors affected by pretrial publicity (see §7.52).

Some defense counsel have sought the alternative of a statewide jury (see §7.47) in cases involving statewide community standards; so far, this has not been successful.

### 1. Form: Motion for Statewide Jury §7.47

*Source:* Adapted from defendant's unsuccessful motion to quash jury panel, *Connecticut v Aniballi* (CP, Fairfield County, Nos. P–CR 2–7139, 2–3838, Oct. 18, 1977). In this case, and in *Connecticut v Pastor* (CP, GA No. 3, Danbury CR 2–3574, 1977), both obscenity cases, defense attorneys moved for statewide juries when state laws required the jury to follow statewide standards. After conviction, the fines were so low that the defendants decided not to appeal, leaving the issue open for litigation and appeal. On statewide grand juries, see chapter 23.

It is defendant's contention that [*he/she*] will be denied a trial by a fair, impartial, and legally constituted jury in this case if the jury panel is limited to electors of [*6*] towns or even all [*23*] municipalities of [*Fairfield*] County. While the jury system in this state is based on a county scheme, [*as described above*], defendant is charged with violation of [*an obscenity*] law. The legislature has specifically declared: [*"Whether a material is obscene shall be judged by ordinary adults applying contemporary community standards. In applying contemporary community standards, the State of Connecticut is deemed to be the community." 1974 Public Acts 74–124.*]

It is defendant's contention that if [*he/she*] is to be tried at all for the alleged offenses, [*he/she*] must be tried by a jury selected from the entire state, not from one county or a portion of one county. Such is the requirement of [*Public Acts 74–124*].

The issue presented here arises because our state legislature has elected to enact statutory standards to be used in determining [*whether or not material is obscene. A review of the statute indicates that this legislation followed in the wake of recent obscenity decisions of the United States Supreme Court. See, e.g.,* Miller v California *(1973) 413 US 15;* Paris Adult Theatre I v Slaton *(1973) 413 US 49.*]

Our legislature elected to define the "community" in clear and precise geographical terms: The community is the state. [*A jury tries an obscenity case as a surrogate for the community. See* Huffman v United States *(DC Cir 1974) 502 F2d 419, 424. Since the prosecution need not as a matter of constitutional law produce "expert" witnesses to testify as to the obscenity of the materials, a juror is entitled to draw on his or her own knowledge of the views of the average person in the community or vicinage from which he or she comes for making the required determination.* Hamling v United States *(1974) 418 US 87.*]

[*The Connecticut legislature, by virtue of Public Acts 74–124, has contemplated that obscenity cases be tried by a jury that is representative of the "community" or "vicinage," defined as the entire state. It presumes that jurors from throughout the state will be available to serve on the jury panel. Compare* Hamling, supra, *418 US at 104–106. Any attempt to limit the jury panel representation to one county or a small portion of one county of the community would be an invalid and undue restriction imposed on the statute and would constitute an arbitrary or a systematic exclusion of truly representative jury members.*]

The legislature's failure to provide a mechanism for summoning a statewide jury panel does not excuse the state from providing a jury panel that is representative of and comes from the "community" or "vicinage" [*in an obscenity case*].

## 2. Publicity-Free Pretrial

### a. Federal Jurisdiction to Decide This Issue §7.48

A Connecticut federal district judge in 1978 held that he had jurisdiction to review the decision of a state judge limiting press access to a pretrial suppression hearing in a state criminal case, and that abstention would be inappropriate. *American-Republican Inc. v Wall* (D Conn, Civ No. H78–348, 1978).

The Court is acutely aware of the consideration of comity and federalism, which counsel caution when such relief is sought. It should be noted, however, that the fundamental premise of *Younger v Harris* (1971) 401 US 37 is that federal equitable intervention is not warranted when the federal plaintiff has a full and fair opportunity to have his constitutional claims litigated in a pending state proceeding. P. Bator, P. Mishkin, D. Shapiro, *Hart & Wechsler's*

*The Federal Courts and the Federal System*, 1977 Supp at 183. This consideration is absent in the present case, because there is no *pending* state proceeding in which the plaintiff is a party who can fully litigate his federal constitutional claims.

In *Huffman v Pursue* (1975) 420 US 592, the Supreme Court noted that "it is typically a judicial system's appellate courts which are by their nature a litigant's most appropriate forum for the resolution of constitutional contentions," 420 US at 609. In the instant case, the plaintiff is unable as a matter of state law to appeal the trial judge's allegedly unconstitutional ruling, because the plaintiff is not a "party" in the pending criminal prosecution. Thus, the normal route to the state's appellate courts for those who have received an adverse ruling from a state trial judge is unavailable to this plaintiff. If this Court were to refrain from exercising jurisdiction under these circumstances, the plaintiff could bring an independent state action seeking the vindication of its constitutional rights. *Dinkins v Kinney* (New Haven County Super Ct, No. 157369, Mar. 15, 1978) at 2. However, a decision to abstain in this case would subvert the established rule of *Monroe v Pape* (1961) 365 US 167, in which the Supreme Court specifically held that "one seeking redress under 42 USC §1983 for a deprivation of federal rights need not first initiate state proceedings" before raising the §1983 claim in federal court. *Huffman*, *supra*, 420 US at 609 n21. Accordingly, the Court finds that *Younger* abstention is inappropriate and that this case is properly before the Court.

### b. Supreme Court Ruling on Merits §7.49

In 1979, the United States Supreme Court held that "a trial judge has an affirmative constitutional duty to minimize the effects of prejudicial pretrial publicity" based, in part, on the danger of prejudicing prospective jurors. In *Gannett v Depasquale* (1979) 443 US 368, Justice Stewart, writing for the five-to-four majority, stated the issue narrowly: "whether members of the public have an independent constitutional right to insist upon access to a pretrial judicial proceeding, even though the accused, the prosecutor and the trial judge all have agreed to the closure of that proceeding in order to assure a fair trial."

The majority held:

> This Court has long recognized that adverse publicity can endanger the ability of a defendant to receive a fair trial. To safeguard the due process rights of the accused, a trial judge has an affirmative constitutional duty to minimize the effects of prejudicial pretrial publicity. And because of the Constitution's pervasive concern for these due process rights, a trial judge may surely take protective measures even when they are not strictly and inescapably necessary.

Justice Stewart explained the special risk from publicity in a pretrial suppression hearing:

The whole purpose of such hearings is to screen out unreliable or illegally obtained evidence and ensure that this evidence does not become known to the jury.

Publicity concerning the proceedings at a pretrial hearing, however, could influence public opinion against a defendant and inform potential jurors of inculpatory information wholly inadmissible at the actual trial.

The Court concluded:

Among the guaranties that the Amendment provides to a person charged with the commission of a criminal offense, and to him alone, is the "right to a speedy and public trial, by an impartial jury." The Constitution nowhere mentions any right of access to a criminal trial on the part of the public; its guaranty, like the others enumerated, is personal to the accused.

The debate on fair trial versus free press will continue, but, under *Gannett*, when defense counsel agrees to closed pretrial proceedings, there will be no basis for a change of venue motion.

## 3. Voir Dire Examination

### a. Venue Motion Ruling Must Precede Voir Dire—State §7.51

*Source:* Opinion of Judge Phillips, *Henley v State* (Tex Crim App 1978) 576 SW2d 66, a highly publicized case concerning six of a mass of homosexual rape and torture murders.

Appellant was tried and on July 15, 1974, a guilty verdict of murder with malice was returned in each of the six causes . . . .

The issue on appeal is not whether the trial court erred by not granting appellant a change of venue, nor whether the trial court erred in delaying its ruling on appellant's motion for change of venue until voir dire had been conducted. The precise question to be decided is this:

If a defendant timely files a properly verified motion for change of venue under Article 31.03, Vernon's Annotated Code of Criminal Procedure, is it an abuse of discretion and a denial of due process for the trial court to overrule the motion without affording defendant a pretrial hearing to present evidence in support of the motion?

A criminal defendant is guaranteed a fair trial by an impartial jury. Article 1, Section 10, Texas Constitution; Sixth Amendment to the United States Constitution; Article 1.05, Vernon's Annotated Code of Criminal Procedure. Due process provides for a change of venue when a defendant demonstrates his inability to obtain an impartial jury or fair trial at the place of venue. *Groppi v Wisconsin* (1971) 400 US 505; *Chapman v California* (1966) 386 US 18; *Sheppard v Maxwell* (1966) 384 US 333.

Articles 31.03 and 31.04[4] [of the code], the provisions controlling the disposition of this case, provide, in pertinent part, as follows:

> A change of venue may be granted in any felony or misdemeanor case punishable by confinement on the written motion of the defendant, supported by his own affidavit and the affidavit of at least two credible persons, residents of the county where the prosecution is instituted, for either of the following causes, *the truth and sufficiency of which the court shall determine:*
>
> 1. That there exists in the county where the prosecution is commenced so great a prejudice against him that he cannot obtain a fair and impartial trial; and
>
> 2. That there is a dangerous combination against him instigated by influential persons, by reason of which he cannot expect a fair trial.
>
> . . .
>
> The credibility of the persons making the affidavit for change of venue, or their means of knowledge, may be attacked by the affidavit of a credible person. *The issue thus formed shall be tried by the judge*, and the motion granted or refused, as the law and facts shall warrant. [Emphasis added.]

. . .

In the instant case . . . the trial court predicated its denial of appellant's motion solely upon the successful qualification of a jury panel. In so doing the court confused the grounds for change of venue with the grounds for juror challenge for cause.

> . . . If obnoxious jurors could be detected and kept from the panel by the question provided for in the Code, then there would be no reason for a change of venue. But . . . the law providing for the change proceeds upon the assumption that, notwithstanding all tests are made, there may be such a prejudice in the county as will render it probable that an impartial juror might serve.

In *Faulkner v State* (Tex Crim App 1901) 43 Tex 311, 65 SW 1093, the Court noted that:

> Prejudice is a sinister quality. It may possess a man and he not be aware of it; or, being aware of it, he may purposely conceal it, in order that he may vent his revenge.

Also see *Cortez v State* (Tex Crim App 1902) 44 Tex Crim 169, 69 SW 537.

---

4. A change of venue motion drafted in compliance with Article 31.03 and supported by properly verified affidavits entitles a defendant to a change of venue as a matter of law, unless the motion is controverted by the State. *Wall v State* (Tex Crim App 1967) 417 SW2d 59; *Flores v State* (Tex Crim App 1973) 493 SW2d 785.

The aforementioned cases recognize the problem of obtaining answers on voir dire affected by conscious or subconscious juror prejudice resulting from widespread inflammatory news coverage. Therefore, a change of venue is a remedy to assure an accused a fair trial when extensive news coverage has raised substantial doubts about the effectiveness of voir dire for obtaining an impartial jury.

Some relevant factors in determining whether outside influences affecting the community climate of opinion as to a defendant are inherently suspect are (1) the nature of pretrial publicity and the particular degree to which it has circulated in the community, (2) the connection of government officials with the release of the publicity, (3) the length of time between the dissemination of the publicity and the trial, (4) the severity and notoriety of the offense, (5) the area from which the jury is to be drawn, (6) other events occurring in the community which either affect or reflect the attitude of the community or individual jurors toward the defendant, and (7) any factors likely to affect the candor and veracity of the prospective jurors on voir dire. See generally Annot, 33 ALR3d 17 (1970). . . .

. . . [T]he successful qualification of a jury panel is not the *sole* criterion in determining whether a defendant is entitled to a change of venue. [Citations.] The primary factor for the court's consideration in ruling on a venue change is whether the "outside influences affecting the community's climate of opinion as to a defendant are inherently suspect." [Citations.]

Appellant was entitled to a change of venue if he could show, even though it would be possible to select a jury whose members were not subject to a challenge for cause, that there were influences in the community which could affect the answers on voir dire, or the testimony of witnesses at trial or that for any other reason a fair and impartial trial could not be held in Bexar County.

. . . If the hearing on a change of venue is postponed until after trial, a great deal of time, effort and money will be wasted if the evidence adduced during the post-trial hearing compels a new trial in another county. Further, it is unlikely that following a jury verdict of guilty in a highly publicized, mass sex-torture killing case the trial court would readily erase the jury's pronouncement and grant appellant another trial. Lastly, such a procedure would allow the trial courts to escape their duty of making an independent assessment of the merits of the change of venue motion and to delegate that responsibility to an appellate court. The dictates of due process and [the state statute] necessitate that a defendant's right to an impartial jury and fair trial be protected *in the first instance* by the trial court. A defendant must not needlessly be denied due process by a trial court and suffer the emotional rigors and expense of a criminal trial, and possibly incarceration pending appeal only to be afforded due process months or even years later by an appellate court. Such a state of affairs is in itself a denial of due process.

Therefore, we are constrained to hold under these cases cited and the facts of this case that the trial court's refusal to grant appellant a pretrial hearing to introduce evidence in support of his motion for change of venue precluded a determination, as contemplated by our law, of the community attitude toward appellant and constituted a deprivation of due process.

On retrial, defendant Henley was again convicted of six murders. *S.F. Chronicle*, June 28, 1979, p. 28.

### b. Voir Dire Must Precede Venue Motion Ruling—Federal §7.52

*Source:* Opinion of Judge Robert L. Taylor, *United States v Mandel* (D Md 1977) 431 F Supp 90, 98–101, denying a change of venue motion before voir dire had been conducted.

Defendants must carry a heavy burden in moving for a change of venue under Fed R Crim P 21(a). As the rule provides, they must "satisfy" the Court that there is "so *great* a prejudice" against them that they "cannot obtain a fair and impartial trial." Transfer has been granted in only a few reported cases. See C. Wright, *Federal Courts* §44 at 183 n5 (3d ed 1976); 8A J. Moore, *Federal Practice* ¶21.03[1]–[3] (2d ed 1965). A change of venue is appropriate only for "exceptional cases." See 1 C. Wright, *Federal Practice and Procedure* §342 (1969).

The Court has confidence in the efficacy of voir dire examination as a protection against prejudicial publicity. By requesting a transfer now, rather than after voir dire examination, defendants contend that the publicity surrounding the previous trial was so "inherently prejudicial" as to render voir dire ineffective. Defendants principally rely upon *Sheppard v Maxwell* (1966) 384 US 333; *Estes v Texas* (1965) 381 US 532; *Rideau v Louisiana* (1963) 373 US 723; and *Irvin v Dowd* (1961) 366 US 717.

The newspaper clippings and television and radio transcripts filed by the defendants have been examined. Much of the publicity was simply straightforward factual reporting, as distinguished from inflammatory publicity.... If we focus only on the publicity which is unfavorable to the defendants, it pales by comparison to the pervasive and extremely incriminating confession of the defendant in *Rideau* [or *Sheppard*].

... The Court is of the opinion that this publicity is not "inherently prejudicial," and that through effective use of voir dire examination an impartial jury can be found to try this case.

Defendants have submitted the results of a public opinion poll in an attempt to demonstrate that actual prejudice exists among prospective jurors to such an extent that an impartial jury cannot be selected. The conclusions drawn in the poll appear to invade the province of the Court and are based upon hearsay information.[8] In the opinion of the Court, a public opinion poll is no substitute

8. The poll attempts to show that a number of potential jurors in this District have formed an opinion about the guilt or innocence of the defendants. It concludes, among other things, that the effects of the publicity will dissipate significantly over a period of at least four to six months. Out of an abundance of precaution, the poll will not be released to the public until a verdict is rendered by the jury.

for voir dire examination. *Cf. United States v Partin* (ED La 1970) 320 F Supp 275.

*COMMENT:* Mandel was convicted and his conviction was affirmed by an equally divided court. (4th Cir 1979) 602 F2d 653.

### 4. Recent Developments §7.59

See §7.21.

## II. DISMISSAL ON JURY GROUNDS

### A. When Dismissal Appropriate §7.61

In the exceptional case in which the defendants are outraged by many unconstitutional features of jury selection, or are convinced that a fair jury cannot be impaneled in the vicinage because of publicity about them or their cases, and they do not want a change of venue, counsel should consider a motion to dismiss the charges. This approach proved successful in cases arising out of opposition to the Vietnam war (§7.64), out of the events at Wounded Knee (§§7.62, 7.65), and out of a long delay by a county in changing the jury selection system to conform to existing state and federal law (§7.67).

At the same time, there is something to be said for the idea that both the community and the principle of democratic self-government lose when local citizens cannot judge a person accused of violating the law in their vicinage and thereby establish community standards of conduct. See Kershen, "Vicinage," 30 *Okla L Rev* 1, 126–154 (1977), and the discussion of the jury as the conscience of the community in chapter 22.

### B. Motion to Dismiss for Inability to Obtain a Fair Trial §7.62

*Source:* Motion to dismiss for inability to obtain a fair trial, *South Dakota v Waubun Nuwi Nini* (Minnehaha County Cir Ct, 2d Cir, 1975).

Now come the above named Defendants, by their counsel, and move this court to dismiss the informations stating:

1. That the alleged offenses charged in these informations arose from a confrontation between Indian people and police at the Minnehaha County Courthouse on April 30, 1974, during trial proceedings in a case involving alleged offenses at a Custer, South Dakota, confrontation between Indian people and police.

2. That at the time of the alleged offenses in the instant case, there was also considerable continuing publicity on the occupation of Wounded Knee a year earlier due to the ongoing conspiracy trial of Dennis Banks and Russell Means in Saint Paul, Minn., and a continuous series of cases in Sioux Falls itself.

3. That all three of the above confrontations received massive media coverage and were all closely associated by the media and in the public mind with the American Indian Movement (AIM).

4. That the media coverage of these AIM-police confrontations has included great emphasis on statements by AIM members which the press interpreted to be admissions, confessions or threats, on alleged criminal conduct for which they were never indicted, prior criminal records, opinions as to their guilt and character assassinations by editorial writers and public officials and great concern for the alleged victims.

5. That the community became extremely hostile to Indian people and especially to those associated with AIM and their supporters.

6. That this hostility has not abated due in part to the courthouse which was allowed to stand unrepaired for six months as a reminder of the confrontation. It was further encouraged by Attorney General elect William Janklow's election campaign promises to "stop AIM violence." This campaign greatly prejudiced defendants by propagandizing the prosecutor's opinion as to the contested issue of who was responsible for the outbreak of violence in these confrontations in violation of all professional ethical standards.

7. That a recent opinion poll verifies that a large percentage of Minnehaha County residents firmly believe defendants are guilty.

8. That under the circumstances it is impossible to obtain an impartial, indifferent juror uninfluenced by this hostility.

WHEREFORE, for all the reasons stated above, and based on all evidence presented in motions thus far, and upon evidence, authorities, and argument to be presented in a memorandum in support of this motion and upon the hearing of this motion and other pretrial motions, Defendants pray this court dismiss these informations.

*COMMENT:* For the opinion granting the motion to dismiss in this case, see §7.65.

## C. Opinions on Granting Motions to Dismiss §7.63

Civil and criminal cases can be dismissed in the interest of justice on jury issues.

In civil cases, dismissal can be ordered under the doctrine of forum non conveniens, which is based on the right of the court, in the exercise of its equitable powers, to refuse the imposition on its jurisdiction of the trial of cases, even though the venue is properly laid, if it appears that for the convenience of litigants and witnesses and in the interest of justice the action should be instituted in another forum where the action might have been brought. The application of the doctrine rests in the sound discretion of the court and the factors to be considered in the doctrine are the private interests of the litigant and the interest of the public. These can include the virtual impossibility of selecting an impartial, cross-section jury.

### 1. Dismissal for Community Prejudice §7.64

Historically, few defendants have been willing to gamble everything on a motion to dismiss, and have instead filed motions for change of venue and for delay of trial in order to minimize the effects of adverse pretrial publicity on prospective jurors. However, in *United States v Cotton*, an unusual set of defendants developed an unusual set of facts in the antiwar protestors' case known as the "Milwaukee 14." The defendants demanded a speedy trial and then moved for dismissal of all charges on the ground that community prejudice made it impossible to select an impartial jury.

In August 1968, a group of Catholic priests and laymen broke into a Selective Service office, removed the records showing I-A classifications of registrants, and burned them outside the office, singing "We Shall Overcome." They were charged in the state court with arson, burglary, and theft, and simultaneously in the federal court with conspiracy to obstruct the Selective Service System and conspiracy to destroy federal records. In the state court, 12 of the 14 defendants, representing themselves, were convicted on all three counts and sentenced to two years on the theft and arson charges, to run concurrently, and four years' probation on the burglary charge, to run consecutively.

On June 9, 1969, three days after the defendants were sentenced in the state court, the federal trial began. The federal indictment included another defendant, Mr. Hagedorn, who was not charged in the state case but was included in the conspiracy charges because he was allegedly involved in the group's plans. Two attorneys handled the cases in the federal district court until counsel were discharged by their clients two days before the trial so that the defendants could represent themselves.

The unusual procedural stance of the defendants (except for Hagedorn) was that they refused to apply for a change of venue, they demanded a speedy trial, and they moved for a dismissal because of community prejudice. Faced with this situation, the federal judge conducted an extensive voir dire of 142 prospective jurors. Following this he granted Mr. Hagedorn's motion for change of venue and ruled on the remaining defendants' motion for dismissal.

*Source:* Opinion of Judge Myron L. Gordon from the bench, granting defendants' motion for dismissal, *United States v Cotton* (ED Wis, No. 68-CR-113, Sept. 9, 1969), as reported in 28 *Law Guild Practitioner* 101 (1969).

**Court:** About ten days ago, I denied motions for dimissal because of the claimed community prejudice; and my reasoning at the time was that the existence of community prejudice for purposes of deciding an application for a change of venue did not necessarily mean that that ruling would govern at the time of the trial. In other words, there is a different evaluation between applying for a change of venue and secondly asking for dismissal. I felt it was my duty to attempt to find an impartial panel of jurors, notwithstanding my previous ruling that Mr. Hagedorn should have a change of venue. And as you will recall, I invited as I had your counsel previously, I also invited you gentlemen to apply for a change of venue; and when that was not done, I then felt it my responsibility to attempt to pick a jury which would present a sufficient panel, so that an ultimate jury of 12 uninfluenced minds could hear this cause.

Now, there are three generally recognized ways of curing the impact on a fair trial that is made when there is broad, hostile news coverage of an event. One is the change of venue, and the litigants have a Constitutional right to be tried in the district in which the event occurred and in the state in which it occurred; and they indicated earlier that they are not waiving that right.

Another technique, a generally recognized way of curing the impact of hostile news coverage on a fair trial is to delay a trial. The mere passage of time, we know, dulls memories and dulls feelings; but once again, the defendants here chose, as they had the right to do, to have a prompt trial; and the government shared that view; and some months ago, this trial date was reached at a time when the government's attorneys and the then attorneys for these defendants conferred. Since that time, the defendants have reiterated their demand for a speedy trial; and there has never been any occasion or opportunity for a delay beyond this time of the trial; so, that technique was unavailable as a means of assuring a fair trial.

That left as the third and only means that I know to reach a fair trial here: to screen the jurors' intent to find a sufficient number of persons who would qualify. The latter was the only method open; and I, as you know, have questioned 142 prospective jurors, almost all of them individually. The first group of five were questioned as a group; but subsequent to that five, every juror was interrogated separately—that is, in the absence of the other jurors.

I have certain comments I want to make with reference to those interrogations of the jurors. I think it's striking that only one had never heard of the Milwaukee 14, and one other had, I believe, only heard of the Milwaukee 14 upon coming to Court. If I believed that they—that this was a clue that potential jurors could possibly be found, I think it would be the Court's obligation to continue the search far beyond the 142 jurors whom we've now questioned during the past three days; but I am of the view that the jury should be made up not of just a hermit or a recluse or a person who is shut out from life, but should rather be a cross-section of the community. I think, as . . . Walter Schneider, a prospective juror, said, that—in response to a question: "Of course, everybody's heard of this!" I think it's also interesting that the greatest number, by far, who had heard discussion of the event, stated that the views given by others were hostile. Approximately one out of every four or five jurors called was, by his own evaluation, free of bias; but [for] only very few of those persons could I fully agree [with] a juror's own assessment of his lack of bias.

I think it's remarkable that although a large number had heard of the Milwaukee 14 and had heard opinions about them, . . . almost every single one of the 142 jurors examined professed that he gave no personal opinions. In other words, almost every juror said: "I heard discussions by others, but I didn't participate. I expressed no opinions." And I find this somewhat incredible. It seems to me it's contrary to human nature to have heard so much and said so little.

I am also concerned with the fact that many of the prospective jurors—I think most of them were experienced as jurors, and I think that many of them were familiar with the rule that a case is to be tried on the evidence in the courtroom. Ordinarily, we interrogate jurors in a group; and as a matter of fact, the judge tells them they are not to—they are to put aside everything they may have heard of the event and try the case on the evidence alone. And I perceive that this sophisticated response to my inquiries was made by a large number of jurors who professed impartiality. I felt that many of them were aware of what the right answer would be from their past experience; and I think that, in a great many instances, influenced their responses.

I am also impressed with the large number who knew about the recent state court trial and of the conviction, let alone of the sentence that was made in the state court only a short number of days ago; and in my opinion, the effect of that must clearly be very adverse. It is the obligation of this Court to give these defendants a fair trial. In a trial, we carefully avoid allowing the prosecution to offer into evidence proof of prior convictions, at least not until the defendants have been submitted to the witness stand and, then, under only limited circumstances. Here, practically every juror knew about a prior conviction of these defendants.

I also thought it rather curious that although radio and television and the press expressed very firm and frequent opinions, not a single juror professed to having seen or heard such editorializing by the news media. This could mean that the public doesn't listen to or read editorials, or it could mean that people don't realize that they're being conditioned by such opinions.

Many jurors prefaced their admissions of prejudice against these defendants by starting to say: "I'm a good American," or: "I was in the service, and I have sons in the service," or words to that effect, which impressed me as meaning that an attitude has been extant in this community that what these defendants have done is in contravention to those attitudes, that is, those concepts of good Americanism and love of Country and the use of the antithesis device persuades me that there would be community reaction against the defendants.

I was also struck by the fact that some jurors would remove the cloak by taking a deep breath and bursting out with a statement like: "I am going to be very honest with you," and they would proceed to acknowledge prejudice. I have fear that others in this community, particularly the members who were interrogated, would not remove the cloak which surrounded their views. Roughly, four out of five jurors who were questioned have been removed for apparent bias.

There may have been a misunderstanding with regard to those jurors who were not removed upon the first screening. They were not individuals, all of whom the Court believed were unbiased. Rather, they were those who professed impartiality. And as to those, the Court was reserving his judgment regarding those qualifications. So, when Mr. Lerner—when you suggested we had 28 or 30 jurors—

**Mr. Lerner:** I did not mean to say found qualified by the Court—ones the court was still considering.

**Court:** The latter statement was correct. I was still considering them. But I am glad you understand that I was not and did not purport to indicate that they or others had satisfied me . . . of their ability to be qualified as jurors in this case.

In attempting to select an unbiased jury in the face of the mass of adverse publicity which surrounded these defendants, it is the Court's duty to ascertain each prospective juror's knowledge and attitude, rather than to accept his subjective assessment as to his own impartiality. In *United States v Largo* (7th Cir 1965) 346 F2d 253, 257, the following was said by Judge Swygert: "It was not the province of the juror to make the ultimate determination whether the article might or could have prejudiced him. The judge, after further questioning, should have made that final decision." And similar views are expressed in the reported case of *Irvin v Dowd* (1960) 366 US 717, 722, 723, and in *Silverthorne v United States* (9th Cir 1968) 400 F2d 627, 639.

I have concluded that the barrage of continuing hostile publicity which related to these defendants for the past nine months, including headlines and cartoons and editorials, coupled by the adverse news of their recent state court conviction, that that barrage has created or at least sustained such intense public reaction that the Court cannot assure the defendants a completely fair and impartial trial in this state—in this district at this time. As the Supreme Court said in *Sheppard v Maxwell* (1965) 384 US 333, 362:

> Given the persuasiveness of modern communications and the difficulty of effacing prejudicial publicity from the minds of the jurors, the trial courts must take strong measures to ensure that the balance is never weighed against the accused.

Now, I want to incorporate into these remarks, by reference, the exhibits regarding community prejudice as well as my decision thereon in the *Hagedorn* case. The conditions recited therein, in my opinion, are still true; and the examination of the 142 jurors has only reinforced this belief.

Notwithstanding the undoubtedly sincere belief of the number of prospective jurors that they could be fair in spite of their knowledge, I entertain the very serious doubt as to the correctness of their subjective attitudes.

> I am not satisfied that there will be a fair jury and, therefore, that there will be a fair trial. Under these circumstances, justice demands that there be no trial; and accordingly, the charges against the ten defendants are hereby dismissed.

The prosecution, after waiting five months, filed notices of appeal in the court of appeals and the US Supreme Court and filed a separate suit in the nature of mandamus against both the defendants and the district judge. The court of appeals considered the mandamus action and dismissed it. The US Supreme Court denied certiorari on the mandamus suit and affirmed the decision to dismiss the charges, on other grounds. Justice Douglas dissented, claiming that the issue of "whether the District Court properly dismissed the indictment, because there could be no 'fair trial' in the district at that time and that if a continuance was granted, appellees would be denied a speedy trial guaranteed by the Constitution . . . is an important question we should hear and decide." *United States v Cotton* (1970) 397 US 45.

## 2. Dismissal for Inability to Select Impartial Jurors §7.65

*Source:* Memorandum decision of Richard Braithwaite, Circuit Judge, dated May 5, 1975, *South Dakota v Waubun Nuwi Nini* (Minnehaha County Cir Ct, 2d Cir, 1975), granting motion quoted in §7.62.

On April 25th defendants filed a Motion to Dismiss for Inability to Obtain a Fair Trial. This was their fourth such Motion. The first one, filed last December, was the subject of an evidentiary hearing. In denying that Motion the court stated:

> I do not doubt that there is prejudice in Minnehaha County against AIM and against Indian people. I am not persuaded by the evidence that this is so pervasive that these defendants will never be able to obtain a fair trial—or even that at this time they cannot obtain a fair trial. Voir dire is a tool that will disclose far better than the evidence I have before me now whether these defendants can obtain a fair trial in Minnehaha County in March of 1975.

A second Motion shortly before commencement of the trial was denied on the same basis. On April 2d the defendants made a third Motion after the first three jurors examined by counsel had been excused for cause. They took the position that the voir dire had adequately disclosed an impartial jury could not be obtained.

Defendants now interpose the same Motion claiming that the weeks of voir dire have proved their point.

*Irvin v Dowd* (1961) 366 US 717, laid down the rule that community bias and prejudice must be traced to the jury box. Later pronouncements of the

Supreme Court have modified that rule so that such tracing need not be done where bias has so infiltrated the community as to render the existence of community prejudice against the defendant highly probable. *Rideau v Louisiana* (1963) 373 US 723; *Estes v Texas* (1965) 381 US 532; *Sheppard v Maxwell* (1965) 384 US 333.

The law is clear; its application is most certainly not. The difficulty with the cases cited by the defendants is that their fact situations differ greatly from each other and bear very little similarity to the facts here involved. All that can be gleaned from the plethora of cases I have read is that the law previously enunciated must be applied to the facts in each case on an individual basis. I now proceed to do that.

SDCL 23–43–31 defines actual bias in terms of a state of mind in reference to the case or a party which satisfies the court the juror cannot try the case impartially. *State v Flack* (1958) 77 SD 176, provides that the court is not bound by any specific statement of a juror but rather is to determine state of mind based upon the totality of the voir dire, including juror's appearance, conduct and demeanor. A trial judge is neither mystic, omniscient or medically trained to discern a person's thought processes. Measuring state of mind is at best an educated guess; more frequently it is a gut reaction based upon a judge's experience with witnesses.

Since trial commencement I have examined 107 jurors. 27 of those were excused before any questioning by counsel. An additional 6 were excused on the basis of hardship either during or shortly prior to their voir dire by counsel. 15 of the remaining 74 have not yet been subject to individual voir dire. Of the 59 jurors, 12 have been passed for cause—one over the objection of the State and 7 over defense objection. 47 have been determined by the court to have actual bias. That is approximately 80% of those examined. SDCL 23–43–31(2) says that actual bias can be found in a state of mind with reference to the case or a party. There were only 3 jurors excused because their bias was evidenced by opinions as to guilt. The bias of the remaining 44 was evidenced in other ways, but it was sufficiently clear that in only a handful of instances did the State object to the juror's excuse.

In view of the entire voir dire I have grave doubts concerning the jurors already tentatively seated. Not as to their honesty and sincerity but as to whether, even with a concerted effort, they can stand indifferent to the defendants in the case.

Voir dire has shown the difficulty of accurately assessing the extent of knowledge and opinions of a prospective juror. Phrases as "now that you mention it" or "now I remember" heavily larded the jury selection process. Many expressed a skeleton recollection of the events of April 30th only to reveal under additional questioning that there was considerable flesh on the bones. And there is no assurance that even the extensive questioning already done has uncovered everything in the recesses of the mind and that testimony during the trial will not trigger additional recollections.

Every juror examined had heard of the events of April 30th on that very day; each had seen television news broadcasts about it; nearly everyone had read about it in the newspaper; each had heard and participated in discussions of the events—yet very few ever formed or expressed any opinion about it beyond that it was too bad. That neither jibes with my understanding of human nature or my recollection of the atmosphere prevailing in Sioux Falls last May. Whether the prospective jurors simply do not recall—or whether they have simply repressed what occurred at a time when emotions were running high—certainly reliving the events of that day during the course of testimony at the trial could well trigger the same response those events did last year.

Though the news media gave extensive coverage I am surprised at what the jurors did not notice. Though nearly every juror saw TV news films and read the *Argus Leader* (all of which contained pictures of property damage actually taking place) very few recall seeing any such pictures. Though AIM was repeatedly connected with April 30th events, very few recall of reading or seeing such a connection. For whatever reason, the jurors did not see and hear what was there or else do not recall it. At a minimum that coverage has had a subliminal effect and at least to that extent their minds have been conditioned.

A juror's decision must be based on what he hears in court. Where he has been subjected to considerable publicity outside the courtroom, he may have difficulty separating the two sources. That is troublesome enough when the evidence is compacted into a short trial; it is grossly magnified when the trial is a lengthy one. A juror is more likely to confuse what he heard a year ago with what he heard two months ago—than he is to confuse what he heard a year ago with what he heard in the previous week.

Another striking revelation of voir dire was the depth of feeling people have about this courthouse and the system of justice which it symbolizes. Though every juror questioned had to some extent (many to a great extent) observed what the news media had to say about the events of April 30th, relatively few remembered anyone was injured. And most of those did not recall it until their memories were refreshed. For whatever reason they found damage to this courthouse the most significant thing about that day.

It is essential that the community bias be against a defendant personally. It is sufficient if that bias is toward a group of which the defendant is a member. See *Ham v South Carolina* (1973) 409 US 524. All of the defendants were at this courthouse on April 30th; all of them are members of AIM; all of them have expressed strong opinions that this state is racist; all have expressed the opinion that a courthouse in this state is a symbol of injustice where Indians are concerned.

Further, bias in the community from which the jurors are drawn has been fortified during the course of this trial by news media publicity highlighting: (1) exclusion of the public from voir dire, (2) cost of this trial to the taxpayers, and (3) a reshowing of films of the actual disturbance.

It is my belief an impartial trial cannot be obtained in this county at this time. I can conceive of only three possible solutions to that situation.

The first is to change venue to another county. The defendants have consistently maintained that they do not seek and would not consent to a change of venue under the State Constitution. Under our State Constitution they have an absolute right to a trial in this county and under the *Nelson* case (infra) transfer to another county cannot be forced upon them.

A second possibility is to continue the case. If this trial had been commenced shortly after the disturbance I would feel this solution to be viable because passage of time might change the atmosphere sufficiently that an impartial jury could be obtained. But we are now a year from the event. I do not think the passage of time would work any appreciable change. Memories held a year after the event—or that can be refreshed after that period of time—will be no more [dull] in another 6 months—or 12—or 18. Perhaps somewhere down the line an impartial jury could be obtained but only at the expense of the defendants' constitutional right to a speedy trial. Such a price may not be exacted from them.

The only other alternative available is dismissal. Article VI Sec. 7 of our State Constitution provides an accused is entitled to a (1) speedy (2) public trial by (3) an impartial jury (4) of the county in which the offense allegedly was committed. These four basic rights are conjunctive—not alternative. A defendant is entitled to all of them and may not be required to forgo any single one in order to ensure the others.

Our Supreme Court spoke succinctly and graphically to this point in the case of *In re Nelson* (1902) 19 SD 214:

> The jury must not only be impartial. It must also be of the county in which the crime is alleged to have been committed. Until the accused shall have been tried by such a jury, or shall have waived his right by consenting to a change of place of trial, he cannot be lawfully convicted. If such a jury cannot be secured, there will be no tribunal before whom he can be tried and the ends of justice in an individual instance may be defeated. But however regrettable such a result might be, its possibility or even probability cannot be invoked to justify a disregard of so plain a provision of the State Constitution.

The Information charging Mrs. Tiger with encouraging a riot and the Informations charging each defendant with injury to a public building will be dismissed.

## 3. Dismissal for Denial of Speedy Trial

### a. General Rule §7.66

In *Strunk v United States* (1973) 412 US 434, the Court faced the issue of dismissal in a case involving a ten-month delay between return of the indictment and the date of arraignment. The Court upheld the judicial determination that the accused had been denied a speedy trial despite three facts: that the defendant was responsible for a large part of the delay, that he neither claimed nor showed that the preparation of his defense was prejudiced by the delay, and that the United States attorney's office was understaffed. The Court then held that dismissal is the only possible remedy for deprivation of the constitutional right to speedy trial; reduction of sentence will not suffice.

### b. Due to Stale Jury Lists §7.67

*Source:* Opinion of Justice Polsky, *New York v Hasson* (Sup Ct 1976) 390 NYS2d 507, dismissing indictment for failure to build and use an up-to-date jury list.

On the intended eve of trial the defendant moves for the dismissal of the indictment in the interest of justice and because of a claimed denial of a speedy trial. Underlying this motion is a challenge to the array of prospective jurors and assertions that the entire petit jury panel of Richmond County is hopelessly and irredeemably tainted by methods of jury qualifications and selection which are contrary to established constitutional and statutory requirements.

Of considerable importance to the motion to dismiss the indictment—which is the relief sought by the defendant if he prevails on the challenge to the array— is the context in which the issue arises at this late date.

I

The charges in this case . . . arise out of incidents allegedly occurring in early 1972 while the defendant herein was appearing as the attorney for a police officer charged with an offense in the Richmond County Criminal Court. In August 1973 the Deputy Attorney General began presenting evidence to the Grand Jury of the Extraordinary, Special and Trial Term of the Supreme Court, Richmond County, concerning alleged efforts by the defendant and others to improperly influence the testimony of certain witnesses in the 1972 Criminal Court case.

On Oct. 24, 1973 the Grand Jury voted to indict Mr. Hasson for bribery of a witness and two counts of perjury. An indictment was not signed and filed until April 22, 1974, approximately six months after a true bill had been voted . . . . [T]he case was set down for trial in early February, 1975.

On Jan. 21, 1975 the Supreme Court of the United States held in *Taylor v Louisiana* (1975) 419 US 522, that a statutory procedure whereby women were granted automatic exemption from jury service violated the constitutional right of a defendant to be tried before a jury selected from a fair cross-section of the community. The defendant promptly moved before the late Justice Murtagh to dismiss the indictment because of the New York statutory exemption of women from jury service and their consequent under-representation on the grand jury which voted the indictment. Counsel also challenged the composition of the petit jury venire . . . .

[Judge Murtagh] held the New York statutory exemption unconstitutional.

In a brief memorandum Justice Murtagh denied the motion to dismiss the indictment, holding that there was "no proof whatever of a deliberate and intentional exclusion of women from grand jury service."

After the conclusion of a pre-trial "Wade" hearing, extensive discussions were had between counsel and the court in an effort to arrive at a stipulated method of obtaining an array in which women would be fairly represented. Negotiations were unsuccessful and the case was adjourned to await reconstitution of the Richmond County venire or pool of qualified jurors to bring it into compliance with constitutional requirements.

II

. . . Some further delay was occasioned by the death of Justice Murtagh and the reargument before me of certain pre-trial motions. In the late Spring of 1976, in order to accommodate the trial schedule of the court and both counsel, it was agreed that trial would commence in mid-October—later changed to November 1. Just prior to that date the People requested an adjournment because of the illness of a witness. A hearing was held on the People's application and an adjournment of trial was denied. During the course of the hearing, defense counsel informed the court that he had become aware that jurors in Richmond County were required to fill out a qualifications questionnaire which contained questions not contained in the form presently approved in Judiciary Law, section 661 or by Joint Rule 620.17 of the First and Second Judicial Departments. The defense requested a hearing to determine what happened to prospective jurors who gave the "wrong" answer to any of the questions.

In the course of the hearing it became glaringly apparent that the present jury selection process failed to approach constitutionally acceptable standards. The defendant then filed formal papers challenging the array and moved to dismiss the indictment. At the thus-expanded hearing held on the challenge to the array, testimony was given by the County Clerk, by his former deputy who supervised the jury selection process from 1939 through 1975, and by one of the assistant clerks who has participated in the process since 1969. Among the exhibits received in evidence at the hearing were the jury qualification questionnaires and records of service of the 103 persons summoned for jury duty on this case and drawn from the pool of approximately 18,000 qualified jurors. Although this group of 103 persons is the end-product of the selection system here challenged, it would help place the issues in focus to at this point summarize the salient characteristics of this venire:

| *Age* | *Number* |
|---|---|
| 20-29 | 2 |
| 30-39 | 16 |
| 40-49 | 26 |
| 50-59 | 31 |
| 60-69 | 2 |

| *Year Initially Qualified* | *Number* |
|---|---|
| Pre-1950 | 7 |
| 1951-1955 | 9 |
| 1956-1960 | 13 |
| 1961-1965 | 12 |
| 1966-1970 | 41 |
| 1971-1974 | 14 |
| 1975-1976 | 7 |

Prior Service

Including prior grand jury service, the average prospective juror had been drawn and summoned for jury duty on 6.9 prior occasions. It should be noted however that on numerous occasions the juror had been excused without actually serving.

Sex

Of the 103 persons in the panel, sixteen, or 15.5% are female. The mean age of the women on the panel is 60 and the average is between 55 and 56. Of the seven persons qualified as jurors since the Taylor decision, four are female and three male.

III

Selection of the Jury Pool

The present jury pool of approximately 18,000 qualified jurors was created from an initial group of 8,700 persons qualified in 1939-1940 from the voter enrollment in alternately selected election districts. Thereafter as additional jurors were needed, either to increase the size of the pool or to replace persons who died or moved, further random selections were made from randomly selected election districts. During this period a significant but presently unascertainable number of volunteers not chosen from voter registration lists were also added to the pool of qualified jurors.

Sometime in late 1972 or early 1973, the Office of Court Administration supplied the county clerk with a computer printout of 10,000 randomly selected registered voters. All such voters, at the time, were over the age of twenty-one. This list in part was used during 1973 and 1974 for the notice by the county clerk to persons to come in for examination as to their qualifications. The testimony indicates that approximately one-third of the persons so summoned responded. Persons found qualified were added to the jury pool along with whatever volunteers had been obtained.

In May of 1975, another list of 10,000 names was obtained from the Office of Court Administration. This list was similar to the earlier list in that it contained a randomly selected group of Richmond County registered voters. However, it also included new registrants over the age of 18. With the list were preprinted mailing labels for each of the 10,000 registrants. In order to summon these people to qualify, all that had to be done was to affix the mailing label to existing postcard type notices and run them through a postage meter. Instead, because of budgetary considerations, it was decided to convert to an entirely voluntary system of obtaining additional jurors to supplement the pool. Articles appearing in the local newspaper and word of mouth generated enough volunteers so that no new jurors have needed to be summoned since the spring of 1975. The evidence indicates that these walk-in volunteers were at least 80 percent male. There is also testimony, somewhat contradicted, that

500 or 1000 women, their names obtained from the voter registration list, were summoned during one week in 1975 and those who did not have children under sixteen and were otherwise qualified were added to the pool.

IV

In the 21 months following Justice Titone's decision noting the constitutional imbalance in the Richmond County pool of jurors, and in the 20 months since Justice Murtagh adjourned this trial in anticipation of a reconstitution of the pool of qualified jurors, the County of Richmond has failed to take any meaningful action.

With the exception of one week in 1975 when an effort was made to add women to the panel no attempt was made to correct the impermissible sexual bias in the pre-*Taylor* pool of qualified jurors. Viewing the conflicting testimony in a manner most favorable to the People, no more than 1000 women were specially summoned. Assuming none claimed exemption and all were otherwise qualified, the addition of these persons to the existing panel of about 18,000 persons would result in the raising of the proportion of women from 15 percent up to 20 percent of the total . . . .

V

The challenge to the panel of 103 jurors drawn for this Criminal Term of the Supreme Court is allowed (CPL 270.10). The panel consisting of only 15.5 percent women was drawn from and reflected a larger group of qualified jurors which failed to represent a fair cross-section of the community.

VI

Having rejected the panel drawn for the Term, is there any way that a constitutionally acceptable panel can be drawn from the present roll of approximately 18,000 qualified jurors? One possibility would be to separate the ballots of the male and female jurors and draw fifty jurors of each sex. Such a make-shift procedure, while not comporting with New York statutes, might do as a temporary improvisation to meet constitutional requirements.

I reject this for two reasons. While such improvisation could be justified in dealing with trials occurring shortly after the *Taylor* decision, there is no reason why almost two years later a court should have to invent an impromptu method of giving a defendant a constitutionally acceptable jury.

More significant perhaps is the fact that the underrepresentation of women on the panel of qualified jurors is only one of many defects in the Richmond County jury qualification process.

Although it has been over two years since persons between the ages of 18 and 21 have been eligible for jury service, no person in that age group has yet been summoned to qualify for jury duty . . . .

A further problem lies in noncompliance with Rule 620.2(g) of the Appellate Division, which provides:

"There shall be a continuous search for persons qualified and liable for jury service in order to obtain as many prospective jurors as possible and to *limit as much as possible, repetition of jury service*." [Emphasis added.]

The records of prior service of the 103 members of the challenged array demonstrate that the procedure of replacement of qualified jurors on an "as needed" basis has resulted in the creation of a panel of "professional" jurors.

There is no need for me to address the problem of whether—since *Taylor*—the qualifying of volunteer jurors is permissible. I do think however that serious problems are created by the use of volunteers on the magnitude present here.

In sum, I find the system and procedures for selecting qualified persons for the jury pool precludes the obtaining of a fair cross-section of the community as to age and sex, and is further overly imbalanced by persons who have previously served.

I find that the entire petit jury panel of Richmond County is hopelessly and irredeemably tainted by methods of qualification and selection which are contrary to established constitutional requirements, state law and court rules.

VII

. . . In spite of past nonperformance, I will assume with the use of technology available through the Office of Court Administration, that a new pool and drawing of an array can be accomplished in a relatively short time.

I do not believe that a further delay would be appropriate.

The trial of this case was put off for almost two years upon the specific premise that the mandates of the Supreme Court of the United States, the Legislature of the State of New York, and the Rules of the Appellate Division would be complied with. The grant of a further opportunity to the responsible County officials to comply with clear and unambiguous requirements of law would be to sanction almost two years of inaction.

In the context of the remoteness in time of the events underlying this prosecution and the defendant's readiness for trial in February, 1975 and the considerable opportunity given the County to correct the unlawful condition, I believe the State has failed to fulfill its obligation of providing a forum for the resolution of the charges it has brought.

The motion to dismiss the indictment in the interest of justice and, also, because of the denial of the right to a speedy trial is granted.

*COMMENT:* Under the 1978 New York jury act, the problem of stale jury lists may be avoided. See §2.26.

## 4. Refusal to Dismiss for Pretrial Publicity §7.68

In the Massachusetts bank robbery trial of Susan Saxe, the defense moved to dismiss on the ground of pretrial publicity. The defendant described herself as a "revolutionary, a feminist, an amazon and lesbian" after pleading guilty to possession of firearms in Philadelphia.

Soon after, she faced trial for robbery and first-degree murder in Massachusetts, where state and federal practice at that time prohibited lawyer-conducted voir dire. The defense claimed saturation media coverage of Saxe, submitting:

1. A statistical summary of testimony regarding the publicity surrounding the case
2. Results and statistical summary of an opinion poll in Suffolk County conducted by the defense in conjunction with the National Jury Project
3. A complete list of the questions asked in the opinion poll
4. A comprehensive compilation of the news clippings, television transcripts, press releases, and other publicity concerning the defendant

The trial judge granted a hearing on defendant's motion to dismiss and conducted an extensive hearing, in which Dr. Jay Schulman criticized the inadequacy of voir dire customarily conducted by the trial judge. Walter H. McLaughlin, Chief Justice of the Superior Court, Suffolk County, Massachusetts, wrote a lengthy opinion discussing testimony presented at the hearing, granting the defense motion for additional peremptory challenges, i.e., 16 for the defense only, but denying the motion to dismiss. His important but unreported opinion, dated April 14, 1976, is reprinted in full below and in §8.67 (subheadings have been added, some footnotes have been omitted, and other footnotes have been inserted into the text). *Note:* Massachusetts revised its jury law in 1979; see Mass Rules of Crim Proc 37.

Thereafter the defense did not seek a change of venue or delay of trial, and conducted an extensive voir dire. After trial, the jury voted nine to three for acquittal. *Massachusetts v Saxe* (Suffolk Super Ct ##51775–51777). In January 1977 defendant pleaded guilty to manslaughter and armed robbery and was sentenced to 12 to 14 years.

MEMORANDUM OF LAW IN SUPPORT OF COURT'S ORDER RE DEFENDANT'S MOTION TO DISMISS ON THE GROUNDS OF PRETRIAL PUBLICITY

**[Extent of Pretrial Publicity]**

The defendant comes before the court seeking dismissal of the indictments on the grounds that pretrial publicity has so prejudiced the popular mind against her that she cannot obtain a fair trial in Massachusetts. She points to an extensive and comprehensive compilation of the myriad news clippings, television transcripts, press releases and other publicity concerning her as well as the results of a public opinion poll conducted at her direction and an expert analysis of this data in support of her motion. Finally, the defendant contends that the publicity in this case is of such a nature that all of the remedial devices commonly used in similar situations to obviate the impact of prejudicial publicity are likely to be ineffectual and that dismissal of the indictments is the only remedy.

This defendant first became generally known very shortly after the State Street Bank and Trust Company in Brighton was robbed and a policeman, Officer Schroeder, shot and killed on September 23, 1970. Since that day, a total of approximately 424 newspaper articles has appeared, both within and without the Commonwealth, concerning the defendant. The great majority of these items sought to characterize the defendant through the use of numerous derogatory appellations. Also, many of the articles link the defendant with social privilege and money, political violence, or other crimes never shown to be connected with her and others dwell on the death of Officer Schroeder, his police service, and his family.

It cannot be denied that newspaper publicity of this sort, regardless of intent, cannot but serve to impassion, inflame, and prejudice. Indeed, much of the information reported emanated from government sources, both state and federal, a circumstance which may be particularly prejudicial to criminal defendants. See *United States v Bando* (2d Cir 1957) 244 F2d 833, 837–838; *Delaney v United States* (1st Cir 1952) 199 F2d 107, 113–114.

Following this immediate publicity, public awareness of the defendant was rekindled time and again, both in the papers and in television and radio, by succeeding events such as the separate trials of her two codefendants, William Gilday, Jr. and Stanley Bond; the violent death of Stanley Bond; the death of Officer Schroeder's brother; the arrest of the defendant; and subsequent court hearings concerning her. Consequently, the court accepts as fact that the publicity generated by this case has been extensive, rather continuous, and prejudicial.

Such publicity in and of itself does not immediately require the conclusion that the defendant cannot be tried by a jury uncontaminated by prejudice. In similar circumstances, courts have granted a continuance until the effects of the publicity have abated (see *Commonwealth v Gilday* (Mass 1975) 327 NE2d 851), a change of venue (Massachusetts General Laws, chap 227, §51, gives a criminal defendant in Massachusetts the right to ask for change of venue on the grounds that an impartial trial cannot be had in the county where the case is pending), or conducted an extensive voir dire of the venire to eliminate potential jurors who have been biased irrevocably (see *Commonwealth v Gilday* (Mass 1975) 327 NE2d 851). The defendant, however, argues that such measures will only palliate the effects of the adverse publicity rather than guarantee her the fair trial to which she is entitled under the Fifth and Sixth Amendments of the United States Constitution. The defendant suggests that the only alternative is dismissal of the indictments against her.

**[Opinion Poll on Pretrial Publicity Conducted by Defendant]**

In order to substantiate her claim that an impartial jury cannot be sworn, the defendant, in conjunction with the National Jury Project, initiated an opinion poll within Suffolk County to determine the extent and influence of the publicity concerning her. Based on a sample randomly selected by computer from all individuals within the county between eighteen and seventy years of age, 405 telephone interviews were completed during late August and early September of 1975 and the results tabulated. The demographic composition of the group interviewed approximated that of Suffolk County as a whole. Among other things, the poll established that of 91 percent, 79 percent recognized her name without a description of the case and 12 percent recognized the description. Seventy-six percent of those polled thought that the defendant had probably taken part in the crime. Sixty-two percent felt that the burden was upon the defendant to prove her innocence. Fifty-nine percent thought they could be fair and impartial jurors; however, of this 59 percent, 74 percent felt that Susan Saxe probably took part in the crime, 57 percent stated that the burden was upon the defendant to prove her innocence, and 42 percent felt that she should be severely punished. From these figures, the defendant's expert witness who supervised the poll constructed a hypothetical jury of twelve members drawn solely from those people who stated that they could be fair and impartial jurors. Of these twelve, the poll established that nine thought the defendant probably did take part in the crime, seven thought that she deserved severe punishment.

**[Court Opinion on Validity of Opinion Poll]**

These results cannot be accepted at face value. Their impact is reduced by a number of factors. First, another expert witness produced by the defendant testified that polls of this sort are inherently subject to a seven percent plus or minus error in their results. Transcript of Hearing on Motion to Dismiss, February 17, 1976, at 119 (hereinafter cited as Tr. at ___). That even greater error may exist in this poll is suggested by the fact that 25 percent of those who had not heard of the *Saxe* case thought she was guilty anyway. Tr. at 65–66. Such a non sequitur does not lead the Court to place as great a faith in the veracity and meaningfulness of the answers given to the poll as the defendant would suggest. The same expert witness also testified that the use of volunteer interviewers was "standard but controversial." Tr. at 121. The controversy is accentuated in this instance by the fact that no supervision existed to ensure that the responses recorded by the volunteers were those actually given by the respondents. Tr. at 91–92. Moreover, the introductory questions contained in the poll may well have predisposed many towards making harsher judgments of the defendant in response to the later questions than would otherwise have been the case. (See, e.g., [the following questions]:

1. Crime is a fairly widespread problem nowadays. Would you say you agree or disagree?
2. Anyone on the FBI's most wanted list is a dangerous criminal. Would you say you agree or disagree?
3. It is right for revolutionaries in this country to take violent action in order to bring about social change. Would you say you agree or disagree?
4. There should be stiffer penalties for killing a policeman than for other types of killings. Would you say you agree or disagree?

5. If the authorities go to the trouble of bringing someone to trial, that person is probably guilty. Would you say you agree or disagree?

6. The increasing number of militant lesbians and homosexuals are creating problems. Would you say you agree or disagree?

7. If someone who is accused of a crime disappears for a long time to avoid arrest, that is a pretty sure sign the person is guilty. Would you agree or disagree?

. . . .)

The court does not mean by this analysis to belittle the results of the defendant's poll. Rarely has the court seen a pretrial publicity motion as thoroughly researched and documented and as effectively presented as this one. However, a crucial overriding consideration exists which must be taken into account when weighing the value of such evidence. The most serious difficulty with these studies is that their results are elicited outside of the courtroom, before the voir dire and before instructions are given to the jurors by the presiding judge. Given a different setting, the ability of such polls to reproduce that setting or predict what a jury will decide is open to question. However, despite these objections, the court accepts that at least a majority of the potential Suffolk County venire has been somewhat prejudiced against the defendant.

**[Effect of Court-Conducted Voir Dire]**

The defendant suggests that this prejudice has been so thoroughly inculcated that any voir dire conducted by this court will not sufficiently eliminate it from those affected, citing *Irvin v Dowd* (1961) 366 US 717, 727, as quoted in *United States ex rel. Bloeth v Enno* (2d Cir 1962) 313 F2d 364, 372 in support.

To further buttress her arguments, the defendant produced an expert witness, Dr. Jay Schulman, Director of the National Jury Project, who testified to the same effect. In particular, Dr. Schulman raised the point that no voir dire—no matter how thorough and no matter by whom conducted—could ferret out all underlying prejudice. Tr. at 135–141. In effect, he stated that it was perhaps impossible for an entirely fair, unbiased, and impartial jury ever to be selected in any case. He noted that curative measures such as a continuance, voir dire by counsel instead of the trial judge, and an increase in the number of peremptory challenges allowed defendants may be effective in some instances, but suggested that the problem is particularly acute in this case because of the particularly massive amount of publicity which has been disseminated. Dr. Schulman concluded that the venire in this case would be so strongly biased against the defendant that no voir dire would suffice to guarantee her a fair trial unless additional peremptory challenges were accorded to her in the ratio of three to every one of the Commonwealth's. Tr. at 414–443; 154–156.

The court is inclined to accept many of the opinions ventured by Dr. Schulman, but with the following thought in mind: that he also testified that in spite of the results obtained by the polls in the *United States v Mitchell*, *State v Attica Brothers*, and *United States v Swinton* cases, and the opinion of defense counsel in those cases that a fair trial could not be had, the verdict in each (except for a few of the defendants in the *Attica* trial) was not guilty. Tr. at 157. This contradiction between the implications of those polls and the subsequent verdicts reaffirms the court's belief that "No such simulated cases can reproduce the great responsibility which exists when 'in the solemnity of a courtroom a defendant is tried and his liberty or his life are at stake.'" *Commonwealth v McAlister* (Mass 1974) 313 NE3d 113, 117, quoting from *Commonwealth v Blackburn* (1968) 354 Mass 200. The court now turns to an examination of the prevailing law in this area.

### 5. Recent Developments §7.71

See §7.21.

**PART IV**

# Preparing for Voir Dire

# Chapter 8

# *Establishing Jury Selection Procedures*

**I. Voir Dire Questioning of Jurors §8.1**

**II. Challenges Resulting from Voir Dire**
A. Cause Challenges
  1. Based on Bias §8.2
  2. Number Permitted §8.3
B. Peremptory Challenges
  1. Grounds §8.4
  2. Number Specified: State and Federal §8.5
  3. Methods of Exercising
    a. Traditional §8.6
    b. Arizona Struck System §8.7
    c. Recent Developments §8.9

**III. Purposes of Voir Dire**
A. General Goal §8.10
B. To Move the Jury as a Group §8.11
C. To Uncover Prejudices §8.12
D. To Eliminate Extreme Positions §8.13
E. To Discover "Friendly" Jurors §8.14
F. To Exercise "Educated" Peremptories §8.15
G. To Cause Jurors to Face Their Own Prejudices §8.16
H. To Teach Jurors Important Facts in the Case §8.17
I. To Expose Jurors to Damaging Facts in the Case §8.18

J. To Teach Jurors the Law of the Case §8.19
K. To Converse with Jurors Directly and Individually §8.20
L. To Expose Opposing Counsel §8.21
M. To Provide Time and Space for Citizens to Become Jurors §8.22
N. To Rehabilitate Jurors after Questioning by Opposing Counsel §8.23
O. To Prepare for Summation §8.24

**IV. Procedures for Conducting Voir Dire**
A. Preliminary Screening §8.27
B. Introductory Questioning by Judge §8.28
C. Customary Modern Procedures for Further Questioning §8.29
  1. In State Courts §8.30
  2. In Federal Courts §8.31
  3. In American Bar Association Standards §8.32
  4. In Capital Cases §8.33
D. Procedures Requiring Reversal §8.34
E. Recent Developments §8.35

**V. Effects of Full Voir Dire §8.37**

**VI. Pretrial Steps to Ensure Adequate Voir Dire §8.40**
A. Requests and Motions
  1. Form: Letter to Trial Judge §8.41
  2. Motions for Suggested Voir Dire Procedures
    a. Form in State Criminal Case—General §8.42
    b. Form in Federal Criminal Case—General §8.43
    c. Form for Individual Voir Dire Out of Presence of Others §8.44
    d. Form for Counsel Participation in Voir Dire §8.45
  3. Motion for Hearing on Procedures §8.46
  4. Motions for Continuances §8.47
  5. Motions for Additional Peremptory Challenges §8.48
B. Legal Arguments in Support of Full Voir Dire by Counsel §8.50
  1. Form: Memorandum in Support of Motion for Certain Voir Dire Procedures §8.51
    a. Sample: Factual Issues in the Instant Case Touch Common Prejudices §8.52
    b. Form: Parties Are Entitled to Probing Voir Dire §8.53
    c. Form: Many Potential Jurors Harbor Strong Prejudices §8.54
    d. Form: Jurors Will Not Reveal Their Own Prejudices §8.55
    e. Form: Open-ended, Specific Questions Must Be Asked §8.56
    f. Form: Broad Questioning Provides Basis for Challenges §8.57
    g. Form: Court Rules Provide for Attorney-conducted Voir Dire §8.58
    h. Form: Counsel-conducted Voir Dire Is Expedient and Effective §8.59
    i. Form: Time Factory Not Decisive §8.60

j. Form: Risks in Judicial Voir Dire Avoided by Participation of Counsel §8.61
k. Form: Group Voir Dire Inconsistent with Due Process §8.62
l. Form: In Camera Voir Dire Protects Selection Process §8.63
m. Form: In Camera Voir Dire Protects against Pretrial Publicity §8.64
n. Form: In Camera Voir Dire Protects Privacy Rights §8.65
o. Form: Jurors Must Be Questioned on Issues in This Case §8.66
p. Jurors Must Be Questioned on Pretrial Publicity §8.67
q. Form: Jurors Must Be Questioned on Racial Prejudice §8.68
r. Form: Jurors Must Be Questioned on Conflicting Social Values §8.69
s. Form: Jurors Must Be Questioned on Self-Defense §8.70
t. Other Issues on Which Courts Have Upheld Voir Dire §8.71
u. Form: Conclusion §8.72
v. Recent Developments §8.73

2. List: Issues on Which Courts Have Upheld or Ordered Voir Dire §8.79
3. Appendix to Memorandum: Expert Testimony
a. On All Aspects of Juror Voir Dire §8.80
b. In Highly Publicized Cases
(1) On Jurors' Lying about Prejudices §8.81
(2) On Prejudice against Defendant as One of a Group §8.82
(3) On Obstacles to Discovering Jurors' Predispositions §8.83
c. In Many Cases
(1) On Individual Questioning Being More Effective §8.85
(2) On Questioning Jurors Privately §8.86
(3) On Prejudice against Black People §8.87

C. Results of Hearings on Motions for Extensive Voir Dire §8.90
D. Recent Developments §8.95

## I. VOIR DIRE QUESTIONING OF JURORS §8.1

The American College Dictionary (1962) defines voir dire as follows:

1. an oath administered to a proposed witness or juror by which he is sworn to speak the truth in an examination to ascertain his competence. 2. the examination itself, *i.e.*, the preliminary examination of a prospective witness or juror touching his competence.

Trial attorney Charles Garry of San Francisco explained the meaning of voir dire to a nervous woman prospective juror in *California v Newton* (see §3.22):

**Q** You say you are upset?
**A** Yes.
**Q** What are you upset about?
**A** Well, maybe upset isn't the right word.
**Q** Nervous?
**A** Nervous and prone to doing a lot of self-thinking, I guess.
**Q** Well, that is a good thing.
**The Court:** Good for all of us to do a lot of self-thinking.
**Q** Well, just relax a little bit, Mrs. Anderson, if you will, and let me carry on with this voir dire. Voir dire means in plain English, you speak. This is your chance to speak so that we lawyers can get an evaluation of your state of mind.

Voir dire also describes the questioning of jurors during trial about incidents or publicity that may affect their impartiality. See *United States ex rel. Greene v New Jersey* (3d Cir 1975) 519 F2d 1356.

## II. CHALLENGES RESULTING FROM VOIR DIRE

### A. Cause Challenges

#### 1. Based on Bias §8.2

The grounds of particular challenges for cause are actual bias or implied bias.

Actual bias is present when the juror has a state of mind in reference to the case, or to either of the parties or their witnesses, that will prevent him or her from acting with entire impartiality and without prejudice to the substantial rights of either party.

The Supreme Court has dealt with this question several times. In *Dennis v United States* (1950) 339 US 162, counsel for the defendant Communist Party leader (charged with contempt of the House Committee on Un-American Activities) questioned each juror individually on voir dire and then challenged for cause all employees of the federal government on the District of Columbia panel. The Court (at 168) reaffirmed that "the trial court has a serious duty to determine the question of actual bias" but rejected the challenge. In *United States v Wood* (1936) 299 US 123, 133, the Court similarly concluded that the defense had proved no actual bias on the part of the government employees in trying someone for petty larceny from a private corporation, but held that "[a]ll persons otherwise qualified for jury service are subject to examination as to actual bias." The Seventh Circuit Court of Appeals, in its exhaustive consideration of the question in the *Chicago Eight* case (see §3.54), held that "[j]ury service by a person with actual bias in a particular case would violate the right to an impartial jury." *United States v Dellinger* (7th Cir 1972) 472 F2d 340, 367.

A challenge for implied bias may be based on certain relationships between the prospective juror and any of the parties or their witnesses or the victim (see proposed voir dire questions in §§9.9–9.10; Note, 10 *Rutgers Camden L J* 464 (1979) (recent victim of similar crime challenged for cause)).

### 2. Number Permitted §8.3

Whenever actual or implied bias can be shown to the satisfaction of the trial judge, a cause challenge must be granted. Counsel for each side may exercise as many challenges for cause as are justified by the answers given to their questions by prospective jurors.

A lawyer may challenge numerous jurors for cause unsuccessfully and still benefit from the opportunity to do so, since all the prospective jurors within earshot are learning the rules of the litigation game in the process. (Compare §§8.44, 8.63–8.65 on questioning jurors out of the presence of others.)

The value of the right to question jurors at length in order to pursue challenges for cause has now been proved statistically in a pilot study of seven major trials, reported in §8.37. The study shows that intensive and extensive voir dire leads judges to grant many more cause challenges than are granted when voir dire is limited. The importance of these findings cannot be overstated.

See transcripts of voir dire in chapter 17 for examples of successful challenges for cause.

## B. Peremptory Challenges

### 1. Grounds §8.4

Counsel for each side can exercise peremptory challenges when they suspect bias, "on grounds normally thought irrelevant to legal proceedings" such as "the race, religion, nationality, occupation or affiliations of people summoned for jury duty," appearance, association, and the like, and it is "exercised without a reason stated, without inquiry and without being subject to the court's control." *Swain v Alabama* (1965) 380 US 202, 220. But see successful objections to peremptory challenges against all blacks, described in chapter 20.

In a few jurisdictions, the trial judge may limit voir dire to subjects that could lead to challenges for cause and may forbid questioning to assist counsel in making peremptory challenges. This practice can be changed by amending existing statutes or court rules, or by seeking changes in unwritten practice.

See chapters 16 and 17 for examples of voir dire leading to peremptory challenges and chapter 19 for discussion of wise use of peremptory challenges.

### 2. Number Specified: State and Federal §8.5

In federal criminal cases, the number of peremptory challenges depends on the seriousness of the offense and the nature of the party. Under the Federal Rules of Criminal Procedure Rule 24(b), in capital cases, each side has 20 peremptories; in noncapital felonies, the prosecution has 6 and the defense 10; in misdemeanors, each side has 3. In federal civil cases, each side has 3 peremptories. 28 USC §1870.

In state criminal and civil cases, the number of peremptories varies quite widely. For state criminal trials in the 50 states, see §4.53; for state civil trials in the 50 states, see §4.54.

### 3. Methods of Exercising

#### a. Traditional §8.6

Rules on the exercise of peremptory challenges vary from federal district to district, from state to state, sometimes from county to county, and even from trial judge to trial judge in the same county. The style of the trial judge always shapes the final procedures. One judge may permit the prosecution in a criminal case to save up its challenges until the defense has exhausted its challenges. The defense in this situation must concentrate on estimating the precise point at which the best possible defense jury is in the jury box. This may be several rounds before it has used all of its peremptories, which was the situation in the *Camden 28* trial under Judge Clarkson Fischer, see §3.55. Another judge may require that the plaintiff be fully satisfied with the jury before it tenders the jury to the defense, allowing the plaintiff subsequently to challenge only those prospective jurors who come into the box as a result of defense challenges to their predecessors. This procedure was followed in the *Gainesville 8* trial, see §3.53. It obliges the defense to use peremptory challenges in each round depending on what the plaintiff did in the same round.

### b. Arizona Struck System §8.7

The trial judge determines at the outset the number of peremptory challenges each party will have. In personal injury cases, there are often several defendants and sometimes there is more than one plaintiff. In a fairly typical case, the judge will give three peremptories to each party, which will mean three for plaintiff and six for the two defendants. This means nine potential jurors will be struck. Many states (including Wisconsin) require two alternates on 12-person juries. This adds up to 23 potential jurors. The judge or jury commissioner draws 23 jurors' names, and seats the jurors in the courtroom. As jurors are challenged for cause or ask to be excused for cause (e.g., for knowing one of the parties), the judge excuses them and seats new jurors, always keeping the number 23.

When all the challenges for cause have been made, the remaining 23 jurors' names are listed on a piece of paper, which becomes the official jury list. When the voir dire is finished by both sides, the judge gives the list to plaintiff's counsel, who literally strikes a name from the list, and initials it, and then hands the list to one of the defense attorneys. Each party must use all three peremptory challenges allotted by the judge, striking alternately with the other parties, until 14 names remain. The final list of 14 is initialed by both sides, and then the clerk stands up, reads the names of the jurors who remain, and instructs them to stay. All jurors whose names are not read are excused, without having any idea which party struck them, or why. Later the two alternates are selected out of the remaining 14.

Some lawyers prefer the Arizona struck system because it gives them the opportunity to talk to each of the people on the panel so that when the final jury is selected, they know its composition. They do not have the problem that arises when a new juror comes in, after many questions have been asked and answered. The judge usually asks, "Have you heard all the questions that have been asked"; the juror answers, "Yes"; the judge says, "Do you have any different answers"; and the newly seated juror says, "No." This leaves the attorney no opening for further voir dire, and no information on which to make educated peremptory challenges.

The commentary to ABA Standard 2.6 also makes this point:

> The approach of striking jurors, as opposed to other types of peremptory challenge, the Court observed in *Swain*, has been praised "as a fairer system to the defendant and prosecutor and a more efficacious, quicker way to obtain an impartial jury satisfactory to the parties." Ibid. It is true that each party, at the time he exercises each peremptory challenge, is confronted with the total number of persons from whom the final jury will be formed, and thus is always in a position to exclude the person most objectionable to him. Under the other systems, by contrast, there is always the chance of some other person or persons coming on the panel who are more objectionable than those already challenged. At the same time, the system of striking jurors is arguably more time consuming in that in every case it is necessary to examine and qualify a large group of jurors, while under other systems the parties may reach an early accord on the jury without exercising all of their challenges. Comment, 24 *U Chi L Rev* 751, 757 (1957).

The authorities relied on in the commentary include: "The Jury System in the Federal Courts," 26 *FRD* 409, 468 (1961); 1 Busch, *Law and Tactics in Jury Trials* (1959); Comment, 24 *U Chi L Rev* 751, 755, 757 (1957); Note, 58 *Yale L J* 638 (1949); Orfield, *Criminal Procedure From Arrest to Appeal* 406 (1947); and Smith, "Criminal Justice in America: A Reply," 11 *ABAJ* 797, 798 (1925).

## C. Recent Developments §8.9

It is now possible to keep up with the law on jury selection the same way you keep up with the law in any other field—by reading the relevant advance sheets, subscribing to services on trial advocacy or criminal law, and reading daily newspapers and legal newspapers. The *Index to Legal Periodicals*, *Current Law Index*, and *Legal Resource Index* provide provocative (and sometimes descriptive) titles to law review articles, comments, and notes in this field, indicating what is happening at the cutting edge of the law. It is a good idea occasionally to ask your law librarian for an index to journals on psychology, applied psychology, and the social sciences, to pick up new ideas from these disciplines.

Increasingly, lawyers are learning to use *Lexis* and *Westlaw* in order to find the latest cases and interesting parallels in other fields of law. It is always necessary to Shepardize all citations.

The Annual Supplement to these volumes will use recent developments sections throughout the book to describe new cases, ideas, and articles that are worthy of note, and to warn of cases overruled and of rules and statutes amended or repealed.

## III. PURPOSES OF VOIR DIRE

### A. General Goal §8.10

The goal in questioning prospective jurors is different from the goal in questioning witnesses, although the method of achieving the goal is the same, namely, questioning. A witness is questioned so that he or she will reveal to the jury one version of events so that the attorneys can reconstruct what took place and argue from the facts that the plaintiff should recover or that the defendant is not guilty. Jurors, on the other hand, are not questioned about objective facts but about their own attitudes. They are questioned so that they will give clues to one attorney about their thinking habits and prejudices without revealing to the other attorney very much about themselves.

In addition, the attorneys begin to share with the jury some of the burdens they carry as they face the realities of human behavior that are revealed in courts of law. Lawyers, like many other workers who deal with people in trouble, must analyze the facts of negligent or criminal behavior, even when the particular client is blameless or innocent. Often *someone* committed an act that we label "negligent," "deliberate," "inhuman" or "unspeakable." The lawyer must learn to use objective tools to determine who did the act, how they did it, and, often, why they did it (intent). The lawyer must begin to share with the jury this ability to think objectively at the earliest moment in the trial, because objective thinking is a skill that is not learned quickly. Many jurors have never before been required to overcome their initial emotional responses to facts of violent death, major injuries, or sexual passion, and to lay aside their prejudices and intuitions. They have never been told not to listen to rumors or hearsay, or to make decisions on the basis of stated rules. It is the responsibility of the lawyer to help each juror scrub up for the intellectual operation that will take place in the courtroom, to transform each juror from lay person to judge of the facts.

In order to face this challenge, lawyers work hard on voir dire. The reason they care about the rules concerning the conduct of voir dire is that success hangs in the balance. See the simple statistics collected by psychologist Richard Christie, in §8.37.

The most common prosecution objections to voir dire questions are objections to the form of a question or that it is not related to any ground of challenge for cause, such as bias. Both sides can also object to questions on the grounds that they attempt to preinstruct the jurors on the law, do not correctly state the law, or ask the juror to prejudge the evidence. See, e.g., chapter 23 for criticisms of the use of lengthy voir dire.

## B. To Move the Jury as a Group §8.11

*Source:* Speech by Theodore Koskoff before the American Trial Lawyers Association.

The trial of a law suit is a study in applied psychology. Most of the time the lawyer is attempting to move a group of people (the jury) in a certain direction. The jury itself has its own motives in moving in one direction or another. The task is to motivate a group. Motivational techniques in moving a group as a group are different from moving 12 individuals. To move a group one must appeal to common denominator motivations like decency, honor, humanity, justice, the jurors' oath, etc. This must be done from the voir dire through to the summation. As the voir dire is our first contact with the jury, that first impression of both client and lawyer on the jury is most important. It must immediately, through sincerity, honesty, and no obviously trick questions, be a good impression.

The voir dire is an exclusionary process. It is not really designed to try to pick what the examiner thinks are "good" jurors for his case. No one ever knows who the really good ones are. The process is designed, at least in part, to get rid of the "bad" ones.

See Attorney Koskoff's closing argument to a jury based on their promises made during voir dire, in chapter 21.

## C. To Uncover Prejudices §8.12

The impartiality required of a fair juror is "not a technical conception," as Chief Justice Hughes observed in *United States v Wood* (1936) 299 US 123, 145–146: "It is a state of mind. For the ascertainment of this mental attitude of appropriate indifference, the Constitution lays down no particular tests and procedure is not chained to any ancient and artificial formula." Instead, the "defendant in a criminal case has the right to 'probe for the hidden prejudices of the jurors.'" *Lurding v United States* (6th Cir 1950) 179 F2d 419, 421.

## D. To Eliminate Extreme Positions §8.13

*Source:* Affidavit of Hans Zeisel, *In re Coordinated Pretrial Proceedings in Antibiotic Antitrust Action* (D Minn, No. 4–71, Civ 4350).

The legal formula for selecting our jurors is to aim at a jury that can be "impartial and fair." This is an important and meaningful guideline for selection, but by itself it is not sufficient, partly because, strictly speaking, the concept of complete impartiality cannot be realized as long as humans are called upon to judge. No person sitting as juror can completely remove his own experiences and values, however hard he may try.

The real and realistic aim of our jury selection method is not to achieve the impossible complete impartiality but rather to minimize the range of predispositions that may influence the jury's verdict. Conceptually, we can rank the members of a jury in a spectrum that ranges from those most predisposed toward the plaintiff to those most predisposed toward the defendant. The purpose of the voir dire proceedings is to eliminate from the jury that will sit on the case the extreme positions on both sides of the spectrum.

Additional excerpts from Professor Zeisel's affidavit are in §§8.83 and 8.85.

## E. To Discover "Friendly" Jurors §8.14

A delicate problem arises when a juror friendly to one side is discovered. It becomes important to keep the other side from figuring out that juror's predilections and using a peremptory challenge on him or her. For example, in the *Panther 21* case (see §3.25), the prosecutor asked one juror his occupation. "Artist," was the reply. The prosecutor did not ask further questions about the juror's work. Unfortunately for them, defense counsel did, only to be told that the prospective juror had shown one of his paintings at a benefit for the defendants in the case. Of course, the prosecution used a peremptory challenge on the artist.

For excerpts of questioning of not-unfriendly jurors, see chapters 15 and 16.

## F. To Exercise "Educated" Peremptories §8.15

If the juror's answers lead a lawyer to question further in order to make a challenge for cause, and that challenge fails, the lawyer may have to use a peremptory challenge because opposing counsel will probably want that juror to remain on the jury. A San Francisco lawyer who has tried 20 felony cases and won several has challenged 15 or 16 jurors for cause, but never successfully. However, he has then used peremptory challenges and has never run out of peremptories. On the whole, he has been satisfied with the juries selected in this way.

CAVEAT: In a few jurisdictions the rules do not permit voir dire questioning for the purpose of exercising peremptory challenges, but only to challenge for cause.

The Seventh Circuit Court of Appeals explained the theory behind the use of peremptories in reversing convictions of the *Chicago Eight* conspiracy defendants due, *inter alia*, to improper limitations on voir dire (*United States v Dellinger* (7th Cir 1972) 472 F2d 340, 368, see §3.54):

But beyond this, an answer which falls short of an admission of bias may nevertheless aid counsel in deciding to exercise a peremptory challenge. The Supreme Court has stated that the peremptory challenge, although not required in the Constitution, is "one of the most important of the rights secured to the accused," and that "[t]he denial or impairment of the right is reversible error without a showing of prejudice." *Swain v Alabama* (1965) 380 US 202, 219. The peremptory challenge is provided in the federal system by Federal Rule of Criminal Procedure 24(b).

If this right is not to be an empty one, the defendants must, upon request, be permitted sufficient inquiry into the background and attitudes of the jurors to enable them to exercise intelligently their peremptory challenges. Cf. *United States v Esquer* (7th Cir 1972) 459 F2d 431, 434; *United States v Lewin* (7th Cir 1972) 467 F2d 1132; *Spells v United States* (5th Cir 1959) 263 F2d 609, 611; *cert. denied* 360 US 920.

In its memorandum in support of defendant's motion for counsel to participate in voir dire, filed March 26, 1972, in *United States v McNeil* (see §3.51), the American Civil Liberties Union of Northern California argued that

a thorough voir dire also enables counsel to exercise "educated" peremptories, thus reducing community distrust of the judicial process and making justice satisfy the appearance of justice. Since the peremptory challenge is "one of the most important of the rights secured to the accused" (*Pointer v United States* (1894) 151 US 395, 408), it would seem logical that educated peremptories would be preferred. Thus a thorough voir dire will enable counsel to depart from the traditional practice of challenging all [members of minority groups], all young people, etc., and instead enable him to exercise some individualized judgments as to jurors. See Youtt, "Voir Dire Has Its Proper Uses," 57 *ABAJ* 38, 40 (1971) ("the roulette wheel should best be left on the gaming table, not brought into the trial court").

## G. To Cause Jurors to Face Their Own Prejudices §8.16

The important purpose of a voir dire that probes juror prejudices is spelled out in detail in questions on racism (in §§9.30–9.49), on effects of pretrial publicity (in §§9.21–9.23, 11.82), and in other sections of the basic voir dire questions in chapter 9. Extensive examples of colloquies between counsel and prospective jurors in which the attorneys seek to probe prejudices are provided in chapters 15–17.

## H. To Teach Jurors Important Facts in the Case §8.17

*Source:* Malcolm Burnstein in *The Relevant Lawyers* 53 (Ginger ed 1972).

One of the points that we want the jury to keep in mind [in the case of a black defendant charged with murdering a white policeman] is the fact that Officer Grey didn't think one gun was enough for him; he had two. So we asked the jurors, "Would it disturb you in any way if you learned that the dead police officer was carrying a second gun?" We're asking the jurors whether they can be fair to the prosecution, right? That's essentially how the question sounded, but we're really telling the jurors that here's the kind of a cop who doesn't think that a single gun is enough for him. And, of course, the irony is that it was the second one that killed him.

We also talked about the fact that the defendant had been drinking. We asked, "If you learn during the course of the trial that the defendant had been drinking, would that prejudice you in any way? Do you take a drink yourself, Mr. Smith, every once in a while?"

## I. To Expose Jurors to Damaging Facts in the Case §8.18

On voir dire jurors should be asked their attitudes toward the accident or crime at issue. Counsel should also bring to the attention of the jury the most damaging features of the case against the client, if these facts will probably be brought to their attention by one of the parties. By doing so, the lawyer takes some of the shock out of the opponent's case. For examples of questions used by various attorneys, see §9.20.

When appropriate, counsel should point out that during the trial gruesome pictures may be exhibited to the jurors and should ask whether under such circumstances the jurors could be fair to the parties. Jurors who maintain they can be fair are at least put on their honor to do so, and that should be stressed in the closing argument. See, for example, excerpts from attorney Howard Moore's closing argument in the *Angela Davis* case, in chapter 21.

In *California v Burt* (see §3.24), defense counsel Charles Garry brought out many of the more damaging facts about the defendants during voir dire.

**Q. (By Mr. Garry)** Assuming that the evidence was to show that Mr. Burt believes that capitalism is on its way out, and it serves no human purposes, that it is destructive to human dignity and that it destroys human endeavor, and he believes that socialism is the only answer, would that factor create within you a prejudgment against him that would color your ability to be able to analyze and evaluate the testimony?

**Mr. Canty:** Again, your Honor, I object to the question. To put it in the form of an assumption is to do the same thing, but it is an attempt to preinstruct the juror as to what he expects the evidence to be. I see no relevance to that question. Counsel can ask a general question.

**Mr. Garry:** He has asked questions about Mr. Beaty [the prosecution witness] being in prison, Mr. Beaty being this and that. I did not object, because I think these questions are material and relevant.

**The Court:** I agree with you. I am a little concerned about the form of the question itself, however. Sir, if a Defendant's political views were different from your own, would you hold that against the Defendant?

Over prosecution objection, Garry was also permitted to ask:

If it should develop in the evidence that Mrs. Burt has done work in prison, the system to assist prisoners, would that fact bias or prejudice you in any way against her?

The judge sustained the prosecution's objection to the following question after Garry had asked it:

If the evidence showed that both of my clients believe that the United States' participation in the war in Vietnam was an act of aggression, that . . . we were committing genocide, and we were war criminals, and the leaders of our country that participated were war criminals, would that create within you a prejudgment against them?

For further excerpts from the transcript of the *Burt* voir dire, see chapters 15 and 17; voir dire questions in §9.20.

See also questions asked on voir dire by defendant Angela Davis acting as her own co-counsel, in chapters 15 and 17.

## J. To Teach Jurors the Law of the Case §8.19

Voir dire provides the first opportunity for the lawyers to teach the jurors some of the rules of evidence and other rules of law involved in the particular case.

Jurors know they are not mere observers of the chess game unfolding before them. They have indicated, in posttrial interviews, their frustration at not understanding what is really going on in the courtroom until the trial is virtually over, at which point the judge explains to them some of the rules of law they are supposed to follow. Jurors welcome information from the lawyers, as well as from the judge, at the beginning of the case, so they will have a framework for figuring out how to make the final move required of them at the close of the trial.

Trial lawyer Theodore Koskoff is of the opinion that, despite the court's instructions to jurors in criminal cases, they understand neither the presumption of innocence nor the burden of proof of the state. They can repeat what the judge tells them but it amounts to tunnel thought that they do not apply in the reasoning process. As these are the two most important principles for jurors to understand in criminal cases, they must be the most important areas to voir dire. See examples of voir dire on these points in §§11.10–11.13, 17.10, 17.22. In civil cases, the hard issues are liability and amount of damages. See examples in §§10.31–10.42, and chapter 16.

## K. To Converse with Jurors Directly and Individually §8.20

One purpose of voir dire is to reveal the attorney and the client to each juror individually, so that a relationship can be established that will cause the juror to look at the party as a fellow human being with a serious problem and to listen in a friendly manner to the lawyer's presentation of the case. Lawyers have expressed their determination to retain the right to conduct voir dire for this reason, among others. Attorney Theodore Koskoff, of Bridgeport, Connecticut, expressed this idea in a speech before the American Trial Lawyers Association:

> It is admittedly a lot easier to get the juror to identify with your client in a civil case than in a criminal case. In a criminal case the best technique is to get the juror to identify with his important part in the judicial process and at least to like *you* and, if possible, your client and to be convinced of the sincerity of your case.

Attorney Malcolm Burnstein of Oakland, California, says simply:

> You have five or ten minutes at the most to talk to a prospective juror and try to develop some kind of personal relationship. The prosecutor almost invariably asks every juror the same questions. I always try to find some little personal comment or joke with each juror, about where they work or where they were born or something. You've got to be different with each one, to get a personal relationship going. It's just crucial.

The art of persuasion is practiced best on a known audience. Lawyers cannot really select their jury audiences, they can only eliminate a few of the least sympathetic members. As to the rest, the task is to learn as much as possible about them *as individuals* in order to suggest the most effective ways to present the case to them, and the pitfalls to avoid.

In Louisiana, the accused's right to "full voir dire examination" explicitly "includes . . . the right to address, hear and observe the veniremen directly and as individuals." *Louisiana v Dixon* (La 1979) 365 So2d 1310.

## L. To Expose Opposing Counsel §8.21

Attorney Doris Walker describes how the voir dire examination of a prospective juror in the *Angela Davis* case (see §3.23) backfired on the prosecution in "An Interview with Doris Brin Walker," *Conspiracy*, May 11, 1972, p.11.

Another example of white racism on the part of the prosecution that comes most readily to mind is the manner in which the chief prosecutor handled the voir dire of the one black person on the jury panel. That person was a woman, the wife of a man who operated a beer and wine saloon and who had recently lost his license because he lacked the money to renew it. Prior to his losing his license, there had been some charges concerning gambling in the saloon; they had been disposed of, and had absolutely nothing to do with the license renewal. The prosecutor, during the voir dire, inquired at great length into the gambling charges and other aspects of the juror's husband's involvement with law enforcement authorities, with the Alcoholic Beverage Control Board, and with the State of California.

All of this related to the juror's husband, not to the juror herself. It was purportedly for the purpose of establishing the existence of bias in the juror's mind against the State of California and thus against the prosecution. But in the course of the examination, it became clear to the other prospective jurors, as well as to everyone in the courtroom, that the prosecution was totally insensitive to the humiliating nature of the questions he was asking the juror and to her responses. She stood up to him in the most courageous manner, manifesting great staunchness and a determination not to permit him to establish a nonexistent bias against the State, thus forcing him to accept her or to use a peremptory challenge against her.

It was one of the most moving experiences that I have had in a courtroom. The situation between the prosecution and this juror was very tense, and it soon became apparent that all the rest of the prospective jurors in the box were becoming emotionally and psychologically involved. When the prosecutor did indeed exercise a peremptory to excuse that juror, the defense pointed out the white racism manifested in the voir dire proceeding and in excusing her. It was very helpful, even an auspicious beginning for the case because it dramatized in a spontaneous way an example of white racism, which might otherwise have remained an abstraction in the minds of the jury.

## M. To Provide Time and Space for Citizens to Become Jurors §8.22

The juror is under tremendous pressures that have seldom been mentioned by judges and commentators. One of these pressures is being asked to determine the fate of another human being who is not known by the juror and who has done the juror no personal wrong. While many people enjoy making decisions, many do not. Both kinds of people abhor making decisions quickly in matters about which they have no previous knowledge. A juror walks into the jury box the first time with no previous knowledge of courtroom procedure; no previous close acquaintanceship with the lawyer for either side; no previous acquaintanceship with the judge, bailiff, or court clerk; and no familiarity with the parties or witnesses. The juror is at first amazed, and later may become angered, by a judge's continual harping on the need for speed in the trial and deliberations.

These sentiments were expressed very clearly by Ralph Davis, called for jury duty in Los Angeles County in 1973, whose comments appear in "Black Jurors," 30 *Lawyers Guild Practitioner* 111, 114 (1974):

> [The judge] said there is no need for a case to take four hours to try. Imagine, four hours to try a man on armed robbery and sodomy, from 11 a.m. to 1 p.m. and the next day from 10 to 11 a.m. Here is a man who brought out the fact that he had been convicted once for armed robbery and who could go up for twenty or thirty years [because this was a second offense].
>
> Just think of that—four hours could send a man to the penitentiary for thirty years. How much pressure is that on one human being to deliberate the fate of a man who could go to the penitentiary for thirty years?

Davis, who had expressed his anger at being peremptorily challenged several times, and who assumed this was because of his race, concluded: "Really, I will never go again. They would have to give me contempt and give me five days because that is just too much pressure for just one individual to have to go through."

For further comments of Davis, see §1.55.

## N. To Rehabilitate Jurors after Questioning by Opposing Counsel §8.23

"[F]ull voir dire examination includes the right to examine a prospective juror for purposes of demonstrating his impartiality . . . . " *Louisiana v Claiborne* (La Sup Ct 1981) 397 So2d 486, 489. Claiborne's conviction for possession of a firearm as a convicted felon was reversed on the basis of the following colloquy on voir dire:

[PROSECUTING ATTORNEY]: Will anyone here hold the State to a greater burden of proof than that? You, sir, can you do that?

BY JUROR #160: I don't know if I'm saying this at the right time, but as far as this [inaudible] I don't think I could be a good witness because . . .

BY THE COURT: A little louder, sir . . . .

BY JUROR #160: There could be some doubt in my mind. The fact that I've known situations where police planted a gun on somebody . . .

BY THE COURT: Planted a gun on somebody?

BY JUROR #160: Right. She mentioned a situation that the guy . . . I heard her say this two times that he want to prove that the gun is not his. He was only in possession of the gun. So I get the impression that the gun didn't belong to him or it was not registered to him.

BY THE COURT: Well, you can't get the impression until you hear the evidence.

[PROSECUTING ATTORNEY]: What I said, Your Honor, was that it's not necessary to prove ownership.

BY THE COURT: That's right.

[PROSECUTING ATTORNEY]: Only that he was in possession.

BY THE COURT: Right.

[PROSECUTING ATTORNEY]: Are you saying that you want possession to be equal to ownership, that it would take ownership before you would . . .

BY JUROR #160: It could be possible . . .

BY THE COURT: Well, if they prove to you that the police framed this guy and put their gun in his pocket, well, you cut him loose. But if they don't prove that the police slipped the gun wherever it was, then that's a horse of a different matter. Then you've also got to find out if he's guilty of this other offense, aggravated [battery] . . . .

[PROSECUTING ATTORNEY]: Sir, would you be less than fair to the State based on the police testifying?

BY JUROR #160: I wouldn't be unfair to anyone, but I mention the fact that it might be on my mind.

[PROSECUTING ATTORNEY]: Yes, sir, I appreciate that. Thank you very much. Well, you understand the definition of possession of arms, and you understand the things that are necessary to prove that?

BY JUROR #160: Yes.

After a short period during which other prospective jurors were being polled on their beliefs, the state returned to questioning the juror:

[PROSECUTING ATTORNEY]: Sir, let me ask you one question. But as far as police officers testifying would you look at at [sic] like you would anybody else?

BY A JUROR: Yes, I mentioned about this particular case here. I didn't say anything about police officers. I said there could be some doubt in my mind.

[PROSECUTING ATTORNEY]: What I'm trying to get down to is that if I put on a police officer and he's going to be the one testifying about the crime would you disbelieve what he says, automatically?

BY THE JUROR: No.

[PROSECUTING ATTORNEY]: So you can look at him and not let your other experiences . . .

[DEFENSE ATTORNEY]: Your Honor, this has been asked and answered about four times now.

[PROSECUTING ATTORNEY]: No, sir, I'm asking it a little differently. I am trying to ask him if it's going to interfere with him judging the police officer.

BY THE JUROR: Now, you asked me about this at first. I think I told you that it's possible that there would be some doubt in my mind. Now, that's about . . . I can't.

[PROSECUTING ATTORNEY]: But now I'm asking you would you let it interfere.

BY THE JUROR: Any time you have doubt I guess that's an interference. Wouldn't it be a interference if you there's a possibility that you could have a doubt? Would that be a interference?

BY THE COURT: Well, would that doubt would be predicated on what you hear and see here, or is that doubt going to be predicated on what you believe universally? We're talking about what you're going to see and hear here, whatever it is. I don't know what it is. Just what you see and hear here.

BY THE JUROR: Okay, yes, all right.

BY THE COURT: Whatever doubt or whatever you have in your mind would that be based on what you see and hear here? That would satisfy it.

[PROSECUTING ATTORNEY]: Or, would that doubt interfere with what he sees and hears here today, would be the question.

BY THE JUROR: Well, I've already said that. I don't know.

[PROSECUTING ATTORNEY]: I just thought you might be able to put it aside.

BY THE JUROR: Well, I don't know if I can or not. I merely stated the fact when you aked me if it would interfere. Well, I don't know.

[PROSECUTING ATTORNEY]: Your Honor, I would ask for a challenge for cause.

BY THE COURT: I'll excuse him.

[DEFENSE ATTORNEY]: I'd like to traverse.

BY THE COURT: Oh, I don't think we need to hear any more. I've had enough.

[DEFENSE ATTORNEY]: Note an objection.

397 So2d at 487–489.

The appellate court said (at 489) that its reversal was "buttressed by the numerous cases in which this court has condoned a trial court practice of permitting prosecuting attorneys to employ voir dire examination to rehabilitate and establish the impartiality of prospective jurors who initially expressed an opinion or impression of the defendant's guilt or innocence." Since the prosecutor had exhausted his peremptory challenges, defense counsel argued successfully that the cause challenge against Juror #160 had given the prosecutor one more peremptory than he was entitled to.

## O. To Prepare for Summation §8.24

Theodore Koskoff explained to a seminar by the American Trial Lawyers Association that from the day a lawyer steps into the courtroom to try a case, the lawyer's mind must have a place to start thinking in terms of summation. "To this end, many lawyers keep a notebook which they feed during the course of the trial with summation notes.

Such notes are invaluable." Koskoff's skeleton closing argument, based on voir dire colloquies, appears in chapter 21.

## IV. PROCEDURES FOR CONDUCTING VOIR DIRE

### A. Preliminary Screening §8.27

Preliminary screening by a jury commissioner or other official usually eliminates persons not qualified for jury duty under a statute or rule regarding lack of citizenship, ordinary intelligence, or natural faculties. This function may also be performed by the trial judge. (Other traditional grounds for exemption, such as youth (aged 18 to 20), short residence in the jurisdiction, particular occupation, or past conviction of a felony, are now being challenged in some jurisdictions and cases—see chapter 6.)

### B. Introductory Questioning by Judge §8.28

The trial judge has the duty to examine and select a fair and impartial jury. At the outset, most judges briefly state what the case is about; remind the jurors of the basic rules of law (such as the preponderance of the evidence, finding liability, and assessing damages in a civil case, or the presumption of innocence and the burden of proof in a criminal case); identify the parties and the attorneys; ask the jurors if they are acquainted with anyone in the case; and ask each juror to describe his or her residence, education, and occupation, state the occupation of spouse and grown children, and perhaps give a brief self-description. Judges usually conclude this phase by asking the prospective jurors if they know any reason why they cannot be fair and impartial jurors after considering the nature of the case, the parties involved, and the rules pertaining to their duties. See §§9.7, 10.46–10.48.

The answers to the general questions asked by the judge usually determine whether a right to challenge for cause exists as a matter of law, on the surface.

Procedures vary from this point on.

### C. Customary Modern Procedures for Further Questioning §8.29

The customary modern method of conducting the balance of the voir dire is for counsel to propose a particular method and for the trial judge to grant the request or motion unless it violates a statute or court rule. See §§8.41–8.48.

### 1. In State Courts §8.30

A good example of the modern procedure is provided by defendant's motion for individual voir dire out of the presence of other prospective jurors in *Wisconsin v Carothers* (Racine County Ct, No. 170-56, Nov. 13, 1974). The case concerned the contract murder of a prominent white druggist in Racine, Wisconsin, where jurors are customarily middle-class, Lutheran, northern European whites. Before the *Carothers* trial was held, a white pharmacy employee was charged with participation in the murder. The main prosecution witness in that trial was a black informer. There was a great deal of pretrial publicity. When the jury acquitted, the local newspaper printed the names and addresses of the 12 jurors on the front page. Calvin Carothers, Jr., an indigent black defendant, was charged with the same murder and would face the same informer witness. Defendant Carothers was represented by a new public defender staff under contract to the county. The media published a good deal of unfavorable material on the case over a long period of time, but defense counsel concluded that the trial judge would probably deny a motion for change of venue, which was strongly opposed by the prosecution. The defense argued that the only acceptable alternative would be extensive individual voir dire.

The trial judge granted the defense motion and instituted the following procedure:

The venire of 100 sitting in the courtroom were questioned by the judge to eliminate those obviously disqualified. The remainder were sequestered in a hotel until called in a panel. Thirty panelists were selected at a time and were sequestered separately. Each time jurors were eliminated the same process was followed with new panels.

Individual voir dire took place in the judge's conference room which had limited space. Present were the judge, the two trial prosecutors, one defense attorney, the defendant, the court staff, a reporter from the local paper, a few interested citizens (on request), and one prospective juror at a time. From time to time, other members of the defense team sat in.

For the questioning, the following procedure was adopted: (1) introduction of juror and explanation of basic voir dire procedure by judge; (2) questions by one prosecutor; (3) discussion of those questions and answers between defense attorney and juror; (4) questions by second prosecutor; (5) further discussion with defense attorney; (6) questions by judge; (7) questions by one prosecutor; (8) final discussion with defense attorney. All motions to strike were made after the individual had been excused.

Individual voir dire sessions were held with 150 individuals from four panels during two weeks. The result was a jury that had faced a reporter during voir dire in the conference room and would probably not be afraid of what the local press might say about the verdict. The trial lasted one and a half weeks. After about six hours of deliberation, the jury acquitted.

The defense team consisted of Mark Cross and Charles Swanson, who prepared all motions and instructions, Dennis W. Reeve, who coordinated the factual and investigative material, James E. Nash, lead investigator, and William D. Whitnall, the trial advocate. (After acquittal, the public defender hired the defendant as an investigator-trainee.)

Efforts to limit voir dire, particularly attorney participation and individual questioning, have been rejected repeatedly.

After the California Supreme Court, in *California v Crowe* (1973) 106 Cal Rptr 369, held that the judge alone could conduct voir dire, California Penal Code §1078 was amended in 1974 to read: "It shall be the duty of the trial court to examine the prospective jurors to select a fair and impartial jury. He shall permit reasonable examination of prospective jurors by counsel for the people and for the defendant, *such examination to be conducted orally and directly by counsel*." (Emphasis added.) The California Rules of Court now provide:

> Upon request of counsel, the trial judge shall permit such counsel to supplement the judge's examination by oral and direct questioning of any of the prospective jurors. The scope of such additional questions or supplemental examination shall be within reasonable limits prescribed by the trial judge in his sound discretion.

Superior Court Rule 228: Municipal Court Rule 516 (adopted Jan. 1, 1975).

Connecticut adopted an amendment to the Connecticut Constitution providing: "The right to question each juror individually by counsel shall be inviolate." Conn Const art IV (Dec. 22, 1972), amending art I, §19.

Modern judges also modify the approach they take to their role in voir dire. For example, in a Detroit Recorder's Court case, the judge began the voir dire one way, then strengthened the procedure as required by the circumstances. Congressman George W. Crockett, Jr., then on the Recorder's Court, was trying a black defendant charged with raping a white woman. The defense was going to be admission of the sexual act, with the claim that the woman acted voluntarily. The defendant was represented by a young white woman lawyer. Judge

Crockett conducted a short voir dire of the jurors, without going into the specifics of the case. He turned the questioning over to the defense attorney, who asked few questions and got few significant responses.

Judge Crockett could see that the prospective jurors were not at all aware of the kind of testimony that would come before them for judgment, and he decided to probe more deeply. He asked one of the white women if she realized that the charge was rape, and that the defendant and complaining witness were of different races. Would that affect her ability to listen to the evidence and decide the case fairly? The woman began to look inside herself a little.

He turned to a black woman on the jury and talked about the defense that would be given, that the act was voluntarily committed. Would she be able to listen to this evidence without embarrassment and be able to decide on the basis of the evidence alone? He asked a couple of innocuous questions and then returned to the racial and factual questions.

When he turned the questioning back to the prosecutor and the defense lawyer, the latter picked up on his cue and proceeded to conduct a vigorous and profound voir dire. As a result, several jurors, both black and white and of both sexes, asked to be excused on the ground that they could not promise to decide the case solely on the basis of the evidence put before them and without prejudice of any kind. The ensuing trial was conducted in an atmosphere of frank recognition of the realities in society as well as the facts in the particular case.

## 2. In Federal Courts §8.31

In an antitrust case, *MCI v AT&T* (see §3.73), the federal district court judge concluded the preliminary, formal questioning described in §§8.27–8.28, and then asked each juror to say a few words about himself or herself. Jurors who said too little were asked a few quiet questions by the judge, which resulted in more information being given. Plaintiff's counsel felt that he knew a great deal about the jurors from these short autobiographical statements, since the items covered, the order in which they were covered, and the style of delivery were all quite revealing.

In a highly publicized criminal case during the Vietnam war (*United States v Ahmad*, known as "the Berrigan Case"), seven defendants were charged with conspiracy and with several substantive crimes in demonstrating their opposition to that war as illegal and immoral. (Cr. No. 14950, tried before Hon. J. Dixon Herman, U.S. District Judge, Middle District of Pennsylvania, Harrisburg Division, and a jury.) The defendants moved for dismissal of the indictment on the ground of prejudicial pretrial publicity, engendered, they claimed, in large part by the government. That motion was denied. However, there was no dispute that the case had been the subject of nationwide and international publicity.

Counsel were of the opinion that unusual precautions were required to secure a petit jury that would represent a cross-section of the community and would not be affected by the extensive publicity that had attended the case or by the political sympathies that necessarily exist when political issues such as the Vietnam war lie in the background of the case. They requested the opportunity to participate in the selection of the jury.

Counsel for the defense and for the prosecution set forth in writing hundreds of questions to be put to the prospective jurors by the trial judge. Judge Herman put many of these questions himself to a group of prospective jurors, and then to individual ones outside the presence of the others. He then gave government counsel the opportunity to examine the prospective jurors individually outside the presence of others with respect to their education, employment, views on the war, their views on political issues, and many other matters deemed appropriate by the court. Defense counsel then engaged in similar examinations.

During the course of the examinations, many jurors were excused for cause on application of the government, or the defense, or by decision of the court in the absence of any request by counsel. Forty-seven jurors were selected, subject to peremptory challenges by the respective parties. The 7 defendants were given 28 challenges, the government 6.

After the jury had been selected, the court proceeded in a similar manner to select six alternate jurors. The defendants were given seven peremptory challenges to the panel of alternates and the government one. The process of selecting the petit jury took approximately four weeks with an additional two weeks for the selection of the alternates.

Intensive individual voir dire by counsel was not uncommon in federal courts in 1950. See *Dennis v United States* (1950) 339 US 162, and cases cited in §8.79.

### 3. In American Bar Association Standards §8.32

In February 1975, the American Bar Association House of Delegates approved a resolution that "the American Bar Association supports the concept of voir dire by counsel as a matter of right in federal civil and criminal cases." In August 1976, the House of Delegates recommended that Rule 47(a) of the Federal Rules of Civil Procedure be amended to provide:

> (a) Examination of Jurors. The court shall permit the parties or their attorneys to conduct oral examination of prospective jurors. The court may inquire of prospective jurors as a supplement to the examination by the parties.

For current ABA policy, see Standards Relating to Fair Trial and Free Press §3.4 and Standards Relating to Trial by Jury §2.4.

### 4. In Capital Cases §8.33

Procedures for conducting voir dire in the guilt phase of a trial that could result in the death penalty require careful consideration of the current state of capital punishment law and challenges to the death penalty. *Any* voir dire questions about capital punishment in the *guilt* phase may increase the likelihood of a guilty verdict. See lengthy discussion in §§11.61–11.82.

## D. Procedures Requiring Reversal §8.34

In the famous *Chicago Eight* case arising out of the demonstrations at the 1968 Democratic Party Convention during the Vietnam war, the method of conducting voir dire was a ground for reversal of the convictions. (See *United States v Dellinger* (7th Cir 1972) 472 F2d 340, 366, described in §3.54.)

The trial judge, the late Julius Hoffman, told the parties they could propose questions that he would ask on voir dire. He asked the entire venire the following questions:

> Whether the prospective jurors were acquainted with employees of the FBI, or of the Justice Department;
> Whether they were acquainted with defendants, their counsel, or their associates;
> Whether they could agree to follow the law as given to them;
> Whether they could keep an open mind until time to reach a verdict;
> Whether they could treat the testimony of a government agent the same as that of any other witness;
> Whether prior jury service would prevent them from being impartial;
> Whether there was any reason they could not be fair and impartial jurors in this case.

Of those questioned, 56 requested to be excused on one or more of these grounds, and the judge excused them.

The Seventh Circuit Court of Appeals described the procedure in a long and careful analysis of Judge Hoffman's conduct:

> The jury box was filled and the court questioned the first 12 individually. The court asked standard questions, primarily relating to marital and family

status, occupation of prospective juror and spouse, employer and length of employment of prospective juror and spouse, number of children, their schools and occupations.

Two veniremen who said they worked for the federal government were asked whether being a government employee would influence their judgment. Another was asked, "Do you feel that the fact that your father is a member of the Chicago Police Force and has been for many years would affect your judgment as a juror if you were selected in this case?" All said they could still be impartial.

After interviewing each of these first 12, the court inquired of the group whether any had close relatives or friends who were employed by any law enforcement agency or other agency of the local, state or federal government. When five answered yes, the court asked each whether this would influence his judgment. All answered that it would not. The court did not ask this question of the succeeding veniremen who entered the jury box.

Defense counsel repeated defendants' request that the judge ask the questions they had submitted. The court responded, "I have reached the conclusion that those I haven't asked are not germane to the issues presented here by the indictment and the pleas of not guilty thereto."

The jury was selected after 24 persons had been individually questioned, the defense had exercised 10 of their 17 peremptory challenges, and the government two. Appellants accepted the tendered jury but "under the greatest of protest" because the court had not asked questions they considered necessary for fully exercising their challenges.

The court of appeals explicitly rejected the district judge's rationale for his voir dire behavior, in footnote 42 of its opinion:

> One of the district judge's comments at the hearing in November, 1970, concerning communications between the judge and the deliberating jury (see Part V) indicates that he limits voir dire as a practice:
>
> > I restrict voir dire of prospective jurors very carefully. I think there is more time wasted in many American courts on voir dire than for any reason I know of.
>
> We are sympathetic with the district judge's view, but expedition is clearly subsidiary to the duty to impanel an impartial jury. See Judicial Conference Committee on the Operation of the Jury System, 26 F.R.D. 409, 465–467 (1960).

For a list of issues on which appellate courts have ordered or upheld voir dire, see §8.79.

## E. Recent Developments §8.35

See §8.9.

## V. EFFECTS OF FULL VOIR DIRE §8.37

Social psychologist Richard Christie made an effective argument for full voir dire by lawyers in an affidavit in support of plaintiffs' motion for fair jury selection procedures in *Hampton v Hanrahan* (see §3.71), the civil suit for damages against police officers in Chicago for the deaths of Black Panther Party leaders Fred Hampton and Mark Clark:

> Sheer skill aside, the roles played by a judge, the lawyers for the plaintiffs, and the lawyers for the defendants tend to determine the content of their questions. The respective lawyers, intent as they are in uncovering bias prejudicial to their client's interests, are more likely to look for and follow up any indication of bias on the part of a prospective juror. The judge is more concerned with maintaining an impartial posture and making certain that the potential juror satisfies statutory requirements.
>
> The advantages of having members of the venire questioned by parties representing different interests go beyond the content of the questions asked. In permitting the trial judge to conduct voir dire, there is a great probability that prospective jurors will respond to the judge's questions rather less than candidly. The judge's stature makes him an important authority figure in the eyes of the average venireperson, and the prospective juror will be reluctant to parade his prejudice in front of this figure cloaked with the robes of authority. In answering the judge's inquiry he will be more concerned with looking good than telling the truth. This tendency is present even when the examination is conducted by lawyers, but it will not be as pervasive. Reports from psychological studies indicate that respondents avoid contradicting the interviewer or displeasing her or him when the interviewer is perceived as having higher status than the subject. In such cases it is likely that the question will result in biased information. The greater the distance between the social status of the interviewer and that of the respondent, the greater is the probability of obtaining biased answers.
>
> Also, the non-verbal communications of a venireperson are more revealing when lawyers conduct the voir dire. If a potential juror is biased for one side, his behavior is likely to vary in the way in which he responds to questions asked by the respective lawyers. The juror is apt to display signs of tension, evasion, or overt non-verbal indicators of hostility in responding to the lawyer representing the side against which he is biased. Similarly, he is more likely to emit cues of approval in responding to the lawyer representing the side which he favors. Such subtle indicators of bias are rarely elicited by judges who are almost unanimously perceived by jurors as being fair and impartial in their treatment of members of the venire. Such indicators of bias are, of course, insufficient to disqualify a potential juror. They do serve to sensitize a lawyer as to possible bias and thus to influence the content of the questioning and also to assist in assigning priorities for the peremptory strikes.

Christie's conclusions were based on a previous statistical study.

*Source:* Affidavit of Richard Christie, 1974, *In Re Coordinated Pretrial Proceedings in Antibiotic Antitrust Action* (D Minn, 1974) 410 F Supp 659.

1. I, Richard Christie, having been duly sworn, depose as follows. I am Professor of Social Psychology in the Graduate Faculties of Columbia University in the City of New York .... During the past 24 years I have sponsored or cosponsored over 50 doctoral dissertations and served on over 350 doctoral dissertation committees .... I am a Fellow of the American Psychological Association and the American Sociological Association .... My own research has resulted in three books, two research monographs, and over 30 journal articles and chapters in other books ....

*COMMENT:* These salient items in Dr. Christie's career are excerpted from a much longer statement of the credentials that prove his expertise.

**3. Analysis of the Voir Dire in Recent Trials Established the Necessity of Extended Individual Voir Dire Conducted by the Lawyers for Both Sides.**

One way of testing the validity of the assertion that an individual voir dire conducted by the lawyers with extensive questioning is more effective in eliminating biased members of the venire [than a brief judge-conducted voir dire] is to examine the court's disposition of venire-persons in cases satisfying these criteria as contrasted to cases in which these criteria are not met. The standard for comparison is how many challenges for cause raised by lawyers for the prosecution and defense during voir dire and based on information elicited during the voir dire are sustained by the judge. The assumption is that a challenge for cause by a lawyer is based upon the lawyer's belief that a venireperson is biased toward the defendant and that if the judge concurs he also believes that there are reasonable grounds for believing that the person is in fact biased. Thus the number of challenges for cause sustained by the court correlates to how successful the voir-dire procedures are in exposing the biases of the venirepersons.

... [T]he [following] analysis was restricted to seven trials in which I was involved with the defense in varying ways and therefore knew some of the details of jury selection. In the Harrisburg 7, Gainesville 8, and Wounded Knee trials I was part of the defense team working on jury selection; I consulted with the Camden 17 defense team, exchanged information with the Pentagon Papers defense, and was approached (although not retained) by the defense in the Mitchell-Stans trial.

*COMMENT:* The Harrisburg trial of the *Berrigan Brothers* is described in §8.35, the *Gainesville Eight* case in §3.53, the *Camden* case in §3.55, and the *Pentagon Papers* case in §3.52. On *Wounded Knee* trials, see §§8.81, 8.90; on *Mitchell-Stans*, see §8.86.

Court transcripts were available for all of these trials except for the Harrisburg 7 and Gainesville 8 trials. In the latter two it was possible to work from notes taken by members of the defense teams. These materials were examined to determine the procedures used in the voir dire and the disposition of each and every venireperson who appeared in court and was examined.

The procedures used in these cases fell into three natural groupings.

A. Three trials, those of the Gainesville 8, Pentagon Papers I, and Pentagon Papers II (the first jury was dismissed because of the long delay in the trial) are viewed as similar in procedure. All involved a group voir dire which was conducted by the judge in which the lawyers were not permitted to ask questions. The judge's questions were narrow in scope and did not deal with the attitudes of the members of the venire.

B. The second grouping consists of the Mitchell-Stans, Camden 17, and Wounded Knee trials. These are classified as intermediate on the three criteria.

In the Mitchell-Stans trial there was an initial group voir dire by the judge and those surviving the screening were examined individually in the judge's chambers, with the lawyers being permitted to suggest questions to the judge. Except for questioning about exposure to the mass media the questioning was not extensive.

The Camden 17 trial started with a group voir dire (over defense objections). However, after one potential juror went into a tirade about the defendants' guilt, those remaining were examined individually. Lawyers were permitted to suggest questions but extensive questioning was not permitted.

In the Wounded Knee trial, there was an individual voir dire conducted by the judge. The voir dire was extensive and included many of the questions suggested by the lawyers for the two sides. In addition, the lawyers were permitted to suggest additional questions after the judge completed asking his standard set of questions.

C. The final trial, that of the Harrisburg 7, is an example of a voir dire which more fully satisfies the . . . criteria [of individual, extensive voir dire by counsel]. Venirepersons were examined individually, first by the judge and then by lawyers for the prosecution and defense. A wide latitude in questioning was allowed so that the prospective juror's group memberships, attitudes toward the Vietnam War, and similar matters were elicited.

[The analysis of these three groups of cases is presented in table I.]

. . . Causes for excuse [by the judge, the second column of figures in table I] vary from jurors living too far from the scene of the trial, . . . [because of] having moved outside the federal district since entry onto the jury roles, being physically incapacitated, being responsible for the care of a sick member of the family, [or facing] occupational hardship, [to] statements of opinion as [to] the guilt or innocence of the defendants, etc. The largest number excused for saying that they had an opinion occurred in Harrisburg where 23 were excused on such grounds. In the Wounded Knee trial Judge Nichol correctly anticipated a long trial and excused a large number of jurors for occupational hardships associated with disruption of employment.

The fourth column contains the number of venirepersons eliminated by

**Table I: Disposition of Veniremen Appearing for Voir Dire in Seven Trials**

| *Trial* | *Number Examined* | *[Initially] Excused by Judge* | *Number [Remaining] Eligible* | *Eliminated by Challenges* | | *Number on Jury* |
|---|---|---|---|---|---|---|
| | | | | *Peremptory* | *[For Cause] Sustained* | |
| **Group I** | | | | | | |
| Gainesville 8 | 54 | *18* | 36 | *24* | *0*[1] | 12 |
| Pentagon Papers I | 38 | *4* | 34 | *18* | *4* | 12 |
| Pentagon Papers II | 69 | *38* | 31 | *18* | *1*[2] | 12 |
| **Group II** | | | | | | |
| Mitchell-Stans | 61 | *19* | 42 | *26* | *4* | 12 |
| Wounded Knee | 93 | *48* | 45 | *26* | *7* | 12 |
| Camden 17 | 61 | *34* | 27 | *8*[3] | *7* | 12 |
| **Group III** | | | | | | |
| Harrisburg 7 | 109 | *36* | 73 | *34* | *27* | 12 |

1 No transcript was available. Two defense lawyers remembered one challenging a partially aphasic venireman and thought the challenge was successful. Defense team notes indicate, however, that the judge deferred decision and finally did not grant the challenge.

2 Does not include three veniremen improperly approached by a defense volunteer and two peace officers who are listed on the transcript as successfully challenged for cause. In neither case was the excuse for duty based on events in the courtroom.

3 All of the peremptories were not exercised.

peremptory challenges. In all cases the prosecution had the statutory six with all of the judges using their discretionary powers in allotting at least eight extra peremptories to the defense. The highest number of peremptory challenges allotted to the defense was 28 in the Harrisburg 7 trial. This reflected Judge Herman's awareness of strong opinion against the anti-war Catholic defendants in a district composed predominantly of conservative Protestants.

The fifth column is the crucial one for the present analysis. Only five persons were successfully challenged for cause in all three trials in Group I, two by the prosecution and three by the defense. The limited nature of the questioning simply did not give the lawyers enough information on which to base a successful challenge when the judge conducted a group voir dire in which the lawyers were not allowed to participate.

A total of 18 veniremen were eliminated in the three trials falling under Group II where there were varying blends of group and individual voir dire and the lawyers were permitted to suggest questions to the judge which he might or might not ask.

Finally, in the Harrisburg 7 trial where, of the seven trials, there were the best conditions for examining the members of the venire, *i.e.*, extended individual voir dire conducted mainly by the lawyers, a total of 23 were successfully challenged by the defense and four by the prosecution. In fact, more persons were successfully challenged for cause in Harrisburg 7 than in the other six trials combined.

The correspondence between the number of sustained challenges for cause in the three groupings and the predicted ordering is apparent. This is true despite the fact that in addition to the three major procedural differences on which attention was focused there were a number of idiosyncratic factors associated with each trial and the manner in which it was conducted. The trials were held in courts which differed in the sociological characteristics of the population from which the juries were drawn and the judges were not always consistent with one another in the standards which they applied in excusing venirepersons—indeed, a close reading of the transcripts suggests that individual judges were not completely consistent within a trial in the standards they employed in excusing jurors.

Thus, although the findings are based on a limited number of trials, they are striking enough to suggest that they might well be generalized to other trials. In a case where there is an extended individual voir dire conducted by the lawyers, both the prosecution and the defense are best able to successfully challenge for cause those members of the venire who have shown through the voir dire that they are indeed biased.

## VI. PRETRIAL STEPS TO ENSURE ADEQUATE VOIR DIRE §8.40

In a less hurried society, the attainment of justice was expected to be time-consuming, and citizens commonly attended trials as interesting historical events in their community and as a method of adding drama to their lives, rather than rushing home to watch fictional drama on television. In that seemingly far-off time, lawyers were permitted extensive voir dire of prospective jurors, and it is possible that jurors were more open in that time than they are today, showing their biases and prejudgments more clearly. In any event, the emphasis was on the thoroughness of jury questioning rather than on efficiency, speed, or saving money in jury fees.

The trial lawyer today in virtually any case, whether major or minor, faces a judge who has been inundated with literature from judicial and bar sources indicating that he or she must not permit lawyers to conduct a voir dire that is too extensive, because it is a waste of time and money and is not necessary in order to attain justice (see chapter 23). In some states the trial judge faces a fairly recent decision by a fairly high appellate court indicating that lawyer voir dire should be limited. See, e.g., *California v Crowe* (Cal 1973) 106 Cal Rptr 369.

This chapter deals with the situation in which a trial judge refuses to permit lawyers to ask questions on specific subjects the lawyers think are related to the case or the judge refuses to ask questions requested by the lawyers. Chapters 15–17 present examples of attorney approaches when extensive voir dire is permitted.

When a judge usually conducts the entire voir dire or sharply limits voir dire by lawyers, what is the best approach? Probably the first step is to read carefully *United States v Dellinger* (7th Cir 1972) 472 F2d 340, *cert. denied* (1973) 410 US 970, which contains a lengthy and careful analysis of voir dire. The American Bar Association's *Standards Relating to Trial by Jury* (1968) and *Standards Relating to Fair Trial and Free Press* (1968) are also instructive (see §8.32).

Despite the heading of this section, there is no way to "ensure" proper voir dire; there are only procedures for raising the issue early and often and preserving it if needed on appeal. The word "adequate" is used because few voir dire questions are "constitutionally required," although the Supreme Court recognizes that some questions fall in that protected category. See §2.8.

The lawyer determined to try a case before a jury that is capable of listening, deliberating, and then voting without reliance on prejudgments may have to file innovative pretrial papers concerning the conduct of the voir dire. On the need for extensive voir dire, see §§8.56 8.57. On the need for intensive voir dire, see §8.53. On the need to question each prospective juror individually, see §8.62; on the related need to conduct voir dire out of the presence of other jurors, see §§8.63–8.65. Arguments in favor of lawyers participating actively in voir dire are presented in §§8.58–8.59, 8.61. Any or all of these points can be raised in a motion for extensive and intensive individualized voir dire conducted by counsel (see §8.44). The motion can request a hearing for the taking of expert testimony on the need for this type of voir dire (see §8.46). A supporting memorandum of points and authorities should accompany the motion, with material from §§8.51–8.73. The motion will be strengthened by supporting affidavits from experts who may later testify at the hearing (see, e.g., §§8.80–8.87). The outcome of two efforts along these lines is recounted in §8.90.

A lawyer with less time or confidence in pretrial motions can simply prepare to argue during voir dire for more questioning in sensitive areas, for individual questioning, and for more direct participation by counsel. Even if there is no possibility of convincing the trial judge, it is essential to preserve these points for appeal.

Both approaches depend on preparation of a comprehensive list of questions that are demonstrably relevant to one or more recognized purposes of voir dire (see §§8.10–8.24) and that have been asked in other trials (see questions in chapters 9–11).

## A. Requests and Motions

### 1. Form: Letter to Trial Judge §8.41

*Source:* Dean A. Robb of Michigan often sends a letter like the following to a trial judge sometime before trial is scheduled.

Dated:__________

Honorable __________
United States District Judge
_____ Federal Building
____________________

Re: __________ v __________, Case No. __________
Dear Judge __________:

We are delivering, for your consideration, our suggestions and requests about the conduct of voir dire in this case.

I understand [*from my co-counsel,* __________] that you are not of the Judge [*Name of judge who permits attorney voir dire*] school of voir dire, which permits attorneys to conduct the voir dire, and that you usually just want supplemental follow-up questions from the lawyers. Would you consider trying our method or proposal in this case?

*COMMENT:* This forthright comparison of your trial judge with another judge who permits attorney voir dire may strike some judges well and others badly.

Counsel proposes the use of a questionnaire, described in chapter 12, to get individual information from jurors without taking court time.

**PLAINTIFF'S PROPOSAL FOR VOIR DIRE**

1. The entire panel will be given the enclosed questionnaire to fill out while we are meeting with you on preliminary matters and discussing settlement, last-minute motions, or whatever.
2. The Court will read or in some appropriate manner acquaint the jury with this case, the [*Federal Employers Liability Act*], and read plaintiff's and defendant's claims. (Plaintiff's suggested claim is enclosed.)
3. After you have thoroughly examined the jury on the enclosed questions (that will, we hope, locate jurors who have had experiences that might affect their attitudes or opinions), you will then let the attorneys participate directly in the voir dire by follow-up questions. I've tried to separate the questions in the enclosed pleading for your convenience.

Sincerely,
[*Attorney's Name*]

## 2. Motions for Suggested Voir Dire Procedures

### a. Form in State Criminal Case—General §8.42

*Source:* The basic form used by attorney Neal Bush of Detroit in his criminal defense work.

**DEFENDANT'S MOTION FOR SUGGESTED VOIR DIRE PROCEDURES**

NOW COMES __________, Defendant, by and through [*his/her*] attorney, __________, and for the reasons stated in the accompanying memorandum of law and the attached declaration of [*Dr. Craig Haney*], moves this Court to select and instruct the jurors in this cause as follows:

1. Voir dire procedure in selection:

a. The jury should be selected by qualifying for cause a number of jurors equal to the number of jurors to be seated, including alternates, plus the number of peremptory challenges available to the prosecution and the defense;

b. The qualifying process should be conducted by questioning of groups of three or four prospective jurors at a time. Any prospective juror who believes he or she may know something about this case should be questioned individually out of the presence of other prospective jurors;

*COMMENT:* As to public and press attendance at all voir dire questioning, see §8.44

c. The attorneys for both sides should be permitted to participate in the voir dire, including direct questioning of prospective jurors;

d. The scope of the voir dire should be broad enough to determine factual as well as legal prejudice and permit intelligent exerecise of peremptory challenges;

e. Challenges for cause should be made and determined at the completion of the questioning of each group; and

f. When the qualification process has been completed, the jurors should be excused until 9:00 a.m. the following day, at which time peremptory challenges will be exercised according to the "Arizona" struck system.

*COMMENT:* See description in §8.7.

As he or she is qualified, each juror will be given a number, and at the completion of the striking, the 12 jurors with the lowest numbers will be designated as the jury, with the other(s) as the alternate(s).

2. Preliminary instructions:

Prior to and after the jury has been selected, the jurors should be given preliminary instructions of law appropriate to the case. *Cf.*, *e.g.*, [*Michigan Criminal Jury Instructions*, §§1:2:01–1:2:12, 1:3:01–1:3:14 and 2:1:06–2:1:07].

WHEREFORE, Defendant prays this Court for an Order adopting the procedures suggested herein.

Respectfully submitted,

________________________

Attorney for Defendant

Dated:____________

### b. Form in Federal Criminal Case—General §8.43

*Source:* The motion filed by defense counsel in *United States v Berkowitz*, see §3.56. The Craig Haney declaration referred to appears in §8.80.

**DEFENDANTS' MOTION FOR**
**SUGGESTED VOIR DIRE PROCEDURES**

NOW COME DEFENDANTS, by and through their attorneys, and for the reasons stated in the accompanying memorandum of law and the declaration of [*Dr. Craig Haney*] request:

1. The following procedure for the voir dire examination:

a. A small group of 12 potential jurors should be brought into the courtroom and asked the general questions specified in defendants' proposed voir dire. Jurors who cannot sit on a lengthy case should be excused at this time;

b. All jurors should then leave the courtroom. Each juror should then be questioned in court individually, out of the presence of other jurors, concerning areas identified as sensitive in the voir dire;

*COMMENT:* On the right of the public and the press to be present, see §8.44

c. Attorneys for all parties should be permitted to participate in the voir dire concerning the sensitive areas;

d. After each juror is questioned in this manner, any cause challenge should be made and determined;

e. A potential juror who is qualified at this point should be told that he or she will be notified when to return to the courtroom;

f. The same procedure should be completed for additional groups of 12 until enough potential jurors are qualified for cause to use the Arizona struck system; and

g. Exercise of peremptory challenges should begin at 9:00 a.m. on the day after a sufficient number of jurors are qualified for cause.

[*Use the following paragraph where appropriate:*]

2. This Court has determined that the defendants should have [*15*] peremptory challenges. Such additional peremptory challenges for multiple defendants are provided for in Rule 24(b) of the Federal Rules of Criminal Procedure. However, Rule 24(b) does not provide for additional peremptory challenges for the prosecution. Therefore, defendants object to the prosecution being given three (3) additional peremptory challenges.

Respectfully submitted,

______________________

Attorney for Defendants

Dated:____________

### c. Form for Individual Voir Dire Out of Presence of Others §8.44

*Source:* Adapted from the notice of motion and motion in limine in support of defendant's successful motion for individual voir dire, out of the presence of other prospective jurors, Oct. 1974, *Wisconsin v Carothers*, described in §8.30.

[*Calvin Carothers, Jr.*] by [*his/her*] attorney, [*William D. Whitnall*], [*Racine County Public Defender*], moves this Honorable Court [*in limine*] for an order permitting the defendant by [*his/her*] attorney to undertake individual voir dire of prospective members of the jury outside the presence or hearing of other members of the jury panel.

This motion is made in order to prevent the questions asked of a prospective juror and any answers given from prejudicing any other members of the panel or influencing in any way the answers to questions put to other members of the panel.

Hearing time, date, and place on this motion are to be set by the Court.

*COMMENT:* The Supreme Court will require that the press and public be permitted to be present at all voir dire questioning of jurors, in the absence of specific findings arising out of affirmative requests for privacy by specific jurors. *Press-Enterprise Co. v Superior Court* (1984) 104 S Ct 819. This decision builds on earlier holdings that "the press and general public have a constitutional right of access to criminal trials . . . embodied in the First Amendment, and applied to the States through the Fourteenth Amendment." *Globe Newspaper Co. v Superior Court* (1982) 457 US 596. Open trials enhance both the basic fairness of the criminal trial and the appearance of fairness so essential to public confidence in the system. *Richmond Newspapers, Inc. v Virginia* (1980) 448 US 555, at 569–571. "The presumption of openness may be overcome only by an overriding interest based on findings that closure is essential to preserve that interest. The interest is to be articulated along with findings specific enough that a reviewing court can determine whether the closure order was properly entered." *Press-Enterprise Co v Superior Court, supra*, at 824.

The proper procedure is for the trial judge to inform the array,

> once the general nature of sensitive questions is made known to them, that those individuals believing public questioning will prove damaging because of embarrassment, may properly request an opportunity to present the problem to the judge *in camera* but with counsel present and on the record. By requiring the prospective juror to make an affirmative request, the trial judge can ensure that there is in fact a valid basis for a belief that disclosure infringes a significant interest in privacy. This process will minimize the risk of unnecessary closure. The exercise of sound discretion by the court may lead to excusing such a person from jury service.

*Press-Enterprise Co. v Superior Court, supra* at 825.

### d. Form for Counsel Participation in Voir Dire §8.45

*Source:* Adapted from unsuccessful motion to permit the defendant's attorneys to supplement voir dire examination, Apr. 25, 1972, *United States v Russo* (see §3.52).

Defendant, by and through [*his/her*] undersigned counsel, moves this court, pursuant to Federal Rules of Criminal Procedure 24(a), to permit [*his/her*] attorney to supplement the court's voir dire examination by further inquiry, restricted to the following areas:

(1) Inquiry as to what information the juror has accumulated about this case, and the impact caused by this pretrial knowledge on the juror's impartiality;

(2) Inquiry as to what attitudes the juror has regarding [*the morality or legality of the current war in Vietnam,*] and the impact caused by this attitude on the juror's impartiality;

(3) Inquiry as to what attitudes the juror has regarding [*the limitations on the right of the government to conduct its operations in secrecy,*] and the impact caused by this attitude on the juror's impartiality;

(4) Inquiry as to what attitudes the juror has regarding the credibility of [*government*] witnesses, [*and the credibility of the government in general,*] and the impact caused by this attitude on the juror's impartiality.

This motion is based on the files and records of this case, the attached memorandum of points and authorities, and the argument to be offered at the hearing on this motion.

*COMMENT:* With slight modification, and a reference to Rule 47(a) of the Federal Rules of Civil Procedure, this form can be used in federal civil cases.

The defense in one of the criminal cases arising out of the events at Wounded Knee, South Dakota, filed motions and memorandums, which resulted in a hearing on voir dire procedures proposed by defendant. *United States v Baker* (WD SD, No. 73–5021, 1974). The defense questioned an expert on the need for voir dire by counsel rather than by the trial judge. Bruce Dennis Sales was both an assistant professor of psychology at the University of Nebraska (director of the law-psychology graduate studies program), and an attorney working in psycholinguistics, the study of the human use of language. Sales described the difference in reaction to judicial questioning and lawyer questioning in civil or criminal cases:

> What we are talking about now is three levels of communicating to you, of answering to you. There is one level in what the juror says, the verbal level.

There is a second level that's called paralinguistics, that refers to his breathing rate, his stress, his pauses; all of which indicate anxiety and tension, the indications that are used to identify lying.

And then the third level of communication is the kinesics, more commonly referred to as the gestures. It is those two levels, the pause and the stress, the paralinguistics and the kinesics, which will come through to you, but will be able to be repressed when talking to the judge, because the judge is perceived as a neutral.

### 3. Motion for Hearing on Procedures §8.46

In a few recent state and federal cases, counsel have sought hearings on motions for thorough voir dire. In one case, the motion was later denied but relatively extensive and intensive voir dire was nonetheless permitted (see discussion of *United States v McNeil* in §3.51). In another case, the motion was granted but the defense won on another point before the jury was selected (see discussion of *United States v Baker* in §8.90). In a state case, the motion was granted without a hearing (see discussion of *Wisconsin v Carothers* in §8.30). In all these cases, defense counsel were convinced that the exercise was quite productive. For statistics on the relationship between lengthy voir dire and the granting of challenges for cause, see §8.37.

The memorandum filed in support of the motion for a particular manner of conducting voir dire should focus on the facts and legal issues in the particular case. Material from §§8.51–8.72 may be used in the pretrial memorandum, although some sections will require revamping from their present form as briefs or petitions for certiorari.

A pretrial motion seeking a hearing on the method of conducting voir dire will be strengthened by supporting declarations by experts. These may be, in effect, first drafts of the testimony the same experts will give at the hearing, if the trial judge agrees to a hearing (see §§8.80–8.87). Often the experts selected for this purpose will have been working on previous pretrial motions on the need for a change of venue, challenging grand or petit jury lists, etc. (see chapters 6 and 7).

When requesting a pretrial hearing on voir dire procedures, if counsel list as expected witnesses prominent trial lawyers who are known to the trial judge, the chances that the judge will grant a hearing may be improved. On the other hand, many judges believe that they have more knowledge about the conduct of trials in general and of voir dire in particular than any of the lawyers who practice before them, and they do not feel the need to listen to alleged expert trial lawyers.

### 4. Motions for Continuances §8.47

A defendant in a criminal case has the constitutional right to a speedy trial guaranteed in the Sixth Amendment. A defendant may choose not to waive that right and to seek dismissal of charges because a fair jury cannot be impaneled in his jurisdiction due to hostile pretrial publicity (as was done effectively in *United States v Cotton* (ED Wis, No. 68–CR–113, 1969); see chapter 7). When the defendant is denied a speedy trial, for whatever reason, the only constitutionally acceptable response is dismissal of charges. *Strunk v United States* (1973) 412 US 434.

However, most defendants approach the problem the other way, seeking change of venue (see chapter 7), and, if that fails, continuances in the assigned jurisdiction, accompanied by extensive voir dire questioning on the effects of pretrial publicity. Plaintiffs also seek continuances and extensive voir dire under appropriate circumstances.

In the appeal of the *Chicago Eight* conspiracy case (see §3.54), the court noted: "On August 27, 1969, defendants again moved for continuance because of contemporaneous publicity concerning defendant Seale's arrest. In denying the latter motion the court said that a careful voir dire examination was the proper procedure for safeguarding against prejudicial publicity." The Seventh Circuit Court of Appeals then held that the defendants had never waived this issue:

> Since the district court had denied several motions for continuance, two of which related to pretrial publicity, a motion for continuance on the eve of trial may well have been futile, and failure to make it should not prejudice defendants in seeking the protection which would be afforded by an adequate voir dire. The same should be true with respect to their election not to seek a change of venue.

*United States v Dellinger* (7th Cir 1972) 472 F2d 340, 371–372.

When the trial judge denies a motion for a continuance until the effect of publicity on the case has died down, counsel may move for more extensive and intensive voir dire than is customary in order to safeguard against such prejudicial publicity. See §§8.66–8.67.

### 5. Motions for Additional Peremptory Challenges §8.48

Defense motions for additional peremptory challenges were successful in the following cases (additional challenges in parentheses): *United States v Olin* (N 78-38 (WD NY 1979)) (2); *United States v Goldfarb*

(No. 8-80572 (ED Mich 1979)) (14); *United States v Sturman* (ND Ohio 1976) (14); *Massachusetts v Saxe* (No. 51775 (Suffolk Co. Mass Super Ct. 1976) (10), see §7.68; *South Dakota v Means* (No. 11826 (SD Cir Ct 1976)) (10); *United States v Mitchell* (Nos. 75-1381, 75-1382, 75-1384, 76-1441 (DC Cir 1976)) (5); *United States v Ehrlichman* (No. 74-1882 (DC Cir 1976)) (5); *United States v Means* (409 F Supp 115 (D ND 1976)) (16); *New York v Hill & Pernesalice* (Erie Co., NY Sup Ct 1975) (10); *United States v Means* (3rd Div Minn 1973) (10); *United States v Anderson* (No. 602-71 (D NJ 1973)) (15), see §3.55; *United States v Ahmad* (No. 14950 (MD Pa 1971)) (18).

The value of applying for additional peremptories in a case with many parties, or special circumstances, was demonstrated in a study of one of the Watergate cases.The Zeisel-Diamond study of the effects of voir dire and other jury factors in the trial of former Attorney General Mitchell and former Commerce Secretary Stans involved an extensive voir dire, on which peremptory challenges were based.

*Source:* Zeisel and Diamond, "The Jury Selection in the Mitchell-Stans Conspiracy Trial," 1 *Am B Foundation Research J* 151, 157–160 (1976); reprinted by permission.

The court, in its understandable desire to compensate for the considerable, one-sided pretrial publicity, allowed the defense 23 peremptory challenges (20 for the jury and 3 for the alternates) as against only 11 (8 and 3) for the government.

[At the time] Rule 24(b) of the Federal Rules of Criminal Procedure [entitled] the defense to 10 peremptory challenges. As a rule, multiple defendants are deemed a single party for purposes of challenges. The court, however, in its discretion, may allow each defendant 10 challenges, which it did in the present case to counteract adverse pretrial publicity (*United States v Bonanno* (1956) 177 F Supp 106). The rule allows 6 challenges to the government. When the judge announced his intention to allow 20 challenges to the defense, the prosecution argued that the disparity between 6 and 20 challenges could not be justified and would predetermine the outcome of the case. Thereupon, apparently in an effort to secure the 20 challenges for its side, the defense offered to see the government challenges increased to 8—to which the court agreed.

Rule 24(c) entitles both sides to three peremptory challenges if, as in this case, six alternate jurors are to be selected.

The panel of prospective jurors . . . exposed to these challenges had shrunk to 52 members. Of the original 196, the court had excused 135 for cause, which left 61; since only 52 were needed for this last phase, the court dismissed the 9 supernumerary jurors without further questioning.

The government exercised only 6 of its 8 available jury challenges. The defense exercised all of its 20 available challenges. Each side then had 3 more peremptory challenges for the selection of the six alternate jurors. The defense again used all of its challenges; the government used none, a decision it would come to regret.

Three graphs show how these challenges were executed and how they affected the composition of the jury .... [graph 2 shows] the resulting successive shifts in the composition of the juror panel in terms of its demographic characteristics, graph 3 the resulting shifts in terms of characteristics more specifically related to the issues in the trial.

**GRAPH 2. Composition of the juror panel at the various stages of the selection process**

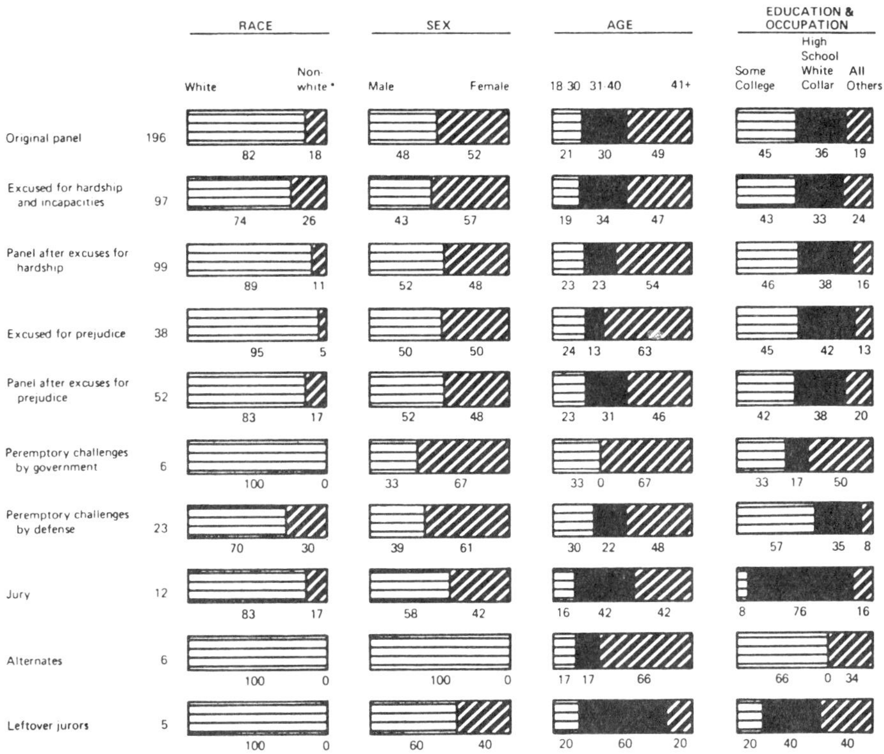


* 94% Black

Graph 2 shows ... [that the] racial composition of the jury panel hardly varies from the original distribution down to the jury eventually selected. In the original panel the proportion of nonwhites was 18 percent; on the jury it was 17 percent, the equivalent of two jurors .... Neither did the composition by sex and age undergo significant changes. What did change was the composition by education and occupation. Forty-five percent of the original panel had some college education. On the jury their proportion was reduced to 8

GRAPH 3. Peremptory challenges and jury composition by political indicators (in percent)

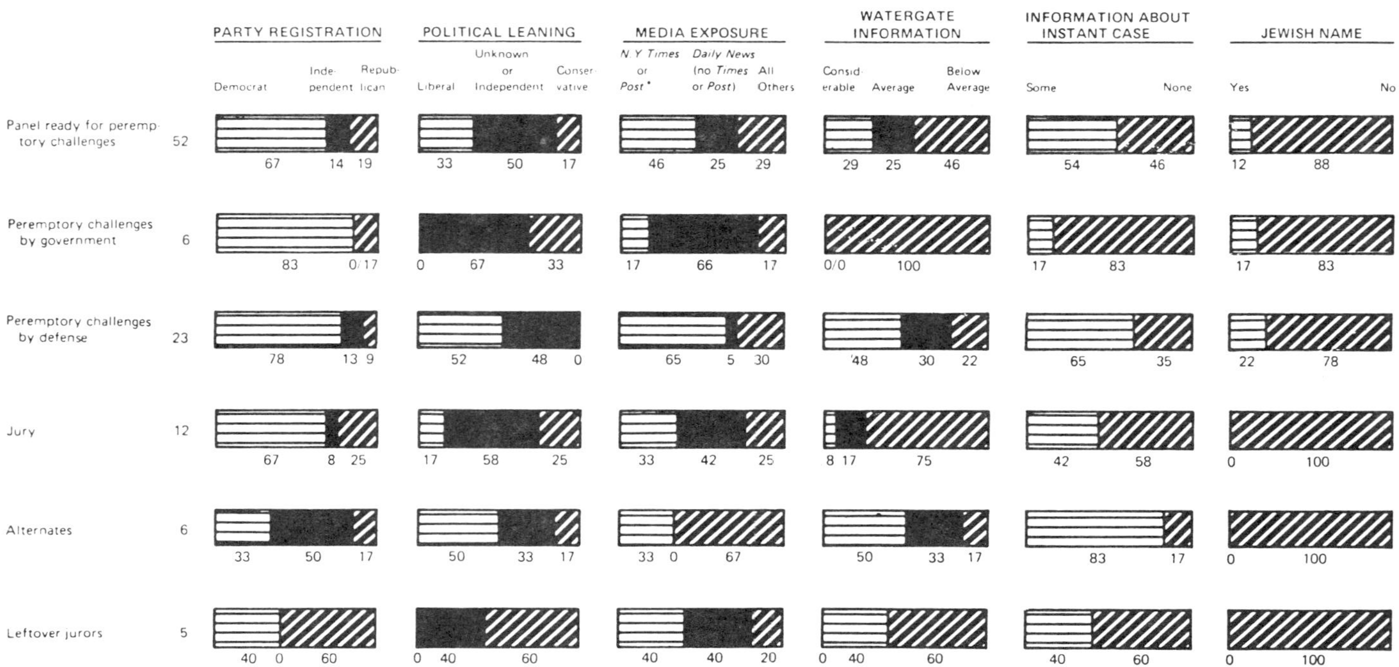


*Considered "liberal" newspapers.

percent: one juror with one year of college. In their stead, the middle group—white-collar occupations with at least some high school—had expanded from 36 percent in the original panel to 76 percent on the jury. The dramatic shift can be traced to the very last of the selection phases, the peremptory challenges by the defense.

... During the private questioning period the prospective jurors revealed details about their political leanings, their media exposure, and what they knew about Watergate and the instant trial. [Graph 3] shows how that information affected the peremptory challenges and thereby the composition of the jury and the panel of alternative jurors.

... Again the jury had a higher percentage of conservatives (25 percent) than the total remaining panel (13 percent). The defense also effectively curtailed readers of the *New York Times* or *Post*. Its major achievement, though, was to reduce the number of jurors well informed about Watergate from 32 percent in the total panel to 8 percent, a single juror.

The state court trial judge granted additional peremptories in the *Saxe* case (see §§7.68 and 8.67).

## B. Legal Arguments in Support of Full Voir Dire by Counsel §8.50

The following materials may be used in pretrial motions, memoranda, and supporting papers concerning the conduct of voir dire. They may also be used if a party laid a proper basis for extensive voir dire, and later seeks to raise voir dire issues on appeal (see chapter 23). Several styles of memorandum and brief writing are included for easier adaptability.

Counsel may also want to attach as an appendix the results of a public opinion survey (described in chapter 5) in support of the motion for extensive voir dire. In a misdemeanor case, it is wise to prepare a short, well-outlined memo that simply states the proposition or rule of law and gives one or two citations that are right on point. A lengthy discussion before a busy trial judge will be counterproductive.

### 1. Form: Memorandum in Support of Motion for Certain Voir Dire Procedures §8.51

*Sources:* Attorney Kenneth Mogill of Detroit has developed a basic form for use in state criminal cases that can be adapted for use in civil cases, and Detroit attorneys in the *Berkowitz* case submitted a Memorandum in Support of Defendants' Motion for Certain Voir Dire Procedures (see description of case in §3.56). These and other materials are the basis for §§8.51–8.65.

MEMORANDUM IN SUPPORT OF [*DEFENDANT'S/PLAINTIFF'S*] [*MOTION/REQUEST*] FOR CERTAIN VOIR DIRE PROCEDURES

### a. Sample: Factual Issues in the Instant Case Touch Common Prejudices §8.52

I. THE FACTUAL ISSUES IN THIS CASE REQUIRE THE SETTING ASIDE OF COMMON PREJUDICES

This case involves a [*two-count*] [*Information/Indictment*] charging [*Mr./Ms.* ________] with [*first-degree murder*] [*and possession of a firearm in the commission of a felony*]. If [*convicted*] as charged, this Court will be compelled to [*sentence*] [*him/her*] to [*life imprisonment at hard labor and in solitary confinement*]. [*MCLA 750.316.*]

Trial of this case will raise numerous factual questions as to which careful voir dire is necessary in order to obtain a fair and impartial jury. Jurors' attitudes and feelings about [*weapons, alcohol, marijuana, and other drugs*] will all be significant in determining their ability to be fair in this case.

Feelings about a [*murder*] charge and sitting in judgment of one accused of this crime will be important. Attitudes about [*the use of deadly force in defense of another*] will be central to jurors' abilities to be impartial in this particular case.

There will be important testimony of [*Mr./Ms.* ________]'s emotional tate around the time of the events at issue. This testimony will have a substantial impact on the jurors, and it raises important questions as to jurors' attitudes about emotional stress and anxiety and human behavior under those conditions.

At the time of the incident involved herein, [*Mr./Ms.* ________] had [*been off work*] [*on a medical leave for a period of time*]. Testimony as to this fact will raise the question of jurors' attitudes and prejudices about [*unemployment and idleness*].

[*Witness's Name*], [*Mr./Ms.*]'s [*girl/boy*] friend, will probably be a witness, and there is likely to be testimony that, [*although unmarried, they have slept together*]. Jurors' attitudes about [*sex and personal relationships*] may affect their views of [Mr./Ms. ________] and [Ms./Mr. ________].

These circumstances and others involve areas where many people have strong attitudes and deep-seated feelings that can unconsciously tilt them against the [*accused*]. Unless such attitudes are fully probed, there is a significant risk that jurors selected to sit in judgment of [*Mr./Ms.* ________] may unconsciously take into the jury room impressions, preconceptions or feelings undermining [*his/her*] right to a decision based only on the testimony presented in court. In order to minimize this possibility, [*Defendant/Plaintiff*] has suggested to this Court certain procedures designed to create an effective atmosphere for learning what feelings and attitudes the jurors bring into the courtroom and identifying them for the Court and the parties. If applied, these procedures will significantly reduce the possibility of an unfair jury.

### b. Form: Parties Are Entitled to Probing Voir Dire §8.53

II. TO ASSURE [*DEFENDANT'S/PLAINTIFF'S*] RIGHT TO A FAIR TRIAL BY AN IMPARTIAL JURY, BROAD VOIR DIRE IS NECESSARY

"*Voir dire* plays a critical function in assuring the criminal defendant that his Sixth Amendment right to an impartial jury will be honored." *Rosales-Lopez v United States* (1981) 451 US 182, at 188.

Voir dire plays the same critical function in assuring civil plaintiffs and defendants that their constitutional rights will be honored under the Seventh Amendment, and, in state cases, the Fourteenth Amendment. "Without an adequate *voir dire* the trial judge's responsibility to remove prospective jurors who will not be able impartially to follow the court's instructions and evaluate the evidence cannot be fulfilled. See *Connors v United States* (1895) 158 US 408, 413. Similarly, lack of adequate *voir dire* impairs the defendant's right to exercise peremptory challenges where provided by statute or rule, as it is in the federal courts." *Rosales-Lopez v United States, supra*.

In California, the right to voir dire for peremptory challenges was recently affirmed in *California v Williams* (1981) 174 Cal Rptr 317.

The right to question prospective jurors can be traced back to medieval English common law, where two "triers" questioned jurors. The purpose of voir dire was to obtain an impartial jury. As Lord Coke stated, the juror must "'be indifferent as he stands unsworn,'" *Reynolds v United States* (1878) 98 US 145, 154.

The right to jury trial was enshrined in the United States Constitution and in the constitution of each of the states (see [*State*] Constitution [*date*], art____ §____), in the specific amendments and in the principles of due process. See *Ristaino v Ross* (1976) 424 US 589, 595, n6.

*COMMENT:* See §3.30 on *Ristaino*.

This "American tradition . . . necessarily contemplates an impartial jury drawn from a cross-section of the community." *Thiel v Southern Pac. Co.* (1946) 328 US 217, 220. See also:

[*Insert recent strong decisions from the jurisdiction in which the instant case is pending, and add, particularly in a federal case:*]

*Abbot v Mines* (6th Cir 1969) 411 F2d 353, 354; *United States v Bear Runner* (8th Cir 1974) 502 F2d 908, 911; *Krause v Rhodes* (6th Cir 1977) 570 F2d 563.

### c. Form: Many Potential Jurors Harbor Strong Prejudices §8.54

[*DEFENDANT/PLAINTIFF*] IS ENTITLED TO UNCOVER UNCONSCIOUS PREJUDICES

Justice Stevens recently summarized the basic problem in jury selection in the United States in this era:

> An impartial tribunal is an indispensable element of a fair criminal trial. See *In re Murchison* (1955) 349 US 133, 136, *Irvin v Dowd* (1961) 366 US 717, 722. Before any citizen may be permitted to sit in judgment on his peers, some inquiry into his potential bias is essential. Such bias can arise from two principal sources: a special reaction to the facts of the particular case, or a special prejudice against the individual defendant that is unrelated to the particular case. Much as we wish it were otherwise, we should acknowledge the fact that there are many potential jurors who harbor strong prejudices against all members of certain racial, religious, or ethnic groups for no reason other than hostility to the group as a whole. Even when there are no "special circumstances" connected with an alleged criminal transaction indicating an unusual risk of racial or other group bias, a member of the Nazi Party should not be allowed to sit in judgment on a Jewish defendant.

Stevens, J, in *Rosales-Lopez v United States* (1981) 451 US 182, at 196, 197, dissenting with Brennan and Marshall, JJ.

Voir dire is a procedure to prevent potential jurors with strong prejudices from sitting in judgment on people they hate or love. In the famous treason case of the *United States v Aaron Burr* (1807) 25 Fed Cas 49, Chief Justice Marshall, sitting as the trial judge, discussed voir dire at length. His remarks regarding personal bias underscore the need for judicial protection of a rigorous voir dire:

> Why do personal prejudices constitute a just cause of challenge? Solely because the individual who is under their influence is presumed to have a bias on his mind which will prevent an impartial decision of the case, according to the testimony. He may declare that notwithstanding these prejudices he is determined to listen to the evidence, and be governed by it; but the law will not trust him . . . . He will listen with more favor to that testimony which confirms, than to that which would change his opinion.

The *Burr* case recognizes that every juror has some preconceived opinions. During trial the juror is bombarded with data, recollections, impressions, and conflicting stories. As Justice Holmes observed in *Frank v Mangum* (1915) 237 US 309, 349 (dissenting opinion): "this is not a matter of polite presumptions; we must look facts in the face. Any judge who has sat with juries knows that in spite of forms they are extremely likely to be impregnated by the environing atmosphere."

[*In a case involving Jewish defendants, the following might be added:*]

The "environing atmosphere" in the *Frank* case resulted in a Georgia mob lynching the New York Jewish defendant as he was being moved to the prison where he would be executed after the Supreme Court affirmed his conviction, despite his protestations of innocence.

It is a simple psychological truth that much evidence at any trial will fall within areas of prejudice and that the jurors will, in Chief Justice Marshall's words, have "preconceived opinions which will resist these impressions." Consequently the purpose of voir dire is to probe deeply into the jurors' minds to root out the conscious and subconscious preconceptions that will keep them from viewing the evidence objectively.

While a probing voir dire is often the key to obtaining a fair trial, it is absolutely necessary when problems of pretrial publicity, personal prejudice, or important political issues are present. *Murphy v Florida* (1975) 421 US 794; *Sheppard v Maxwell* (1966) 384 US 333; *United States v Dellinger* (7th Cir 1972) 472 F2d 340. The reason for giving even greater attention to voir dire in these cases is evident:

> The possibility of prejudice is real, and there is consequent need for a searching voir dire examination in situations where, for example, the case carries racial overtones, or involves other matters concerning which either the local community or the population at large is commonly known to harbor strong feelings that may stop short of bias in law yet significantly skew deliberations in fact. In a case involving such sentiment, the trial court must take into account and govern the voir dire accordingly.

*United States v Robinson* (DC Cir 1973) 475 F2d 376, 380–381.

### d. Form: Jurors Will Not Reveal Their Own Prejudices §8.55

A trial court must permit proposed voir dire questions that are "designed to uncover prejudice," *United States v Clancy* (7th Cir 1960) 276 F2d 617, 632, "probe for the hidden prejudices of the jurors," *Lurding v United States* (6th Cir 1950) 179 F2d 419, 421, or concern a "particular subject affecting the basic fairness of the trial," *United States v Eastwood* (5th Cir 1973) 489 F2d 818, 820, unless it may safely assume that the prejudices are not present or are irrelevant. *United States v Dellinger* (7th Cir 1972) 472 F2d 340, 368.

Prejudice can be defined as a state of mind that causes the bearer to react in a preconceived manner to a topic, and to close his mind to facts and opinions that do not fit a preconceived stereotype. Prejudice is also a feeling of hostility or superiority toward a person who looks, thinks, or acts differently from oneself. Most prejudices are subconscious. People think they are fairminded and objective, yet they feel uneasy or distrustful in the company of people of other races, nationalities, or political viewpoints. Until a juror recognizes his or her own inner feelings or stereotypes, he or she cannot try to combat them. These truisms have been demonstrated by innumerable scientific studies on which we plan to introduce expert testimony.

This point was at the heart of the Court of Appeals decision in *United States v Dellinger, supra*. In that case feelings for and against the Vietnamese war, as well as differing concepts of patriotism, were involved. The court held that the trial court could not assume that persons with serious prejudices "could recognize such prejudices and lay them aside."

*COMMENT:* Judge Gordon conducted voir dire in *United States v Cotton* (ED Wis 1969, No. 68 CR 113), the prosecution of Catholic priests and laymen who broke into a Selective Service office during the Vietnam war and destroyed Selective Service System records. He found that "approximately one out of every four or five jurors called was, by his own evaluation, free of bias; but only [as to a] very few of those persons could I fully agree [with] a juror's own assessment of his lack of bias." Judge Gordon cited *United States v Largo* (7th Cir 1965) 346 F2d 253, for the proposition that "it is the Court's duty to ascertain each prospective juror's knowledge and attitude, rather than to accept his subjective assessment as to his own impartiality." (The *Cotton* opinion is reprinted in 28 *Lawyers Guild Practitioner* 101 (1969).)

It is reversible error for the trial court to rely on the assessment by a venireperson of his or her own biases or preconceptions. *United States v Lewin* (7th Cir 1972) 467 F2d 1132; *United States v Polizi* (9th Cir 1974) 500 F2d 856. See also "The Jury System in the Federal Courts: Report on the Judicial Conference Committee on the Operation of the Jury System," 26 FRD 409 (approved by the Judicial Conference of the United States, September 1960).

Courts have consistently recognized that jurors are often unaware of preconceptions they may have about a case or their lack of qualifications to serve on a jury. *United States v Bear Runner*, *supra*, 502 F2d at 912; *United States v Dellinger*, *supra*, 472 F2d at 367. As the court explained in *Kiernan v Van Schaik* (3d Cir 1965) 347 F2d 775, 770: "We do not believe a prospective juror is so alert to his prejudices. Thus it is essential to explore the backgrounds of the jurors to some extent in order to discover actual bias, or cause."

In *Silverthorne v United States* (9th Cir 1968) 400 F2d 627, 638, the court stated:

> We agree with the language of the *en banc* majority in *United States ex rel. Bloeth v Denno* (2d Cir 1963) 313 F2d 364, *cert. denied,* 372 US 987, that in the absence of an examination designed to elicit answers which provide an objective basis for the court's evaluation, "merely going through the form of obtaining jurors' assurances of impartiality is insufficient [to test that impartiality]."

313 F2d at 372.

### e. Form: Open-ended, Specific Questions Must Be Asked §8.56

Open-ended questions are necessary to stimulate responses that will provide insight into a juror's true attitudes. The usual practice of many judges who refuse to ask open-ended questions was criticized in *California v Crowe* (1973) 106 Cal Rptr 369, 380 n31, where the court noted the "danger that a biased juror may be unwilling to confess that bias openly, . . . and questions to which there is a 'right' and a 'wrong' answer may be less likely to reveal such bias than more open-ended questions."

General voir dire questions such as "Can you be fair and impartial?" have been carefully considered by appellate courts. In *Dellinger*, *supra*, 472 F2d at 348, the court recognized the difficult problem of reaching the jurors' true attitudes and concluded that:

> Natural human pride would suggest a negative answer to whether there was a reason the juror could not be fair and impartial. A juror might well answer negatively in good faith, without stopping to consider the significance or firmness of impressions he might have gained from news reports. We think the question is not adequate to bring out responses showing that jurors had gained information and formed opinions about relevant matters in issue if in truth any had. This broad question should not be relied on in a situation where there is a probability of exposure.

See also *Goins v McKeen* (6th Cir 1979) 605 F2d 947, 953.

The *Dellinger* court went on (472 F2d at 367):

> The government argues that the court is obligated to inquire only into matters that would disqualify the juror for cause, and that the court's first group of questions were adequate to produce disclosure of any relevant prejudice. We disagree. The government's position must rest upon an assumption that a general question to the group whether there is any reason they could not be fair and impartial can be relied on to produce a disclosure of any disqualifying state of mind. We do not believe that a prospective juror is so alert to his own prejudices. Thus it is essential to explore the backgrounds and attitudes of the jurors to some extent in order to discover actual bias, or cause. See *Kiernan v Van Schaik* (3d Cir 1965) 347 F2d 775, 779.

The court noted in footnote 39:

> Jurors are drawn from the general body of the community for a short term of service, . . . and then return to their customary occupations with neither training nor traditions of impartiality. They must often be unaware of their own disqualification in specific cases.

The different responses to open-ended and closed questions can be illustrated by two questions: (1) "Have you ever had an unfortunate experience with a black person that makes you biased in this case?" This will almost always exact a negative response; it is a closed question. (2) "Have you ever had an unfortunate experience with a black person?" This may get some jurors to discuss any unpleasant experience and thereby discover and possibly confront their own prejudices. Other examples of open-ended questions are, "Do you think your life would have been much different if you had been born black? How so?" "These questions I have asked you—have they triggered any feelings or ideas you would like to tell us about?"

Due process requires an effective voir dire, which in turn compels searching questioning of each juror individually by means of open-ended questions and sometimes by hostile probing.

In *Dellinger* the court of appeals noted, 472 F2d at 371–372:

> After the government tendered the panel, but before the defense began exercising peremptories, defendants made a motion to reopen the voir dire "to include questions . . . concerning the exposure of the veniremen to press, radio & TV reporting concerning the facts surrounding this case." The court denied the motion on the grounds that it had asked a general question of the entire venire about whether they could be impartial.

The court of appeals held that the general question was insufficient and that the trial court had a duty to determine specifically what the jurors had heard or read and what impact the exposure had had on them. After that trial, juror Ruth Petersen admitted that her "one worry" was that her son might become friendly with "hippies." Furthermore, she admitted being offended by Abbie Hoffman's long hair. (Exhibit 11 to Motion for Judgment Notwithstanding Verdict, *United States v Dellinger*, *supra*.) Obviously these considerations had nothing to do with the evidence in the case but they made it difficult if not impossible for the jury to follow the instructions that the verdict must be based solely on the evidence introduced in court.

### f. Form: Broad Questioning Provides Basis for Challenges §8.57

The Supreme Court of the United States has made it clear that "the denial or impairment of the right" to exercise one's challenges to prospective jurors "is reversible error without a showing of prejudice." *Swain v Alabama* (1964) 380 US 202, 219. Of course, the questions to be asked on voir dire are a matter of the trial court's discretion, but this discretion is "subject to the essential demands of fairness." *Aldridge v United States* (1931) 283 US 308, at 313. As a result, a requested voir dire question should be asked if an anticipated response would afford the basis for a challenge. *United States v Blount* (6th Cir 1973) 479 F2d 650.

Furthermore, to enable defendants to exercise their peremptory challenge rights in an intelligent and informed manner, in-depth questioning into areas that are relevant to the case is required. As the Seventh Circuit explained in reversing the convictions in *Dellinger*, *supra*, at 367–368:

> But beyond this, an answer which falls short of an admission of bias may nevertheless aid counsel in deciding to exercise a peremptory challenge. The Supreme Court has stated that the peremptory challenge, although not required in the Constitution, [footnote omitted] is "one of the most important of the rights secured to the accused," and that "[t]he denial or impairment of the right is reversible error without a showing of predudice." *Swain v Alabama* (1965) 380 US 202, 219, . . . If this right is not to be an empty one, the defendants must, upon request, be permitted sufficient inquiry into the background and attitudes of the jurors to enable them to exercise intelligently their peremptory challenges . . . .

While the trial judge is vested with large discretion in determining the scope of voir dire examination,

[*Cite cases from the appropriate jurisdiction, e.g.:*]

*Michigan v Rose* (1934) 268 Mich 529; *Fedorinchik v Stewart* (1939) 289

Mich 436; *Kuisell v Farrar* (1967) 6 Mich App 560, [*Michigan*] courts, too, have recognized the need for voir dire to be broad enough to: (1) determine whether there exist grounds to challenge for cause; and (2) allow counsel a reasonable opportunity to exercise peremptory challenges.

### g. Form: Court Rules Provide for Attorney-conducted Voir Dire §8.58

III. TO ASSURE AN IMPARTIAL JURY, PROSPECTIVE JURORS MUST BE QUESTIONED DIRECTLY BY COUNSEL

Federal Rules of Criminal Procedure 24(a) provides:

> The court may permit the defendant or his attorney and the attorney for the government to conduct the examination of prospective jurors or may itself conduct the examination. In the latter event the court shall permit the defendant or his attorney and the attorney for the government to supplement the examination by such further inquiry as it deems proper or shall itself submit to the prospective jurors such additional questions by the parties or their attorneys as it deems proper.

Counsel recognize that the court's discretion is a broad one and that, in ordinary circumstances, a defendant has no constitutional right to a personal voir dire of the jury. *Hamer v United States* (9th Cir 1958) 259 F2d 274, 279, *cert. denied* (1959) 359 US 916.

*COMMENT:* This section can be adapted to a federal civil case and to a state criminal or civil case, citing state statutes or court rules. In Connecticut, and elsewhere, there is a state constitutional right to lawyer voir dire of the jury, as described in §8.30.

### h. Form: Counsel-conducted Voir Dire Is Expedient and Effective §8.59

*COMMENT:* In cases raising difficult issues (such as attitudes toward sexual behavior, interracial relations, or church attendance), attorneys may be able to convince a judge that he or she will feel more comfortable if the lawyers ask these "bad" questions rather than requiring the judge to do so. The judge may see value in this option, particularly in a year when the judge faces reelection, or during a campaign against the judiciary by a local "judge watch" committee.

The effectiveness of voir dire as a means of selecting an impartial jury is maximized if questions are posed directly by the attorneys for both sides. The psychological and sociological reasons for this conclusion, discussed in the attached declaration of [*Dr. Craig Haney* (see §8.80)], are compelling:

(1) Since jurors look on the judge as an important authority figure, whom they are reluctant to displease, they tend to respond to judicial questions with less candor than to questions posed by counsel;

(2) Lawyers, as advocates who have acquired a thorough working knowledge of the details of the case, are in a better position to determine what questions should be posed to jurors and are better equipped and more inclined than the judge to follow up initial responses with the type of probing, "individualized" questions needed to explore and expose prejudices; and

(3) The nonverbal communication of a prospective juror (such as displays of tension, evasion, or hostility) is much more revealing when questions are posed by advocates rather than the neutral judge.

See also Padawer-Singer and Singer, *Voir Dire by Two Lawyers: An Essential Safeguard*, 57 Judicature 386 (1974).

The Fifth Circuit has recently recognized the value of attorney-conducted voir dire, concluding that voir dire has "little meaning if it is not conducted by counsel." *United States v Ledee* (5th Cir 1977) 549 F2d 990, 993; *United States v Corey* (5th Cir 1980) 625 F2d 704, 707. Recent and ancient decisions of several state courts have also mandated participation in direct questioning by the parties. Cf., e.g., *Oden v Nebraska* (1958) 90 NW2d 356; *Griffin v Arkansas* (1965) 398 SW2d 900; *Donovan v Illinois* (1891) 28 NE 964.

The American Bar Association Project Standards for Trial by Jury, §2.4, and on the Function of the Trial Judge, §5.1, would require an opportunity for direct questioning of jurors by counsel in a criminal case. In addition, the American Bar Association's House of Delegates in 1976 proposed a revision to Rule 47(a) of the Federal Rules of Civil Procedure to permit attorney-conducted voir dire. Cf., Corboy "Opening Statement," 6 *Litigation* 1–2 (1980).

### i. Form: Time Factor Not Decisive §8.60

The most frequently mentioned justification for court-conducted voir dire is to save the time of the court, the jurors, the parties, and the attorneys. See *United States v Bryant* (DC Cir 1972) 471 F2d 1040; *American Bar Association Report on Minimum Standards for Criminal Justice, Approved Draft* (1968). A 1977 Federal Judicial Center survey, however, "revealed no substantial difference in judge's estimates of time consumed by voir dire with or without the direct participation of attorneys." Corboy, "Opening Statement," 6 *Litigation* 1 (1980). And when a trial judge rejects questions proposed by attorneys, resultant appeals expend more than the time originally saved in a trial.

In a case this serious, where the [*accused*] is facing [*a potential mandatory life sentence*] if [*convicted as charged*], mere economy of time, even if that is the case, is an insufficient consideration upon which to risk a decision based on bias rather than a fair weighing of the evidence.

[*Use where appropriate, i.e., where the judge knows that both sides have done a great deal of pretrial work:*]

Perhaps such an argument has merit in the formulation of a general rule for routine cases; however, in a case such as this one, in which both sides have expended a massive amount of time and energy, all the preparation in the world would be futile if the jury's decision is based on bias and not on a fair weighing of the evidence.

Another argument advanced by proponents of court-conducted examination is that this method obviates counsel's abuse of voir dire by asking improper questions. *United States v Mesarosh* (WD Pa 1953) 116 F Supp 345, 349, rev'd on other grounds (1956) 352 US 1. Such possible abuse can, however, be eliminated effectively by careful supervision by the Court. See Vance, "Voir Dire Examination of Jurors in Federal Civil Cases," 8 *Vill L Rev* 76 (1962). In the instant case, defense counsel has prepared written questions to ask on voir dire, and is prepared to submit them to the Court on request, thus providing the Court the opportunity to rule in advance on the propriety of any proposed inquiry. Opposing counsel can also be counted on to assure that voir dire questions are kept within proper bounds.

### j. Form: Risks in Judicial Voir Dire Avoided by Participation of Counsel §8.61

In order to conduct a searching inquiry a judge must be as familiar with the case at the outset of the trial as counsel for both sides. A skillful attorney is on top of the case at the outset in a way a trial judge, coming straight from another case, cannot be. The court does not have hours, days, and weeks to devote to one case.

In addition, the trial judge who rejects counsel's request to conduct voir dire must accept the additional burden of reviewing possibly hundreds of proposed voir dire questions submitted by counsel, and determining which are proper, which are generally all right but should be rephrased by the court, and which are improper. Each denial or rephrasing by the court creates a possible point for appeal. This is exactly what happened in *United States v Dellinger* (7th Cir 1972) 472 F2d 340, *cert. denied* (1973) 410 US 970.

California Supreme Court Justice Stanley Mosk's warning in this area should be noted:

> When it is counsel who interrogates prospective jurors he has no legal basis for claiming dissatisfaction with the ultimate product of the selection process in which he participated. But if the court alone interrogates veniremen, taking some questions suggested by counsel and, as here, imperiously rejecting others, an issue for appellate review emerges. In such circumstances we must recreate the scene, ascertain if the rejected queries should have been permitted, and if so, undertake to determine whether the exclusion was prejudicial. This is unlike the usual case in which we weigh the prejudicial effect of evidence; here the issue is the prejudicial inclinations of jurors. For a reviewing court, in this context, to attempt an analysis of the juror's undisclosed predilections in order to reach a conclusion on potential prejudice would require an omniscience which I for one disclaim. The courthousekeeping seal of approval on denial of counsel's right to interrogate prospective jurors presages new bases for appeal with which reviewing courts will be grappling in innumerable future cases. A substantial portion of the time saved at trial may thus be expended on appeal.

*California v Crowe* (1973) 106 Cal Rptr 369, 386–387 (Mosk, J, dissenting).

The unique circumstances of this case present most compelling reasons to allow personal voir dire by counsel [*in the limited areas requested*]. Bias or prejudice on the part of prospective jurors about the sensitive issues in each of these areas will be exposed only by diligent and probing follow-up questions.

The difference between voir dire by the lawyer and voir dire by the judge based on written questions propounded by the lawyers is similar to the difference between depositions and interrogatories in discovery. Counsel seeking discovery invariably prefers the former because of their greater flexibility. The lawyer is often in touch with jurors' feelings in court regarding the [*defendant/plaintiff*] and the particular case. When personally questioning jurors, counsel can decide when to push a juror or to try a different tactic to uncover prejudice.

Effective voir dire often requires questioning akin to cross-examination of a hostile witness, rather than merely examination of a juror. In other words, the questioner must be prepared to play a hostile role in order to probe deeply into the juror's thinking on unpopular subjects like racial prejudice.

It would be unseemly for a judge to play this role. He must at all times preserve not only the fact of fairness but also the appearance of fairness (as required by the United States Supreme Court in *Aldridge v United States* (1931) 283 US 308). The judge should not have to risk the jurors' animosity. Few, if any, judges have indicated a willingness to perform the necessary but unpleasant probing function.

On the other hand, counsel must perform this probing function, with its attendant risk, explaining later that the cross-examination was necessary to conduct a proper voir dire.

*COMMENT:* See description of Charles Garry's antagonistic technique in chapter 15.

An example of the need for such unpleasant probing occurred in the New Haven trial of Erica Huggins, a leading member of the Black Panther Party (*Connecticut v Huggins* (New Haven Super Ct, No. 15681, 1971)). Her white attorney, Catherine Roraback, developed the tactic of asking questions while standing directly behind her black client in order to make the juror look at Ms. Huggins and recognize that the attorney had a friendly and respectful attitude toward her client. After one juror had answered innumerable questions from the judge and three of the lawyers and had consistently stated that she could be fair, Ms. Roraback moved behind her client, and the following exchanges took place:

> **Roraback:** Is there anything about your attitude or experiences we haven't covered in all of these questions that would make you unable to listen to the evidence in this case and reach an unbiased verdict?
>
> **Juror:** (Looking directly at the defendant for the first time) She's guilty!
>
> **Judge:** (Startled) What did you say?
>
> **Juror:** She's guilty!

The juror was promptly excused for cause.

Ginger, "What Can Be Done To Minimize Racism in Jury Trials," 20 *J Pub L* 427, 437 (1971).

### k. Form: Group Voir Dire Inconsistent with Due Process §8.62

IV. TO MAXIMIZE TRUTHFUL ANSWERS, PROSPECTIVE JURORS MUST BE QUESTIONED INDIVIDUALLY

In some courts, the trial judge asks a question to the total panel or to all [12] prospective jurors. The judge waits for individual jurors to raise their hands and volunteer answers. [*Defendant/Plaintiff*]suggests that this system violates our commonsense knowledge that peer group pressure makes jurors reluctant to act differently from their fellow jurors. This is not to say that no juror will ever offer an answer. However, we can be sure such a process will not produce the results of individual voir dire. [*Defendant/Plaintiff will call ex-juror(s) from previous* [*federal*] *trials in this district to further substantiate this point.*]

This proposition has been recognized by numerous courts. In a recent Massachusetts case, the defendant attacked the trial judge's practice of collective questioning followed by questioning at the side bar of individual jurors who came forward. He contended this was not equivalent to individual voir dire as required by Mass. GLC 234, §28. "We agree," the Supreme Judicial Court of Massachusetts said, in *Massachusetts v Shelley* (1980) 409 NE2d 732, at 740.

> Collective questioning on sensitive issues may not elicit a response from some jurors who would respond in private. That the collective questioning provides no "positive ripple among the venire," [citing cases] does not conclude the issue whether individual voir dire is necessary. Nor is the issue settled when, as here, a few jurors come forward and are excused. Some more private form of questioning is necessary. Unless some evidence appears that other jurors can hear a side bar conference, that method of individual voir dire is generally acceptable. However, the preferable practice is questioning outside the presence of the jury.

> *COMMENT:* For preferred United States Supreme Court procedure for questioning individual jurors on sensitive issues, see *Press-Enterprise Co. v Superior Court* (1984) 104 S Ct 819; §8.44

In *California v Barrett* (1929) 207 Cal 47, the court condemned the practice of collective examination of the jury panel and found prejudicial error. In *California v Estorga* (1928) 206 Cal 81, the judge asked the panel as a group whether they held any prejudice and took their silence as a negative reply. Although the appellate court did not find this reversible error in the face of an admission of guilt, as early as 1928 they did find error and sharply criticized such questioning. The federal court of appeals also condemned such a practice in *Patriarca v United States* (1st Cir 1968) 402 F2d 314, 318, *cert. denied* (1969) 393 US 1022: "[W]e feel bound to concede that such a single question posed to the panel en bloc, with an absence of response, achieves little or nothing by way of identifying, weighing, or removing any prejudice from prior publicity."

The Sixth Amendment guaranty of the right to assistance of counsel has been interpreted to mean the right to effective aid of counsel. *Avery v*

*Alabama* (1940) 308 US 444, 446; *California v Chacon* (1968) 69 Cal 2d 765, 777. The right to fair trial has been interpreted to include the right to jury challenge. *Pointer v United States* (1894) 151 US 396, 408. The right to challenge includes the right to an effective voir dire. *Ham v South Carolina* (1973) 409 US 524, 532. Reliance on group questioning is not effective to bring out prejudices. It is a rare juror who will raise a hand and admit racial prejudice. Group questioning fails to bring out subtle prejudice because it does not confront the individual. Consequently, questions about racism directed generally to the panel en bloc do not ensure an effective voir dire and do not live up to the "essential demands of fairness" required by *Ham*, *Ristaino v Ross* (1976) 424 US 589, and *Rosales-Lopez v United States* (1981) 451 US 182.

*COMMENT:* Defense attorney Malcolm Burstein described the problem of group voir dire in a first-degree murder case:

> The bad aspect of having all the jurors in the room is that the others soon learn what answers to give. In our current trial, we asked, "What's your attitude toward capital punishment?" One of the early jurors decided it would be nice to say he was "neutral." From then on just about every one of the 181 jurors questioned took the position that he or she was neutral on capital punishment. I don't even understand what being neutral about capital punishment means . . . .

In Ginger, *The Relevant Lawyers* 52 (1972).

[*Small-group/Individual*] questioning out of the presence of other potential jurors induces more candid responses from jurors and minimizes the impact of each individual's biases on the entire jury panel. In his attached declaration, [Dr. Haney] analyzes why small-group or individual voir dire is more effective. He found that:

1. Jurors respond more truthfully and extensively when interviewed individually or in small groups, out of the presence of others.
2. In a large group setting, a juror's responses affect the responses and perceptions of others and have an impact on the later interaction of jurors during their deliberations.

*COMMENT:* See Haney declaration in §8.80

In addition, individual or small-group voir dire minimizes intrusions on the privacy of prospective jurors.

The Supreme Court has accepted the proposition that individual voir dire promotes candor. The principle was well-stated in *Irvin v Dowd* (1961) 366 US 717, 728: "No doubt each juror was sincere when he said that he would be fair and impartial . . . but the psychological impact requiring such a declaration before one's fellow is often its father."

Additional judicial support is provided by *Coppedge v United States* (DC Cir 1959) 272 F2d 504. In *Coppedge*, a case involving check forgery and various other criminal offenses, one of the defendants refused to take the witness stand, and his attorney stated in the jury's presence that this refusal was prompted by his client's fear of retaliation by Coppedge, another defendant. Furthermore, newspaper articles published during the course of the trial portrayed Coppedge as a ruthless thug. Several jurors admitted to having read these articles. As a result, Coppedge's counsel requested the court to interrogate the jurors individually regarding their ability to remain impartial. The judge denied this request, and Coppedge was convicted. His conviction was reversed on several grounds, one of which was the court's failure to question out of the presence of the other jurors the jurors who had read the inflammatory articles. The court's language is instructive:

> It is too much to expect of human nature that a juror would volunteer, in open court, before his fellow jurors, that he would be influenced in his verdict by a newspaper story of the trial. *Coppedge*, 272 F2d 504, at 508.
>
> . . . Had one or more of [the jurors] said they would be influenced [by the inflammatory articles], and especially if they had then explained why, the damages to the defendant would have been spread to the listening other jurors. In view of the nature of the articles the court should have made a careful, individual examination of each of the jurors involved out of the presence of the remaining jurors, as to the possible effect of the articles.

## l. Form: In Camera Voir Dire Protects Selection Process §8.63

Several courts have also addressed themselves to the impact on other veniremen of responses uttered in a group setting and have concluded that isolated questioning is necessary in order to avoid a "contagion of bias" among the veniremen. See, generally, *Krause v Rhodes* (6th Cir 1977) 570 F2d 563.

COMMENT: *Krause v Rhodes* is described in §3.72.

Not only is there more candor when there is an individual or small-group voir dire, but if one potential juror states something potentially prejudicial in response to a question, other jurors will not be tainted because the remark will not have been made in their presence.

*COMMENT: In camera* voir dire examination is absolutely required in certain circumstances. Even when general voir dire is conducted of the jurors as a group, experienced trial lawyers have learned to request *in camera* voir dire in judge's chambers when they become suspicious about a prospective juror during voir dire in the courtroom. Some judges seem to be very surprised by such a request, but counsel may be able to persuade them to call the questionable person aside for more in-depth questioning. Often when jurors get into chambers, they become uncomfortable enough for the judge to exercise judicial discretion and remove them without counsel having to make a formal challenge.

For example, in a recent wrongful death case in Detroit, an undercover narcotics officer was in the jury box. Liability had been determined; the second jury would determine only damages. During voir dire in the courtroom, plaintiff's counsel noted that this officer's voice "got really strange." He said, "I'm having real problems, and I would have real problems sitting on this case."

The initial reaction of plaintiff's counsel was to make a challenge for cause. Instead, they took the juror into chambers, where he broke down into tears, which was a real surprise to everyone. He explained that his problem was trying to put a dollar value on a human life, which is what the judge had told him he was going to have to do in this case. He said, "I can't deal with it. I can't deal with death. I don't know how I can do it, or how I would ever be able to do it."

After this revelation, neither side moved to challenge him for cause, and the judge did not excuse him.

Throughout the trial, his face showed he was visibly pained. The jurors elected him foreman. Then the jury brought in a verdict that was acceptable to plaintiff. It was a little lower than expected, but it was all right. This juror clearly carried out his responsibility, despite his difficulty in doing so.

For the proper procedure to assure *in camera* examination without unconstitutional limitations on open trials and free press, see discussion of *Press-Enterprise Co. v Superior Court* (1984) 104 S Ct 819, in §8.44

### m. Form: In Camera Voir Dire Protects against Pretrial Publicity §8.64

Although the court has discretion in determining how voir dire is to be conducted, it is best if the in-depth voir dire examination concerning pretrial publicity is not done with a panel, because, as stated in *Patriarca v United States* (1st Cir 1968) 402 F2d 314, 318, *cert. denied* (1969) 393 US 1022:

> such a single question posed to the panel, *en bloc*, with an absence of response, achieves little or nothing by way of identifying, weighing or removing any prejudice from prior publicity. In cases where there is, in the opinion of the court, a significant possibility that jurors have been exposed to potentially prejudicial material, and on request of counsel, we think that the court should proceed to examine each prospective juror apart from other jurors and prospective jurors, with a view to eliciting the kind and degree of his exposure to the case or the parties, the effect of such exposure on his present state of mind, and the extent to which such state of mind is immutable or subject to change from evidence.

As stated in *Silverthorne v United States* (9th Cir 1968) 400 F2d at 637–638, "[w]hen pretrial publicity is great, . . . [t]he judge must insure that the voir dire examination of the jurors affords a fair determination that no prejudice has been fostered." See also *Aldridge v United States* (1931) 283 US 308. The examination should be of individuals, out of the presence of other jurors and potential jurors. *United States v Accardo* (7th Cir 1965) 298 F2d 133; *Semler v United States* (9th Cir 1964) 332 F2d 6, *cert. denied* (1964) 379 US 831.

In *United States v Addonizio* (3d Cir 1971) 451 F2d 49, 67, the Third Circuit stated that individual voir dire is the optimum form of question where there is exposure to potentially prejudicial material:

> We feel impelled to add, however, that we find much merit in the method of *voir dire* recommended in the American Bar Association's Standards Relating to Fair Trial and Free Press, §3.4(a) (Approved Draft, March 1968). As an exercise of our supervisory powers over the district courts in this circuit, therefore, we recommend that in cases hereafter in which there is, in the opinion of the court
>
> > a significant possibility that individual talesmen will be ineligible to serve because of exposure to potentially prejudicial material, the examination of each juror with respect to his exposure shall take place outside the presence of other chosen and prospective jurors. . . . The questioning shall be conducted for the purpose of determining what the prospective juror has read and heard about the case and how his exposure has affected his attitude towards the trial. . . . Standards, §3.4(a).

This view was reiterated in *United States v Starks* (3d Cir 1975) 515 F2d 112, 125. See also *United States v Khoury* (5th Cir 1976) 539 F2d 441.

This section of the standards has also been approved by the Judicial

Conference of the United States and has been cited with approval by other [*federal*] courts, including

[*Insert a citation to a leading or recent opinion from the appropriate jurisdiction, e.g.:*]

the Sixth Circuit Court of Appeals. See *United States v Bryant* (6th Cir 1973) 471 F2d 302.*

---

*The procedure suggested in this motion was approved by the Sixth Circuit in *United States v Giacalone* (6th Cir 1978) 588 F2d 1158.

*COMMENT:* See §8.44 for method of protecting rights of public and press.

### n. Form: In Camera Voir Dire Protects Privacy Rights §8.65

The final principle in support of individual or small-group voir dire is the protection of the privacy of the venirepersons.

In this case there will be questions posed to prospective jurors concerning areas of highly personal attitudes.

[*Here give examples from the instant case, such as the following from the* Berkowitz *case, see §3.56:*]

There will also be questions concerning pretrial publicity, anti-Semitism, people's attitudes toward government, government spending of tax money, and feelings toward people who work for governments.

If people give forthright answers, there is a greater possibility that they may be embarrassed by their answers if all the other prospective jurors are present.

*COMMENT:* Mary Timothy, foreperson of the jury in the *Angela Davis* case (see §3.23), suggests:

> Jurors have a right to privacy. They have a right to a private voir dire. Only the basic questions of name, residence in county, citizenship should be asked in public. The press has no need to know anything about a juror beyond that. There is no need for any of the other jurors to know any more about their fellows, unless the information is given voluntarily. All the other questions should be asked in private conference with only the judge, the attorneys, the defendant and the court reporter present.
>
> There would be double advantage: The personal privacy of the individual would be protected and the juror being questioned would feel freer to disclose any problems he or she might have.

*Jury Woman* 306 (1974) (available from Volcano Press, 330 Ellis Street, San Francisco, California 94102).Mrs. Timothy was very concerned about jurors' right to privacy. She apparently was not concerned about conflicting rights to public trials and to freedom of the press. Nonetheless, the views of the conscientious and courageous foreperson of the jury in a major trial like the *Davis* case must be pondered.

In 1984 the United States Supreme Court established a procedure to protect the public's right to public trials and the jurors' right to privacy. *Press-Enterprise Co. v Superior Court* (1984) 104 S Ct 819; see §8.44.

### o. Form: Jurors Must Be Questioned on Issues in This Case §8.66

V. TO PROTECT AGAINST PREJUDGMENT, PROSPECTIVE JURORS MUST BE QUESTIONED ON SPECIFIC ISSUES IN THIS CASE

In its definitive analysis of voir dire in a "big case," the Seventh Circuit Court of Appeals held, in *United States v Dellinger* (7th Cir 1972) 472 F2d 340, 368, 369:

> The government is correct that collateral or unrelated issues should not be raised [on voir dire]. *United States v Daily* (7th Cir 1943) 139 F2d 7. But this does not mean that all questions must relate directly to the indictment or pleas in the case. Some questions may appear tangential to the trial but are actually so integral to the citizen juror's view of the case, especially one with publicly controversial issues, that they must be explored. For example, in *Daily*, this court acknowledged the right of a defendant of the Jehovah's Witness faith to limited inquiry into the jurors' prejudice against Jehovah's Witnesses, even though his religious faith was not an issue before the court. Similarly, in *United States v Clancy* (7th Cir 1960) 276 F2d 617, 632, *rev'd on other grounds* (9161) 365 US 312, a case in which the defendants were tried for evasion of wagering taxes, we found no error in the district court's refusal to ask questions tendered by defendants, but we noted that the trial court had substituted two questions "designed to uncover prejudice against gamblers and religious scruples against gambling." At a minimum, when requested by counsel, inquiry must be made into matters where the likelihood of prejudice is so great that not to inquire would risk failure in assembling an impartial jury.
>
> What these essential inquiries are, of course, varies with each case.

[*Here add points such as those discussed in* §§*8.67–8.80.*]

### p. Jurors Must Be Questioned on Pretrial Publicity §8.67

Some of the best discussions on the use of extensive voir dire to counter the effects of massive pretrial publicity appear in the appellate decision reversing the convictions in the *Chicago 8* case and in the trial court opinion issued before the state trial of *Susan Saxe* in Massachusetts.

Rather than drafting a model memo on this issue, lengthy excerpts from these opinions are presented, from which counsel undoubtedly can find material to use in a short memo.

*Source:* Opinion of Seventh Circuit Court of Appeals, *United States v Dellinger* (7th Cir 1972) 472 F2d 340, 370–377 (see §3.54). (Footnotes have been deleted or inserted into the text.)

The disorders from which this case arose generated worldwide publicity. There was frequent and continuing local press coverage. [Examples omitted.] [W]e can only speculate as to why defendants did not submit questions concerning pretrial publicity, or why they did not object to the lack of questioning until the government had tendered the panel. . . . Even if the court was not required to go into the subject in the absence of a request, albeit recognizing its importance, we see no reason why the court could not have reopened voir dire for this purpose when the matter was brought to its attention. Indeed, the court's stated reason for denying the motion was not untimeliness, but rather that it considered the subject to have been covered.

Most of the prejudicial pretrial publicity cases that have been before the Supreme Court have been attacks on state convictions in highly publicized cases. These appear to be cases of high sensationalism where the Court has granted certiorari to explore the minimal protections required by the due process clause.

. . . That the publicity surrounding the instant case was tremendous cannot seriously be questioned. Although we do not perceive the "deep and bitter prejudice" in the community that was present in *Irvin* we are certain that the publicity could well have had a prejudicial impact on the persons summoned for jury service. Even the government concedes the possibility that the veniremen had formed opinions before they entered the courtroom. Under these circumstances, we must conclude that the court had a duty to inquire into pretrial publicity on voir dire.

Despite the district court's earlier assurance that the voir dire would cover pretrial publicity, the only explicit reference to publicity was to that which might occur during the trial. The court's only reference to pretrial publicity occurred when, in response to defendants' request to reopen the voir dire, it said that it had covered pretrial publicity in its general inquiry into whether there was any reason the veniremen could not be fair and impartial.

This broad question was not expressly pointed at impressions a juror may have gained from reading or hearing about the relevant events. Natural human pride would suggest a negative answer to whether there was a reason the juror could not be fair and impartial. A juror might well answer negatively in good faith, without stopping to consider the significance or firmness of impressions he might have gained from news reports.

We think the question is not adequate to bring out responses showing that jurors had gained information and formed opinions about relevant matters in issue if in truth any had. This broad question should not be relied on in a situation where there is a probability of exposure. In contrast, in all the Supreme Court cases mentioned above, the trial court inquired specifically into pretrial publicity. See *Irvin v Dowd* (1961) 366 US 717, 727–728; *Beck v Washington* (1962) 369 US 541, 556–557; *Rideau v Louisiana* (1963) 373 US 723; *Sheppard v Maxwell* (1966) 384 US 333, 354 n9.

. . .

. . . Specific questioning with respect to pretrial publicity or prior knowledge of the case occurred in *United States v Shaffer* (7th Cir 1961) 291 F2d 689, *cert. denied* (1961) 368 US 915, and *Allen v United States* (7th Cir 1924) 4 F2d 688. That the prospective jurors in the above cases were explicitly asked about prior knowledge of the case is not an inconsequential distinction. It makes the crucial difference of the prospective jurors being alerted to the problem of pretrial publicity in evaluating their own fitness to serve as jurors.

The two cases seemingly closest to the situation before us are *Silverthorne v United States* (9th Cir 1968) 400 F2d 627, and *Patriarca v United States* (1st Cir 1968) 402 F2d 314, *cert. denied* (1969) 393 US 1022. In *Silverthorne*, the court reversed a conviction where, unlike the instant case, the prospective jurors were asked if they had heard anything about the case, but the court "made no effort to ascertain what information the jurors had accumulated and, consequently, had no way of objectively assessing the impact caused by this pretrial knowledge on the juror's impartiality." 400 F2d at 638. In *Patriarca*, the trial court asked a question substantially identical to the one asked here. Unlike this case, however, the trial judge informed counsel of the question he planned to ask and counsel responded that it was "fine." Because "the court did all that was requested," the appellate court did not reverse, but it criticized that question as being ill-directed at the issue of publicity:

> We feel bound to concede that such a single question posed to the panel en bloc, with an absence of response, achieves little or nothing by way of identifying, weighing, or removing any prejudice from prior publicity.

Finally, contrary to the government's argument, it is undoubtedly possible to question the prospective jurors about pretrial publicity without exposing other members of the venire to the publicity. The procedure of individual questioning recommended by the American Bar Association, *Standards Relating to Fair Trial and Free Press* §3.4 (Approved Draft, 1968), is of course one method. But even without individual questioning, the court could probe the impact of pretrial publicity without requiring the veniremen to describe what they had heard.

> . . . We conclude that the failure to inquire into the effect of pretrial publicity upon the jurors was error.

Factual situations like those described in chapter 7 (requiring change of venue or dismissal of the indictment because of pretrial publicity) also justify extensive voir dire, if the other motions are denied.

In 1978, in a civil jury case, the Seventh Circuit held that the defendant's "right to an impartial jury guaranteed by the Sixth Amendment was impaired by the district court's failure to sufficiently probe the jury." In *Fietzer and Kautz v Ford Motor Co.* (7th Cir 1978) 622 F2d 281, the decision was based in part on failure to probe for possible prejudice against Ford. But the court was also concerned about the trial court's denial of Ford's request to ask the jurors whether they were aware of a newspaper article that appeared three days before the trial in the newspaper with the largest circulation in Wisconsin on the front page, headlined "Fuel Tank Peril Cited in Mavericks, Comets," concerning findings by the National Highway Traffic Safety Administration on fuel tank defects in Comets and Mavericks. The appellate court continued, 622 F2d at 286:

> Additionally, we believe that the better practice in this case would have been for the trial court to question the jurors about the pretrial publicity rather than to ignore it. Specifically, the court should have asked the jurors if any one of them had read or had heard about the article and, if so, whether anything read or heard stood out in his or her mind. After determining the juror's degree of exposure to and interest in the article, the court then would have been able to have inquired whether he or she had formed an opinion about Ford's relative negligence in the case.

The trial judge in the bank robbery trial of Susan Saxe (see §7.68) granted a hearing on defendant's motion to dismiss on the grounds of pretrial publicity. In denying the motion to dismiss, the Chief Justice of the Supreme Court, Suffolk County, Massachusetts, wrote a lengthy opinion discussing testimony presented at the hearing, and granted the defense motion for additional peremptory challenges.

*Source:* Chief Justice McLaughlin's important unreported opinion (April 14, 1976) is reprinted in full below and in §7.68 (subheadings have been added, some footnotes have been omitted, and other footnotes have been inserted in the text).

**[Standard of Fair Trial After Extensive Publicity]**

While many cases exist in Massachusetts concerning the contamination of jurors by publicity during trial (see, e.g., *Commonwealth v Beneficial Fin. Co.* (1971) 360 Mass 188, 296–298; *Worcester Telegram & Gazette, Inc. v Commonwealth* (1968) 354 Mass 578; *Commonwealth v Swenor* (1975) Mass App Adv

Sh 239, 248–252 (Goodman, J, dissenting)), the court is aware of very few which directly address themselves to the issue in a pretrial context. For example, in *Commonwealth v Beneficial Fin. Co.* (1971) 360 Mass 188, the Supreme Judicial Court was principally concerned with the scope of the voir dire conducted by the trial judge in a case accompanied by extensive pretrial publicity. The court noted that the decision not to ask the further questions requested by the defendants was within the sound discretion of the judge. 360 Mass at 295–296.

Subsequently, in *Commonwealth v Gilday* (Mass 1975) 327 NE2d 851, the Supreme Judicial Court held that the judge took every measure which was required by the reasonable exercise of his discretion in securing a fair trial for the defendant in spite of extensive pretrial publicity. Among the measures taken were the "resourceful and thorough" interrogation of the jurors, the resolution of all doubts in favor of the defendant, the instruction of all potential jurors in the strongest language as to publicity and its possible effect on them, and the sequestering of the jury after impaneling. The court rejected the argument that a showing that there was a possibility of prejudice requires a new trial in all circumstances. 327 NE2d at 862.

The prevailing standard in the Commonwealth in this area appears to be that announced in the earlier case of *Commonwealth v Blackburn* (1968) 354 Mass 200: whether there is a reasonable likelihood that pretrial publicity has been so prejudicial that a fair trial cannot be had. 354 Mass at 204. However, at the same time, the Supreme Judicial Court noted:

> Obviously it is not necessary in the interests of a fair trial that all citizens who have read of or been interested in a crime be excluded from the jury or that the trial take place where few such citizens will be found. Intelligent persons read and take an interest in events; because of the same endowments they are likely to give due regard to the evidence and to disregard rumor, report, and suspicion when in the solemnity of a courtroom a defendant is tried and his reputation and his liberty or his life are at stake. [Citations deleted.] The trial judge should and does have substantial discretion in the premises.

354 Mass at 204–205.

[**Summary of *Irvin*, *Rideau*, *Murphy***]

The "fairness" standard announced in *Blackburn* comports substantially with the guidelines established by the federal cases, principally by *Irvin v Dowd* (1961) 366 US 717. *Irvin v Dowd* reiterates that the right to a jury trial guarantees to the criminally accused a fair trial by a panel of impartial, indifferent jurors whose verdict must be based on the evidence developed at the trial. 366 US at 722. The failure to accord an accused a fair trial violates even the minimal standards of due process. *Id.*

> It is not required, however, that the jurors be totally ignorant of the facts and issues involved. In these days of swift, widespread and diverse methods of communication, an important case can be expected to arouse the

> interests of the public in the vicinity, and scarcely any of those best qualified to serve as jurors will not have formed some impression or opinion as the merits of the case. This is particularly true in criminal cases. To hold that the mere existence of any preconceived notion as to the guilt or innocence of an accused, without more, is sufficient to rebut the presumption of a prospective juror's impartiality would be to establish an impossible standard. It is sufficient if the juror can lay aside his impression or opinion and render a verdict based on the evidence presented in court. [Citation deleted.]

*Id.* at 722–723. At the same time, a juror's assurances of his impartiality are not solely dispositive of an accused's rights; it remains open to the defendant to demonstrate the existence of such an opinion in the mind of the juror as will raise the presumption of partiality. *Id.* See also *United States v Denno* (2d Cir 1963) 313 F2d 364, 372.

In *Irvin*, the petitioner succeeded in raising a presumption of partiality and his conviction was accordingly voided by the Supreme Court. Among other things, the petitioner pointed to the barrage of publicity that preceded his trial (including published reports of his confession to six murders and 24 burglaries and his unaccepted offer to plead guilty to avoid the death sentence) and the fact that of 430 persons in the voir dire, 370 prospective jurors or almost 90 percent of those examined on the point entertained some opinion as to the petitioner's guilt—ranging in intensity from mere suspicion to absolute certainty. 366 US at 725–727. Of the twelve jurors finally placed in the jury box, eight out of the twelve thought the petitioner was guilty. *Id.* at 727.

The Court concluded,

> With such an opinion permeating their minds, it would be difficult to say that each could exclude this preconception of guilt from his deliberations. The influence that lurks in an opinion once formed is so persistent that it unconsciously fights detachment from the mental processes of the average man. [Citation deleted.] Where one's life is at stake—and accounting for the frailties of human nature—we can only say that in the light of the circumstances here the finding of impartiality [by the trial judge] does not meet constitutional standards.

*Id.* at 727–728.

The teachings of *Irvin v Dowd* were applied subsequently in *Rideau v Louisiana* (1963) 373 US 723; *Estes v Texas* (1965) 381 US 532; *Sheppard v Maxwell* (1966) 384 US 333; and most recently in *Murphy v Florida* (1975) 421 US 794.

In *Rideau*, a twenty-minute film of the defendant's confession during police interrogation to the murder for which he was later convicted was broadcast three times by a television station in the community where the crime and the trial took place. In reversing the defendant's conviction, the Supreme Court did not even examine the voir dire for evidence of actual prejudice, because it considered the trial under review but a hollow formality. The real trial had occurred when tens of thousands of people in a community of 150,000 witnessed the defendant admit his guilt before the cameras. 421 US at 799. In the later cases of *Estes* and *Sheppard*, the convictions were reversed because of inflammatory pretrial publicity, the circus atmosphere in which the trials were conducted, and the intrusion of the media into the courtroom during the trial. The proceedings in *Estes* and *Sheppard* were found to be "entirely lacking in the solemnity and sobriety to which a defendant is entitled in a system that subscribes to any notion of fairness and rejects the verdict of a mob." 421 US at 799.

In *Murphy*, the Supreme Court was once again confronted with a case in which there had been extensive media coverage prior to trial, especially of the defendant's flamboyant life style and previous conviction for murder and the robbery of the Star of India sapphire from a museum in New York. During the voir dire, 78 potential jurors were questioned. Of these, 30 were excused for miscellaneous personal reasons; 20 were challenged peremptorily; 20 were excused by the trial court as having prejudged the defendant; and the remaining eight served as the jury and two alternatives. 421 US at 796.

The Court discussed the *Irvin*, *Rideau*, and *Sheppard* cases in *Murphy*, noting the circumstances of each. However, the Court stated, "[Those cases] cannot be made to stand for the proposition that juror exposure to information about a state defendant's prior convictions or to news accounts of the crime with which he is charged alone presumptively deprives the defendant of due process." *Id.* at 799.

To resolve the due process issue involved in *Murphy*, the Supreme Court turned to examine "any indication in the totality of circumstances that petitioner's trial was not fundamentally fair." *Id.* Relying heavily on the language quoted above from *Irvin v Dowd*, the Court scrutinized the voir dire in *Murphy* and concluded that it indicated "no such hostility to the petitioner by the jurors who served in his trial as to suggest a partiality that could not be laid aside." *Id.* The Court also noted that the general atmosphere in the community or courtroom was not sufficiently inflammatory to require the conclusion that his trial had been prejudiced. *Id.* at 802.

The court concluded,

> The length to which the trial court must go in order to select jurors who appear to be impartial is another factor relevant in evaluating those jurors' assurances of impartiality. In a community where most veniremen will admit to a disqualifying prejudice, the reliability of the others' protestations may be drawn into question; for it is then more probable that they are part of a community deeply hostile to the accused, and more likely that they may unwittingly have been influenced by it. In *Irvin v Dowd*, for example, the Court noted that 90% of those examined on the point were inclined to belief in the accused's guilt, and the court had excused for this cause 268 of the 430 veniremen. In the present case, by contrast, 20 of the 78 persons questioned were excused because they indicated an opinion as to petitioner's guilt. This may indeed be 20 more than would occur in the trial of a totally obscure person, but it by no

> means suggests a community with sentiment so poisoned against petitioner as to impeach the indifference of jurors who displayed no hostile animus of their own.

*Id.* at 802–803. It should be noted that a trial court has considerable discretion in accepting prospective jurors' opinions of their impartiality. *Irvin v Dowd* (1961) 366 US 717, 723–725; *Commonwealth v Gilday* (Mass 1975) 327 NE2d 851, 863; *Commonwealth v Beneficial Fin. Co.* (1971) 360 Mass 188, 295–296.

[**Importance of Extensive Voir Dire**]

In all the cases discussed above—including *State of South Dakota v Waubun Nuwi Nini* [see §7.65], not included above but cited in the defendant's brief—one of the most important criteria was the indications of prejudice provided by a review of the voir dire conducted by the trial judge. And in this court's opinion, the most single important circumstance involved in the motion before it is the fact that the voir dire of the prospective jurors in this case has not yet taken place. The court is not aware of any case in which a motion to dismiss on the grounds of prejudicial pretrial publicity has been granted prior to the voir dire. The obvious reason for this is that the critical question is what lies in the mind of a potential *juror* and not in that of the public generally. To find the answer to that crucial question, this court will conduct an extensive and thorough voir dire examination, within the solemnity and sobriety of the courtroom, to determine exactly to what extent the venire has been prejudiced against the defendant and whether that prejudice is so pervasive as to require the conclusion that the defendant cannot obtain a fair trial. Moreover, this court does not intend to allow any trial of the defendant to be so corrupted by media influence and popular pressure that any review of the voir dire would be necessary. Consequently, while the court is cognizant of the legal principles cited by the defendant, it does not believe that they control in this situation or that they, at this time, require dismissal of the indictments against the defendant.

Another factor which makes it premature for the court to grant the defendant's motion at this time is the fact that the defendant's evidence firmly establishes the existence of prejudice only within the environs of Suffolk County. The poll conducted by the defendant was limited in its scope to the potential venire within this county. The court notes in this regard that Massachusetts General Laws, chap 277, §51, gives a criminal defendant in Massachusetts the right to ask for a change of venue on the grounds that an impartial trial cannot be had in the county where the case is pending. The defendant has so far chosen to ignore this avenue, even despite this court's suggestion that such might be a possible solution.

*COMMENT:* §51 has been repealed and replaced by Rule 37 of Massachusetts Rules of Criminal Procedure, drawn from Federal Rules of Criminal Procedure 20, 21, and 22.

**[Remedies: Extensive Voir Dire Plus Additional Defense Peremptory Challenges]**

In order to fully protect the defendant's rights, the court will accord the defendant the opportunity to establish "the actual existence of such an opinion in the mind of the juror as will raise the presumption of partiality." To this end, the court, as stated earlier, intends to conduct extensive questioning of the venire on its own, as well as to allow interrogation, within the bounds of propriety, by the parties themselves. See Massachusetts General Laws, chap 234, §28.

*COMMENT:* §28 was amended in 1973 and 1975 to require judges and permit attorneys to conduct extensive voir dire when necessary.

The court also intends to grant to the defendant, under its inherent power to order changes for the purpose of securing a fair trial (*Crocker v Justices of the Superior Court* (1911) 208 Mass 162, 175, 178–180; see *Commonwealth v Beneficial Fin. Co.* (1971) 360 Mass 188, 227; *Fanciullo v B. G. & S. Theatre Corp.* (1937) 297 Mass 44, 51), another sixteen (16) peremptory challenges in addition to those already granted by statute. See Massachusetts General Laws, chap 234, §§26B, 29. The court is aware of that part of the statute which provides, "In every criminal case the commonwealth shall be entitled to as many such [peremptory] challenges as equal the whole number to which all the defendants in the case are entitled." Massachusetts General Laws, chap 234, §29. This excerpt could be interpreted to expressly limit the inherent common law power of the court to order changes in court procedure in order to secure a fair trial. See *Fine v Commonwealth* (1942) 312 Mass 252, 254–255. However, it is the opinion of the court that were this statutory directive to be applied in this instance, it would work to excessively infringe upon and limit, and thereby violate, the defendant's right to due process in contravention of the Fifth and Sixth Amendments to the United States Constitution. See *Murphy v Florida* (1975) 421 US 794, 799. The court considers that under the unique circumstances of this case the fundamental right of the defendant to a fair trial outweighs the statutory mandate. Thus, the defendant will be accorded a total of thirty-two (32) peremptory challenges. The Commonwealth will be allowed the normal statutory limit of sixteen (16), and there will be no change in the procedure concerning challenges for cause. See Massachusetts General Laws, chap 234, §28.

In conclusion, it has been this court's experience that the great majority of potential jurors, impressed, even awed, by the seriousness and importance of their possible function, speak honestly and frankly about any prejudice or bias in the course of voir dire examination. Furthermore, this court must determine what is in their minds, what they, and not the public in general, believe for they ultimately are the ones to establish guilt or innocence. With this in mind and in addition to the extraordinary and unusual measures set out above, this court is convinced that there can be no substitute for a thorough and searching voir dire examination to determine the existence of prejudice. Until such prejudice [is] presented, other measures are not only premature, but also unwarranted.

### q. Form: Jurors Must Be Questioned on Racial Prejudice §8.68

## A. Race, Like Pretrial Publicity, Creates Prejudiced Expectations

*COMMENT:* Similar wording may be used when the defendant's sex or nationality is an issue.

Pretrial race prejudice is analogous to pretrial prejudice based on publicity concerning the crime. In both instances the juror comes into the jury box with a preconceived bias determined by outside sources. In both instances the jurors have formed opinions before they come into the courtroom. The court cannot erase the influence of society on the juror in these areas. The court cannot remake the jurors' minds. Therefore intensive questioning is necessary to determine the extent of such pretrial influence in order to remove from the jury box those infected with prejudgment or racism.

Trial judges in several recent cases involving black defendants active in political groups have therefore permitted extensive voir dire by lawyers, and have expanded their previously held views about the proper limits on voir dire. See excerpts from lengthy voir dire in [*California v Newton*] and lists of questions asked in other recent cases [*in the Appendix.*]

*COMMENT:* An appendix to the brief, memorandum, or petition should present relevant excerpts from chapters 15–17 and questions from chapter 9 of this book.

Pretrial publicity creates no greater prejudice than already exists in the area of race. Racial stereotypes are so prevalent in United States society and specifically in [*California*] that [*the State Bar of California has established a Special Committee on Disadvantaged Persons of Special Concern to the Bar to study racism in the law, following passage of Resolution 10-15 by the 1969 Conference of Delegates*].

*COMMENT:* Similar descriptions from other states or on sexism may be inserted. For example, in 1971 the Resolutions Committee of the California Conference of Delegates recommended that a proposal for creation of a permanent committee on women "be referred to the Board of Governors of the State Bar of California so that it may consider a program of action to help break down the barriers which prevent a meaningful number of women from entering the practice of law and which also prevent their full utilization and proper compensation." 1971 Conference of Delegates, *Report of Resolutions Committee on Resolution 13–7*, at 21.

In this situation it is incumbent on the judicial process to ensure a voir dire that will confront racial prejudices. We intend to present expert testimony to prove that people hold conscious and subconscious racial views and accept racial stereotypes, that individual and extensive voir dire is necessary to uncover these attitudes, and that further voir dire is necessary to cause the jurors to confront their views and stereotypes.

**B. Defendant Has a Constitutional Right To Conduct Voir Dire in the Area of Racism**

The United States Supreme Court, in *Ham v South Carolina* (1973) 409 US 524, held that due process requires interrogation of jurors on the subject of racial prejudice. Ham follows case law covering over a hundred years and many races and ethnic groups. See, e.g., *California v Reyes* (1855) 5 Cal 347 (Chicanos); *California v Car Soy* (1880) 57 Cal 102 (Chinese); *California v Potigian* (1924) 64 Cal App 257 (Armenians); *Potter v Texas* (1919) 216 SW 886 (Jews); *Pennsylvania v DePalma* (1920) 110 A 756 (Italians); *Aldridge v United States* (1931) 283 US 308, 314–315.

In *Ristaino v Ross* (1976) 424 US 589, the Court said that under its supervisory powers it would have required a *federal* trial court to conduct voir dire questioning directed to racial prejudice in the case of a black defendant charged with violent crimes against a white security guard, and that this would have been the wiser course for a *state* trial court to follow, despite defense counsel's failure to explain why such questioning was necessary.

*COMMENT:* See §3.30.

Following *Ham*, the conviction of a Native American defendant for killing a calf on a reservation was reversed by the Eighth Circuit Court of Appeals due to inadequate voir dire on racial prejudice at a time when feeling in the area was running high over the Indian occupation of Wounded Knee (although the defendant's act was not related to that event). *United States v Bear Runner* (8th Cir 1974) 502 F2d 908. The trial court refused to ask specific questions propounded by the defense, instead asking generally:

> When I asked you if you were in the position of the Defendants, now, I want to rephrase that in this way. I would want to know if you were either a defendant or if you were the government's attorney in this case or in any case, would you want anyone on the jury who has the frame of mind that you now have? Is there anyone who would not want anyone on the jury with the frame of mind that you each individually now have?

502 F2d at 911. The court of appeals explained:

> We take judicial notice of the fact that the criminal charges against those American Indians involved in Wounded Knee were moved by the court out of the Deadwood locale. We conclude under these circumstances there existed a sincere concern over prejudicial issues and that a general rhetorical question asking if the jurors would be fair and unbiased toward the defendant was of questionable sufficiency. Cf. *United States v Dellinger* (7th Cir 1972) 472 F2d 340, 366–368, *cert. denied* (1973) 410 US 970. Under these circumstances it would have been a much better practice for the court, or counsel with the court's permission, to have examined each of the prospective jurors on an individual basis in these sensitive areas.

502 F2d at 912–913. The Third and Seventh Circuit Courts of Appeals likewise interpreted *Ham* to require reversal in cases where jurors were not permitted to be interrogated about possible racial prejudice. *United States v Robinson* (3d Cir 1973) 485 F2d 1157; *United States v Booker* (7th Cir 1973) 480 F2d 1310.

These decisions underscore the fact that an extensive voir dire on racism is essential to guarantee a fair trial for a minority defendant and to guarantee that the community will know that a fair trial was conducted and accept the outcome of the trial as being fair. See Note, "The Case for Black Juries," 79 *Yale L J* 531 (1970); *Rosales-Lopez v United States* (1981) 451 US 182.

*COMMENT:* For material on the need for intensive voir dire on possible prejudice against Latinos, Puerto Ricans, and people with Spanish surnames, contact the Mexican American Legal Defense Fund, in major cities.

### r. Form: Jurors Must Be Questioned on Conflicting Social Values §8.69

The Seventh Circuit Court of Appeals delineated the elements in the famous *Chicago 8* case that required considerable voir dire, in reversing the convictions in *United States v Dellinger* (7th Cir 1972) 472 F2d 340, 368–369 (see §3.54):

> Many elements of this case might have aroused the jurors' prejudices. One of the central themes was the protest against the nation's involvement in war in Vietnam.
>
> Perhaps secondary, but significant, were the conflicts of values represented by the so-called youth culture—hippies, yippies and freaks—in contrast with the more traditional values of the vast majority

of the community, presumably including most citizens summoned for jury service. Again, we are not unaware that many otherwise qualified members of the community could not be impartial toward, and in fact are often offended by, persons who wear long hair, beards, and bizarre clothing and who seem to avoid the burdens and responsibilities of regular employment. Several defendants would exemplify this conflict.

A similar conflict of values was symbolized in the confrontation between the city police and the demonstrators. A juror's basic sympathies with the actors in these events could easily impair his ability to consider alternative views of the case as presented in court. A venireman's relationship with law enforcement officers would be an important factor to be inquired about in evaluating his ability to be an impartial juror.

In our view, some minimal inquiry into at least these three basic areas was essential to a fair trial of this extraordinary case, at least when defendants requested such inquiry.

### s. Form: Jurors Must Be Questioned on Self-Defense §8.70

As mentioned above, self-defense is a central aspect of the defense in this case.

*COMMENT:* When a related issue, e.g., defense of a third person, is present, this can be rephrased: " . . . defense of a third person is a central aspect . . . . Addressing the closely related area of self-defense, . . . "

Addressing this issue, the Indiana Supreme Court recently stressed the necessity of permitting inquiry into this area when the defense is raised:

> Like the death penalty, the State's burden of proof, and the insanity defense, the law of self-defense is not without its controversial features, e.g., the "no retreat" rule, the right under certain circumstances, to use deadly force to protect oneself, the State's burden to disprove a claim of self-defense, once evidence tending to show such has been introduced. Consequently, each party must be afforded a reasonable opportunity to conduct "pertinent inquiry" to ascertain whether the prospective jurors possess, or are likely to possess, conscientious scruples or other mental obstacles likely to interfere with a proper application of the law of self-defense.

*Everly v Indiana* (Ind 1979) 395 NE2d 254, 256.

### t. Other Issues on Which Courts Have Upheld Voir Dire §8.71

Use material from the list and citations in §8.79.

### u. Form: Conclusion §8.72

For the foregoing reasons, justice requires this Court to grant defendant[s]' motion for certain voir dire procedures.

### v. Recent Developments §8.73

See §8.9.

## 2. List: Issues on Which Courts Have Upheld or Ordered Voir Dire §8.79

The following list of issues on which trial and appellate courts have permitted or ordered voir dire examination is not exhaustive. It is based on reported opinions in which appellate courts have reversed jury verdicts for inadequate voir dire, and a few trial court opinions on voir dire issues. It should provide a good starting place for research on the particular issue in your case or the rulings of courts in your jurisdiction. For further issues on which courts have permitted voir dire, see the lists of questions that have actually been permitted by trial court judges, usually without written opinions, reported in chapter 9 (basic questions in all cases), in chapter 10 (questions in civil cases), and in chapter 11 (questions in criminal cases). Follow-up questions flowing out of initial questions are reported in chapters 15–17.

*Sources:* Adapted from memorandum on subject matter and scope of voir dire, Mar. 8, 1976, *United States v Soliah* (see §8.82); memorandum of points and authorities in support of plaintiffs' proposed jury selection methods, *Hampton v Hanrahan* (ND Ill, ED, No. 70 C 1384) (see §3.71); memorandum in support of defendants' proposed jury selection methods, *United States v Berkowitz* (see §3.56).

1. General personal information. *Walker v Greenberger* (1944) 63 Cal App 2d 457. [See §9.8.]
2. Effect of pretrial publicity. *Murphy v Florida* (1975) 421 US 794; *Sheppard v Maxwell* (1966) 384 US 333; *Feitzer and Kautz v Ford Motor Co.* (7th Cir 1980) 622 F2d 281.
3. Juror's bias or prejudice in relation to:
   a. Political attitudes and beliefs. Because of the serious duty of

the trial court to impanel a fair jury, questions concerning bias stemming from political belief or association must be allowed when relevant. *Dennis v United States* (1950) 339 US 162; *Morford v United States* (1950) 339 US 258. When the parties are associated with a political movement and politics is very much a part of the case, recent decisions have required at least inquiry into the effect that a party's political beliefs or activities will have in terms of impartiality. E.g., *United States v Dellinger* (7th Cir 1972) 472 F2d 340; *United States v Lebron* (2d Cir 1955) 222 F2d 531; *United States v Nertess* (2d Cir 1944) 139 F2d 923; *United States v Malinowski* (ED Pa 1972) 347 F Supp 347, *aff'd* (3d Cir 1972) 472 F2d 850, *cert. denied* (1973) 411 US 970; *United States v Anderson* (DC NJ Crim No. 602-71, May 19, 1973 (*Camden 28* case—see §3.55)); *New York v Presley* (1964) 254 NYS2d 400. In *Dellinger* and *Anderson*, which both involved antiwar activities, inquiry into the attitudes of potential jurors about the Vietnam war was allowed. See §§3.54 and 3.55. However, some courts have held that political prejudice is not a proper area of inquiry absent special circumstances. E.g., *New Jersey v Longo* (1937) 3 A2d 127.

b. Religious beliefs and affiliations. Questions concerning religious prejudice are usually allowed, certainly if there are religious issues in the case. See, *e.g.*, *Wasy v Indiana* (1955) 123 NE2d 462; *United States v Clancy* (7th Cir 1960) 276 F2d 617, 637; *Yarborough v United States* (4th Cir 1956) 230 F2d 56; *California v Simon* (1927) 80 Cal App 675. The potential juror's religion is usually allowed. E.g., *United States v Anderson, supra*. The Supreme Court has held that it is permissible and appropriate to ask voir dire questions concerning religion and personal moral beliefs. *Witherspoon v Illinois* (1968) 391 US 510; *United States v Dailey* (7th Cir 1943) 139 F2d 72; *California v Barr* (Livermore Muni. Ct. Cr. No. 362173–8, Feb. 16, 1984), see §11.58.

c. Sexual roles. *Anderson, supra*; *Dellinger, supra*; *Dresch v Elliot* (1910) 122 NYS 14.

d. Social or economic position or class. Inquiry is usually permitted. 47 *Am Jur 2d* 852. On questions concerning prejudice against unions and union activity, see *Gaytou v Buering* (Wis 1900) 81 NW 1003; *Metallic Gold Mine Co. v Watson* (Colo 1911) 117 P 609; *St. Louis R. Co. v Hooser* (Tex 1906) 97 SW 708; *Massachusetts v Sacco* (1926) 255 Mass 369; *California v Barr, supra*.

e. Youth. *Dellinger, supra. Anderson, supra.* See §9.58.

4. Juror's attitudes on:

a. Credibility of police witnesses. *Brown v United States* (DC Cir

1964) 338 F2d 543 (Burger, J); *Anderson, supra*; *United States v Cleveland* (7th Cir 1973) 477 F2d 310; *Chavez v United States* (10th Cir 1958) 258 F2d 816, *cert. denied sub nom. Tenario v United States* (1958) 359 US 916; *Michigan v Milkovich* (1971) 188 NW2d 124; *Sellers v United States* (DC Cir 1960) 271 F2d 475. In *Anderson, supra*, where one of the important issues concerned the role of an informer, the potential jurors were also asked whether they thought it was possible that the FBI would provoke a crime. See §§9.72, 9.82, 9.104.

It is reversible error to refuse to allow the question: "Would you give greater credence to the testimony of a law enforcement officer merely because he is an officer as compared to other witnesses?" *Brown v United States* (DC Cir 1964) 338 F2d 543; *Chavez, supra*. But cf. *United States v Brewer* (10th Cir 1970) 427 F2d 409 (not abuse of discretion in bank robbery case to refuse question whether jurors would be quicker to believe bank employees because of their involvement than someone else).

b. Evidence. *California v Deriso* (1963) 222 Cal App 2d 478; *California v Tuthill* (1947) 31 Cal 2d 92; *California v Bennett* (1926) 79 Cal App 76 (permissible to ask whether a juror has a bias or prejudice about the law or the evidence that will be involved in the case); *California v Moore* (1923) 64 Cal App 328; *California v Allen* (1969) 275 Cal App 2d 428; *Marshall v United States* (1959) 360 US 310 (inability of juror to disregard inadmissible evidence heard). See also Anno, 3 L Ed 2d 2004.

c. Helping fleeing fugitive. *California v Khau Din* (1919) 39 Cal App 695.

d. Notoriety of a party. *United States v Hoffa* (7th Cir 1961) 367 F2d 698, 711, vacated on other grounds (1967) 387 US 231.

e. Prior conviction of other offenses or experiences of crime. *California v Hillery* (1965) 62 Cal 2d 692; *California v Ranney* (1931) 213 Cal 70; *United States v Poole*, (3d Cir 1971) 450 F2d 1082.

f. Right to remain silent. "Will you require the defendant to testify and to tell his side of what happened?" *California v Flavin* (1913) 21 Cal App 244. See §11.11.

g. Rules of law. Refusal to allow questions on whether jurors can accept the proposition of law that a defendant is presumed to be innocent, has no burden to establish his innocence, and is clothed throughout trial with that presumption has been held reversible error. *United States v Blount* (6th Cir 1973) 479 F2d 650. See §§11.10–11.11. Questions regarding jurors' acceptance of the basic rules of law involved in a case must be asked, and in such a form as to "permit the intelligent exercise of challenges by counsel." *United States v Anderson* (6th Cir 1977) 562 F2d 394, at 398.

Prejudicial error to refuse questioning on defense of necessity. *California v Jimmie Ray Williams* (Sup Ct 1981) 174 Cal Rptr 317.

5. Jurors' experience with:
   a. Crime. *United States v Poole* (3d Cir 1971) 450 F2d 1082. See §§11.5–11.6.
   b. Organizations related to the case. *California v Reyes* (1855) 5 Cal 347; 31 ALR 411; 158 ALR 1362. See §§9.16, 9.17.
   c. Persons involved in the case. *Boothe v Baltimore Steam Packet Co.* (ED Va 1957) 149 F Supp 861 (party); *Progner v Eagle* (4th Cir 1967) 377 F2d 461 (attorney); *Cook v United States* (5th Cir 1967) 379 F2d 966; *United States v Lewin* (7th Cir 1972) 467 F2d 1132; *United States v Baldwin* (9th Cir 1979) 607 F2d 1295 (potential witness).

      Refusal to allow questions on whether jurors have been employed by the organization that employs the chief prosecution witness has been held reversible error. *United States v Lewin, supra.*

      Refusal to allow questions on whether jurors are acqainted with or related to chief prosecution witnesses has been held reversible error. *Cook v United States, supra.* See §9.9.
   d. Prior conviction of other offenses or experiences of crime. *California v Hillery* (1965) 62 Cal 2d 692; *California v Ranney* (1931) 213 Cal 70; *United States v Poole, supra.*
   e. Prior jury duty. *California v Wismer* (1922) 58 Cal App 679. See §9.15.
6. Juror's fear of retaliation by a party. *Coppedge v United States* (DC Cir 1959) 272 F2d 504.
7. Length of case. "Will you allow yourself to be influenced by the length of your deliberations, or by the fact that other jurors may disagree with you?" *California v Bennett*, (1926) 79 Cal App 76. See §9.96.

### 3. Appendix to Memorandum: Expert Testimony

#### a. Sample: Affidavit on All Aspects of Juror Voir Dire §8.80

The following affidavit of Dr. Craig Haney is frequently appended to motions seeking certain voir dire procedures in criminal cases, because it discusses the major points customarily included in such motions. Similar affidavits are often filed in civil suits seeking changes in voir dire procedures.

*Source:* Affidavit of Dr. Craig Haney in support of defendant's motion regarding voir dire procedures, *Maryland v Sails* (Circuit Court, Prince Georges County, Md, No. 82–352), a capital felony case. For the remainder of the affidavit, on death qualification of jurors, see §11.81.

I. DR. CRAIG HANEY, under penalty of perjury, make the following declaration:

1. I am currently employed as an Associate Professor of Psychology at the University of California at Santa Cruz. I teach undergraduate courses in research methodology, social psychology, and in psychology and law. I received a Bachelor's Degree from the University of Pennsylvania, a Master's Degree and Ph.D. in Psychology from Stanford University, and a J.D. degree from the Stanford Law School. I have received many scholarship and fellowship awards, and I have published over 30 scholarly articles in the area of psychology and law. I am also the author of a forthcoming book, *Social Psychology and the Criminal Law*.

*COMMENT:* You may want to append to the affidavit a copy of Dr. Haney's curriculum vita.

2. Over the past ten years, I have served as a consultant to numerous law enforcement and legal agencies and organizations including the Palo Alto Police Department, the California Assembly Committee on Criminal Justice, and the United States Department of Justice. I am also a member of the Faculty of the National Judicial College in Reno, Nevada. In addition, I have been qualified and have testified as an expert in several United States District Courts, and the state courts of California, New Mexico, Oklahoma, and Washington.

3. One area of psychology and law in which I have specialized extensively concerns the effects of voir dire conditions and procedures on the attitudes and beliefs of jurors. I have observed part or all of the jury selection process in approximately 75 criminal trials. (I would estimate that roughly half of those were capital cases.) In addition, I have conducted numerous interviews with persons who were successfully challenged in the course of jury selection, as well as posttrial interviews with actual jurors. I have also conducted controlled experimental research on the effects of the death qualification process. I served as an expert witness in the hearing on which the California Supreme Court's opinion in *Hovey v Superior Court* [(1980) 28 C3d 1] was based, and also testified when these issues were presented before Judge Eiseley in United States District Court, in the *Grigsby v Mabry* rehearing, July 1981. (ED Ark 1983) 569 F Supp 1273.

4. Upon the request of counsel, I have reviewed the customary voir dire procedures used in [*Circuit*] Courts of the [*State of Maryland*]. This review included an examination of relevant [*Maryland*] statutes and court rules, and a careful analysis of official transcripts from several recent [*Maryland*] [*capital*]

cases. I have also examined a file of newspaper publicity pertaining to the crime with which the defendant in this case is charged. I have formed an opinion as to the effect that customary voir dire conditions will have on the ability of the Court and counsel to identify bias among prospective jurors and to excuse jurors who cannot be impartial in [*State of Maryland*] *v* [*Harlow Brian Sails*].

[*In a noncapital case, delete the following sentence.*]

I have also formed an opinion about the likely effects of the "death qualification" process on the jury that will hear and decide [*Mr. Sails'*] case.

5. Based on my observations of the effects of courtroom procedures on prospective jurors, my own systematic research on these and related issues, and my knowledge of the relevant psychological literature, I believe that: (a) the conditions that prevail during standard group voir dire as it is customarily practiced in [*Maryland*] seriously jeopardize the Court's ability to impanel a fair and impartial jury in this case

[*In a noncapital case, delete (b)*]

, and (b) the process of death qualification further undermines the impartiality of the jury and will likely predispose them to convict [*Mr. Sails*].

GENERAL CONSIDERATIONS

6. The first step in understanding the difficulties involved in selecting a fair and impartial jury is a recognition of the degree to which many prospective jurors enter the courtroom with strong biases and prejudices that are likely to affect their ability to be impartial in a given case. These types of biases have been repeatedly documented in the context of criminal proceedings. For example, surveys of prospective jurors conducted by the National Jury Project in jurisdictions across the country reveal that anywhere from 23 to 58 percent of persons eligible for jury service would require a criminal defendant to prove innocence, despite a judge's instructions to the contrary. The surveys also show that anywhere from 13 to 39 percent of persons eligible for jury service believe that if the prosecution has gone to the trouble of bringing a defendant to trial, that person is probably guilty. Typically, between 55 and 65 percent of persons eligible for jury service believe that a criminal defendant who fails to take the witness stand and testify is probably guilty.[1]

7. These survey results are confirmed by other independent national studies. The National Center for State Courts commissioned a survey of 1800 households nationwide, and found that 37 percent of the population believe it is the responsibility of the defendant to prove his or her innocence in a criminal case.[2] In 1979, the George Fine Organization, on behalf of the *Washington Post*, conducted a survey of 1808 randomly selected respondents throughout the United States. This study showed that 31 percent of those questioned agreed with the statement that if the government brings someone to trial that person is probably guilty of some crime. Fully 52 percent of the respondents in this

study felt that the defendant in a criminal trial should be required to take the witness stand and prove innocence.[3]

8. Thus, it is likely that in any jurisdiction, a substantial proportion of prospective jurors will enter the courtroom holding opinions and beliefs that do not conform with fundamental principles of American constitutional law.

9. These biases which prospective jurors can be expected to hold in any case are frequently exacerbated by the features of a particular case. The [*heinous*] nature of the crime with which [*Mr. Sails*] is charged is likely to evoke very strong emotional reactions among prospective jurors. These reactions will be exacerbated by a growing national preoccupation with the rise in violent crime in our communities and the widely held belief that the courts and constitutional rights of defendants are largely responsible for our inability to curtail crime.

10. Unfortunately, these biases cannot be compensated for by instructions from the trial court. Numerous studies show that jurors comprehend surprisingly little of the information that is contained in judicial instructions.[4] Even after service as a trial juror, a substantial proportion of people fail to endorse basic concepts like presumption of innocence, burden of proof, and reasonable doubt. Even when jurors do comprehend judicial instructions and conscientiously strive to follow them, they may not be sufficiently aware of their own prejudices to know when and how to control them.

11. In short, there is little doubt that many prospective jurors enter the courtroom with prejudicial attitudes and erroneous opinions concerning the criminal justice system, law and order, racial minorities, and the like. These attitudes can have an effect on a juror's ability to listen to and evaluate evidence. If a fair and impartial jury is to be selected, these attitudes must be elicited and probed during voir dire examination so that prospective jurors whose attitudes and opinions will interfere with their evaluation of evidence can be excused.

## THE SOCIAL PSYCHOLOGY OF VOIR DIRE

12. Voir dire is essentially an interview situation with all problems and benefits inherent in obtaining information with this kind of format. The Court and the attorneys ask questions and, based on the answers the prospective jurors give, they must decide who to select to participate in the trial. However, in any interview situation, the quality of the information obtained is controlled by the conditions under which the interview is conducted, the type of information that is sought, and the interviewee's perceptions of the consequences of the interview.

13. The courtroom is an intimidating place for most prospective jurors. Most people are uncomfortable speaking in front of large groups. Yet, standard group voir dire as it is practiced in [*Maryland*] requires prospective jurors to do precisely that. Moreover, during voir dire in the instant case, prospective jurors will be asked to voice their opinions about sensitive subjects such as their attitudes toward [*racial minorities*] and their feelings and opinions about [*violent*] crime and the criminal justice system. Moreover, they will also be asked to respond to questions regarding issues they may never have thought about before—including the concepts of presumption of innocence and burden of proof.

They also know that they will be included or excluded as jurors based on their responses to these questions.

14. Extensive empirical research in social psychology has documented the degree to which attitudes and behavior are shaped and influenced by situational conditions.[5] That is, if one wants to predict and explain behavior, then the characteristics of the setting in which the behavior takes place may be far more important than the personality traits of the people involved. In a typical voir dire, jurors answer questions in front of a group of strangers, which includes other jurors, attorneys, the judge, courtroom personnel, and other spectators.

*COMMENT:* The press may also be present, and must be permitted to attend. See *Press-Enterprise Co. v Superior Court* (1984) 104 SCt 819; §8.44.

For a half a century social psychologists have been studying the effect of the presence of others on individual behavior. For example, in one series of laboratory studies on the independence of judgment in a group setting, over a third of the subjects typically went along with the majority on matters as clear and objective as judging the lengths of lines quite different in size.[6] When the experimental stimuli are statements of opinion endorsed by the majority of the group, the proportion of agreement is much higher.

15. Thus, the immediate environment exerts a powerful influence on what people say and do. This voir dire setting makes jurors highly sensitive to the consequences which they expect their words and actions will bring,[7] and may inhibit even the most conscientious jurors from responding frankly and openly. Individuals are concerned with winning approval and disapproval from others. They devote considerable time and energy learning what factors will have a positive influence on how they will be received or evaluated and they try to behave in a manner which will give a favorable impression.[8]

16. During standard voir dire, in many [*Maryland*] courts, most questions are asked of the prospective jurors by a trial judge. Psychological studies indicate that respondents avoid contradicting or displeasing an interviewer, especially when he is perceived as having higher social status than the subject. The greater the distance between the social status of the interviewer and that of the respondent, the greater is the probability of obtaining biased answers. In the courtroom, of course, the judge is the most highly respected authority figure; he has a far higher status than any of the jurors. Jurors are acutely aware of subtle cues or indications from judges in the courtroom, and they base a number of important inferences upon them.[9]

17. For example, if the trial judge begins voir dire, as is customary, by telling the jury panel that the Court is seeking a "fair and impartial" jury, then the prospective jurors learn that their responses "should" reflect that they are fair and impartial jurors. By contrast, if the judge indicates instead that the Court seeks open and honest responses during voir dire, then the prospective jurors will be more likely to respond frankly to questions regardless of whether their responses display impartiality.

18. Problems can also arise if, during the voir dire, prospective jurors become

aware of specific qualities which the court is looking for in a juror. If, for example, the Court indicates its desire to impanel jurors who are not prejudiced against [*black*] people, prospective jurors may place an inordinate importance on appearing to be without [*racial*] prejudice. This is because the prospective juror experiences what social psychologists have termed "evaluation apprehension," or a heightened concern for what respected authority figures think of them.[10]

19. The expressed attitudes of prospective jurors are also greatly affected, and can be modified, by what they learn about the beliefs of other prospective jurors.[11] It is not uncommon for jurors to adopt what is called a "social desirability response set."[12] That is, jurors will attempt to respond during voir dire in a socially appropriate manner instead of simply being truthful. These behavior patterns encourage prospective jurors to modify their own answers to conform with those they have heard expressed earlier by other jurors. The tendency to conform in a group has been well documented in the social psychology literature. The effect of this tendency is that opinions given in public often differ from opinions given in private.[13]

20. Voir dire is an unfamiliar and uncertain situation for prospective jurors. The courtroom is a highly formal situation in which most people feel uncomfortable. Under conditions of uncertainty and unfamiliarity, people are highly susceptible to "social comparison information"—indications from other persons about the appropriateness of their behavior, attitudes and feelings.[14]

21. During voir dire, a prospective juror's ability to reveal feelings or facts that may greatly influence the decision-making process is seriously inhibited by the prospective juror's needs to appear to be as good or as acceptable as other potential jurors. For example, some prospective jurors will knowingly cover up their feelings when questioned in a group voir dire situation. Others will unconsciously try to conform as closely as possible to other members of the group, especially with members who appear to be the most "respectable" members of the group. Other prospective jurors may contrive to be seated or excused by adjusting their responses to the results observed during the questioning of those who precede them. Socially acceptable responses to voir dire questions are established early in the jury selection process. These questions appear continuously throughout the examination so that less and less honest information is elicited from prospective jurors as standard group voir dire proceeds.

22. The social psychological influences discussed *supra* operate in standard group voir dire to mask or distort juror responses on precisely those issues which are of primary importance, such as [*racial*] attitudes and attitudes about [*the presumption of innocence*]. Prospective jurors who are concerned about how they will be evaluated by others in the courtroom, or who are answering in a socially desirable fashion in order to obtain the Court's approval, are unlikely to admit [*racial*] prejudice or to concede disagreement or confusion concerning the basic tenets of American justice.

## IMPROVING GENERAL VOIR DIRE CONDITIONS

23. In light of these social psychological considerations, there are a number of concrete steps that the Court can take to improve general voir dire conditions and increase the likelihood that a truly fair and impartial jury will be impaneled in [*Maryland v Sails*].

24. The trial judge can directly influence the voir dire process so as to minimize the impact of the social psychological forces that inhibit the selection of a fair and impartial jury. The trial judge can begin voir dire by encouraging prospective jurors to be open and honest in their responses and not indicate any kind of disapproval for certain answers, even when those answers might indicate bias that requires the person to be excused for cause. Jurors who are excused for cause can be thanked openly for their frankness.

25. Once the judge has set (and continues to support) the general atmosphere of candor and openness, major responsibility for conducting the actual voir dire questioning should be transferred to the attorneys rather than remaining with the Court. Prospective jurors perceive far less social distance between themselves and the attorneys, are far less intimidated by counsel, and are far less likely to perceive and respond to pressures towards socially desirable responses and approval-seeking. The social psychological realities of voir dire mean that attorneys will have the best chance of uncovering attitudes, biases, and prejudices that may jeopardize fairness and impartiality. Also, because attorneys are more acquainted with the details of the evidentiary presentations that will follow, they are better able to identify specific biases most threatening to a fair hearing of their case. Forcing attorneys to suggest questions to the Court on a juror-by-juror basis is cumbersome and ineffective.

26. Another barrier to effectively identifying bias or prejudice during voir dire is the excessive use of fixed-response or leading questions. A fixed-response question is one in which the answer is limited to a single response, such as "yes" or "no," "agree" or "disagree." In social science research, such fixed-response questions are often asked to elicit narrow or particularized factual information from a particular respondent. Although leading questions can be useful in obtaining information about a juror's residence, age, or occupation, such questions are not useful in eliciting more substantial information about a prospective juror's attitudes. In other contexts, all lawyers and judges know that leading questions can suggest or control the content of the response elicited. Thus, a leading voir dire question, such as "Is there anything about the [*race*] or [*background*] of the defendant which would prevent you from being fair and impartial?" indirectly informs the prospective juror that the "correct" answer is "no." It also provides the court with virtually no information regarding the existence of biases and the subtle impact such biases may have on the juror's decision-making. Indeed, many prejudiced persons consider themselves to be completely fair-minded people who simply are "aware of the inferiority of certain [*minority*] groups." Only open-ended questions that require jurors to formulate their thoughts in a sentence or two will separate those persons who

are actually fair from those who are merely unaware of their invidious stereotypes.[15]

27. Accordingly, it is imperative that the voir dire include questions that are nonleading and that require the prospective juror to respond with a few sentences rather than a single word. Nonleading questions allow respondents to explain their opinions and attitudes in their own words, thus penetrating stereotyped and socially desirable responses. Only nonleading questions will uncover the underlying attitudes and prejudices that are unlikely to surface in perfunctory responses given to standard closed-ended questions.

28. . . .Voir dire which includes nonleading questions can take less time than most customary voir dire. A single open-ended question which allows a prospective juror to speak a few sentences will often reveal far more information than numerous and lengthy leading questions.

29. The [*racial status*] of the defendant in this case poses a special challenge to the Court's ability to impanel a fair and impartial jury. Invidious [*racial stereotypes*] may influence some jurors' perceptions of the evidence and predisposition to convict. Yet, many prospective jurors will be reluctant to reveal their [*racial*] attitudes during voir dire. Recent research indicates that there may be at least 12 different dimensions along which [*whites*] express their [*racism*].[16] Thus, it is difficult to identify such prejudice in a single voir dire question. For example, one of the most widely accepted ways of measuring [*racial*] prejudice uses 120 different questions to do so.[17] While it would be, of course, unrealistic to administer such an extensive series of questions to prospective jurors, this methodology suggests that in order to identify [*racial*] prejudice, it is necessary to ask prospective jurors a number of questions that allow for the emergence of a *pattern* of [*racial*] beliefs and feelings. These might include: "What contact have you had with [*black*] people at your job or in your neighborhood?" or "Would you please describe your experiences with people of other [*racial*] groups?" Responses to questions of this type will give the Court and the attorneys a clearer picture of the degree to which a juror may be affected by [*racial*] prejudice and the juror's ability to fairly assess the facts presented in a case like this one, involving a [*black*] defendant.

30. Finally, voir dire questioning of individual prospective jurors out of the presence of other panelists can help to minimize the impact of many of the social psychological factors described above. Individual voir dire minimizes those problems in several ways: (a) a smaller "audience" reduces prospective jurors' concern for their peers' opinions of them; (b) questioning of jurors individually minimizes opportunities for jurors to pick up cues from others about socially approved responses; (c) prospective jurors will be less able to contrive to be either seated or excused because they will not have the opportunity to observe others being questioned; and finally, (d) the questioning of jurors out of the presence of others eliminates the possibility that panelists will be exposed to or "contaminated" by the prejudicial statements or revelations of other prospective jurors.[18]

*COMMENT:* Paragraphs 31–44 discuss death qualification. See §11.81.

. . .

[45]. I respectfully urge the Court to consider these issues in light of the seriousness of the charges that [*Mr. Sails*] faces in the present case.

The foregoing is true and correct to the best of my knowledge.

DATED: [*December 6, 1982*] ______________________

DR. CRAIG HANEY

---

1. Based on surveys conducted in connection with criminal proceedings in the following jurisdictions: Sonoma County, California; Walla Walla County, Washington; Prince Georges County, Maryland; Spokane County, Washington; Middlesex County, New Jersey; Monterey County, California; Newark, New Jersey; El Paso, Texas; Northern District of California; Suffolk County, Massachusetts; Berks County, Pennsylvania; Lehigh County, Pennsylvania; Southern District of New York, and others.

2. "The Public Image of the Courts: Highlights of a National Survey of the General Public, Judges, Lawyers and Community Leaders," prepared for the National Center for State Courts by Yankelovich, Skelley and White, Inc. (March 1978), p.6.

3. Turner, Charles, "Tabulation of Attitude Data on Criminal Justice Issues from a National Survey," Washington, D.C., National Research Council—National Academy of Sciences, unpublished manuscript (June 1979).

4. See, e.g., Strawn, D., and R. Buchanan, "Jury Confusion: A Threat to Justice," 59 *Judicature* 478 (1976) (50 percent of instructed jurors did not understand that the defendant did not have to present evidence of innocence); Sales, B.D., et al., *Making Jury Instructions Understandable* (1982) (average comprehension level among 1000 jurors of attempted murder trial instructions was 51 percent). The subjects in both studies cited here were actual jurors.

5. E.g., Mischel, W., *Personality and Assessment* (1968); Sarbin, T., "Contextualism: A world view for modern psychology," in J. Cole, ed., *Nebraska Symposium on Motivation* (1976).

6. Asch, S.E., "The effects of group pressure upon the modification and distortion of judgments," in H. Guetzkow, ed., *Groups, Leadership and Men* (Carnegie Press, 1951).

7. For a discussion of the effect that perceived consequences have on the attitudes and beliefs, see Collins, B., and Hoyt, M., "Personal responsibility for consequences; An integration of the forced compliance literature," *Experimental Social Psychology* 558–593 (1972).

8. Arkin, R.M., et al., "Social anxiety, self-presentation and the self-serving bias in causal attribution," 38 *J Personality and Social Psychology* 23 (1980).

9. E.g., "Judges' Non-verbal Behavior in Jury Trial: A Threat to judicial impartiality," 6 *Va L Rev* 1226 (1975).

10. E.g., Rosenberg, M., "When dissonance fails: On eliminating evaluation apprehension from attitude measurement," *J Personality and Social Psychology* 28 (1965).

11. On how knowledge about the beliefs of others affects our own attitudes and beliefs, see, Haney, C., "Consensus information and attitude change: Modifying the effects of counter-attitudinal behavior with information about the behavior of others," *J Personality and Social Psychology* (in press).

12. Marlowe, D., and Crowne, D., "Social desirability and response to perceived situational demands," 25 *J Consulting Psychology* 109 (1968).

13. See Hare, A. Paul, *Handbook of Small Group Research* (Free Press, 1976), and studies cited therein.

14. E.g., Festinger, L., "A theory of social comparison processes, 7 *Human Relations* 117 (1954); Schacter, S., *The Psychology of Affiliation* (1959).

15. For a general discussion of people's inability to identify or specify accurately the various factors that influence and affect their thoughts and actions, see Nisbett and Wilson, "Telling more than we can know: Verbal reports on mental processes," 84 *Psychological Rev* 231 (1977).
16. Brigham, Woodmansee, and Cook, "Dimensions of Verbal Racial Attitudes; Interracial Marriage and Approaches to Equality," *J. Social Issues* 9–12 (1976).
17. Id. at 9–11.
18. Cf. Neitzel and Dillehay, "The effects of variations in voir dire procedures in capital murder trials," *Law & Human Behavior* (in press). This study suggests that individual voir dire is a far more effective procedure for uncovering serious biases and prejudices that lead to successful cause challenges.

## b. In Highly Publicized Cases

### (1) On Jurors' Lying about Prejudice §8.81

*Source:* Direct examination of Dr. Jay Schulman, sociologist, by attorney John Thorne of San Jose, during hearing in support of defendants' motion to permit counsel to conduct voir dire examination and to conduct it individually outside the presence of other prospective jurors, because of prejudice against Native Americans, *United States v Baker* (WD SD, No. Cr. 73-5021, 1974).

**Q.** Do you have any figures on the number of people who said they were unaware of the events at Wounded Knee and did not follow the events in South Dakota and Minnesota?

**A.** Well I should point out that we have done two surveys. I and a group of people working with me have done a survey on the Southern Judicial District of South Dakota and the Third Judicial District of Minnesota. And in the Southern Judicial District of South Dakota 95 percent of the sample that we talked with were aware of the events at Wounded Knee and had followed them carefully. It's something like 75 percent of the people in the Third Judicial District of Minnesota. Now the importance of this information is that when Judge Nichol, for example, interrogated the people in the Third District, only perhaps 40 percent of the people said that they had followed the case closely and were aware of the events at Wounded Knee. There is then a discrepancy of some 35 percent which needs to be dealt with, and many of these people in my judgment, were saying that they did not have an awareness of the events at Wounded Knee because they wanted to serve on a jury .... One-third of the people we have interviewed say that they lied during the voir dire; deliberately lied.

**Q.** You mean they consciously told you—

**A.** Consciously lied under oath.

. . .

**Q.** Assuming prejudiced persons versus nonprejudiced persons in any given area, do you have an opinion as to whether or not those persons who have prejudice tend to deliberately consciously lie about the existence of prejudice over persons who do not have prejudice?

**A.** Well this is also a complicated question. People who are highly prejudiced either way, for or against the government; for or against black people; for or against Indian people are more likely to lie about the absence of such prejudice than people who do not feel that they have prejudice. So that people who are prejudiced one way or the other, are more likely to lie, saying that they do not have a prejudice. The other side of the coin is, that people who tend to be fair-minded are much more likely to bring to the attention of the court the fact that they may have a bias, and therefore are more likely to be excused for cause than people who oftentimes in fact have prejudice.

For the trial judge's decision on the extent of voir dire following this hearing, see §8.90.

In his extensive study of midwestern civil and criminal jury trials, Professor Dale Broeder uncovered numerous instances of jurors who did not answer voir dire questions entirely truthfully. See Broeder, "Voir Dire Examinations: An Empirical Study," 38 *S Cal L Rev* 503, 506, 511, 512 (1965).

### (2) On Prejudice against Defendant as One of Group §8.82

An unusual problem arose in the case of Steven Soliah in terms of the group to whom he was linked in the press. He was indicted for the April 2, 1975, robbery of a Carmichael, California, bank in which a bank customer was killed by a shotgun blast fired by one of the robbers. Soliah had achieved national fame when he was arrested with Patricia Hearst. Numerous news stories appeared, linking him with the Symbionese Liberation Army or the Carmichael bank robbery and discussing in detail his romantic involvement with Hearst. Federal Judge Thomas MacBride conducted an extensive voir dire examination, and allowed the attorneys to participate in the questioning, which lasted four weeks. The jurors were sequestered during the four-week trial and acquitted Soliah of all charges. Jurors told defense counsel later that they had stood eight-to-four for acquittal at the outset. The group dynamic leading to unanimous vote for acquittal arose out of the harmonious relations developed during sequestration and the jurors' desire to have them continue. *United States v Soliah* (ED Cal, No. S 75–523, Apr. 21, 1975). Soliah's attorneys were Sheldon Otis and Steffan Imhoff of San Francisco, assisted by Emily DeFala, Kit Delicos, Marsha Greenfield, and members of the National Jury Project led by Neal Bush and Beth Bonora.

*Source:* Excerpts from affidavit of Dr. Alice Marie Padawer-Singer, January 4, 1976, *United States v Soliah*, on results of prejudicial pretrial publicity on prospective jurors, submitted in support of motion for change of venue.

III. Sensational pretrial publicity, which links the defendant with people who are "cold blooded murderers," "revolutionaries," etc., changes the way jurors perceive a defendant, reduces the credibility of the defendant and raises the resistance of jurors to anything said by or on behalf of the defendant. It predisposes jurors to see the defendant as guilty and to vote for guilty in jury deliberations.

PREJUDICIAL PRETRIAL PUBLICITY LINKING THE DEFENDANT WITH OTHER DEFENDANTS ACCUSED OF OTHER CRIMES, WITH GROUPS SUCH AS THE SLA, PRECLUDES THE POSSIBILITY THAT STEVEN SOLIAH CAN RECEIVE A FAIR AND IMPARTIAL TRIAL IN THE EASTERN DISTRICT OF CALIFORNIA

**Ways in which some articles are written make it arduous without rereading to reconstitute the events and to distinguish in many articles which crimes are discussed, who are the defendants in these cases, which are (in reality) separate cases.** Upon reading at a normal pace, the effect is that every person mentioned was involved in each of the crimes. In the usual scanning of everyday newspaper reading, these separate items mesh so that each defendant is perceived as guilty of more crimes than he is accused of in reality. For instance the article in the *Sacramento Union* on September 20, 1975, under one headline "Court Revokes Patty Hearst's Bail," discusses the following: Patty Hearst and charges against her, articles found in the Harrises' home, arraignment of the Harrises, arraignment of Wendy Yoshimura and charges against her, arrests of Soliah, Soliah's sister Kathy, "a known revolutionary," then back to Hearst's encounter with her mother, etc.

**It is my opinion that the association of the name of Steven Soliah with the SLA, the Harrises, Patty Hearst, Kathy Soliah, and others makes a profound negative impression on the persons in the Eastern District of California who may be called to jury duty. Such pairing prejudices the credibility of statements which may be made by or on behalf of Steven Soliah.** An experiment on the effect of pairing pictures of faces demonstrated that the impression of a particular face and consequently of a person changed radically depending on the type of pairing. (Cline, "The Influence of Social Context on the Perception of Faces," 25 *J Personality* 142 (1956).) "A person's facial expression (and to generalize his behavior in general) are perceived to reflect underlying characteristics, but always in reference to the total context in which these expressions occur." (Jones and Gerard, *Foundations of Social Psychology* (1967).) People assign characteristics to others and generalize about others on the basis of a few salient points made about that person.

**Negative characteristics said about other defendants, persons in the SLA linked to Soliah in the news media, and about Soliah himself further prejudice Soliah's credibility.** A classical psychological study (Asch, "The Doctrine of Suggestion, Prestige and Imitation in Social Psychology," 55 *Psych*

*Rev* 250 (1958)) demonstrated that the meaning of a statement as perceived by an audience, changes depending on who purportedly made that statement. Other classic, well-known, and highly respected studies on first impression formation (Asch, "Forming Impressions of Personality," 41 *J Abnormal & Soc Psych* 258 (1946); Kelley, "The Warm-Cold Variable in First Impressions of Persons," 18 *J Personality* 431 (1950); Anderson and Barrios, "Primacy Effects in Personality Impression Formation," 63 *J Abnormal & Soc Psych* 346 (1961)) showed that people attribute different characteristics to a person when good qualities about that person are mentioned first before negative qualities than when negative qualities precede good ones. The early impressions bias the interpretation of later statements and facts. Examples abound in the press of prejudicial characterization: "From Patty Hearst to Tania the Teenage Terrorist" in the *Sacramento Union*, September 19, 1975; "Soliah's sister Kathy a known revolutionary," September 20, 1975, *Sacramento Union*; Soliah's sisters described as "armed and dangerous," September 22, 1975, *Sacramento Union*; the pairing of headlines on September 24 reading: "Patty Tells of Fantasy and Terror" and underneath "Patty Says She Lived with Steven Soliah," etc. This type of pairing distorts the perceptions of the public and makes Steven Soliah look guilty. It is similar to the method used by advertising agencies (but for different purposes and in the opposite direction) in pairing a pretty girl with a facial cream advertised for its power of rejuvenation.

**Fear-appeals, appeals to the bizarre, descriptions of sex practices not generally accepted countrywide generate fear of the defendants in the public and intense dislike which further prejudice the presentation of the case on behalf of Steven Soliah.** On September 18 the *Sacramento Union* called the arrests of Patricia Hearst, Steven Soliah, William and Emily Harris, and Wendy Yoshimura "bizarre," the *Bee* called it a "bizarre kidnap-crime wave." The characterization of bizarre referring to the crimes and to the defendants, heightens prejudices of many in the population who distrust strangers, unknown people who are different from them. The ingroup-outgroup distinction thus becomes the basis "for most of the social thinking of the ethnocentric individual." "A primary characteristic of ethnocentric ideology is the 'generality' of outgroup rejection." (Levinson, "The Study of Ethnocentric Ideology," in *The Authoritarian Personality* (Adorno et al. eds. 1969).)

Additional research data have observed that attraction is influenced by similarity: racial similarity, attitudinal similarities, membership group similarity, etc. (Byrne, "Interpersonal Attraction and Attitude Similarity," 62 *J Abnormal & Soc Psych* 713 (1961); Byrne, "Interpersonal Attraction as a Function of Affiliation Need and Attitude Similarity," 14 *Human Relations* 283 (1961); Byrne et al., "Effect of Economic Similarity—Dissimilarity on Interpersonal Attraction," 4 *J Personality & Soc Psych* 220 (1966); McWhirter and Jecker, "Attitude Similarity and Inferred Attraction," 1 *Psychonomic Sci* 225 (1967); Byrne and McGraw, "Interpersonal Attraction Toward Negroes," 17 *Human Relations* 201 (1964); Byrne and Wong, "Racial Prejudice, Interpersonal Attraction and Assumed Dissimilarity of Attitudes," 65 *J Abnormal & Soc Psych* 246 (1962); Byrne and Ervin, "Attraction Toward a Negro Stranger as a Function of Prejudice, Attitude Similarity and the Stranger's Evaluation of the Subject," 22 *Human Relations* 397 (1969); Smith, "Similarity of Values and Its Relation to Acceptance and the Projection of Similarity," 43 *J Psych* 251 (1957); Smith et al., "Race, Sex and Beliefs as Determinants of Friendship Acceptance," 5 *J Personality & Soc Psych* 127 (1967).)

The fear appeals such as mentioning the neighbors' request for anonymity reported in the *Sacramento Union* on October 2, the pairing of the *Bee*'s headline "Harrises Linked to Bomb Attempt on S.F. Police Car" with a picture of Steven Soliah below, September 21, the mention in "The Private Life of Patty Hearst" (National Mirror, Inc.) that "A check on the backgrounds of all the known SLA members clearly indicates that they were a little out of step with the rest of humanity.

If they weren't sexually abnormal, they were emotionally unstable, guilt-ridden or like de Freeze, violent and dangerous," or the enumeration of characteristics of Patty Hearst:

> HER HANG UP FOR SEX, DRUGS AND VIOLENCE
> PATTY'S LOVE AFFAIR AT SIXTEEN
> FROM KIDNAP VICTIM TO SLA MISTRESS
> WHY PATTY WANTED TO KILL HER MOTHER
> WHY PATTY HID OUT IN A LESBIAN COMMUNE, etc.,

and many other examples of prejudicial publicity in Appendix B constitute prejudicial materials of the most virulent sort since they appeal to a variety of prejudices and arouse fear in the public.

Such strong emotions hinder the power to think and evaluate evidence clearly, as required of jurors. This may operate on the conscious and the unconscious level. For instance a juror may sincerely believe that he is not prejudiced since his views coincide with those generally held in his community. "A Southern White whose attitudes towards Negroes coincide with those of his reference group does not see himself as prejudiced." (Jones and Gerard, *Foundations of Social Psychology* (1967).) Other psychological studies report that greater persuasion follows when the impression is given of having "overheard" something, an impression given by newspapers when they allude to sources not identified (see Appendix B). (Walster and Festinger, "The Effectiveness of 'Overheard' Persuasive Communications," 65 *J Abnormal & Soc Psych* 395 (1962).) Once a belief sets in on the basis of various messages, greater resistance to change or to be persuaded in the opposite direction takes place. (Janis et al., "Effects of Preparatory Communication on Reactions to a Subsequent News Event," 15 *Pub Op Q* 487 (1951).)

**Mentioning the sentences before the defendants have been tried and found guilty or not guilty is a strong form of prejudicial publicity.** It lends the impression that the defendants are indeed guilty. It gives a reference or "anchor," a standard against which to judge the defendants. For instance in the *Sacramento Union* of October 3, Dep. Dist. Atty. Samuel Mayerson is quoted as saying: "the counts of kidnaping and kidnaping for the purpose of robbery" carried the "possible maximum sentences of life imprisonment" but that was up to a jury and judge.

**The strongest form of present prejudicial publicity consists of reporting a fingerprint identification or an identification on the scene of the crime. [The above is sufficient ground for granting a change of venue.]** On October 30, the *Sacramento Union* reported that investigators "found Soliah's fingerprints on the licence plate of an automobile used in the Carmichael robbery." On the same day, U.S. Atty. Dwayne Keyes said, "Mr. Soliah was positively identified as being in the bank." This prejudicial type of publicity is similar to that studied in my research on Free Press–Fair Trial and in previous research as reported by Wilcox, *Free Press and Fair Trial* (Bush ed. 1970). Some of the findings in the Free Press–Fair Trial study are given below:

**SENSATIONAL PRETRIAL PUBLICITY AFFECTS JURORS' PERCEPTION AND BEHAVIOR AGAINST THE DEFENDANT**

1. More jurors who had been "exposed" to prejudicial publicity find the defendant *not sincere at all*.

| "Exposed" | "Not Exposed" |
|---|---|
| 43% | 29% |

2. More jurors report that newspaper accounts of a case are *discussed in deliberations* when these accounts contain prejudicial publicity.

| "Exposed" | "Not Exposed" |
|---|---|
| 49% | 33% |

3. More jurors report that *newspaper accounts influence other jurors against the defendants* when they have been exposed to prejudicial publicity.

| "Exposed" | "Not Exposed" |
|---|---|
| 22% | 10% |

4. Even when there is no motive for the crime mentioned in a trial, more jurors report they "know" the motive, when these jurors have read prejudicial pretrial publicity.

| "Exposed" | "Not Exposed" |
|---|---|
| 30% | 19% |

5. *More guilty votes and verdicts result* when jurors have been exposed to prejudicial pretrial publicity.

| "Exposed" | "Not Exposed" |
|---|---|
| 80% | 39% |

(Juries with guilty verdicts or final votes with majority for guilty)

Psychological Literature References re Voir Dire:

Kahn and Cannell, *The Dynamics of Interviewing* (1957).

Miller et al., "The Tendency to Agree: Situational Determinants and Social Desirabilty," *J Experimental Research in Personality*, Oct. 1965, p. 78.

Crowne and Marlowe, *The Approval Motive: Studies in Evaluative Dependence* (1964).

Gordon, *Interviewing: Strategy, Techniques, and Tactics* (1975).

Richardson et al., *Interviewing, Its Forms and Functions* (1963).

Maller, "The Effect of Signing One's Name," 3 *Schools & Soc'y* 882 (1930).
Lambert et al., "Evaluational Reactions to Spoken Languages," 60 *J Abnormal & Soc Psych* 44 (1960).
Anisfeld et al., "Evaluational Reactions to Accented English Speech," 65 *J Abnormal & Soc Psych* 223 (1962).

### (3) On Obstacles to Discovering Jurors' Predispositions §8.83

*Source:* Excerpts from affidavit of Hans Zeisel, dated July 3, 1974, *In Re Coordinated Pretrial Proceedings in Antibiotic Antitrust Action* (D Minn 1974) 410 F Supp 659.

6. The more important issue is the degree of depth to be allowed in the questioning. At this point, it will be helpful to consider the obstacles in the path of efforts to discover the true predispositions of a juror. There are several types of obstacles to such discovery and they will vary in seriousness with the nature of the case, with the parties involved, and with other circumstances.

The first obstacle is the self-esteem of a juror who, not unnaturally, likes to think of himself or herself as able to be fair and impartial. Barring, therefore, extraordinarily clear situations to the contrary, such as knowing one of the litigants, or having had a bad personal experience with the very same issue, jurors will automatically answer in the affirmative a general question as to their ability to be fair and impartial.

The second obstacle is prevarication, if the juror either desires to serve on the case or would like to be released. His answer as to fairness and impartiality may then be determined by such a desire rather than by what the juror knows to be the truth.

The third obstacle, and often the most serious one, is the juror's genuine inability to gauge the extent of his or her own prejudice. The juror may deny in good faith any prejudice until he is confronted with certain searching questions that will reveal the true state of affairs to the juror as well as to the court.

7. How serious these three types of obstacles are will depend on the case and on the litigants, and on the composition of the particular jury venire. If case and litigants are simple and nondescript, and if one may assume therefore that there is little predisposition toward either side, the task of the voir dire proceedings may be simple too. But if this be a litigation in which the issue or the litigants or both have been in the limelight for some time; or if the issue or the litigants or both are likely to have touched the lives of the ordinary citizen in one way or another; or if the emotions of the jurors are likely to be affected differentially by the case; or if the nature of the predisposition is not pronounced and clear, but resides in deeper layers not easily discovered—if any or all of these circumstances pertain, the voir dire proceedings will serve their purpose only if they are conducted in some depth.

. . .

9. It is nevertheless true that the predispositions of the jurors will not come into play in every jury trial. As we mentioned before, in roughly one-third of all cases, the evidence is so clear that the jury's first ballot is tantamount to its verdict, in spite of differences in predispositions that may have existed among the jurors. These predispositions are likely to come into play only in cases where the evidence is not completely clear, but to some extent contradictory.

The closer a case is to the fifty-fifty line from which, in theory, the preponderance of the evidence is to be gauged, that is, the smaller the preponderance of the evidence is, the greater will be the role of the juror predispositions in the formulation of the verdict. But since, as a rule, it is not possible to say in advance how clear or how close the trial evidence will be, it is the better part of wisdom to be prepared for the close case and to select the jury accordingly with care, so that jurors with extreme predispositions can be discovered.

Additional excerpts from Professor Zeisel's affidavit are in §8.85.

### c. In Many Cases

#### (1) On Individual Questioning Being More Effective §8.85

*Source:* Excerpts from affidavit of Hans Zeisel, dated July 3, 1974, *In Re Coordinated Pretrial Proceedings in Antibiotic Antitrust Action* (1974) 410 F Supp 659.

HANS ZEISEL, being first duly sworn, deposes and says:

1. I am Emeritus Professor of Law and Sociology at the University of Chicago Law School. I am co-author with Professor Harry Kalven, Jr., of *The American Jury* (1966), the standard work on the operation of our jury system.

Since the publication of that volume I have continued my studies of the jury system and of the various modifications of it that have come into operation. In particular I have been studying also the problem of juror selection. I am presently engaged in a study of the jury selection process in Cook County, [Illinois,] comparing the procedures in the federal court with those in the state court.

Following is a list of my subsequent publications on various aspects of the jury system:

*Some Data on Juror Attitudes towards Capital Punishment*, Center for Studies in Criminal Justice, the University of Chicago, 1968.

"Dr. Spock and the Case of the Vanishing Women Jurors," 37 *University of Chicago Law Review* 1-18 (1969).

"Jury," *Encyclopedia Britannica* (with Harry Kalven, Jr.) 1971.

" . . . And Then There Were None: the Diminution of the Federal Jury," 38 *University of Chicago Law Review* 710-724 (1972).

*Six-Man Juries, Majority Verdicts—What Difference Do They Make?*

Occasional Papers from the Law School of the University of Chicago (1973).

" 'Convincing Empirical Evidence' on the Six-Member Jury" (with Shari S. Diamond), 41 *University of Chicago Law Review* 281-295 (1974).

Bradford L. Ferguson, Esq., a member of the law firm of Dorsey, Marquart, Windhorst, West & Holliday, of Minneapolis, Minnesota, approached me and asked whether I would give him my expert opinion of the merits and likely effects of the various modes of conducting the voir dire proceedings prior to the empaneling of the jury. What follows is this opinion.

2. The primary determinant of the verdicts our juries render is the evidence presented to them; more precisely, the evidence as the individual jurors perceive it. This is to say that not all jurors will perceive the evidence in the same way. This is so because jurors bring different experiences and values with them into the court. The fact that only about one-third of all first ballots are unanimous is clear proof that often the very same "evidence" is perceived or evaluated differently by different jurors. If no such differences existed, one juror would be as good as twelve or six. The system thus expects and even appreciates this variety of experiences, values and perceptions of the individual jurors—but only up to a point.

. . .

4. The traditional means of discovering the jurors who hold extreme positions is to have them answer certain questions. The method of questioning varies in our courts along two dimensions: first, and most importantly, it differs as to the type and number of questions the jurors will be asked; they may be few in number and more or less stereotyped—or they may be numerous and go into detail and depth. The other dimension is the mode of questioning—who will be the questioner, and how will the questions be asked? The judge may be the questioner or it may be counsel, or it may be the judge supplemented by counsel; also, jurors may be questioned en bloc or individually, and in the latter case, they may be questioned in the courtroom or in chambers.

5. As to the mode of questioning, I have a firm view on but one aspect of it: Individual questioning of each juror will more effectively elicit the desired true answer than en-bloc questioning. As to whether it is better to interview the juror in chambers (as it was done in the Mitchell-Stans trial) or in open court, must depend on the degree of privacy the questions deemed necessary are likely to touch on. I do not know as yet for sure whether the widely prevalent notion that the lawyers are bound to be more effective in asking questions than the judge is correct. But it is of some interest to note that a recently voted-on change of the constitution of the State of Connecticut made it impossible for a court to abridge the right of counsel to conduct his own voir dire in state court trials.

. . .

Executed July 3, 1974 at Chicago, Illinois.

[Signed] Hans Zeisel
Declarant

An additional excerpt from Professor Zeisel's affidavit is in §8.83.

### (2) On Questioning Jurors Privately §8.86

*Source:* Excerpts from study by Hans Zeisel with Shari Siedman Diamond on the *Mitchell-Stans* trial, "The Jury Selection in the Mitchell-Stans Conspiracy Trial," 1 *Am B Foundation Research J* 151, 155–156 (1976):

Altogether, 38 prospective jurors were excused for evidence of prejudice; 16 during the public en banc phase of questioning. Of these, 12 prospective jurors confessed to some sort of prejudice, while for 2 the prejudice was inferred: 1 had been found guilty of unlawful refusal to testify before a grand jury, and the other reported he had been "harassed by the FBI."

Although the public questioning gave ample opportunity to the prospective jurors to confess prejudice, the private, individual questioning elicited prejudice in 22 more cases, one and a half times as many as had been excused during the public questioning. Prejudice was inferred for two of these jurors: one juror's close relative had been investigated by the state prosecutor; another juror was a member of Common Cause, an organization that had filed a civil suit against one of the defendants.

In three excuses, one during the public phase and two during the private one, the "cause" appeared somewhat remote. One woman had first claimed hardship for fear that a prolonged absence might create difficulties in her job. The judge suggested that she try to resolve them by talking to her employer, which she was able to do. But when the marshal, who had overheard her saying on the telephone to her employer, "Yes, I should like to serve as juror on this case," reported this remark to the court, the juror was excused. The other two prospective jurors were excused because they disliked hunting and because Mr. Stans was a hunter.

The excuses for hardship, incapacity, and prejudice, and the dismissal of 9 supernumerary jurors, left 52 prospective jurors in the panel from which the two sides were to exercise their peremptory challenges.

*COMMENT:* For a discussion of the Supreme Court's new rules for protection of press freedom and juror privacy, see *Press-Enterprise Co. v Superior Court* (1984) 104 S Ct 819, discussed in §8.44.

### (3) On Prejudice against Black People §8.87

*Source:* Testimony of Dr. William Pierce in hearing on defendant's motion to allow counsel for defendant to participate in voir dire, Mar. 29, 1973, denied after hearing, *United States v McNeil* (1973) 357 F Supp 342 (see §§3.51, 8.90).

**Q.** I asked you about social desirability. Maybe you will explain that term.
**A.** Yes. It simply means that people tend to answer in a socially acceptable

manner whether or not they are aware that they're doing this or not . . . especially in public where their answers are heard by people that they don't know.

**Q.** Could you give us an example of a situation where a person would be more likely or less likely to verbalize his prejudices?

. . .

**A.** . . . [I]t would be clear that if a person was in a room with people of different ethnic backgrounds and a highly charged issue such as race was brought up, that they would tend to make their answers more socially acceptable, independent of what their conscious attitude about it was, negative or positive.

**Q.** Well, let me give you a hypothetical, then, Doctor.

Assume a jury trial, 12 jurors and the defendant is on trial for gambling. A question is posed to the group as a whole: Do you hold any prejudices against gambling?

Now, is that, in your mind, any different than a situation where you have a black defendant in, let's say, a draft case, and the question is posed to the jury: Do you have any prejudice against black people?

. . .

**A.** Yes, I think there is a very real difference there. The content of the question is very important. For instance, if there are socially acceptable positions, pro and con, on an issue like gambling, one would not be in a stressful situation to answer or to hide his answer, since it's acceptable to be for gambling or it's acceptable not to be for gambling. However, in the other incident where race is an issue, obviously it's less socially acceptable, given the spirit of the time or whatever one wants to call it, to say that I am a racist or to say that I have negative feelings about a member of a cultural group.

In essence, then, it depends on the content, and whether that content has appropriate freedom for one to be positive and negative without the indication of social disapproval or social ostracizing.

. . .

**Q.** Assume a case where there are 12 white jurors; assume further that we have a black defendant, and assume also that the heart of the case is the defendant's own credibility, and that the defendant takes the stand.

Now, would the defendant's race be an important factor in the jury's determination of the evidence?

**A.** Yes, I would think it certainly would be, given what I have said before, that people do hold certain stereotypes or prejudices, that person . . . would have a very high profile, obviously, because he is a sinner now, sit him down and he is on the stand. Therefore, his race would have a very high stimulus value which would tend to pull on attitudes and prejudices and stereotypes that people may have. Interestingly enough, it's not . . . only whether or not that person is nominated as a particular ethnic group; in other words, it's not just enough to see that person is black or Chicano or Asian or white, people tend to respond on a covert level to physical features, so that whether or not that person is light-skinned or dark-skinned, whether or not that person has a heavy Afro-American style hair-do or close-cropped hair, whether or not that hair tends to be more wavy or more kinky, whether that person's lips tend to be broad or thin, whether their nose tends to be wide or narrow, these are also variables that pull for people's attitudes and stereotypes, their myths, their socially reinforced misconceptions of another ethnic group.

**Q.** All right. Going right along with the same hypothetical: Assume that the black defendant's major witnesses were also black. Would that factor be an important situational factor in this case?

**A.** It certainly would be, based on much of what I have just said. What would be in operation for that black defendant would also be in operation for other black people that would come up, and it would probably have an accumulative effect rather than an isolated one.

**Q.** All right.

Can racial stereotypes, in your opinion, affect a juror's deliberations once he walks into the jury room itself?

**A.** [O]nce the door is closed it becomes a little bit less public. So we have to make that distinction, I think between public and private. On the other hand, I think that it's important also to note that just the attitudes and prejudices and stereotypes that may be either triggered off or maintained by the person anyway are going to affect his decision. I have already stated just physical features can be an important factor in one's perception of another person. That perception automatically is going to have some influence, whatever, on his decision-making abilities about it, because it's going to prevent him, on the one hand, from seeing things more objectively. It's going to enhance, on the other, and reinforce his already frame of reference about that particular ethnic group.

**Q.** . . . My last question to you is this: In your opinion, can a juror, a white juror holding racial stereotypes, be a fair juror in certain circumstances?

**A.** I think that we have to take into consideration two things. One, that there is a level of racial and ethnic feelings that we all have about other groups of people.

Two. In what way does this interfere with one's ability to be able to be objective more or less about what's presented to him in terms of information. I think to me that's the important issue, not whether people have racism or stereotypes, we know they do. To the extent that one of any race, and this is in the question of a white person, can minimize the interference of stereotypical thinking, prejudice or racism, to the greater extent, he can become a more impartial and objective person on the jury. The answer is yes.

**Cross-examination by Mr. Carey:**

. . .

**Q.** Let me pose to you a hypothetical question:

If you have 12 white jurors and one black defendant, isn't it also possible that in the consideration of the evidence the fact of the defendant's race might help him obtain a more favorable verdict than he otherwise would?

**A.** Yes. I think that's possible in terms of how people would react contemporarily to the issue of race. As a matter of fact, a student of mine just completed a study that indicated that probably in present day, whites are less likely and willing to present their honest views about black people probably because of the racial situation.

Now, that would imply, I think that there would be certain people who may tend to feel guilt, feel a certain sense of responsibility for the social injustices to black people that would tend to, in an emotional way, respond rather than in an objective way. I would think that that would be a concern in a voir dire, for instance, . . . for [the] prosecution . . . to voir dire, to see that they were not getting people who were that emotionally involved so that they could not hear the evidence correctly.

So I think the answer to the question is that it could be possible, yes.

## C. Results of Hearings on Motions for Extensive Voir Dire §8.90

In two federal cases in which counsel filed pretrial motions seeking to participate directly in extensive voir dire, the results are inconclusive for reasons unrelated to the motions, since defendants won on legal issues before trial commenced, once after and once before jury selection.

In *United States v McNeil* (see §3.51), the trial judge granted a hearing on the motion. The hearing, involving three defense witnesses, took approximately four hours (see excerpts from testimony of expert witness, §8.87). The judge wrote a four-page opinion denying the motion (ND Cal 1973) 357 F Supp 342. Thereafter, the defense submitted 150 questions, many asked in the *Newton* (see §3.22) and *Pentagon Papers* (see §3.52) cases, and a few original ones (see chapter 9). The prosecution filed a list of five questions.

The spirit in which the judge conducted the voir dire was perhaps as important as the actual questions asked. He did ask many questions individually, and he returned to this practice at the suggestion of defense counsel whenever he strayed from it on important issues. He did express concern that each juror speak individually about his or her own feelings, and he repeatedly said that it was important for the jurors to think deeply about the questions and to answer them fully and truthfully. At the conclusion of a series of questions, the judge did turn to counsel and ask whether there were additional questions they wanted asked. Frequently there were two or three, and, as often happens, defense counsel ended up actually facing the jurors as they formally asked the judge to repeat their questions to the jurors.

Early in the voir dire the defendant, who was charged with refusal to be drafted during the Vietnam war, reached the conclusion that two of the prospective jurors were racists and would have to be removed from the jury, although their answers would not have justified challenges for cause. After four hours of voir dire, both men asked to be excused on the ground that they could not be impartial about someone who had not done his duty in the armed services, as both of them had done. They did not admit that they were racially prejudiced against the black defendant. The judge congratulated them on their honesty and thanked them for stepping down. This led others in the jury box to take the same step later. It was not a universal teacher, however: one employee of a weapons development agency refused to disqualify himself and had to be excused peremptorily.

The voir dire consumed approximately six hours, longer than customary in that jurisdiction. Although no blacks were seated on the jury destined to try a black draft refuser, one alternate was black, and the defense team was not displeased with the jury.

In *United States v Baker*, the hearing on defendants' motion for extensive voir dire by counsel covered 119 transcript pages, including expert testimony (see §8.45). Judge Warren K. Urbom issued a very valuable bench opinion allowing six hours (two for government, four for defense) for voir dire to select 12 jurors and 3 alternates.

**The Court:** Before this hearing I held a conference with counsel, and at that time made a rather full statement of the competing factors which seemed to me to be at war with one another in a motion such as this . . . .

Having heard this very interesting testimony my attitude remains the same. I think that a part of the voir dire in a case in which these two defendants are members of a minority race, and there is involved an incident receiving widespread publicity that there is a different flavor than in other cases. That doesn't mean it is altogether different, but there is a different flavor. Because of that I intend to grant to counsel a limited right to conduct voir dire examination of prospective jurors. I say limited because, although an argument has been made, and properly can be made, that time ought to be of no consequence, I think it is a matter of consequence. I think the fact that we have well over 100 cases now pending out of this Wounded Knee incident necessarily means that time is a factor. On a broader scale I think that time is a factor even if those 100 cases did not exist, for the ponderous movement of cases through the courts is and has long been a concern, not merely to the people involved in the trial, not merely the courts—the citizenry at large.

Cases should move deliberately but they should move with a fair balance of thoroughness, striving for perfection and a time limitation . . . . I will make a rather full explanation of the way the voir dire will be conducted, and that will stand as a ruling on the motion, in a sense a qualified granting of the motion, and in a sense an overruling of the motion.

There will be three alternate jurors selected. The United States will have 6 peremptory challenges; the defendants jointly will have 10. We will call 35 jurors, seating them in a manner which I have outlined . . . . There will be 15 in the jury box. There will be 5 in chairs directly in front of the jury box, parallel to the jury box. There will be 8 along and in front of the railing, . . . 7 along the right-hand . . . . That will comprise 35. Those will be the 35 from whom peremptory challenges will be made, if there are no challenges for cause sustained. There will be 15 additional prospective jurors seated in the first row of the spectators' seats. That makes a total of 50; and those entire 50 will be selected by lot at the outset. Then the judge will conduct the voir dire at its beginning covering such subjects as these: The occupation, the residence, spouse, spouse's occupation, children, education of the prospective juror, past service of the prospective juror as a juror; acquaintanceship, if any, with the lawyers and the defendants, acquaintanceship, if any, with any known prospective witnesses, involvement in any past criminal charge, political affiliation, religious affiliation, relationship with the United States, that is, law enforcement officers and other relationship[s] touching the general relationship with the United States; some but not detailed questions about relationship to Wounded Knee affair; but the subjects of possible racial prejudice and pretrial publicity will either not be touched or will be touched lightly, but essentially will be left to counsel.

Then counsel will be permitted to conduct voir dire . . . under these limitations:

[First,] the Court reserves the prerogative of intercepting any question or line of questions which the Court concludes are calculated, whether deliberately or otherwise, to build with the juror and the counsel, or the juror and any party, whether the United States or the defendant, a special rapport relationship, thus creating the possibility of being favorably inclined to a party or unfavorably inclined to a party.

Secondly, the voir dire will be conducted in the presence of prospective jurors who have been identified . . . as being one of the initial 35 called, may be examined individually, but in the presence of . . . the remainder of the 50 who at that stage are still among the prospective jurors.

Third, counsel will be limited by time, a predetermined time. Within that time frame counsel may conduct their examination as they choose. By that I mean they may interview a specific juror or the whole panel [of 35] massively, as they choose . . . or any of those 35 who have been replaced by one or more of the 15 in excess of the 35 initially identified because of excuse for cause. But at the end of that predetermined time period counsel's questioning will cease. The Court may then conduct further examination if the Court chooses to do so. Counsel may submit additional questions they may have for the judge's deciding whether those questions will be asked or not by the judge. At the end of that questioning challenges for cause as to those in the group of 35 will be made and ruled upon; and as to any challenges which then are sustained, persons from the additional 15 sitting behind the railing . . . will fill in, in the order in which they were called . . . . Then counsel may question those jurors who replace ones excused for cause for a predetermined time period, and the Court may conduct such further examination it chooses of those jurors; then challenges for cause will be entertained and ruled upon as to those persons. If additional jurors are needed they then will be identified and called from the entire panel by lot, and a similar questioning process will go on as to them.

. . . I shall allow the United States with respect to questioning the 35 a total of 2 hours. I shall allow the defendants collectively—the same will be true if there is only one defendant—4 hours.

With respect to the amount of time that will be permitted counsel to examine persons called to replace someone challenged successfully for cause, or excused for cause, . . . I shall at this moment leave rather unresolved, although . . . that means approximately 7 minutes for the defense counsel per juror, and half that for the Government; but I suspect we can better come to a positive decision on how specifically to handle that when we know better exactly what we are faced with in terms of numbers.

. . . The United States will be permitted 2 peremptory challenges with respect to alternates; defendants collectively 2. Obviously if there is an excuse for cause from that 7, again they will be filled from the 15 who sit behind the rail.

After issuing this opinion, the judge granted a pretrial motion to dismiss on legal grounds, foreclosing any validation of the procedure he proposed.

In *Wisconsin v Carothers*, described in §8.30, the trial judge (without a hearing) granted the defendant's motion for individualized voir dire out of the presence of other jurors; the voir dire took two weeks. Defense counsel was convinced that the intensive and lengthy voir dire produced different jurors than would have been selected by customary means. The trial ended in the defendant's acquittal.

## D. Recent Developments §8.95

See §8.9.

# Chapter 9

# *Basic Questions*


**I. Compilation of a Useful List**
A. Sources of Questions §9.1
B. Ways to Use List §9.2
C. Abbreviations Used §9.3
D. Common Areas of Inquiry §9.4
E. Number of Questions to Submit §9.5

**II. Preliminary Questions Concerning Each Juror**
A. Introductory Statement §9.7
B. Demographic §9.8
C. Relationship with Persons in Case
  1. To Parties and Witnesses §9.9
  2. To Counsel §9.10
D. Employment and Volunteer Work
  1. Employment Background §9.11
  2. Relationship to Intelligence Work and Classification System §9.12
  3. Relationship to Federal Government's Security Clearance Program §9.13
E. Connections with Law Enforcement Agencies §9.14
F. Jury Experience §9.15
G. Organizational Affiliations §9.16
H. Political Affiliations §9.17
I. Military Service §9.18
J. Additional Questions §9.19

**III. Most Damaging Features of Case §9.20**

**IV. Pretrial Publicity on Case**
A. Prior Discussions of Case §9.21
B. Prior Knowledge or Opinion of Case §9.22
C. Influence of Newspapers and Other News Media §9.23
D. Has Juror Been Touched by a Party's Demographic Study? §9.24
E. Recent Developments §9.25

**V. Racial or Ethnic Prejudgment**
A. Attitudes toward Black People
1. Feelings toward Black People in General §9.30
2. "Unfortunate Experience" with Black Person §9.31
3. Opinion on "Black Power" §9.32
4. Attitude on Children Having Black Friends §9.33
5. Parties Who Speak Different Language §9.34
B. Attitudes toward La Raza/Latino People §9.36
C. Attitudes toward Native Americans §9.38
1. In Overtly Political Cases §9.39
a. Attitudes toward Law Enforcement §9.40
b. Attitudes toward Native Americans' Reactions to Treaty Breaking §9.41
c. Attitudes toward Specific Incident §9.42
2. In Nonpolitical Cases §9.43
3. Native Americans Who Speak Different Language §9.44
D. Attitudes toward Racial Prejudice
1. Attitudes toward Commissions Reporting on Civil Disorders §9.46
2. Attitudes toward White Racism §9.47
3. Subjective and Objective Racism §9.48
4. Attitudes on Fair Housing §9.49
E. Recent Developments §9.50

**VI. Prejudgment of Women**
A. Women Parties §9.51
B. Lifestyles §9.52
C. When Rape Is an Issue §9.53

**VII. Attitudes toward Plaintiff or Defendant**
A. In General §9.56
B. Toward Party's Views on White Racism §9.57
C. Toward Party's Age §9.58
D. Toward Plaintiff's or Defendant's Organization
1. Knowledge or Opinion of Organization §9.59
2. Prejudice against Views of Organization §9.60

3. Views of Organization on War §9.61
4. Views on Boycotts by Organization §9.62
5. Views on Language Used by Organization §9.63
6. Knowledge and Opinion of Communist Party §9.64

E. Toward Party's Lifestyle §9.66
F. Toward Party's Religion §9.67
G. Recent Developments §9.68

**VIII. Attitudes toward Credibility of Witnesses**
A. Plaintiff or Defendant §9.70
B. Black Person §9.71
C. Law Enforcement Officer §9.72
D. Government Official §9.73
E. Other Witnesses §9.74
F. False Testimony §9.75
G. Evaluating Witness's Testimony §9.76
H. Eyewitness Identification §9.77
I. Recent Developments §9.78

**IX. Attitudes toward Police**
A. Questions on "Support Your Local Police" §9.80
B. In the Ghetto §9.81
C. Individual Police Officer and Juror §9.82
D. Recent Developments §9.83

**X. Attitudes toward Constitutional Rights**
A. Democratic Functioning of Government §9.85
B. Dissent and Militants §9.86
C. Right to Organize for Social Change or for Peace §9.87
D. Right to Bear Arms §9.88
E. Recent Developments §9.89

**XI. Individual Responsibility of Juror**
A. Attitudes toward Jury Trial §9.90
B. Juror's Confidence in Own Fairness §9.91
C. Would Juror Stand by Own Opinion? §9.92
D. Would Juror Fear Reaction If Verdict Goes One Way? §9.93
E. Jurors Taking Notes §9.94
F. Recent Developments §9.95

**XII. General Trial Problems**
A. Length of Case §9.96
B. Juror Health
1. General §9.97
2. Hearing §9.98

C. Juror Empathy and Emotion §9.99
D. Recent Developments §9.100

**XIII. Attorneys' Actions**
A. Role of Attorneys §9.102
B. Women Attorneys §9.103
C. FBI Activity §9.104

**XIV. Media Coverage and Court "Gag Rule" §9.105**

**XV. Final Questions**
A. Did Counsel Prejudice Juror against Party? §9.108
B. Next-to-Last Questions §9.109
C. Final Question §9.110

**XVI. Common Issues in Civil and Criminal Cases**
A. Multiple Plaintiffs or Defendants §9.115
B. Public Official Is Party §9.116
C. Homosexual Parties or Witnesses §9.117
 1. General Knowledge of Homosexuality §9.118
 2. Attitudes toward Homosexuality §9.119
 3. Terms §9.120
 4. Juror's Personal Contact with Homosexuals §9.121
 5. Believing Testimony of Homosexual §9.122
 6. Homosexuals and Public Accommodations and Facilities §9.123
 7. Armed Services §9.124
 8. Showing Affection in Public §9.125
 9. Gay Liberation Movement §9.126
 10. Openness/Closetry §9.127
 11. Demonstrations §9.128
 12. Sick, Immoral, and Unnatural §9.129
 13. Media and Pornography §9.130
D. Opponents of Nuclear War and Nuclear Power §9.131
 1. Nuclear War Protesters §9.132
 2. Nuclear Power Dangers §9.133
 3. Antinuclear/Antiwar Advocates §9.134
E. Anti-Klan/Anti-Nazi Parties §9.136
 1. KKK/Nazi Activities §9.137
 2. KKK/Nazi Policies §9.138
 3. Anti-Ku Klux Klan Act of 1871 §9.139
F. International Human Rights Law §9.140
G. Other Issues §9.145

## I. COMPILATION OF A USEFUL LIST

### A. Sources of Questions §9.1

The questions in this chapter provide a comprehensive, well-organized list for use in any case in which jury prejudgment is potentially a serious problem. The list is compiled from many civil and criminal sources: *California v Newton* (the Huey Newton murder trial, see §3.22), *United States v Russo* (the *Pentagon Papers* case, §3.52), *United States v Briggs* (the *Gainesville Eight* trial of Vietnam Veterans Against the War, see §3.53), *California v Burt* (one of the *Venceremos* trials, see §3.24), *California v Davis* (the *Angela Davis* case, see §3.23), *United States v Sherpix* (an obscene film trial, see §11.35), *United States v Ramos* (a case involving homosexual defendants, see §9.117), *Michigan v DeSaussure* (the *Detroit Black Panther* case, see §3.27), California state criminal cases involving Latino defendants, *Michigan v Jeanette Smith* (a case involving a battered wife defendant, see §11.51), *Brewster v Martin Marietta* (see §3.41), *Administrative Discharge Board in the Case of DK3 Tangela Gaskins* (a court-martial case, see §3.91), *Stokes v Detroit* (see §10.80), *United States v McNeil* (see §3.51), and *California v Block* (see §3.29).

The list includes some questions asked of grand jurors (under a former New York state statute permitting voir dire of grand jurors) in *New York v Shakur* (the *Panther 21* trial, see §3.25). Names of attorneys who handled these cases appear with the descriptions of the cases. Also included are comments made by attorney Theodore Koskoff to the American Trial Lawyers Association, and questions supplied by attorneys William Sebastian Moore, Dennis Roberts, James Herndon, Hugh M. Davis, Jr., Ernest Goodman, Richard Soble, Paul Harris, Edmundo Espinosa, Don C. Keenan, Louis S. Katz, Daniel Russo, David Weitzman, Warren Wilson, Ann Fagan Ginger, Priscilla Camp, and Gerri Russell. Professor Robert Blauner has suggested some open-ended questions to be used in place of the traditional adversary-type questions. Questions submitted by the prosecution in a few of these cases also appear.

All questions asked of one or more prospective trial jurors in the extensive and intensive voir dire conducted in the highly publicized murder trial, *California v Newton* (see §3.22), are included. Defense attorney Charles R. Garry convinced the trial judge in Oakland that community feeling against the Black Panther Party for Self-Defense and against Huey Newton, its Minister of Defense, was so strong that a fair jury could be selected only after the most probing questions on racism and on the presumption of innocence by the lawyers for both sides. In the *Newton* case, 152 citizens were called and 99 were questioned over a period of two weeks in order to select 12 trial jurors and 4 alternates; the voir dire covered 1,500 transcript pages. As a result of the questioning, 41 persons were successfully challenged for cause on the ground of prejudice, only 2 of these for racial prejudice alone.

Garry did not ask all the questions of any one juror. How he used the questions is demonstrated in the transcript excerpts given in chapters 15 and 17. His ultimate goal was a jury that could admit it had some prejudgments and some prejudices but that would listen with as much objectivity as possible to the evidence, including the testimony of the defendant, the closing arguments by counsel, and the jury instructions. To achieve this goal, Garry often found it useful to treat jurors as it they were witnesses for the opposition and, in effect, to cross-examine them. (See description in chapter 14, and an analysis of Garry's technique by sociologist Robert Blauner in §18.5.)

It should be noted that, after *Newton*, the California Supreme Court attempted to limit attorney voir dire, in *California v Crowe* (Cal 1973) 506 P2d 193. However, Garry's voir dire after *Crowe* in the *Venceremos* case, *California v Burt* (see §3.24), was extensive (see excerpts in chapter 17). On national judicial and bar association efforts to limit voir dire by lawyers, see chapter 23.

The questions from *Newton* are supplemented by questions asked in other state and federal cases by defense counsel who had aggressively pursued other pretrial motions (discussed in chapters 6–8), many of whom built on Garry's list.

The voir dire in a wrongful death case by Dean Robb of Traverse City and Detroit, Michigan, is the source for many of the basic questions for civil cases. *Stroud v General Motors* was a successful suit for damages for the death of a wife and mother of three young children in an accident caused by one of defendant's corporate employees. Robb represented the plaintiffs in the trial, which took place in a small town. See §3.42. His tactic was to take control of the courtroom in which several of the six jury members had prior jury experience with both counsel, see chapter 14. The voir dire questions and answers are rich in ideas for use or consideration in any civil voir dire. See the entire voir dire in chapter 16.

Attorneys frequently called jurors by name at the beginning of questions. For greater adaptability to other cases, these references and the names of defendants have been deleted. Names of witnesses, places, criminal charges and other specifics have been deleted or placed in brackets. Questions have been edited to eliminate duplication, ambiguities, and the kind of grammatical shorthand that can be understood in speech at the time but is inexplicable later in print.

The letter provided for each question indicates the case in which the question was used, *e.g.*, P=*Pentagon Papers* case. The key is given in §9.3. A blank is left at the beginning of each question for counsel to use in numbering questions to copy for a particular case.

## B. Ways to Use List §9.2

Counsel may want to reproduce the following pages, mark up the copy, cross out and write in the margins, rearrange questions, and number them to suit a particular case on the blank before the question. Attorneys may want to change the language of the question to suit the idiom of the region and the court. The questions contain many phrases in brackets, or instructions for filling in organization names or specific charges, many *he/her*, *his/her*, *life/liberty* choices. This editorial approach is deliberate. It is intended to encourage thinking about whether to include each question when making a list of proposed voir dire questions to submit in a case, rather than simply including all questions because one is in a hurry. Defense of the right of counsel to ask voir dire questions directly, and to question prospective jurors individually and in depth, includes a disciplined approach to preparation of questions to be asked in each particular case.

Many attorneys believe that a prerequisite to an effective voir dire is an effective challenge to the trial jury list (see chapter 6). Even if the challenge is unsuccessful, which it often is, it has the effect of educating the judge and the public, including potential jurors, about the pervasive influence of bias and prejudice in the society. In several major trials the judges, after denying motions to expand jury lists, seemed clearly to permit much broader questioning of the jury panel than they customarily permitted in order to elicit indications of prejudgments based on the race, social class, sex, lifestyle, or political ideology of the parties. Thus, without such a challenge, a well-drawn list of voir dire questions may be useless.

Once the edited list of voir dire questions is prepared, it may be submitted to the judge in any court in which the trial judge asks questions propounded by counsel and limits or denies counsel's right to question prospective jurors directly. Since the questions in the following sections are marked to show in which cases they were used (see abbreviations in §9.3), the list can be used as precedent for asking the same or similar questions in counsel's current cases.

Counsel may include a request that all questions be used and offer an explanation of the need for conscientious probing of "the crevices" of the jurors' minds (see the memorandum of points and authorities on this subject in chapter 8). In *United States v McNeil* (see §3.51), counsel moved the court

> to ask the attached questions to prospective jurors. The defendant strongly requests that jurors be questioned individually because questions directed to the group as a whole are not likely to receive a truthful response, if any response at all is given. The defendant also requests that the court attempt to ask open-ended questions instead of questions that only require yes or no answers.

If questions must be submitted in writing for the judge to ask, counsel should include all follow-up questions (in this list, a, b, etc.), and indicate, "If the answer to the last question is 'yes,' the following question should be asked."

For development of a line of questions starting from a question on this list, see the excerpts from the transcripts of voir dire in chapters 15–17.

Over time, a lawyer will want to add questions from other sources that prove useful and to delete ones that prove ineffective.

## C. Abbreviations Used §9.3

The following abbreviations, which precede each voir dire question in this chapter, show the case in which the question was used and the section of this book in which each case is described.*

A *Brewster v Martin Marietta*; see §3.41
B *United States v Briggs* (Gainesville Eight); see §3.53
C Questions traditionally asked by the trial judge
D *California v Davis* (Angela Davis case); see §3.23
E *Michigan v DeSaussure* (Detroit Black Panther case); see §3.27
F *Stroud v General Motors*; see §3.42
G *Administrative Discharge of Tangela Gaskins*; see §3.91
H *United States v Ramos*; see §9.117
J *Michigan v Jeanette Smith*; see §11.51
K *Stokes v Detroit*; see §10.80
M *United States v McNeil*; see §3.51
N *California v Newton* (Huey Newton case); see §3.22
O *United States v Sherpix*; see §11.35

*Some capital letters are used as abbreviations for other (civil) cases in chapter 10.

P *United States v Russo* (Pentagon Papers case); see §3.52
S *New York v Shakur* (Panther 21 case); see §3.25
V *California v Burt* (Venceremos case); see §3.24
W *California v Block*; see §3.29

## D. Common Areas of Inquiry §9.4

The following checklist, supplied by Michigan attorneys Dean Robb and Hugh M. Davis, Jr., is helpful in organizing voir dire questions. This chapter and chapters 10 and 11 contain specific questions in each area suggested by the checklist.

1. Education and formal specialized training.
2. Details about what a juror does at work: supervises others; fine detail work; works alone; how much decision-making involved in everyday life.
3. Family: father and mother work? How important does the family seem to be to this juror?
4. Prior jury service: how long; how many cases; if possible, the lawyers and judges involved; facts to see how well this juror understood what the cases were all about.
5. Other experiences with courts, lawyers, claims: prior accidents and injuries (a good opening to distinguish between civil and criminal legal principles, both to educate and commit).
6. Experiences with doctors, hospitals, the healing arts.
7. Spare-time activities: hobbies; community service; reading; church affiliation, political affiliation, where possible.
8. Neighborhood: what it is like: rural, semirural, urban? Likes the neighborhood?
9. Military connections, law-enforcement or government connections.
10. Pretrial publicity on this or similar cases?
11. Acquaintance with *any* of the witnesses in the case?

## E. Number of Questions to Submit §9.5

When trial judges keep the voir dire in their own hands, requiring counsel to submit lists of questions they will pass on and then ask, how many questions should counsel submit?

One approach is to list only eight or ten questions, carefully phrased, that will provide the demographic information from which the trial lawyer or trial team can make predictions concerning the prospective jurors' biases and prejudgments. It is customarily followed in cases in which an individual expert (psychologist, psychiatrist, or sociologist) helps select the jury based on sociological or psychological factors (see chapters 18 and 19).

The other approach is to submit a list of all the questions the lawyer believes are necessary to ascertain the nature and extent of each prospective juror's prejudgment. If this list is submitted after denial of a motion and memorandum supporting the right to extensive and intensive voir dire, oral argument on the motion, and the taking of expert testimony (described in chapter 8), it is likely that the trial judge will ask many of the questions on the list. That was the experience in *United States v McNeil* (see §3.51), and defense counsel were convinced that the judge asked many more of the defendant's desired questions than he would have if the questions had not been submitted or if the motion had not been argued. It is certainly a common experience to see trial judges shift their attitudes on the permissible extent of voir dire. If they start asking probing questions of one prospective juror, they often begin to get a feeling for what a good voir dire requires, and to press the jurors almost as far as a trial lawyer would.

After his first six months of practice, Thomas Ginger, then trying criminal cases in Jackson, Mississippi, concluded that in a short trial, a long voir dire was not helpful. The jurors had no time to absorb the significance of the process in which they were leading figures, or to think deeply about the presumption of innocence, which is the issue stressed in most voir dire questioning.

## II. PRELIMINARY QUESTIONS CONCERNING EACH JUROR

### A. Introductory Statement §9.7

Attorney Dean Robb of Detroit, Michigan, gave the following introduction to his voir dire questions in *Underhill v Traverse City*, in which he represented plaintiffs in a wrongful death action against a municipality (see §10.22).

> Members of the Jury:
>
> I am [*Attorney's name*] and during the course of this trial, [*my partner*, ____________, and] I [*am/are*] going to be representing the family of [____________] [*and Baby Boy/Girl* ____________].
>
> This part of the proceeding—voir dire—is always one in which everyone is a little nervous and a little bit uptight, and sometimes a little impatient,

wondering when the trial will get started. Let me assure you the trial has started and this is an important part of it for all the parties concerned.

The first thing I'd like you all to understand, from our point of view, is that we'd like to talk to you to determine whether or not, in this case, you would be a suitable juror. This is not an attempt to inquire and pry into your personal views and your personal affairs in any unfair way. Do you all agree that you'd be willing to accept this as part of our joint duty?

Secondly, I've heard this and I am sure you've heard it many, many times—over radio: "This is a test. This is a test." I want to turn that around. "THIS IS NOT A TEST." There are no wrong answers when you're answering either the judge's questions or our questions about your past work, your past experiences, or your views on certain things. All you need to do is to think with us and answer questions with us as completely and openly as possible to help us jointly determine whether or not, in this case, you would be an appropriate juror for both sides. What we're attempting to do here is to find out what people's experiences have been and what opinions you have. Everyone has opinions so there's nothing wrong with that. OK?

Attorney Robb gave the following introduction to the attorney portion of the voir dire questioning in *Michigan v Jeanette Smith*, a state murder trial in which defendant raised a "battered wife" defense, see §11.51.

The purpose of the questions I will be asking you is to understand how you feel about various issues. Since everyone is certainly entitled to their own views, there are no right or wrong answers to these questions. Please let me know if you'd like me to clarify or repeat any of the questions so there won't be any confusion in our conversation. We are talking with each juror separately because some of the questions involve sensitive issues. I'm sure you understand why we need to know your true feelings on these issues, and I hope you understand that none of my questions are intended to make you uncomfortable. Most people feel a little nervous in this situation, but let me assure you that we're only interested in your honest reactions—there are no right or wrong answers.

*COMMENT:* Attorney Robb often goes through the list of jurors' names, checking pronunciation and seating. This helps fix the names in his mind, and is another step in taking control of the courtroom. See §14.12.

1. F ____. Members of the jury, my name is [*Attorney*]. First I might ask if I got everyone's name straight? Box No. 1, you're [*Mr./Mrs./Ms.*]____________, No. 2, ____________, [*and so on*].

*COMMENT:* While it is common, and acceptable, practice to ask jurors their marital status, the California Court of Appeal recently upheld the refusal of a prospective woman juror to tell whether she had a husband since no men jurors were being asked whether they had wives. The Salinas Municipal Court judge who found the juror, a bankruptcy lawyer, in contempt was reversed (2-1). *Bobb v Municipal Court of Monterey* (Cal App 1983) 192 Cal Rptr 270.

## B. Demographic §9.8

All the methods of analyzing prospective jurors include consideration of demographic factors. See generally chapters 4, 5, and 19.

1. C ___. Where were you born?
2. C ___. What is your educational background?
3. C ___. Where did you receive your grammer school, high school, and any further education?
   [*If juror attended college*]
4. N ___. What subjects did you take in college?
5. N ___. What college was that?

*COMMENT:* In the *Pentagon Papers* case, the government requested that the very specific matters in questions 6-8 be asked of each juror.

6. P ___. What has been your residence for the last ten years?
7. P ___. What has been your employment for the last ten years?
8. P ___. What college degrees do you hold?
   a. What was your major field of study?
   b. Please give the names and locations of the colleges you attended.

*COMMENT:* Plaintiffs' personal injury lawyers often ask:

9. ___. Could you tell me a little bit about the area you live in?
   a. What made you decide to select ___________?
   b. Was it important for you to locate a place where there are [*various racial and ethnic groups*], or did you consider that at all?

*COMMENT:* In a typical personal injury or product liability case, counsel may ask questions 9 and 10.

---

A=*Brewster*; B=*Briggs*; C=questions traditionally asked or permitted by the trial judge; D=*Angela Davis* case; E=*Detroit Black Panther* case; F=*Stroud*; G=*Gaskins*; H=*United States v Ramos*; J=*Michigan v Jeanette Smith*; K=*Stokes*; M=*United States v McNeil*; N=*Huey Newton* case; O=*United States v Sherpix*; P=*Pentagon Papers* case; S=*Panther 21* case; V=*Venceremos* case; W=*California v Block*; see §§9.1 and 9.3

10. A ___. How far did you go in school?
[*When appropriate*]
a. Where and what did you study beyond high school—any courses in science, engineering, algebra, higher mathematics, or law?
[*If a student*]
b. What kind of work are you planning on doing?

11. A ___. How far did your spouse go in school; where and what did [*he/she*] study beyond high school—any courses iother lawyers committed to open-ended business or personnel spouse is a management, or law?
[*If spouse is a student*]
a. What kind of work is [*he/she*] planning on going into?
[*If spouse is employed*]
b. What kind of work does your [*spouse*] do?
c. Where?
d. Is your [*spouse*] a member of a union?

12. G ___. Did you attend public or private schools?
a. Was that prior to the college level, private school?

13. G ___. What type of schooling, and by that I mean was it religious, military, or some other possible classification?

*COMMENT:* Tort lawyers, and other laywers committed to open-ended questions, may also ask:

14. ___. Since you left school (or completed your formal education) I'd like to know what other types of education you've had. Some people take occasional night school courses or correspondence courses, or classes through their church or other organizations. I'm interested in weekend seminars, self-help courses, or anything at all you took to further your knowledge, or education, or productivity?
[*If some courses*]
a. What interested you in those courses?
b. What did you feel you gained from them?

*COMMENT:* In preparing profiles of ideal and unacceptable jurors, sociologists have found the answers to questions 15–18 significant indicators. See chapter 5.

---

A=*Brewster*; B=*Briggs*; C=questions traditionally asked or permitted by the trial judge; D=*Angela Davis* case; E=*Detroit Black Panther* case; F=*Stroud*; G=*Gaskins*; H=*United States v Ramos*; J=*Michigan v Jeanette Smith*; K=*Stokes*; M=*United States v McNeil*; N=*Huey Newton* case; O=*United States v Sherpix*; P=*Pentagon Papers* case; S=*Panther 21* case; V=*Venceremos* case; W=*California v Block*; see §§9.1 and 9.3

15. B ___. What is your religious preference?
16. B ___. Do you attend church regularly?

*COMMENT:* In a case involving an exercise of religion or conscience, e.g., nuclear weapons protesters charged with trespass or obstructing traffic, counsel may add questions from *California v Barr.* See §§9.67 and 11.58

17. N ___. How old are you?
18. O ___. What are the ages, sexes, residences, and occupations of your children, if any?
19. A ___. What do your children do for a living?

*COMMENT:* As to younger children, counsel may ask:

20. ___. What school do they attend—that is public or parochial school?
    a. Why did you select that school for them?

*COMMENT:* Attorneys who conduct the voir dire as if it were an interview for a job (see chapter 14) often ask a series of self-evaluation questions. One purpose is to get the juror to relax, while discussing very personal traits and ideas.

As the judge explained to you, this is an attempt to learn something about you quickly. I'm going to ask you to try to describe yourself to me now, to save a little time.

1. ___. What would you describe as your greatest strengths? Or if you would rather, tell me about some weakness?
2. ___. Would you describe yourself as more of a leader or a follower?
3. ___. What descriptive words or adjectives would you use to describe yourself?
4. ___. How do other people describe you, your [*spouse/best friend*]?
5. ___. Do you believe in the philosophy that people bring their own misfortunes on themselves?
    [*If yes*]
    a. Why do you feel this way?
6. ___. Do you have a personal philosophy you can describe?

---

A=*Brewster*; B=*Briggs*; C=questions traditionally asked or permitted by the trial judge; D=*Angela Davis* case; E=*Detroit Black Panther* case; F=*Stroud*; G=*Gaskins*; H=*United States v Ramos*; J=*Michigan v Jeanette Smith*; K=*Stokes*; M=*United States v McNeil*; N=*Huey Newton* case; O=*United States v Sherpix*; P=*Pentagon Papers* case; S=*Panther 21* case; V=*Venceremos* case; W=*California v Block*; see §§9.1 and 9.3

## C. Relationship with Persons in Case

### 1. To Parties and Witnesses §9.9

1. F ___. The[*Plaintiff(s)/Defendant(s)*] are from [*Name of city*], and [*is/are*] present in the courtroom. Would you please stand and face the jury?
2. N ___. Are you related in any way to [*Plaintiff/Defendant/Victim*]?
3. N ___. [*Do/Did*] you know [*him/her*]?
4. N ___. [*Do/Did*] you know [*his/her*] [*father/mother/brother/sister/wife/children*]?
5. F ___. [*Mrs./Mr.*___________], would you advise as to [*your/your spouse's*] maiden name?

*COMMENT:* In *Stroud*, the widower-plaintiff pronounced and spelled his deceased wife's maiden name. The judge repeated the pronunciation and the spelling and asked: "Is there anybody on the jury panel who is related to or acquainted with Mrs. Stroud; if so, would you please raise your hand?" He then announced, for the record: "There are no hands." When jurors raised their hands in answer to such group questions, he identified those jurors and questioned them further on that point.

6. F ___. Is there anybody on the jury panel who is now or has in the immediate past been an employee of [*Name of defendant employer*]?
7. F ___. Is it a present employment?
8. F ___. Was that employment in any kind of administrative or executive capacity?

*COMMENT:* For additional questions relating to a juror's employment history, see §9.11.

9. F ___. Is there anybody on the jury panel who is a stockholder of [*Name of defendant corporation*]?
10. N ___. Do you know [*Names of witnesses for other side*]?
11. N ___. Are you acquainted with any of the following witnesses: [*Names of all witnesses for both sides*]?

*COMMENT:* If the judge does not ask these preliminary questions,

---

A=*Brewster*; B=*Briggs*; C=questions traditionally asked or permitted by the trial judge; D=*Angela Davis* case; E=*Detroit Black Panther* case; F=*Stroud*; G=*Gaskins*; H=*United States v Ramos*; J=*Michigan v Jeanette Smith*; K=*Stokes*; M=*United States v McNeil*; N=*Huey Newton* case; O=*United States v Sherpix*; P=*Pentagon Papers* case; S=*Panther 21* case; V=*Venceremos* case; W=*California v Block*; see §§9.1 and 9.3

counsel should do so. As to the last question, counsel should turn to opposing counsel and, in the presence of the jury, ask whether opposing counsel knows of any other possible witnesses whose names have not been included.

### 2. To Counsel §9.10

*COMMENT:* The following questions are particularly necessary in a small community with relatively few lawyers.

1. F ___. There are a number of attorneys assisting in the trial of this case. They are [*Names of counsel for plaintiff(s) and defendant(s)*]. Is there anybody on the jury panel who is related to any of these attorneys?
2. F ___. Is there anybody on the jury panel who has any legal matter presently pending in which you are represented by any of the attorneys in this case?
3. F ___. Do you consider [*him/her*] your attorney? [*If response is affirmative*]
4. F ___. I think it would be better if you would step down, don't you? Is that fair, Your Honor?
5. F ___. Is there anybody on the jury panel who has now, or has in the past, had any litigation in which any of the attorneys in this case represented the party opposing you?
6. A ___. Do you know any of the attorneys or any members of their families, any of the partners or law associates or employees or law offices?
7. F ___. I can ask you all this: Are you on a nodding basis or a social basis with any of the lawyers?
8. F ___. Is your relationship with [*Name of attorney*], such that you would have a tendency to want to be on [*his/her*] side of the issues that may be raised here just because of this acquaintanceship?
9. F ___. You wouldn't feel that you could discount or ignore that, is that a fair statement?

*COMMENT:* Two murder convictions were reversed because the trial judge denied the defendants' challenge for cause against a woman who

---

A=*Brewster*; B=*Briggs*; C=questions traditionally asked or permitted by the trial judge; D=*Angela Davis* case; E=*Detroit Black Panther* case; F=*Stroud*; G=*Gaskins*; H=*United States v Ramos*; J=*Michigan v Jeanette Smith*; K=*Stokes*; M=*United States v McNeil*; N=*Huey Newton* case; O=*United States v Sherpix*; P=*Pentagon Papers* case; S=*Panther 21* case; V=*Venceremos* case; W=*California v Block*; see §§9.1 and 9.3

had associated with the district attorney. She had met him three years before the trial and had campaigned in his successful bid to become district attorney, and he was a member of her political club. *Provenzano v New York* (Albany County Sup Ct, App Div, 1979), reported in *NY Times*, June 8, 1979, at B2.

A different problem arises when counsel is truly a stranger to jurors, because he or she is from out of town, or even from out of state. Don C. Keenan from Atlanta often handles cases in other jurisdictions. On voir dire, he discloses this:

10. ____. [*Mr./Mrs./Ms.* ____________], I am the attorney for ____________, the [*plaintiff/defendant*]. Now, as you know, my office is not down the street, or even in this [*state*]. Rather, it is located in [*Atlanta, Georgia*]. Does that bother you or cause you any concern?

*COMMENT:* If your client is also from out of state, you should question the jurors for any possible prejudice on this score.

11. ____. My client, ____________, is from ____________. The [*defendant truck driver*] is a resident of this state. Would the fact that you and the [*defendant*] happen to live in the same state make you tend to believe the testimony of my client less than the [*defendant*]?

## D. Employment and Volunteer Work

### 1. Employment Background §9.11

1. N ____. Can you tell me what kind of work you do?
2. B ____. What are your duties?
3. N ____. How long have you been doing that kind of work?
4. A ____. What other occupations or jobs did you have before this one; when and where?
5. A ____. Do you supervise other people?
   [If yes]
   a. How many people do you supervise?
   b. How long have you had these responsibilities?
   c. What are your responsibilities as a [*supervisor/foreman/manager*]?

---

A=*Brewster*; B=*Briggs*; C=questions traditionally asked or permitted by the trial judge; D=*Angela Davis* case; E=*Detroit Black Panther* case; F=*Stroud*; G=*Gaskins*; H=*United States v Ramos*; J=*Michigan v Jeanette Smith*; K=*Stokes*; M=*United States v McNeil*; N=*Huey Newton* case; O=*United States v Sherpix*; P=*Pentagon Papers* case; S=*Panther 21* case; V=*Venceremos* case; W=*California v Block*; see §§9.1 and 9.3

6. A ___. Who does your spouse work for?
   a. How long has [*he/she*] worked there?
   b. What kind of work is done there?
   c. Does [*he/she*] supervise other people; how many?
7. F ___. What did [*he/she*] do before that?

*COMMENT:* Many experts in jury selection feel that the question of supervising others is one of the key issues. See discussion in chapter 19 on selecting one or more "leaders" when hoping for a hung jury.

8. N ___. Do you belong to any union?
9. O ___. If you are an active or retired government employee, will the fact that the government is prosecuting this case cause you to be partial toward the government?

*COMMENT:* Question 9 is particularly relevant in trials in the District of Columbia and in state capitals. The question was submitted by the defense, but not asked by the federal judge, in *United States v Sherpix*. (See §11.35)

Questions 10–12 should certainly be asked when a juror says he or she is not employed or is retired.

10. M ___. Are you doing any volunteer work now, or have you done any?
    [*If so*]
    a. In what organizations?
11. M ___. Are you active in any union or veterans or senior citizens groups?
    [*If yes*]
    a. Which ones?
12. M ___. Is your spouse active in any of these kinds of groups?

*COMMENT:* When counsel has access to jury questionnaires completed by prospective jurors (see chapter 12), counsel may want to explain, as was done in *Stroud*:

We have some information from the jury questionnaire, not too much, but [Mr. ___________], if I could just spend a few minutes going through your work life for a little bit—you're a self-employed carpenter now?

Questions 13–16 should be asked if juror is self-employed.

---

A=*Brewster*; B=*Briggs*; C=questions traditionally asked or permitted by the trial judge; D=*Angela Davis* case; E=*Detroit Black Panther* case; F=*Stroud*; G=*Gaskins*; H=*United States v Ramos*; J=*Michigan v Jeanette Smith*; K=*Stokes*; M=*United States v McNeil*; N=*Huey Newton* case; O=*United States v Sherpix*; P=*Pentagon Papers* case; S=*Panther 21* case; V=*Venceremos* case; W=*California v Block*; see §§9.1 and 9.3

13. F ___. How long have you been self-employed?
14. F ___. Does that mean that you don't employ anyone else, you just take contract jobs for others?
15. F ___. Do you have a regular employer or do you work out of the union hall?
16. F ___. What did you do before that?

*COMMENT:* Several defendants, including both blacks and whites, were charged with misuse of funds of the Office of Economic Opportunity, for which they had worked. Defense counsel formulated a series of questions on juror attitudes toward welfare, War on Poverty programs, and the ability of blacks to manage money. Several jurors asked to be excused because of their overwhelming prejudice against anyone working in such programs, according to jury consultant Maureen McLaughlin, in "How To Read a Juror," *Barristers*, summer 1978, at 44.

### 2. Relationship to Intelligence Work and Classification System §9.12

In *Newton*, the general background questions included question 1.

1. N ___. Are you doing any intelligence work where you are working now?

*COMMENT:* In the *Pentagon Papers* case, the probing went deeper because the federal government's classification system was a substantive issue in the case.

2. P ___. Have you or any relative, close friend, or neighbor ever had a relationship, through employment, business, or otherwise, with the [*Department of Defense*], or its branches or agencies? [*If yes*]
   a. When and where?

*COMMENT:* The same questions were asked about the State Department, National Security Agency, the United Nations, the Rand Corporation, and contractors doing business with the Department of Defense.

---

A=*Brewster*; B=*Briggs*; C=questions traditionally asked or permitted by the trial judge; D=*Angela Davis* case; E=*Detroit Black Panther* case; F=*Stroud*; G=*Gaskins*; H=*United States v Ramos*; J=*Michigan v Jeanette Smith*; K=*Stokes*; M=*United States v McNeil*; N=*Huey Newton* case; O=*United States v Sherpix*; P=*Pentagon Papers* case; S=*Panther 21* case; V=*Venceremos* case; W=*California v Block*; see §§9.1 and 9.3

3. P ___. Have you ever worked with classified material?
[*If yes*]
a. What was the nature of the materials?
b. When and where?
4. P ___. Have you ever read anything, in your employment or otherwise, about the maintenance of security materials?
5. P ___. What does the term *classified* mean to you?
6. P ___. Could you accept the proposition that the government of the United States classifies materials that do not relate to the national defense if evidence of that fact were produced in court during this trial?
7. P ___. Would you be able to return a finding of [*not guilty/other*] if the government failed to convince you [*beyond a reasonable doubt/other standard*] that the documents in evidence, even though classified, did not relate to [*national defense*] as that term will be defined by the court at the end of the case?
8. P ___. Could you accept the instruction of this court that the classification of the documents by the government does not determine the issue of whether they relate to national defense, but that the government has the burden of proving that they do, [*beyond a reasonable doubt/other standard*], by proofs other than classification?
9. P ___. If the evidence so demonstrated, could you accept the proposition that the government of the United States stamped as "top secret" materials that bear no relationship to the national defense?

### 3. Relationship to Federal Government's Security Clearance Program §9.13

1. N ___. Do you have a security clearance on your job?

*COMMENT:* In the *Pentagon Papers* case, since the government's security system was a substantive issue in the case, all of the following questions were asked.

2. P ___. Have you ever applied (or had an application submitted by your employer) for a security clearance?

---

A=*Brewster*; B=*Briggs*; C=questions traditionally asked or permitted by the trial judge; D=*Angela Davis* case; E=*Detroit Black Panther* case; F=*Stroud*; G=*Gaskins*; H=*United States v Ramos*; J=*Michigan v Jeanette Smith*; K=*Stokes*; M=*United States v McNeil*; N=*Huey Newton* case; O=*United States v Sherpix*; P=*Pentagon Papers* case; S=*Panther 21* case; V=*Venceremos* case; W=*California v Block*; see §§9.1 and 9.3

[*If yes*]
a. When and under what circumstances?

3. P ___. Has any member of your family ever applied (or had an application submitted by an employer) for a security clearance?
[*If yes*]
a. When and under what circumstances?
b. What clearance was sought and for what reasons?
c. Was clearance granted?
d. Do you still have a security clearance?
[*If yes*]
(1) What type of clearance?
(2) For what purpose?

## E. Connections with Law Enforcement Agencies §9.14

1. N ___. Are you connected with any police department?
2. N ___. Were you ever connected with any type of police force?
3. N ___. Do you have any immediate relatives who are connected with the police?
4. N ___. And you said you work with the police in [*Name of city*]?
5. N ___. Does your job cause you to work with the Sheriff's Office of [*Name of county*]?
6. P ___. Have you or any member of your family worked as a volunteer or employee for a law enforcement agency on the local, state, or federal level?
[*If so*]
a. When and where?
7. P ___. Have you or any member of your family worked for a local, state, or federal prosecutor's office?
[*If so*]
a. When and where?
8. P ___. Have any of your neighbors or close friends worked as a volunteer or employee for a law enforcement agency or prosecutor's office on the local, state, or federal level?

*COMMENT:* See also questions in §§10.13, 10.62, 10.80–10.81.

---

A=*Brewster*; B=*Briggs*; C=questions traditionally asked or permitted by the trial judge; D=*Angela Davis* case; E=*Detroit Black Panther* case; F=*Stroud*; G=*Gaskins*; H=*United States v Ramos*; J=*Michigan v Jeanette Smith*; K=*Stokes*; M=*United States v McNeil*; N=*Huey Newton* case; O=*United States v Sherpix*; P=*Pentagon Papers* case; S=*Panther 21* case; V=*Venceremos* case; W=*California v Block*; see §§9.1 and 9.3

## F. Jury Experience §9.15

On the right to information on jurors available to the government, see chapters 12 and 13.

1. P ___. Have you ever appeared as a witness before a grand jury?
   [*If yes*]
   a. When and where?
2. C ___. Have you ever appeared as a witness in a criminal prosecution?
   [*If yes*]
   a. Where and when?
3. C ___. Have you ever served on a grand jury?
   [*If so*]
   a. Where and when?
4. N ___. Have you ever had any jury experience before?
   [*If so*]
   a. On how many juries have you served?
5. N ___. Were these in criminal or civil cases?
   a. Was there a verdict?
6. N ___. What kind of case was it?
7. N ___. Was it state or federal?
8. N ___. Did any of the [*civil/criminal*] cases you heard in previous jury duty place any burdens on your capacity to be able to sit on future cases, or did it make you cynical about [*civil/criminal*] trials?
9. N ___. Was there anything about your previous jury experience that would lead you to feel that you may have some prejudices either for or against [*other side, e.g., the prosecution*]?
10. N ___. In your previous jury trial, were the persons involved in the [*assault and battery*] on [*the police officers*] white or black?

*COMMENT:* The *Stroud* case was tried in a small town. Attorney Dean Robb asked questions 11–25 of jurors who had been excused in prior cases or had sat on other juries involving the same attorneys or parties.

11. F ___. There's two of you I excused in a recent case, and I don't know whether I'm going to excuse you yet or not. The fact that you were excused in the last trial by this side, with pretty

---

A=*Brewster*; B=*Briggs*; C=questions traditionally asked or permitted by the trial judge; D=*Angela Davis* case; E=*Detroit Black Panther* case; F=*Stroud*; G=*Gaskins*; H=*United States v Ramos*; J=*Michigan v Jeanette Smith*; K=*Stokes*; M=*United States v McNeil*; N=*Huey Newton* case; O=*United States v Sherpix*; P=*Pentagon Papers* case; S=*Panther 21* case; V=*Venceremos* case; W=*California v Block*; see §§9.1 and 9.3

much the same cast of characters here except [*Corporation name*] is the [*defendant*], would you resent that?

12. F ___. Did you resent it when you were excused the last time?
13. F ___. You understood it?
14. F ___. Did you go out of here and say, "That blankety-blank [*Attorney's name*]?
15. F ___. You understand why we sometimes excuse people?
16. F ___. Sometimes we excuse the wrong people?
17. F ___. [*Mr./Mrs./Ms.*], did you harbor any feelings? You didn't harbor any feelings? You didn't take it personally?
18. F ___. You understand sometimes we excuse jurors for reasons that even we don't understand at times?
19. F ___. It might be, you know, if I had the feeling you didn't like my looks or something, that might be a good reason, but you understand that that is nothing personal? This questioning of you has nothing to do with whether you're a good person and a fair person generally, right?
20. F ___. So you didn't hear anything that was asked that made you feel that you couldn't fairly sit?
21. F ___. And the issue that caused you to be excused before is not certainly present now?
22. F ___. Maybe my most dangerous juror is No. [*6*] here, [*Mr./Mrs./Ms.*]. Since you've heard of me before, is there anything about your experiences working on that other case where I was an attorney, that would make it difficult for you to sit on this case?
    a. You don't think so?
23. F ___. Do you have any regrets about being a juror on that other trial?
24. F ___. Did you feel that you did right in that other trial?

## G. Organizational Affiliations §9.16

1. P ___. Have you or any member of your immediate family ever been a member of any veterans' organizations?
   [*If so*]
   a. What organizations and who was a member?
2. P ___. Have you ever held an office in any of these organizations?

---

A=*Brewster*; B=*Briggs*; C=questions traditionally asked or permitted by the trial judge; D=*Angela Davis* case; E=*Detroit Black Panther* case; F=*Stroud*; G=*Gaskins*; H=*United States v Ramos*; J=*Michigan v Jeanette Smith*; K=*Stokes*; M=*United States v McNeil*; N=*Huey Newton* case; O=*United States v Sherpix*; P=*Pentagon Papers* case; S=*Panther 21* case; V=*Venceremos* case; W=*California v Block*; see §§9.1 and 9.3

3. P ___. Do you belong to any fraternal or other societies?
   [*If so*]
   a. Have you ever held an office in any of these organizations?
4. P ___. Do you belong to any organizations or groups that have as one of their primary purposes advocating or promoting legislation, either federal, state or local?
   [If so]
   a. To what organization or group do you belong?
5. P ___. Do you attend meetings of that organization or group?
6. P ___. Are you active in the organization or group or its activities?
7. P ___. Based on any of these activities, have you formed an opinion that would affect your ability to fairly and impartially judge the evidence and law presented in this case?
8. N ___. Have you ever heard of the [*John Birch Society/Moral Majority/Other*]?
9. N ___. Do you belong to it?
10. N ___. Have you ever received any of their literature?
11. N ___. Do you believe in the philosophy of the [*John Birch Society/Moral Majority/Other*]?

*COMMENT:* In the *Pentagon Papers* case, the government proposed question 12.

12. P ___. Have you, or any member of your family or your close friends, belonged or contributed to the American Civil Liberties Union?

*COMMENT:* The following questions were asked in *California v Barr* (protesters against Livermore Nuclear Weapons Laboratory; see §11.58).

13. ___. Are you active in any senior citizens groups?
14. ___. Have you heard of an organization called [*Children for Peace*]?
15. ___. Are any of your friends who work at [*Livermore Defense Laboratory*] members of the group studying [*how to convert it to nonmilitary purposes*]?

*COMMENT:* Although many prospective jurors had friends working at the Livermore Laboratory, and none had friends in this group, bringing its existence to the attention of the jurors (and the press) was considered helpful to the defense.

---

A=*Brewster*; B=*Briggs*; C=questions traditionally asked or permitted by the trial judge; D=*Angela Davis* case; E=*Detroit Black Panther* case; F=*Stroud*; G=*Gaskins*; H=*United States v Ramos*; J=*Michigan v Jeanette Smith*; K=*Stokes*; M=*United States v McNeil*; N=*Huey Newton* case; O=*United States v Sherpix*; P=*Pentagon Papers* case; S=*Panther 21* case; V=*Venceremos* case; W=*California v Block*; see §§9.1 and 9.3

It is important to question jurors on membership in purely local organizations that may be active on issues involved in your case.

### H. Political Affiliations §9.17

1. N ___. What political organization do you belong to?
2. N ___. Aren't you a registered [*Republican*]?
3. N ___. You are not a member of the [*American Independence*] Party, are you?

*COMMENT:* In *McNeil*, when defense counsel indicated that in a letter that might be introduced in evidence the defendant had called Richard M. Nixon a derogatory name, the federal judge asked question 4 at the defendant's request.

4. M ___. Did you sign the nominating petition for President Richard M. Nixon in 1970?

*COMMENT:* In *California v Barr* (protesters charged with obstructing traffic at Livermore Laboratory; see §11.58), the following questions were asked:

5. ___. Do you belong to a political party?
   [*If yes*]
   a. Are you active in the party?
   b. Does your party have a position on [*nuclear weapons*]?
   [*If yes*]
   c. Could you tell me what the party's position is?

### I. Military Service §9.18

1. N ___. Were you in the service?
   [*If yes*]
   Were and when?
2. N ___. What branch of the service?
3. P ___. Were you on active duty?
   [*If so*]
4. N ___. What rank did you have in the [*Navy*]?
5. N ___. How long were you in the service?

---

A=*Brewster*; B=*Briggs*; C=questions traditionally asked or permitted by the trial judge; D=*Angela Davis* case; E=*Detroit Black Panther* case; F=*Stroud*; G=*Gaskins*; H=*United States v Ramos*; J=*Michigan v Jeanette Smith*; K=*Stokes*; M=*United States v McNeil*; N=*Huey Newton* case; O=*United States v Sherpix*; P=*Pentagon Papers* case; S=*Panther 21* case; V=*Venceremos* case; W=*California v Block*; see §§9.1 and 9.3

6. N ___. While you were in the service, was your service outfit integrated?
7. N ___. Were you ever on any courts martial?
[*If yes*]
a. As a member of the court?
8. N ___. While you were in the [*Navy*], were you ever on [*shore patrol*] duty?
[*If yes*]
a. That is the role of the police officer, isn't that right?

*COMMENT:* In *McNeil*, the defense submitted questions 9–10, but the federal judge did not ask them.

9. M ___. Did you volunteer for the armed forces?
[*If so*]
a. Where and when?
10. M ___. Were you drafted?
[*If so*]
a. When and where?

*COMMENT:* Pursuing a personal profile of the juror, counsel may ask:

11. ___. Why did you decide on a military career?
a. What did you like best about it?
b. What did you like the least?

*COMMENT:* In the *Gainesville Eight* trial, the defense submitted question 12.

12. B ___. Has anyone in your immediate family or anyone close to you been injured or killed in the military?
[*If so*]
a. When and where?
b. What was the extent of the injury?

*COMMENT:* In the *Pentagon Papers* case, the trial judge did ask additional questions posed by the defense on the prospective jurors' military service related to Vietnam, and to the service of friends there. The judge also asked questions proposed by the defense on juror's contributions to Vietnam relief funds and to prisoner of war organizations.

---

A=*Brewster*; B=*Briggs*; C=questions traditionally asked or permitted by the trial judge; D=*Angela Davis* case; E=*Detroit Black Panther* case; F=*Stroud*; G=*Gaskins*; H=*United States v Ramos*; J=*Michigan v Jeanette Smith*; K=*Stokes*; M=*United States v McNeil*; N=*Huey Newton* case; O=*United States v Sherpix*; P=*Pentagon Papers* case; S=*Panther 21* case; V=*Venceremos* case; W=*California v Block*; see §§9.1 and 9.3

In that case, the government asked the judge to ask question 13 of those who had been in the armed forces.

13. P ___. Is there anything about that experience that would cause you to be prejudiced against the government or against the defendants?

*COMMENT:* The following questions were asked in *California v Barr* (protesters against Livermore Nuclear Weapons Laboratory; see §11.58).

14. ___. If your [*son/daughter/grandson/granddaughter*] thought about going into the [*Army*], how would you feel about that?
15. ___. If your [*son/daughter/grandson/granddaughter*] thought about becoming a conscientious objector, how would you feel about that?

*COMMENT:* For questions on attitudes toward the laws of war, including the Nurnberg Principles, which are part of the *U.S. Army Field Manual,* see §§9.140 and 11.58.

## J. Additional Questions §9.19

This section is being reserved for additional questions, to be presented in supplements to this volume.

## III. MOST DAMAGING FEATURES OF CASE §9.20

Lawyers frequently use the voir dire to present, in a dispassionate manner, the most damaging features of the anticipated case against their clients. The goal is to desensitize the jurors so they will listen analytically to the testimony of opposition witnesses, rather than reacting emotionally due to shock or surprise. When the opposition is expected to introduce objects coated with blood or photographs of bloody victims, it is essential that you prepare the jurors in advance to remember their function as triers of the facts, not as moralists or sensation-mongers. (See also §11.27).

Questions 1–4, which are examples from the *Burt* (see §3.24) and *Davis* (see §3.23) cases, should suggest questions to be framed in other

---

A=*Brewster*; B=*Briggs*; C=questions traditionally asked or permitted by the trial judge; D=*Angela Davis* case; E=*Detroit Black Panther* case; F=*Stroud*; G=*Gaskins*; H=*United States v Ramos*; J=*Michigan v Jeanette Smith*; K=*Stokes*; M=*United States v McNeil*; N=*Huey Newton* case; O=*United States v Sherpix*; P=*Pentagon Papers* case; S=*Panther 21* case; V=*Venceremos* case; W=*California v Block*; see §§9.1 and 9.3

cases. They are, of course, too specific to be used, even with some modifications.

1. V ___. Benton Douglas Burt here is 30 years old. He has spent some 15 years of those 30 years either in the penitentiary or in juvenile custody. Ten of those 15 years were in the penitentiary. Would that factor alone create within you a prejudgment that he must have done something wrong in this case?

2. V ___. The evidence will undoubtedly show the fact that Mrs. Burt went to Cuba some time ago, and while in Cuba, she worked in a work brigade there cutting sugarcane as a donation, and when she got back, she made speeches on what she found there, what she believed. Would that factor create within you an antagonism that may interfere with your being able to evaluate the testimony properly?

3. V ___. One factor that I want to call attention to is that both Mr. and Mrs. Burt believe that the capitalistic system is not working to the benefit of all the people, and they believe in a socialist society. Would that factor create within you an antagonism of any kind?

4. D ___. The prosecutor, Mr. Harris, has already talked about photographs, and I don't know which photographs he will be allowed to introduce before this jury. But we know that there exist many, many photographs. It is our contention that those photographs don't have anything to do with this case. He has no photographs showing Ms. Davis being involved in these [*violent*] incidents.

   But we are fearful that these photographs may disturb you to such a point that you may feel you have to do something about the situation shown in the pictures.

   As Mr. Harris said, some of those photographs are pretty gruesome. We hope you will never have to look at them, because we think that might have some effect on you emotionally.

   Now, if the judge should let you look at these photographs and if you become emotional about them, will you try as desperately as you can to put aside that emotion and try to reach the real issue that is involved: What has this got to do with Ms. Davis?

---

A=*Brewster*; B=*Briggs*; C=questions traditionally asked or permitted by the trial judge; D=*Angela Davis* case; E=*Detroit Black Panther* case; F=*Stroud*; G=*Gaskins*; H=*United States v Ramos*; J=*Michigan v Jeanette Smith*; K=*Stokes*; M=*United States v McNeil*; N=*Huey Newton* case; O=*United States v Sherpix*; P=*Pentagon Papers* case; S=*Panther 21* case; V=*Venceremos* case; W=*California v Block*; see §§9.1 and 9.3

*COMMENT:* Detroit attorney Ernest Goodman used question 5 in *Michigan v DeSaussure*, a Black Panther case (see §3.27).

5. E ___. The prosecutor has indicated that he will offer evidence in this case of weapons, such as files, shotguns, and explosives. Now, the defendants are not being charged with possessing rifles, guns, and explosives; these in and of themselves are not part of the offense charged against them. If such items are introduced in connection with the prosecutor's theory of the case, if they are brought here or described to you, would that fact alone make you believe that these defendants are guilty of a crime unless it was part of the proof that these defendants were guilty of [*conspiring to kill Detroit police officers or the other crimes charged*],—the mere fact of the presence of these items in the case, would that prejudice you against these defendants?

*COMMENT:* Attorney Dennis Roberts of Oakland has used the more general questions 6–9.

6. ___. If there is evidence of violence in this case, possibly with serious physical injury, would that fact alone prejudice you against the [*defendant/plaintiff*]?
7. ___. Would the presence of violence, bloodshed, or injury shock or embarrass you so as to interfere with your objective judgment?
8. ___. Would evidence of serious physical injuries hamper your consideration of all the other evidence?
9. ___. If the evidence shows that the defendant was near the scene of the crime charged, would this create in your mind an assumption that because he was there, he probably is guilty?

## IV. PRETRIAL PUBLICITY ON CASE

### A. Prior Discussions of Case §9.21

1. N ___. Have you heard anybody discussing this case?
2. N ___. Have you discussed it with anybody?
3. N ___. Immediately after this event took place, you met with a friend of yours, [*who is an Oakland police officer*], isn't that right?

---

A=*Brewster*; B=*Briggs*; C=questions traditionally asked or permitted by the trial judge; D=*Angela Davis* case; E=*Detroit Black Panther* case; F=*Stroud*; G=*Gaskins*; H=*United States v Ramos*; J=*Michigan v Jeanette Smith*; K=*Stokes*; M=*United States v McNeil*; N=*Huey Newton* case; O=*United States v Sherpix*; P=*Pentagon Papers* case; S=*Panther 21* case; V=*Venceremos* case; W=*California v Block*; see §§9.1 and 9.3

*COMMENT:* See further voir dire on this point in chapters 15 and 17.

The following questions from *Newton*, a criminal case, can be modified for use in civil cases by using "liable" or "negligent" instead of "guilty," etc.

4. N ____. You have never discussed this case with anybody who said to you, "Well, I think the defendant is innocent" or "I think the defendant is guilty"?
5. N ____. And you, yourself, have not expressed an opinion?
6. N ____. It's also true that most of the people who have discussed the case with you were on the side of the police rather than on the side of the defendant, isn't that correct?
7. N ____. Did you ever say in these group discussions, "Look, everybody, this is a country where we live by laws. Let's hold our views until the case is tried and let's see what the evidence shows." Did you ever make that statement to them?
8. N ____. As you sat in these discussions, did you at any time defend the fact that [*Mr./Ms. Smith*] may be innocent and we shouldn't be maligning this [*man/woman*]?
9. N ____. In these group discussions with these [*white*] fellow-workers of yours, which side of the coin were you on? On the side of the police or on the side of [*Mr./Ms. Smith*]?

*COMMENT:* In the *Pentagon Papers* case, the government proposed question 10.

10. P ____. Have you, or has any close friend or relative, attended any meeting, rally, or function of any kind at which [*either*] defendant spoke?
    [*If so*]
    a. When, where, and what meeting?

## B. Prior Knowledge or Opinion of Case §9.22

Theodore Koskoff of Bridgeport, Connecticut, described the customary examination of a prospective juror concerning his prior knowledge of the case in a speech before the American Trial Lawyers Association:

> Usually the juror doesn't remember too many specific things, but, with a little prompting, finally indicates he has formed an opinion. Now the judge

A=*Brewster*; B=*Briggs*; C=questions traditionally asked or permitted by the trial judge; D=*Angela Davis* case; E=*Detroit Black Panther* case; F=*Stroud*; G=*Gaskins*; H=*United States v Ramos*; J=*Michigan v Jeanette Smith*; K=*Stokes*; M=*United States v McNeil*; N=*Huey Newton* case; O=*United States v Sherpix*; P=*Pentagon Papers* case; S=*Panther 21* case; V=*Venceremos* case; W=*California v Block*; see §§9.1 and 9.3

leans towards the witness and says: "If I told you to put that opinion out of your mind and confine yourself to the evidence in the courtroom, would you do it?"

The juror then says: "Certainly I will."

This is, of course, absurd. A previously-held opinion is a good ground for a challenge of the juror for cause even where he promises to put that opinion out of his mind. The Supreme Court, at least in one case, recognized the absurdity of doing otherwise. In *Irvin v Dowd* (1961) 366 US 717, the voir dire lasted four weeks. Two hundred sixty-eight jurors were excused for cause. Ninety percent of those asked entertained some opinion as to guilt. Eight of the twelve finally chosen thought the defendant was guilty. The Court said:

> With such an opinion permeating their minds, it would be difficult to say that each could exclude this preconception of guilt from his deliberations. The influence that lurks in an opinion once formed is so persistent that it unconsciously fights detachment from the mental processes of the average man.... No doubt each juror was sincere when he said that he would be fair and impartial to petitioner, but psychological impact requiring such a declaration before one's fellows is often its father. [366 US at 727–728.]

This is an area requiring extensive questioning of each juror.

1. N ___. Had you ever heard of this case before you came here for jury duty?
2. N ___. And is there anything about what you have seen since you came for jury duty that would lead you to feel that you may have an opinion on this case one way or the other?
3. N ___. I am going to ask you several questions and the purpose of my questions is to get down to your inward self and your own qualifications to be a fair and impartial juror. You understand that?
4. N ___. First of all, do you have an opinion of this case?
5. N ___. Have you at any time ever expressed an opinion about this case, one way or the other?
6. N ___. Within your own mind, have you ever said, "Well, I think this person is [*guilty/liable*]," or, "I think this person is [*innocent/not negligent*]"? Have you ever gotten that far?
7. N ___. Have you formed any opinion from the news media, television and radio, that would be a burden that the [*plaintiff/defendant*] would have to overcome?

---

A=*Brewster*; B=*Briggs*; C=questions traditionally asked or permitted by the trial judge; D=*Angela Davis* case; E=*Detroit Black Panther* case; F=*Stroud*; G=*Gaskins*; H=*United States v Ramos*; J=*Michigan v Jeanette Smith*; K=*Stokes*; M=*United States v McNeil*; N=*Huey Newton* case; O=*United States v Sherpix*; P=*Pentagon Papers* case; S=*Panther 21* case; V=*Venceremos* case; W=*California v Block*; see §§9.1 and 9.3

[*If the juror has an opinion*]

8. N ___. Would you have any difficulty overcoming that opinion that has already been set in your mind?
9. N ___. When is the first time that you got the opinion about the defendant's [*guilt/liability*] fixed in your mind?
10. N ___. And it is also a fact, is it not, that you carried that opinion until about a week ago when you became a prospective juror in this case?
11. N ___. In other words, there has been nothing in these many months from the time of the incident on [*May 3d*] up until a week ago that changed your opinion that [*Mr./Ms. Smith*] had done what they said [*he/she*] did?
12. N ___. Well, don't you think that is a tremendous burden for you to have to overcome in a [*case/charge*] that is as serious as the one that the [*plaintiff/defendant*] is facing?
13. N ___. In other words, after this long period of time that you have had this opinion, you would have to see the evidence contrariwise before your opinion would change, isn't that right?
14. N ___. But there has been a period of months in which your mind has been conditioned as to certain facts and you have accepted them as true?

*COMMENT:* For parallel questions to ask on voir dire in death penalty cases, see §11.82.

15. N ___. As far as you are concerned, you have held this opinion that it was an open and shut case for the last [*nine*] months, and there has been nothing that you have read or seen that has changed your opinion except the fact that the judge indicated that you should have an open mind?
16. N ___. In what way do you have an open mind? What has come into your own thinking that has eliminated the fixed opinion that you had that this was an open and shut case?
17. N ___. I am somewhat interested in how you can unwind. I don't mean unwinding in the sense of relaxing. I am talking about unwinding the previous subconscious mind to a point where you will undo in your own subconscious mind what has dwelled in there for the past [*nine or ten*] months: the fact that this is

A=*Brewster*; B=*Briggs*; C=questions traditionally asked or permitted by the trial judge; D=*Angela Davis* case; E=*Detroit Black Panther* case; F=*Stroud*; G=*Gaskins*; H=*United States v Ramos*; J=*Michigan v Jeanette Smith*; K=*Stokes*; M=*United States v McNeil*; N=*Huey Newton* case; O=*United States v Sherpix*; P=*Pentagon Papers* case; S=*Panther 21* case; V=*Venceremos* case; W=*California v Block*; see §§9.1 and 9.3

an open and shut case, that [*Mr./Ms. Smith*] is [*negligent/ guilty as charged*]—how are you going to unwind that?

18. N ___. There has been no evidence, no articles, nothing intervening that would change your mind, isn't that right?
19. N ___. In other words, as far as you are concerned, from [*the date of the incident*] until the present time, [*date of trial*], there has been nothing to change that so-called superficial opinion that you had that [*Mr./Ms. Smith*] [*killed Officer Clark/caused or contributed to the accident/injury*]?
20. F ___. Is there anybody on the jury panel who has reason to believe from what I've told you briefly about the facts of this case, that you have any personal knowledge about it?
21. F ___. Anyone who has reason to believe you have any personal knowledge about [*the parties*]?

## C. Influence of Newspapers and Other News Media §9.23

1. P ___. How did you first hear or read about this case?
2. P ___. What have you heard or read about this case?
3. F ___. May I inquire what newspapers you usually read?

*COMMENT:* In the *Pentagon Papers* case, the government proposed questions 4–5.

4. P ___. Do you subscribe to, or regularly read: The *New York Times*? The *Washington Post*? *Saturday Review*? *Atlantic Monthly*? *Look* Magazine? *Harpers*? *Ramparts*? *Esquire*?
5. P ___. Have you read any newspaper or magazine articles or seen any television program about [*either*] defendant or about any counsel?
   [*If so*]
   a. What articles or programs?
   b. About which defendant or counsel?
6. N ___. Was there anything in the newspaper that you read that led you to believe [*Mr./Ms. Smith*] was [*guilty or not guilty/liable or not*]?
7. N ___. Did you form any opinion about this case when you read the stories in the [*Tribune*] over a period of several months?

---

A=*Brewster*; B=*Briggs*; C=questions traditionally asked or permitted by the trial judge; D=*Angela Davis* case; E=*Detroit Black Panther* case; F=*Stroud*; G=*Gaskins*; H=*United States v Ramos*; J=*Michigan v Jeanette Smith*; K=*Stokes*; M=*United States v McNeil*; N=*Huey Newton* case; O=*United States v Sherpix*; P=*Pentagon Papers* case; S=*Panther 21* case; V=*Venceremos* case; W=*California v Block*; see §§9.1 and 9.3

8. N ___. In other words, when you read about this case in the news media, you got the impression that [*Mr./Ms. Smith*] did it [*commited the crime/caused the accident*] and it was an open and shut case?
9. N ___. Weren't those stories you read on this case in the [*Tribune*] slanted on the side of the [*prosecutor/defense*]?
10. N ___. Well, what has come over your thinking that would lead you to feel that you are now able to overcome the fixed opinion that was indelibly put into your mind through the [*Tribune*] that you read?
11. N ___. In other words, whatever you read didn't prejudice you as to the facts of the case against the [*defendant/plaintiff*], is that what you are saying?
12. P ___. Have you ever read or heard any commentary concerning the guilt or innocence of the defendant by [*President Lyndon Johnson/Richard Nixon/Ronald Reagan*]?
[*If so*]
a. What do you recall [*their*] having said or written?

## D. Has Juror Been Touched by Party's Demographic Study? §9.24

In the *Gainesville Eight* prosecution of members of the Vietnam Veterans Against the War, the defense conducted a sociological study of the community before jury selection to determine the best and worst jurors from the defense viewpoint (see chapter 5). As a result, the prosecution requested the trial court to ask

> all prospective jurors whether any juror or any member of the juror's family has been contacted since July, 1972 by any person or persons purporting to be conducting a poll or survey in which questions dealing either generally or specifically with the following areas were asked:
>
> 1. The choice of newspapers, magazines, radio and television stations and the degree of contact with these media.
> 2. Knowledge of the defendants and this case.
> 3. The greatest Americans in the past ten years.
> 4. Trust in government.
> 5. Ages and activities of respondents' children.

---

A=*Brewster*; B=*Briggs*; C=questions traditionally asked or permitted by the trial judge; D=*Angela Davis* case; E=*Detroit Black Panther* case; F=*Stroud*; G=*Gaskins*; H=*United States v Ramos*; J=*Michigan v Jeanette Smith*; K=*Stokes*; M=*United States v McNeil*; N=*Huey Newton* case; O=*United States v Sherpix*; P=*Pentagon Papers* case; S=*Panther 21* case; V=*Venceremos* case; W=*California v Block*; see §§9.1 and 9.3

6. Religious attitudes and commitment.
7. Spare time activities.
8. Organizational memberships.
9. Attitudes concerning private property, support of the government, use of police force, presumed innocence of persons charged with crime and other questions reflecting attitudes relating to the trial.
10. Questions dealing with tolerance for protest activities.

## E. Recent Developments §9.25

It is now possible to keep up with the law on jury selection the same way you keep up with the law in any other field—by reading the relevant advance sheets, subscribing to services on trial advocacy or criminal law, reading daily newspapers and legal newspapers, and participating in continuing education programs of bar associations. The *Index to Legal Periodicals*, *Current Law Index*, and *Legal Resource Index* provide provocative (and sometimes descriptive) titles to law review articles, comments, and notes in this field, indicating what is happening at the cutting edge of the law. It is a good idea occasionally to ask your law librarian for an index to journals on psychology, applied psychology, and the social sciences, to pick up new ideas from these disciplines.

Increasingly, lawyers are learning to use *Lexis* and *Westlaw* in order to find the latest cases and interesting parallels in other fields of law. It is always necessary to Shepardize all citations.

The Annual Supplement to these volumes will use recent developments sections throughout the book to describe new cases, ideas, and articles that are worthy of note, and to warn of cases overruled and of rules and statutes amended or repealed.

# V. RACIAL OR ETHNIC PREJUDGMENT

## A. Attitudes toward Black People

### 1. Feelings toward Black People in General §9.30

The following questions can be adapted quite easily for use concerning other ethnic groups.

1. N ___. Let me hear, in your own words, how you feel about black

A=*Brewster*; B=*Briggs*; C=questions traditionally asked or permitted by the trial judge; D=*Angela Davis* case; E=*Detroit Black Panther* case; F=*Stroud*; G=*Gaskins*; H=*United States v Ramos*; J=*Michigan v Jeanette Smith*; K=*Stokes*; M=*United States v McNeil*; N=*Huey Newton* case; O=*United States v Sherpix*; P=*Pentagon Papers* case; S=*Panther 21* case; V=*Venceremos* case; W=*California v Block*; see §§9.1 and 9.3

people generally and what your relationships with them have been?

2. N ___. Do you equate shabbiness with black people?
3. N ___. What is your general attitude toward black people?
4. N ___. Have you ever made a statement to anyone that Negroes should be able to help themselves just like anybody else does?
5. N ___. In your opinion, how do you think black people have been treated in this society?

*COMMENT:* The prosecutor objected to question 5, and the court sustained the objection on the ground that the question was too broad.

6. N ___. Well, do you think that the black people of [*Alameda*] County have a legitimate complaint when they accuse the white society of white supremacy and white racism?

*COMMENT:* The prosecutor objected to question 6, and the court sustained the objection on the ground that it was improper voir dire.

7. N ___. Do you think there is any difference between black people and white people?
8. N ___. You don't have any prejudice against black people? [*If juror answers "no"*]
9. N ___. Let me break it down. You believe that black people have the same rights that other people do, is that right?
10. N ___. And you don't believe then, I take it, that black people have been denied substantial rights over a period of many, many years?
11. N ___. In other words, you feel that, if the black people had the same opportunity, it is up to them to make a go of it?
12. N ___. Do you feel black people by and large have had the same opportunity as whites?
13. N ___. When is the last time you had blacks in your home as social guests?
14. N ___. There will be evidence that [*the plaintiff/defendant*] was [*married*] to a white [*woman/man*]. Would this in any way affect your ability to judge fairly and openly all the evidence in this case?

*COMMENT:* Under a unique New York State statute (which no longer

A=*Brewster*; B=*Briggs*; C=questions traditionally asked or permitted by the trial judge; D=*Angela Davis* case; E=*Detroit Black Panther* case; F=*Stroud*; G=*Gaskins*; H=*United States v Ramos*; J=*Michigan v Jeanette Smith*; K=*Stokes*; M=*United States v McNeil*; N=*Huey Newton* case; O=*United States v Sherpix*; P=*Pentagon Papers* case; S=*Panther 21* case; V=*Venceremos* case; W=*California v Block*; see §§9.1 and 9.3

exists), defense counsel asked questions 15–35 of *grand* jurors in *New York v Shakur*, the *Panther 21* case in New York City (see §3.25).

15. S ___. What is your contact with black people?
16. S ___. Do you have any black employees in your home or store?
17. S ___. Would you know anything about black rhetoric, culture, or speech?
18. S ___. If a certain [*Black Panther*] said, "We should off those pigs," would you know what that meant?
19. S ___. Do you believe that blacks have a greater propensity for criminal behavior than whites?
20. S ___. Over the past years have you noticed a change in the number of crimes being committed in this city?
21. S ___. Has it been severely on the increase?
22. S ___. Has it disturbed you?
23. S ___. Do you feel this increase is due primarily to blacks in the city?
24. S ___. Have you noticed an increased number of blacks and Puerto Ricans coming into your neighborhood?
25. S ___. Have you been disturbed by the changes in your neighborhood?
26. S ___. Have you thought of moving out of it?
27. S ___. Do you feel that as the city has changed that property values have increased?
28. S ___. Do you object to the number of blacks and Puerto Ricans on the welfare rolls in the city?
29. S ___. Do you think they are entitled to welfare?
30. S ___. Do you have children?
31. S ___. Do they go to the public schools?
32. S ___. [*If in private schools*] Is this a result of your feelings towards the number of blacks and Puerto Ricans in the school system?
33. S ___. Have you had discussions with your family or friends about law and order?
34. S ___. Have you had discussions with your family or friends about politics?
35. S ___. Have you had discussions with your family or friends about the whole question of civil rights and militancy regarding blacks in [*New York City*]?

---

A=*Brewster*; B=*Briggs*; C=questions traditionally asked or permitted by the trial judge; D=*Angela Davis* case; E=*Detroit Black Panther* case; F=*Stroud*; G=*Gaskins*; H=*United States v Ramos*; J=*Michigan v Jeanette Smith*; K=*Stokes*; M=*United States v McNeil*; N=*Huey Newton* case; O=*United States v Sherpix*; P=*Pentagon Papers* case; S=*Panther 21* case; V=*Venceremos* case; W=*California v Block*; see §§9.1 and 9.3

*COMMENT:* Attorney Theodore Koskoff of Connecticut suggests asking question 36.

36. ___. Do you agree with people who say admitting black students to white schools won't work because black students don't have the background to keep up?

*COMMENT:* To make a record on prosecution peremptories against black jurors, the defense must get the juror's race on the record without alienating jurors in the process. The attorney in *California v Wheeler* (1978) 148 Cal Rptr 890, 894, made the point this way:

**Q.** As I admonished the jury earlier, I asked questions that might seem to be personal and prying. My client is black; obviously you are black, too.
**A.** Yes, I am.

One black juror went further: "We are not trying color. We are trying a case." See chapter 20.

*COMMENT:* The following questions were asked in *Stokes v City of Detroit* by plaintiff's attorney Richard A. Soble (see §10.80).

37. K ___. For a trial that has two parties of different races, do you feel that the jurors are predisposed to one party or the other because of their race?
    a. In other words, will a white juror be predisposed toward favoring a white party, and a black juror predisposed toward favoring a black party?
    [*If yes*]
    b. Why do you think this is the case?
    c. Would you, as a potential juror, be predisposed one way or the other because of the race of the parties?
38. K ___. Do you believe that there can be a fair trial when one party is black and the other party is white?
39. K ___. Do you feel that blacks involved in a lawsuit can get a fair trial?

*COMMENT:* Voir dire concerning jurors' racism is not a new area of questioning. The following questions asked by trial judges are drawn from cases dating as far back as 1855.

---

A=*Brewster*; B=*Briggs*; C=questions traditionally asked or permitted by the trial judge; D=*Angela Davis* case; E=*Detroit Black Panther* case; F=*Stroud*; G=*Gaskins*; H=*United States v Ramos*; J=*Michigan v Jeanette Smith*; K=*Stokes*; M=*United States v McNeil*; N=*Huey Newton* case; O=*United States v Sherpix*; P=*Pentagon Papers* case; S=*Panther 21* case; V=*Venceremos* case; W=*California v Block*; see §§9.1 and 9.3

40. ___. Could you give the defendant, who is black, as fair and impartial a trial as you could a white man, and give him the same advantage and protection as you would a white man upon the same evidence? *Pinder v Florida* (1891) 27 Fla 370, 8 So 837.

41. ___. Have you got any prejudice against a black person as a black person that would induce you to return a verdict on less or slighter evidence than you would return a verdict of guilty against a white man under the same circumstances? *Hill v Mississippi* (1916) 112 Miss 260, 72 So 1003.

42. ___. Defendant sought to ask a prospective juror if "he believes he could, as a juror, do equal and impartial justice between the State and a black man." *North Carolina v McAfee* (1870) 64 NC 339.

43. ___. a. Would you fairly try this case on the basis of the evidence and disregard the defendant's race?
b. You have no prejudice against blacks? Against black people?
c. You would not be influenced by the use of the term "black"? *Ham v South Carolina* (1973) 409 US at 525.

44. ___. a. Are you under any obligation not to extend the same rights, privileges, protection and support to men of foreign birth as to native-born American citizens?
b. Have you any prejudice whatever against foreigners? *California v Reyes* (1855) 5 Cal 347, 349.

45. ___. Have you any bias or prejudice against that class of citizens of which class the defendant is one?
*Watson v Whitney* (1863) 23 Cal 375, 379.

46. ___. a. Other things being equal, would you take the word of an Asian as soon as you would that of a white man?
b. If the defendant, an Asian, should be sworn as a witness in his own behalf, would you give his testimony the same credit that you would give to the story told by a white person, under the same circumstances?
*California v Car Soy* (1880) 57 Cal 102, 103.

---

A=*Brewster*; B=*Briggs*; C=questions traditionally asked or permitted by the trial judge; D=*Angela Davis* case; E=*Detroit Black Panther* case; F=*Stroud*; G=*Gaskins*; H=*United States v Ramos*; J=*Michigan v Jeanette Smith*; K=*Stokes*; M=*United States v McNeil*; N=*Huey Newton* case; O=*United States v Sherpix*; P=*Pentagon Papers* case; S=*Panther 21* case; V=*Venceremos* case; W=*California v Block*; see §§9.1 and 9.3

## 2. "Unfortunate Experience" with Black Person §9.31

1. N ___. Have you ever had an unfortunate experience with [*a black person*] in the community that you live in or at any other place?

*COMMENT:* To a juror who answered yes and described the incident involving a "colored boy," defense attorney Garry continued with questions 2–5.

2. N ___. Was it a little boy?
3. N ___. You are talking about a man?
4. N ___. You are not using the word, *boy,* in a derogatory fashion because he happens to be colored, are you?
5. N ___. You do know that black people, when they get to be adult, don't like to be called boys?

*COMMENT:* To another juror who answered yes to question 1, Garry responded with questions 6–7.

6. N ___. Was there a criminal proceeding as a result of this experience or incident?
7. N ___. You were the prosecuting witness?

## 3. Opinion on "Black Power" §9.32

1. N ___. Have you heard of the words *black power*?
2. N ___. Do you know what *black power* means?
3. N ___. Do you have any objection to the term when the black people say, "We want black power"?
4. N ___. Just the fact of the words *black power*, and the talk about black power by black people, does that create revulsion in your own mind?

*COMMENT:* Professor Robert Blauner, a sociologist who observed and participated in jury selection in the *Newton* case, believes that open-ended questions, like 5 and 6 below, might produce better results (see §8.7):

5. ___. Tell me what feelings [*black power*] brings to your mind?
6. ___. Tell me what some of those subjective feelings of [*racism*] are?

---

A=*Brewster*; B=*Briggs*; C=questions traditionally asked or permitted by the trial judge; D=*Angela Davis* case; E=*Detroit Black Panther* case; F=*Stroud*; G=*Gaskins*; H=*United States v Ramos*; J=*Michigan v Jeanette Smith*; K=*Stokes*; M=*United States v McNeil*; N=*Huey Newton* case; O=*United States v Sherpix*; P=*Pentagon Papers* case; S=*Panther 21* case; V=*Venceremos* case; W=*California v Block*; see §§9.1 and 9.3

*COMMENT:* The New York City grand jurors questioned in the *Panther 21* case were asked question 7.

7. S ___. Do you have an opinion on the idea that black people should have a role in their own destiny and control their own institutions?

### 4. Attitude on Children Having Black Friends §9.33

1. D ___. Do your children attend school with blacks?
2. D ___. Do you approve of your children having black friends?

*COMMENT:* When the *Newton* voir dire questions were used in a Portland trial, the prospective jurors answered most of them calmly and indicated no racial prejudice or prejudgment. When counsel reached the question, "What would you do if your son or daughter started to date or socialize with black people?" the answers suddenly changed. The jurors said they would forbid such relationships. Counsel then repeated the basic questions on racism, and the second time most of the prospective jurors admitted their prejudices. This suggests emphasis on these questions, and perhaps also on questions about the juror's friendships, if any, in the black community.

### 5. Parties Who Speak Different Language §9.34

Problems arise when the plaintiff or defendant and their witnesses use one kind of language, and the judge, jurors, and the other side use another. It is very difficult for jurors to trust someone who uses words and phrases they cannot understand. This potential distrust is magnified when the jurors can understand the words and phrases by themselves but not in the context in which a stranger is using them (for example in slang expressions or ghetto English). Jurors who do not quite understand someone—due to a regional accent or the extensive use of a "secret language" (slang)—may have greater distrust or suspicion of that person than they would of one speaking a totally foreign language. Federal District Judge Charles W. Joiner recently recognized black English formally and directed a school board to devise a plan to help teachers deal with it. *Martin Luther King, Jr., Pupils v Ann Arbor*

---

A=*Brewster*; B=*Briggs*; C=questions traditionally asked or permitted by the trial judge; D=*Angela Davis* case; E=*Detroit Black Panther* case; F=*Stroud*; G=*Gaskins*; H=*United States v Ramos*; J=*Michigan v Jeanette Smith*; K=*Stokes*; M=*United States v McNeil*; N=*Huey Newton* case; O=*United States v Sherpix*; P=*Pentagon Papers* case; S=*Panther 21* case; V=*Venceremos* case; W=*California v Block*; see §§9.1 and 9.3

*School Dist. Bd.* (ED Mich, July 12, 1979) reported in *NY Times*, Aug. 21, 1979. His decision supports voir dire questioning on this subject.

Use of the word "nigger" became important in jury selection in a southern Alabama case in which a black defendant was charged with killing a white man. When defense counsel asked prospective jurors whether they had ever used that word, it "came as quite a jolt . . . and led to a number of people being excused for cause." McLaughlin, "How To Read a Juror," *Barristers*, summer 1978, at 44.

One of the points made repeatedly by counsel representing members of the Black Panther Party was that their clients and witnesses frequently use different words from those of most white judges, jurors, police officers, and witnesses, or use the same words to convey different meanings. In addition, many northerners have difficulty understanding a strong southern accent, and vice versa.

The point was made sharply in a motion to expand void dire further in order to determine the existence and extent of possible racism, filed May 1, 1975, in *California v Bingham* (the *San Quentin Six* case (Marin County Super Ct, No. 4094, Jan. 17, 1974); see §2.21). Some of the questions proposed in the motion and the appendix were:

1. ___. Do you believe that black people have a culture of their own that is different from that of white people?
2. ___. Do you believe that black people, especially ghetto blacks, have a different vocabulary from white people?
3. ___. Do you know what is meant by "playing the dozens"?
4. ___. Do you know what is meant by "ribbin"?
5. ___. Do you know what is meant by "jivin"?
6. ___. Do you know the meaning of "signifying"?
7. ___. Do you know the meaning of "shuckin"?
8. ___. Do you know the meaning of "run a game"?
9. ___. Do you know the meaning of "to put someone down"?
10. ___. Do you know the meaning of "scab" when used by a black person?
11. ___. Do you know the meaning of "a fish" when used by a black person?
12. ___. Do you know the meaning of "phat tip" when used by a black person?
13. ___. Do you know the meaning of "vamp on"?

---

A=*Brewster*; B=*Briggs*; C=questions traditionally asked or permitted by the trial judge; D=*Angela Davis* case; E=*Detroit Black Panther* case; F=*Stroud*; G=*Gaskins*; H=*United States v Ramos*; J=*Michigan v Jeanette Smith*; K=*Stokes*; M=*United States v McNeil*; N=*Huey Newton* case; O=*United States v Sherpix*; P=*Pentagon Papers* case; S=*Panther 21* case; V=*Venceremos* case; W=*California v Block*; see §§9.1 and 9.3

14. ____. Do you know the meaning of the word "nigger" when used by a black person?
15. ____. Do you know the meaning of a "field nigger" when used by a black person?
16. ____. Do you know the meaning of a "house nigger" when used by a black person?
17. ____. Do you know the meaning of "fire on" when used by a black person?
18. ____. Do you know the meaning of "throwin iron" when used by a black person?
19. ____. Do you know the meaning of "knobs" when used by a black person?
20. ____. Do you know the meaning of "pimp socks" when used by a black person?
21. ____. Do you know the meaning of "right on"?
22. ____. Do you know the meaning of "deal with" when used by a black person?
23. ____. Do you know the meaning of "kill" when used by a black person?
24. ____. Do you know the meaning of "taking care of business" when used by a black person?
25. ____. Do you know the meaning of "bootlicker" when used by a black person?
26. ____. Do you the meaning of "Uncle Tom" when used by a black person?
27. ____. Do you know the meaning of "handkerchief head" when used by a black person?

*COMMENT:* For definitions and further lists of words, see Foster, Glossary to *Ribbin', Jivin', and Playin' the Dozens: The Dilemma of Inner City Schools* (1975).

## B. Attitudes toward La Raza/Latino People §9.36

San Francisco Bay Area jurors have been asked the following questions in La Raza cases:

---

A=*Brewster*; B=*Briggs*; C=questions traditionally asked or permitted by the trial judge; D=*Angela Davis* case; E=*Detroit Black Panther* case; F=*Stroud*; G=*Gaskins*; H=*United States v Ramos*; J=*Michigan v Jeanette Smith*; K=*Stokes*; M=*United States v McNeil*; N=*Huey Newton* case; O=*United States v Sherpix*; P=*Pentagon Papers* case; S=*Panther 21* case; V=*Venceremos* case; W=*California v Block*; see §§9.1 and 9.3

1. ____. Do you believe that it is important for a person to have a strong sense of cultural identity?
2. ____. Do you take pride in your heritage?
3. ____. Do you think Mexican culture is equal to American culture?

The following questions, drafted by attorneys Paul Harris and Edmundo Espinosa of San Francisco, have been asked in cases involving La Raza—Latinos, Chicanos, and others.

1. ____. Do you own a grocery store?
2. ____. Do you work at a grocery store or supermarket?
3. ____. Do you have any feelings about the [*current/recent*] Farmworker boycott of [*lettuce, grapes*]?
4. ____. Do you think Chicanos should try to lose their accents?
5. ____. Do Chicano families have too many children?
6. ____. Have you ever walked or driven down [*24th*] Street [*near Folsom and Mission*] at night?
7. ____. Did you feel uncomfortable or tense at these times?
8. ____. If you had a grocery store, would you watch Chicano patrons closer than Anglo patrons?
9. ____. Do you think Chicanos lie more frequently than Anglos?
10. ____. Have you ever heard jokes derogatory to Chicanos?
11. ____. How would you feel if your child became close friends with a Chicano?
12. ____. How would you feel if your child became close friends with a Chicano of the opposite sex?
13. ____. How would you feel if your child married a Latino?
14. ____. Why do you think there are more Latino boxers than Anglo boxers?
15. ____. Do you know what the word *barrio* means?
[*If no answer, counsel should explain*]
16. ____. If you had a store in the barrio, would you want more theft insurance than in an Anglo section of town?
17. ____. How would you feel if your child had a Chicano teacher?
18. ____. Would you prefer to go to an Anglo doctor rather than a Chicano doctor?
19. ____. Would you be offended if a Chicano called you an "Anglo"?
20. ____. Do you believe that for most people it makes a difference in

---

A=*Brewster*; B=*Briggs*; C=questions traditionally asked or permitted by the trial judge; D=*Angela Davis* case; E=*Detroit Black Panther* case; F=*Stroud*; G=*Gaskins*; H=*United States v Ramos*; J=*Michigan v Jeanette Smith*; K=*Stokes*; M=*United States v McNeil*; N=*Huey Newton* case; O=*United States v Sherpix*; P=*Pentagon Papers* case; S=*Panther 21* case; V=*Venceremos* case; W=*California v Block*; see §§9.1 and 9.3

America if they grow up Chicano or if they grow up white? [*If yes*]

a. Can you tell me what the difference is?

21. ___. Do you know that the US Census Bureau shows that almost one of every [*three*] La Raza families has an income under [*$4,000*] a year?

*COMMENT:* Up-to-date statistics can be obtained from the Sociology Department in a local college, or directly from the Census Bureau.

22. ___. Do you think this is because they do not work as hard or have less initiative?
23. ___. Do you think your life would have been much different if you had been born Hispanic? How so?
24. ___. Some people say that most white people think of Chicanos as lazy. Do you think most white people believe that?
25. ___. Would you say that you were raised in an atmosphere free of prejudice?
26. ___. In school did you learn about any of the great achievements of Latinos in American history?
27. ___. Do you believe that there will come a time in this country when race will have no more significance than hair color? How soon?

## C. Attitudes toward Native Americans §9.38

Many of the questions counsel will want to ask when representing Native American clients are similar to questions needed in cases involving black, brown, and yellow clients (see §§9.30–9.33, 9.36, 9.59–9.60, 9.71–9.73, 9.82). These questions are not repeated here.

The questions in §§9.39–9.43 were either asked (in an important *Wounded Knee* occupation case) or should have been asked (in a non-*Wounded Knee* case) and are specifically appropriate in Native American cases.

For further materials from *Wounded Knee* cases, contact Meiklejohn Civil Liberties Institute, the repository of a major collection of litigation materials from the several cases, Box 673, Berkeley, California 94701.

---

A=*Brewster*; B=*Briggs*; C=questions traditionally asked or permitted by the trial judge; D=*Angela Davis* case; E=*Detroit Black Panther* case; F=*Stroud*; G=*Gaskins*; H=*United States v Ramos*; J=*Michigan v Jeanette Smith*; K=*Stokes*; M=*United States v McNeil*; N=*Huey Newton* case; O=*United States v Sherpix*; P=*Pentagon Papers* case; S=*Panther 21* case; V=*Venceremos* case; W=*California v Block*; see §§9.1 and 9.3

### 1. In Overtly Political Cases §9.39

Federal Judge Fred J. Nichol asked many questions concerning prospective jurors' attitudes toward Native Americans in one of the cases arising out of the Wounded Knee events in which Dennis Banks and Russell Means, two American Indian Movement leaders, were charged with five felonies. *United States v Banks* (D SD, WD, Nos. CR 73–5034, CR 73–5035, CR 73–5062, CR 73–5063, 1974). The case was moved to St. Paul, Minnesota. After a lengthy trial, it was sent to the jury, but one of the jurors had to be excused because of a sudden illness. All the alternates had already been excused and had publicly indicated their views toward an acquittal. The government refused to accept the judge's suggestion for deliberation and decision by the remaining 11-member jury. On September 16, 1974, Judge Nichol criticized the government for this refusal, repeated earlier criticisms of the FBI, said Assistant United States Attorney R. D. Hurd had deceived him about one of the government witnesses, and dismissed all felony charges against both defendants. See Tilsen, "US Courts and Native Americans at Wounded Knee," 31 *Lawyers Guild Practitioner* 61 (1974).

The questions in §§9.40–9.41 may be used in almost any case involving a Native American client that requires jurors to begin to understand United States history in a different way from that commonly taught, and to understand Native American culture. Questions in §9.42 can be adapted to many kinds of demonstrations. Typical questions asked to probe racial prejudice are omitted here.

#### a. Attitudes toward Law Enforcement §9.40

These questions were asked by federal Judge Fred J. Nichol in *United States v Banks* (see §9.39).

1. ___. Do you have any favorable impression or unfavorable impression about the Bureau of Indian Affairs?
2. ___. Does the mere fact that law enforcement officials attempted to clear certain of these defendants and others associated with them from [*Wounded Knee*] lead you to come to the conclusion that just the fact that the law enforcement officials

A=*Brewster*; B=*Briggs*; C=questions traditionally asked or permitted by the trial judge; D=*Angela Davis* case; E=*Detroit Black Panther* case; F=*Stroud*; G=*Gaskins*; H=*United States v Ramos*; J=*Michigan v Jeanette Smith*; K=*Stokes*; M=*United States v McNeil*; N=*Huey Newton* case; O=*United States v Sherpix*; P=*Pentagon Papers* case; S=*Panther 21* case; V=*Venceremos* case; W=*California v Block*; see §§9.1 and 9.3

were there was a sign that they must have been doing something wrong?

3. ___. Would you be inclined to give the testimony of the United States Marshal, an FBI agent, or some official like a BIA Policeman, would you be inclined to give their testimony more weight because of the official position that they held, than you

4. ___. Now, would you make any distinction between, for example, Indian individuals who held an official position, such as say a tribal chairman—would you be inclined to give his testimony more weight than you would the testimony of an Indian who did not hold such an official position, or would you treat them the same?

*COMMENT:* See also questions in §§9.14, 10.13, 10.62, 10.80–10.81.

### b. Attitudes toward Native Americans' Reactions to Treaty Breaking §9.41

These questions were asked by federal Judge Fred J. Nichol in *United States v Banks* (see §9.39).

1. ___. You have heard of various treaties, Indian treaties, I assume. Have you heard of the Sioux Treaty of 1868?

2. ___. In your college and studies, did you form any impressions as to whether or not the United States government has lived up to those treaties, and maybe conversely, whether the Indians have lived up to their treaty; have you formed any impression about whether the treaties have been abided by?

3. ___. Have you heard that at least there are some people who claim that many of the treaties, including the Treaty of 1868, have been broken by the United States government in the past? Have you ever heard that statement?

4. ___. Now, do you feel that it is possible that through your study of history that there has been in the past, at least, a dealing of the United States government with Indians that was not completely fair, and that was in violation of some of these treaties?

5. ___. You had indicated that you did feel some sympathy with the Indian cause. Has that sympathy been caused by what you

---

A=*Brewster*; B=*Briggs*; C=questions traditionally asked or permitted by the trial judge; D=*Angela Davis* case; E=*Detroit Black Panther* case; F=*Stroud*; G=*Gaskins*; H=*United States v Ramos*; J=*Michigan v Jeanette Smith*; K=*Stokes*; M=*United States v McNeil*; N=*Huey Newton* case; O=*United States v Sherpix*; P=*Pentagon Papers* case; S=*Panther 21* case; V=*Venceremos* case; W=*California v Block*; see §§9.1 and 9.3

observed in your business, or has it been based on the fact that the United States government hasn't always treated the Indians right and, therefore, you've got kind of a conscience and you think in order to right that conscience that might make you sympathetic [*and that the Indians had some right to go on the reservation and commit certain acts which the government is now charging as a crime*]? Is it a matter of conscience, or is it because of your experience, your general sympathy with them? Which is it?

6. ___. In other words, does your conscience bother you a little bit about the way your ancestors may have treated the Indians?

7. ___. Now, do you feel that an individual or a group of Indians or any other group of people who may have had the feeling in the back of their mind of trying to right certain alleged wrongs that occurred in the past should not be prosecuted for crimes that might have been committed in connection with that matter, or if they committed crimes, do you think they should be prosecuted?

8. ___. Now, one of the matters that's charged in the indictment deals with alleged civil disorders. Do you believe that riots and insurrections are usually caused by outside agitators?

### c. Attitudes toward Specific Incident §9.42

These questions were asked by federal Judge Fred J. Nichol in *United States v Banks* (see §9.39).

1. ___. [*The Harris*] poll made during [*the occupation of Wounded Knee*], I believe nation-wide, . . . had indicated that a rather substantial, maybe even a majority of the people in the United States favored—at least at one time—favored the Indian's side with reference to the [*occupation or takeover of Wounded Knee*], so I'm asking you, did you feel that you would be inclined to go along with what may have been the majority of the people polled?

2. ___. Are you aware of the significance of [*Wounded Knee*] as to what it was that did happen at [*Wounded Knee*] [*some time ago*]?

---

A=*Brewster*; B=*Briggs*; C=questions traditionally asked or permitted by the trial judge; D=*Angela Davis* case; E=*Detroit Black Panther* case; F=*Stroud*; G=*Gaskins*; H=*United States v Ramos*; J=*Michigan v Jeanette Smith*; K=*Stokes*; M=*United States v McNeil*; N=*Huey Newton* case; O=*United States v Sherpix*; P=*Pentagon Papers* case; S=*Panther 21* case; V=*Venceremos* case; W=*California v Block*; see §§9.1 and 9.3

3. ___. Did you form any impression as to whether the Indians [*at Wounded Knee*] were right or wrong as far as events that you heard on the radio or TV?

## 2. In Nonpolitical Cases §9.43

In *United States v Bear Runner* (8th Cir 1974) 502 F2d 908, the defendant had been convicted of larceny for killing a calf on an Indian reservation not far from the Wounded Knee demonstrations temporally or geographically. The defense had submitted the following voir dire questions (502 F2d at 910):

1. ___. Do you accept the idea that customs, actions, and needs of those persons raised and living in an Indian culture can be different from the customs, actions and needs of those persons raised in a white culture?
2. ___. Do you accept the idea that these customs, actions, and needs of those persons raised and living in an Indian culture are just as valid as those customs, actions, and needs of persons raised in a white culture?
3. ___. Would any of you jurors have difficulty in accepting the idea that Indians have a right to an do hunt wildlife such as deer or rabbits, on the reservation; that under reservation rules and regulations they are allowed to do this hunting at any time during the year, day or night?

*COMMENT:* The trial judge had refused to ask these questions. The court of appeals reversed and sent the case back for a new trial on the ground that the trial court should "have examined each of the prospective jurors on an individual basis in these sensitive areas." See excerpts from opinion in §8.68.

In *United States v Banks* (see §9.39), federal Judge Fred J. Nichol asked the following general questions on voir dire:

1. ___. By the way, do you have any Indians working in the plant with you?
2. ___. Now, do you have any associations with them such as going and having coffee, or having a beer, or going bowling, or something like that with your Indian employees?

---

A=*Brewster*; B=*Briggs*; C=questions traditionally asked or permitted by the trial judge; D=*Angela Davis* case; E=*Detroit Black Panther* case; F=*Stroud*; G=*Gaskins*; H=*United States v Ramos*; J=*Michigan v Jeanette Smith*; K=*Stokes*; M=*United States v McNeil*; N=*Huey Newton* case; O=*United States v Sherpix*; P=*Pentagon Papers* case; S=*Panther 21* case; V=*Venceremos* case; W=*California v Block*; see §§9.1 and 9.3

3. ___. Do you have any view or think that alcohol, for example, would affect Indians differently than it would non-Indians?
4. ___. We've always heard this statement occasionally, those of us that are white, for example that—well, all Indians or all blacks look alike. Have you ever encountered any difficulty distinguishing among individuals of another race? You've heard that story before, haven't you?
5. ___. I suspect that we have people that have different impressions of Indians. You said that you felt that you would be fair, but do you subscribe to a belief that you heard some persons express, that Indians are generally drunk and dirty?
6. ___. Do you subscribe to a belief that sometimes has been indicated that most Indians want the government to take care of them?
7. ___. Have you ever been on an Indian reservation in your life?
8. ___. [*To person who had been on Indian reservation*] Did you have any consciousness that this must be a reservation and, if so, did you observe the manner in which the Indians might have been living on the reservation?
9. ___. Could I ask you whether you have any impression of Indians from, say, watching westerns where the Indians seem to be the bad guys, and the whites seem to be the good guys?
10. ___. In other words, your impressions about Indians have not been affected by what you might have seen in western movies or things like that?
11. ___. Do you feel that there sort of is an obligation, that Indians might be better off, for example, if they would conform harder, or try harder to conform to the lifestyle of the area of the white people?
12. ___. Do you think Indians would be better off if they tried harder to conform to the American way of life? Now, by American way of life, I know we are appropriating the word "American." That isn't quite fair because I guess the Indians were here before, but I am thinking of what we as a white community would refer to as the American way of life. Do you think an Indian should conform to our style of living or try harder to do so?

---

A=*Brewster*; B=*Briggs*; C=questions traditionally asked or permitted by the trial judge; D=*Angela Davis* case; E=*Detroit Black Panther* case; F=*Stroud*; G=*Gaskins*; H=*United States v Ramos*; J=*Michigan v Jeanette Smith*; K=*Stokes*; M=*United States v McNeil*; N=*Huey Newton* case; O=*United States v Sherpix*; P=*Pentagon Papers* case; S=*Panther 21* case; V=*Venceremos* case; W=*California v Block*; see §§9.1 and 9.3

### 3. Native Americans Who Speak Different Language §9.44

Federal Judge Fred J. Nichol asked the following questions in *United States v Banks* (see §9.39).

1. ___. Have you ever had any contact with persons who do not speak English at all or who do not speak English fluently?
2. ___. The reason I ask that is there may be witnesses in this case that will either speak it very poorly or may have to have an interpreter. Now, in the event they have to have an interpreter where they may only speak the [*Sioux*] language and do not speak Engligh and the interpreter interprets from the [*Sioux*] language into the English language, would you still accord the testimony, as you heard it from the interpreter, the same credibility as a person who did speak English fluently?
3. ___. Do you feel that there is an obligation, for example, on the part of [*Indians*] to learn the English language?

## D. Attitudes toward Racial Prejudice

### 1. Attitudes toward Commissions Reporting on Civil Disorders §9.46

A shocking rise in attacks on blacks, Asians, Latinos, Jews, and other racial and ethnic groups has been reported in the press and in a carefully documented study by the California Governor's Task Force on Civil Rights, *Report on Racial, Ethnic and Religious Violence in California 1982*, Summary and Recommendations (Dec. 1982, Documents and Publications, Box 1015, North Highlands, CA 95660). This study is a good source from which questions can be developed, whether or not jurors have seen it.

Immediately after publication of the Kerner Commission report on civil disorders in 1968, few Americans called for jury duty had heard of it. (See Blauner, §18.7.) The passage of time certainly has not increased this proportion. In addition, the lustre of this government commission has been tarnished by the conviction and imprisonment of its chairman on federal charges. However, the report continues to provide counsel with a carefully documented analysis on which to base

---

A=*Brewster*; B=*Briggs*; C=questions traditionally asked or permitted by the trial judge; D=*Angela Davis* case; E=*Detroit Black Panther* case; F=*Stroud*; G=*Gaskins*; H=*United States v Ramos*; J=*Michigan v Jeanette Smith*; K=*Stokes*; M=*United States v McNeil*; N=*Huey Newton* case; O=*United States v Sherpix*; P=*Pentagon Papers* case; S=*Panther 21* case; V=*Venceremos* case; W=*California v Block*; see §§9.1 and 9.3

questions concerning racism, separatism, and police prejudice that arise in every case involving a party from a nonwhite group.

1. N ___. Have you ever heard of the report of the National Advisory Commission on Civil Disorders, otherwise known as the Kerner Commission?
2. N ___. Do you agree with the commission when it states that white Americans have never fully understood what black Americans can never forget, that white society is deeply implicated in the ghetto, white institutions created it, white institutions maintain it, and white society condones it?

*COMMENT:* The district attorney objected to question 2, and the judge sustained the objection, ruling that this was improper voir dire. A few days later the defense asked question 3 and there was no objection.

3. N ___. Do you go along with the fact that the Kerner Commission report states that the predominant and first complaint of all black people in the ghettos of the United States is against police oppression, and that police brutality goes along with that?

### 2. Attitudes toward White Racism §9.47

1. N ___. Do you know what white racism is?
2. N ___. Do you believe that there is white racism in the United States?
3. N ___. White racism is the feeling that white people have that they are the dominant group over the black people or people of color. In some circles, it is called white supremacy. Does that give you some idea of what we are talking about?
4. N ___. Do you think that most white people are prejudiced against black people?
5. N ___. Do you belong to any clubs or any organizations [*outside of your trade union*] that have black members?
6. N ___. In other words, you recognize that you have a little bit of white racism, or it might be there and you try to compensate for it; is that right?
7. N ___. Would you say that we have had many, many years of white power?

---

A=*Brewster*; B=*Briggs*; C=questions traditionally asked or permitted by the trial judge; D=*Angela Davis* case; E=*Detroit Black Panther* case; F=*Stroud*; G=*Gaskins*; H=*United States v Ramos*; J=*Michigan v Jeanette Smith*; K=*Stokes*; M=*United States v McNeil*; N=*Huey Newton* case; O=*United States v Sherpix*; P=*Pentagon Papers* case; S=*Panther 21* case; V=*Venceremos* case; W=*California v Block*; see §§9.1 and 9.3

8. N ___. In other words, you are willing to accept the fact that the United States has been a racist society?
9. N ___. Then do you have any objection to the black people saying, "We want to share some of that power; we are getting tired of being pushed around"?
10. N ___. Would you say that in [*Alameda*] County the white people consider themselves supreme over the black people?

*COMMENT:* The district attorney objected to question 10. The court sustained the objection, noting that the defense may ask the prospective juror only how she feels.

11. N ___. Let me put it this way: Do you believe that conditions and the things that happen to black people in the community, black brothers and sisters, do you think that they concern you?
12. N ___. You have heard people say that, "I don't discriminate; I don't dislike Negroes and colored people," but they go on with it, and say something else. Do you have that kind of a reservation in your thinking?
13. N ___. Well, do you think that the people in the ghetto of [*West Oakland*] have complaints, justifiable complaints, against the white people?

*COMMENT:* The prosecution objected to question 13, but the court allowed the question.

14. N ___. I am asking: do you think the white people have done enough?

### 3. Subjective and Objective Racism §9.48

1. N ___. You understand that white racism can come out either objectively or subjectively?
2. N ___. Do you know what I mean by subjective or objective?
3. N ___. Objective racism is the outward manifestation of racism. An example would be restaurant owners putting up a big sign saying that they don't want any blacks in their restaurant. Subjective racism is a feeling people have inwardly. They may not say it to anybody else.

    What we are trying to do is find out whether any of you have

A=*Brewster*; B=*Briggs*; C=questions traditionally asked or permitted by the trial judge; D=*Angela Davis* case; E=*Detroit Black Panther* case; F=*Stroud*; G=*Gaskins*; H=*United States v Ramos*; J=*Michigan v Jeanette Smith*; K=*Stokes*; M=*United States v McNeil*; N=*Huey Newton* case; O=*United States v Sherpix*; P=*Pentagon Papers* case; S=*Panther 21* case; V=*Venceremos* case; W=*California v Block*; see §§9.1 and 9.3

any prejudices, and if you have, to what extent they can affect your judgment of the case. Can you decide the case on its merits rather than on the built-in prejudices that all human beings have in one way or the other? That is the question.

4. N ___. Now let me ask you personally: do you have any racial prejudices, whether they are objective or subjective?

5. N ___. In determining white racism, we determine it from two standpoints. One of them is whether the racism is objective, something you can put your finger on, like the owner of a bar saying, "I don't want any black people in my bar." They use a little stronger language than that, but that gives you some idea of a person expressing objective racism.

The other kind of racism is subjective. It is a feeling within you that a person of a darker color, or a black person, is inferior, that they don't take advantage of their educational opportunities. Subjective racism may mean an inward feeling that if the Irish and Italians can make a go of it and become a credit to this country, why can't the black people do the same when they've been here over 300 years. Someone might not stress this feeling, or say it out loud, but he would have the feeling inside. You might have a subjective or inward feeling, and say to yourself, "I'd hate to have my daughter or my son marry a black." You may not advertise it, but when you see your daughter coming home with a black boyfriend, it makes you cringe. That's a subjective feeling. You may not want to say anything to your daughter because you don't want to alienate her. But it's the feeling you have within yourself. It's a subjective feeling.

I am saying all this to you so that you can decide whether you have any form of white racism within you. You are being voir dired, that means "you speak." It is your chance to say what inward feelings you have. You are the only one who can tell us these things, whether you have any form of white racism in you. And if you do have that in you, only you can tell us whether it is objective or subjective. These are the kinds of things that [*Mr./Ms. Smith*] is entitled to know.

That is why I am asking: Do you have any racial prejudices, whether they are objective or subjective?

---

A=*Brewster*; B=*Briggs*; C=questions traditionally asked or permitted by the trial judge; D=*Angela Davis* case; E=*Detroit Black Panther* case; F=*Stroud*; G=*Gaskins*; H=*United States v Ramos*; J=*Michigan v Jeanette Smith*; K=*Stokes*; M=*United States v McNeil*; N=*Huey Newton* case; O=*United States v Sherpix*; P=*Pentagon Papers* case; S=*Panther 21* case; V=*Venceremos* case; W=*California v Block*; see §§9.1 and 9.3

6. N ___. Whatever racism you may have may be subjective, but you can't put your finger on what it is?
7. N ___. Is this subjective prejudice that you may have such that you recognize it and can make allowances for it?

*COMMENT:* Defendant Angela Davis, acting as co-counsel in her case, interrogated one juror extensively on racism using quite different questions and style. See chapter 15.

### 4. Attitudes on Fair Housing §9.49

Fair housing acts forbidding racial discrimination in selling and renting have been the subjects of initiative and referendum elections in many cities, counties, and states. In California, older prospective jurors who voted in the 1964 election would probably still remember the passage of an initiative to repeal the Rumford Fair Housing Law (Calif Const art I, §26). The proposition was declared unconstitutional in *Mulkey v Reitman* (Cal 1966) 413 P2d 825, *aff'd* (1967) 387 US 369. Voters in other areas probably remember their elections on fair housing issues more recently.

1. N ___. Do you recall in [*1964*] when [*California*] had what we call [*Proposition 14*] on the ballot to repeal the [*Rumford*] Fair Housing Law?
   [*If yes*]
2. N ___. Did you vote yes or no on that proposition?

*COMMENT:* The district attorney objected to question 2; the judge sustained the objection, ruling that defense counsel can ask how a juror feels, but not how he voted.

3. N ___. As a matter of fact, your community of [*Fremont*] is a community that voted overwhelmingly in support of [*Proposition 14*], isn't that right?
4. N ___. Are you in favor of a fair housing law or not?
   [*If yes*]
   a. In other words, you don't believe that a person has a right to discriminate in selling or renting his house because of race, color or creed?

---

A=*Brewster*; B=*Briggs*; C=questions traditionally asked or permitted by the trial judge; D=*Angela Davis* case; E=*Detroit Black Panther* case; F=*Stroud*; G=*Gaskins*; H=*United States v Ramos*; J=*Michigan v Jeanette Smith*; K=*Stokes*; M=*United States v McNeil*; N=*Huey Newton* case; O=*United States v Sherpix*; P=*Pentagon Papers* case; S=*Panther 21* case; V=*Venceremos* case; W=*California v Block*; see §§9.1 and 9.3

5. N ___. I want to know whether you are in favor of an open housing law that says that no person, whether he or she owns the property or doesn't own the property, no person has the right to discriminate against someone in selling or renting the house because of race, color, creed, or national origin. Are you in favor of such a law?

[*If yes*]

a. Fine. No matter what color?

[*If no*]

b. In other words, your feeling is that each person should decide morally on discrimination in housing, and the state should not intervene to stop discrimination as an immoral and illegal act, is that what you are saying?

c. But you don't feel that the immorality goes to the very heart of the right of humanity to see that that kind of conduct doesn't take place, and the state should step in and stop it?

6. N ___. Do you have any black neighbors?

7. N ___. Have you or your family ever moved out of a neighborhood because black people were moving in?

8. N ___. You understand that I am asking this question because there are white people who have moved when black people moved into the neighborhood?

*COMMENT:* The judge ordered a prospective juror to disregard question 8 because it was a statement, not a question. But this proved to be an important question in the voir dire of another prospective juror in the *Newton* case.

9. N ___. Is the neighborhood you live in an integrated neighborhood?

10. N ___. There are no black people living in your neighborhood, are there?

11. N ___. Are there any black people living in the apartment house you are living in?

12. N ___. Do you have any idea why no black people live in that apartment house?

*COMMENT:* The prosecutor objected to question 12, and the court asked Garry to rephrase his question.

---

A=*Brewster*; B=*Briggs*; C=questions traditionally asked or permitted by the trial judge; D=*Angela Davis* case; E=*Detroit Black Panther* case; F=*Stroud*; G=*Gaskins*; H=*United States v Ramos*; J=*Michigan v Jeanette Smith*; K=*Stokes*; M=*United States v McNeil*; N=*Huey Newton* case; O=*United States v Sherpix*; P=*Pentagon Papers* case; S=*Panther 21* case; V=*Venceremos* case; W=*California v Block*; see §§9.1 and 9.3

13. N ___. I believe you volunteered that you have some property where you have colored tenants; did I hear you say that?
14. N ___. Now, you said you own some property in [*Michigan*]?
15. N ___. None of your property was involved in the so-called riots in 1967 in [*Detroit*], was it?
16. E ___. You say that in some of the areas of [*Detroit*] the housing is pretty bad?
17. E ___. Are the homes in this condition all occupied by black people, or are there poor white people in [*Detroit*] whose homes you have been to?
18. E ___. Do you have any feelings, in reacting to what you've seen of the conditions under which these people live, that it is due to the fault of the individual people; I mean, that it is their fault that they live in these conditions? Do you have any reaction of that sort?
19. E ___. How do you view the problem as to whose fault it is or why the people live in these conditions?
20. E ___. And I guess you are stating that perhaps because of your [*union*] background, you can see the desirability of organizing to change this sort of condition?
21. E ___. Do you think that the people there [*in the slum housing areas*] ought to wait for those at the top of society (maybe I should include myself, you know I am a lawyer) to come down and change things?

*COMMENT:* The following questions have been asked in San Francisco trials:

22. ___. Are there any Latinos living in your neighborhod?
23. ___. Why do you think no Chicanos live in your neighborhood?
24. ___. Do any Chicano children go to school with your children?

## E. Recent Developments §9.50

See §9.25.

---

A=*Brewster*; B=*Briggs*; C=questions traditionally asked or permitted by the trial judge; D=*Angela Davis* case; E=*Detroit Black Panther* case; F=*Stroud*; G=*Gaskins*; H=*United States v Ramos*; J=*Michigan v Jeanette Smith*; K=*Stokes*; M=*United States v McNeil*; N=*Huey Newton* case; O=*United States v Sherpix*; P=*Pentagon Papers* case; S=*Panther 21* case; V=*Venceremos* case; W=*California v Block*; see §§9.1 and 9.3

# VI. PREJUDGMENT OF WOMEN

## A. Women Parties §9.51

As women enter the mainstream of economic and political life in the United States, increasing numbers of women are suing for injuries and damages and are charged with violations of state and federal law. Chapter 4 discusses some problems to anticipate in cases in which women will be present in the courtroom—as parties, attorneys, witnesses, or judges. And see questions in §§11.27–11.29, 11.51–11.56. The following questions are directed to men and women panel members in cases in which women are parties.

Questions 1 and 2 were asked in *California v Barr* (protesters against Livermore Nuclear Weapons Laboratory; see §11.58).

1. ____. You have probably noticed that several of the [*defendants/plaintiffs*] in this case are women. [*Several are mothers, and we also have a few grandmothers.*] Will you have any difficulty in listening impartially to testimony they give as to why they participated in the [*events*] leading up to this case?
2. ____. Are you embarrassed that women in their [*sixties and seventies*] have been [*arrested*] for [*demonstrating for peace/other causes*]?
3. A ____. Do you feel that the laws of this country may incorrectly favor minority groups or women?
   [*If yes*]
   a. How?
4. A ____. Have any of you been accused by anyone of racial or sex bias?
   [*If yes*]
   a. Please describe the circumstances.
5. A ____. Do any of you, or your immediate family or close friends, belong to any organization that denies membership to women?
   [*If yes*]
   a. Describe.

*COMMENT:* Counsel may decide to follow the Charles Garry cross-examination approach at this point and ask:

b. What organization is that?

---

A=*Brewster*; B=*Briggs*; C=questions traditionally asked or permitted by the trial judge; D=*Angela Davis* case; E=*Detroit Black Panther* case; F=*Stroud*; G=*Gaskins*; H=*United States v Ramos*; J=*Michigan v Jeanette Smith*; K=*Stokes*; M=*United States v McNeil*; N=*Huey Newton* case; O=*United States v Sherpix*; P=*Pentagon Papers* case; S=*Panther 21* case; V=*Venceremos* case; W=*California v Block*; see §§9.1 and 9.3

c. Why does it deny membership to women?
d. Why do you belong to it?

*COMMENT:* These questions and answers lead into additional questions:

6. ___. Are you opposed to the Equal Rights Amendment?
7. ___. What do you think of the women's movement?

*COMMENT:* Eisenberg and Seymour, in "Defending Battered Women: A Model Voir Dire," 16 *Trial* 30 (1980) recommended asking women jurors:

1. ___. What do you do?
2. ___. Do these activities take up much of your time?
3. ___. Do you approve of women working while they are married?
4. ___. Do you think your job is as important as your husband's?
5. ___. Do you think your judgment is as good as your husband's?
6. ___. Do you think your husband would make a better juror than you?

*COMMENT:* It is easy to draft voir dire questions concerning juror reactions to women workers. A good basic list can be drafted from a letter to columnist "Dear Abby" by a woman protesting such old husband's tales and attitudes as:

> Sorry, but we don't hire single girls; they'll just leave us to get married.
> Sorry, we don't hire married women; they'll just leave us to have babies.
> Sorry, we don't want to employ mothers; they ought to be home with their children.
> Sorry, we don't give jobs to women whose husbands are working; they don't need the money.

*San Francisco Chronicle*, Dec. 17, 1976, p.61. See Soler, "Woman's Place . . .'; Combatting Sex-Based Prejudices in Jury Trials Through Voir Dire," 15 *Santa Clara Lawyer* 535 (1975).

## B. Lifestyles §9.52

When a woman's sexual relations or marital status may be referred to in a derogatory fashion by prosecution witnesses or may become an

---

A=*Brewster*; B=*Briggs*; C=questions traditionally asked or permitted by the trial judge; D=*Angela Davis* case; E=*Detroit Black Panther* case; F=*Stroud*; G=*Gaskins*; H=*United States v Ramos*; J=*Michigan v Jeanette Smith*; K=*Stokes*; M=*United States v McNeil*; N=*Huey Newton* case; O=*United States v Sherpix*; P=*Pentagon Papers* case; S=*Panther 21* case; V=*Venceremos* case; W=*California v Block*; see §§9.1 and 9.3

issue in a civil suit, counsel may adapt questions asked in *United States v Soliah*, the case of a male bank robbery defendant who was a companion of kidnapped Patricia Hearst (ED Cal, No. S 75-523, Apr. 21, 1975; see §8.82).

1. ___. How do you feel about a man and a woman living together who are not married to each other?
2. ___. If the evidence presented at trial were to show that [*Steven Soliah*] lived with, or slept with [*Patty Hearst*], would that fact alone cause you to return a verdict of guilty to the bank robbery charge?

If the defendant is a white woman who has borne children out of wedlock, especially if the father was black, counsel may need to ask questions on jurors' attitudes toward women who bear children out of wedlock and also on women who have sexual relations across color lines. If the prosecution is expected to make derogatory references to one or both of these situations, jurors will be much better prepared to put these facts in perspective if they have already learned about them. Jury consultant Maureen McLaughlin describes one case in which this problem arose, although nothing about the children was relevant to the crime charged, "How To Read a Juror," *Barristers*, summer 1978, at 44.

## C. When Rape Is an Issue §9.53

The issue of sexual assault against a woman may arise in a civil suit for damages or in a criminal case. It is discussed in depth in Schneider and Jordan, *Representation of Women Who Defend Themselves in Response to Physical or Sexual Assault* (Center for Constitutional Rights, 853 Broadway, New York, New York 10003). See also Sharon L. McCombie, ed., *The Rape Crisis Intervention Handbook: A Guide for Victim Care* (Plenum Publishing, 1980) and A. Nicholas Grath with H. Jean Birnbaum, *Men Who Rape* (Plenum Publishing, 1979).

In the Joan Little case, jury selection required ten days. Little, a black woman prisoner, was charged with murdering her white male jailer. The defense team questioned jurors about their attitudes on race and rape, police and jails, politics and fear, asking questions such as:

---

A=*Brewster*; B=*Briggs*; C=questions traditionally asked or permitted by the trial judge; D=*Angela Davis* case; E=*Detroit Black Panther* case; F=*Stroud*; G=*Gaskins*; H=*United States v Ramos*; J=*Michigan v Jeanette Smith*; K=*Stokes*; M=*United States v McNeil*; N=*Huey Newton* case; O=*United States v Sherpix*; P=*Pentagon Papers* case; S=*Panther 21* case; V=*Venceremos* case; W=*California v Block*; see §§9.1 and 9.3

1. ___. Do you think that most women who are raped may have encouraged the attack?
2. ___. Do you think male jailers take advantage of female prisoners?

A jury composed of five blacks and seven whites was eventually chosen (one of the white jurors became ill and was replaced by a black alternate during trial). The trial lasted for five weeks, during which the prosecution argued that Little had lured the jailer into her cell in order to kill him. Little testified that the jailer, armed with an icepick, forced her to perform an act of oral sex; he dropped the icepick; she grabbed it and stabbed him in self-defense. After deliberating for an hour and 18 minutes, the jury acquitted Little of all charges. *North Carolina v Little* (Wake County Super Ct, Aug. 15, 1975).

## VII. ATTITUDES TOWARD PLAINTIFF OR DEFENDANT

### A. In General §9.56

The most difficult problem to overcome in the trial may be the client's appearance and demeanor, which may be objectionable to the majority of the jurors, even when no racial or religious factors are present. For example, defense counsel in the *Chicago Eight* federal conspiracy trial (see §3.54) requested the judge to ask questions 1–2 of prospective jurors.

1. ___. Do you have any hostile feeling toward persons whose lifestyles differ considerably from your own?
2. ___. Would you let your son or daughter marry a [*hippie/yippie*]?

*COMMENT:* Defense counsel pursued the line shown in questions 3–6.

3. ___. If your children are male, do they have long hair or wear what you consider to be unorthodox clothing?
4. ___. Do you know who the Jefferson Airplane, Country Joe and the Fish, Phil Ochs, or the Fugs [*Jefferson Starship*, *David Bowie*, *The Clash or Michael Jackson*] are?
5. ___. Do you consider marijuana habit forming?
6. ___. Do you believe that young men who refuse to participate in the armed forces because of their opposition to war are cowards, slackers, or unpatriotic?

---

A=*Brewster*; B=*Briggs*; C=questions traditionally asked or permitted by the trial judge; D=*Angela Davis* case; E=*Detroit Black Panther* case; F=*Stroud*; G=*Gaskins*; H=*United States v Ramos*; J=*Michigan v Jeanette Smith*; K=*Stokes*; M=*United States v McNeil*; N=*Huey Newton* case; O=*United States v Sherpix*; P=*Pentagon Papers* case; S=*Panther 21* case; V=*Venceremos* case; W=*California v Block*; see §§9.1 and 9.3

*COMMENT:* The Seventh Circuit Court of Appeal reversed the convictions in the *Chicago Eight* case on the ground, inter alia, that the trial judge had improperly restricted defense voir dire. *United States v Dellinger* (7th Cir 1972) 472 F2d 340.

In the *Gainesville Eight* trial, the defense submitted questions 7–8.

7. B ___. How do you feel about people whose personal appearance, clothing and general lifestyle is different from that of most Americans?
8. B ___. How do you feel about people who smoke marijuana?

*COMMENT:* When parties or witnesses are disabled, and it is important that the jurors listen to their testimony attentively, it will be necessary to give the jurors time to get accustomed to the disabled person's appearance before the taking of testimony begins. Otherwise, jurors will be looking at the disabled person furtively or openly, trying to satisfy their natural curiosity about why the person is in a wheelchair, is wearing braces, or whatever. On first seeing a disabled person, it is common for people to be engulfed by feelings about the unfairness of the way accidents happen or illness strikes.

Somehow during voir dire counsel needs to prepare the jurors for this aspect of the case so they will be able to face the disabled person directly and evaluate the person's testimony accordingly.

## B. Toward Party's Views on White Racism §9.57

1. N ___. Assuming it is a fact that my client, [*Mr./Ms. Smith*], believes that no white person can be fair and impartial in this particular case, would that in any way prejudice you?
2. N ___. Assume that my client, [*Mr./Ms. Smith*], believed that white supremacy and white racism cause the problems in the ghetto in [*Alameda County*], would that factor create within you a prejudice or prejudgment against [*Mr./Ms. Smith*]?

## C. Toward Party's Age §9.58

1. E ___. Now could you, members of the jury, accept the possibility that young people of the age of these [*plaintiffs/defendants*],

---

A=*Brewster*; B=*Briggs*; C=questions traditionally asked or permitted by the trial judge; D=*Angela Davis* case; E=*Detroit Black Panther* case; F=*Stroud*; G=*Gaskins*; H=*United States v Ramos*; J=*Michigan v Jeanette Smith*; K=*Stokes*; M=*United States v McNeil*; N=*Huey Newton* case; O=*United States v Sherpix*; P=*Pentagon Papers* case; S=*Panther 21* case; V=*Venceremos* case; W=*California v Block*; see §§9.1 and 9.3

who are [*17 to 22*], might look at society and feel that it is important to make very basic changes?

2. E ___. Do you have any feeling about young people, as distinguished from older people, trying to find different approaches and wanting to change things more quickly than, let's say, people of your age group?

*COMMENT:* When counsel is older than client, counsel may ask question 3.

3. E ___. Do you feel that [*we older people*] are of such experience that people like [*ourselves*] ought to judge young people because they are too young, and [*we*] ought to decide what is right and wrong for people? Do you have any feelings like that?
4. E ___. Do you feel, in view of your background and experience, that you can judge people coming from the background of these[*defendants/plaintiffs*], and from their age group: do you feel that you're in a position to do that?
5. E ___. Do you think that there is an important difference in background between yourselves and these [*defendants/plaintiffs*]?
6. E ___. Do you think that you can understand the differences between yourself (and other persons of your age, racial or ethnic group) and these [*defendants/plaintiffs*]?

*COMMENT:* It is also necessary to ask questions about older parties when they participate in litigation in an unexpected role. For example, when people in their seventies or eighties demonstrate for peace and get arrested, jurors of the same or of middle age may feel at first that the grey-haired defendants were acting in a manner not appropriate for their age. Questions need to be asked on voir dire to shake loose any stereotypes about what kinds of political action are "proper" for older people. See §9.51

## D. Toward Plaintiff's or Defendant's Organization

### 1. Knowledge or Opinion of Organization §9.59

Extensive voir dire was permitted on attitudes toward and knowledge of the Black Panther Party in the *Newton* case. The following questions

---

A=*Brewster*; B=*Briggs*; C=questions traditionally asked or permitted by the trial judge; D=*Angela Davis* case; E=*Detroit Black Panther* case; F=*Stroud*; G=*Gaskins*; H=*United States v Ramos*; J=*Michigan v Jeanette Smith*; K=*Stokes*; M=*United States v McNeil*; N=*Huey Newton* case; O=*United States v Sherpix*; P=*Pentagon Papers* case; S=*Panther 21* case; V=*Venceremos* case; W=*California v Block*; see §§9.1 and 9.3

will suggest appropriate questions to ask when a client is a member, or allegedly a member, of a Puerto Rican party or organization, or other organizations sometimes involved in civil or criminal cases, such as peace and environmental groups engaged in civil disobedience.

1. N ___. Now, have you ever heard of the [*Black Panther Party*]?
2. N ___. Have you ever heard anybody discussing the [*Black Panther Party*]?
3. N ___. Have you ever seen anything in the news media criticizing the [*Black Panther Party*]?
4. N ___. Have you ever seen anything in the [*Oakland Tribune*] about Police Chief [*Gain*] criticizing the [*Black Panther Party*]?
5. N ___. Have you heard or read anything about the [*Black Panther Party*] that would lead you to feel you may have prejudices against people who belong to that [*party/organization*]?
6. N ___. Have you ever made the statement that the [*Black Panthers*] ought to be destroyed and every one of its members put in jail?
7. N ___. You have never discussed with any of your fellow men that those [*Panthers*] ought to be done away with?
8. N ___. You mean to say that you have heard that the [*Black Panthers*] cause trouble?
9. N ___. Do you mean you heard on the news that the [*Black Panthers*] were involved in troublemaking, is that right?
10. N ___. Have you made statements similar to that?
11. N ___. Do you have any preconceived opinions about what the [*Black Panther Party*] stands for?
12. N ___. Would you say that you are already committed to the belief that the [*Black Panthers*] are trouble makers, though?
13. N ___. Have you within your mind associated the members of the [*Black Panther Party*] with guns?
14. N ___. Do you feel any revulsion against the [*Black Panther Party*]?
15. N ___. Do you believe that the [*Black Panther Party*] is a group of [*black racists*]?
16. N ___. Do you believe that any member of the [*Black Panther Party*] is not a credible person?
17. N ___. You would consider that any person who was a member of the [*Black Panther Party*] would not have a very good character?

---

A=*Brewster*; B=*Briggs*; C=questions traditionally asked or permitted by the trial judge; D=*Angela Davis* case; E=*Detroit Black Panther* case; F=*Stroud*; G=*Gaskins*; H=*United States v Ramos*; J=*Michigan v Jeanette Smith*; K=*Stokes*; M=*United States v McNeil*; N=*Huey Newton* case; O=*United States v Sherpix*; P=*Pentagon Papers* case; S=*Panther 21* case; V=*Venceremos* case; W=*California v Block*; see §§9.1 and 9.3

18. N ___. You would have difficulty believing any member of the [*client's organization*] testifying under oath because of [*his/her*] questionable character as far as you have determined it, isn't that right?
19. N ___. Does the name [*Black Panther Party*] bring any revulsion in your own feelings?
20. N ___. Do you have any conscientious feelings against the platform of the [*Black Panther Party*]?
21. N ___. Do you hold the [*Black Panther Party*] responsible for any violence?
22. N ___. And has the thought also entered into your head that once we do away with organizations like the [*Black Panther Party*], the threat to the white community will cease? Has that thought ever entered your mind?
23. N ___. Well, the thought entered into your mind that the [*Black Panther Party*] has tended toward violence. Do you still hold that view?
24. N ___. Do you think that the [*Black Panther Party*] is just a political party?
25. N ___. Well, then, do I take it that you would treat the [*Black Panther Party*] by the same standard you treat the [*Christian Endeavor*] or [*YMCA or YWCA*]?
26. N ___. Would you be prejudiced by the fact that my client is a member of the [*Black Panther Party*]?
27. N ___. In other words, it won't make any difference to you that the defendant is a member of the [*Black Panther Party*]?
28. N ___. Now let's talk a little bit about what you have referred to as [*black racism*]. What information has come to your mind that denotes the fact that the [*Black Panther Party*] is a [*black racist*] organization?
29. N ___. Isn't it a fact that you have never seen any accounts by any [*Black Panther Party*] member or heard from their platform any things showing that they have ever advocated [*black racism*]?
30. N ___. And, as a matter of fact, if you have studied their literature and their pamphlets you have found the opposite to be true; is that right?
31. N ___. It's true, is it not, that when you equated the [*Black Panther Party*] as the spokesmen for and advocating the cause of the

A=*Brewster*; B=*Briggs*; C=questions traditionally asked or permitted by the trial judge; D=*Angela Davis* case; E=*Detroit Black Panther* case; F=*Stroud*; G=*Gaskins*; H=*United States v Ramos*; J=*Michigan v Jeanette Smith*; K=*Stokes*; M=*United States v McNeil*; N=*Huey Newton* case; O=*United States v Sherpix*; P=*Pentagon Papers* case; S=*Panther 21* case; V=*Venceremos* case; W=*California v Block*; see §§9.1 and 9.3

[*black*] people with the Ku Klux Klan advocating the cause of white people, that this was not really based on facts at your disposal?

32. N ___. Do you have an opinion as to whether the organization [*Venceremos*] is a peaceful organization, or do you associate it within your own mind as an organization that participates in illegal activity?

*COMMENT:* Questions 33–43 were asked in the voir dire of members of a New York City *grand* jury asked to indict 21 members of the Black Panther Party of New York.

33. S ___. Have you heard of the [*Black Panther Party*] before your appearance in court?
[*If yes*]
a. In what connection?
34. S ___. Have you heard about pending indictments against certain members of the [*Black Panther Party*] in this country?
35. S ___. Do you feel that the [*Black Panther Party*] is a militant organization?
36. S ___. Is it your view that black militancy means change through violence?
37. S ___. Do you feel that, if the [*Black Panther Party*] as an organization is unable to achieve its objectives by legal means, that they will then be achieved by violent or unlawful means?
38. S ___. Do you feel that, under the circumstances, members of the [*Black Panther Party*] are more disposed towards violence than any other person?
39. S ___. Would you agree with the goal of the [*Black Panther Party*] for community control of the police?
40. S ___. How about schools or sanitation?
41. S ___. If you heard testimony that the [*Black Panthers*] were Marxist-Leninist revolutionaries, would that in and of itself render you more prone to vote for an indictment for an unrelated crime?
42. S ___. In other words, even though there was testimony to the effect that a prospective defendant was a revolutionary, that wouldn't influence you in deciding to [*indict*] [*him/her*] for the crime of [*robbery*] or [arson]?

---

A=*Brewster*; B=*Briggs*; C=questions traditionally asked or permitted by the trial judge; D=*Angela Davis* case; E=*Detroit Black Panther* case; F=*Stroud*; G=*Gaskins*; H=*United States v Ramos*; J=*Michigan v Jeanette Smith*; K=*Stokes*; M=*United States v McNeil*; N=*Huey Newton* case; O=*United States v Sherpix*; P=*Pentagon Papers* case; S=*Panther 21* case; V=*Venceremos* case; W=*California v Block*; see §§9.1 and 9.3

43. S ___. Do you think [*Eldridge Cleaver's*] leaving this country was an act of political exile?

### 2. Prejudice against Views of Organization §9.60

1. N ___. Do you have any objections to the [*Black Panther Party*] elucidating their opinions vocally to the press and to the public at large that the [*black*] people of the [*ghetto*] are being oppressed?
2. N ___. Did anything about what the [*Black Panther*] spokesman said affect you to the point where you would be in a state of shock?
3. N ___. What he said made you angry?
4. N ___. Did it start you to thinking?
   [*To Spanish-surname juror who had been to Cuba*]
5. N ___. Well, let me ask you this, if the evidednce shows that my client, [*Mr./Ms. Smith*], and [*his/her*] organization think that Fidel Castro has done a good job in Cuba, would that prejudice you against [*him/her*]?
6. N ___. If my client says that the white people are causing all the misery for black people, does that make you mad?
   would the testimony of other persons, particularly Indians?
7. N ___. If it were a fact that the [*client's organization*] says, among other things, that the white community are the oppressors and that blacks are a colony, and that they are victims of conditions in the ghettos, and if they say that the police are their oppressors, would that fact in itself create within you a revulsion and a prejudice toward any member of the [*organization*]?
8. N ___. Assuming the evidence will show that the [*client's organization*] is an organization originally created for the purpose of [*self-defense against the oppression of the police in the ghettos of Oakland*], would that create a prejudice within you?

*COMMENT:* The district attorney objected to question 8, but the judge allowed the question, restated: "Assume it's true that."

Professor Robert Blauner recommends an open-ended style of questioning as an effective technique. See §18.7. In reference to a previous prospective juror who stated that "the Black Panthers make a mockery

---

A=*Brewster*; B=*Briggs*; C=questions traditionally asked or permitted by the trial judge; D=*Angela Davis* case; E=*Detroit Black Panther* case; F=*Stroud*; G=*Gaskins*; H=*United States v Ramos*; J=*Michigan v Jeanette Smith*; K=*Stokes*; M=*United States v McNeil*; N=*Huey Newton* case; O=*United States v Sherpix*; P=*Pentagon Papers* case; S=*Panther 21* case; V=*Venceremos* case; W=*California v Block*; see §§9.1 and 9.3

of the law," Blauner suggests asking the next prospective juror: "What do you think about this opinion"?

9. E ___. The question is, if it were shown in the evidence that these people believe that capitalism is not a proper way to organize society and that capitalism has brought about many of the problems of society, and that they believe in socialism as a better method, would you hold that against them in any way? Would you feel you wouldn't be able to sit fairly in judgment because they hold such beliefs?

### 3. Views of Organization on War §9.61

The verbs in this section have been put in the past tense for easier current use by readers. Parallel questions could refer to El Salvador, Nicaragua, Guatemala, South Africa, the Middle East, or to protesters against war in general, nuclear war, or nuclear weapons.

1. N ___. Now I believe you said that [*one of your sons*] was in [*Vietnam*]?
2. N ___. And do you know that the [*Black Panther Party*], as one of its creeds, opposed the war in [*Vietnam*]; they thought it was a bad war and we had no business there?
3. N ___. Would that attitude influence you so you would be prejudiced against a member of that organization?
   [*If no*]
   a. In other words, you don't care what the beliefs of the [*Black Panthers*] were on [*Vietnam*]?
4. N ___. The fact that [*plaintiff/defendant*] is a member of a party that believes the [*Vietnam*] war was a white man's war, that we should have gotten out of there, that they were killing people of color—assuming those to be their beliefs—would that prejudice you?

*COMMENT:* In the *Pentagon Papers* case, the government proposed questions 5–12.

5. P ___. Do you hold any opinion about United States military involvement in the defense of [*South Vietnam*] which would prevent

A=*Brewster*; B=*Briggs*; C=questions traditionally asked or permitted by the trial judge; D=*Angela Davis* case; E=*Detroit Black Panther* case; F=*Stroud*; G=*Gaskins*; H=*United States v Ramos*; J=*Michigan v Jeanette Smith*; K=*Stokes*; M=*United States v McNeil*; N=*Huey Newton* case; O=*United States v Sherpix*; P=*Pentagon Papers* case; S=*Panther 21* case; V=*Venceremos* case; W=*California v Block*; see §§9.1 and 9.3

you from acting, or would make it difficult for you to act, as a fair and impartial juror in this case?

6. P ___. Have you or any of your close friends or relatives attended or participated in any marches, demonstrations, meetings, or other activities conducted to protest United States military involvement in the defense of [*South Vietnam*]?

7. P ___. Have you or any of your close friends or relatives ever advocated or participated in any activities designed to cause obstruction of United States military involvement in the defense of [*South Vietnam*]?

8. P ___. Have you or any of your close friends or relatives ever belonged, or contributed financially, to any organization, a purpose of which was to oppose, protest, or obstruct United States military involvement in the defense of [*South Vietnam*]?

9. P ___. Have you or any of your close friends or relatives ever advocated, or participated in any activities designed to give aid to the [*Viet Cong*] or [*North Vietnamese*]?

10. P ___. Do you hold the belief that the use of military force to oppose communist conquest is wrong, or that the use of military force for any purpose is wrong?

11. P ___. Have you or any of your close friends or relatives ever had any dispute or disagreement with the Selective Service System? If so, would that cause you to be prejudiced against the government or against the [*defendants/plaintiffs*]?

12. P ___. Do you hold any opinion about US policies, foreign or domestic, which would tend to prevent you from acting as a fair and impartial juror in this case?

*COMMENT:* Trial judges found questions on conscientious objection to military service too remote to ask prospective jurors in the *Pentagon Papers* case (concerning publication of secret government documents regarding the war in Vietnam) and in the draft refusal case of a black registrant who had not completed a conscientious objector's form. But such questions were permitted in *California v Barr;* see §§9.18 and 11.58.

---

A=*Brewster*; B=*Briggs*; C=questions traditionally asked or permitted by the trial judge; D=*Angela Davis* case; E=*Detroit Black Panther* case; F=*Stroud*; G=*Gaskins*; H=*United States v Ramos*; J=*Michigan v Jeanette Smith*; K=*Stokes*; M=*United States v McNeil*; N=*Huey Newton* case; O=*United States v Sherpix*; P=*Pentagon Papers* case; S=*Panther 21* case; V=*Venceremos* case; W=*California v Block*; see §§9.1 and 9.3

### 4. Views on Boycotts by Organization §9.62

1. N ___. Some time ago did you see an ad in the [*Oakland Tribune*] regarding the [*housewives' boycott*]?
2. N ___. Do you know about the [*housewives' boycott*]?
3. N ___. Do you approve or disapprove of that boycott?

*COMMENT:* The district attorney objected to question 3; the court sustained the objection, saying the question was "too far afield." Questions concerning boycotts of grapes and lettuce by the United Farm Workers union have been permitted, however, in San Francisco criminal trials of Latino or Chicano defendants. (See other questions concerning Latino defendants in §9.36.)

### 5. Views on Language Used by Organization §9.63

1. N ___. Do you know that the [*Black Panthers*] referred to certain police officers as "pigs"?
2. N ___. And would the fact that the [*Black Panthers*] referred to certain police officers as "pigs" prejudice you in any respect?
3. N ___. Now, it is very, very important to the [*defendant*] whether you have any prejudgments in this matter. You have expressed yourself, and very frankly and candidly, on how you react toward someone calling a police officer a "pig." Now would your reaction be such that it would create within you a prejudgment to a point where there would be a resentment on your part against the [*defendant*], a rejection of [*Mr./Ms. Smith*] as a person when [*he/she*] takes the witness stand?
4. E ___. There's going to be some evidence introduced here that deals with the question of language, and language is something that affects us all and that can trouble us sometimes when we express our ideas. If it is shown here during the course of the trial that the literature and the words used by these [*defendants*] and other members of their organization include the expression "pigs," as representing the oppressor in society, do you believe that the use of that term would affect your judgment?

---

A=*Brewster*; B=*Briggs*; C=questions traditionally asked or permitted by the trial judge; D=*Angela Davis* case; E=*Detroit Black Panther* case; F=*Stroud*; G=*Gaskins*; H=*United States v Ramos*; J=*Michigan v Jeanette Smith*; K=*Stokes*; M=*United States v McNeil*; N=*Huey Newton* case; O=*United States v Sherpix*; P=*Pentagon Papers* case; S=*Panther 21* case; V=*Venceremos* case; W=*California v Block*; see §§9.1 and 9.3

5. E ___. Can you, as the [*prosecutor*] pointed out earlier, differentiate words of different meanings to different people under different circumstances?

6. E ___. Can you realize that you might not yourself use a word or even want to use such words but yet keep your mind open to understand what the [*defendants*] mean by those words? As an example, the word, "honky," has often been used in recent years and, of course, for white people it is more difficult to take this word than for black people. Can you keep your minds open to the language used by these young people?

7. E ___. Let me ask you this: Does the slogan, "Power to the People," which is the slogan of the [*12*] people here and of a party they are associated with, does that bother you, offend you in any way; do you feel that that is wrong?

8. E ___. Associated with this slogan of, "Power to the People," is frequently seen the arm with the fist upright, like this. Have any of you ever seen that symbol?
[*If yes*]

9. E ___. You know, perhaps you have noticed that as I made this gesture I had to stand up straight. Do you feel that this symbol of "Power to the People," as I have described it to you, offends you or makes you feel there is something about it that suggests perhaps violence or that it is in itself criminal action for a man to stand up and do this, a black man especially? Do any of you feel that there is something wrong about that?

*COMMENT:* And see questions on community, regional, and ethnic language in §§9.34, 9.36, and 9.44.

Every group has its own buzz words whose meaning is quite clear to the initiated and quite meaningless, if not offensive, to others. In a case involving antiwar demonstrators, for example, it may be helpful to discuss on voir dire the kinds of language your clients are likely to use in their testimony, including "warmongers," "the arms race," "civil disobedience," "passive resistance," "hawks," etc.

When the women's movement is in issue, it is worthwhile to define what your client or witnesses mean by "male chauvinist pig," "feminism," etc.

---

A=*Brewster*; B=*Briggs*; C=questions traditionally asked or permitted by the trial judge; D=*Angela Davis* case; E=*Detroit Black Panther* case; F=*Stroud*; G=*Gaskins*; H=*United States v Ramos*; J=*Michigan v Jeanette Smith*; K=*Stokes*; M=*United States v McNeil*; N=*Huey Newton* case; O=*United States v Sherpix*; P=*Pentagon Papers* case; S=*Panther 21* case; V=*Venceremos* case; W=*California v Block*; see §§9.1 and 9.3

### 6. Knowledge and Opinion of Communist Party §9.64

For extensive voir dire on the juror's ideas about the Communist Party by defendant Angela Davis, acting as her own cocounsel, see chapter 17.

1. D ___. Do you associate communism with riots?
2. D ___. Has [*the plaintiff's/defendant's*] Communist party membership affected your thinking in any way as a result of what you read about the events [*at issue in this case*]?
3. D ___. And your being against members of the Communist party means that you would be against [*the plaintiff/defendant*] if [*he/she*] admitted that [*he/she*] was a member of the Communist party, wouldn't you?
4. D ___. And you understand that [*the plaintiff/defendant*] is not charged with being a member of the Communist party?
5. D ___. Would you give the testimony of a Communist as much weight as you would the testimony of a non-Communist?
6. D ___. Do you have any opinion that Communists are as inclined to tell the truth under oath as anybody else?
7. D ___. Don't you believe that a Communist will lie under oath, if necessary, in order to carry out [*his/her*] aim of overthrowing the government [*of the state of California*]?

## E. Toward Party's Lifestyle §9.66

A battered woman was acquitted of second degree murder for the fatal stabbing of her husband in *Michigan v Jeanette Smith* (Circuit Court for County of Kalkasa, Mich., No. 416), see §11.51. Defense counsel Dean Robb asked the following questions of prospective jurors. (For additional questions from this case, see §11.51.)

1. J ___. The evidence in this case will be that [*Mrs. Smith*] moved to [*Las Vegas*] when she separated from [*her husband*]. Have you ever been out there?
   [*If no*]
   Would the fact that [*Mrs. Smith*] moved there lead you to form any particular opinions about her character or credibility?

---

A=*Brewster*; B=*Briggs*; C=questions traditionally asked or permitted by the trial judge; D=*Angela Davis* case; E=*Detroit Black Panther* case; F=*Stroud*; G=*Gaskins*; H=*United States v Ramos*; J=*Michigan v Jeanette Smith*; K=*Stokes*; M=*United States v McNeil*; N=*Huey Newton* case; O=*United States v Sherpix*; P=*Pentagon Papers* case; S=*Panther 21* case; V=*Venceremos* case; W=*California v Block*; see §§9.1 and 9.3

*COMMENT:* See also questions on the lifestyle of women parties to litigation in §9.52.

## F. Toward Party's Religion §9.67

When religious belief is an important factor in your client's life, or when an ethical or moral principle is at the root of your client's actions, it is wise to ask some questions on voir dire that go beyond demographic questions about the jurors' attendance at church or sending their children to parochial schools.

A black woman Muslim defendant was acquitted by a conservative, all-white San Diego jury in a welfare fraud case in *California v Mary Barnes* (San Diego Super Ct, 1977). Defense counsel was permitted to ask a few voir dire questions concerning the defendant's religion, which figured in the case.

1. ___. Do you know what a Black Muslim is?
2. ___. Is there anything about this religious belief that is going to interfere with your sitting as a juror in this case?

Attorney Gerri Russell wanted to ask further questions, particularly to dispel any juror hostility that might have arisen because members of an offshoot Muslim sect were being charged with terrorist acts in a contemporaneous trial in Washington, D.C. The trial judge did not permit this, on First Amendment grounds. However, Russell felt the questions asked had been important in preparing the jury for this aspect of the case.

The following question was posed to jurors in a wrongful death case tried to a six-person jury a small Michigan town. *Stroud v General Motors* (see §3.42).

1. F ___. This question is for all of you, although it rarely hits a person. There are some people in every community and every county in this land who believe that death and tragedy are preordained; in other words, that it's God's will—or it's a Supreme Being's will. Some people even believe that you shouldn't bring a lawsuit, that you should not bring a civil suit for wrongful killing of another. Do any of you hold that view?

---

A=*Brewster*; B=*Briggs*; C=questions traditionally asked or permitted by the trial judge; D=*Angela Davis* case; E=*Detroit Black Panther* case; F=*Stroud*; G=*Gaskins*; H=*United States v Ramos*; J=*Michigan v Jeanette Smith*; K=*Stokes*; M=*United States v McNeil*; N=*Huey Newton* case; O=*United States v Sherpix*; P=*Pentagon Papers* case; S=*Panther 21* case; V=*Venceremos* case; W=*California v Block*; see §§9.1 and 9.3

*COMMENT:* The following questions were asked in *California v Barr* (protesters against Livermore Nuclear Weapons Laboratory; see §11.58).

1. ___. The First Amendment to the United States Constitution protects everyone's right to practice or exercise his or her religion or conscience. Do you believe in that right?
2. ___. Have you thought about what it means to have the right to practice or exercise your religion?
3. ___. Can you be fair in judging people who practice their religion by protesting?
4. ___. Are you opposed to people who act out their convictions?
5. ___. Are you a member of any church?
   [*If yes*]
   a. Does your church take a position on [*nuclear weapons*]?
   b. Do you agree with the position of your church?

*COMMENT:* If a juror mentions a connection with the Catholic Church, the following questions may elicit a more significant response.

6. ___. Have you heard about the Catholic bishops' statement on nuclear weapons and war?
7. ___. Have you heard about the pope's statement to scientists?

*COMMENT:* This statement was made November 12, 1983, to the Pontifical Academy of Sciences, that scientists "must make a choice that will enable [them] to work for the good of people, for the building up of peace. By refusing certain fields of research . . . scientists of the whole world ought to be united in a common readiness to disarm science . . . and to form a . . . force for peace."

If a juror mentions a connection with the Mormon Church, question 8 may be particularly appropriate.

8. ___. Have you heard of the Mormon Church's opposition to the placement of nuclear weapons in Utah?
9. ___. Have you ever prayed over a difficult decision in your life?
10. ___. Do you believe that the fate of the defendants will rest in your hands?

*COMMENT:* Source material for voir dire on religious attitudes may be drawn from various national and state civil rights reports such as

A=*Brewster*; B=*Briggs*; C=questions traditionally asked or permitted by the trial judge; D=*Angela Davis* case; E=*Detroit Black Panther* case; F=*Stroud*; G=*Gaskins*; H=*United States v Ramos*; J=*Michigan v Jeanette Smith*; K=*Stokes*; M=*United States v McNeil*; N=*Huey Newton* case; O=*United States v Sherpix*; P=*Pentagon Papers* case; S=*Panther 21* case; V=*Venceremos* case; W=*California v Block*; see §§9.1 and 9.3

the Governor's Task Force on Civil Rights' *Report on Race, Ethnic and Religious Violence in California 1982* (available from Documents and Publications, Box 1015, North Highlands, CA 95660).

### G. Recent Developments §9.68

See §9.25.

## VIII. ATTITUDES TOWARD CREDIBILITY OF WITNESSES

### A. Plaintiff or Defendant §9.70

1. N ___. Would you have any fault to find with the law that says that a person who takes the witness stand, regardless of what his profession is, has equal dignity with any other person who takes the witness stand?
2. N ___. If the [*plaintiff/defendant*] in this case were to testify, would you give [*him/her*] the same credence that you would give to any other witness?
3. N ___. If and when it is necessary to the [*plaintiff/defendant*] to testify in [*his/her*] own behalf, would you give the same credence to [*his/her*] testimony that you would to a person who is not a [*plaintiff/defendant*]?

### B. Black Person §9.71

1. N ___. Would you give more credence to the testimony of a white person than you would the testimony of a black person?
2. C ___. Would any juror be prejudiced by the fact that [*Witness*] is white and [*Party*] is black?
   [Asked in *King v United States* (DC Cir 1966) 362 F2d 968.]
3. J ___. Do you feel that jurors give greater credibility to witnesses who are of the same racial or ethnic group?

### C. Law Enforcement Officer §9.72

*COMMENT:* See §§9.14, 9.80–9.82, 9.104, 11.56 for further related questions.

---

A=*Brewster*; B=*Briggs*; C=questions traditionally asked or permitted by the trial judge; D=*Angela Davis* case; E=*Detroit Black Panther* case; F=*Stroud*; G=*Gaskins*; H=*United States v Ramos*; J=*Michigan v Jeanette Smith*; K=*Stokes*; M=*United States v McNeil*; N=*Huey Newton* case; O=*United States v Sherpix*; P=*Pentagon Papers* case; S=*Panther 21* case; V=*Venceremos* case; W=*California v Block*; see §§9.1 and 9.3

1. P ___. Would you give greater credence to the testimony of a law enforcement official because of the fact that [*he/she*] is such an official as compared with the testimony of the [*plaintiff/defendant*] or other person?
2. N ___. Now, as between the testimony of a police officer who would testify, and the [*plaintiff/defendant*] who would testify, would you give more credibilty to the testimony of a police officer than you would to the [*plaintiff/defendant*]?
3. S ___. Do you feel that testimony of a black police officer who may have infiltrated the [*Black Panther Party*] is entitled to more merit than any other witness?
4. S ___. Would you give more credence to the testimony of a police officer than to any other person?
5. S ___. Would you give more credence to the testimony of an informer than to any other person?
6. N ___. In other words, just because a witness happens to be a police officer wouldn't give [*him/her*] any halo indicating that [*he/she*] is telling the truth, would it?
7. N ___. Would you give the testimony of a police officer more credence, more reliability, than you would that of a [*black*] person?
8. N ___. You appreciate the fact that there can be a situation in which a police officer would not tell the truth, isn't that right?
9. N ___. Would you give the testimony of a [*Black Panther*] as much credence as you would a police officer?
10. ___. How did Watergate affect your impressions of the FBI?

*COMMENT:* This question is sometimes used when an FBI agent is expected to testify for the prosecution.

## D. Government Official §9.73

1. P ___. If the [*prosecution/defense*] were to call high ranking officials, either civilian or military, would you give any more weight to their testimony by virtue of their position than any witnesses called by the [*defense/plaintiff*]?

*COMMENT:* Concerning this style of questioning, attorney Theodore Koskoff of Bridgeport, Connecticut, in a speech to the American Trial Lawyers Association, stated:

A=*Brewster*; B=*Briggs*; C=questions traditionally asked or permitted by the trial judge; D=*Angela Davis* case; E=*Detroit Black Panther* case; F=*Stroud*; G=*Gaskins*; H=*United States v Ramos*; J=*Michigan v Jeanette Smith*; K=*Stokes*; M=*United States v McNeil*; N=*Huey Newton* case; O=*United States v Sherpix*; P=*Pentagon Papers* case; S=*Panther 21* case; V=*Venceremos* case; W=*California v Block*; see §§9.1 and 9.3

In a much-criticized decision the court would not permit jurors to be asked whether they would attach more importance to the testimony of a government witness than a nongovernment witness. The court's discretion was upheld here because of what it said was a "lack of probative value." *Abeyta v United States* (10th Cir 1966) 368 F2d 544. But in an almost identical situation in the District of Columbia the same action was held to be error. *Brown v United States* (DC Cir 1964) 338 F28 543.

## E. Other Witnesses §9.74

1. P ___. Do you feel that a witness called by the [*prosecution/defense*] is more impartial and more credible that one called by the [*defense/plaintiff*] by virtue of that fact?
2. B ___. Would you give the same credibility to witnesses with long hair and beards as to any other witnesses?
3. N ___. You heard that juror say that [*he/she*] would have difficulty believing a member of the [*Black Panther Party*] or the [*Hell's Angels*]—[*he/she*] put them all in the same category. You don't share that view, do you?

*COMMENT:* Attorney Dennis Roberts of Oakland suggests asking question 4.

4. ___. You wouldn't accept the combined testimony of the [*prosecution's/defense's*] witnesses just because there are more of them, would you?

*COMMENT:* Detroit attorney Ernest Goodman used question 5 in *Michigan v DeSaussure* (see §3.27).

5. E ___. One question was raised earlier by the prosecutor. He asked you to assume that one of the persons who was to testify as a witness for the prosecution was a person who had formerly been a defendant in the case and later became a prosecution witness. He asked you whether you thought there is anything wrong with such a witness, and you said there was not. I would like to ask you about that possibility, if it arises in this case. Would you be prepared to examine the circumstances under which a person who was a defendant later became a prosecution witness? Would you be prepared to keep an open

A=*Brewster*; B=*Briggs*; C=questions traditionally asked or permitted by the trial judge; D=*Angela Davis* case; E=*Detroit Black Panther* case; F=*Stroud*; G=*Gaskins*; H=*United States v Ramos*; J=*Michigan v Jeanette Smith*; K=*Stokes*; M=*United States v McNeil*; N=*Huey Newton* case; O=*United States v Sherpix*; P=*Pentagon Papers* case; S=*Panther 21* case; V=*Venceremos* case; W=*California v Block*; see §§9.1 and 9.3

mind with respect to that man so that we can understand all the circumstances, how it happened, and what his motives were?

## F. False Testimony §9.75

1. G ___. Do you think a person can be frightened or coerced into giving false testimony?
2. G ___. Do you think a person could be coerced or frightened into giving a false statement—not in a formal proceeding, but, let's say, to an investigator?
3. G ___. Do you think it's likely?
4. G ___. It would depend on the investigator and on the interviewee's frame of mind, is that correct?
5. G ___. Do you think it might also depend on the circumstances under which the statement was obtained?
6. G ___. If a person being interviewed by some law enforcement or investigative agency is frightened that some sort of charge would be made against [*him/her*], do you believe such an individual might give a statement simply to avoid any charges, even though the statement wasn't true?

## G. Evaluating Witness's Testimony §9.76

1. G ___. In considering any statement or testimony made by a witness at a proceeding, what types of factors would you look at in evaluating that witness's testimony?
2. G ___. Let's put it this way: When someone tells you about an event, I imagine you evaluate what that person is telling you based on what you know about that person. Would that be fair? Maybe I'll expand on it a little bit. If you know that person tends to exaggerate whenever he or she tells you something, would you consider that in evaluating whatever you're told?
3. G ___. In making your own determination as to whether or not you're going to believe what you're told, you would probably consider everything you knew about that person—past experiences, the way that person's acting, all the factors, tangible and in-

A=*Brewster*; B=*Briggs*; C=questions traditionally asked or permitted by the trial judge; D=*Angela Davis* case; E=*Detroit Black Panther* case; F=*Stroud*; G=*Gaskins*; H=*United States v Ramos*; J=*Michigan v Jeanette Smith*; K=*Stokes*; M=*United States v McNeil*; N=*Huey Newton* case; O=*United States v Sherpix*; P=*Pentagon Papers* case; S=*Panther 21* case; V=*Venceremos* case; W=*California v Block*; see §§9.1 and 9.3

tangible, that you see, that you feel, that you hear, when you speak to somebody—would that be a fair statement?

4. G ___. And I imagine you'll do the same thing when you hear a witness testifying in this proceeding, right?

## H. Eyewitness Identification §9.77

The following questions were posed by respondent's counsel, Kenneth Lee Chotiner, now a judge of the Los Angeles Municipal Court, in a court-martial of a sailor accused of homosexual activity. *Administrative Discharge Board in the Case of DK3 Tangela Gaskins* (see §3.91). Chotiner was denied use of the Navy's standard questionnaire for courts-martial but was permitted to voir dire the three members of the board as if selecting a jury.

1. G ___. As an attorney, what type of practice did you have, what areas of law?
2. G ___. I heard you say "we." Were you in a partnership, a member of a firm?
3. G ___. Did you practice any criminal law?
4. G ___. In any of the cases that you handled, did you encounter any eye-witness identification problems?
5. G ___. So, then, would it be fair to say that you are aware that people can be mistaken in what they see and in what they identify?
6. G ___. And each of the people may believe that he or she is absolutely correct?
7. G ___. Do you believe it is possible for someone to misinterpret what they see?

## I. Recent Developments §9.78

See §9.25.

# IX. ATTITUDES TOWARD POLICE

## A. Questions on "Support Your Local Police" §9.80

1. N ___. Do you believe that the local police should be supported?

---

A=*Brewster*; B=*Briggs*; C=questions traditionally asked or permitted by the trial judge; D=*Angela Davis* case; E=*Detroit Black Panther* case; F=*Stroud*; G=*Gaskins*; H=*United States v Ramos*; J=*Michigan v Jeanette Smith*; K=*Stokes*; M=*United States v McNeil*; N=*Huey Newton* case; O=*United States v Sherpix*; P=*Pentagon Papers* case; S=*Panther 21* case; V=*Venceremos* case; W=*California v Block*; see §§9.1 and 9.3

2. N ___. Do you think the local police need any special help or support?
3. N ___. Do you or any members of your family carry placards or bumper strips on your automobiles saying "Support Your Local Police"?

*COMMENT:* It should be noted that jurors may become upset when asked by counsel whether they have stickers on their cars or homes. In at least one case in which the defense committee had visited the jurors' neighborhoods (see chapter 13), two prospective jurors were questioned about stickers seen on cars parked in front of their homes. Both jurors denied that their cars carried such stickers. (Neighbors or friends with stickers on their cars could have parked in front of the jurors' homes.) More important, the other prospective jurors seemed disturbed by the intrusion on their privacy indicated by such information in the hands of defense counsel. This reaction must be weighed against the value of probing questioning into "the juror's inwards," as Charles Garry puts it.

According to Attorney Victoria Heldman of Detroit, of the general questions lawyers ask, some say they obtain the most information about prospective jurors from questions about newspapers, magazines, and bumper stickers. Jurors give the lawyers "some real funny looks" when asked what bumper stickers they have on their cars. They often look at the judge, who looks back indicating that they are going to have to answer. Finally they answer reluctantly. The lawyers have no way of learning whether the answers are truthful, but the question often breaks the ice. The lawyer gets an incisive look into how a juror feels about disclosing something.

## B. In the Ghetto §9.81

The California *Governor's Task Force on Civil Rights* reported a deep-rooted hostility toward law enforcement officers in many California minority communities. The task force found that this hostility is based on the perception that minorities receive abusive treatment and inadequate protection at the hands of police officers. Governor's Task Force on Civil Rights, *Report on Racial, Ethnic and Religious Violence in California 1982*, Summary and Recommendations, pp. 2–3 (Dec. 10,

---

A=*Brewster*; B=*Briggs*; C=questions traditionally asked or permitted by the trial judge; D=*Angela Davis* case; E=*Detroit Black Panther* case; F=*Stroud*; G=*Gaskins*; H=*United States v Ramos*; J=*Michigan v Jeanette Smith*; K=*Stokes*; M=*United States v McNeil*; N=*Huey Newton* case; O=*United States v Sherpix*; P=*Pentagon Papers* case; S=*Panther 21* case; V=*Venceremos* case; W=*California v Block*; see §§9.1 and 9.3

1982) (available by order number DFEH 201 from Documents and Publications, Box 1015, North Highlands, CA 95660).

1. N ___. You have never been a [*black*] person, of course, but do you know how the police behave in the [*ghetto*] in [*West Oakland*] of [*Alameda County*]?
2. N ___. Do you think that there is such a thing as police brutality in the [*ghetto*] of [*Oakland*]?
3. N ___. Do you think it is possible that there is such a thing as police brutality?
4. N ___. Would you believe that it's possible to have police brutality in the [*black ghetto*]?
5. N ___. And I take it you are not personally aware of any such conduct on the part of the police?
6. N ___. You don't think that the aggression and the attitudes of the police toward the [*black ghetto*] and the members of the [*black ghetto*] create the same atmosphere as fascism created in Europe and with which the fascists tried to permeate the world?
7. N ___. If the evidence were presented to you that the police in this instance were the instigators and the plotters to destroy the [*plaintiff/defendant*], would you find that difficult to believe, as you sit there right now [*as a former police officer*], one who [*has friends*] in the police department?

*COMMENT:* The prosecutor objected to question. 7. The court asked the juror if he could answer before hearing the evidence, and he said no.

8. N ___. Now, have you ever watched night programs on television about ghetto problems, the problems of the so-called riots, or about Negro or black history and culture? Have you ever seen any of those on television?
   [*If yes*]
   a. Do you recall whether these programs made any kind of impression on you about whether there is a problem in the ghetto of hunger and deprivation and police brutality?
9. N ___. You haven't heard the [*plaintiff's/defendant's organization*] on television talking about police brutality?
10. N ___. Assuming that the [*Black Panther Party*], as one of its complaints, states that there is an excessive amount of police

A=*Brewster*; B=*Briggs*; C=questions traditionally asked or permitted by the trial judge; D=*Angela Davis* case; E=*Detroit Black Panther* case; F=*Stroud*; G=*Gaskins*; H=*United States v Ramos*; J=*Michigan v Jeanette Smith*; K=*Stokes*; M=*United States v McNeil*; N=*Huey Newton* case; O=*United States v Sherpix*; P=*Pentagon Papers* case; S=*Panther 21* case; V=*Venceremos* case; W=*California v Block*; see §§9.1 and 9.3

brutality against black people in the [*ghetto*] of [*Oakland*], do you believe that to be a justified complaint?

11. B ___. Can you conceive of government officials breaking the law?
12. ___. Did you hear about the California case in which a jury awarded three million dollars to the families of two black men slain in their bedrooms by white police officers? [*Roman and Guillory v City of Richmond* (ND Cal) (June 3, 1983)]
    [*If yes*]
    a. What did you think about the verdict? (See §10.80).

## C. Individual Police Officer and Juror §9.82

1. N ___. You know that a police officer was allegedly [*killed/injured/attacked*] in this case?
2. N ___. And your [*brother/son*] is a police officer, is he not?
3. N ___. Is he a [*patrolman*], or does he have a rank of some kind?
4. N ___. Are you friendly with him?
5. N ___. How often do you see him?
6. N ___. Do you go to each other's homes?
7. N ___. Would you find it embarrassing with your [*brother/son*] if you were to be on the jury that [*acquitted*] [*Mr./Ms. Smith*]?
8. N ___. Do you have any friends in the police department?
9. N ___. Now, would the fact that a police officer is a member of your [*union*], or affiliated with your union, or a fellow worker for the [*city*], would that factor give a police officer a head start in this case? I want you to think about this a little bit because it is an important question.
10. N ___. The fact that you are a [*municipal*] worker and you have friends in the police department, the very group that is going to [*prosecute*] this case, that would not in any way affect you, is that your statement?
11. N ___. I am somewhat interested in how you can be an impartial juror when you were already told by a friend of yours in the [*police*] department what his version of the facts of this case are. Would you explain that to me, please?

## D. Recent Developments §9.83

See §9.25.

---

A=*Brewster*; B=*Briggs*; C=questions traditionally asked or permitted by the trial judge; D=*Angela Davis* case; E=*Detroit Black Panther* case; F=*Stroud*; G=*Gaskins*; H=*United States v Ramos*; J=*Michigan v Jeanette Smith*; K=*Stokes*; M=*United States v McNeil*; N=*Huey Newton* case; O=*United States v Sherpix*; P=*Pentagon Papers* case; S=*Panther 21* case; V=*Venceremos* case; W=*California v Block*; see §§9.1 and 9.3

## X. ATTITUDES TOWARD CONSTITUTIONAL RIGHTS

### A. Democratic Functioning of Government §9.85

*COMMENT:* See also §§9.131–9.140.

1. P ___. Do you believe that the government of the United States has withheld information from the citizens of this country about how or why we became involved in [*Vietnam/Lebanon/Nicaragua/Grenada*]?
2. P ___. Do you believe that under our system of law, the government has a right to withhold information from the citizens of this country about how or why we became involved in [*Vietnam*]?
3. B ___. Are you familiar with the Declaration of Independence? Do you believe in it?

*COMMENT:* You may want to quote some of the words, or paraphrase them: That governments are instituted among people to secure their inalienable rights to life, liberty, and the pursuit of happiness, deriving their just powers from the consent of the governed. "That whenever any Form of Government becomes destructive of these ends, it is the Right of the People to alter or to abolish it, . . ."

4. P ___. If the documents in evidence contain information critical of certain actions by the government of the United States, would you still be willing to accept the documents as evidence and weigh them together with all other evidence in deciding the issues in this case, being fair to both the [*prosecution and the defense*]?

### B. Dissent and Militants §9.86

Juror attitudes toward the free exercise of religion (see §9.67) or toward freedom of speech, press, assembly, or petition may be significant indicators in many types of civil and criminal cases. The following questions were asked in state and federal felony cases. For the use of a First Amendment defense to state misdemeanor charges, see *California v Barr*; §11.58.

1. P ___. Do you recognize that all Americans have the right to speak out against any policy of the government with which they

---

A=*Brewster*; B=*Briggs*; C=questions traditionally asked or permitted by the trial judge; D=*Angela Davis* case; E=*Detroit Black Panther* case; F=*Stroud*; G=*Gaskins*; H=*United States v Ramos*; J=*Michigan v Jeanette Smith*; K=*Stokes*; M=*United States v McNeil*; N=*Huey Newton* case; O=*United States v Sherpix*; P=*Pentagon Papers* case; S=*Panther 21* case; V=*Venceremos* case; W=*California v Block*; see §§9.1 and 9.3

disagree under the First Amendment to the United States Constitution?

*COMMENT:* Free speech or press guaranties in many state constitutions are broader than the federal First Amendment. See, e.g., Calif Const Art I §§1–4. Particularly in state court cases, use both federal and state provisions.

2. P ___. Do you think that demonstrations are a proper method for people to employ to attempt to protest or alter a policy of the government, such as our involvement in [*Vietnam/Nicaragua/the Middle East*]?
3. P ___. Do you have any quarrel with people who actively protest or demonstrate?
4. M ___. Would you be prejudiced against or angry at a person who consistently took part in public rallies against war?
5. P ___. Have you ever been inconvenienced by a demonstration against [*war/nuclear weapons/etc.*]?
   [*If so*]
   a. What were the circumstances?
6. P ___. Has any member of your family to your knowledge participated in or witnessed a demonstration against war?
   [*If yes*]
   a. What were the circumstances?
7. P ___. Have you ever been present at or witnessed a demonstration against the war in [*Vietnam*]?
   [*If yes*]
   a. Where and when?
   b. Were there any law enforcement officers present?
      [*If yes*]
      (1) How many?
   c. Was anyone arrested that you saw?
   d. Did anything you observed affect your opinion of persons opposed to the war in [*Vietnam*]?
8. S ___. What does the word *militant* mean to you?
9. S ___. Do you know any person whom you could characterize as "militant"?
10. S ___. Do you think that being a militant in and of itself is a crime?

---

A=*Brewster*; B=*Briggs*; C=questions traditionally asked or permitted by the trial judge; D=*Angela Davis* case; E=*Detroit Black Panther* case; F=*Stroud*; G=*Gaskins*; H=*United States v Ramos*; J=*Michigan v Jeanette Smith*; K=*Stokes*; M=*United States v McNeil*; N=*Huey Newton* case; O=*United States v Sherpix*; P=*Pentagon Papers* case; S=*Panther 21* case; V=*Venceremos* case; W=*California v Block*; see §§9.1 and 9.3

## C. Right to Organize for Social Change or for Peace §9.87

1. E ___. Now there are some people who feel that change ought to be made for poor people through means of charity, through somebody coming in and helping them. Would any one of you feel that there is anything wrong when young people organize in the belief that the only way that you can really change a society that is bad is to obtain the power to do so? Do any of you feel that people should not seek to make changes that way, and that they should only make changes by asking for help or assistance?
2. E ___. Do you think there is anything wrong if the people that live at the bottom of society seek a part of the power at the top of society in order to make changes in their own way with their own power and by their own means? Do you think there is something wrong with that way of doing it?
3. E ___. Do you think that perhaps people who live in poorer circumstances deserve their poverty, and that the only way that people can achieve change is by individually asking for help?
4. E ___. Do you think that the people who seek to organize to change their basic condition in the society in which they live, so that they can become a part of it, do you think these people have always been able to make changes by just claiming their right to do it and by asking for it?
5. E ___. And would you understand that these people living around [*16th and Myrtle*] who have poor housing conditions, which some of the people on the jury panel have described already, that these young people that want to help themselves might find similar difficulties in trying to accomplish something for themselves?
6. E ___. Do you have an opinion whether it's right or wrong for the people to seek the power that organization gives in order to change society by use of their own power?
7. E ___. Do you think when workers seek to organize a union, say the mines in the early part of the century, they would be able just to say to the employers, "We want a union," and get together and form a union and that they would get a union? Do you think that's the process by which such things take place?

---

A=*Brewster*; B=*Briggs*; C=questions traditionally asked or permitted by the trial judge; D=*Angela Davis* case; E=*Detroit Black Panther* case; F=*Stroud*; G=*Gaskins*; H=*United States v Ramos*; J=*Michigan v Jeanette Smith*; K=*Stokes*; M=*United States v McNeil*; N=*Huey Newton* case; O=*United States v Sherpix*; P=*Pentagon Papers* case; S=*Panther 21* case; V=*Venceremos* case; W=*California v Block*; see §§9.1 and 9.3

8. E ___. What do you feel about the black people like the [*defendants*] here organizing to obtain some power in society to change their conditions by the use of that power?

*COMMENT:* Attorney Ernest Goodman of Detroit asked questions 9–14 of a prospective juror who had been involved in early union work at Ford Motor Company.

9. E ___. So, at least as you remember, in connection with the efforts of the [*Ford*] workers to organize the [*Ford Motor*] Company (even though there was a law that permitted them to organize) that while the workers may have been *called* the violent people involved in the situation, *actually* the violence that occurred was the result of the conditions that caused it, is that right?

10. E ___. After the company recognized the union and, as a result, an agreement was entered into, the working conditions were changed as a result of the efforts of the workers?

11. E ___. After a period of time the workers began to control to some extent the environment in which they worked, did they not?

12. E ___. Do you consider the process by which the workers achieved the right to organize and bargain collectively with their employers a process in which the workers obtained some of the power that the [*Ford Motor*] Company had held for itself?

13. E ___. If they left it to the employer over the years, nothing really would happen; so the workers did obtain a certain amount of power through the union, and they were able to negotiate with the company on the basis of equality, and the conditions then changed so that today at the [*Ford Motor*] Company it would be hard to remember the exact conditions that existed 40 years before; is that your view?

14. E ___. But at the time you engaged in this struggle in [*1940*], even some of your friends looked on you with some trepidation as though you weren't the right kind of a guy and you were called names sometimes, weren't you?

*COMMENT:* In representing peace activists, similar historical references are appropriate in drafting voir dire questions. See §§11.57, 11.58.

---

A=*Brewster*; B=*Briggs*; C=questions traditionally asked or permitted by the trial judge; D=*Angela Davis* case; E=*Detroit Black Panther* case; F=*Stroud*; G=*Gaskins*; H=*United States v Ramos*; J=*Michigan v Jeanette Smith*; K=*Stokes*; M=*United States v McNeil*; N=*Huey Newton* case; O=*United States v Sherpix*; P=*Pentagon Papers* case; S=*Panther 21* case; V=*Venceremos* case; W=*California v Block*; see §§9.1 and 9.3

### D. Right to Bear Arms §9.88

1. N ___. Do you own a firearm?
2. N ___. Do you have any objection to anybody that does own a firearm and keeps one for his own protection in his home?
3. N ___. Do you believe in the citizen's right of self-defense?
4. N ___. Do you belong to any group that is training its members or its affiliates in the use of firearms?
5. B ___. Do you have any quarrel with the [*Florida*] law that it is lawful to use reasonable force to defend yourself or another when attacked?
6. B ___. Have you had any experience with weapons or firearms of any kind? What sort of experience?
7. B ___. How do you feel about long-hairs or people in the [*antiwar*] movement owning guns?
8. S ___. Have you ever owned a gun?
9. S ___. Do you have any quarrel with the constitutional right to bear arms?
10. S ___. Do you have any view that because someone does bear arms he is more prone to commit a crime?
11. S ___. Do you have an opinion on the right of a black person to bear arms in self-defense?

*COMMENT:* On women's right to self-defense, see §11.51.

### E. Recent Developments §9.89

See §9.25.

## XI. INDIVIDUAL RESPONSIBILITY OF JUROR

### A. Attitudes toward Jury Trial §9.90

1. E ___. I would like to ask all members of the jury, although you are all in different age groups, and are a good cross-section of our community, whether you understand that the purpose of the jury trial as it developed in England and later on in this country, is to enable a person charged with a crime to be tried

---

A=*Brewster*; B=*Briggs*; C=questions traditionally asked or permitted by the trial judge; D=*Angela Davis* case; E=*Detroit Black Panther* case; F=*Stroud*; G=*Gaskins*; H=*United States v Ramos*; J=*Michigan v Jeanette Smith*; K=*Stokes*; M=*United States v McNeil*; N=*Huey Newton* case; O=*United States v Sherpix*; P=*Pentagon Papers* case; S=*Panther 21* case; V=*Venceremos* case; W=*California v Block*; see §§9.1 and 9.3

by his or her peers, that is, people of the same general background. Do any of you feel that this is not a good principle, that the people should not be judged by their own peers but by those who are better educated or more experienced—do any of you have any opinion of this kind about the jury?

2. G ___. Would you wait until you heard absolutely everything and saw all the evidence before you would make any decision, or even make any tentative decision about how to vote?

## B. Juror's Confidence in Own Fairness §9.91

1. N ___. Is there anything about this case that bothers you in any way?
2. N ___. Assuming that some loved one of yours were [*standing trial/seeking compensation for injuries*] in place and instead of my client [*for the same crime/accident*], would you feel satisfied with [*12*] jurors of the same mind as yours to stand judgment in the case of your friend or loved one?
3. N ___. If you are chosen in this case, do you know of any reason why you could not sit as an impartial juror?
4. N ___. You don't know of anything in your own mind's eye that we cannot penetrate that will lead to some crevice of prejudice that I have not been able to reach?
5. N ___. Is there anything that I have said about the [*Black Panther Party*] that creates a doubt in your own mind about whether you could be fair and impartial?
6. F ___. If the situation were turned around, would you want someone with the frame of mind that you presently have about what you've heard about this case to be sitting as a juror?

*COMMENT:* Questions 7–14 were posed to the jury by defense counsel in *Stokes v City of Detroit*, a police misconduct case (Circuit Court for Wayne County, Michigan, No. 78 819 767 CZ).

7. K ___. Will you consider and judge the [*plaintiff's/defendant's*] testimony by the same rules and standards you would use in judging the testimony of any other witness in this case?
8. K ___. If you find that the evidence produced does not support a finding that the [*defendant*] is [*at fault for plaintiff's injuries*]

A=*Brewster*; B=*Briggs*; C=questions traditionally asked or permitted by the trial judge; D=*Angela Davis* case; E=*Detroit Black Panther* case; F=*Stroud*; G=*Gaskins*; H=*United States v Ramos*; J=*Michigan v Jeanette Smith*; K=*Stokes*; M=*United States v McNeil*; N=*Huey Newton* case; O=*United States v Sherpix*; P=*Pentagon Papers* case; S=*Panther 21* case; V=*Venceremos* case; W=*California v Block*; see §§9.1 and 9.3

would you hesitate to award a judgment for the [*defendants*]?

9. K ___. Will you require the [*prosecution/plaintiff*] to prove [*his/her/its*] case according to every requirement of the law that [*I/the judge*] give[*s*] you in [*my/his/her*] charge?

10. K ___. Do you realize that you are bound to reach a verdict based solely on the evidence introduced during the trial?

11. K ___. Do you understand that the comments of the lawyers are not evidence in this case?

12. K ___. Will you allow any natural, human sympathy that you feel for the [*defendant/prosecution/plaintiff*] and [*his/her*] injury to interfere with your returning a just verdict based on the evidence?

13. K ___. If you were the [*plaintiff/defendant*] in this action, would you object to a person with your frame of mind and background—whatever it might be—sitting as a juror in this case?

14. K ___. Do you realize that the court will instruct you as to the law, but that you are the sole and exclusive judge(s) of the facts?

## C. Would Juror Stand by Own Opinion? §9.92

1. N ___. And if you are chosen as a juror, will you stand by your opinion based on the evidence that comes into the trial, isn't that right?

2. N ___. You won't let anybody shake that opinion; if you believe that the [*defendant is innocent or guilty/defendant is liable*], you will stick with your own opinion?

3. N ___. You won't let anybody push you around, is that right?

4. N ___. Now if you are chosen as a juror in this case, will you stand on your own individual analysis of the evidence and not be swayed by any emotions of other jurors? You can be swayed by facts, but will you stand on your own individual judgment if you are chosen as a trial juror?

In civil disobedience cases in which defendants are emphasizing their own individual sense of responsibility to take action, defense counsel often ask:

5. ___. The defendants on trial are entitled to [*12/6*] independent verdicts, not 3 or 4 verdicts by 3 or 4 of the most talkative

---

A=*Brewster*; B=*Briggs*; C=questions traditionally asked or permitted by the trial judge; D=*Angela Davis* case; E=*Detroit Black Panther* case; F=*Stroud*; G=*Gaskins*; H=*United States v Ramos*; J=*Michigan v Jeanette Smith*; K=*Stokes*; M=*United States v McNeil*; N=*Huey Newton* case; O=*United States v Sherpix*; P=*Pentagon Papers* case; S=*Panther 21* case; V=*Venceremos* case; W=*California v Block*; see §§9.1 and 9.3

jurors who may be able to sway the other jurors into their way of thinking. Do you accept that idea?

a. Can you remember, in your deliberations in the jury room, that each juror's opinion is important, that everyone should talk and no one should cut anyone off?
b. Do you agree that no one person should control the show, no matter what their job, age, education, etc.?

*COMMENT:* In *McNeil*, questions 6–7 were submitted to the federal judge, but were not asked.

6. M ___. Do you find it difficult to make up your mind who is right and who is wrong in a family dispute or a problem at the office?
7. M ___. When faced with a difficult decision, would you rather leave it to someone else so you won't be blamed if the wrong decision is made?

*COMMENT:* In the *Gainesville Eight* case, the defense proposed question 8.

8. B ___. If your vote in the jury room is 11 to 1, would you be willing to vote your conscience even though you were sequestered and away from your family for a long time?

*COMMENT:* The following question was asked in *California v Barr* (see §11.58).

9. ___. Do you realize that after you have heard all of the evidence and the judge's instructions, you have the right to come to your own decision and to vote your own conscience?

## D. Would Juror Fear Reaction If Verdict Goes One Way? §9.93

1. N ___. Now, would it be embarrassing to you or your [*husband/wife*] if you sat on a jury in a case that's been as charged up as this one has over a period of several months and the jury [*acquitted this defendant*]? Would it be embarrassing to you or your [*husband/wife*] at work?
2. N ___. Assuming that you were picked as a juror in this case, and

---

A=*Brewster*; B=*Briggs*; C=questions traditionally asked or permitted by the trial judge; D=*Angela Davis* case; E=*Detroit Black Panther* case; F=*Stroud*; G=*Gaskins*; H=*United States v Ramos*; J=*Michigan v Jeanette Smith*; K=*Stokes*; M=*United States v McNeil*; N=*Huey Newton* case; O=*United States v Sherpix*; P=*Pentagon Papers* case; S=*Panther 21* case; V=*Venceremos* case; W=*California v*

you brought in a verdict of [*not guilty*], would you find it embarrassing in the neighborhood that you are living in in [*Hayward*]?

3. N ___. If you were to bring in a verdict of [*not guilty*], would you have any embarrassment at all with any of your fellow workers?

## E. Jurors Taking Notes §9.94

Wisconsin recently adopted a rule requiring every judge to allow jurors to take notes unless the judge expressly rules otherwise on the record and gives a reason. The previous practice had been for judges to forbid jurors from taking notes. The question arises: should restrictions be placed on the types of notes jurors can take?

In a recent product liability case tried in Wisconsin, five plaintiffs represented five people killed in an airplane crash suing two defendants presenting drastically different theories. It was very complicated, and the judge said he thought the jurors should be able to take notes.

Counsel for plaintiffs disagreed, but the judge's rule held, and the jurors took notes.

Plaintiffs' counsel did not think to ask during voir dire, "Does anyone take shorthand?"

Unknown to the judge and counsel, a secretary who took rapid shorthand got on the jury. She filled seven shorthand pads with the actual transcript of the trial. She never paid attention to what was happening. Counsel would look over at her and her head was always down so she could write. She did not *listen* to a word. She did not take notes during opening or closing arguments, but she took down literally everything else. She even took down the bailiff's announcements about recesses.

She took her notes into the jury room during deliberations.

The judge was shocked and agreed afterward that it was horrible. He said, "I never would allow that again." But he felt he could not stop it once it began. Counsel were convinced that, after that experience, that judge would excuse any juror who took shorthand notes, and they resolved to ask the shorthand question in any trial in which note-taking was permitted.

---

A=*Brewster*; B=*Briggs*; C=questions traditionally asked or permitted by the trial judge; D=*Angela Davis* case; E=*Detroit Black Panther* case; F=*Stroud*; G=*Gaskins*; H=*United States v Ramos*; J=*Michigan v Jeanette Smith*; K=*Stokes*; M=*United States v McNeil*; N=*Huey Newton* case; O=*United States v Sherpix*; P=*Pentagon Papers* case; S=*Panther 21* case; V=*Venceremos* case; W=*California v Block*; see §§9.1 and 9.3

### F. Recent Developments §9.95

See §9.25.

## XII. GENERAL TRIAL PROBLEMS

### A. Length of Case §9.96

*COMMENT:* In the *Pentagon Papers* case the trial judge asked question 1 at defendants' request.

1. P ___. If this trial lasts in excess of [*two and one-half months*], is there anything about that length of time that could prevent your giving this case your full and undivided attention?
2. F ___. I should have asked all of you, and I don't think the Court would mind my asking: Do any of you have any really serious pressing personal problems, like someone really ill in the hospital or something at work or at home, that's just too distracting for you to lend us your ear for [*a couple of days*]?
3. F ___. We hope to finish this case this [*week*], maybe even [*tomorrow*], because of [*the liability being admitted*], but are any of you in that circumstance?

*COMMENT:* In *United States v Soliah* (see §8.82), defense counsel Sheldon Otis and Steffan Imhoff filed a motion in support of their challenges for cause of certain jurors. The following argument was made challenging one juror:

> For reasons previously orally argued to this court, Mr. Jinks should be excused from sitting on this case. He will suffer serious financial hardship, he will be forced to pay a baby sitter to stay with his children because his wife works.
>
> Mr. Jinks is willing to serve on this case even though it will be a lengthy trial and even though he will be sequestered. But, a review of this record should lead this court to the conclusion that Mr. Jinks, his family, and the community as a whole will be better served if this court exercises its discretion and relieves Mr. Jinks from the burden of serving as a juror in this case.

After the motion was filed, this juror asked the judge to be excused for hardship, and this was done (see §17.20).

---

A=*Brewster*; B=*Briggs*; C=questions traditionally asked or permitted by the trial judge; D=*Angela Davis* case; E=*Detroit Black Panther* case; F=*Stroud*; G=*Gaskins*; H=*United States v Ramos*; J=*Michigan v Jeanette Smith*; K=*Stokes*; M=*United States v McNeil*; N=*Huey Newton* case; O=*United States v Sherpix*; P=*Pentagon Papers* case; S=*Panther 21* case; V=*Venceremos* case; W=*California v Block*; see §§9.1 and 9.3

## B. Juror Health

### 1. General §9.97

The health of a juror may determine his or her behavior in the tense atmosphere of jury deliberations. Maureen McLaughlin, an Atlanta jury consultant, wrote in "How To Read a Juror," *Barristers*, summer 1978, at 44, that the strongest juror for the defense on one of her cases voted to convict simply because she was suffering from lower back pain and wanted to go home to bed. Questions on health are quite appropriate and may elicit useful information, as McLaughlin demonstrated from one of her cases:

**Q.** Do you have any health problems that would make it difficult for you to be a juror in this case?
**A.** I've had some trouble with my heart.
**Q.** With you heart?
**A.** Yes. I had a mild heart attack six weeks ago.

On the healthy jurors' attitudes toward sick or disabled parties and witnesses, see §9.56.

### 2. Hearing §9.98

Disabled people are participating more fully in society today, though often at their own expense. A deaf person who could read sign language, John G. O'Brien, was sworn in as a juror in a Washington state criminal case (marijuana-selling) in Seattle after he answered no to the question: "Do you think there would be a problem in hearing all of the evidence presented to you?" *SF Chronicle*, May 16, 1979. A deaf person, Charles Peck, who had to provide (and pay) his interpreter was sworn in as a trial juror in a state criminal case (prostitution-solicitation) tried in Oakland, California, after both sides agreed to allow the interpreter to accompany the 12 jurors into the jury room during deliberations (but not to express his own opinion on the case). *SF Chronicle*, Oct. 25, 1979.

---

A=*Brewster*; B=*Briggs*; C=questions traditionally asked or permitted by the trial judge; D=*Angela Davis* case; E=*Detroit Black Panther* case; F=*Stroud*; G=*Gaskins*; H=*United States v Ramos*; J=*Michigan v Jeanette Smith*; K=*Stokes*; M=*United States v McNeil*; N=*Huey Newton* case; O=*United States v Sherpix*; P=*Pentagon Papers* case; S=*Panther 21* case; V=*Venceremos* case; W=*California v Block*; see §§9.1 and 9.3

## C. Juror Empathy and Emotion §9.99

1. C ___. In this case you will be hearing evidence about someone being [*killed/injured*]. You may hear some details about the [*death/accident*], perhaps see some pictures of [*him/her*] after [*he/she died*]. That sort of evidence is not very nice to look at, and I'd like to ask: Do you consider yourself a squeamish person?
2. C ___. Have you had much experience dealing with people who are very ill, or dying?
   [*If yes*]
   a. Could you describe that?
3. C ___. Have you ever witnessed a violent death?
   [*If yes*]
   a. How did it make you feel?
4. C ___. Have any of your friends lost loved ones unexpectedly, or through violence?
   [*If yes*]
   a. Did you play any role in comforting them?
5. C ___. Do you feel you are the type of person to whom other people bring their troubles?
6. C ___. What role do you think emotion plays in your decision–making processes?
7. C ___. Do you consider yourself something of a student of human nature, or is such an interest a waste of time?

## D. Recent Developments §9.100

See §9.25.

# XIII. ATTORNEYS' ACTIONS

## A. Role of Attorneys §9.102

1. G ___. It's quite likely that there will be a number of motions, objections, different procedural things that take place in this hearing, possibly by the [*recorder/plaintiff*], and possibly by the [*de-*

---

A=*Brewster*; B=*Briggs*; C=questions traditionally asked or permitted by the trial judge; D=*Angela Davis* case; E=*Detroit Black Panther* case; F=*Stroud*; G=*Gaskins*; H=*United States v Ramos*; J=*Michigan v Jeanette Smith*; K=*Stokes*; M=*United States v McNeil*; N=*Huey Newton* case; O=*United States v Sherpix*; P=*Pentagon Papers* case; S=*Panther 21* case; V=*Venceremos* case; W=*California v Block*; see §§9.1 and 9.3

*fense*]; would the fact that any motions or objections are being made by any of the attorneys here cause you to judge [*Ms./ Mr.* __________] more severely simply because of what we as attorneys may be doing?

2. G ___. In other words, even if we get you pretty mad, you are not going to take it out on [*my client*] in any way; is that right?

*COMMENT:* In a civil disobedience case in California involving hundreds of defendants and several defense lawyers, the following questions were asked.

3. ___. When you look at the legal team here, and there are [*number*] attorneys, and [*number*] defendants sitting here, and a lot of people behind us, and over there is the [*district attorney/ prosecutor*], does that make you feel that things are imbalanced?
   a. You realize, of course, that the [*D.A./Prosecutor*] has an office and staff of people to help him?

*COMMENT:* In *Stroud*, one juror, whose father was an attorney, was questioned about his attitude toward lawyers.

1. F ___. Now, going back to everyone a little bit—have any of you had any particularly bad experiences with courts or lawyers?
2. F ___. You had a bad experience with your old man? Do you want to enlarge on that a little bit?
3. F ___. What kind of lawyer was your dad?
4. F ___. Well, if he was better than us, will that—you wouldn't judge us because he'd have done a better job?
5. F ___. Where did he practice?
6. F ___. Is he still practicing?
7. F ___. I see, but you don't feel—well, do you feel that you're kind of an expert in law growing up [*in a lawyer's family*]?

Defense counsel in the *Gainesville Eight* case proposed questions concerning their role.

8. B ___. During this case, lawyers for the [*defendants/plaintiff*] may be making objections to testimony or evidence offered by the government. Do you understand that this is their job so that you will not hold it against the [*defendants/plaintiff*]?

---

A=*Brewster*; B=*Briggs*; C=questions traditionally asked or permitted by the trial judge; D=*Angela Davis* case; E=*Detroit Black Panther* case; F=*Stroud*; G=*Gaskins*; H=*United States v Ramos*; J=*Michigan v Jeanette Smith*; K=*Stokes*; M=*United States v McNeil*; N=*Huey Newton* case; O=*United States v Sherpix*; P=*Pentagon Papers* case; S=*Panther 21* case; V=*Venceremos* case; W=*California v Block*; see §§9.1 and 9.3

*COMMENT:* Mississippi attorney William Sebastian Moore uses this question:

9. ___. Do you realize that the [*district/defense*] attorney and myself are both equals, both lawyers, both equal in the eyes of the law, each doing our best to represent our clients?

## B. Women Attorneys §9.103

Some women and men jurors may welcome women who become lawyers for poor criminal defendants but resent women who become part of the law-and-order team. The reverse is also true: Men and women may feel that women have the right to uphold the law but that they certainly should not get involved with criminals. Women prosecutors and defense lawyers are working out the best kinds of voir dire to conduct in order to select jurors who will not decide cases on the basis of the sex of the lawyers.

On the civil side, some jurors will accept a woman lawyer representing an injured plaintiff or a civil defendant in a "good cause," but will be antagonistic to a woman corporate lawyer representing a traditional client.

Readers are requested to send examples of voir dire questions that were used successfully to attack such prejudices, for inclusion in Supplements to these volumes.

When men and women lawyers work together in a case, particularly when both men and women are clients, jurors may be very curious about the relationships between the lawyers, and women jurors in particular are likely to notice how the men lawyers relate to women colleagues and clients. If a husband-and-wife or a father-and-daughter team is involved, but their names are different, it may be thoughtful to let the jurors know about the relationship so they will not be surprised if the intimacy of the lawyers becomes evident at some point during trial.

*COMMENT:* In *McNeil*, one of defense counsel was a woman who used a professional last name different from her married name. Since the defendant had started using a different last name when he returned

---

A=*Brewster*; B=*Briggs*; C=questions traditionally asked or permitted by the trial judge; D=*Angela Davis* case; E=*Detroit Black Panther* case; F=*Stroud*; G=*Gaskins*; H=*United States v Ramos*; J=*Michigan v Jeanette Smith*; K=*Stokes*; M=*United States v McNeil*; N=*Huey Newton* case; O=*United States v Sherpix*; P=*Pentagon Papers* case; S=*Panther 21* case; V=*Venceremos* case; W=*California v Block*; see §§9.1 and 9.3

from Canada after failing to be inducted into the U.S. Army, it was thought possible to sensitize the jurors to the idea that a name change was not necessarily an improper act. The trial judge agreed to ask the prospective jurors:

10. M ___. Would it affect your thinking to learn that one of the lawyers for the [*defendant/plaintiff*] uses two different names at the same time—one, [*Ms. Jones*], in her professional and political life; and another, [*Mrs. Smith*], in her private life?

*COMMENT:* One woman juror seemed to respond negatively to the question, and the defense excused her peremptorily, fearing she would draw a conclusion about McNeil's name change, ignoring the presumption of innocence. In any case in which one of the clients or one or more counsel are women, some questions should certainly be propounded to check for sexist attitudes by jurors that might affect their deliberations. See §4.35.

## C. FBI Activity §9.104

In the *Gainesville Eight* trial, the government proposed questions 1–4.

1. B ___. There has been publicity since this trial commenced regarding events occurring here in the Federal Building involving special agents of the Federal Bureau of Investigation.
   a. Have any of you heard or read about these events?
   b. If so, does this publicity influence you in any way in favor of the [*defendants/plaintiffs*]?
   c. Does this publicity influence you in any way against the FBI?
   d. Does your knowledge of these events influence you against the prosecution or against the government?
   e. Has this information in any way altered your state of mind regarding this case? If so, how?
   f. Will you recall this publicity during the trial of this case?
2. B ___. There has been publicity since these proceedings began about activities occurring in front of the Federal Building during the

A=*Brewster*; B=*Briggs*; C=questions traditionally asked or permitted by the trial judge; D=*Angela Davis* case; E=*Detroit Black Panther* case; F=*Stroud*; G=*Gaskins*; H=*United States v Ramos*; J=*Michigan v Jeanette Smith*; K=*Stokes*; M=*United States v McNeil*; N=*Huey Newton* case; O=*United States v Sherpix*; P=*Pentagon Papers* case; S=*Panther 21* case; V=*Venceremos* case; W=*California v Block*; see §§9.1 and 9.3

hours when this court was not in session in which this case was discussed.
[*Repeat subquestions a–f of question 1*]

3. B ___. Statements have been made in the public media by participants in this trial since these proceedings began.
[*Repeat subquestions a–f of question 1*]

4. B ___. There has been publicity since these proceedings began reciting the contents of a telegram sent to a member of the United States Congress.
[*Repeat subquestions a–f of question 1*]

## XIV. MEDIA COVERAGE AND COURT "GAG RULE" §9.105

The defense in the *Gainesville Eight* trial requested that the federal judge ask questions 1–6.

1. B ___. Did you read the article in the [*Gainesville Sun*] of [*July 22, 1973*], headlined [*"No Political Theater in Arnow's Courtroom"*], in which there is reference to:
   a. The [*defendants*] having been charged with [*conspiring to bomb the Republican Convention*]?
   b. The Court's views on [*what is patriotism and the views of one of the defendants as to what is patriotism*]?
   c. The statement attributed to [*the Court*] that [*defendants*] will not be allowed to turn the courtroom into a political theater?

   [*If any juror answered "Yes," the juror must be questioned individually and outside the presence of the other jurors as follows:*]

2. B ___. What do you recall of the article?
3. B ___. Did you realize the article was about the case you were chosen for?
4. B ___. Did you discuss the article with anyone?
   [*If yes*]
   a. Who?
   b. What did you say?
   c. What did [*he/she*] say?

---

A=*Brewster*; B=*Briggs*; C=questions traditionally asked or permitted by the trial judge; D=*Angela Davis* case; E=*Detroit Black Panther* case; F=*Stroud*; G=*Gaskins*; H=*United States v Ramos*; J=*Michigan v Jeanette Smith*; K=*Stokes*; M=*United States v McNeil*; N=*Huey Newton* case; O=*United States v Sherpix*; P=*Pentagon Papers* case; S=*Panther 21* case; V=*Venceremos* case; W=*California v Block*; see §§9.1 and 9.3

5. B ___. Did you have any feelings about this article?
   [*If yes*]
   a. What were they?

6. B ___. Are you prepared to accept the court order that despite what you have read in the paper:
   a. [*Defendants*] have not been charged by the government with having [*conspired to bomb the Republican Convention*]?
   b. The Court's views [*as to what is patriotism*] and the views of one of the [*defendants*] [*as to what is patriotism*] are irrelevant?
   c. You have to make your decision exclusively on what you hear in the courtroom?

7. B ___. Have you read the article in the [*Gainesville Sun*] of [*July 22, 1973*] headlined [*"Gag Rule Clamped on Gainesville 8 Trial Here"*], or have you otherwise heard about the court order limiting extrajudicial statements of [*defendants*] and attorneys, limiting [*demonstrations*], ruling that the [*defendants*] [*could not know your names until today*], ordering you not to [*disclose your addresses*], and ordering that you would be [*escorted to and from the courtroom by United States Marshals daily*]?
   [*If any juror answers "Yes," the juror must be questioned individually and outside the presence of the other jurors as follows:*]

8. B ___. What do you recall of the article?

9. B ___. Did you realize the article was about the case you were chosen for?

10. B ___. Did you discuss the article with anyone?
   [*If yes*]
   a. Who?
   b. What did you say?
   c. What did [*he/she*] say?

11. B ___. Did you have any feelings about the article?
   [*If yes*]
   a. What were they?

12. B ___. Other than the general feelings you have spoken of, what do you conclude from the court order?

---

A=*Brewster*; B=*Briggs*; C=questions traditionally asked or permitted by the trial judge; D=*Angela Davis* case; E=*Detroit Black Panther* case; F=*Stroud*; G=*Gaskins*; H=*United States v Ramos*; J=*Michigan v Jeanette Smith*; K=*Stokes*; M=*United States v McNeil*; N=*Huey Newton* case; O=*United States v Sherpix*; P=*Pentagon Papers* case; S=*Panther 21* case; V=*Venceremos* case; W=*California v Block*; see §§9.1 and 9.3

[*If the jurors answer "No," each juror must be asked the following:*]

13. B ___. Do you understand that your name has not been disclosed until today, that you cannot give your address, and that you are to be escorted to and from the courthouse daily by United States Marshals?

14. B ___. Has that caused you to form any opinions about the [*defendants*]?

## XV. FINAL QUESTIONS

### A. Did Counsel Prejudice Juror against Party? §9.108

1. N ___. I have asked you many questions. At certain points you may feel I was trying to invade your own private thinking. Did the questions I asked you infuriate you in such a way that you couldn't be a fair and impartial juror?

2. N ___. You understand why I am asking these questions?

### B. Next-to-Last Questions §9.109

The defense in *McNeil* asked the federal judge to ask question 1.

1. M ___. Is there anything else you want to tell us that will help the court discover whether you have any stereotypes or prejudgments in your mind that will affect your decision-making?

2. N ___. These questions I have asked you—have they triggered off within your mind anything you want to volunteer to us?

In *Michigan v Jeanette Smith*, a self-defense against sexual harassment murder trial, defense counsel asked, as a last question:

3. J ___. Is there anything that I haven't asked you about that might have some bearing on your feelings about this case?

### C. Final Question §9.110

It is both polite and politic to conclude the voir dire as many lawyers do, by saying: "I certainly appreciate your patience and your honesty

A=*Brewster*; B=*Briggs*; C=questions traditionally asked or permitted by the trial judge; D=*Angela Davis* case; E=*Detroit Black Panther* case; F=*Stroud*; G=*Gaskins*; H=*United States v Ramos*; J=*Michigan v Jeanette Smith*; K=*Stokes*; M=*United States v McNeil*; N=*Huey Newton* case; O=*United States v Sherpix*; P=*Pentagon Papers* case; S=*Panther 21* case; V=*Venceremos* case; W=*California v Block*; see §§9.1 and 9.3

in discussing these matters, and I have no further questions at this time. Thanks for your assistance."

An experienced trial lawyer, Louis S. Katz of San Diego, suggests that a modification of this closing may provide valuable information. He often ends his formal voir dire with "Thank you, Mr. Jones, we have no further questions." The juror is put off guard and Katz then says, "Oh, by the way," and asks another question or repeats an earlier question using different wording. He has frequently received an answer he didn't expect or has observed a reaction (facial or otherwise) indicating the juror's true attitude toward the subject that was not revealed earlier.

## XVI. COMMON ISSUES IN CIVIL AND CRIMINAL CASES

### A. Multiple Plaintiffs or Defendants §9.115

Question 1 was submitted by the defense, but not asked by the federal judge, in *United States v Sherpix*.

1. O ___. Each [*defendant/plaintiff*] is entitled to your separate and independent judgment. Will you treat each [*defendant/plaintiff*] individually, separately, and fairly?

*COMMENT:* For more information on questions concerning multiple parties, see §11.33.

### B. Public Official Is Party §9.116

The following questions were asked by the trial judge in *United States v Mitchell* (the *Mitchell-Stans* case, reported in Zeisel and Diamond, "The Jury Selection in the Mitchell-Stans Conspiracy Trial," 1 *Am B Foundation J* 151 (1976). They indicate the breadth of voir dire questioning on general and specific areas in a prosecution of (former) government officials.

After excusing prospective jurors who claimed that lengthy sequestration would impose undue hardship, the trial judge, in open court, asked basic questions individually—name, address, occupation, military service, relationship with parties or counsel—and then asked the following questions jointly, in open court:

---

A=*Brewster*; B=*Briggs*; C=questions traditionally asked or permitted by the trial judge; D=*Angela Davis* case; E=*Detroit Black Panther* case; F=*Stroud*; G=*Gaskins*; H=*United States v Ramos*; J=*Michigan v Jeanette Smith*; K=*Stokes*; M=*United States v McNeil*; N=*Huey Newton* case; O=*United States v Sherpix*; P=*Pentagon Papers* case; S=*Panther 21* case; V=*Venceremos* case; W=*California v Block*; see §§9.1 and 9.3

1. ___. Has any member of the panel, or any close relative or friend, known any attorneys in or had any dealings with the US Attorney's office for the [*Southern*] District of [*New York*]?
2. ___. Is any member of the panel a close relative or a close friend—of, or friendly with anybody employed in the US Attorney's office?
3. ___. Or with other law enforcement agencies?
4. ___. Has any member of the panel served on a jury before, appeared as a witness in a trial, or been involved in legal action with the US government?

   [*If a juror answered yes to any of these, but the connection with the case was not close*]
5. ___. Would this [*fact/relationship*] prejudice you in favor of either side?

   [*Last question asked in open court*]
6. ___. Has any juror formed any preconceived ideas that would preclude him or her from following the court's instructions on the law in this case?

The *Mitchell-Stans* jurors who survived the general questioning were examined individually and privately in the judge's robing room, in the presence of the clerk, the prosecutors, and a varying number of defense attorneys. All questions were asked by the judge. His questions were occasionally supplemented by follow-up questions suggested for the particular juror by the defense attorneys or the prosecutor.

Sometimes, if the panel members gave more than a simple yes or no answer, the judge would pursue the point through questions that arose naturally in the ensuing dialogue.

1. C ___. What is your party registration?
2. C ___. Have you been involved in campaign activities such as rallies, demonstrations, or fund raising?

*COMMENT:* In *United States v Chapin* (DC Cir 1975) 515 F2d 1264, 1269–1270, the appellate court indicated that defense counsel would have been permitted to ask questions on whether jurors were registered voters and, if so, in which party, if they had persisted after the trial judge forbade all questions on political affiliations, since District of Columbia voter registration lists by party are now compiled and made

---

A=*Brewster*; B=*Briggs*; C=questions traditionally asked or permitted by the trial judge; D=*Angela Davis* case; E=*Detroit Black Panther* case; F=*Stroud*; G=*Gaskins*; H=*United States v Ramos*; J=*Michigan v Jeanette Smith*; K=*Stokes*; M=*United States v McNeil*; N=*Huey Newton* case; O=*United States v Sherpix*; P=*Pentagon Papers* case; S=*Panther 21* case; V=*Venceremos* case; W=*California v Block*; see §§9.1 and 9.3

public. Typical questions were asked about exposure to media coverage of Watergate, including questions on what publications the prospective jurors read regularly and their knowledge of the main Watergate figures.

3. ___. Have you formed any opinions about [*the main figures in Watergate*]?
4. ___. Do you have any opinion about the honesty of public officials generally?

*COMMENT:* Two questions concerned issues specifically connected with incidents in the instant case:

5. ___. Have you ever asked for assistance from a person in public life?
6. ___. Do you have any prejudice against hunting or someone who goes hunting?

*COMMENT:* The last question was:

7. ___. If you were the prosecutor or defendant in this case, would you be satisfied with yourself as a juror?

*COMMENT:* On the trial judge's refusal to pursue at length certain lines of inquiry suggested by answers to some of these questions, and the possible effect of this on the verdict in the case, see the article by Zeisel and Diamond cited above.

## C. Homosexual Parties or Witnesses §9.117

Several of the following questions were prepared for submission in *United States v Ramos* (District of Columbia Super Ct, No. 49352–70, dismissed Jan. 1971). Two gay couples were refused service at a bar-restaurant, because they were openly gay. The men returned with a group of friends to stage a civil rights protest. They brought signs and placards with them. A fight erupted, and 12 members of the group were arrested and charged with assault and battery and disorderly conduct. The case was dismissed on a motion by the government before the jury was selected in January 1971.

The questions in the *Ramos* case were prepared (with the help of the

---

A=*Brewster*; B=*Briggs*; C=questions traditionally asked or permitted by the trial judge; D=*Angela Davis* case; E=*Detroit Black Panther* case; F=*Stroud*; G=*Gaskins*; H=*United States v Ramos*; J=*Michigan v Jeanette Smith*; K=*Stokes*; M=*United States v McNeil*; N=*Huey Newton* case; O=*United States v Sherpix*; P=*Pentagon Papers* case; S=*Panther 21* case; V=*Venceremos* case; W=*California v Block*; see §§9.1 and 9.3

defendants) by Renee Hanover of Chicago, John Kenneth Zwerling of Alexandria, Virginia, Larry Feingold of Washington state, Michael Fayad and Mary Helen Mautner of Washington, D.C., and Peter Wiseman and Chuck Daniels, then at Howard University Law School. The questions were prepared for a jury that was anticipated to be predominantly black, as are most juries in the District of Columbia.

The other questions in this section were asked in the court-martial case against Tangela Gaskins, a sailor accused of homosexual conduct (see §3.91); Gaskins denied the charge and won the court-martial. For other questions from the *Gaskins* voir dire of the three-person court-martial, see §§9.77, 9.118–9.130, and §§10.97–10.99.

### 1. General Knowledge of Homosexuality §9.118

1. H ___. What ways do you think homosexuals are different from heterosexuals?
2. H ___. Do you think homosexuals are more suited to certain types of work than others?
   [*If yes*]
   a. What kind of work do you think this would be?
3. H ___. If they are qualified, should homosexuals be considered capable as: executives, plumbers, members of a jury, lawyers, truck drivers, generals, teachers, policemen, tree trimmers?
4. H ___. Do you think that homosexuals feel that they are oppressed or discriminated against in this society?
5. H ___. Do you think homosexuals have anything to complain about?
6. G ___. Do you think that it is possible to tell a homosexual by looking at him or her?
7. G ___. Do you think there are any particular characteristics that a homosexual displays that nonhomosexuals do not display?
8. G ___. Do you think you have ever seen a homosexual?
9. G ___. What I'm getting at is that you didn't see someone walking down a street, or in a bar, whatever, and say to yourself, "That's a gay, a lesbian, a dyke," whatever?
10. G ___. If so-called homosexual acts were alleged against an individual, would you take into consideration the manner in which that individual was brought up, and by that I mean, for example, whether displays of affection were common in that family, or

A=*Brewster*; B=*Briggs*; C=questions traditionally asked or permitted by the trial judge; D=*Angela Davis* case; E=*Detroit Black Panther* case; F=*Stroud*; G=*Gaskins*; H=*United States v Ramos*; J=*Michigan v Jeanette Smith*; K=*Stokes*; M=*United States v McNeil*; N=*Huey Newton* case; O=*United States v Sherpix*; P=*Pentagon Papers* case; S=*Panther 21* case; V=*Venceremos* case; W=*California v Block*; see §§9.1 and 9.3

were not common; would this type of information be of interest to you in reaching a decision as to whether that sailor had in fact committed a homosexual act?

## 2. Attitude toward Homosexuality §9.119

1. G ___. Whatever your feelings may be with respect to homosexuality, or, I should say, opinions—that might be a better word: Does it make any difference to you whether the subject is a woman or a man?
2. G ___. Do you mind telling us what your opinions are with respect to homosexuality?
3. G ___. Let's assume that John Doe is acquitted of a criminal charge. Do you think that the fact of acquittal will cause John Doe's neighbors to completely forget about whatever the charge was?
4. G ___. Let's take on a range of criminal charges—from being drunk out on a street and being arrested by the police in the housing area, to something such as robbery, kidnapping or rape, something serious. Do you think this is something that persons, neighbors, or those who know him, would tend to recall, over the years, as different conversations might take place or different things might happen, that they would remember that even though John Doe was acquitted, that he was charged with committing that robbery down at the corner bank? "I wonder if he did it?" Do you think it would be normal for people to have those types of reactions even though somebody was acquitted?

   We've been talking about a situation where a person was acquitted of a criminal charge. Do you think the same type of situation would be true where the person had an allegation of homosexuality made against him or her?

## 3. Terms §9.120

1. H ___. What term or terms do you and your friends use when referring to homosexuals?

---

A=*Brewster*; B=*Briggs*; C=questions traditionally asked or permitted by the trial judge; D=*Angela Davis* case; E=*Detroit Black Panther* case; F=*Stroud*; G=*Gaskins*; H=*United States v Ramos*; J=*Michigan v Jeanette Smith*; K=*Stokes*; M=*United States v McNeil*; N=*Huey Newton* case; O=*United States v Sherpix*; P=*Pentagon Papers* case; S=*Panther 21* case; V=*Venceremos* case; W=*California v Block*; see §§9.1 and 9.3

2. G ___. What does the term "straight" mean to you?
3. G ___. And by that, you mean a nonhomosexual person, is that right?
4. G ___. What does the term "gay" mean to you?
5. G ___. Does that mean man, woman, either or both?
6. G ___. What does the term "lesbian" mean to you?
7. G ___. Would there be a term that would be applied to a male homosexual, as far as you know?

### 4. Juror's Personal Contact with Homosexuals §9.121

1. H ___. What would be your first reaction if you found out your son or daughter was homosexual?
2. G ___. Did you think any less of someone because you believed they were homosexual?
3. G ___. Have you ever observed any person whom you believe to be a homosexual?
4. G ___. At any time in your life?
5. G ___. Let's try to draw a hypothetical here. Assuming that you are not married, as you are. Let's say that you're dating a woman, you're in love with her, you're planning to get married. Someone says, "She's a lesbian." What kind of reaction do you think you'd have? And also assuming you had what you would consider to be a normal relationship during the time you've known her and dated her and been courting her?
6. G ___. Do you think you'd feel anger at the person making such an allegation?

### 5. Believing Testimony of Homosexual §9.122

1. H ___. If two people, a homosexual and a heterosexual, were both under oath in a court of law and testifying in a trial, do you feel you would give equal consideration to the testimony each of them gave?
2. H ___. Would you believe a homosexual's testimony about the actions of a policeman?
3. H ___. If a policeman and a homosexual gave different stories about the same event, which one would you be more likely to believe?
   a. Why?

---

A=*Brewster*; B=*Briggs*; C=questions traditionally asked or permitted by the trial judge; D=*Angela Davis* case; E=*Detroit Black Panther* case; F=*Stroud*; G=*Gaskins*; H=*United States v Ramos*; J=*Michigan v Jeanette Smith*; K=*Stokes*; M=*United States v McNeil*; N=*Huey Newton* case; O=*United States v Sherpix*; P=*Pentagon Papers* case; S=*Panther 21* case; V=*Venceremos* case; W=*California v Block*; see §§9.1 and 9.3

## 6. Homosexuals and Public Accommodations and Facilities §9.123

1. H ___. Do you think that the management of a facility that discriminates against homosexuals would admit to such discrimination publicly?
2. H ___. Should they tell others who might be refused service to stay out of the facilities?
3. H ___. Do you think that a segregated bar, restaurant, or other public facility that refuses to serve homosexuals should be allowed to keep its liquor license and municipal licenses?
4. H ___. Do you think that the management of a public facility that discriminates against homosexuals might misunderstand the intentions of a group of homosexuals who attempt to integrate that facility?
5. H ___. Do you think that the management of a public facility that discriminates against homosexuals would become agitated when such discrimination is objected to by homosexuals?
6. H ___. Do you think that the regular male heterosexual patrons of a neighborhood bar would resent or have hostile attitudes toward the presence of men who were recognizable as being homosexual?

## 7. Armed Services §9.124

1. H ___. Do you know that homosexuals who serve in the armed services, hold civil service positions in many departments, and are employed in public education have risked losing their positions if their homosexuality is revealed?
2. G ___. In order for you to be able to decide the case of a person in military service charged with homosexual conduct, you would want more than that the person had a good military record, this was the only act alleged, and it was between consenting adults—you would want more information than that?
3. G ___. What is your understanding of a homosexual act as used in the [*Navy*]?
4. G ___. Are you aware of so-called pornographic material being available aboard ship and aboard a naval base?

---

A=*Brewster*; B=*Briggs*; C=questions traditionally asked or permitted by the trial judge; D=*Angela Davis* case; E=*Detroit Black Panther* case; F=*Stroud*; G=*Gaskins*; H=*United States v Ramos*; J=*Michigan v Jeanette Smith*; K=*Stokes*; M=*United States v McNeil*; N=*Huey Newton* case; O=*United States v Sherpix*; P=*Pentagon Papers* case; S=*Panther 21* case; V=*Venceremos* case; W=*California v Block*; see §§9.1 and 9.3

5. G ____. Do you know if *Hustler* is sold in the Base Exchange?
6. G ____. Are you aware of such magazines being kept aboard ship in what is loosely referred to as a "Porn Locker"?
7. G ____. Do you feel that there should be any restrictions on use of such a locker as between men and women in the [*Service*]?
8. G ____. Do you have any feelings as to whether or not the magazines of the nature we've been discussing, *Playboy*, *Oui*, *Penthouse*, *Playgirl*, the various others, should be restricted aboard ship depending on the grade or rank of an individual?
9. G ____. Do you feel that such material should be restricted from the ship?
10. G ____. In other words, if they are old enough to be in the [*Service*], they are old enough to look at whatever they want to look at. Is that right?
11. G ____. But if the [*Service*] does allow it, then there should be no restrictions. Is that correct?
12. G ____. Have you seen female sailors walking hand-in-hand or arm-in-arm?

### 8. Showing Affection in Public §9.125

1. H ____. How do you react if you see a man and a woman hugging each other at a bus station after one of them has come back from a trip?
2. H ____. Now suppose that they were two women or two men, and they hugged each other at the bus station after one of them came back from a trip—how would you react to that?
3. H ____. Do you think it is OK for a boy and a girl in high school to walk home from school holding hands?
4. H ____. How about two girls?
5. H ____. How about two boys?
6. H ____. Do you think it is OK for a man to wink at a woman he finds attractive?
7. H ____. How about a woman winking at a man for the same reason?
8. H ____. How about a man winking at another man?
9. H ____. If a homosexual couple is having coffee and talking at a restaurant, should they be allowed to hold hands, or do you think they should wait until they are in private?

---

A=*Brewster*; B=*Briggs*; C=questions traditionally asked or permitted by the trial judge; D=*Angela Davis* case; E=*Detroit Black Panther* case; F=*Stroud*; G=*Gaskins*; H=*United States v Ramos*; J=*Michigan v Jeanette Smith*; K=*Stokes*; M=*United States v McNeil*; N=*Huey Newton* case; O=*United States v Sherpix*; P=*Pentagon Papers* case; S=*Panther 21* case; V=*Venceremos* case; W=*California v Block*; see §§9.1 and 9.3

10. H ___. Is it all right for a husband and wife to hold hands while they are in a restaurant?
11. H ___. Do you think it is OK for two people of the same sex to [*shake hands/hold hands/kiss on the cheek/kiss on the lips/have sex with each other if they are in prison and there is no one of the opposite sex around/love each other/make love with each other*]?
12. G ___. Do you think there's anything wrong with seeing women physically expressing affection toward each other?
13. G ___. Suppose these two mythical women hug each other, they give each other an embrace and they also kiss eath other. Would you necessarily think that that was a homosexual act?
14. G ___. In other words, if it was something that was really passionate and prolonged that it might be, but if it were a warm embrace and a kiss, something of that nature, that it wouldn't be. Would that be correct?
15. G ___. Do you have any brothers and sisters?
    [*If yes*]
    a. Are they of approximately the same age, let's say within a five year span, either older or younger?
    b. Would there be displays of affection between you and your sisters and your brother and your parents and your family?
16. G ___. Are you a sports fan?
    [*If yes*]
    a. What sports?
17. G ___. [*Do you/have you*] participate[*d*] in any sports?
    [*If yes*]
    a. Which ones?
18. G ___. Have you ever noticed in watching sports on television, or maybe through your active participation in sports, that, among men, quite often when someone made a good hit or made a good move in a game, or whatever, that it would be common for team-mates to pat that person on the rear?
    [*If yes*]
    a. Do you think there's anything homosexual about that?
19. G ___. Have you watched women's sports, women's teams play, or anything like that?

---

A=*Brewster*; B=*Briggs*; C=questions traditionally asked or permitted by the trial judge; D=*Angela Davis* case; E=*Detroit Black Panther* case; F=*Stroud*; G=*Gaskins*; H=*United States v Ramos*; J=*Michigan v Jeanette Smith*; K=*Stokes*; M=*United States v McNeil*; N=*Huey Newton* case; O=*United States v Sherpix*; P=*Pentagon Papers* case; S=*Panther 21* case; V=*Venceremos* case; W=*California v Block*; see §§9.1 and 9.3

20. G ___. Have you ever seen—I don't know if you'd call it a sport, but have you ever seen roller derby on television, for example?

21. G ___. Have you ever seen any contact sports between women?
[*If yes*]
a. Have you noticed what could be characterized as displays of affection if a particularly good play were made or when one wins and the other loses, possibly they throw their arms around each other at the end of the tennis match—have you seen that sort of thing?

22. G ___. Did you think there was anything of a homosexual nature in what you saw?

## 9. Gay Liberation Movement §9.126

1. H ___. If homosexuals are a minority group and as such are discriminated against, do you think homosexuals should stick together as a group and oppose discrimination?

## 10. Openness/Closetry §9.127

1. H ___. If you were a homosexual, would you let people know it, or would you keep it a secret?

2. H ___. If you were a light-skinned black, would you try to pass for white if you thought that would get you a better job or more white friends?

3. H ___. If you were a Jew, would you want people to think you were a Christian if you thought that would help you get a house in the neighborhood you wanted?

4. H ___. Should homosexuals try to pass as heterosexuals?

5. H ___. Should they try to be heterosexuals as much as they can?

## 11. Demonstrations §9.128

1. H ___. Have you ever heard of a sit-in as a method of bringing about an end to segregated facilities?
[*If yes*]
a. What people used such a measure?

---

A=*Brewster*; B=*Briggs*; C=questions traditionally asked or permitted by the trial judge; D=*Angela Davis* case; E=*Detroit Black Panther* case; F=*Stroud*; G=*Gaskins*; H=*United States v Ramos*; J=*Michigan v Jeanette Smith*; K=*Stokes*; M=*United States v McNeil*; N=*Huey Newton* case; O=*United States v Sherpix*; P=*Pentagon Papers* case; S=*Panther 21* case; V=*Venceremos* case; W=*California v Block*; see §§9.1 and 9.3

2. H ___. Do you think that homosexuals who engage in a sit-in at a place that refuses to serve them might ever be in physical danger?
[*If yes*]
a. From what?

3. H ___. Do you believe that the police would favor one side or the other in a sit-in?

4. H ___. In a confrontation between militant blacks and the management of a public facility owned by whites, do you think the police would fairly consider both sides?

## 12. Sick, Immoral, and Unnatural §9.129

1. H ___. Have you ever heard of the biblical cities of Sodom and Gomorrah?
[*If yes*]
a. Do you know what the Bible says happened to these cities?
b. Do you know why those cities were punished by God?

2. H ___. Could you be impartial toward homosexuals in a court of law when your religion teaches that homosexuality is wrong?

3. G ___. Do you believe that it is a stigma on a person to be characterized as a homosexual, or a lesbian? I'm specifying a woman homosexual.

4. G ___. Do you think this would hold such an individual up to ridicule, possible hatred, cause that person to lose friends, to be shunned by the family, that type of thing?

5. G ___. If that person maintained that he or she was not a homosexual and that term were put on a person, do you think that it would be damaging to that individual?

## 13. Media and Pornography §9.130

1. G ___. Have you ever seen any material—any magazines or newspapers—that you believed was homosexual in nature?

2. G ___. Have you ever seen or been aware of any of your male friends reading any material that may have had a homosexual cartoon, homosexual story, or anything of a homosexual nature?

---

A=*Brewster*; B=*Briggs*; C=questions traditionally asked or permitted by the trial judge; D=*Angela Davis* case; E=*Detroit Black Panther* case; F=*Stroud*; G=*Gaskins*; H=*United States v Ramos*; J=*Michigan v Jeanette Smith*; K=*Stokes*; M=*United States v McNeil*; N=*Huey Newton* case; O=*United States v Sherpix*; P=*Pentagon Papers* case; S=*Panther 21* case; V=*Venceremos* case; W=*California v Block*; see §§9.1 and 9.3

3. G ___. If one of your friends were to read such material, or let's say look at a cartoon in *Penthouse* or *Playboy* that might depict a homosexual act, whether between women or between men, would you feel that this was at all indicative of your friend's sexual preference, the fact that he was reading such a cartoon?
4. G ___. If you saw a woman reading, let's say, a copy of *Playgirl*, what would your reaction be toward that woman, assuming this is a woman whom you had not met before, you didn't know anything about her?
5. G ___. If you happened to be looking over that woman's shoulder and saw that the particular page she was looking at depicted a cartoon showing some sort of homosexual act, would that cause you to form any type of opinion, based strictly on the limited facts that I've given you?
6. G ___. I hope this doesn't embarrass you in any way—Have you ever looked at *Playboy*, *Penthouse* or any of the magazines I've mentioned?
7. G ___. Did they offend you?
8. G ___. In other words, using women as objects of sexual gratification?
9. G ___. If a woman were to be reading such a magazine, what opinion would you have of her or what reaction would you have?
10. G ___. If a woman were reading such magazines as we have discussed, would you feel that she was a homosexual because she was reading those magazines?
11. G ___. Don't they read them for the articles, like all the men?

*COMMENT:* And see §9.124 concerning the presence of such magazines in "porn lockers" on board ship.

## D. Opponents of Nuclear War and Nuclear Power §9.131

Opponents of the United States development, production, use, and sale of nuclear weapons occasionally sue for injunctive or other relief based on alleged violations of the United States Constitution, treaties, or statutes. Opponents of construction and operation of nuclear power plants occasionally sue for damages to themselves or to their property due to radiation. Both groups are frequently arrested during on-site

A=*Brewster*; B=*Briggs*; C=questions traditionally asked or permitted by the trial judge; D=*Angela Davis* case; E=*Detroit Black Panther* case; F=*Stroud*; G=*Gaskins*; H=*United States v Ramos*; J=*Michigan v Jeanette Smith*; K=*Stokes*; M=*United States v McNeil*; N=*Huey Newton* case; O=*United States v Sherpix*; P=*Pentagon Papers* case; S=*Panther 21* case; V=*Venceremos* case; W=*California v Block*; see §§9.1 and 9.3

demonstrations; usually there is no charge of violence or assault. The questions in §9.133 were asked in *California v Block* (Sacramento County Justice Ct, CR Nos. 3235–3245, 1979), in which 11 defendants were charged with trespass and resisting arrest as a result of a March 31, 1979, demonstration during which 13 people climbed and sat on a fence at the Rancho Seco Nuclear Power Plant. After a seven-week trial, the jury found one defendant not guilty, found one guilty, and deadlocked on nine. The case was set for retrial and subsequently removed to Sacramento Municipal Court, where the judge stated he would grant the defense of necessity, if urged. The district attorney dismissed the case; see §3.29. See also questions in §§9.67, 9.85–9.87, 9.140, 11.57–11.58.

### 1. Nuclear War Protesters §9.132

In numerous trespass-type cases arising out of civil disobedience demonstrations against Honeywell Corporation in Minneapolis, the following questions have been asked, often by misdemeanor defendants representing themselves. They also asked the questions in §11.57.

1. ___. Do you think that it's possible that corporations and government agencies don't always act in the best interests of all of us?
2. ___. What do you think people should do when they disagree with the actions of the government or corporations, actions that affect people's lives?
3. ___. What do you think people should do when they feel that people's lives are being threatened by the actions of the government or of a corporation?
4. ___. Do you think people have an obligation to speak out when they disagree with the actions of a corporation? Should they act when they feel that the environment and people's lives are endangered?
5. ___. What do you think of demonstrations?
6. ___. Have you ever taken part in a demonstration of some kind?
7. ___. Have you ever signed a petition?
8. ___. Do you believe that people who take part in demonstrations are just out to cause trouble?

---

A=*Brewster*; B=*Briggs*; C=questions traditionally asked or permitted by the trial judge; D=*Angela Davis* case; E=*Detroit Black Panther* case; F=*Stroud*; G=*Gaskins*; H=*United States v Ramos*; J=*Michigan v Jeanette Smith*; K=*Stokes*; M=*United States v McNeil*; N=*Huey Newton* case; O=*United States v Sherpix*; P=*Pentagon Papers* case; S=*Panther 21* case; V=*Venceremos* case; W=*California v Block*; see §§9.1 and 9.3

9. ___. What do you think about nuclear war?
10. ___. Are you afraid of nuclear war?
11. ___. Do you feel helpless to prevent a nuclear war?
12. ___. Recently, the American Catholic Bishops made a statement urging disarmament and renewed peace efforts. What do you think about this?

## 2. Nuclear Power Dangers §9.133

The following questions were asked early in *California v Block* (see §3.29 and §9.131).

1. W ___. Do you own stock in [*Name of utility or other company*]?
2. W ___. What do you know about [*Name of utility or other company*]?
3. W ___. Are you aware that [*Name of utility*] is a public utility and not like an ordinary private company?
4. W ___. Do you know that [*Name of utility*]'s rates must be approved by [*Name of state or federal agency*]?
5. W ___. Do you agree that the people should maintain control over [*Name of utility*] because of its peaceful nature?
6. W ___. Do you agree that it is appropriate to challenge [*Name of utility*]'s statements, policies, etc.?
7. W ___. Would you be willing to believe testimony that [*Name of utility*] has not been honest in statements it has made concerning the [*safety/other*] of the [*Name*] plant?

Thereafter, the following questions were asked.

1. W ___. What do you think of when I say "nuclear power"?
2. W ___. Are you familiar with the Three Mile Island [*catastrophe/events*]?
3. W ___. Do you know what radiation sickness is?
4. W ___. Do you know that you can't see radiation?
5. W ___. Do you know that radiation is invisible and odorless?
6. W ___. Have you seen the movie *China Syndrome*?
7. W ___. Do you know the difference between low-level and high-level radiation?
8. W ___. Did you attend any meeting at [*Name of site*]?
9. W ___. If you were told by expert scientists in this trial that there is a

A=*Brewster*; B=*Briggs*; C=questions traditionally asked or permitted by the trial judge; D=*Angela Davis* case; E=*Detroit Black Panther* case; F=*Stroud*; G=*Gaskins*; H=*United States v Ramos*; J=*Michigan v Jeanette Smith*; K=*Stokes*; M=*United States v McNeil*; N=*Huey Newton* case; O=*United States v Sherpix*; P=*Pentagon Papers* case; S=*Panther 21* case; V=*Venceremos* case; W=*California v Block*; see §§9.1 and 9.3

danger to you and your family of cancer and other diseases from low-level radiation leaking from [*Name of site*], would you have a hard time believing that information because it may be upsetting?

10. W___. How would you view such testimony?
11. W___. Have you ever worked with or been around X rays?
12. W___. Did you know that X-ray technicians wear badges and are protected by lead shielding against radiation?
13. W___. Do you have an opinion about the safety of X rays?
14. W___. What is your opinion?
15. W___. Do you have an opinion about whether nuclear power is safe?
16. W___. Do you know if there is an evacuation plan for people living near the [*Rancho Seco*] plant?
17. W___. Have you seen the [*Rancho Seco*] evacuation plan in the [*library*]?
18. W___. Are you aware that nuclear power affects the whole world?
19. W___. Are you aware that a disaster at [*Rancho Seco*] could affect everyone?
20. W___. Do you have any reservations about the use of your tax money to finance and subsidize [*nuclear power*]?

*COMMENT:* This question can be coupled with a question on reservations about using taxes for district attorney's staff, judge, jury fees, etc., to prosecute the instant case.

### 3. Antinuclear/Antiwar Advocates §9.134

The following questions were asked in *California v Barr* (protesters against Livermore Nuclear Weapons Laboratory; see §11.58).

1. W___. Did you see the TV special, *The Day After,* first shown in November 1983?
   [*If yes*]
   a. What did you think of it?
   b. Did you discuss it with anyone?
2. W___. Did you see *The Last Epidemic*?
   a. *On the Beach*?
   b. *Dr. Strangelove?*

---

A=*Brewster*; B=*Briggs*; C=questions traditionally asked or permitted by the trial judge; D=*Angela Davis* case; E=*Detroit Black Panther* case; F=*Stroud*; G=*Gaskins*; H=*United States v Ramos*; J=*Michigan v Jeanette Smith*; K=*Stokes*; M=*United States v McNeil*; N=*Huey Newton* case; O=*United States v Sherpix*; P=*Pentagon Papers* case; S=*Panther 21* case; V=*Venceremos* case; W=*California v Block*; see §§9.1 and 9.3

[*If yes*]

c. Is there anything you saw in [*that movie/those movies*] that would make it impossible for you to judge this case fairly?

3. W____. Do you agree or disagree with the United States being part of the United Nations?
4. W____. Do you support the administration's policy on [*national defense/nuclear weapons/etc.*]
5. W____. How do you feel about the research and development of nuclear weapons?
6. W____. Do you feel that the government is correct in allocating funds for nuclear weapons at the [*Livermore Laboratory*]?
7. W____. Do you see any danger in the unlimited development of nuclear weapons?
8. W____. Do you believe there are any circumstances under which nuclear weapons may be used on civilian targets?
7. W____. Do you see any danger in the unlimited development of nuclear weapons?
8. W____. Do you believe there are any circumstances under which nuclear weapons may be used on civilian targets?
9. W____. Have you ever thought about nuclear weapons or the use of them and been frightened or had a nightmare?

*COMMENT:* One of the defendants would testify that she had had this experience after growing up in a military family that had moved several times and always had a bomb shelter.

10. W____. Have you ever heard of [*The Doomsday Clock*]?

*COMMENT:* While this question was permitted on voir dire, a reproduction of the clock, with its hands standing at 2 minutes to midnight in 1984, was not admitted as an exhibit and defense counsel were not permitted to show it to the jury.

11. W____. How do you feel about nuclear weapons in relation to the issues of war and peace?
12. W____. Would your attitudes about [*nuclear weapons*] affect your ability to decide this case fairly?

---

A=*Brewster*; B=*Briggs*; C=questions traditionally asked or permitted by the trial judge; D=*Angela Davis* case; E=*Detroit Black Panther* case; F=*Stroud*; G=*Gaskins*; H=*United States v Ramos*; J=*Michigan v Jeanette Smith*; K=*Stokes*; M=*United States v McNeil*; N=*Huey Newton* case; O=*United States v Sherpix*; P=*Pentagon Papers* case; S=*Panther 21* case; V=*Venceremos* case; W=*California v Block*; see §§9.1 and 9.3

13. W___. Have you heard the term [*nuclear winter*] which describes [*the devastating climatic effects of nuclear explosions*]?
14. W___. You heard the prospective juror from [*the San Francisco Water Department*] say he worked with [*Livermore Laboratory*] on water quality. Have you ever been concerned about the water quality at the [*Lab*] or in the [*City of Livermore*]?
15. W___. Do you worry about the possibility of accidents at [*Livermore Weapons Laboratory*] that would endanger the community?
16. W___. How do you feel about laws that limit the kinds of weapons a country can use?
17. W___. Would you be able to be impartial in this case, knowing that the [*Livermore Weapons Laboratory*] is [*part of the University of California*]?
18. W___. Do you believe that a great university such as the [*University of California*] should support humanistic values?
    [*If yes*]
    a. Why?
19. W___. Do you believe that a good purpose is served by the [*University*] developing [*nuclear weapons*]?
20. W___. Do you believe that the [*Laboratory*] promotes peace?

*COMMENT:* Defense counsel concluded after getting several "Yes" answers, that the question should be posed: "Do you believe that the Laboratory promotes war?"

## E. Anti-Klan/Anti-Nazi Parties §9.136

When people are arrested for participating in demonstrations against the Ku Klux Klan or the American Nazi Party, they are frequently charged with misdemeanors or felonies against the peace and/or the police. In *California v Wagner* (Ventura County Super Ct, Nos. A028732–028734, 1979), the defendants were charged with unlawful assembly, assaulting police officers, resisting arrest, etc., as a result of their participation in a large demonstration (200–300 people) in July 1978 against the Ku Klux Klan. The Klan had put out fliers advertising a showing of the old movie *Birth of a Nation*, which depicts the KKK as the savior of the South after the Civil War. The Klan announced that proceeds from the movie would go to a white woman who had

A=*Brewster*; B=*Briggs*; C=questions traditionally asked or permitted by the trial judge; D=*Angela Davis* case; E=*Detroit Black Panther* case; F=*Stroud*; G=*Gaskins*; H=*United States v Ramos*; J=*Michigan v Jeanette Smith*; K=*Stokes*; M=*United States v McNeil*; N=*Huey Newton* case; O=*United States v Sherpix*; P=*Pentagon Papers* case; S=*Panther 21* case; V=*Venceremos* case; W=*California v Block*; see §§9.1 and 9.3

allegedly been raped by young Chicanos. When the Klan began shouting racist epithets, before the movie, the crowd broke into the auditorium, and the police drove the people out. The crowd continued to march peacefully for three hours. A large police contingent then ordered the crowd to disperse, and the arrests followed.

One misdemeanor trial of three defendants resulted in acquittals on some counts and guilty verdicts on others. In another trial, defendant Lynn was acquitted. In the third trial, the jury was hung eight to three for conviction of defendant Guzman on two counts. All of the convictions were appealed on nonjury issues. *California v Wagner* (Ventura County Super Ct, App Div, Nos. 911–913).

In each of the trials in the fall of 1979, defense counsel David Weitzman of Berkeley and Daniel Russo of Santa Rosa, California, conducted an intensive voir dire on the nature of the Klan, its activities, and its ideology. They asked many of the general questions in §§9.7–9.18, as well as the questions on attitudes toward the crime charged (see §§11.5–11.7), on pretrial publicity (see §§9.21–9.24), and on burden of proof (see §§11.10–11.13). Counsel then expanded on the questions on racial prejudgment (see §§9.30–9.33, 9.36, 9.46–9.49) and attitudes toward defendant (see §9.56) with the questions on the Klan in §§9.137–9.138.

In their opening arguments, defense counsel discussed at length the policies and practices of the Klan. They cross-examined prosecution witnesses, particularly police officers, on their knowledge of the Klan. They asked defense witnesses on direct examination whether they knew about violent activities of the Klan. These questions were relevant to prove that the defendants had no intent to violate the law. All of the information about the Klan was discussed in the closing arguments.

Post-trial conversations with some jurors indicated that specific information about the Klan provided by the defense throughout the three-week trial helped convince the jurors who voted for acquittals of some defendants on some charges.

### 1. KKK/Nazi Activities §9.137

The following questions were asked in *California v Wagner* (see §9.136).

1. ____. Did you hear that the [*Ku Klux Klan*] had a recruitment rally

A=*Brewster*; B=*Briggs*; C=questions traditionally asked or permitted by the trial judge; D=*Angela Davis* case; E=*Detroit Black Panther* case; F=*Stroud*; G=*Gaskins*; H=*United States v Ramos*; J=*Michigan v Jeanette Smith*; K=*Stokes*; M=*United States v McNeil*; N=*Huey Newton* case; O=*United States v Sherpix*; P=*Pentagon Papers* case; S=*Panther 21* case; V=*Venceremos* case; W=*California v Block*; see §§9.1 and 9.3

and fundraiser in [*this area*] on the day of the incident that led to [*defendant's arrest/plaintiff's damage suit*]?

2. ___. Were you aware of [*Klan*] activity in the area around that time?
3. ___. Did you hear about [*Klan*] efforts to recruit in the schools?
4. ___. Did you read in the [*local newspapers*] about the [*Klan*] sending people to [*Oxnard*] in [*1978*] in order to set up a [*Klan*] chapter there?
5. ___. What do you know about the [*Ku Klux Klan*]?
6. ___. Have you ever known anyone who was a member of the [*Klan*], or associated with it?
7. ___. Do you have any feelings about the [*Ku Klux Klan*]?
8. ___. If the evidence shows that my client participated in a demonstration against the [*Klan*], will this information bias you against [*him/her*]?

*COMMENT:* For additional information on Klan activity, policy, and the character of Klan members, see *Intelligence Report*, a publication of KLANWATCH a project of the Southern Poverty Law Center, P.O. Box 548, Montgomery, Alabama 36195.

### 2. KKK/Nazi Policies §9.138

The following questions were asked of many prospective jurors in *California v Wagner* (see §9.136).

1. ___. Are you aware that the [*Ku Klux Klan*] has, as its main idea, the idea of racism or white supremacy?
2. ___. If racism is talked about in this trial, will it make you uncomfortable?
3. ___. Do you have any acquaintances who consistently feel that minority people are inferior to white people?
4. ___. Do you have any acquaintances who consistently feel that minority people are their enemies?
5. ___. If the evidence were to show that there are individuals and groups who actively work toward keeping minorities [*down/in their place*], could you accept this?

*COMMENT:* At some point in a juror's answers, it may be helpful to repeat certain questions, e.g., those on objective and subjective racism

---

A=*Brewster*; B=*Briggs*; C=questions traditionally asked or permitted by the trial judge; D=*Angela Davis* case; E=*Detroit Black Panther* case; F=*Stroud*; G=*Gaskins*; H=*United States v Ramos*; J=*Michigan v Jeanette Smith*; K=*Stokes*; M=*United States v McNeil*; N=*Huey Newton* case; O=*United States v Sherpix*; P=*Pentagon Papers* case; S=*Panther 21* case; V=*Venceremos* case; W=*California v Block*; see §§9.1 and 9.3

(see §9.48). After thinking about the KKK for a few minutes, jurors may be more truthful or precise about their racial attitudes.

In each of the Ventura KKK trials, at least one prospective juror was a member of the Klan, had been asked to join, or had a relative who was a member. Defense counsel questioned these prospective jurors intensively on what they knew about the Klan's current policies and activities, and what they knew of its history, in order to educate the other prospective jurors in the courtroom. The trial judge granted challenges for cause against all but one Klan-related juror, who testified he had been a Klansman in Indiana many years ago and now thought the Klan was wrong. The defense used a peremptory challenge on this man.

### 3. Anti-Ku Klux Klan Act of 1871 §9.139

The following questions flow naturally from the voir dire in *California v Wagner* (see §9.136–9.138) and current discussions on how best to defeat KKK/Nazi ideology. Counsel who ask similar questions on voir dire are urged to send the citations to the author for inclusion in the next updating of this chapter.

1. ___. Have you ever heard of the Ku Klux Klan Act of 1871, passed by Congress after the Civil War to stop the killing of black people, and of their white friends in the South—the beatings and lynchings by Klansmen wearing white hoods?
2. ___. The Ku Klux Klan Act makes it a crime for two or more people to conspire to deprive someone of his or her rights because of race or color, and it sets a punishment of life imprisonment if the victim dies. Do you agree with this law?

*COMMENT:* For text of the Ku Klux Klan Act, see 17 Stat 11, now codified in 18 USC §§241–242 (criminal) and 42 USC §§1981–1985 (civil). The wording of 18 USC §241 is paraphrased in question 2 above.

3. ___. The Ku Klux Klan Act makes it a crime for people to wear hoods to disguise themselves and then to drive around or go on someone else's property in order to keep black people from exercising their rights. Do you agree with this law?

---

A=*Brewster*; B=*Briggs*; C=questions traditionally asked or permitted by the trial judge; D=*Angela Davis* case; E=*Detroit Black Panther* case; F=*Stroud*; G=*Gaskins*; H=*United States v Ramos*; J=*Michigan v Jeanette Smith*; K=*Stokes*; M=*United States v McNeil*; N=*Huey Newton* case; O=*United States v Sherpix*; P=*Pentagon Papers* case; S=*Panther 21* case; V=*Venceremos* case; W=*California v Block*; see §§9.1 and 9.3

*COMMENT:* Question 3 is paraphrased from 18 USC §241, which provides, in pertinent part:

> If two or more persons conspire to injure, oppress, threaten, or intimidate any citizen in the free exercise or enjoyment of any right or privilege secured to him by the Constitution or laws of the United States, or because of his having so exercised the same; or
>
> If two or more persons go in disguise on the highway, or on the premises of another, with intent to prevent or hinder his free exercise or enjoyment of any right or privilege so secured . . . [those persons shall be punished by ten years' imprisonment and/or $10,000 fine, and, if death results, the punishment shall be life imprisonment.]

4. ____. The Ku Klux Klan Act makes it a crime for any government official to deprive someone of his or her rights because of race or color, and sets a punishment of life imprisonment if the victim dies. Do you agree with this law?

*COMMENT:* Question 4 is paraphrased from 18 USC §242, which provides, in pertinent part:

> Whoever, under color of any law, statute, ordinance, regulation, or custom, willfully subjects an inhabitant of any State, . . .to the deprivation of any rights, privileges, or immunities secured or protected by the Constitution or laws of the United States, or to different punishments, pains, or penalties, on account of such inhabitant being an alien, or by reason of his color, or race, than are prescribed for the punishment of citizens . . . [shall be punished by one year's imprisonment and/or $1,000 fine and, if death results, by life imprisonment.]

## F. International Human Rights Law §9.140

Many civil and criminal cases today turn on acceptable standards of conduct by government agencies and government contractors. One source of standards for government conduct is international human rights law. United States courts are increasingly using this source in appropriate cases, e.g. *Filartiga v Pena Irala* (2d Cir 1980) 630 F2d 876 (tort action for torture committed in Paraguay by defendants found in the United States).

Protesters often indicate that their actions were based on their determination not to be in complicity with actions of the United States government violating international law. In *Californa v Barr,* several

---

A=*Brewster*; B=*Briggs*; C=questions traditionally asked or permitted by the trial judge; D=*Angela Davis* case; E=*Detroit Black Panther* case; F=*Stroud*; G=*Gaskins*; H=*United States v Ramos*; J=*Michigan v Jeanette Smith*; K=*Stokes*; M=*United States v McNeil*; N=*Huey Newton* case; O=*United States v Sherpix*; P=*Pentagon Papers* case; S=*Panther 21* case; V=*Venceremos* case; W=*California v Block*; see §§9.1 and 9.3

of the defendants charged with "willfully and maliciously obstructing the highway" at the Lawrence Nuclear Defense Laboratory said they did not act maliciously but rather out of commitment to the principles of the Nurnberg Judgment, and a determination not to be in complicity with U.S. nuclear weapons policy. See §11.58. The defense in *Barr* asked several prospective jurors:

1. W___. Have you ever heard of Lt. Calley and the My Lai incident during the Vietnam War?

The next questions would have been:

2. W___. Did you see the movie *Judgment at Nuremberg* ?
3. W___. Did you know that Lt. Calley was convicted of violating the laws of war?

This, in turn, would have led to questions about the limits on the laws of war expressed in the Nurnberg Principles. However, all but one of the jurors said they had never heard of Lt. Calley, and the one had only heard enough to lead to a brief second question. Juror ignorance prevented pursuit of this issue, and trial judge Clifford B. Bachand ruled that defendants could not explain their reliance on the Nurnberg Principles.

Lawyers in the United States, having the Bill of Rights and similar provisions in state constitutions to turn to, have been slow to study and use international human rights standards that are now part of U.S. domestic law, having been included in treaties ratified by the Senate and signed by the president. Lawyers in Northern Ireland and other areas lacking the rudiments of democratic government frequently use U.N. standards that have been codified in international covenants and conventions. They go beyond the U.S. Bill of Rights and are often on point in U.S. litigation.

Few U.S. lawyers recall that the U.S. Army, Navy, Air Force, Marines, and National Guard are all governed by the standards adopted in the trial of Nazi war criminals in Nurnberg after World War II, for example, which are quoted in the Department of the Army Field Manual, "The Law of Land Warfare" (FM 27–10) (18 July 1956):

---

A=*Brewster*; B=*Briggs*; C=questions traditionally asked or permitted by the trial judge; D=*Angela Davis* case; E=*Detroit Black Panther* case; F=*Stroud*; G=*Gaskins*; H=*United States v Ramos*; J=*Michigan v Jeanette Smith*; K=*Stokes*; M=*United States v McNeil*; N=*Huey Newton* case; O=*United States v Sherpix*; P=*Pentagon Papers* case; S=*Panther 21* case; V=*Venceremos* case; W=*California v Block*; see §§9.1 and 9.3

Section II. CRIMES UNDER INTERNATIONAL LAW

498. Crimes Under International Law

Any person, whether a member of the armed forces or a civilian, who commits an act which constitutes a crime under international law is responsible therefor and liable to punishment. Such offenses in connection with war comprise:

a. Crimes against peace.

b. Crimes against humanity.

c. War crimes.

Although this manual recognizes the criminal responsibility of individuals for those offenses which may comprise any of the foregoing types of crimes, members of the armed forces will normally be concerned only with those offenses constituting "war crimes."

499. War Crimes

The term "war crime" is the technical expression for a violation of the law of war by any person or persons, military or civilian. Every violation of the law of war is a war crime.

These standards become relevant to individual civilians because "complicity in the commission of . . . crimes against peace, crimes against humanity, and war crimes [is] punishable." [Sec. 500] These crimes are committed when the act is done with knowledge of its illegality, and no lines are drawn in principle that free average citizens or workers from criminal responsibility for an act of which they have full knowledge. Responsibility extends not merely to the prohibited conduct but also to complicity in it, and the test formulated at Nurnberg was whether moral choice was in fact possible. Today, as nuclear weapons are deployed and as new weapons are developed that violate international law, according to international law experts of all nations, moral choice commences with the first knowledge of their deployment or development. See Mary M. Kaufman, "The Individual's Duty under the Law of Nurnberg: The Effect of Knowledge on Justiciability," 27 *Lawyers Guild Practitioner* 15 (1968).

For protesters like those in *California v Barr*, the Nurnberg Principles explain their motives and their (noncriminal) state of mind. See §11.58.

As the Army Field Manual points out, in Sec. 511: "The fact that domestic law does not impose a penalty for an act which constitutes a crime under international law does not relieve the person who committed the act from responsibility under international law."

---

A=*Brewster*; B=*Briggs*; C=questions traditionally asked or permitted by the trial judge; D=*Angela Davis* case; E=*Detroit Black Panther* case; F=*Stroud*; G=*Gaskins*; H=*United States v Ramos*; J=*Michigan v Jeanette Smith*; K=*Stokes*; M=*United States v McNeil*; N=*Huey Newton* case; O=*United States v Sherpix*; P=*Pentagon Papers* case; S=*Panther 21* case; V=*Venceremos* case; W=*California v Block*; see §§9.1 and 9.3

The crimes are defined in the Nurnberg Principles:

(a) Crimes against peace:
   (i) Planning, preparation, initiation or waging of a war of aggression or a war in violation of international treaties, agreements or assurances;
   (ii) Participation in a common plan or conspiracy for the accomplishment of any of the acts mentioned under (i).

(b) War crimes:
Violations of the laws or customs of war which include, but are not limited to, murder, ill-treatment or deportation to slave-labour or for any other purpose of civilian population of or in occupied territory, murder or ill-treatment of prisoners of war or persons on the seas, killing of hostages, plunder of public or private property, wanton destruction of cities, towns, or villages, or devastation not justified by military necessity.

(c) Crimes against humanity:
Murder, extermination, enslavement, deportation and other inhuman acts done against any civilian population, or persecutions on political, racial or religious grounds, when such acts are done or such persecutions are carried on in execution of or in connection with any crime against peace or any war crime.

Sohn, *Cases of United Nations Law* 970–981 (1956).

See practical ideas on the use of these international law principles in domestic cases in "Proceedings: Conference on International Human Rights Law in State and Federal Courts," 17 *USF L Rev* 1 (1982).

The following questions flow naturally from these questions asked in *California v Wagner* (see §§9.136–9.138) and the current discussions on how best to defeat KKK/Nazi ideology. They are also suggested by the hearings on ratification of five international human rights covenants or conventions pending before the United States Senate Committee on Foreign Relations since November 1979. Professors Richard Lillich and Frank Newman in *International Human Rights: Problems of Law and Policy* (1979), discuss at length the use of international documents before ratification. Their casebook also contains the complete text of all of the documents mentioned in this section.

1. ___. Have you heard the term "international human rights"?
2. ___. Perhaps you have heard the President talk about the United

A=*Brewster*; B=*Briggs*; C=questions traditionally asked or permitted by the trial judge; D=*Angela Davis* case; E=*Detroit Black Panther* case; F=*Stroud*; G=*Gaskins*; H=*United States v Ramos*; J=*Michigan v Jeanette Smith*; K=*Stokes*; M=*United States v McNeil*; N=*Huey Newton* case; O=*United States v Sherpix*; P=*Pentagon Papers* case; S=*Panther 21* case; V=*Venceremos* case; W=*California v Block*; see §§9.1 and 9.3

States having a policy of supporting human rights or international human rights all over the world?

3. ____. During the crisis over United States hostages being held in the American Embassy in Iran, do you recall hearing that President Carter quoted the United Nations Universal Declaration of Human Rights when the United States appealed to the World Court for release of the hostages?

4. ____. Did you know that the Senate Committee on Foreign Relations is considering ratification of the Convention Against Genocide, already ratified by many nations, which makes it a crime to do any act, or make any attempt, to destroy black people or any racial or national group?

*COMMENT:* The Convention Against Genocide, signed by the United States at the United Nations many years ago, provides in part:

Article I. The contracting parties confirm that genocide, whether committed in time of peace or in time of war, is a crime under international law which they undertake to prevent and to punish.

Article II. In the present Convention, genocide means any of the following acts committed with intent to destroy, in whole or in part, a national, ethnical, racial or religious group, such as:
(a) Killing members of the group;
(b) Causing serious bodily or mental harm to members of the group;
(c) Deliberately inflicting on the group conditions of life calculated to bring about its physical destruction in whole or in part;
(d) Imposing measures intended to prevent births within the group;
(e) Forcibly transferring children of the group to another group.

Article III. The following acts shall be punishable:
(a) Genocide;
(b) Conspiracy to commit genocide;
(c) Direct and public incitement to commit genocide;
(d) Attempt to commit genocide;
(e) Complicity in genocide.

Article IV. Persons committing genocide or any of the other acts enumerated in article III shall be punished, whether they are constitutionally responsible rulers, public officials, or private individuals.

---

A=*Brewster*; B=*Briggs*; C=questions traditionally asked or permitted by the trial judge; D=*Angela Davis* case; E=*Detroit Black Panther* case; F=*Stroud*; G=*Gaskins*; H=*United States v Ramos*; J=*Michigan v Jeanette Smith*; K=*Stokes*; M=*United States v McNeil*; N=*Huey Newton* case; O=*United States v Sherpix*; P=*Pentagon Papers* case; S=*Panther 21* case; V=*Venceremos* case; W=*California v Block*; see §§9.1 and 9.3

5. ___. Do you agree with the law now pending before the Senate Committee on Foreign Relations, that makes it illegal to advocate racial or religious hatred that incites discrimination, hostility, or violence? It is the International Covenant on Civil and Political Rights.

*COMMENT:* The American Bar Association testified for ratification of this Covenant and of the International Convention discussed in question 6 below. The Covenant referred to in question 5 states in article 20, ¶2, "Any advocacy of national, racial or religious hatred that constitutes incitement to discrimination, hostility or violence shall be prohibited by law."

6. ___. Knowing that many groups, including the American Bar Association, support ratification of the International Convention against all forms of racial discrimination, can you agree that we, in the United States, should also declare it illegal to "promote and incite racial discrimination" and should "prohibit organizations" that do so?

*COMMENT:* The International Convention on the Elimination of All Forms of Racial Discrimination was signed by the United States when it was drafted at the United Nations, and it is now before the Senate Committee on Foreign Relations for ratification. It provides, in article 4:

> [Parties to this Convention] condemn all propaganda and all organizations which are based on ideas or theories of superiority of one race or group of persons of one colour or ethnic origin, or which attempt to justify or promote racial hatred and discrimination in any form, and undertake to adopt immediate and positive measures designed to eradicate all incitement to, or acts of, such discrimination and, to this end, with due regard to the principles embodied in the Universal Declaration of Human Rights and the rights expressly set forth in article 5 of this Convention, inter alia:
>
> (a) Shall declare an offence punishable by law all dissemination of ideas based on racial superiority or hatred, incitement to racial discrimination, as well as all acts of violence or incitement to such acts against any race or group of persons of another colour or ethnic origin, and also the provision of any assistance to racist activities, including the financing thereof.
>
> (b) Shall declare illegal and prohibit organizations, and also organized and

A=*Brewster*; B=*Briggs*; C=questions traditionally asked or permitted by the trial judge; D=*Angela Davis* case; E=*Detroit Black Panther* case; F=*Stroud*; G=*Gaskins*; H=*United States v Ramos*; J=*Michigan v Jeanette Smith*; K=*Stokes*; M=*United States v McNeil*; N=*Huey Newton* case; O=*United States v Sherpix*; P=*Pentagon Papers* case; S=*Panther 21* case; V=*Venceremos* case; W=*California v Block*; see §§9.1 and 9.3

all other propaganda activities, which promote and incite racial discrimination, and shall recognize participation in such organizations or activities as an offence punishable by law;

(c) Shall not permit public authorities or public institutions, national or local, to promote or incite racial discrimination.

"Racial discrimination" is defined in article 1.

As trial lawyers use these international human rights documents in their cases and make the citations available to the author, those citations will be provided in supplements to this section.

## G. Other Issues §9.145

This section is being reserved for additional issues to be presented in Supplements to this volume.

## Chapter 10

# *Questions in Civil Cases*


**I. Compilation of a Useful List**
A. Sources of Questions §10.1
B. Ways to Use This List §10.2
C. Abbreviations Used §10.3

**II. Points to Explore in a Typical Case §10.4**

**III. Introductory Questions for Judge to Ask §10.5**

**IV. Juror Attitudes Toward Jury Duty**
A. Hard Questioning on Voir Dire §10.6
B. Jurors' Sympathy for Parties §10.7
C. Recent Developments §10.8

**V. Juror Attitudes Toward Defendants**
A. Corporate §10.10
B. Insurance Companies §10.11
C. Municipalities §10.12
D. Police Officers §10.13
E. Other Defendants §10.14

**VI. Juror Attitudes Toward Plaintiffs**
A. Seriously Injured §10.21
B. Family of Deceased Housewife §10.22

C. Bar Owner §10.23
D. Absent Plaintiff §10.24
E. Other Plaintiffs §10.25

**VII. Juror Attitudes Toward Rules of Law**
A. Liability
1. Based on Negligence §10.31
2. Admitted §10.32
3. Vicarious §10.33
4. Standard of Care §10.34
B. Damages
1. As Compensation for Injury §10.36
a. Physical and Emotional §10.37
b. Emotional §10.38
2. Amount of Award §10.39
3. Comparative Fault §10.40
4. Other Problems §10.41
C. Proof
1. Burden §10.46
2. Standard §10.47
3. Contrasted with Criminal Cases §10.48
D. Presumptions
1. General Meaning §10.50
2. Due Care §10.51
3. Other Presumptions §10.52
E. Doctrines
1. Sudden Emergency §10.56
2. Other Doctrines §10.57

**VIII. Specific Types of Cases**
A. Personal Injury
1. Automobile Accidents
a. Typical Case §10.61
b. Police Emergency Case §10.62
c. Other Cases §10.63
2. Product Liability
a. General Questions about Manufacturer §10.65
b. Automobile Accidents §10.66
c. Airplane Accidents §10.67
d. Motorcycle Accidents §10.68
e. Other Cases §10.73
3. Medical Malpractice
a. Plaintiff's Questions §10.75
b. Defendant's Questions §10.76
4. Failure to Make Safety Inspection §10.78

5. Police Misconduct
   a. Plaintiff's Questions §10.80
   b. Defendant's Questions §10.81
6. Other Cases §10.82

B. Employment Discrimination
1. Upgrading, Firing, Hiring §10.91
2. Sexual Harassment
   a. Attitudes toward Filing Suit §10.92
   b. Attitudes toward Employers/Management §10.93
   c. Attitudes toward Awarding Recovery for Sexual Harassment §10.94
3. Other Grounds §10.95

C. Military Discharge
1. General Questions §10.97
2. Attitudes toward Service Personnel §10.98
3. Allegations of Homosexual Conduct §10.99

D. Other Types of Cases §10.101

# I. COMPILATION OF A USEFUL LIST

## A. Sources of Questions §10.1

The questions in this chapter, together with basic questions in chapter 9, provide a comprehensive, well-organized list for consideration in any civil case in which jury prejudgment is potentially a serious problem. Some of the typical issues and many types of cases are discussed, but coverage is not encyclopedic. The breadth and detail of the questions reproduced here indicate what judges have asked, or permitted counsel to ask, in this period. As you work, you will draft numerous questions that go to the heart of your case, building on the comprehensive approach now widely accepted in most jurisdictions in this country.

The questions were compiled from many sources, including a series of personal injury and product liability cases tried successfully in Michigan state and federal courts; police misconduct, employment discrimination, sexual harassment, and medical malpractice cases tried in several jurisdictions; and a successful defense against administrative discharge from the Navy in San Diego (see §10.3). Attorneys Dean Robb, Richard Goodman, Hugh M. Davis, Jr., Victoria Heldman, Charles Barr, Ronald DeNardis, Marion R. Jenkins, Connye Harper, Joan Lovell, Robert A. Obringer, Richard Parker, Richard Schaden, Richard A. Soble, James A. Tuck, William Goodman, and Allyn Ravitz, all of Michigan, and Kenneth Chotiner, now a municipal court judge in Los Angeles, and Huge Manes of Los Angeles, supplied sets of voir dire questions on many topics.

## B. Ways to Use This List §10.2

Counsel may want to reproduce the following pages, mark up the copy, cross out and write in the margins, rearrange questions, and number them to suit a particular case. Attorneys may want to change the language of the questions to suit the idiom of the region and the court. The questions contain many phrases in brackets or instructions for filling in names or specific issues, many *he/she*, *his/her* choices. This approach is intended to encourage *thinking* about whether to include each question when making a list to use in a case, rather than simply including all the questions because one is in a hurry. Defense of the right of counsel to ask voir dire questions directly and to question prospective jurors individually and in depth includes a disciplined approach to preparation of the questions to be asked in each particular case.

Once the edited list of voir dire questions is prepared, it may be submitted to the judge in any court in which the trial judge asks questions propounded by counsel and limits or denies counsel's right to question prospective jurors directly. Since the questions in the following sections are marked to show in which cases they were used (see abbreviations in §10.3), the list can be used as precedent for asking the same, or similar, questions in counsel's current cases.

Over time a lawyer will want to add questions from other sources that have proved useful and to delete ones that prove ineffective.

See further discussion in §9.2.

### C. Abbreviations Used §10.3

The following abbreviations, which precede each voir dire question in this chapter, show the cases in which the question was used and the section of this book in which each case is described.*

A *Brewster v Martin Marietta*; see §3.41
C Questions traditionally asked by the trial judge
F *Stroud v General Motors*; see §3.42
G *Administrative Discharge Board in the Case of DK3 Tangela Gaskins*; see §3.91
I *Haefele v Ruscio*; see §10.68
J *Hammers v Zurich-American*; see §10.11
K *Stokes v City of Detroit*; see §10.80
U *Underhill v Traverse City*; see §10.22
W *Storck v Ward's*; see §10.36
X *Schafer v North American Honda*; see §10.10
Y *Turner v Consolidated Rail Corp.*; see §10.37
Z *Nale v Ford Motor Co.*; see §10.38

## II. POINTS TO EXPLORE IN A TYPICAL CASE §10.4

Dean Robb of Michigan provided this introductory list of subjects to explore in almost any personal injury case.

1. Everyone is different and is capable of different reactions to similar occurrences.
   a. A wrongdoer is not entitled to pick the strongest victim.
   b. A devastating injury to one might be minor to another.

*Some capital letters are used as abbreviations for other (criminal) cases in chapters 9 and 11.

   c. Disability can result from pain alone, and that pain is personal and individual.
2. Attitudes toward medicine, doctors, psychiatrists, hospitals.
   a. The human body is an integral whole, not a series of medical specialties.
   b. Psychiatrists are doctors first.
   c. Jurors' feelings toward psychologists, mental health institutions, and psychiatrists must be brought to the surface.
3. Attitudes toward physical and mental pain.
   a. One is as real as the other.
   b. Negative physical findings of an objective nature do not rule out disability.
   c. A catastrophic injury may not cause immediate hospitalization.
   d. A person may return to work after an injury and find it impossible to continue working.
   e. A person who looks well may nonetheless be seriously and permanently injured.
   f. Try to imagine how difficult it is for a young man or woman to face a permanent injury that will haunt them for the rest of their lives.
4. Attitudes toward plaintiff's earnings compared to the juror's earnings, particularly when a well-paid worker is the plaintiff, e.g., a railroad worker or teamster.

## III. INTRODUCTORY QUESTIONS FOR JUDGE TO ASK §10.5

In a 1978 product liability trial, *Feitzer v Ford Motor Co.*, the federal district court judge asked the prospective jurors certain stock questions such as name, age, address, occupation, spouse's occupation, level of education, and acquaintance with the attorneys involved in the case. The judge added the following questions, as a matter of routine in such cases:

1. Would the juror be available for a trial lasting one week or more?
2. Were any jurors hard of hearing?
3. Did they work for or have close dealings with Ford?
4. Whether the juror had had a claim for personal injuries either as the result of an automobile accident or any other kind of incident?
5. Whether there was any reason whatsoever why the person could not sit as a juror and decide the case fairly and impartially based upon the evidence submitted?
6. Whether any juror worked on a swing shift or the night shift?

*Fietzer v Ford Motor Co.* (7th Cir 1980) 622 F2d 281, 285. (The judge's refusal to ask additional probing questions requested by plaintiff resulted in reversal and a third trial; see §10.66.)

Richard Schaden and Victoria Heldman of Detroit routinely seek to conduct the voir dire in their product liability cases. When this fails, they ask the trial judge to ask certain basic questions, which include:

1. ____. Have you or anyone in your family sued or been sued for money damages?
   [*If yes*]
   a. When?
   b. What kind of case?
   c. What are your feelings or attitudes as a result of that experience?
2. ____. What are your attitudes concerning people who are injured and seek money damages?
3. ____. How do you feel about corporations that are sued for money damages?
4. ____. Do any of you own stock in any manufacturing company?
   [*If yes*]
   a. Which ones?
5. ____. Have you or anyone in your family been seriously injured?
   [*If yes*]
   a. How?
   b. When?
   c. Was a lawsuit filed arising out of the injury?
6. ____. Have you or any close friend or member of your family been laid off recently?
   [*If yes*]
   a. From what work?
   b. Do you believe that a lawsuit like this makes companies have to lay people off?
   c. [*Why/Why not*]?

In a personal injury case brought under the Federal Employer's Liability Act, attorney Dean Robb proposed that the federal district judge ask the following introductory questions.

---

A=*Brewster*; C=questions traditionally asked by trial judge; F=*Stroud*; G=*Gaskins*; I=*Haefele*; J=*Hammers*; K=*Stokes*; U=*Underhill*; W=*Storck*; X=*Schafer*; Y=*Turner*; Z=*Nale*; see §10.3

1. ____. Members of the jury: Have you seen around this courthouse or anywhere else the statue of Minerva, the Princess of Justice? You may recall that first of all, Minerva is a woman; second, she is holding a scale in her hand; third, she is blindfolded. This Roman goddess is a present-day symbol for the way we will be asking you to decide this case.
   a. Why do you feel that she is blindfolded?
   b. Why is she holding a scale in her hand?

*COMMENT:* Robb thinks this in an interesting way for the trial judge to make a preliminary instruction on the fact that everyone comes into court equal; that justice is blind; that a trial is not a popularity contest between lawyers. The jurors should weigh the evidence and the decision carefully on the scale, based on proof given in open court, and the jurors should not go behind the evidence to make up tricky excuses or defenses.

## IV. JUROR ATTITUDES TOWARD JURY DUTY

### A. Hard Questioning on Voir Dire §10.6

For many years personal injury lawyers generally agreed that they should be very careful in questioning prospective jurors. As Dean Robb puts it:

> We had a ballet dancer's approach to hard questioning of jurors and fighting with judges. We had the idea that if you were outrageous in the voir dire, fighting with the judge and with the jurors, the jurors you ended up with would punish you for taking such a long time in selection, since the other lawyer conducted a brief voir dire.
>
> The most telling story in response to the tough approach to voir dire is about a case handled by Richard Goodman of Detroit. A woman juror was coming down in the elevator in the Wayne County Circuit Court building after the verdict in one of his product liability cases. She said to a friend, "I knew the way Mr. Goodman was so fussy about picking on us that we were not only picked by him; we were picked by God."

It is worth remembering that the lawyer does not have to worry about the people who do not get selected, unless they are really close to someone who stays on the jury. The trial lawyer must know that the juror being kept on the jury is someone the other jurors are going

---

A=*Brewster*; C=questions traditionally asked by trial judge; F=*Stroud*; G=*Gaskins*; I=*Haefele*; J=*Hammers*; K=*Stokes*; U=*Underhill*; W=*Storck*; X=*Schafer*; Y=*Turner*; Z=*Nale*; see §10.3

to feel should have been kept, since a spirit develops during voir dire when it is conducted in the courtroom with all prospective jurors present. The lawyer can win or lose points with the jurors depending on how the voir dire is conducted—points that will tell later in the jury's deliberations. Robb illustrated this with stories from two of his cases:

> I had a prospective juror who was answering every question perfectly. Soon virtually everyone in the courtroom knew he was lying to me. He was sort of surly and smart alecky, but nothing that would show in the record. I think eventually even the judge agreed with me that this man should be challenged.
>
> But there was no basis for a cause challenge because he was answering everything perfectly. Everyone knew he wanted to stay on the jury, and everyone felt he was biased, or at least lacked impartiality.
>
> I didn't know exactly what to do, but finally I almost hollered at him: "Are you telling me the truth? Are you really serious about your answers?" I could feel that the other jurors were with me, as if they were saying, "Get him, Robb; get that So-and-So!"
>
> So I just broke him down, and he finally admitted he was determined to stay on the jury even though he was partial to the other side. And I got him off on a cause challenge.
>
> In another case, the federal judge would not let me ask all the questions I wanted to. So I looked at the jurors as I asked the judge: "Could you ask the jurors whether there is anyone on this panel who does not believe this is a proper way to handle problems in society, when someone claims to have money coming as the result of an injury, and the other person says they don't."
>
> The judge said, "That is a ridiculous question," and he lectured me, and the whole jury, about how crazy the question was. Then he said, "But I'll ask it anyway."
>
> And two jurors raised their hands!
>
> The judge was caught. And I still don't know for sure whether that was their cute way of getting off, or whether they really did not agree with the idea of personal injury litigation.

## B. Jurors' Sympathy for Parties §10.7

1. F ___. One of the issues in this case, ultimately the only issue, will be replacing all the different values of the mother-housewife with dollars, with money. I guess the first thing I want to know from each of you is that you won't decide this case on the basis of sympathy. Mr.___________? Ms.___________?

---

A=*Brewster*; C=questions traditionally asked by trial judge; F=*Stroud*; G=*Gaskins*; I=*Haefele*; J=*Hammers*; K=*Stokes*; U=*Underhill*; W=*Storck*; X=*Schafer*; Y=*Turner*; Z=*Nale*; see §10.3

2. F ___. The reason I say that we're here for dollar substitutes, which the law requires and which is the only remedy, although a poor one, is that we don't want a verdict based on sympathy. Mrs. ________, Mr. ________: do you understand that?

3. I ___. I realize that you jurors could feel sympathy for the plaintiffs, [*Name and Name*], because of their injuries, but you could also feel sympathy for the defendant, because [*he/she*] didn't mean to cause this injury. This sympathy also has no place in the lawsuit. Do you agree?

### C. Recent Developments §10.8

It is now possible to keep up with the law on jury selection the same way you keep up with the law in any other field—by reading the relevant advance sheets, subscribing to services on trial advocacy or criminal law, and reading daily newspapers and legal newspapers. The *Index to Legal Periodicals*, *Current Law Index*, and *Legal Resource Index* provide provocative (and sometimes descriptive) titles to law review articles, comments, and notes in this field, indicating what is happening at the cutting edge of the law. It is a good idea occasionally to ask your law librarian for an index to journals on psychology, applied psychology, and the social sciences, to pick up new ideas from these disciplines.

Increasingly, lawyers are learning to use *Lexis* and *Westlaw* in order to find the latest cases and interesting parallels in other fields of law. It is always necessary to Shepardize all citations.

The Annual Supplement to these volumes will use recent developments sections throughout the book to describe new cases, ideas, and articles that are worthy of note, and to warn of cases overruled and of rules and statutes amended or appealed.

## V. JUROR ATTITUDES TOWARD DEFENDANTS

### A. Corporate §10.10

The following questions are often posed in product liability cases.

1. C ___. Do you feel it is wrong to bring a lawsuit against a corporation?

---

A=*Brewster*; C=questions traditionally asked by trial judge; F=*Stroud*; G=*Gaskins*; I=*Haefele*; J=*Hammers*; K=*Stokes*; U=*Underhill*; W=*Storck*; X=*Schafer*; Y=*Turner*; Z=*Nale*; see §10.3

2. F ___. Sympathy hasn't anything to do with this lawsuit, do you agree, and [*Corporation*] doesn't get any breaks because it is a corporation, and it doesn't get punished because it is a corporation?

*COMMENT:* Attitudes toward defendant car or motorcycle manufacturers were reflected in the voir dire proposed by defense counsel Ronald DeNardis of Detroit, Michigan, in the product liability case of *Schafer v American Honda Motor Co.* (Wayne County Circuit Ct, No. 27 816 757 ND). Questions 3 through 5 are a few of the questions DeNardis asked.

3. X ___. Have any of you had any particularly bad experiences or any particularly good experiences with an automobile company or motorcycle company that might influence your thinking on this case?
4. X ___. Would the fact that the defendant here is a corporation instead of a living person prevent you from giving the defendant a fair trial as you would any other person?
5. X ___. Do you feel that a corporate defendant should be held to a higher standard of care than an individual defendant?

## B. Insurance Companies §10.11

In a typical personal injury action, plaintiff was hurt by an overhead crane that had been inspected by the defendant insurance company's agent. The agent did not make a proper recommendation to the crane company and did not pursue the insurance company to make sure it followed the recommendations he did make. The judge conducted the voir dire, granting the attorneys (five defense and one plaintiff's attorney) flexibility to ask their own questions. The jury found the insurance company liable for not following through on the safety inspection after they had established a duty to do so and awarded the plaintiff 2 million dollars. *Hammers v Zurich-American Ins. Co.* (Wayne County Cir. Ct., No. 74 015 631 NM, Nov. 13, 1978). Plaintiff was represented by Richard M. Goodman of Detroit.

1. J ___. Has any juror ever been employed by an insurance company?
2. J ___. Does anybody have any close friends or relatives that have been employed by an insurance company?

---

A=*Brewster*; C=questions traditionally asked by trial judge; F=*Stroud*; G=*Gaskins*; I=*Haefele*; J=*Hammers*; K=*Stokes*; U=*Underhill*; W=*Storck*; X=*Schafer*; Y=*Turner*; Z=*Nale*; see §10.3

3. J ___. Does anybody have any friends or relatives employed by the defendant [*Name of company*]?
4. J ___. Has anybody been an insurance agent, claims adjustor, or underwriter or worked in any other capacity for an agency?
5. J ___. Does anybody have any close friends or relatives that have been employed as agents, claims adjustors, underwriters, or in any other capacities by an agency?
6. J ___. Has anyone read any advertising by any insurance company in any magazine or newspaper suggesting that personal injury lawsuits are financially bad for the economy?
7. J ___. Has anyone ever read any advertising by insurance companies suggesting that lawyers receive an unfair share in the recovery of personal injury lawsuits?
8. J ___. Has anyone read any advertising by insurance companies suggesting that the legal system that supports recovery for injuries is unfair?
9. J ___. Is there anyone who could not find an insurance company liable for money damages if evidence shows that they negligently inspected a [*steel warehouse*] and [*an employee*] was [*seriously*] injured as a result?
10. J ___. Is anybody insured by [*Name of insurance company*]?
11. J ___. Does anyone own stock in any insurance company?
12. J ___. Does anyone own stock in [*Name of insurance company*]?

In *Borkoski v Yost* (Mont S Ct 1979) 594 P2d 688, the court held that the circumstances in that case were such that plaintiff's attorney should have been permitted to pursue a line of inquiry during voir dire to determine whether any prospective jurors were biased against plaintiff as the direct result of a national advertising campaign by leading insurance companies to the effect that large jury awards are in fact paid by the general public and result in higher insurance premiums for everyone. However, since the jury found the defendant physicians not liable, any error was harmless and did not provide a basis for reversal. The opinion contains a thoughtful discussion of the issue of insurance company advertising, plaintiffs' response through voir dire, and judicial actions in many jurisdictions on defense objections to such questions. See several articles on this subject in 10 *St Mary's L J* 395 (1979).

---

A=*Brewster*; C=questions traditionally asked by trial judge; F=*Stroud*; G=*Gaskins*; I=*Haefele*; J=*Hammers*; K=*Stokes*; U=*Underhill*; W=*Storck*; X=*Schafer*; Y=*Turner*; Z=*Nale*; see §10.3

## C. Municipalities §10.12

1. U ___. Does anyone feel that they will hesitate in rendering a full, fair and complete verdict because of some feeling that it may affect the city financially?
2. U ___. Do you understand that if you did, it would be unfair and prejudicial and cannot be part of or a consideration in your mind?
3. U ___. You are a resident, aren't you? This suit is against [*Name of city*] because they are legally liable for the actions of [*Name of city*] [*police officers*].
   a. Would you have any problem finding [*City*] was liable because you are a resident?
   b. Do you think you can treat the [*Name of plaintiff*] family with the same consideration as you treat [*City*]?

## D. Police Officers §10.13

See questions in §§9.14, 9.72, 9.80–9.82, 10.80, and 11.56.

## E. Other Defendants §10.14

This section is reserved for additional issues, which will be discussed in supplements to this volume.

# VI. JUROR ATTITUDES TOWARD PLAINTIFFS

## A. Seriously Injured §10.21

Plaintiff's attorney Richard M. Goodman asked the following questions in a Michigan personal injury suit involving permanent injury to a crane operator. Defendant insurance company was found liable (see §10.11).

1. J ___. In our case we have [*an impaired quadriplegic*], a person with a [*spinal cord*] injury at [*collar bone level*], which impairs movement from [*collar bone down*]. Would anyone be prevented from rendering a verdict in excess of [*two million*] dollars before hearing the evidence against the defendant?

---

A=*Brewster*; C=questions traditionally asked by trial judge; F=*Stroud*; G=*Gaskins*; I=*Haefele*; J=*Hammers*; K=*Stokes*; U=*Underhill*; W=*Storck*; X=*Schafer*; Y=*Turner*; Z=*Nale*; see §10.3

2. J ___. Does anyone have any close friends or relatives who are [*quadriplegic*]?

## B. Family of Deceased Housewife §10.22

1. F ___. The one thing that I maybe should have asked all of you—it's going to be a big part of at least my presentation in this case—is how to approach the death of a woman-housewife who at the time of injury was not working but, like many of you, may later work. Would you, everything else being equal—just man killed, woman killed, and liability—would you give the same kind of award, (I don't mean the same dollar amount, but in the same area) for the death of a housewife-mother, as you would, say, for the death of a working father in a family unit? Do you all understand the question?
2. F ___. And not undervalue the housewife in terms of her economic and service contribution to the household unit?
3. F ___. You are married and have a family?
   [*If yes*]
   a. And generally a pleasant marriage?
   b. Well, if you had your druthers, you'd still stay married though?

   [If jury member has been divorced and remarried]
   c. The fact that you've been divorced only indicates a fact of life today—but you now are married, and you understand what I'm talking about when I'm talking about replacing economically the value of a housewife?
4. F ___. We have to put in proofs about replacement value in a death case—the cost of what the services of what a woman does around the house, things that seem almost crude when you're talking about the death of a human being, but we're only doing that because the law requires it, do you understand?
   a. Do you believe you can listen to the proof about "replacement value" and come to a fair decision?
5. F ___. [*To women jurors*] As a woman approaching the case, you certainly have some value or idea of what the housewife's

---

A=*Brewster*; C=questions traditionally asked by trial judge; F=*Stroud*; G=*Gaskins*; I=*Haefele*; J=*Hammers*; K=*Stokes*; U=*Underhill*; W=*Storck*; X=*Schafer*; Y=*Turner*; Z=*Nale*; see §10.3

duties are, I'm sure. And when you hear someone say, "I don't work, I'm just a housewife," you can't help but laugh?

6. F ___. So you would have no trouble from anything you've heard being a fair and impartial juror in this case?

In *Underhill v City of Traverse City* (Grand Traverse Cir Ct, June 1979), Dean Robb, representing plaintiffs, began with a factual statement and then asked a series of questions. After trial, the six-person jury rendered a unanimous verdict for plaintiff for the death of his wife, a pregnant housewife.

[*Jackie Underhill*] was pregnant at the time of her [*death*] with a [*1050*] gram baby [*boy*]. The proofs will show that this child was viable or able to live outside the mother's womb at the time of its death.

1. U ___. Do any of you have any problem awarding damages to the family for the loss of this child?
2. U ___. Does anyone feel that this child's estate should not be awarded damages?
3. U ___. Is everyone willing to accept the opinion of the doctors that this [*boy*] was viable at [*1050*] grams?
4. U ___. Do you feel that you might reduce your award because [*plaintiff*] is a young man who in your mind might get remarried [*after the death of his wife and unborn son*]?
5. U ___. You understand that fact or issue is not relevant to your consideration?
6. U ___. You understand that your verdict, if you agree with us, is [*Jackie*]'s and [*Baby boy*]'s legacy to their family?
   a. It's their justice and has nothing to do with [*Husband-widower*] and [*Son*]?

## C. Bar Owner §10.23

1. F ___. The testimony will be that [*Mr.* ____________] owns and operates the [*Name of bar*]. Have any of you been there? Seen it?
2. F ___. They serve drinks there, and I guess the only question I'd have to ask all of you—first of all, how many of you drink at least socially, occasionally?

---

A=*Brewster*; C=questions traditionally asked by trial judge; F=*Stroud*; G=*Gaskins*; I=*Haefele*; J=*Hammers*; K=*Stokes*; U=*Underhill*; W=*Storck*; X=*Schafer*; Y=*Turner*; Z=*Nale*; see §10.3

3. F ___. How many of you don't?
4. F ___. Have you ever drunk?
5. F ___. The question is: would religious or ethical feelings about drinking, the fact that [*Mr.* ___________] and [*his brother-in-law*] have run this place for [*a couple of*] years—the testimony will be that [*Mr.* ___________ *is trying to get out of that business*]—but that's what they've been doing. Do you have any prejudice against someone that makes his living that way?
6. F ___. Would that be true with you also, [*Mrs.* ___________]? [*Mrs.* ___________]?
7. F ___. Even though you don't drink, you don't belong to—my mother belonged to the WCTU, for example, the Women's Christian Temperance Union. She didn't like tavern owners. You don't have feelings like that?
8. F ___. And you would leave any feelings you have because you don't drink out of any decision you reach in this case?
9. F ___. [*Mrs.* ___________], you drink occasionally?
10. F ___. I talked to you about this before, [*Mr.* ___________]. I guess you said you weren't opposed to other people drinking but you, personally, on ethical or religious grounds didn't drink yourself. You're not campaigning to keep bars out of your township or working on that?
11. F ___. [*Mrs.* ___________], I forgot what you said this morning when we talked about it before: What is your feeling about [*Plaintiff*] working in a bar. It wouldn't make any difference?
12. F ___. You don't have any strong feelings that way?

## D. Absent Plaintiff §10.24

1. U ___. If you were a juror in a case like this one, what would you think if [*plaintiff*] were not in the courtroom during most of the trial?
   a. Why do you think that someone would not be in court while their suit was being tried?
   b. Would you want to be in court under these circumstances?
   c. Why or why not?

---

A=*Brewster*; C=questions traditionally asked by trial judge; F=*Stroud*; G=*Gaskins*; I=*Haefele*; J=*Hammers*; K=*Stokes*; U=*Underhill*; W=*Storck*; X=*Schafer*; Y=*Turner*; Z=*Nale*; see §10.3

## E. Other Plaintiffs §10.25

See §10.14.

# VII. JUROR ATTITUDES TOWARD RULES OF LAW

## A. Liability

### 1. Based on Negligence §10.31

1. C ___. Do each of you understand that this a civil case and not a criminal case?
2. I ___. Do you understand that finding someone was "negligent" under the law doesn't mean that they did something on purpose?
   a. It can also mean they weren't careful enough. Would you have a hard time finding the defendant was negligent if [*he/she/it*] said [*he/she/it*] didn't do anything on purpose?
3. I ___. Do you have any problem with the law that a person who is careless should be responsible for compensating someone who was injured because of that carelessness?
   a. Do you think you would have a hard time finding the defendant responsible or negligent in a situation in which [*he/she/it*] did not mean to cause the injury?
4. I ___. No one deliberately causes a [*collision*], but under our system of law, a person whose carelessness causes a [*collision*] must be held responsible for the consequences of their actions. If there are injuries as a result of someone's carelessness, that person can be held responsible. What do you think about this?
5. I ___. Do you think [*drivers*] should be held responsible for careless mistakes if those mistakes injure someone else?

*COMMENT:* When a trial court judge will not permit counsel to ask questions on voir dire, counsel should word the proposed questions as the judge would ask them, so the judge does not need to revise them. This was done in question 6, which is based on the law in some jurisdictions.

6. Y ___. Will you follow my instructions that an injury or disability need not be caused solely by the employer's negligence, but that you must only find that the injury or disability results [*in whole or in part*] from [*employer*] negligence?

---

A=*Brewster*; C=questions traditionally asked by trial judge; F=*Stroud*; G=*Gaskins*; I=*Haefele*; J=*Hammers*; K=*Stokes*; U=*Underhill*; W=*Storck*; X=*Schafer*; Y=*Turner*; Z=*Nale*; see §10.3

*COMMENT:* Counsel must be prepared at this point to explain causation: that is, there can be more than one cause for a condition, and plaintiff is entitled to recover full damages as long as the *employer's* negligence is one of the causes.

7. Y ___. Can you accept the fact that if the defendant[*s*] is [*are*] found responsible for the injuries to [*plaintiff*] that they are responsible for all consequences of the injury, even though they might not be expected in the normal course of events?

## 2. Admitted §10.32

1. F ___. I'm getting to the point that defendants are admitting liability, to make the jury feel as if defendants are trying to be super-reasonable, and therefore should gain some benefit from now admitting liability, rather than making us prove it. Do you follow me, [*Mr./Mrs.* __________]?
2. F ___. You won't lean over backwards and give [*Defendants*] any break because they say now that they are at fault? Do you understand me?
3. F ___. In other words, you won't let the fact that they say they're at fault now sway you in terms of cutting down the amount of damages, since the only thing left in this case is how much you're going to award this family, not whether or not you award them anything, which is different from most trials?
4. F ___. You realize that this is the only jury that will decide this case, that will decide the value of [*her/his*] life ended by [*the corporation*]'s fault. Now, do you understand that fault and cause have been admitted?
5. F ___. We won't look into that any further because we are not permitted to bring in any details of the accident since defendant has admitted liability. Will that trouble you any, that you won't know the details?

## 3. Vicarious §10.33

1. U ___. [*Name of person who drove the car*] is not a Defendant in this lawsuit. [*Name of city*] is the [*employer*] of [*Officer*

A=*Brewster*; C=questions traditionally asked by trial judge; F=*Stroud*; G=*Gaskins*; I=*Haefele*; J=*Hammers*; K=*Stokes*; U=*Underhill*; W=*Storck*; X=*Schafer*; Y=*Turner*; Z=*Nale*; see §10.3

____________], as well as the owner of the [*car*]. Do you understand that as [*his/her*] [*employer*], the [*city*] is responsible for [*his/her*] actions?

[*If yes*]

a. Do you agree with that proposition?

2. U ___. Do you think the [*city*] should be held liable for an accident involving an [*employee*] while in the course of employment?
3. U ___. Do you have any problem with the [*city*] being held responsible for an accident a [*police officer*] has while on duty when someone is injured?
4. U ___. How would you feel if the damages were being paid by the [*city*] itself?
5. U ___. Would you feel any different if the money came from the [*city's*] insurance company?
6. U ___. Do you think the [*city*] is insured for this kind of accident caused by its [*officers*]?

*COMMENT:* The following question was phrased by plaintiffs' counsel to be asked by the judge.

1. C ___. It is plaintiff's claim that the injury to [*him/her*] was caused by [*both breach of contract and the negligence of Drs. (A) and (B)*]. Under [*State*] law, as I will instruct you at the end of the case, Dr. [*A*] may be liable for the negligence of Dr. [*B*] because Dr. [*B*] was the agent of Dr. [*A*]. Do any of you think that unfair?
   a. Would any of you have any problem following my instruction on the law with respect to such liability?

### 4. Standard of Care §10.34

1. U ___. Do you understand that it will be you who decide what the community standard of care will be in terms of [*police driving in emergency situations*]?
2. U ___. That is your task and responsibility as citizen judges, do you understand that?
3. U ___. Can you accept this responsibility?
4. U ___. Can you independently judge this incident?
   a. This [*police officer*]?

---

A=*Brewster*; C=questions traditionally asked by trial judge; F=*Stroud*; G=*Gaskins*; I=*Haefele*; J=*Hammers*; K=*Stokes*; U=*Underhill*; W=*Storck*; X=*Schafer*; Y=*Turner*; Z=*Nale*; see §10.3

## B. Damages

### 1. As Compensation for Injury §10.36

1. A ___. Have you or anyone in your family sued or been sued for money damages?
   [*If yes*]
   a. When?
   b. What kind of case?
   c. What are your feelings or attitudes as a result of that experience?
2. A ___. What are your attitudes about people who are injured and seek money damages?
3. I ___. As you know, no amount of money can restore [*Plaintiffs'*] health; however, our system of law provides that they can each be given money to repay them for the loss of their health, earning ability, and enjoyment of life. Are you at all uncomfortable with this?
   a. Why or why not?
4. I ___. How do you feel about awarding money for pain and suffering to someone who is injured?
   a. Why do you feel that way?
5. I ___. How do you feel about awarding money to a person who is disfigured from an injury?
   a. Why do you feel that way?
6. I ___. How do you feel about awarding money to someone because of emotional distress, such as anxiety, depression over problems caused by the injury, or sadness?
   a. Why do you feel that way?
7. I ___. How do you feel about awarding money to someone because of their loss of enjoyment of many of life's pleasures due to their injury?
   a. Why do you feel that way?
8. I ___. What concerns do you have about giving people financial compensation for injuries they have suffered?
   a. How do you think those feelings might affect you as you sit as a juror?

---

A=*Brewster*; C=questions traditionally asked by trial judge; F=*Stroud*; G=*Gaskins*; I=*Haefele*; J=*Hammers*; K=*Stokes*; U=*Underhill*; W=*Storck*; X=*Schafer*; Y=*Turner*; Z=*Nale*; see §10.3

9. I ___. Do you think you are a little suspicious of people who sue?

10. U ___. In this case, we are allowed damages that are "reasonable and just under the circumstances." Damages are made up of four elements: loss of society and companionship, loss of services, loss of [*parental*] training and guidance, and the replacement value of the [*mother's*] services.

    Do any of you have any trouble awarding money damages for these elements of damage?

11. U ___. For which of these areas do you think [*deceased's*] family should be compensated?

12. U ___. What would you want to know about [*deceased*], [*her/his*] [*husband/wife*] and [*her/his*] [*children/daughter/son*] in order to evaluate how much money you would award in each of these areas?

13. U ___. Which do you think is the most important area the family should be compensated for?
    a. Why is that most important?

14. U ___. Which is the next most important?
    a. Why?
    [*For each area*]

15. U ___. Why do you think the family should be compensated for this?

16. U ___. How much money would you award the family to compensate for [*Name*]'s death?
    a. Why that amount?

*COMMENT:* In a Detroit police misconduct case, counsel for the family of the deceased phrased the issue as follows:

1. C ___. Do you feel that a family should be compensated for the loss of the deceased's love, society, companionship, and affection, as well as the medical and funeral expenses if a member of their family was wrongfully killed?

Plaintiff sustained injuries from a defective chair that was made exclusively in Japan for the defendant retailer. Plaintiff's counsel, Richard A. Soble of Detroit, requested questions 9–13 be asked of the jury. *Storck v Montgomery Ward & Co.* (US District Court, ED Mich, No. 79 72758).

---

A=*Brewster*; C=questions traditionally asked by trial judge; F=*Stroud*; G=*Gaskins*; I=*Haefele*; J=*Hammers*; K=*Stokes*; U=*Underhill*; W=*Storck*; X=*Schafer*; Y=*Turner*; Z=*Nale*; see §10.3

1. W ___. State any illnesses or diseases you may have had that have created disabling effects.
   a. Have your spouse or children had any illnesses or diseases that have had disabling effects?
2. W ___. Have you ever been seriously injured?
   [*If yes*]
   a. Please indicate the nature and duration of your injuries.
3. W ___. Do you have any reluctance in awarding damages for the economic losses that the plaintiff has sustained, such as medical bills or loss of work?
4. W ___. Do you have any reluctance, should you find that the plaintiff is entitled to damages, in awarding noneconomic damages, such as damages for pain and suffering?
5. W ___. In terms of noneconomic damages, such as pain and suffering, do you have any problem with the concept that these areas of damages cannot be proved exactly and that you will be left to your good judgment in evaluating the amount of money damages to be awarded for such losses?

*COMMENT:* Dean Robb has found it helpful to ask a few questions to insure that no jurors are opposed to damage actions for religious reasons. Such jurors might include Christian Scientists, Amish people, or followers of faith healers.

1. F ___. This question is for all of you, although it rarely hits a person. There are some people in every community and every county in this land who believe that death and tragedy are preordained; in other words, that it's God's will—or it's a Supreme Being's will. Some people even believe that you shouldn't bring a lawsuit, that you should not bring a civil suit for wrongful killing of another. Do any of you hold that view?
2. F ___. Do you know what I'm talking about?
3. F ___. Do you think it's proper that this family ask the person [*—or in this case a corporate person—*] to repay with money and try to substitute with money as best it can, the death of their [*mother*] and their [*wife*]?
4. F ___. Do any of you have any reservations about that?

---

A=*Brewster*; C=questions traditionally asked by trial judge; F=*Stroud*; G=*Gaskins*; I=*Haefele*; J=*Hammers*; K=*Stokes*; U=*Underhill*; W=*Storck*; X=*Schafer*; Y=*Turner*; Z=*Nale*; see §10.3

### a. Physical and Emotional §10.37

A locomotive engineer was injured in a railroad car collision and brought suit in US District Court under the Federal Employer's Liability Act. *Turner v Consolidated Rail Corp.* (ED Mich 1981, No. 974–510). Jurors' attitudes toward emotional injury were highlighted in the voir dire questions requested by plaintiff's counsel, Dean Robb of Michigan. The case was settled during trial for $275,000 and plaintiff's right to return to work.

1. Y ___. Have any of you studied law?
2. Y ___. Have any of you studied medicine?
3. Y ___. Do any of you have any close relative or friend who is a:
   a. Lawyer
   b. Doctor
   c. Psychologist
   d. Psychiatrist
   e. Social Worker
4. Y ___. Do you feel that you would treat the testimony of a medical doctor who is a psychiatrist any differently than you would a nonpsychiatrist medical witness?
5. Y ___. Do you believe that a physical injury may cause an emotional or psychological injury?
6. Y ___. Can you imagine that the emotional consequences of an injury could be as serious or more serious than just the physical injury?
7. Y ___. How do you feel about the proposition that some people react differently to pain than other people?
8. Y ___. How do you feel about the proposition that some people can withstand severe injury with no emotional consequences while other people can suffer less injury and suffer severe emotional consequences?
9. Y ___. Can you accept and follow the proposition of law that the law protects and permits you as a juror to award damages for emotional or mental injury on the same basis as physical damage or physical injury?

### b. Emotional §10.38

A discharged Ford Motor Company employee claimed damages for the emotional and physical injuries suffered due to the sexual harass-

---

A=*Brewster*; C=questions traditionally asked by trial judge; F=*Stroud*; G=*Gaskins*; I=*Haefele*; J=*Hammers*; K=*Stokes*; U=*Underhill*; W=*Storck*; X=*Schafer*; Y=*Turner*; Z=*Nale*; see §10.3

ment by her foreman. Joining here as co-plaintiff was her husband who worked nearby and witnessed his wife being sexually harassed. The husband sought damages as a result of the impact of the employer's unlawful actions on their marriage. Both plaintiffs were successful in proving their claims. The jury awarded over $147,000 to the wife and $32,000 to her husband. (*Nale v Ford Motor Co.*, Macomb County (Michigan) Circuit Court Case No. 76–6200–CZ, 1980). Attorney Allyn Ravitz of Detroit prepared the following voir dire questions.

1. Z ___. Do you believe that for a victim of discrimination the emotional wounds can be a lot deeper than the financial wounds?
2. Z ___. Do you think the law ought to award compensation for indignity and anguish in the form of money damages?
3. Z ___. Do you think a person should be entitled to financial compensation for "hurt feelings"?
4. Z ___. Do you think it is unfair to make the employer pay for the emotional damages a [*woman*] suffered if that [*woman*] is the type who would have a much more severe reaction than an average [*woman*]?
5. Z ___. If the judge were to instruct you that the manner of [*Plaintiff's*] damages has to be what [*she*] herself suffered and not what some other [*woman*] would have suffered, would you be willing to award [*her*] money to compensate [*her*] for [*her*] own particular suffering?
6. Z ___. Would you have a problem awarding large amounts for emotional damages, even if the damages far exceeded any wage damages of the plaintiff?
7. Z ___. Has anyone on the jury seen a psychologist or psychiatrist, or had close family or friends who did?
   [*If yes*]
   a. Would that experience prejudice you against the testimony of a psychologist?
8. Z ___. Do any of you have any prejudices against the science of psychology?
9. Z ___. Do you believe it is possible for a person to significantly alter or fix the results of a psychological test?

When a juror answers "Yes" to a general question about having been

A=*Brewster*; C=questions traditionally asked by trial judge; F=*Stroud*; G=*Gaskins*; I=*Haefele*; J=*Hammers*; K=*Stokes*; U=*Underhill*; W=*Storck*; X=*Schafer*; Y=*Turner*; Z=*Nale*; see §10.3

injured in an automobile accident, personal injury lawyers customarily pursue the point:

1. ____. Did you feel that you were compensated for your pain and suffering or your emotional distress?
   a. How did you feel about that?
2. ____. Why didn't you file a claim for the injury you received?
3. ____. When you spent a month in the hospital as a result of your injury, did you feel that caused you any emotional distress?
   a. How did you feel about the fact that you were not compensated for that?

## 2. Amount of Award §10.39

Dean Robb asked questions 1–6 in a damage suit by a young father and mother who were injured in a motorcycle accident, see §10.68.

1. I ____. Have you ever heard or read about a million dollar lawsuit?
2. I ____. What do you think about a lawsuit where someone is awarded a million dollars?
   a. Do you ever think to yourself, "One million dollars is too much, no matter what happened to the person"?
   b. Did you ever say to yourself, "What could happen to someone that they would deserve a million dollars?"
3. I ____. Do you think you could ever award someone a million dollars?
4. I ____. There has been some publicity lately about jury awards, and some controversy about awards being too high. Do you ever get the feeling that people are sometimes getting large amounts they don't deserve?
   [*If yes*]
   a. Why do you think this happens?
   b. What do you think causes this situation?
   c. Do you think that there are cases where large awards are justified and proper?
5. I ____. Do you have any limits in your mind as to the amount you would be willing to award someone for an injury?
6. I ____. If the evidence indicates that [*Plaintiffs*] have lost several [*million*] dollars' worth of future wages, and have suffered severe

---

A=*Brewster*; C=questions traditionally asked by trial judge; F=*Stroud*; G=*Gaskins*; I=*Haefele*; J=*Hammers*; K=*Stokes*; U=*Underhill*; W=*Storck*; X=*Schafer*; Y=*Turner*; Z=*Nale*; see §10.3

emotional and physical damages, would you be able to award that sum, even though it might seem like a large amount of money?

Robb asked the following questions in the wrongful death suit by a young father and three children for the death of the young mother, see §3.42.

1. F ___. I want to ask each of you, since a money award is the only remedy the law has for the wrongful killing of another—do you believe a [*housewife-mother's*] life could be worth [*$667,281.32*]? Could her life be worth that much money to [*her husband and three children*] if we prove it to you?
2. F ___. Do any of you feel you couldn't award that much money for the death of a [*woman-mother-housewife*]?
3. F ___. You would follow the law on this, and follow the evidence, and if we prove to you, it doesn't have to be this exact amount, which is our claim, but if we prove to you that our damages are in this area—what I'm really saying is, would you give that, even though you think it is an awful lot of money?
4. F ___. This is for life for the kids; this is for life for the father, and if we prove that, the size of the award alone is not going to keep you from deciding they should receive it if you think it is justified?
5. F ___. [*Mrs. __________*], do you have any reservations about that?
6. F ___. Do you think that's too much money for a woman?
7. F ___. We have asked jurors that question who have said they wouldn't give anybody that kind of money for anything. That's why we're asking these questions. Do you understand?
8. F ___. And let me ask you this: There is sometimes a tendency on the part of some people to assume that just because we mention a figure—I remember [*Defense Counsel*] was questioning one of the jurors and in effect [*he/she*] was saying, "We have no right to commit you to a figure ahead of time." You understand that?
9. F ___. But we do have a right to know whether you think a certain figure, an outside figure, is too much. We mentioned the figure of our claim here of a total of [*$667,281.32*], and of course,

---

A=*Brewster*; C=questions traditionally asked by trial judge; F=*Stroud*; G=*Gaskins*; I=*Haefele*; J=*Hammers*; K=*Stokes*; U=*Underhill*; W=*Storck*; X=*Schafer*; Y=*Turner*; Z=*Nale*; see §10.3

you haven't heard the evidence, you don't know what the loss was and so forth. But that figure alone does not trouble you if you think that was the kind of loss that was sustained to this family unit?

10. F ___. And even if you're confronted with an array of figures, large figures and small figures, could you make up your own mind as to what you think is right and not be swayed by some chart or multiplication table or something of that sort?

### 3. Comparative Fault §10.40

In a jurisdiction providing for contributory negligence, if a prospective juror seems troubled by questions of fault as between two drivers involved in a collision, ask:

1. U ___. The law says that even if [*Plaintiff*] was in some way at fault in the [*collision*], [*her/his*] family can still receive money compensation from the [*other driver*]. However, the amount the family would receive would be decreased by the percentage [*she/he*] was at fault. Can you accept the law on this point?

*COMMENT:* Counsel can then proceed to ask other questions about the amount of damages. See §10.39.

In a jurisdiction rejecting contributory negligence, defense counsel often asks:

1. C ___. Do you have any quarrel or reservations with the law of this state that a person who was at fault in the slightest degree may not recover from a defendant in a civil lawsuit?

### 4. Other Problems §10.41

## C. Proof

### 1. Burden §10.46

The defense counsel in *Tangela Gaskins* (see §3.91), an administrative discharge hearing for alleged homosexual activity, asked the following questions of the hearing officers. In a military proceeding, the prose-

A=*Brewster*; C=questions traditionally asked by trial judge; F=*Stroud*; G=*Gaskins*; I=*Haefele*; J=*Hammers*; K=*Stokes*; U=*Underhill*; W=*Storck*; X=*Schafer*; Y=*Turner*; Z=*Nale*; see §10.3

cutor or charging party is referred to as the Recorder and the charged party as the Respondent.

1. G ___. Do you believe that the [*respondent/plaintiff*] has a greater burden than the [*recorder/defendant*] in presenting [*her*] evidence?

Let me put it another way. If we were to have a balanced scale with the two pans, and the [*recorder's*] evidence perhaps weighted one of the pans a little lower than the other pan, do you feel that the [*respondent*] would simply have to bring those pans even again, or would have to bring [*her*] pan all the way to the table before you would believe the [*respondent*]? Assuming we got our balance and the [*recorder*] puts in evidence so this is the [*recorder's*] side and it fills just a little bit, do you think that to negate what the [*recorder*] has done, it would simply be necessary to balance out again as far as testimony is concerned, or do you think it would be necessary for the [*respondent*] to go absolutely as far as [*she*] could before you would be convinced that the [*recorder*] may have been wrong?

### 2. Standard §10.47

1. U ___. Mr. [*Name*], you understand that this is not a criminal case. No one is going to jail and no one is going to be found guilty?
2. U ___. You have probably heard the legal term "beyond a reasonable doubt." Did you know that term applies only to criminal cases?
3. U ___. Did you know that in order to prove our case, [*plaintiff*] has to convince you by what is called a preponderance of the evidence—that is, you have to believe that what we say is simply more likely to be true that what the [*defendant*] says?
4. U ___. Do you think you can follow this standard?

### 3. Contrasted with Criminal Cases §10.48

1. C ___. Does each of you understand that in a criminal case, if the prosecutor wins, the defendant is found guilty of the crime and is sentenced by the court, but that is not true in a civil case? In a civil case, if the plaintiff wins the case, the defendant is

A=*Brewster*; C=questions traditionally asked by trial judge; F=*Stroud*; G=*Gaskins*; I=*Haefele*; J=*Hammers*; K=*Stokes*; U=*Underhill*; W=*Storck*; X=*Schafer*; Y=*Turner*; Z=*Nale*; see §10.3

not found guilty of anything and cannot be punished, but the plaintiff is awarded damages. Does each of you understand that?

## D. Presumptions

### 1. General Meaning §10.50

1. C ___. A presumption is a substitute for evidence and is used as an aid to logical reasoning when there is no evidence on point. For example, there is a presumption that [*an automobile was in the possession of its owner at the time of an accident*]. This is not evidence, but will serve until it is overcome by competent evidence. Can you accept this legal tool?

### 2. Due Care §10.51

1. U ___. [*Name*] was killed in this accident. [*She/he*] was driving the other car involved in this collision. Under our law, since [*she/he*] is dead and cannot testify, [*she/he*] has a presumption of due care. That means [*she/he*] is presumed not negligent unless the [*defendant*] can prove to you that [*she/he*] was negligent. Do you understand it is the [*city's*] responsibility to prove [*her/his*] fault, if any?
2. U ___. Will you accord [*her/him*] this presumption of due care?
3. U ___. Do you have any problem with presuming [*she/he*] was not negligent unless they can prove [*she/he*] was?

### 3. Other Presumptions §10.52

See §10.14.

## E. Doctrines

### 1. Sudden Emergency §10.56

1. U ___. We have a law or doctrine that may be applied in this case called the sudden emergency doctrine. That is, if a person is confronted with an emergency, not of [*his/her*] own making,

---

A=*Brewster*; C=questions traditionally asked by trial judge; F=*Stroud*; G=*Gaskins*; I=*Haefele*; J=*Hammers*; K=*Stokes*; U=*Underhill*; W=*Storck*; X=*Schafer*; Y=*Turner*; Z=*Nale*; see §10.3

[*he/she*] is not guilty of contributory negligence if [*he/she*] fails to exercise the best possible judgment, or even takes evasive action that should not have been taken or would not have been taken except for the stres of the emergency.

Do you have any problem with this rule of law?

### 2. Other Doctrines §10.57

See §10.14.

## VIII. SPECIFIC TYPES OF CASES

### A. Personal Injury

#### 1. Automobile Accidents

##### a. Typical Case §10.61

1. F ___. Have any of you or close members of your family been in a serious automobile accident or any kind of tragedy where there was a very serious loss?
   [*If yes*]
   a. How old were you at the time?
   b. Was there a lawsuit arising out of that?
   c. Where did it occur?
2. F ___. Have you ever been an eye-witness to a death?
3. F ___. Would the fact that [*Juror's relative*] was killed under circumstances where there was no liability on anybody else's part, while here clearly there was liability on the part of [*the corporation*], would that fact influence you?
   a. You don't think there's any carry-over in your feelings about it?
4. U ___. Anyone ever witness a traffic accident?
   [*If yes*]
   a. What were the circumstances?
   b. What did you do?
   c. Were there different perceptions by the witnesses?
   [*If juror was automobile accident victim*]
5. I ___. This lawsuit is about a situation that is somewhat similar to

A=*Brewster*; C=questions traditionally asked by trial judge; F=*Stroud*; G=*Gaskins*; I=*Haefele*; J=*Hammers*; K=*Stokes*; U=*Underhill*; W=*Storck*; X=*Schafer*; Y=*Turner*; Z=*Nale*; see §10.3

the situation you described. How do you think your experience would affect you if you were chosen to serve as a juror in this case?

a. Do you think you would tend to side with the defendant because you also [*hit*] someone?
b. Why not?
c. Would you be able to hold the defendant responsible for [*his*] actions if you found that [*he*] was at fault in this situation?
d. Would you feel at all uncomfortable about sitting in a case where the situation was so similar to a collision you were involved in?

6. U ___. Do you drive?
7. U ___. What kind of car do you drive?
8. U ___. In general, do you think when there is a traffic accident, more often than not both drivers are at fault?
9. U ___. What do you think about people suing after car accidents?
   a. Do you ever think that your insurance rates go up because of large money verdicts?
10. U ___. Now that we have "no fault" auto insurance in [*Michigan*], why do you think there are still suits following auto collisions?

### b. Police Emergency Case §10.62

For additional questions on police officers, see §§9.14, 9.72, 9.80–9.82, 10.80–10.81, 11.56.

1. U ___. Did you ever drive or ride in vehicles which went on an emergency call?
   [*If yes*]
   a. Please describe frequency and type of vehicle.
2. U ___. Do you now or have you ever known anyone who was a police officer, a sheriff, or in the highway patrol?
3. U ___. Do you know anyone who works as an ambulance driver?
4. U ___. Do you know anyone who works for the fire department?
5. U ___. How do you know this person?
   a. What is [*Name*]'s job.

---

A=*Brewster*; C=questions traditionally asked by trial judge; F=*Stroud*; G=*Gaskins*; I=*Haefele*; J=*Hammers*; K=*Stokes*; U=*Underhill*; W=*Storck*; X=*Schafer*; Y=*Turner*; Z=*Nale*; see §10.3

b. Have you ever talked with [*Name*] about [*his/her*] job? What has [*she/he*] said?
c. Does [*he/she*] ever go on emergency calls?
d. Has [*she/he*] ever talked to you about what it is like to drive that fast on emergency calls?

6. U ___. What do you think about the job of being a police officer?
7. U ___. Have you ever wanted to be a police officer?
   a. [*Why/why not*]?
8. U ___. Police officers are allowed to exceed the speed limit in an emergency. If a police officer has an accident on the way to an emergency, do you think it is just as likely to be the police officer's fault as it is to be the other person's fault?
   a. [*Why/why not*]?
9. U ___. Do you think the fact that a police officer has lights and siren on means that if [*he/she*] is involved in a collision, it is not [*his/her*] fault?
10. U ___. Do you think you would look at an accident differently if the driver were an ambulance driver?
11. U ___. Do you think you might be more willing to question the judgment of a *private* ambulance driver?
12. U ___. We all see TV police shows where there are high-speed chases—you understand these are carefully staged—with highly trained stunt people, not regular police officers? Do you feel all police officers can drive like that?
13. U ___. Do you feel a police officer can be at fault in an accident?
14. U ___. Would you treat both drivers fairly and give each equal consideration?
15. U ___. Do you feel that if there were a collision involving a police car, you would assume it was the other person's fault and/or give the benefit of the doubt to the policeman?
16. U ___. It will be claimed in this lawsuit that Officer [*Name*] was on an "emergency run" and therefore [*he/she*] could violate the basic speed laws as long as [*he/she*] did not endanger life or property, under the applicable law that permits an officer to exceed the statutory speed limit as long as he or she does not endanger life or property, while requiring driving with due regard for safety. Do you feel that because a police officer

A=*Brewster*; C=questions traditionally asked by trial judge; F=*Stroud*; G=*Gaskins*; I=*Haefele*; J=*Hammers*; K=*Stokes*; U=*Underhill*; W=*Storck*; X=*Schafer*; Y=*Turner*; Z=*Nale*; see §10.3

may be on an emergency run [*he/she*] should still be held responsible if [*he/she*] endangers life or property or drives without due regard for the safety of others?

17. U ___. Do you understand that it is up to you, the jury, to determine whether the run Officer [*Name*] was on at the time of the collision was an emergency?

### c. Other Cases §10.63

See §10.14.

## 2. Product Liability

### a. General Questions about Manufacturer §10.65

1. W ___. The [*chair*] in the injury to [*Plaintiff*] was made in [*Japan*] exclusively for [*Name of company*]. Do you feel it is wrong to hold [*Company*], the seller of this [*chair*], responsible for any defects that existed in the [*chair*] when they sold it?
2. W ___. Have you had any dealings with [*Company*]?
3. W ___. Have any of you or your family or close friends ever worked in a [*retail*] store such as [*Company*]?
   [*If yes*]
   a. What was the name of the store, and the job or jobs performed in that store?
4. F ___. Now, none of you have had any particular personal acquaintanceship with [*General Motors*] other than we all have?
5. F ___. Anybody always buy [*General Motors*] products, [*General Motors*] cars?
   [*If yes*]
   a. So far it's been [*Chevrolet*]?
   b. You mean all your life?

### b. Automobile Accidents §10.66

The Seventh Circuit Court of Appeals held that all the following questions should have been asked in voir dire in *Fietzer and Kautz v Ford Motor Co.* (1980) 622 F2d 281, at 286.

---

A=*Brewster*; C=questions traditionally asked by trial judge; F=*Stroud*; G=*Gaskins*; I=*Haefele*; J=*Hammers*; K=*Stokes*; U=*Underhill*; W=*Storck*; X=*Schafer*; Y=*Turner*; Z=*Nale*; see §10.3

1. ___. Have you, or any members of your family, been involved in a [*rear-end collision*]?
2. ___. Have you, or any members of your family, been involved in a [*collision*] that resulted in [*burn*] injuries?
3. ___. Have you, or any members of your family, ever owned a [*Mercury Comet*]?
4. ___. Did you read or hear about an article [*about defects in Mercury Comets*]?
5. ___. If so, does anything stand out in your mind that you read or heard about?
6. ___. Have you formed an opinion about [*defendant Ford Motor Co.*]'s relative negligence in the accident that occurred leading to this case?

Defendant manufacturer proposed the following questions in a product liability suit against American Honda (see §10.10).

1. X ___. Do any of you feel that a manufacturer has a duty to manufacture an accident-proof product?
2. X ___. Have any members of the jury, their immediate families, close relatives, or friends, been employees of an automobile company or a motorcycle company or in any way connected with the operation of same?
   [*If yes*]
   a. Please outline the connection.
3. X ___. Would any members of the jury harbor any bad feelings toward [*Honda Motor Company*] because it is a [*Japanese*] company?
4. X ___. Do any members of the jury harbor any bad feelings or prejudice toward people who speak with accents?
5. X ___. Do any members of the jury harbor any bad feelings or prejudice toward people who come from the [*Far East*]?
6. X ___. Have any members of the jury had their own personal lives or the lives of their close families, relatives, or friends affected adversely by the recent automobile slump?
   [*If yes*]
   a. Please describe the problem and tell us whether it would affect your decision in this case in any way.

---

A=*Brewster*; C=questions traditionally asked by trial judge; F=*Stroud*; G=*Gaskins*; I=*Haefele*; J=*Hammers*; K=*Stokes*; U=*Underhill*; W=*Storck*; X=*Schafer*; Y=*Turner*; Z=*Nale*; see §10.3

7. X ____. Do any of you feel that [*Japanese*] auto makers and foreign auto makers are responsible for the automobile slump that has developed in recent years?
[*If yes*]
a. Please describe your feelings and advise us whether they would affect your decision in this case in any way.

8. X ____. Have any members of the jury had their own personal lives, or the lives of their close family, relatives, and friends, affected as a result of an automobile company's layoff of employees due to the automobile slump?
[*If yes*]
a. Describe what happened and whether this would affect your decision in this case in any way.

9. X. ____. Have any members of the jury or their families, relatives, or close friends ever owned a [*Honda*] product?
[*If yes*]
a. Would that affect your decision in this case in any way?

10. X ____. Have any members of the jury or their close friends or relatives had any experience with [*American Honda*] employees or representatives?
[*If yes*]
a. Describe the experience and advise whether this would affect your decision in this case in any way.

### c. Airplane Accidents §10.67

Most jurors, like most people, are enchanted by the idea of airplanes. They sound romantic and exciting. But, in some areas, most people still have never flown in an airplane. Attorneys Victoria Heldman and Richard Schaden of Detroit were amazed to discover that most people voir dired in airplane damage cases in Wayne County had never flown in an airplane.

This problem is multiplied in cases involving corporate aircraft, corporate jets, and small private aircraft. Most jurors have never even seen such an airplane up close. They have never flown in a small airplane. Those who have flown on a major airline know that you walk

---

A=*Brewster*; C=questions traditionally asked by trial judge; F=*Stroud*; G=*Gaskins*; I=*Haefele*; J=*Hammers*; K=*Stokes*; U=*Underhill*; W=*Storck*; X=*Schafer*; Y=*Turner*; Z=*Nale*; see §10.3

from the hallway in an airport into a tube into an airplane chair, and that's that. They have no idea about the size and nature of small aircraft, so the lawyers have to educate the jurors about small planes.

In all airplane cases, plaintiffs' lawyers try to draw out of the jurors on voir dire what they really think about airplanes. Attorney Heldman says that most people think: airplanes fall out of the sky and hurt people; an airplane is an unnatural thing; it is not natural for a person to fly, or, it is not natural for airplanes to stay in the air. When they crash, people always die; it's a chance the passengers took.

Plaintiffs' attorneys have to smoke out and deal with these common prejudices in airplane cases. They need jurors who understand a few things: Airplanes are not supposed to crash. When small airplanes crash, people do not have to die. There are ways of building airplanes to crash without hurting people at all, or keeping injuries to a minimum.

To find fair-minded jurors, lawyers in small plane cases often ask prospective jurors:

1. ___. Are you afraid of flying?

*COMMENT:* Lawyers will rarely get a juror to say he or she is afraid of flying. But when this question is followed by other questions, the truth may emerge.

2. ___. If someone gave you the opportunity to ride in a [*Lear*] jet, would you do it?

*COMMENT:* Some jurors will say, "Oh, my God, no!" Other people's faces will light up, indicating their love of flying. And there will be many reactions in between. In this respect, small airplane damage cases resemble motorcycle damage cases.

Heldman asked the following questions in *Detroit Bank & Trust v Jet Electronics & Technology* (Wayne County Cir. Ct., No. 79 926 983 NP (1982).

1. ___. Have any of you heard of a [*Lear Jet*]?
   [*If yes*]
   a. What have you heard?
   b. Would you ride in one if you had the opportunity? Why or why not?

---

A=*Brewster*; C=questions traditionally asked by trial judge; F=*Stroud*; G=*Gaskins*; I=*Haefele*; J=*Hammers*; K=*Stokes*; U=*Underhill*; W=*Storck*; X=*Schafer*; Y=*Turner*; Z=*Nale*; see §10.3

2. ___. Have you flown in an airplane of any kind? What kind? When?
3. ___. Are you afraid of flying? Why or why not?
4. ___. Do you know any pilots or aircraft mechanics, or anyone in the airplane business?
   a. Who do they work for?
   b. Do you discuss their work?
5. ___. Have you ever seen a "little plane" or business airplane up close?
   a. When, under that circumstances?

### d. Motorcycle Accidents §10.68

Plaintiffs' lawyers have learned that many people are prejudiced against motorcycles and assume that a person who rides a motorcycle is bound to get injured. Although prospective jurors usually say they can be fair and unprejudiced in deciding whether to find a defendant-manufacturer liable in a damage case, plaintiffs' lawyers have smoked them out by asking:

1. ___. If someone offered you a motorcycle as a present, would you take it?
   a. Would you be happy?

*COMMENT:* A juror who so far passed muster as "fair-minded" may now answer truthfully, "No! I would *never* have a motorcycle, even if it were a present!"

That puts the person off the jury.

The plaintiffs' attorney proposed questions 2–16 in *Haefele v Ruscio* (WD Mich #G 80 774 CAI), a suit by a married couple for personal injuries incurred when the motorcycle they were riding was sideswiped by defendant's automobile. On motion of plaintiffs' attorney, Dean Robb, the judge granted plaintiffs the use of a pre-voir dire supplemental questionnaire (see chapter 12), as well as a limited attorney voir dire on sensitive issues (i.e., attitudes concerning motorcycles and money damages). After a six-person jury was selected, defendants settled and paid plaintiffs one million U.S. dollars, the limit of liability on a Canadian insurance policy.

2. I ___. Is there anyone in the jury box who doesn't drive a car?

---

A=*Brewster*; C=questions traditionally asked by trial judge; F=*Stroud*; G=*Gaskins*; I=*Haefele*; J=*Hammers*; K=*Stokes*; U=*Underhill*; W=*Storck*; X=*Schafer*; Y=*Turner*; Z=*Nale*; see §10.3

3\. I ___. Have you ever been on a motorcycle?
- a. How often?
- b. What kind?
- c. What did you think of the experience?
- d. Have you ever owned a motorcycle?

4\. I ___. What do you think about motorcycles?
- a. Do you think they are dangerous?
- b. What kinds of people do you think generally drive motorcycles?

5\. I ___. Do you know anybody who drives a motorcycle?
- a. What kind of motorcycle?

6\. I ___. Have you ever known anyone who was hurt riding a motorcycle?
- a. How did it happen?

7\. I ___. Do you think people who drive motorcycles generally drive less carefully than people in cars?
- a. Do you think people who drive motorcycles generally drive faster than people in cars?

8\. I ___. Do you let your children ride on motorcycles?
- a. Have you ever forbidden your children to ride on a motorcycle?
- b. Why?
- c. Would you rather they didn't?

9\. I ___. Do you have different standards of driving for motorcycle drivers than you do for car drivers?

10\. I ___. How do you feel about motorcycles on the highway?

11\. I ___. Do you think motorcycles have the same right to use the highways that cars have?

12\. I ___. Do you think people who ride motorcycles are courting danger?
- a. Why do you say that?
- b. How do you think this might affect your attitude toward [*Name*], who [*was/were*] riding a motorcycle when [*he/she*] were injured?

13\. I ___. Have you ever heard anyone say that if a person riding a motorcycle gets hurt, it's their own fault for being on a motorcycle to begin with?

---

A=*Brewster*; C=questions traditionally asked by trial judge; F=*Stroud*; G=*Gaskins*; I=*Haefele*; J=*Hammers*; K=*Stokes*; U=*Underhill*; W=*Storck*; X=*Schafer*; Y=*Turner*; Z=*Nale*; see §10.3

a. What do you think about that?
b. Have you ever thought that yourself?

14. I ___. Do you think that because [*Name*]'s injuries might not have been as serious if [*he/she/they*] had been in a car, [*he/she/they*] should get any less money?
a. Why do you think that would be fair?

15. I ___. Would you think that because a motorcycle is not as big as a car, [*Name*] [*is/are*] responsible for [*his/her/their*] own injuries, even if [*he/she/they*] did nothing wrong in driving?
[*If yes*]
a. This is a personal attitude and opinion that you are entitled to, but if you found out that the law did not agree that a person is responsible simply because he or she was riding a motorcycle, do you think you might still tend to feel this way?
b. Would it be hard for you to sit on a jury with this attitude, knowing that the law on this issue was different?

16. I ___. Have you ever had a job driving a truck?
[*If yes*]
a. Have you had any experiences with motorcycles, or do you have any feelings about motorcycle drivers based on this experience?

*COMMENT:* Defendant manufacturer proposed the following questions in *Schafer v North American Honda*, a product liability suit (see §10.10).

1. X ___. Have any members of the jury, their close friends, or relatives ever had any bad experiences with motorcycles?
[*If yes*]
a. Please describe.

2. X ___. Have any members of the jury, their close relatives or friends ever had any bad experience with a motorcyclist?
[*If yes*]
a. Please describe.

3. X ___. Do any members of the jury, their close relatives or friends, own any shares in an [*American*] automobile company or motorcycle manufacturing company?

---

A=*Brewster*; C=questions traditionally asked by trial judge; F=*Stroud*; G=*Gaskins*; I=*Haefele*; J=*Hammers*; K=*Stokes*; U=*Underhill*; W=*Storck*; X=*Schafer*; Y=*Turner*; Z=*Nale*; see §10.3

4. X ___. All of you, no doubt, sympathize with a young [*man/woman*] riding a motorcycle who has an unfortunate accident. Do any of you feel that your sympathy for [*Name*] would prevent you from giving the defendant a fair trial?

5. X ___. Do any members of the jury harbor any bad feelings or prejudice against motorcycle manufacturers?

#### e. Other Cases §10.73

See §10.14.

### 3. Medical Malpractice

#### a. Plaintiff's Questions §10.75

Richard M. Goodman, counsel for a quadriplegic in a medical malpractice suit, was allowed to ask the following questions after the court conducted its initial voir dire. *McDowell v Sinai Hospital* (Wayne County Cir. Ct., No. 80 008 672 NM, 1982).

1. ___. Does anyone here have any strong feelings one way or another about people who bring lawsuits against doctors?
   [*If yes*]
   a. Please explain.
2. ___. Does anyone have, or know anyone who has, [*Name of disease/illness/condition*]?
   [*If yes*]
   a. Please explain what your relationship is with this individual and what, if anything, you know about the treatment.
3. ___. Does anyone feel that limits should be placed on a person's right to sue a doctor?
4. ___. Has anyone here ever worn a [*cervical collar*]?
   [*If yes*]
   a. Please explain why, and for how long.
5. ___. Do you have a family doctor?
   [*If yes*]
   a. What is your doctor's name and how long has this doctor been treating you?

---

A=*Brewster*; C=questions traditionally asked by trial judge; F=*Stroud*; G=*Gaskins*; I=*Haefele*; J=*Hammers*; K=*Stokes*; U=*Underhill*; W=*Storck*; X=*Schafer*; Y=*Turner*; Z=*Nale*; see §10.3

6. ____. Have you ever sought a second medical opinion to confirm or "check" a doctor's diagnosis?
7. ____. Do you think patients should tell their doctors they would like a second opinion if they have any doubt regarding the doctors' diagnosis or recommended treatment?
8. ____. Does anyone know an individual who is disabled.
   [*If yes*]
   a. What is your relationship with the individual?
   b. What type of disability?
   c. How did the person become disabled?
9. ____. Has anyone here ever had surgery?
   [*If yes*]
   a. What was the surgery for?
   b. Who performed the surgery?
   c. Where was the surgery performed, in what hospital?
   d. Were you satisfied with the treatment you received at the time of this surgery?
10. ____. Has anyone ever been admitted to a hospital? If so, how many times and for each admission, please state:
   a. What was the admission for?
   b. What hospital were you admitted to?
   c. Who was the doctor who treated you while you were in the hospital?
   d. Were you satisfied with the treatment you received while in the hospital?
11. ____. Have you, any member of your family, or any close friends ever worked in a hospital or in any other medical setting? If so, please state:
   a. Where did you work?
   b. What was your job?
   c. Why did you leave the job?
12. ____. Has anyone in your family or any close friend ever been admitted to [*Name*] hospital? If so, please state:
   a. Who was admitted into [*Name*] Hospital?
   b. What were they admitted for?
   c. Who was their doctor?
   d. Were they satisfied with their treatment?
13. ____. Do you believe a patient has a right to be fully and honestly

A=*Brewster*; C=questions traditionally asked by trial judge; F=*Stroud*; G=*Gaskins*; I=*Haefele*; J=*Hammers*; K=*Stokes*; U=*Underhill*; W=*Storck*; X=*Schafer*; Y=*Turner*; Z=*Nale*; see §10.3

informed of all possible risks and benefits of treatment a doctor recommends?

14. ____. Who do you believe should decide the proper course of treatment for a patient:
a. The doctor?
b. The patient, after being fully informed by the doctor?
c. The doctor and patient should make the decision together?

15. ____. How many times have you gone to a doctor in the last year?

16. ____. Do you tend to put your faith in the doctors' opinion and advice, and rely on their training and expertise, in deciding what course of treatment you should follow?

17. ____. Do you have any personal friendships with doctors or nurses?
[*If yes*]
a. Who?
b. Where do they work?
c. What do they do?
d. Have you ever discussed with them or heard them discuss medical malpractice lawsuits?
[*If yes*]
e. What was the thrust of the conversation(s)?

18. ____. This case involves claims against the defendants for [*very serious*] injuries. The plaintiff is [*confined to a wheelchair*] for [*the rest of his/her life*]. Assuming the plaintiff is able to prove [*his/her*] case, would you have any difficulty awarding [*him/her*] a substantial verdict, including a verdict in the [*millions*] of dollars?

19. ____. Do you know what a quadriplegic is?

20. ____. Do you feel nervous or self-conscious when you are around a person in a wheelchair?
[*If yes*]
a. Please explain why?

21. ____. Do you know anyone who has a [*spinal cord*] injury?
[*If yes*]
a. What caused the injury?
b. Who cares for the person now?

22. ____. Is there anyone who believes that a doctor need not inform a patient of the potential risks of having or not having surgery?

---

A=*Brewster*; C=questions traditionally asked by trial judge; F=*Stroud*; G=*Gaskins*; I=*Haefele*; J=*Hammers*; K=*Stokes*; U=*Underhill*; W=*Storck*; X=*Schafer*; Y=*Turner*; Z=*Nale*; see §10.3

[*If yes*]
a. Why or under what conditions?

*COMMENT:* In another medical malpractice case, *Neff v Abbott Labs* (Wayne County Cir. Ct., No. 73 244 315 CP, 1978), plaintiff's attorneys, James A. Tuck and Joan Lovell of Detroit, proposed the following voir dire questions.

1. ___. Have you read any magazine articles, newspaper articles or any other kind of literature on the issue of [*malpractice*]?
2. ___. Have you ever signed any petition on the issue of malpractice?
3. ___. Have you seen anything in your doctor's office on the question of malpractice?
4. ___. Have you ever discussed the question of malpractice with your family doctor or friends?
5. ___. Is any member of your family in a medical or paramedical profession?
6. ___. Is any member of your family connected with [*Name*] Hospital?
7. ___. Do you or any member of your family belong to any organization that has taken a policy position on the medical malpractice question?
8. ___. Do you or any member of your family belong to any organization that has issued a statement or resolution regarding medical malpractice?
9. ___. Have you heard anything on television or radio regarding the medical malpractice issue?
10. ___. Do you have any fixed feelings about lawyers who represent people who bring malpractice cases?
11. ___. Do you feel that lawyers are responsible for bringing malpractice cases?
12. ___. Do you believe that malpractice lawsuits have increased the cost of medical care and services to the public?
13. ___. Do you believe that malpractice lawsuits have interrupted the quality of medical care to the public?
14. ___. Do you believe malpractice cases have disrupted the doctor's care to his or her patients?
15. ___. Do you think a lawsuit is the proper method of resolving disputes against doctors and hospitals?
16. ___. Do you think that juries should have the right to make decisions

A=*Brewster*; C=questions traditionally asked by trial judge; F=*Stroud*; G=*Gaskins*; I=*Haefele*; J=*Hammers*; K=*Stokes*; U=*Underhill*; W=*Storck*; X=*Schafer*; Y=*Turner*; Z=*Nale*; see §10.3

about the conduct of medical persons or hospitals or do you think that should be handled by a special board of physicians?

17. ____. Do you think there should be some procedure other than a jury trial by which persons can settle their grievances against doctors and hospitals?

*COMMENT:* Judges in malpractice cases involving more than one doctor may ask the following question:

1. C ____. It is plaintiff's claim that the injury to [*him/her*] was caused by both breach of contract and the negligence of Drs. [*Name*] and [*Name*]. Under [*State*] law, as I will instruct you at the end of the case, Dr. [*Name*] may be liable for the negligence of Dr. [*Name*] because Dr. [*Name*] was the agent of Dr. [*Name*]. Do any of you think that unfair? Would any of you have any problem following my instruction on the law with respect to such liability?

### b. Defendant's Questions §10.76

In *Woods v St. Mary Hospital of Livonaia* (Wayne County Cir. Ct., No. 73 249 888 CM), the eight-year-old plaintiff sustained permanent personal injuries while under the medical care of the defendants. Attorney Robert A. Obringer of Detroit, and five other defense counsel, requested the following voir dire of the jury.

1. ____. Even though this case involves a [*retarded child*], will you keep your natural feelings of sympathy from entering into your deliberations?
2. ____. Do you believe that, because this [*child*]'s condition exists, in and of itself it somehow indicates that one or all of the defendants were negligent or guilty of malpractice?
3. ____. Are there any of you, or members of your families, who have suffered any injury that you believe to have been caused by a doctor?
4. ____. Are there any of you, or members of your families, who have ever had a claim for damages or a lawsuit against a doctor, either as a plaintiff or as a defendant?
5. ____. Have any of you, or members of your families, ever had a

A=*Brewster*; C=questions traditionally asked by trial judge; F=*Stroud*; G=*Gaskins*; I=*Haefele*; J=*Hammers*; K=*Stokes*; U=*Underhill*; W=*Storck*; X=*Schafer*; Y=*Turner*; Z=*Nale*; see §10.3

dispute with a hospital, doctor, or other member of the healing arts regarding fees?

6. ___. Do any of you, or your close relatives, have a [*retarded child*]?

## 4. Failure to Make Safety Inspection §10.78

The following questions were asked by counsel during voir dire in *Hammers v Zurich-American Ins. Co.* (see §10.11).

1. J ___. Has anybody ever been employed by a [*crane*] company?
2. J ___. Has anybody ever been employed by [*Name of company*]?
3. J ___. Has anybody ever been employed in a [*steel manufacturing/ warehousing*] company?
4. J ___. Does anybody have any friends or relatives who have been employed in a [*steel manufacturing/warehousing*] company?
5. J ___. Has anybody ever done any [*steel beam handling*]?
6. J ___. Has anybody ever [*operated*] an [*overhead crane*] with [*pendant controls*]?
7. J ___. Has anybody ever worked with someone operating an [*overhead crane*]?
   a. Has anybody ever owned [*an overhead crane*]?
8. J ___. Has anybody ever been employed as a [*safety inspector*] for an [*insurance*] company?
9. J ___. Does anybody have close friends or relatives that are [*safety inspectors*]?
10. J ___. Does anybody have any special knowledge of [*safety inspection*] work?
11. J ___. Has anyone ever participated in any [*safety engineering*] meetings?
12. J ___. Is anybody a member of or does anybody know anything about [*ASSE, the American Society of Safety Engineers*]?
13. J ___. Does anybody have any special knowledge about [*ANSI, American National Standards Institute*]?
14. J ___. Does anybody have any connection with the [*National Safety Council*]?
15. J ___. Does anybody have any special knowledge about [*materials handling*]?
16. J ___. Does anybody have any special knowledge about the [*materials handling steel industry*]?

---

A=*Brewster*; C=questions traditionally asked by trial judge; F=*Stroud*; G=*Gaskins*; I=*Haefele*; J=*Hammers*; K=*Stokes*; U=*Underhill*; W=*Storck*; X=*Schafer*; Y=*Turner*; Z=*Nale*; see §10.3

17. J ___. Does anybody have any special knowledge about the [*construction*] industry with [*steel beams*]?
18. J ___. Does anybody know anybody who does [*inspection*] work, [*safety or otherwise*]?
19. J ___. Does anybody do any [*actuarial*] work?
20. J ___. Has anybody done any [*supervisory*] work with any [*safety inspection*] company in connection with [*workers compensation*]?
21. J ___. Has anyone attended any safety meetings set up or run by [*insurance*] company [*safety inspection*] departments?
22. J ___. Has anyone seen any films on safety made by [*insurance*] company [*safety inspection*] departments?

### 5. Police Misconduct

#### a. Plaintiff's Questions §10.80

For additional questions on police officers, see §§9.14, 9.72, 9.80–9.82, 10.62, 10.81, 11.56.

Attorney Hugh M. Davis of Detroit represented a private citizen in a police misconduct suit against the Police Department and City of Detroit, *Jennings v Terry* (Wayne County Cir. Ct., No. 75 055 609 NO). Questions 1–2, 11, 12, and 15–17 were asked in voir dire proposed by Davis.

Questions 3–10, 13, 14, and 18–20 were asked in voir dire by Richard A. Soble, plaintiff's attorney in *Stokes v City of Detroit* (Wayne County Cir. Ct., No. 78 819 767 CZ). Mrs. Stokes was suing for the shooting death of her husband during an altercation with two off-duty police officers which took place in the parking lot of a Jack-in-the-Box restaurant at 2:30 a.m. The jury returned a verdict for the plaintiff.

1. ___. Have you ever been in a police car?
2. ___. Have you ever been handcuffed?
3. K ___. Have you or any member of your family or friends been employed by or worked for the defendant city of [*Name*]?
   [*If yes*]
   a. Who? When? In what capacity?
4. K ___. Does your job cause you to work with any law enforcement officer or agency?

---

A=*Brewster*; C=questions traditionally asked by trial judge; F=*Stroud*; G=*Gaskins*; I=*Haefele*; J=*Hammers*; K=*Stokes*; U=*Underhill*; W=*Storck*; X=*Schafer*; Y=*Turner*; Z=*Nale*; see §10.3

5. K ___. Have you, or any members of your family, ever been engaged in private investigatory work?

6. K ___. Would any of the relationships you mentioned cause you to sympathize with, give greater credibility to, or in any manner favor the defendants because they, too, are law enforcement officers?

7. K ___. Are you a member of any group organized principally for the suppression of crime?

8. K ___. Do you think that police officers would never lie under oath?

9. K ___. Do you think police officers should be given the benefit of a doubt when their conduct is challenged and there is a dispute arising out of their conduct?

10. K ___. Do you think that law and order should be maintained at all costs, even if it means sacrificing somebody's constitutional rights?

11. ___. Do you believe that lawsuits against police officers and their governmental employer might actually improve performance by providing a check on those few officers who might be inclined to violence, abuse, or loss of temper?

12. ___. Do you have any feelings of resentment or disapproval against organizations that support civil rights for minorities, like the National Association for the Advancement of Colored People (NAACP) or the Congress for Racial Equality (CORE), or Mexican-American Legal Defense Fund (MALDEF)?

13. K ___. This is a lawsuit brought by a private citizen against a member of the [*police department*]. Do you feel that citizens who believe they have been treated illegally and unfairly should not bring suit against police officers?

14. K ___. Do you believe that a person who complains that he or she has been a victim of police abuse:
   a. Is only trying to get attention?
   b. Is actually trying to cover up for [*his/her*] guilt in the situation?
   c. Is trying to discredit the police and our system of law enforcement?

15. ___. Do you disapprove of the legal principle that the plaintiff may recover damages from the defendants if it is proved, by the preponderance of the evidence, that defendants deprived

---

A=*Brewster*; C=questions traditionally asked by trial judge; F=*Stroud*; G=*Gaskins*; I=*Haefele*; J=*Hammers*; K=*Stokes*; U=*Underhill*; W=*Storck*; X=*Schafer*; Y=*Turner*; Z=*Nale*; see §10.3

plaintiff of rights protected by the Constitution of the United States and [*State*]?

16. ___. Do you feel that people should be compensated for deprivation of their civil and legal rights?
17. ___. Does any member of the jury hold the belief that mental anguish, humiliation, embarassment, fear, loss of privacy, and loss of freedom, if proved by the evidence, should *not* be compensated for in money damages?
18. K ___. If, after hearing the evidence and the instructions of the judge, you found that the defendant[s] had wrongfully [*killed*] the plaintiff, would you hesitate to make them pay money damages to the person suing them?
19. K ___. If the judge were to instruct you that such compensation was proper under the law, would you have any hesitation about making such an award if the evidence warranted it?
20. K ___. Do you believe that a police officer's authority should always be respected and that [*he/she*] should always be obeyed and supported even if [*he/she*] acts illegally?
21. K ___. Is there any member of the jury who has a belief now, without hearing any evidence or the law, that defendants should not be held responsible for the actions complained of even if the claims of the [*Name*] family are proved?

*COMMENT:* Attorney Richard A. Soble of Detroit, Michigan asked the following questions in *Ortho v City of Detroit* (Wayne County Cir. Ct., No. 77 721 245 NO), a case involving an alleged assault by a police officer on a 17-year-old teenager.

1. ___. Have you ever used or heard others use the word "nigger"?
2. ___. What do you feel when you hear the word "nigger"?
3. ___. Is a racial or ethnic remark ever sufficient provocation for a police officer to hit someone?
4. ___. When is it ever justified, in your opinion, for a police officer to strike someone for making a racial or ethnic remark?
5. ___. Do you feel police officers, as part of their training, should be hardened to verbal abuse?
6. ___. Do you feel that police officers should not respond physically to racial or ethnic remarks?
7. ___. There will be testimony that [*a witness*] used the word "nigger."

---

A=*Brewster*; C=questions traditionally asked by trial judge; F=*Stroud*; G=*Gaskins*; I=*Haefele*; J=*Hammers*; K=*Stokes*; U=*Underhill*; W=*Storck*; X=*Schafer*; Y=*Turner*; Z=*Nale*; see §10.3

Will the fact that this word was used cause you to decide this case one way or the other?

a. Will the use of this word prejudice or predispose you toward one side or the other?

8. ____. Do you feel that because [*a witness*] used the word "nigger," plaintiff should not recover for any of the losses suffered by plaintiff's family?

*COMMENT:* Hugh Manes of Los Angeles, whose specialty is police misconduct cases, recommends asking the following in an appropriate case.

1. ____. Can you accept that a police officer could get angry, lose control, overreact, [*and write something in a report that is not true and then stick with the story later*]; can you accept that that could happen?

2. ____. I am not discussing a pattern or practice but only this one incident in which this particular police officer violated the rules of the [*Name*] police department. Do you understand this viewpoint?

*COMMENT:* In effect, plaintiff's counsel here is fighting a police misconduct case as a supporter of law-and-order, attacking only one police officer on one occasion.

### b. Defendant's Questions §10.81

Defense counsel Marion R. Jenkins of Detroit requested the following voir dire in *Stokes* (see §10.80), a police misconduct case.

1. K ____. Have any of you ever been the victim of a crime?
[*If yes*]
a. Did you report it to the police?
b. Were they cooperative and helpful?

2. K ____. Have any of your family or close friends been the victim of a crime?
[*If yes*]
a. Did they report it to the police?
b. Were they cooperative and helpful?

---

A=*Brewster*; C=questions traditionally asked by trial judge; F=*Stroud*; G=*Gaskins*; I=*Haefele*; J=*Hammers*; K=*Stokes*; U=*Underhill*; W=*Storck*; X=*Schafer*; Y=*Turner*; Z=*Nale*; see §10.3

3. K ___. Have you or any member of your family ever been the complaining witness in a trial?
[*If yes*]
a. What type of case was it?
b. Was the issue of police misconduct raised in the trial?
4. K ___. Have you read, heard, or seen anything regarding alleged police misconduct?
[*If yes*]
a. Does that influence your opinion about what you think might have happened in this case?
5. K ___. Have you had any dealings or experiences with police officers that might make it difficult for you to sit in impartial judgment on this case?
6. K ___. The judge will instruct you that a police officer has a duty to use force, whenever necessary, in the course of effecting an arrest. Do you promise to heed that instruction?
7. K ___. Are you a member of any organization that is trying to abolish any division, unit, or facet of the [*City*] Police Department, or any other law enforcement agency?
8. K ___. Did anybody ever apply to a police force for employment, or have any members of anyone's family applied?
9. K ___. Have you ever been involved with the police so that you are now prejudiced against them?
a. Any of your family members?

### 6. Other Cases §10.82

## B. Employment Discrimination

### 1. In Upgrading, Firing, Hiring §10.91

In *Brewster v Martin Marietta* (see §3.41), a four-man, two-woman civil jury awarded $1,270,000 to a pioneer woman sales manager in industrial metals fired from her position. Voir dire questions asked by counsel included the following:

1. A ___. Do any of you own stock in any corporations?
[*If yes*]
a. Which ones?

---

A=*Brewster*; C=questions traditionally asked by trial judge; F=*Stroud*; G=*Gaskins*; I=*Haefele*; J=*Hammers*; K=*Stokes*; U=*Underhill*; W=*Storck*; X=*Schafer*; Y=*Turner*; Z=*Nale*; see §10.3

2. A ___. Have you or any close friend or member of your family been employed by [*Name of company or corporation*]?
[*If yes*]
a. Describe your [*friend's/relative's*] position.

3. A ___. Have you or any close friend or member of your family been employed in the [*industrial metals sales*] business?
[*If yes*]
a. Describe your [*friend's/relative's*] position.

4. A ___. Have you or any close friend or member of your family been employed as a [*sales person*] of any kind?
[*If yes*]
a. Describe the position.

5. A ___. Have you or any close friend or member of your family been fired from a job?
[*If yes*]
a. Was it for cause or without cause?
b. What was the job?
c. How long had [*you/your friend/your relative*] been employed?
d. Did [*you/your friend/your relative*] begin any grievance or lawsuit against the employer?
e. What was the result?

6. A ___. Have you or any close friend or member of your family sued [*your/their*] employer?
[*If yes*]
a. What happened?
b. Do any of you feel that a person who is fired should not sue [*his/her*] former employer?

7. A ___. How do you feel about women working outside the home?
a. Does anyone feel that it is not right for women to be in the job force?
b. [*Why/why not*]?

8. A ___. Do you or any close friend or member of your family work with women?
[*If yes*]
a. Is the woman a supervisor, a fellow employee, or a subordinate?
b. What has been your [*friend's/relative's*] experience in this situation?

---

A=*Brewster*; C=questions traditionally asked by trial judge; F=*Stroud*; G=*Gaskins*; I=*Haefele*; J=*Hammers*; K=*Stokes*; U=*Underhill*; W=*Storck*; X=*Schafer*; Y=*Turner*; Z=*Nale*; see §10.3

9. A ___. Do any of you feel you would not give a plaintiff money damages if the plaintiff proves she was fired in part because her employer discriminated against her because of her sex?
10. A ___. Would any of you feel uncomfortable if you are selected to sit on an employment case that involves claims of sex discrimination?
11. A ___. Would any of you have difficulty returning a money verdict in favor of plaintiff if she shows she was fired illegally or without cause?
12. A ___. Are you or any close friend or member of your family in a union?
    [*If yes*]
    a. What union?
    b. For how long?
    c. Did [*you*] hold any committee or officer positions?
13. A ___. Have you or any close friend or member of your family supervised employees? Describe your [*relative's/friend's*] position. Have any of those subordinates been members of the opposite sex?
14. A ___. How would you react toward testimony of a supervisor or manager? Would you be able to give it the same weight as testimony from other persons, or would you give it more or less weight?
15. A ___. Have you or any close friend or member of your family been placed on probation at work? Describe the situation.

*COMMENT:* On various forms of sex discrimination in employment, see Blumrosen, "Wage Discrimination, Job Segregation, and Women Workers," 6 *Women's Rights L Rptr* 19 (1979–1980), and Note, "Challenges to Sex-Based Mortality Tables in Insurance and Pensions," 6 *Women's Rights L Rptr* 59 (1979–1980).

## 2. Sexual Harassment

### a. Attitudes toward Filing Suit §10.92

All of the following questions not marked with a *Z* were asked by attorneys Connye Harper and Richard Parker of Detroit, Michigan, in a case filed by a black woman who was dismissed for complaining about sexual harassment by a white supervisor at the Bendix Corporation.

---

A=*Brewster*; C=questions traditionally asked by trial judge; F=*Stroud*; G=*Gaskins*; I=*Haefele*; J=*Hammers*; K=*Stokes*; U=*Underhill*; W=*Storck*; X=*Schafer*; Y=*Turner*; Z=*Nale*; see §10.3

1. Z ___. Are any of you currently unemployed?
[*If yes*]
a. Has it been the result of layoffs?
2. ___. Plaintiff in this case claims she was fired for complaining about working conditions. Do any members of the jury feel they could not grant plaintiff recovery if they found she was fired for complaining about working conditions?
3. ___. The working conditions plaintiff complained about involve sexual advances by a [*member of management*]. Is there anyone on the jury who feels that sex in the work place is not the legitimate subject of an employee complaint?
4. ___. This case will involve [*explicit*] sexual language that may be offensive. Do any of you feel you could not sit in unbiased judgment under these circumstances?
5. ___. The plaintiff in this case is a [*black*] woman and the person accused of the advances is a [*white*] male. Does this circumstance render you incapable of making an unbiased decision in this case?
6. ___. Part of the testimony the plaintiff will give in this case involves remarks that some people might consider objectionable, that is, sexual terms that some people might consider objectionable. Would hearing testimony like this—if it came from the mouth of the plaintiff, for example—cause you to be biased in any way?
7. ___. Would any of you be so offended by what society might consider to be bad language that you wouldn't be able to hear clearly the facts and listen to the evidence?

*COMMENT:* The following questions were asked in *Nale v Ford Motor Co.* (see §10.38).

8. Z ___. Are you aware of the problem in the work force called sexual harassment?
9. Z ___. What do you understand sexual harassment to be?
10. Z ___. Which of the following would you find objectionable in a job context:
a. Sexual jokes or pictures?
b. Sexual remarks or teasing?

A=*Brewster*; C=questions traditionally asked by trial judge; F=*Stroud*; G=*Gaskins*; I=*Haefele*; J=*Hammers*; K=*Stokes*; U=*Underhill*; W=*Storck*; X=*Schafer*; Y=*Turner*; Z=*Nale*; see §10.3

c. Subtle sexual hints?
d. Invitations for a date?
e. Sexual gestures?
f. Propositions for sex?
g. Physical touching without your consent?

11. Z ___. Do you know that it is against the law for an employer or supervisor to sexually harass someone?

12. Z ___. Do you think the lawmakers have gone too far when they start making laws interfering with how men and women sexually relate to each other on the job?

13. ___. Does any member of the jury hold the belief that mothers of [*young*] children should not work outside the home?

14. ___. Does any member of the jury hold the belief that [*minorities*] have any more employment rights under the law than [*white*] people do?

15. Z ___. Why do you think women choose to work outside the home?

16. Z ___. Do you know that ___ percent of the women who work are the sole breadwinner for the family?

*COMMENT:* For the current percentage in the community where the case is being tried, consult a local university demographer or the latest U.S. Census.

17. Z ___. Do you believe that women are discriminated against on the job?
a. [*Why/why not*]?

18. Z ___. Do you believe that women are sexually harassed on the job?
a. [*Why/why not*]?

19. Z ___. Have you or any close relatives or friends ever been discriminated against on any job on the basis of race or sex?

20. Z ___. Do any of you feel that the laws designed to prevent and punish discrimination against people in the work force have gone too far?

21. Z ___. Do any of you feel that people are always going to behave in ways that discriminate against other people and there is nothing that can be done to change that?

22. Z ___. Do you believe that women can handle the pressures of the work place as well as men?

---

A=*Brewster*; C=questions traditionally asked by trial judge; F=*Stroud*; G=*Gaskins*; I=*Haefele*; J=*Hammers*; K=*Stokes*; U=*Underhill*; W=*Storck*; X=*Schafer*; Y=*Turner*; Z=*Nale*; see §10.3

23. Z ___. Do you believe that sexual harassment is part of the pressure that women should be expected to handle?
24. Z ___. Do you believe that it is acceptable for a woman to work in [*a factory*] that is predominantly male?
25. Z ___. Do you think that sexual harassment occurs more frequently in [*a factory*] than it would in a [*school/office*]?
26. Z ___. Do you believe that sexual advances are inevitable when men and women are working together?
27. Z ___. Do you see any difference in sexual advances being made by a coworker and someone in position of authority over you?
28. Z ___. Do you think that sexual advances are made as regularly against men as they are against women?
29. Z ___. Do you think a woman applying for a job in [*an automotive factory*] is asking for and expecting sexual attention?
30. Z ___. Do you think a woman can encourage sexual advances on the job by what she [*wears*]?
31. Z ___. Have any of you ever worked in [*a factory*] during the summer months?
32. Z ___. If the evidence were to show that the plaintiff wore [*a halter*] during the month of [*August*] while working for the employer, would it take some evidence to convince you that she was not inviting sexual attention on purpose?
33. Z ___. Do you think women who have been approached sexually can put a stop to those sexual advances by ignoring them?
34. Z ___. Do you think if a woman wants to, she can stop sexual advances from being made by a [*supervisor/employer*]?
[*If yes*]
a. How would she go about doing that, in your opinion?
35. Z ___. Would it surprise you to learn that in the majority of cases where women try to ignore sexual harassment, it remains the same or gets worse?
36. Z ___. Would it surprise you to learn that out of 9000 people responding to a questionnaire about sexual harassment, nine out of ten responded that they had received unwanted sexual attention on the job?
37. Z ___. Do you believe in the old saying, "If you can't stand the heat, get out of the kitchen"?

---

A=*Brewster*; C=questions traditionally asked by trial judge; F=*Stroud*; G=*Gaskins*; I=*Haefele*; J=*Hammers*; K=*Stokes*; U=*Underhill*; W=*Storck*; X=*Schafer*; Y=*Turner*; Z=*Nale*; see §10.3

38. Z ___. Would it surprise you to learn that unwanted sexual attention is the reason many women quit or are fired from their jobs?

### b. Attitudes toward Employers/Management §10.93

All the following questions not marked with a *Z* were asked by attorneys Connye Harper and Richard Parker of Detroit, Michigan, in a case in which a black woman was dismissed for complaining about sexual harassment by a white supervisor at the Bendix Corporation.

1. ___. Do you, or does any member of your immediate family, have any special knowledge about [*personnel policies*] or [*human resources management*]?
2. ___. Has any member of the jury ever worked in the [*personnel*] department of a [*large corporation*]?
3. Z ___. Would it be difficult for you to find the employer guilty of discrimination against [*plaintiff*] if it were shown that [*Name*]'s sexual advances were only one of several factors that resulted in [*plaintiff*] being fired?
4. Z ___. Do you believe an employer like [*Ford Motor Company*] should be responsible for any unlawful acts of sexual harassment that it may be proved that [*Name*] was involved in with [*plaintiff*]?
5. Z ___. Do you think an employer has the duty to inform its supervisors that it will not tolerate discrimination against any of [*his/her*] employees?
6. Z ___. Do you think the employer has a duty to check on supervisors to see whether they are in any way discriminating against people on the job?
7. Z ___. Do you think, once a person is hired by an employer, the employer should be concerned about any of that employee's behavior other than the ability to perform the job?
8. Z ___. Do you think sexual harassment affects a person's ability to perform on the job?
9. Z ___. Do you think that an employer, once informed that a person is sexually harassing other employees, has a duty to protect the victims of the sexual harassment?
10. Z ___. Do you think the employer, once informed that a person is sexually harassing other employees, has a duty to reprimand

---

A=*Brewster*; C=questions traditionally asked by trial judge; F=*Stroud*; G=*Gaskins*; I=*Haefele*; J=*Hammers*; K=*Stokes*; U=*Underhill*; W=*Storck*; X=*Schafer*; Y=*Turner*; Z=*Naie*; see §10.3

and even fire the employee who is violating the discrimination laws?

11. Z ___. By not punishing and interfering with the ability of a supervisor to sexually harass subordinates, do you believe an employer is tacitly approving those actions?

12. Z ___. Do you understand the difference between active and tacit approval?

13. Z ___. Have any of you jurors ever been in the position of a probationary employee?
[*If yes*]
a. Please describe the situation.

14. Z ___. Have any of you ever been in a position of a person making decisions about whether a probationary employee will be permanently hired?
[*If yes*]
a. Please explain.

15. Z ___. Do you think probationary employees are more concerned about the loss of their jobs than nonprobationary employees?

16. Z ___. Do you think persons in [*supervisory/management*] positions with a company would lie about events to protect the employer?

17. Z ___. Would you be more likely to believe a male witness than a female witness?

18. Z ___. Some witnesses who may testify in this case are in management positions. Does that give their testimony more credibility with you than that of a nonmanagement worker?

19. Z ___. Do you think women fabricate charges of sexual harassment just to get even with employers?

20. Z ___. Do you think women use their sexuality to get ahead on the job?

21. Z ___. Do you know of any women who have "slept their way to the top"?
[*If yes*]
a. Please explain.

22. Z ___. Do you think it is possible for a married foreman to be propositioning women subordinates?

---

A=*Brewster*; C=questions traditionally asked by trial judge; F=*Stroud*; G=*Gaskins*; I=*Haefele*; J=*Hammers*; K=*Stokes*; U=*Underhill*; W=*Storck*; X=*Schafer*; Y=*Turner*; Z=*Nale*; see §10.3

### c. Attitudes toward Awarding Recovery for Sexual Harassment §10.94

All of the following questions not marked with a *Z* were asked by attorneys Connye Harper and Richard Parker of Detroit, Michigan, in a case in which a black woman was dismissed for complaining about sexual harassment by a white supervisor at Bendix Corporation.

1. ___. Does any member of the jury have an opinion at the present time with respect to whether or not a person who is fired should sue [*his/her*] former employer?
2. ___. Plaintiff in this case claims she was fired in retaliation for complaining about sexual harassment; does any member of the jury have any fixed opinion of her right to recover in this case?
3. Z ___. Do you believe that for a victim of discrimination the emotional wounds can be a lot deeper than the financial wounds?
4. Z ___. Do you think experiencing unwanted sexual advances can have an emotional effect on a woman?
5. Z ___. Does any member of the jury believe that women are more likely than men to exaggerate or stretch the truth if it is to their advantage to do so?
6. Z ___. Would you be comfortable about finding a man liable for sexual harassment when that could be a potential cause of embarrassment to him with his family and friends or when it might cause him to lose his job?
7. Z ___. Would the fact that [*Ford Motor Company*] is experiencing some financial problems now affect the amount of money you would award the plaintiffs?
8. Z ___. If a person has substantial injuries, emotional or physical, would you award the amount shown by the evidence even if the sums seemed large to you?
9. Z ___. Would you have a problem awarding large amounts for emotional damages, even if those damages far exceeded any wage damages of the plaintiff?
10. Z ___. Do you believe that it is possible for a woman who is experiencing unwanted sexual attention on the job to begin having and continue having physical problems as a result of the emotional stress she feels?

---

A=*Brewster*; C=questions traditionally asked by trial judge; F=*Stroud*; G=*Gaskins*; I=*Haefele*; J=*Hammers*; K=*Stokes*; U=*Underhill*; W=*Storck*; X=*Schafer*; Y=*Turner*; Z=*Nale*; see §10.3

11. Z ___. Do you have any fixed opinion about the right of the employer to discharge an employee?
12. Z ___. Do you believe it should be against the law for a person to touch another person's body without their consent?
13. ___. There have been several recent cases where women have been awarded up to [*one million dollars*] for their claims of sexual harassment. Do you believe that there is no evidence that you could hear that would substantiate an award of that size?

### 3. Other Grounds §10.95.

## C. Military Discharge

### 1. General Questions §10.97

The questions in §§13.97–13.99 are taken almost verbatim from the transcript of the voir dire of the officers called to hear the Tangela Gaskins court-martial proceeding. Additional questions were asked in this case specifically on the issue of homosexuality, see §§9.117–9.129. For a more detailed description of the case, see §3.91.

In a court-martial, the prosecutor or charging party is called the recorder; the service person is called the defendant.

1. G ___. What was your reaction when you found out you were being assigned to this matter?
2. G ___. If this board were to end right now and for some reason you had to close and make a recommendation based strictly on what has been presented in this board or what has not been presented, what recommendation would you make?
3. G ___. And if the recorder does not convince you—if you're not convinced in your own heart, in your own mind that [*defendant*] did what they say [*she/he*] did, do you think you'd vote for retention [*in the service*]?
4. G ___. [*What*] is your understanding of the [*Navy*] regulations and instructions [*on the issue(s) in this case*]?
5. G ___. How did you acquire that understanding?
6. G ___. Was that in preparation for this board?

---

A=*Brewster*; C=questions traditionally asked by trial judge; F=*Stroud*; G=*Gaskins*; I=*Haefele*; J=*Hammers*; K=*Stokes*; U=*Underhill*; W=*Storck*; X=*Schafer*; Y=*Turner*; Z=*Nale*; see §10.3

7. G ___. Would you feel yourself bound to follow the instructions of the Secretary of the [*Navy*] in regard to this board?
8. G ___. From what you have said [*Lieutenant*], about following instructions and regulations, manuals and so on, I assume I would be correct that you would follow an instruction from the Secretary of the [*Navy*] that if an individual is to be administratively separated because of [*homosexuality*], that person should normally be given an [*honorable*] discharge unless the quality of the service warrants otherwise. I assume you would have no hesitation in following that type of an instruction?
9. G ___. Are you familiar with the Secretary of the [*Navy*] Instruction [*1900.9C*]?
10. G ___. What is your understanding of the options that are open to a board of this nature?
11. G ___. And as to misconduct, where a homosexual act is alleged, what options are available with respect to discharge?
12. G ___. You don't know if an honorable discharge can be recommended?
13. G ___. If there were a communication from the [*Chief of Naval Operations*] and Secretary of the [*Navy*] with respect to the type of discharge that could be accorded, would you tend to follow that?
14. G ___. With respect to retention in a case of the nature that's before this board, what is your understanding about when retention would be appropriate or not appropriate—assuming, of course, that you believe that the person had actually done something?

### 2. Attitudes toward Service Personnel §10.98

1. G ___. If [*defendant*] should testify, how would you treat [*her/his*] testimony vis-a-vis the testimony of anyone else who may testify?
2. G ___. In evaluating [*defendant*] and trying to determine what should be done, what recommendation you would make, would you consider all aspects of [*her/his*] military record?

---

A=*Brewster*; C=questions traditionally asked by trial judge; F=*Stroud*; G=*Gaskins*; I=*Haefele*; J=*Hammers*; K=*Stokes*; U=*Underhill*; W=*Storck*; X=*Schafer*; Y=*Turner*; Z=*Nale*; see §10.3

### 3. Allegations of Homosexual Conduct §10.99

1. G ___. What is your attitude toward the woman at sea program?
2. G ___. What was your reaction when yu heard the [*Captain*] tell the ship's company there were allegations of homosexual conduct?
3. G ___. Did you have any reaction such as "So what," or "Here we go again," or "We've got a [*ship/base*] full of faggots," or any kind of reaction at all?
4. G ___. What is your feeling about whether a person should be retained in the [*Navy*] based on allegations of homosexual conduct?
5. G ___. Do you think that because a [*woman*] enters the [*Navy*] or any branch of the military service, that the manner in which [*she*] displayed affection or greeting as a civilian should in any way change because [*she*] is in the military?
6. G ___. Are you saying that a person of lower rank should not be displaying affection to superiors?
   [*If yes*]
   a. When you say "superior," are you speaking in a technical sense, or are you referring to a situation, for example, between enlisted and officer, or petty officer and officer?
   b. For example, would a difference of one or two pay grades fall within your definition of "superior"?
   c. At what point, at what grade spread, would it not make a difference to you?
7. G ___. Are you thinking of a situation where there is a display of affection between two [*women*] of different rank—that this might in some manner influence the person of higher rank for the benefit of the person of lower rank? Are you thinking along that line?
8. G ___. An [*Ensign*] and a [*Lieutenant JG*] are good friends, and one, the [*Ensign*], comes up to the [*Lieutenant JG*] and slaps [*him*] on the back and maybe puts [*his*] arm around [*him*], or something like that. And the way I'm describing this is as a method of greeting. Do you think this is improper?
9. G ___. I mean, if the [*Admiral/C.O.*] were there, it might be improper. But assuming the two people who see each other are good friends—would you feel there was anything wrong with some

A=*Brewster*; C=questions traditionally asked by trial judge; F=*Stroud*; G=*Gaskins*; I=*Haefele*; J=*Hammers*; K=*Stokes*; U=*Underhill*; W=*Storck*; X=*Schafer*; Y=*Turner*; Z=*Nale*; see §10.3

display of acknowledgment, affection, whatever you want to call it—other than a salute or possibly a handshake—between, let's say, an [*Ensign*] and a [*JG*]?

10. G ___. Would it make any difference if this same type of exchange were to take place between two [*enlisted*] individuals, let's say a [*second class*] and a [*third class*]?

11. G ___. Do you think if someone is discharged from the service for misconduct based on a homosexual act or acts, would that type of background for the discharge carry more of a stigma than some other type of administrative discharge?

12. G ___. Before you would want to vote to discharge anyone based on misconduct where homosexual acts were alleged, would you think you could do it based simply on a suspicion you might have, or would you want to be pretty well convinced before putting that type of stigma on anyone?

13. G ___. Assuming you were faced with a situation of an act between consenting adults, a homosexual act, and the sailor involved had a good military record, with no other homosexual allegations made, would you feel you would have to recommend discharge?
[*If yes*]
a. Do you think you would?

14. G ___. In the event you were to vote for a recommendation of "discharge," and the alleged acts did not involve any [*violence/coercion/any acts between individuals of disparate rank*]—if basically, the acts were between consenting adults, what type of discharge would you recommend, [*assuming also that there was no evidence of other such acts in the past and the person had a good military record*]?

## D. Other Types of Cases §10.101

---

A=*Brewster*; C=questions traditionally asked by trial judge; F=*Stroud*; G=*Gaskins*; I=*Haefele*; J=*Hammers*; K=*Stokes*; U=*Underhill*; W=*Storck*; X=*Schafer*; Y=*Turner*; Z=*Nale*; see §10.3

# Chapter 11

# *Questions in Criminal Cases*


**I. Compilation of a Useful List**
A. Sources of Questions §11.1
B. Ways to Use This List §11.2
C. Abbreviations Used §11.3

**II. Attitudes Toward Crime Alleged**
A. Experiences with Crime Alleged §11.5
B. Attitudes toward Crime Charged §11.6
C. Nature of Defense §11.7
D. Other Issues §11.8

**III. Attitudes Toward Burden of Proof and Presumption of Innocence**
A. Preliminary Questions §11.10
B. "Perry Mason Syndrome" §11.11
C. Effect of Security Precautions §11.12
D. Effect of Defendant's Confinement during Trial §11.13
E. Other Evidentiary Questions §11.14

**IV. Attitudes Toward a Party/Witness**
A. Toward Defendant's Prior Criminal Record §11.20
B. Toward Credibility of Defendant §11.21
C. Toward Counsel for Both Sides §11.22
D. Other Issues §11.23

**V. Attitudes Toward Most Damaging Feature of Case**

A. Pictures/Photographs §11.26

B. Women Charged with Acts of Violence

1. Talking to Jurors about Physical Violence §11.27
2. Women and Violence §11.28
3. Need for Extensive Voir Dire §11.29
4. Other Issues §11.30

C. Other Features §11.31

**VI. Attitudes Toward Specific Crime Charged**

A. Conspiracy §11.33

B. Obscenity or Pornography

1. Current Law §11.34
2. Involving a Movie §11.35
3. Involving Dancing §11.36

C. Drunk Driving §11.37

D. Bank Robbery §11.38

E. Sex Perversion §11.39

F. Drug Offenses

1. Marijuana §11.40
2. Other Drugs §11.41

G. Other Crimes §11.45

**VII. Attitudes Toward Specific Defenses**

A. Self-Defense §11.51

B. Sexual Harassment

1. Rape §11.52
2. Assault by Husband §11.53
3. Battery by Husband
   a. Wife Abuse §11.54
   b. Psychological Testimony §11.55
   c. Police Testimony §11.56

C. Defense of Necessity or Lesser Evil §11.57

D. First Amendment Defense §11.58

E. Other Defenses §11.59

**VIII. Attitudes Toward Capital Punishment**

A. Death-Qualified Jurors

1. The Point of Agreement §11.61
2. The Problem §11.62
   a. *Witherspoon* Solution §11.63
   b. *Gregg v Georgia* Solution §11.64
   c. California Solution: *Hovey v Superior Court* §11.65
      (1) Concept of a Neutral Jury §11.66
      (2) Problem of Sociological Proof §11.67
      (3) Dr. Craig Haney Study §11.68

d. Federal Solution: *Grigsby v Mabry* §11.69
e. Proposal for All Capital Punishment Trials §11.70
f. Requirement of a Cross-Section Jury §11.71

B. Recent Developments §11.74

C. Jurors Affected by Pretrial Publicity §11.80

D. Sample Questions

1. Death Qualification §11.81
2. Pretrial Publicity §11.82
3. Other Subjects §11.83

# I. COMPILATION OF A USEFUL LIST

## A. Sources of Questions §11.1

The questions in this chapter, together with basic questions in chapter 9, provide a comprehensive, well-organized list for consideration in any criminal case in which jury prejudgment is potentially a serious problem. Some of the typical issues and many types of cases are discussed, but coverage is not encyclopedic. The breadth and detail of the questions reproduced here indicate what judges have asked, or permitted counsel to ask. As you work, you will draft numerous questions that go right to the heart of your case, building on the comprehensive approach now widely accepted in most jurisdictions in this country.

The lists of questions come from several sources: *California v Newton* (the Huey Newton murder trial, see §3.22), *United States v Russo* (the *Pentagon Papers* case, §3.52), *United States v Briggs* (the *Gainesville Eight* trial of Vietnam Veterans Against the War, see §3.53), *United States v Satcher* (a bank robbery case, see §11.38), *United States v Sherpix* (an obscene film trial, see §11.35), *Michigan v Hartwell* (a sex harassment murder defense, see §3.31), and *Michigan v Jeanette Smith* (a battered wife murder defense, see §11.51). Names of attorneys who handled these cases appear with the descriptions of most of the cases in chapter 3. Also included are comments made by attorney Theodore Koskoff to the American Trial Lawyers Association; questions supplied by attorneys William Sebastian Moore, Dennis Roberts, James Herndon, Michael Kennedy, Joseph Rhine, Lionel Epstein, Alvin Friedman, Charles Duncan, Richard Medalie, Michael Weiss, Michael E. Rose, Steven A. Chase, Warren Wilson, Ann Fagan Ginger, and Priscilla Camp; and points briefed by Doris Brin Walker and Stephen Bedrick in *Smallwood* (see §11.69). Professor Robert Blauner's open-ended questions are commonly used today in place of the traditional adversary-type questions. Questions submitted by the prosecution in a few of these cases are provided for use and study.

## B. Ways to Use This List §11.2

Counsel may want to reproduce the following pages, mark up the copy, cross out and write in the margins, rearrange questions, and number them to suit a particular case. Attorneys may also want to change the language of the questions to suit the idiom of the region and the court. Trial lawyer Warren Wilson of Oakland, California, recommends that all references in voir dire questions to the defendant be to "my client" or to "Mr./Ms. ____________," since references to "the defendant" reemphasize the client's status as someone charged with a crime.

The questions contain many phrases in brackets or instructions for filling in names or specific criminal charges, many *he/she, his/her* choices. This approach is intended to encourage *thinking* about whether to include each question when making a list to use in a case, rather than simply including all questions because you are in a hurry. Defense of the right of counsel to ask voir dire questions directly and to question prospective jurors individually and in depth includes a disciplined approach to preparation of questions to be asked in each particular case.

Once the edited list of voir dire questions is prepared, it may be submitted to the judge in any court in which the trial judge asks questions propounded by counsel and limits or denies counsel's right to question prospective jurors directly. Since the questions in the following sections are marked to show in which cases they were used (see abbreviations in §11.3), the list can be used as precedent for asking the same or similar questions in counsel's current cases.

Over time a lawyer will want to add questions from other sources that have proved useful and to delete ones that prove ineffective.

For further discussion, see §9.2.

### C. Abbreviations Used §11.3

The following abbreviations, which precede most of the voir dire questions in this chapter, indicate the cases in which the question was used and the section in which each case is described.*

B *United States v Briggs* (Gainesville Eight), see §3.53
C Questions traditionally asked by the trial judge
I *Michigan v Hartwell*, see §3.31
J *Michigan v Jeanette Smith*, see §11.51
N *California v Newton* (Huey Newton case), see §3.22
O *United States v Sherpix*, see §11.35
P *United States v Russo* (Pentagon Papers case), see §3.52
R *United States v Satcher*, see §11.38

## II. ATTITUDES TOWARD CRIME ALLEGED

### A. Experiences with Crime Alleged §11.5

1. C ___. Have you been a victim of a crime similar to that charged here?

---

*Some capital letters are used as abbreviations for other (civil) cases in chapter 10.

2. P ___. Is there anything about the nature of the charges contained in the indictment that would prevent your considering this case fairly and impartially?
3. P ___. Have you, or a relative or close friend of yours, ever been the victim of a crime?

*COMMENT:* Refusal to ask this question constituted reversible error in *Pennsylvania v Davis* (Pa Super Ct 1980) 422 A2d 671, 672.

[*If so*]
a. Where and when and what type of crime?

4. P ___. Following the crime, were you interviewed by any member of a law enforcement agency?
[*If so*]
a. Was [*he/she*] a state or federal official?
5. P ___. Was there a prosecution of the offense?
[*If yes*]
A. What was the result?
6. P ___. Were you satisfied that the people responsible for the investigation and/or prosecution of the case acted competently in apprehending the alleged offender and securing [*his/her*] conviction?
[*If not*]
a. Explain your answer.

## B. Attitudes toward Crime Charged §11.6

In the *Pentagon Papers* case, the government proposed questions 1–2.

1. P ___. Are you opposed to laws providing secrecy for documents relating to military, diplomatic, or other matters relating to the national defense?
2. P ___. Would you tend to excuse or overlook offenses if you believed that they were committed for motives, reasons, or purposes you favor or agree with?

## C. Nature of Defense §11.7

Jurors should be asked questions that present the nature of the defense to test whether they hold such strong beliefs about the use of

B=*Briggs*; C=questions traditionally asked by the trial judge; I=*Michigan v Hartwell*; J=*Michigan v Jeanette Smith*; N=*Huey Newton* case; O=*United States v Sherpix*; P=*Pentagon Papers* case; R=*United States v Satcher*; see §§14.1 and 14.3

violence or against alibi evidence that they could not acquit.

1. N ___. If [*His/Her*] Honor instructs you that the crime charged includes several elements, will you vote for acquittal unless you are satisfied that the proof establishes all the elements?

2. N ___. If it appears from the evidence that [*Mr./Mrs. Smith*] was exercising the lawful right of self-defense, would you vote for an acquittal even though you find the defendant was the one who struck the fatal blow?

*COMMENT:* See additional voir dire questions in §§11.51–11.56.

Defense strategy may require that the defendant not testify. If this strategy can be anticipated when the jury is being selected, the jurors should be asked question 3.

3. N ___. You understand, do you not, that the burden of proof is always on the prosecution, and that the defendant need not present any evidence? You also understand, do you not, that the defendant need not testify on behalf of [*him/her*]self?

### D. Other Issues §11.8

This section is being reserved for additional questions on attitudes toward the crime alleged to be presented in supplements to this volume.

## III. ATTITUDES TOWARD BURDEN OF PROOF AND PRESUMPTION OF INNOCENCE

### A. Preliminary Questions §11.10

The clear, simple, absolute nature of the presumption of innocence is extremely difficult to convey to a new juror. For intensive questioning on this point, see examples in chapter 17.

Attorney William Sebastian Moore of Jackson, Mississippi, finds question 1 useful:

1. ___. Do you realize that the indictment in this case is merely a formal legal pleading, a piece of paper filed by the prosecution in order to start these proceedings, and has no greater legal effect than a complaint or declaration in a civil case?

2. C ___. You understand, do you not, that the burden of proof is always

B=*Briggs*; C=questions traditionally asked by the trial judge; I=*Michigan v Hartwell*; J=*Michigan v Jeanette Smith*; N=*Huey Newton* case; O=*United States v Sherpix*; P=*Pentagon Papers* case; R=*United States v Satcher*; see §§14.1 and 14.3

on the prosecution, and that the defendant need not present any evidence in order to be acquitted?

3. C ___. You also understand, do you not, that the defendant need not testify on behalf of [*him/her*]self?

4. C ___. Do you recognize that while in a civil case a mere preponderance of the evidence is sufficient, in a criminal case it is necessary for the prosecution to prove the defendant guilty beyond a reasonable doubt and to a moral certainty?

5. C ___. Do you agree with our principle of law that a defendant in a criminal case should not be convicted unless the jury is convinced of guilt beyond a reasonable doubt and to a moral certainty?

6. R ___. Do you disagree with the law that a person is presumed innocent until proved guilty beyond a reasonable doubt?

7. R ___. Do you disagree with the law that the burden of proving the defendant guilty beyond a reasonable doubt rests with the prosecution?

8. N ___. As far as you are concerned, at the present time [*Mr./Ms. Smith*] stands innocent of the crime that [*he/she*] is charged with, is that right?

9. N ___. If the Court tells you that [*Mr./Ms. Smith*] is presumed to be innocent, you don't have any fault to find with that, do you?

10. N ___. I still don't have an answer whether you are willing to assume that [*Mr./Ms. Smith*] at the present time is presumed to be innocent?

11. N ___. The law says that a defendant who has been charged with a crime is presumed to be innocent. Are you willing to accept that and give that cloak of presumption of innocence to [*Mr./Ms. Smith*]?

12. N ___. At the present time, are you willing to accept the fact that [*Mr./Ms. Smith*] is presumed innocent because you haven't heard any evidence?

13. N ___. Now you would expect the prosecution to be able to give you convincing evidence to prove that [*Mr./Ms. Smith*] is guilty beyond a reasonable doubt, would you not?

14. N ___. You understand that it is not our responsibility to prove [*Mr./Ms. Smith*] is innocent?

15. N ___. In other words, it is not [*Mr./Ms. Smith*]'s duty to prove [*himself/*

---

B=*Briggs*; C=questions traditionally asked by the trial judge; I=*Michigan v Hartwell*; J=*Michigan v Jeanette Smith*; N=*Huey Newton* case; O=*United States v Sherpix*; P=*Pentagon Papers* case; R=*United States v Satcher*; see §§14.1 and 14.3

*herself*] innocent; [*he/she*] doesn't have to do anything, isn't that right?

16. N ___. It is up to the prosecution to prove [*Mr./Ms. Smith*] guilty beyond a reasonable doubt; are you willing to accept that as the standard of American jurisprudence that governs this trial?

17. N ___. Do you believe that the defendant [*killed Officer Clark*] and [*attempted to kill Officer Jones*]?

18. N ___. Would the fact that [*Mr./Ms. Smith*] has been arrested and charged with this crime create an inference in your own mind that there must be some truth or they wouldn't be holding this [*man/woman*] all these months for trial?

19. N ___. And then the fact that a grand jury indicted [*Mr./Ms. Smith*] for this crime, does that create within you a state of mind that [*he/she*] must have done it or they wouldn't have indicted [*him/her*]?

20. N ___. Would the fact that [*Mr./Ms. Smith*] was at the scene of the crime create in your mind an assumption that [*he/she*] must have some elements of guilt?

21. N ___. Did you ever take the position "where there is smoke there must be some fire someplace"?

*COMMENT:* In *California v Garcia* (Monterey County Super Ct, No. CR 4259, Oct. 14, 1974), Charles Garry asked question 22.

22. ___. If you had to vote right now, before the trial had started, would you vote to acquit or to convict my client?
[*If juror answers, "I would have to hear the evidence."*]
    a. No. At this point, the law requires you to vote to acquit. That is what the presumption of innocence means: that the defendant is presumed innocent until the government has proved [*him/her*] guilty beyond a reasonable doubt. Can you obey that rule?

*COMMENT:* Under appropriate circumstances, Oakland attorney Dennis Roberts suggests questions 23–26.

23. ___. Have you read any of the recent attacks on our appellate courts?

24. ___. Are you influenced by them to the extent that it would interfere with your judgment here?

---

B=*Briggs*; C=questions traditionally asked by the trial judge; I=*Michigan v Hartwell*; J=*Michigan v Jeanette Smith*; N=*Huey Newton* case; O=*United States v Sherpix*; P=*Pentagon Papers* case; R=*United States v Satcher*; see §§14.1 and 14.3

25. ____. You are not persuaded then that the rules of law by which you will be guided here—such as the rule of reasonable doubt, the presumption of innocence, the effect of circumstancial evidence [*etc.*]—are mere technicalities, are you?

26. ____. You understand then that these are fundamental concepts in our American system of criminal justice?

*COMMENT:* Mississippi attorney William Sebastian Moore uses questions 27–29.

27. ____. If you heard the evidence and you felt that the defendant was probably guilty, that is, you weren't convinced that [*he/she*] was or wasn't, but you thought the evidence showed [*he/she*] *probably* was guilty, would you be able to return a verdict of not guilty?

28. ____. If you do have a reasonable doubt about my client's guilt and, after listening to the arguments of your fellow jurors when you retire to consider the case, you still have that reasonable doubt, will you stick to your guns and refuse to change your verdict, even though it is an unpopular one or might result in a mistrial?

29. ____. Would the inconvenience of having to spend the night away from your home prevent you from sticking to your guns and refusing to change your verdict, if you still had that reasonable doubt about the guilt of this defendant?

## B. "Perry Mason Syndrome" §11.11

1. N ____. The questions I am going to ask you now are about the so-called Perry Mason syndrome. You, among others, have watched the Perry Mason-Erle Stanley Gardner shows, have you not?

2. N ____. Well, there is a Perry Mason syndrome in that Perry Mason, at the last minute, always finds the person who actually did the crime, and it is never his client. He takes on the burden of finding and presenting the guilty person, and pulls the rabbit out of the hat. I have never seen any one of his pictures or books that failed in that regard. You understand that?

3. N ____. Now, you wouldn't expect my client, [*Mr./Ms. Smith*], to prove who [*killed Officer Clark*], would you?

---

B=*Briggs*; C=questions traditionally asked by the trial judge; I=*Michigan v Hartwell*; J=*Michigan v Jeanette Smith*; N=*Huey Newton* case; O=*United States v Sherpix*; P=*Pentagon Papers* case; R=*United States v Satcher*; see §§14.1 and 14.3

4. N ___. That is not [*his/her*] responsibility. Will you accept that as the standard?
5. N ___. And that [*he/she*] doesn't have to do anything except defend [*himself/herself*]. [*He/She*] doesn't have to take responsibility for bringing out the person who did the crime if, in fact, a crime was committed. Do you understand that?

## C. Effect of Security Precautions §11.12

1. N ___. I am going to ask you a question I have not yet asked any of the prospective jurors: Does the fact that you came into this courtroom and saw all these security measures and bailiffs and guns and all of this business—does that create within you a feeling that [*Mr./Ms. Smith*] must be guilty of something or else [*he/she*] wouldn't be subjected to these kinds of security measures?
2. N ___. Do these security measures create a suspicion that there must be something there or they wouldn't be doing all this?

## D. Effect of Defendant's Confinement during Trial §11.13

1. N ___. You know that my client is not out on bail, that [*he/she*] goes back and forth each time the Court recesses, back into the holding cell. Does that in itself create any prejudices against [*him/her*]?

## E. Other Evidentiary Questions §11.14

This section is being reserved for additional questions on evidentiary issues to be presented in supplements to this volume.

# IV. ATTITUDES TOWARD A PARTY/WITNESS

## A. Toward Defendant's Prior Criminal Record §11.20

In jurisdictions in which the law will probably make it possible for the prosecutor to inform the jury that the defendant has a prior conviction, it may be wise to ask question 1.

---

B=*Briggs*; C=questions traditionally asked by the trial judge; I=*Michigan v Hartwell*; J=*Michigan v Jeanette Smith*; N=*Huey Newton* case; O=*United States v Sherpix*; P=*Pentagon Papers* case; R=*United States v Satcher*; see §§14.1 and 14.3

1. N ___. Would the fact that [*Mr./Ms. Smith*] was convicted of a felony at one time, would that conviction cause you to prejudge [*him/her*] and to disregard [*his/her*] testimony?

*COMMENT:* Attorney Dennis Roberts of Oakland, California, uses question 2.

2. ___. On the other hand, should the defendant elect to testify, and should you discover that [*he/she*] had been in trouble with the law before, would you promise to follow the judge's instructions—that you may *only* consider this previous trouble as a factor in your determination of [*his/her*] credibility as a witness?

*COMMENT:* Attorney Theodore Koskoff of Connecticut states: "Some cases present special problems on the voir dire. If you have an accused whose prior record is likely to come out during the course of the trial, this must be dealt with on voir dire," and he suggests question 3.

3. ___. The judge will tell you that [*his/her*] prior record may be used by you only in the matter of assessing the accused's credibility, but, despite what the judge tells you, would you nevertheless feel, because of [*his/her*] record, that [*he/she*] is more likely to have committed this crime with which [*he/she*] is charged?

## B. Toward Credibility of Defendant §11.21

1. J ___. What is your impression of [*Mrs. Smith*], knowing that [*she*] is on trial here for [*murder*]?
   a. Why is that?
2. N ___. Would you take the attitude that the defendant is on trial here for [*his/her*] [*life/freedom*], so when [*he/she*] takes that witness stand, would you say, "Well, [*he/she*] is liable to say anything because [*he/she*] is on trial for [*his/her*] [*life/freedom*], and I am not going to believe [*him/her*]"?
3. N ___. Would you say that the defendant would be grasping for [*his/her*] [*life/freedom*] and [*he/she*] is liable to catch onto any straws that may come [*his/her*] way?
4. J ___. Do you feel that you would give [*his/her*] testimony the same serious consideration as any other witness's?

---

B=*Briggs*; C=questions traditionally asked by the trial judge; I=*Michigan v Hartwell*; J=*Michigan v Jeanette Smith*; N=*Huey Newton* case; O=*United States v Sherpix*; P=*Pentagon Papers* case; R=*United States v Satcher*; see §§14.1 and 14.3

## C. Toward Counsel for Both Sides §11.22

1. B ___. Some of the defendants will be representing themselves in this case. How will you feel about this?
2. C ___. You are not going to give any more weight to the arguments of my adversary than to mine merely because [*he/she*] bears the impressive title "district attorney," are you?
3. C ___. The District Attorney is referred to as "The people of the state of [*Name of state*]." Actually everybody in the room is "the people." We are the people, not just the D.A. The D.A. is just an employee. Do you agree?

## D. Other Issues §11.23

This section is being reserved for additional questions on parties and witnesses to be presented in supplements to this volume.

# V. ATTITUDES TOWARD MOST DAMAGING FEATURE OF CASE

## A. Pictures/Photographs §11.26

A shocking photo or painting is less shocking the second time it is observed or described than the first, whether in a European art gallery or a porno movie house. Words that become commonplace are not shocking although they may remain offensive.

This principle governs the voir dire of jurors in obscenity cases. If the lawyer, during voir dire, can first establish professionalism and basic decency and then can use the words or describe the scene that will be testified to later, much of the shock value will be blunted. See model questions for an obscenity trial in §§11.34–11.36.

1. J ___. During the course of the trial, the prosecution will present evidence that includes pictures of [*Mr. Smith*] after [*he*] died, and [*a knife*] that was used in the [*stabbing*]. How do you think this type of evidence would affect your judgment of the case as a whole?
   a. Would these pictures make it difficult for you to keep an open mind?

---

B=*Briggs*; C=questions traditionally asked by the trial judge; I=*Michigan v Hartwell*; J=*Michigan v Jeanette Smith*; N=*Huey Newton* case; O=*United States v Sherpix*; P=*Pentagon Papers* case; R=*United States v Satcher*; see §§14.1 and 14.3

b. Do you have any reservations about serving as a juror, knowing that you would have to look at that type of evidence?

## B. Women Charged with Acts of Violence

### 1. Talking to Jurors about Physical Violence §11.27

The problem for the lawyer defending a woman charged with violent crime is that most prospective jurors find it more difficult to find the humanity in such a woman than to find the humanity in a man facing a similar charge. The men and women on the jury cannot be true peers of the defendant. A peer, strictly speaking, would be another woman charged with a similar crime. Instead, the jury box will contain men and women who have never even been in a serious scrape with the law, let alone taken up an axe or bomb or knife.

The customary weapon used by women in our society is speech. When the State charges a woman with using a weapon of violence, women jurors may feel that the very image of womankind is in the dock, and that it is necessary to convict and punish the defendant in order to set a good example. Defense counsel may need to discuss with prospective jurors the nature of physical violence, the concept of women as equal members of society, and the circumstances of the specific defendant that led her to act.

The problem for the defense lawyer is that white middle- and upper-class jurors are much more afraid of physical violence than of psychological and economic violence (such as the decision to lay off large numbers of workers and simultaneously to lobby against increased unemployment compensation). All jurors who value human life recognize that the effects of physical violence are more often irreversible than the effects of psychic or economic violence. This conclusion is undoubtedly good for society. Physical violence cannot be a way of life; it is a way of death and destruction. But throughout history people have destroyed some institutions and some people by violence in order to permit human progress that the institutions or individuals had thwarted.

The most convinced Quaker can be a good juror in a case involving violent crime if the defense lawyer has a sound understanding of the nature and causes of violence in general and the facts to support the particular client's defense. A defense lawyer has the right, and the need, to dispel false notions held by many jurors that violence is committed only by "them"—that "decent God-fearing men and women" do not take up weapons against individuals or groups. (What about the

Minute Men of 1776?) This is imperative when the defendant is a woman.

Unless all of this is raised with the jury on voir dire before any evidence has been introduced, the jurors may hear only the evidence for the prosecution and never permit themselves to hear evidence for the defendant, whether it is evidence that her confession was not voluntarily given, that she did not do the act charged, that she acted without intent, or that she had to act in self-defense. See §§11.51–11.54.

## 2. Women and Violence §11.28

A woman charged with violent crime, such as attacking someone with a gun or throwing a bomb, is highly upsetting to believers in the old-fashioned image of women. Violent women abound in our history: Bonnie (not "over the ocean," but "and Clyde"), Carrie Nation (who used an axe—against saloons, but nonetheless, an axe), Good Queen Bess (who arranged to have heads cut off with some regularity), even Marie Antoinette (whose dainty mind could conceive of people starving to death by the thousands). Did Maid Marian always stand demurely under that greenwood tree while Robin held up the wealthy? Western culture has even permitted itself one bloodthirsty heroine, Joan of Arc, although she may be acceptable only because she acted in defense of her country at the call of heavenly "voices" and perished in a wall of flame lighted by the men she challenged. For a refreshing and eye-opening reconsideration of this, and related questions, see Mary Beard, *Women as a Force in History* (1971).

In fact, in every revolt or war in which people have tried to gain a new right or retain an old one, women have fought beside and in place of men, from the Revolutionary War to the underground railroad before the Civil War, the Haymarket, the Ford hunger march, World War II, and the struggle to get the United States out of Vietnam, to list only a few examples in our country's history. The weapons women used were numerous, and they were not limited to their tongues and their wits.

In personal disputes, women, like men, have attacked relatives, friends, enemies, and strangers. Their motives have been as typical, and as bizarre, as the motives of men. Their ability to explain their true motives has been no greater than, and has faltered as often as, men's.

Some people think the main difference between men and women in their commission of acts of violence may be that women tend to value life more (perhaps because they are so intimately connected with its creation), and have therefore committed fewer such acts. The number of women charged with violent crimes is smaller, but the acts they have committed have not necessarily been less violent than the acts of men. (It is appropriate to ponder why the number of women convicted of violent crimes is rising at this time in the United States, and what, if anything, conscientious male and female lawyers and judges should be doing about it. But that discussion belongs elsewhere. See, e.g., "Female Offenders—A Challenge to the Courts and the Legislature," 51 *ND L Rev* 827 (1975).)

### 3. Need for Extensive Voir Dire §11.29

All the customary reasons for needing extensive voir dire are compounded when the defendant is a woman charged with a violent and highly publicized crime.

Susan Saxe described herself as a "revolutionary, a feminist, an amazon and lesbian" after pleading guilty to possession of firearms in Philadelphia. Soon after, she faced trial for robbery and first-degree murder in Massachusetts, where state and federal practice at that time prohibited lawyer-conducted voir dire (Massachusetts General Laws, chap 234, §28). The defense sought a dismissal of the indictment on the basis of saturation media coverage of Saxe, demonstrated by opinion polls in the trial jurisdiction. In the extensive hearing on the motion, Dr. Jay Schulman criticized the inadequacy of the voir dire customarily conducted by the trial judge. The judge refused to dismiss before voir dire. But he used the court's "inherent power to order changes for the purpose of securing a fair trial" to allow some attorney-conducted voir dire (as well as 16 additional peremptory challenges for the defense only), stating:

> it has been this court's experience that the great majority of potential jurors, impressed, even awed, by the seriousness and importance of their possible function, speak honestly and frankly about any prejudice or bias in the course of voir dire examination. Furthermore, this court must determine what is in their minds, what they, and the public in general, believe for they ultimately are the ones to establish guilt or innocence. With this in mind, and in addition to the extraordinary and unusual measures set out above, this court is convinced that there can be no substitute for a thorough and searching voir dire examination to determine the existence of prejudice.

For facts and full opinion, see §§7.68 and 8.67. Compare the numerous examples of prejudiced jurors consciously hiding their prejudices during short voir dires in typical, nonheadline cases, reported in Broeder, "Voir Dire Examinations: An Empirical Study," 38 *S Cal L Rev* 503 (1965).

In *Saxe*, the defense did not seek a change of venue or delay of trial, but conducted an extensive voir dire. The jury was deadlocked at nine to three for acquittal.

#### 4. Other Issues §11.30

This section is being reserved for additional questions on women charged with acts of violence, to be presented in supplements to this volume.

### C. Other Features §11.31

See §11.30.

## VI. ATTITUDES TOWARD SPECIFIC CRIME CHARGED

### A. Conspiracy §11.33

In conspiracy cases and cases involving multiple defendants, defense counsel Theodore Koskoff of Connecticut proposed one approach at an American Trial Lawyers Association seminar:

> The special problems existent in defending multiple defendant cases, multiple charge cases, and conspiracy cases are problems that, wherever possible, should be exposed and dealt with in the voir dire. The nature of the conspiracy charge and the trial itself always taxes the ingenuity and resourcefulness of the trial lawyer.
>
> Despite the fact that *Bruton v United States* (1968) 391 US 123, held that, during a joint trial of co-conspirators, a codefendant's confession inculpating the defendant violates that defendant's Sixth Amendment rights (confrontation clause) and is not admissible despite limiting instructions, many problems remain with testimony of co-conspirators and the whole concept of conspiracy that should be explored on voir dire.
>
> One of the problems that immediately comes to mind is the common one raised when a co-conspirator pleads guilty and turns state's evidence. In many, if not most, states the plea of guilty by a codefendant is not admissible in evidence on *behalf of the State* in a prosecution against another co-conspirator. I believe in bringing that fact out on behalf of the accused. Ask the jury what effect that plea would have on the guilt or innocence of your client. During the trial and in your summation you will probably be able to show how the testimony of such a person is tainted with promises or expectations of leniency if his testimony shapes up properly. Indeed, the court will charge that such testimony is suspect and particularly where the co-conspirator has not yet been sentenced, you will get an instruction from the court that will help you. So by all means, on voir dire go into these facts.
>
> Many courts do not permit voir dire questions where the questions are framed

as questions of law. Framed in other contexts, they may be admitted. The education of the jury is essential in conspiracy cases. The following subjects should, wherever possible, be covered on voir dire in a conspiracy or multiple defendant case:

A. Where an act is capable of two interpretations, one consistent with guilt and the other consistent with innocence, jurors must draw the inference consistent with innocence. *United States v Currier Lumber Co.* (D Mass 1947) 70 F Supp 219, 221.

B. In considering whether a defendant was a member of the conspiracy, they must do so independently of statements made by others. *United States v Schneiderman* (SD Cal 1952) 106 F Supp 906, 936.

C. If conspiracy has been established, it must be determined that the defendant unlawfully, knowingly and willfully entered into it. The defendant is entitled to an individual judgment on this. *United States v Gisehaltz* (SD NY 1967) 278 F Supp 434, 437.

D. The jury must find that acts of other conspirators were within the scope of the conspiracy and in furtherance of it; the scope of the conspiracy cannot be enlarged by others. *United States v Crimmins* (2d Cir 1941) 123 F2d 271, 273.

E. Guilty intent is necessary, and a defendant does not become a party to aiding and abetting the conspiracy unless he knew of it. *Direct Sales v United States* (1943) 319 US 703, 709.

F. Mere association with conspirators is an insufficient basis for a finding of participation. *United States v Stromberg* (2d Cir 1959) 268 F2d 256, 267.

G. There must be something more than mere knowledge, approval of, or acquiescence in the object of the conspiracy. *Cleaver v United States* (10th Cir 1956) 238 F2d 766, 771. "Something more" is usually defined as a "stake in the venture." *United States v Cianchetti* (2d Cir 1963) 315 F2d 584, 588.

## B. Obscenity or Pornography

### 1. Current Law §11.34

Because the law in this field changes frequently, and because national and community standards change from time to time, trial lawyers must keep abreast of both kinds of developments before preparing voir dire questions in a particular case.

Some pornography cases raise side issues, and sometimes other charges raise pornography issues. For example, in *United States v Thevis*, the trial judge refused to disqualify jurors who thought it was morally wrong to be in the pornography business. He did ask the jurors: "Would you have a problem, because of the nature of the charges, in being fair to the defendants?" Then he explained, "This is not a pornography case. This is a charge of racketeering." *NY Times*, Aug. 21, 1979. Defendants were convicted. *NY Times*, Oct. 22, 1979.

## 2. Involving a Movie §11.35

The following questions were prepared by attorneys Michael Kennedy of New York; Joseph Rhine of San Francisco; and Lionel Epstein, Alvin Friedman, Charles Duncan, and Richard Medalie of Washington, D.C., for use in *United States v Sherpix* (DC DC, No. 268–73, Oct. 1, 1973), a movie obscenity case. The trial resulted in a hung jury.

1. O ___. Have you ever passed or noticed the [*Trans-Lux*] Theatre on [*14th and H Streets, N.W.*] in [*Washington, D.C.*]?
   [*If so*]
   a. Has anything about the exterior of this theatre shocked or offended you in any way?
2. O ___. Have you had occasion to pass any other so-called adult theatres in [*Washington, D.C.*]?
3. O ___. Are you offended by the existence or location of any of these so-called adult theatres?
4. O ___. Does it disturb or bother you that adults in [*Washington, D.C.*] patronize these theatres?
5. O ___. Have you seen any of the advertisements of any of these so-called adult theatres?
   [*If so*]
   a. Has there been anything about the nature or content of the advertisements that has offended you?
6. O ___. Have you read anything about the film [*"Hot Circuit"*]?
7. O ___. Have you had occasion to discuss the film [*"Hot Circuit"*] with anyone?
8. O ___. Do you feel that the availability of sexually explicit or graphic materials is on the increase or the decrease as far as [*Washington, D.C.*] is concerned?
9. O ___. If you feel the availability of sexually explicit materials is on the increase, does this fact disturb or offend you?
10. O ___. Have you personally ever been exposed or have you known of persons who were exposed to sexually explicit or graphic materials?
11. O ___. Have you ever known of anyone being harmed or hurt in any way by exposure to sexually explicit or graphic materials?
12. O ___. Do you know of any evidence or information that indicates a

---

B=*Briggs*; C=questions traditionally asked by the trial judge; I=*Michigan v Hartwell*; J=*Michigan v Jeanette Smith*; N=*Huey Newton* case; O=*United States v Sherpix*; P=*Pentagon Papers* case; R=*United States v Satcher*; see §§14.1 and 14.3

causal connection between exposure to sexually explicit materials and antisocial sexual behavior?

13. O ___. Do you feel that it is appropriate to have one standard of obscenity for adults and another standard for minors?

14. O ___. Do you realize that we deal here exclusively with adults and an adult standard?

15. O ___. Does the fact that our client earns his living and supports his family by occasionally distributing adult films for adults-only theatres disturb or offend you?

16. O ___. Will you be able to treat our client as fairly and impartially as you would treat any other businessman?

17. O ___. Do you belong to any religious, fraternal, political or social organization that has taken a stand on the issue of obscenity or pornography?

18. O ___. If chosen to sit as a juror you will be caused to view a film wherein certain sexual activity is graphically and explicitly portrayed. Does this prospect cause you any discomfort or embarrassment?

19. O ___. Will you be able to view a film, portions of which contain sexually explicit activities, including [*sexual intercourse/mouth and genital contact/ejaculation/homosexual activity/and group sex*], with open eyes and an open mind?

20. O ___. Will you base your judgment about the merits of the film exclusively on the film itself and the evidence as presented here in court and not on your own personal taste and personal standard of what may or may not be obscene?

21. O ___. Do you presently have an opinion about what materials adults should be allowed to see or read?

22. O ___. Will you be able to set aside that opinion and judge this film based on the evidence?

23. O ___. Is there anything about the nature of the charges here, namely showing an allegedly obscene film, that causes you to believe you could not sit as a fair and impartial juror?

24. O ___. Have you read about or heard about any polls, surveys, or studies taken with reference to American adults' views on obscenity or pornography?

25. O ___. Is there anything about your religious background or present

B=*Briggs*; C=questions traditionally asked by the trial judge; I=*Michigan v Hartwell*; J=*Michigan v Jeanette Smith*; N=*Huey Newton* case; O=*United States v Sherpix*; P=*Pentagon Papers* case; R=*United States v Satcher*; see §§14.1 and 14.3

moral views that you feel might affect your judgment in this case?

### 3. Involving Dancing §11.36

In the case of a woman charged with obscene dancing in a live public show, Michael S. Rose of Milwaukie, Oregon, asked the following questions, which he felt elicited some good responses from the prospective jurors. The six-person jury was composed of five men (40 to 55 years of age, one black) and one Native American woman. The black man was chosen foreperson, and after one hour of deliberation, the jury returned a "not guilty" verdict.

1. ____. Do you think the fact that someone would perform naked on stage says anything about that person?
2. ____. On a gut level, do you make any generalizations about the person?
3. ____. What kind of person do you think would dance naked on a stage?
4. ____. Why do you think someone would perform in a show like that?

*COMMENT:* The typical answer was "She's probably broke and needs the money."

5. ____. What don't you like about most TV programming?
6. ____. Have you heard of the "Family Hour" during prime time? [*If yes*]
   a. What do you think about it?

*COMMENT:* These two questions elicited lengthy discussions on sex and violence on TV with several prospective jurors who felt that kind of programming should only be available after children go to bed.

7. ____. What kind of person do you think *really* reads *Playboy*?

## C. Drunk Driving §11.37

Attorney James Herndon of San Francisco finds the following questions useful in drunk driving cases.

---

B=*Briggs*; C=questions traditionally asked by the trial judge; I=*Michigan v Hartwell*; J=*Michigan v Jeanette Smith*; N=*Huey Newton* case; O=*United States v Sherpix*; P=*Pentagon Papers* case; R=*United States v Satcher*; see §§14.1 and 14.3

1. ___. Do you feel that one who drinks alcohol and then drives a car has violated the law, regardless of the effect on him or the amount he consumed?
2. ___. It is often said, "If you drive, don't drink; and if you drink, don't drive." You know that it is not unlawful to drink alcohol in [*California*]?
3. ___. You know that it is not unlawful to drive a car after taking a drink of alcohol, as long as the alcohol does not affect the ability of the driver to operate the vehicle in the manner of an ordinary reasonable person?
4. ___. You would not find my client guilty simply because [*he/she*] drank and then drove a car, would you?
5. ___. Will you wait until all the evidence showing every element of the crime is presented before you reach a decision in this case?
6. ___. Do you drink on social occasions?
7. ___. Do you object to others taking a social drink?
8. ___. Have you ever been a member or supporter of any group that seeks to prohibit the sale or use of alcoholic beverages?
9. ___. Do you know anything about breath analyzing machines?
10. ___. Have you had any experience with such machines?
11. ___. Do you drive an automobile?
    [*If no*]
    a. Is there any reason why you do not?

## D. Bank Robbery §11.38

These questions were prepared by attorney Michael Weiss of San Francisco for use in *United States v Satcher* (ND Cal, No. Cr. 73–0735–OJC, May 7, 1974). Earl La Mar Satcher, a black man, was indicted on charges of bank robbery. Four white women were also implicated.

1. R ___. Do you know anyone who works in a bank?
   [*If yes*]
   a. Would that fact affect your judgment in this case?
2. R ___. Have you heard, read, etc., anything regarding an "integrated" bank robbery that took place in [*Berkeley*] before you came into court today?

B=*Briggs*; C=questions traditionally asked by the trial judge; I=*Michigan v Hartwell*; J=*Michigan v Jeanette Smith*; N=*Huey Newton* case; O=*United States v Sherpix*; P=*Pentagon Papers* case; R=*United States v Satcher*; see §§14.1 and 14.3

[*If yes*]
a. What do you remember?

3. R ___. Did the fact that four young, attractive, white women participated in a bank robbery and were armed shock you?

4. R ___. Have you seen or heard publicity of a bank robbery involving white women and a black man in which Patricia Hearst was involved?
[*If yes*]
a. Would the fact that this bank robbery was similar affect your ability to judge this case?

*COMMENT:* At the conclusion of the trial, the judge directed a verdict of acquittal.

## E. Sex Perversion §11.39

Attorney Steven A. Chase, of San Bruno, California, uses the following type of question in the voir dire of women jurors when the defendant is charged with an act of sexual perversion:

1. ___. Ms. [*Jones*], as you know already, this case deals with what the law refers to as sex perversion. The facts in this case, and the testimony of [*John Smith*], may turn your stomach, but as an impartial trier of the facts, you mustn't let your repulsion about what happened affect your decision as to whether or not it was my client, Mr. [*Doe*], who actually committed this horrible act. Now, may I have your assurance that this factor will not enter into your deliberations on the question of the identity of the person who committed this act?

## F. Drug Offenses

### 1. Marijuana §11.40

Attorney Michael E. Rose of Milwaukie, Oregon, represented a defendant charged with possession, sale, and conspiracy to sell marijuana found in a closed box in the trunk of the car the defendant was driving. Rose asked the following voir dire questions, and the conspiracy charge was dismissed after the State rested; the other two counts ended in a mistrial.

---

B=*Briggs*; C=questions traditionally asked by the trial judge; I=*Michigan v Hartwell*; J=*Michigan v Jeanette Smith*; N=*Huey Newton* case; O=*United States v Sherpix*; P=*Pentagon Papers* case; R=*United States v Satcher*; see §§14.1 and 14.3

1. ___. What kinds of people do you think smoke marijuana?

*COMMENT:* Prospective jurors typically responded that they thought people from all walks of life smoke marijuana. Attorney Rose continued:

2. ___. So you don't think you can tell anything about a person simply because he or she may smoke marijuana?
3. ___. Do you think marijuana use is a serious problem in our society?
4. ___. Have you ever talked with anyone about marijuana?
   [*If yes*]
   a. What did you talk about?
5. ___. What do you think about recent efforts to legalize marijuana, for example, an initiative to legalize the cultivation of marijuana for personal use, which appeared in [*Oregon*] on the ballot in [*November 1980*]?
6. ___. Did you know that 500 years ago, people thought tomatoes were poisonous and the earth was flat?
7. ___. You realize, of course, that whatever feelings you might have about marijuana should play no part in your consideration of this case?
8. ___. Have you ever driven anyone to the airport or train station?
   [*If yes*]
   a. Did you put [*his/her*] luggage in the trunk of your car?
   b. Did you ever open the luggage to see what was inside?

### 2. Other Drugs §11.41

This section is being reserved for questions on other drugs, to be presented in supplements to this volume.

## G. Other Crimes §11.45

This section is being reserved for questions on attitudes toward other crimes, to be presented in supplements to this volume.

# VII. ATTITUDES TOWARD SPECIFIC DEFENSES

## A. Self-Defense §11.51

The following questions were asked in *Michigan v Hartwell* (see §3.31).

---

B=*Briggs*; C=questions traditionally asked by the trial judge; I=*Michigan v Hartwell*; J=*Michigan v Jeanette Smith*; N=*Huey Newton* case; O=*United States v Sherpix*; P=*Pentagon Papers* case; R=*United States v Satcher*; see §§14.1 and 14.3

1. I ___. Have any of you ever been assaulted or has any member of your family or a close friend ever been involved in an assault?
2. I ___. Have any of you ever been jurors in an assault trial?
3. I ___. Do you understand that if you decide that the murder of [*Victim*] was justifiable, you must return a verdict of not guilty?
4. I ___. Do you understand that you can make the determination, after being so instructed by the judge, that a stabbing in self-defense is justifiable?
5. I ___. If you were told that a person who is attacked in [*her*] own home does not have to retreat, does not have to find a place to flee to, and can use all means up to physical means to the point of death to repel an attack—if you were told that is the law in this case, would you be able to abide by that law?
6. I ___. If you found that the defendant acted in self-defense, and used physical means to the point of [*stabbing and killing* [*Victim*]] to protect [*her*]self [*in her own home*], and you were instructed that that was the law and you had to apply it, and you believed that the defendant's testimony was credible, would you then return a verdict of not guilty?
7. I ___. Do you think that a person should be entitled to defend [*her*]self?
8. I ___. Is the concept of self-defense one you can abide, or does it trouble you?
9. I ___. Would you have any problem invoking self-defense if you were assaulted?
10. I ___. Do you believe that a [*woman*] should be allowed to protect [*her*]self from an assault by [*her husband*]?

In a case similar to *Hartwell*, defendant was acquitted by a 12-person jury of second degree murder for the fatal stabbing of her husband. *Michigan v Jeanette Smith* (Kalkasa County Cir Ct, No. 416, April 1979); see §9.66. Defendant was repeatedly battered by her husband during their relationship. The following questions were asked by Dean Robb, counsel for Smith.

1. J ___. What comes to mind when you hear the term, "self-defense"? What does the term mean to you?
2. J ___. Can you think of a situation in which a person would be justified in killing someone?
   [*If yes*]
   a. Give me an example.

B=*Briggs*; C=questions traditionally asked by the trial judge; I=*Michigan v Hartwell*; J=*Michigan v Jeanette Smith*; N=*Huey Newton* case; O=*United States v Sherpix*; P=*Pentagon Papers* case; R=*United States v Satcher*; see §§14.1 and 14.3

[*If no*]

b. Do you have any religious or moral beliefs that a person does not have the right to kill another, even in self-defense?

3\. J ___. Do you think that a person who kills someone should be punished for that action, no matter what the circumstances?

a. Why do you say that?

4\. J ___. Have you ever been in a situation where you had to defend yourself, or thought you might have to defend yourself?

[*If yes*]

a. What happened?

[*If no*]

b. If someone were hitting you, how would you defend yourself?

5\. J ___. Could you use a weapon in self-defense?

6\. J ___. Have you ever been frightened by someone who was acting crazy or irrational?

[*If yes*]

a. What were the circumstances?

[*If no*]

b. How do you think you would handle a situation like that?

7\. J ___. Do you think that a woman would be able to judge if her life were in danger when she was being physically attacked, or do you think women typically overreact in such situations?

a. Why do you say that?

8\. J ___. To what extent does a woman have the right to defend herself if she is being physically attacked or abused?

[*Follow up if necessary*]

a. The judge will give you the law that applies to these situations, but I'm interested in your own beliefs about this type of situation.

9\. J ___. In a life-threatening situation, do you think a woman would use the same means to protect herself as a man would use?

a. [*Why/why not?*]

10\. J ___. Do you think there are situations where a woman would need to use a weapon, and a man would be able to defend himself without one?

11\. J ___. [*To men*] Have you ever arm wrestled with a woman?

---

B=*Briggs*; C=questions traditionally asked by the trial judge; I=*Michigan v Hartwell*; J=*Michigan v Jeanette Smith*; N=*Huey Newton* case; O=*United States v Sherpix*; P=*Pentagon Papers* case; R=*United States v Satcher*; see §§14.1 and 14.3

[*If yes*]
a. Have you ever been beaten by a woman?

12. J ___. [*To women*] Have you ever arm wrestled with a man?
[*If yes*]
a. What happened?
[*If no*]
b. Do you think you could win?

13. J ___. The judge will tell you that the law states that people are justified in using force to defend themselves against the threat of death or serious bodily harm, if their use of force seemed reasonable under the circumstances. Do you think you will be able to consider the circumstances from Mrs. [*Smith*]'s point of view in this case?

14. J ___. Do you understand that you are not being asked to approve of Mrs. [*Smith*]'s actions, but rather to judge whether her actions were reasonable from her point of view?

15. J ___. If after receiving the evidence, you determine that Mrs. [*Smith*] acted in self-defense, would you have any problem voting not guilty?
a. Would your own feelings about the use of weapons make this difficult for you in any way?

## B. Sexual Harassment

### 1. Rape §11.52

Inez Garcia was charged with murder of a man who, she testified, had forced her into sexual relations half an hour earlier. The prosecution repeatedly commented on the length of time between the rape and the defendant's reaction, and the jury convicted her of second-degree murder. The defendant won a new trial because the trial judge committed error in the jury instructions on proof beyond a reasonable doubt. *California v Garcia* (Dist Ct App 1975) 126 Cal Rptr 275. In the defendant's second trial, in February 1977, defense counsel used the discussion in *Washington v Wanrow* (see §4.23) on the need to evaluate the justification of self-defense in light of all facts known to the defendant, including those known "substantially before the killing." The second jury acquitted Garcia in 1977.

---

B=*Briggs*; C=questions traditionally asked by the trial judge; I=*Michigan v Hartwell*; J=*Michigan v Jeanette Smith*; N=*Huey Newton* case; O=*United States v Sherpix*; P=*Pentagon Papers* case; R=*United States v Satcher*; see §§14.1 and 14.3

## 2. Assault by Husband §11.53

The following questions were asked in *Michigan v Hartwell* (see §3.31).

1. I ___. Do you believe that a woman should be allowed to protect herself from an assault by her husband?
2. I ___. Do you believe that a woman should be made to perform any sexual act her husband wants to indulge in?
3. I ___. Do you believe that a woman should be submissive to her husband's abuse of her, both mentally and physically and sexually, to the point of jeopardizing her mental or physical well-being?

Defense attorneys in *Hartwell* conducted an extensive voir dire on assault, self-defense, and sexual abuse. After the evidence was in, Circuit Judge Victor J. Baum gave the following instructions on these subjects:

Let me turn now to the matter of defense against a sexual attack or sexual advance. We are going to be dealing with this matter in a special context, and that is in the context of a defense of self-defense which is made in a case in which the defendant is charged with using force, fatal force, against a husband. I am not giving you rules of law which have general application. What I am saying regarding resistance to a sexual advance applies only to this case and cases like it. What I say has no application in divorce cases and may not even be applicable to the prosecution of a husband for assault on his wife, sexual or nonsexual. For purposes of this case, a married woman has the right to resist overtures by her husband to have sexual relations, whether of a conventional or an unusual nature. A married woman is not compelled by law to submit against her will to sexual contact which she finds offensive. She does not make herself an aggressor by resisting offensive sexual contact.

However, the law limits the amount and kind of resistance to that which she reasonably and honestly believes to be necessary to turn away the unwanted sexual overture.

If she honestly and reasonably believes that mere verbal resistance will accomplish this purpose, she may not use physical force. On the other hand, if she reasonably and honestly believes that the use of physical force is necessary to repel the sexual advance, she may lawfully use the amount of force which she honestly and reasonably believes is necessary. However, she may not use force which is likely to kill, unless she reasonably and honestly believes

---

B=*Briggs*; C=questions traditionally asked by the trial judge; I=*Michigan v Hartwell*; J=*Michigan v Jeanette Smith*; N=*Huey Newton* case; O=*United States v Sherpix*; P=*Pentagon Papers* case; R=*United States v Satcher*; see §§14.1 and 14.3

that she is in danger of losing her own life or suffering great bodily harm at the hands of her husband.

You see that a wife's right to use fatal force in resisting a sexual advance merges with the right to use deadly force in defense of her own life.

Thus, a married woman may not lawfully resist a husband's verbal overture for sexual contact with force, but if he becomes physically aggressive, she may offer physical resistance; and if she honestly and reasonably believes that he is about to inflict grievous bodily harm or to kill her, she may resist with lethal force. She is to be judged by the circumstances as they reasonably and honestly appear to her during the moment or moments of violence.

Let me talk now about character and reputation as it applies to self-defense.

There has been testimony in this case as to the strength, temper, and personal qualities of both, Judy Hartwell, the defendant, and Fred Hartwell, the deceased. Such testimony was received from witnesses personally familiar with both of the parties involved.

There has been additional testimony as to Fred Hartwell's reputation for being of a quarrelsome and turbulent character, especially when he consumed alcohol.

Such evidence is not direct evidence of the conduct of the parties on November 9, 1975, but it is relevant for your consideration in judging whether or not Fred Hartwell was the aggressor just prior to the fatal fight on November 9, 1975. You are to consider this testimony and give it the weight that you think it deserves in trying to establish who was in fact the aggressor.

You are also to consider such evidence in determining whether Judy Hartwell was reasonable in her belief that she was in fear of death or bodily harm.

Remember that legitimate self-defense is a complete defense to the charge of murder in the second degree.

If the Prosecutor does not prove each and every element of the offense of murder in the second degree beyond a reasonable doubt, it is your duty to acquit the defendant.

## 3. Battery by Husband

### a. Wife Abuse §11.54

1. J ___. Have you ever heard of the term, "wife abuse"?
   [*If yes*]
   a. What does the term mean to you?
2. J ___. Do you know of women who have been beaten by their husbands?

---

B=*Briggs*; C=questions traditionally asked by the trial judge; I=*Michigan v Hartwell*; J=*Michigan v Jeanette Smith*; N=*Huey Newton* case; O=*United States v Sherpix*; P=*Pentagon Papers* case; R=*United States v Satcher*; see §§14.1 and 14.3

[*If yes*]
a. Without going into the names of the people involved, could you tell me a little more about that situation?

3. J ____. Do you feel that wife abuse is a problem in this community?
a. Are you aware of social service programs in the local area that provide assistance for women who have been abused?

4. J ____. Have you seen any TV programs or news stories about women who have been abused?
[*If yes*]
a. What have you seen?
b. What was your reaction?

5. J ____. Do you think women might tend to exaggerate the seriousness of physical abuse, or beatings, by their husbands?

6. J ____. Some people think that a woman who is beaten over and over again has only herself to blame. What do you think about that?

7. J ____. Can you think of any reasons why a woman who was beaten by her husband would be unable to leave him?
[*If yes*]
a. Could you give me an example?
[*If no*]
b. Why do you say that?

8. J ____. Do you feel that a man usually wouldn't hit his wife unless she deserved it?
[*If yes*]
a. Could you give me an example?

9. J ____. Have you ever seen a man hit a woman?
[*If yes*]
a. What happened?
b. What was *your* reaction?

10. J ____. As you know, the legal term for the use of physical force against another person is assault. Do you think there is a difference between wife abuse and other cases of assault?
a. Why do you say that?

11. J ____. Have you ever heard the expression, "A man's home is his castle"?
a. What is your reaction when you hear that phrase?
b. Why do you think people say that?
c. Do you agree with that idea?
d. [*Why/why not?*]

---

B=*Briggs*; C=questions traditionally asked by the trial judge; I=*Michigan v Hartwell*; J=*Michigan v Jeanette Smith*; N=*Huey Newton* case; O=*United States v Sherpix*; P=*Pentagon Papers* case; R=*United States v Satcher*; see §§14.1 and 14.3

12. J ____. Some people think a woman has an obligation to stay with her husband—no matter what happens—because marriage is a life-long commitment. What do you think about that?

13. J ____. Have you ever known a person who was unable to leave an unhappy marriage or relationship?
[*If yes*]
a. Why do you think [*he/she*] was unable to leave?
b. What were your feelings about that situation?

14. J ____. Do you think a man is ever justified in hitting his wife?

15. J ____. Some people think that a certain amount of physical force is acceptable in family arguments. What do you think about that?

16. J ____. Have people ever talked to you about their own experiences of being hit or beaten by a spouse or by their parents?
[*If yes*]
a. What was your reaction?

17. J ____. Do you feel that family problems are private matters that should not be discussed outside the family?

18. J ____. Are you familiar with any situations in which a husband has been accused of sexually abusing his wife?

19. J ____. Do you feel that women should be legally protected from sexual abuse in their marital relationship?
a. [*Why/why not?*]

*COMMENT:* See Eisenberg and Seymour, "Defending Battered Women: A Model Voir Dire," 16 *Trial* 30 (1980).

### b. Psychological Testimony §11.55

1. J ____. The defense may present some testimony by a psychologist who is an expert in the area of wife abuse problems. Do you know anyone who is a psychologist, or works as some other type of counselor?
[*If yes*]
a. What type of work does [*he/she*] do?

2. J ____. Have you or any member of your family ever used the services of a psychologist or counselor?
[*If yes*]
a. Did you feel that the psychologist was helpful?

3. J ____. Do you think that psychologists are qualified to analyze and explain why people behave in certain ways?

---

B=*Briggs*; C=questions traditionally asked by the trial judge; I=*Michigan v Hartwell*; J=*Michigan v Jeanette Smith*; N=*Huey Newton* case; O=*United States v Sherpix*; P=*Pentagon Papers* case; R=*United States v Satcher*; see §§14.1 and 14.3

4. J ___. Have you ever read any books or magazine articles written by psychologists?
[*If yes*]
a. What was the [*book/article*] about?
b. Did you find the information useful?

### c. Police Testimony §11.56

1. J ___. The defense may also present some expert testimony on the methods used by police officers in handling the problem of wife abuse. Have you ever heard any criticism of the way the police handle these problems?
[*If yes*]
a. What was said?
b. Did you think it was justified?

2. ___. Did you hear about the California case in which a jury awarded three million dollars to the families of two black men slain in their bedrooms by white police officers who were called to quell a family disturbance? [*Roman and Guillory v City of Richmond, Richmond Police Department, et al.* (ND Cal, C80–4702 and C82–0142 RPA, June 3, 1983)]
[*If yes*]
a. What did you think about that verdict?

3. J ___. In general, do you think that it is appropriate to question or criticize the behavior of police officers?
a. [*Why/why not?*]

## C. Defense of Necessity or Lesser Evil §11.57

Protesters against nuclear war and development of nuclear and other weapons often try to use the defense of necessity to justify their actions. These efforts, if successful, permit testimony going to the substance of defendants' beliefs and motivations, including expert testimony on the rationality of defendants' actions, i.e., that the threat of nuclear accidents or nuclear war is real. This means that voir dire questions on these issues are relevant.

The intermediate appellate court in Pennsylvania reversed the convictions of protesters against nuclear weapons and nuclear power who

B=*Briggs*; C=questions traditionally asked by the trial judge; I=*Michigan v Hartwell*; J=*Michigan v Jeanette Smith*; N=*Huey Newton* case; O=*United States v Sherpix*; P=*Pentagon Papers* case; R=*United States v Satcher*; see §§14.1 and 14.3

had been denied the right to use the defense of necessity by the trial judge. *Pennsylvania v Berrigan* (Pa Super Ct 1984) ____ A2d ____, and *Pennsylvania v Capitola* (Pa Super Ct 1984) ____ A2d ____.

The following questions were asked in *California v Block*, described in §3.29; see chapter 21 for background and closing argument. Defense counsel did not want to disclose the necessity defense during voir dire; rather, they waited until after the prosecution had concluded its case.

1. ___. If you had a problem with a government agency, how would you go about solving that problem?
2. ___. What would you do if the problem were a life-threatening situation?
3. ___. What would you do if you needed results in 24 hours?

*COMMENT:* The California Supreme Court held it was prejudicial error to refuse questioning on the defense of necessity. *California v Jimmie Ray Williams* (1981) 174 Cal Rptr 317 at 328.

People arrested at the Trojan nuclear power plant in Oregon asked the following questions (*Oregon v Hott & Gundle*, Dec. 12, 1977).

1. ___. These defendants had to make a difficult choice. They could stand at the gates to the plant and risk arrest [*for obstructing*]. Or they could obey police orders to leave the area and risk continued daily exposure to low-level radiation and possible malfunctioning of the plant that could lead to huge emissions of radioactivity. That is the choice as they saw it.

   Would you have any problem in applying the defense [*of necessity*] in this case?

Civil disobedients in California suggest the following question:

2. ___. [*California*] law recognizes that actions that would usually be considered criminal are sometimes justified. For example, speeding in order to get a critically ill person to the hospital may be justified, or entering a burning building to save a person, which otherwise would be a trespass. The law recognizes that sometimes a person is faced with a choice between two evils, that is, to obey the law and permit a great evil, or to violate a minor law and help prevent a greater harm. Do you agree with this law?

---

B=*Briggs*; C=questions traditionally asked by the trial judge; I=*Michigan v Hartwell*; J=*Michigan v Jeanette Smith*; N=*Huey Newton* case; O=*United States v Sherpix*; P=*Pentagon Papers* case; R=*United States v Satcher*; see §§14.1 and 14.3

See also First Amendment defense questions in §11.58, and questions in §§9.18, 9.67, 9.86, 9.131–9.134, and 9.140.

For additional questions, and for the latest cases and ideas in civil disobedience cases, contact the Peace Law Project, Meiklejohn Civil Liberties Institute, Box 673, Berkeley, CA 94701 (415) 848-0599.

## D. First Amendment Defense §11.58

Congress can make no law abridging freedom of speech or of the press, or the exercise of religion, or the right of the people peaceably to assemble and to petition the government for a redress of grievances. U.S. Const. amend I. No state or local government can make a law abridging any of these rights under state constitutional provisions, and under the due process clause of the Fourteenth Amendment, which incorporates the First Amendment and makes it applicable to the states. *Gitlow v New York* (1925) 268 US 652.

Since government "can make no law abridging," and cannot punish someone for exercising these rights, no person can be charged with the crime of speaking, publishing, exercising religion, peaceably assembling, or petitioning. And no person charged with any crime can be convicted solely on proof of conduct that was limited to speech, publication, peaceable assembly, petitioning, or exercising religion.

A defendant charged with any crime can raise a First Amendment defense, just as he or she can claim self-defense, defense against others, defense of necessity (see §§11.51, 11.57), claim of right, or other traditional defenses. Success in the use of this defense requires the defendant to raise a reasonable doubt in the minds of the judge and/or jury that the defendant's conduct was protected by the First Amendment. The defense must put the prosecution to its proof that defendant's actions were outside the First Amendment guaranties, beyond a reasonable doubt.

The First Amendment defense may be appropriate in every case in which defendants are charged with obstructing traffic, trespass, conspiracy, loitering, disturbing the peace, malicious mischief, or a hundred other misdemeanors or felonies based on conduct that is protected by the First Amendment. This defense can only be successful when pursued vigorously throughout trial, starting with jury selection. The First Amendment defense is unfortunately unfamiliar to some trial judges and alien to many jurors. It is, of course, limited to acts within the definitions of free speech and press, peaceable assembly and petition, and free exercise of religion.

This is not the forum for a disquisition on the reasons for amending the Constitution to include the rights listed in the First Amendment, the fundamental character of these rights, the inclusion of actions within the definition of "speech" when they constitute "symbolic speech," what is excluded from coverage, the history of the exercise of First Amendment rights and their protection by the U.S. Supreme Court and lower courts, and so on. See generally the classics, Z. Chafee, *Free Speech in the United States* (1941) and Emerson, Haber, and Dorsen, *Political and Civil Rights in the United States* (1967); for a popular treatment, see also Ginger, *The Law, the Supreme Court and the People's Rights* (1974).

This is the place to list the voir dire questions asked in a recent trial in which the defendants used the First Amendment in two ways:

1. To defend their conduct as a lawful exercise of constitutional rights and nothing more
2. To counter prosecution efforts to prove unlawful intent, as required by a statute criminalizing "willful and malicious" conduct, i.e., obstructing a public roadway

One thousand people were arrested at Livermore National Laboratory on June 20 and 22, 1983, as they demonstrated peacefully in the streets with 2500 others. Defendants were charged with "willfully and maliciously obstructing the free movement of any person on a public street" (Cal Pen C §647c) and some were also charged with failing to give their true names in order to evade proper identification by the investigating officer (Cal Pen C §148.9).

A group of 21 defendants facing 25 charges pleaded not guilty and moved for a public jury trial in Livermore, California, eschewing a motion for change of venue while recognizing the difficulty of selecting a jury that could be impartial to a demonstration against the continued existence of the main industry in their community, the nuclear weapons development laboratory.

Defendants filed pretrial motions for extensive discovery, including plans of law enforcement agencies to deal with the massive peaceful demonstrations, and for extensive and intensive voir dire out of the presence of others (based on §§8.42–8.76). The trial judge granted some aspects of each motion, and agreed to videotaping of the entire trial by the defense, except for voir dire, as long as the jurors were never on camera.

Before trial, the district attorney moved to dismiss 12 charges against ten defendants, and one defendant pleaded nolo contendere. Defense counsel conducted a five-day voir dire, going through a pool of 200 to select 12 jurors and 3 alternates. At the close of the prosecution case, defendants argued for dismissal of the "false name" charges against two defendants, and the prosecution moved for dismissal. During trial, the prosecution moved to dismiss charges against one determined, disabled, religious defendant.

After six days of trial, counsel argued the First Amendment in closing argument, as well as no malicious intent, and as to some, no obstruction.

The jury deliberated five full days, requesting rereads of the testimony of five defendants and one prosecution witness. The jury foreman reported the jury was hopelessly deadlocked as to one defendant; the judge asked them to try again; three hours later the jurors returned, convicting all nine. The judge sentenced them to time served (11 days prior to arraignment). No appeal was taken. For further facts and trial tactics, see chapter 22.

Counsel for defendants were Warren Wilson and Priscilla Camp of Oakland, and Ann Fagan Ginger of Berkeley, California. During voir dire, counsel asked the following questions of some or all jurors.

*Source: California v Barr* (Livermore-Pleasanton Municipal Court No. 362173–9, Feb. 16, 1984, Hon. Clifford B. Bachand).

The prosecutor asked:

1. ___. Did you participate in a demonstration at [*Livermore Laboratory*]?
2. ___. Do you know anyone who participated in a demonstration there?

The defense asked:

1. ___. Do you object to people protesting or exercising freedom of [*speech/assembly/religion or conscience*] or [*petitioning the government for a redress of grievances*], all of which are protected by the First Amendment to the United States Constitution?

*COMMENT:* Defense counsel read the First Amendment to jurors during voir dire and asked whether they agreed with it. Later, the trial judge denied defendants' three requested jury instructions seeking to apply the First Amendment to the facts (see description in chapter 22). Instead, he read the precise language of the Amendment as an instruction.

2. ___. If you disagreed with something the government was doing, how would you express your disagreement, if at all?

3. ___. Have [*you/your children*] [*written letters*] about [*public issues*]?
[*If yes to children*]
a. How did you feel about this?
4. ___. Do you believe that writing to the president or to their representatives should have been sufficient for defendants?
5. ___. Do you feel that there is a limit to the intensity of protest?
6. ___. Do you agree that people have a right to demonstrate peacefully in a street or public place?
[*If yes*]
a. What if your [*son/daughter*] participated in a peaceful protest?
b. Even if the demonstration causes temporary public inconvenience?
7. ___. Do you believe that the public parks and streets are a free marketplace of ideas?
8. ___. Did you approve or disapprove of President Reagan signing the bill that made Martin Luther King's birthday a national holiday?

*COMMENT:* Further questions about King's use of civil disobedience were not allowed, and the phrase "civil disobedience" was not permitted in any question.

9. ___. Would you say that you are already committed to the belief that people who [*protest/demonstrate*] are troublemakers?
10. ___. How would you react if access to your place of employment were blocked by a demonstration, or if your arrival at work were delayed by a protest?
11. ___. Were you or any member of your family or close friends in any way inconvenienced by the [*protests*] that took place on [*June 20th*] at [*Livermore Lab*]?
[*If yes*]
a. In what way?
b. Were you angry? Upset? Shocked?
c. Would you be able to judge our clients fairly in view of this?
12. ___. Does it bother you that [*Livermore*] protesters were taking taxpayers' dollars from [*community services/education*] to pay for their arrest and confinement?
[*If yes*]
a. Would your thoughts about this affect your ability to decide this case fairly?

*COMMENT:* Defense counsel got into a colloquy with one juror who said the local schools were lousy, but finally conceded that counsel might be correct that something could also be learned from seeing a demonstration, so the cost should not all be considered antisocial, and could not be attributed to the arrestees rather than to the prosecution.

13. ___. Do you think it was a waste of money to have [*police/sheriff's deputies*] at the [*Lab*] the day of the [*protest*]?
14. ___. What is your attitude about people who demonstrate against the [*development of nuclear weapons*]?
15. ___. Do you think people have a right to speak out when they disagree with the actions of their government?
16. ___. Would the fact that our clients were at the scene of the [*protest*] create in your mind a presumption that they are guilty?
17. ___. Are you willing to follow the judge's instruction even if it is that in order to find the defendants guilty, you must find that each of them acted [*willfully*] and [*maliciously*] in doing what they were charged with doing?

*COMMENT:* In California, the following can be asked:

18. ___. The California Constitution guarantees everyone the inalienable right to defend life and liberty. What do you think that means?
    a. Can you imagine someone thinking they could participate in a peaceful demonstration as part of their right "to defend life"?

*COMMENT:* "All people are by nature free and independent and have inalienable rights. Among those are enjoying and defending life and liberty, acquiring, possessing, and protecting property, and pursuing and obtaining safety, happiness, and privacy." Cal Const Art 1, §1.

It takes a determined lawyer to raise *state* constitutional guaranties in a courtroom in which the judge is ignorant of, or hostile to, mention of the First Amendment, with its well-known *federal* constitutional guaranties. But in this era in which independent state grounds for decisions are becoming more common, efforts to teach jurors both federal and state constitutional protections are in order. In cases in which federal appeals are inappropriate or unwise, raising state constitutional protections becomes essential. If jurors can come to understand both burden of proof and standard of proof concepts, they are able to understand the First Amendment defense and also a defense based on a state constitutional provision, which may be even broader.

Some state criminal codes specify defenses that can be used by people arrested for protesting. For example, Minnesota law provides a defense to a trespass charge that the defendant had "a claim of right" to be on another person's property. In numerous cases arising out of antinuclear demonstrations against Honeywell Corporation in Minneapolis, misdemeanor defendants, often representing themselves, asked the following questions based on First Amendment and other rights.

1. ___. This is an unusual case in that there will not be any disagreement over what happened on the day of the protest action [*we*] are being tried for. The question will be whether [*we*] were acting within [*our*] legal rights. Do you have any problems with this?
2. ___. Is it possible for someone to have certain beliefs or moral principles that they would be justified in following even if they violated some law?
3. ___. Do you believe that concern for humanity's security and safety is worth taking direct and peaceful action for?
4. ___. Have you ever known anyone killed in a war?
   a. Injured?
5. ___. Have you ever received a traffic ticket, or been arrested?
6. ___. Do you believe the law must be followed no matter what?
   [*If yes*]
   a. Could you ever see yourself not following the law?
7. ___. Do you believe that the American colonists who dumped English tea into the Boston Harbor were criminals?
   [*If yes*]
   a. Why?
8. ___. Do you believe the 19th century abolitionists did the right thing when they helped free black slaves prior to the Civil War, even though it was against the law at the time?
9. ___. Did you agree with Reverend Martin Luther King's campaign to oppose racially discriminatory laws by means of nonviolent civil disobedience?

*COMMENT:* The definition of "civil disobedience" should be carefully formulated.

10. ___. What do you think about people who withhold payment of their telephone tax or income tax as a means of protesting [*high military spending*]?

11. ____. Do you think that nonviolent civil disobedience results in chaos and anarchy?

### E. Other Defenses §11.59

See §11.14.

## VIII. ATTITUDES TOWARD CAPITAL PUNISHMENT

### A. Death-Qualified Jurors

#### 1. The Point of Agreement §11.61

There is almost complete unanimity on the need for intensive voir dire in capital punishment cases. Proponents of the death penalty want to ensure that opponents of capital punishment do not sit on juries if that is an option. Opponents of the ultimate penalty want to ensure that strong supporters of capital punishment do not sit, because studies indicate that such people tend to vote for conviction more often than opponents of the death penalty, as well as voting for capital punishment in the penalty phase.

It is ironic that people with such disparate viewpoints on punishment concur on this one purpose of voir dire while arguments rage on most other purposes. But this is the only point of agreement on this complex and potentially deadly issue.

#### 2. The Problem §11.62

In general terms, the process of jury death-qualification excludes venirepersons who express opposition to the death penalty. Recent decisions have challenged death-qualification of jurors as a violation of the United States Constitution's Sixth Amendment right to a fair and impartial jury, as well as a violation of due process and equal protection guaranties of the Fourteenth Amendment. The cases suggest that death-qualification results in: (1) a jury that is more likely to convict a defendant ("guilt-prone") (*Witherspoon v Illinois* (1968) 391 US 510); (2) an impairment of the proper functioning of a jury (*Ballew v Georgia* (1978) 435 US 223); (3) a denial of a jury representing a fair cross-section of the community (*Taylor v Louisiana* (1975) 419 US 522); and (4) a less-than-neutral jury prejudiced by the traditional open court voir dire procedure on death penalty issues, regardless of the jury's composition (*Hovey v Superior Court* (1980) 168 Cal Rptr 128; *Grigsby v Mabry* (ED Ark 1983) 569 F Supp 1273).

Studies, experiments, and surveys are essential evidence in proving the above propositions. The *Hovey* and *Grigsby* opinions and the special issue of *Law and Human Behavior* (Craig Haney, ed., Vol 8, Nos. 1 and 2 (1984)) devoted to death qualification and the *Hovey* decision contain comprehensive descriptions of the current research data.

Attorneys involved in capital punishment cases maintain a network for resources and ideas to keep abreast of the rapid changes in this area of law. In California, the State Public Defender's Office, which does appellate work, at 1390 Market Street, Suite 425, San Francisco CA 94102, publishes a *Death Penalty Update*. Nationally, attorneys are referred to Professor Anthony Amsterdam at New York University Law School.

### a. *Witherspoon* Solution §11.63

The issue in capital punishment cases since the decision in *Witherspoon v Illinois* (1968) 391 US 510, has been the "death-qualification" of jurors. In *Witherspoon*, the trial court excluded venirepersons for cause who expressed general opposition to the death penalty or who voiced conscientious or religious scruples against capital punishment. These persons were not asked whether their opinions or beliefs would prevent them from voting for capital punishment. The US Supreme Court held that "[N]o defendant can constitutionally be put to death at the hands of a tribunal so selected," 391 US at 522–523. The Court held that the death penalty could constitutionally be imposed only when venirepersons were excluded for cause after they had made it unmistakably clear that (1) they would *automatically* vote against the imposition of capital punishment without regard to evidence presented at trial; or (2) their attitude toward the death penalty would prevent them from making an impartial decision about defendant's guilt.

A *Witherspoon*-qualified jury pool includes four groups, consisting of jurors who (1) would automatically vote for the death penalty ("ADP"s), (2) favor the death penalty, (3) are indifferent, and (4) oppose the death penalty. It excludes, for cause, a fifth group consisting of jurors who would not vote for the death penalty in *any* case. The voir dire must differentiate between case-specific questions and broad questions about the juror's attitude in order to make a proper record for exclusion.

The *Witherspoon* concept is that a death-qualified jury is a "neutral" jury capable of fairly imposing the death penalty at the sentencing phase of the trial. Due to inadequate data presented by defendant at trial, *Witherspoon* left unanswered the question whether the death-qualification process results in a "guilt-prone" jury, that is, whether a jury voir dired on capital punishment attitudes and including those merely opposed to the death penalty is one that tends to favor the prosecution at the guilt phase of the trial. And *Witherspoon* did not consider whether this process also unconstitutionally excludes blacks and women, two cognizable classes whose members oppose the death penalty in higher proportions than men or whites, see *Grigsby v Mabry* (ED Ark 1983) 569 F Supp 1273, 1283–87.

### b. *Gregg v Georgia* Solution §11.64

In capital punishment cases, some state statutes depart from the normal criminal procedure for conviction and require a two-tiered jury determination. When the death penalty is a potential sentence, the jury finds the defendant guilty and then the same jury makes an independent determination about sentencing. This bifurcated approach was held constitutional and the most likely system to limit the otherwise substantial risk of having an arbitrary and capricious jury impose capital punishment. *Gregg v Georgia* (1976) 428 US 153.

### c. California Solution: *Hovey v Superior Court* §11.65

The issue of guilt-proneness was raised 12 years after *Witherspoon* in the leading California case, *Hovey v Superior Court* (1980) 168 Cal Rptr 128.

The issue presented in *Hovey* was whether a prospective juror who can be fair and impartial in determining the guilt or innocence of an accused shall be removed for cause at the guilt phase because that juror is unequivocally opposed to the imposition of the death penalty at the penalty phase. The *Hovey* decision accepted the thesis that jurors favoring capital punishment on a California death-qualified jury are guilt-prone. A California death-qualified jury differs from a *Witherspoon* death-qualified jury, as described above, in that California also excludes the group that would automatically vote for the death penalty (ADPs). The *Hovey* research data failed to convince the court by the "substantial doubt" standard, approved by the court, that a California death-qualified jury is guilt-prone. Nonetheless, the Court did hold that in future capital punishment cases, voir dire questions regarding death penalty issues should be asked individually and in sequestration.

The petitioner in *Hovey* had based his motion to limit exclusions for cause on several grounds:

1. Exclusion of jurors who would automatically refuse to impose the death penalty, but who would be fair as to guilt, results in a less-than-neutral jury (*Witherspoon*).
2. Such a death-qualified jury impairs the purpose and functioning of the jury (*Ballew v Georgia* (1978) 435 US 223).
3. The voir dire *procedure* used to select the jury, regardless of the ultimate composition of the jury, creates a less-than-neutral jury.

*Hovey* failed to challenge the jury selection process on the basis that it did not represent a fair cross-section of the community. The opinion repeatedly referred to petitioner's failure to bring the representativeness issue before the court and implied that the challenge would have been sustained had it been pursued. It left to *Grigsby* to prove that excluding the ADP group as well as the group who would never vote for the death penalty left the remaining pool guilt-prone (see §11.69).

### (1) Concept of a Neutral Jury §11.66

Hovey argued that a constitutionally mandated jury is "one drawn from a pool which reasonably mirrors the diversity of experiences and relevant viewpoints of those persons in the community who can fairly and impartially try the case." Such a jury is not possible when a death-qualified jury makes a determination of defendant's guilt. A death-qualified jury, by definition under *Witherspoon*, excludes jurors who would automatically vote against imposition of the death penalty. The death-qualified jury, Hovey argued, produces an unbalanced jury, unrepresentative of the range of community viewpoints and with a tendency to vote in favor of the prosecution more often than would a broader jury pool.

### (2) Problem of Sociological Proof §11.67

The evidentiary basis for the motion in *Hovey* was developed at an extensive evidentiary hearing in another case tried in the same county (*California v Kenneth Lynn Moore and David Lee Moore* (Alameda County Super. Ct. No. 67113, 1979)). The 24 studies, experiments, and surveys introduced at that hearing were considered and discussed at length in the *Hovey* opinion. The research was grouped into four categories: (1) conviction proneness, or juror voting behavior; (2) prior attitudes; (3) demographic characteristics; and (4) differences in juror evaluation of evidence.

The California Supreme Court, in noting the regularity of the findings and the fact that the prosecution failed to introduce contradictory studies, rejected most of the prosecution's methodological critiques of the evidence. The court did find merit in one prosecution criticism, which became the basis for the court's holding, that is, that the petitioner's studies focused on a *Witherspoon*-qualified pool rather than a California-qualified pool. Petitioner had thus proved the wrong proposition. *Witherspoon* included four categories of jurors—(1) automatically vote for the death penalty (ADPs), (2) in favor of the death penalty, (3) indifferent, and (4) oppose the death penalty—whereas the pool of jurors eligible to serve in a capital trial in California consists of the second, third, and fourth categories but not the first. Although Hovey's evidence was more conclusive than the "tentative" and "fragmentary" data presented in *Witherspoon* 12 years before, the defendant again failed on the basis of an inadequate evidentiary presentation as to the size of the ADP group.

### (3) Dr. Craig Haney Study §11.68

The California Supreme Court in *Hovey* (168 Cal Rptr at 178–181) found merit in a study that depicted the adverse effects of voir dire in open court on the issue of the death penalty. The controlled study—conducted by Dr. Craig Haney, of the University of California at Santa Cruz—indicated that the mere *process* of death-qualification alters the jurors' states of mind and affects both guilt and penalty determinations.

Dr. Haney studied the "process affects" of two sample groups. The first group was shown a standard half-hour voir dire on videotape, the second viewed the same videotape and a half-hour tape of death-qualified voir dire questions. Both groups, knowing nothing more about the case than what they had gleaned from the voir dire, were asked a series of questions about their attitudes toward the death penalty, counsel, and defendant's guilt. There were dramatic statistical differences between the two groups.

Dr. Haney found several reasons for the result:

1. The voir dire process focuses attention on penalty before the defendant is found guilty, which causes some jurors to think it more likely that defendant is guilty.
2. People are sensitive to the way others around them behave when in a novel, complicated, and confusing situation; they are easily impressed by authority figures, such as the attorneys and the judge,

so the dismissal of venirepersons who express unequivocal opposition to the death penalty will be interpreted as general disapproval of such attitudes.

3. Repeated displays of concern regarding the death penalty in voir dire questions before presentation of any evidence of guilt implies that court and counsel assume a penalty trial will be necessary.
4. Jurors are desensitized by the voir dire to the idea that capital punishment is the taking of a human life; therefore, they are more likely to impose capital punishment.

The *Hovey* opinion stated:

> The most practical and effective procedure available to minimize the untoward effects of death-qualification is individualized sequestered voir dire. Because jurors would then witness only a single death-qualifying voir dire—their own—each individual juror would be exposed to considerably less discussion and questioning about the various aspects of the penalty phase before hearing any evidence of guilt. Such a reduction in the pretrial emphasis on penalty should minimize the tendency of a death-qualified jury to presume guilt and expect conviction.

168 Cal Rptr at 181.

The *Hovey* decision left unanswered the question whether jurors sequestered and individually questioned on death penalty issues will be any less affected than jurors questioned on these issues in open court. The decision itself acknowledged this shortcoming:

> Of course, this court cannot insure that a rule of sequestered voir dire in capital cases will alleviate all the untoward effects of the current procedures. Unless a juror is able to understand and respond with certainty to the *Witherspoon* questions, the juror may be subjected at the sequestered proceeding to considerable voir dire on his or her attitude toward capital punishment. It is unknown at this point whether such personal voir dire would entail the same dangers of inducing bias as do the current procedures for voir dire.

168 Cal Rptr at 182.

The question is further complicated by the free press right to observe sequestered voir dire questioning discussed in *Press-Enterprise Co. v Superior Court* (1984) 104 S Ct 819; see §8.44.

In a California death penalty case appealed to the state supreme court after *Hovey* (*California v Smallwood* (Los Angeles County Super Ct, Crim No. 21845, November 26, 1980)), the defendant's attorney Doris Brin Walker argued in the habeas corpus petition that despite sequestration in his trial, all the prejudicial aspects of collective death qualification delineated in *Hovey* were present. This was due, in part, to the failure of efforts to sequester jurors passed for cause from jurors not yet questioned, since the groups were allowed to mingle in the halls and talk with each other.

To a greater degree, the prejudice to the defendant in the *Smallwood* case lay in the manner in which the voir dire was conducted despite the sequestration. In his introductory statement to the venire, the trial judge failed to mention the two phases of the trial, the primacy of the guilt phase, and the prosecution's burden of proof. He finally mentioned these points after several hours of voir dire had taken place. Once sequestered voir dire began, the defense counsel himself concentrated on the death penalty qualification with no reference to the guilt phase of the trial. The prosecutor included statements that he would be "wasting time" and it was "foolish to try the case" if even one juror had already decided to vote against the death penalty. Smallwood's counsel argued on appeal that his case serves as an example of how the *Hovey* procedural protections can be abused.

Although California at least provides a greater guarantee that a capital crime defendant will have a fair trial because of the *Hovey* procedural protection of a sequestered voir dire, many defense counsel argue that they should minimize the death-qualification process in light of Dr. Haney's study. Clearly defense counsel must reevaluate the traditional approach to voir dire in capital punishment cases, avoiding situations such as the one that arose in the *Smallwood* trial. They must sensitize trial judges to the damage to the defendant that lurks in the death-qualification process.

This is crucial in a capital punishment case, not only because the stakes are higher, but because death penalty cases raise inherent civil rights issues. Death row inmates represent a cognizable class of poor, young, male, often minority members who are often accused of murdering a person of high social status, almost always white. See "The Jury System in Death Penalty Cases: A Symbolic Gesture," Courtney Mullin, 43 *Law & Contemp Prob* 4, Autumn 1980. A recent study of 17,000 murders reported by the FBI in eight states between 1976 and 1980 found that murderers who kill white victims are much more likely to be sentenced to death than those who slay black victims, and those who slay women are slightly more likely to be sentenced to death than those who slay men. "These findings suggest that the death penalty, as now imposed in the United States, does not meet the Supreme Court's requirement . . .that the penalty not be imposed arbitrarily," according to the authors of the study, Samuel P. Gross of Stanford University

School of Law, and Robert Mauro, a Stanford doctoral candidate in psychology.

The law on every aspect of capital punishment remains fluid, in California after *Hovey* and elsewhere, since the treatment of persons accused of taking life remains a touchstone of attitudes toward all persons accused of crime. See, e.g., the split decision limiting *Hovey* in *California v Stevie Lamar Fields* (Cal Sup Ct 1983) 174 CR 317.

### d. Federal Solution: *Grigsby v Mabry* §11.69

In federal habeas corpus proceedings challenging the convictions of three Arkansas state prisoners, the federal district court, in *Grigsby v Mabry* (ED Ark 1980) 483 F Supp 1372, held that a defendant has a right to show that death-qualified juries are guilt-prone and that trial by such a jury would deny defendants the constitutional right to an impartial jury. The Eighth Circuit affirmed and remanded to the district court for an evidentiary hearing (637 F2d 525 (1980)).

The opinion of Chief Judge G. Thomas Eisele, based on his extensive 1981 hearing on sociological data, was worth the long wait (ED Ark 1983) 569 F Supp 1273. In 49 lucid pages, Judge Eisele presents the history of capital punishment jury selection litigation, the development of constitutional issues, the history and validity of sociological studies from *Witherspoon* through *Hovey* to date, the conclusions to be drawn from the data, and proposals for new methods of conducting voir dire and trying capital punishment cases.

The record in *Grigsby* duplicates the *Hovey* record to a great extent, and Judge Eisele's evaluation of the social scientific studies on death-qualification is as favorable as that of the California Supreme Court in *Hovey*. But the *Grigsby* opinion goes beyond *Hovey* in two respects:

1. Judge Eisele concludes that death-qualification violates a capital defendant's Sixth Amendment right to a jury drawn from a representative cross-section of the community. (569 F Supp at 1278–87.) This conclusion is based in part on empirical data that proves that those who are excluded from capital cases because of opposition to the death penalty differ on important attitudes from the jurors who are allowed to serve, including those mild opponents of the death penalty who are not excluded. See 569 F Supp 1291–1308.
2. The *Grigsby* opinion holds that death-qualified juries are conviction-prone and hence unconstitutional under the Sixth and Fourteenth Amendments.

Judge Eisele also discusses the constitutional problems that are caused by the use of prosecutorial peremptory challenges to purge capital juries of *all* opponents of the death penalty. (See Winick, "Prosecutorial Peremptory Challenge Practices in Capital Cases: An Empirical Study and a Constitutional Analysis," 81 *Mich L Rev* 1 (1982).) He ruled that everyone should sit on a jury to determine guilt or innocence who can fairly judge that issue without being questioned on attitudes about capital punishment. He concluded, from his own experience as a lawyer and trial judge, substantiated by the sociological studies presented, that even some adamant opponents and proponents of capital punishment could fairly judge guilt or innocence, and that their automatic exclusion from the guilt determination phase results in an unrepresentative jury. He also concluded that all questioning on capital punishment clouds jury deliberations at the guilt determination phase.

### e. Proposal for All Capital Punishment Trials §11.70

After studying the judicial precedents and sociological data presented in *Grigsby v Mabry* (ED Ark 1983) 569 F Supp 1273, Judge Eisele proposed two-phase trials:

1. At the guilt determination phase, voir dire on capital punishment should be restricted to one general question:

Q: Can jurors be fair and impartial in determining guilt or innocence in this case?

Only jurors who express doubts on this score should be asked follow-up questions in order to locate those so opposed to capital punishment that they would automatically vote to acquit, thus violating their duty to fairly judge the facts, and those so committed to capital punishment that they would automatically vote to convict, thus similarly violating their duty. 569 F Supp at 1308 (1983).

2. At the penalty determination phase, a second jury should be impaneled, but only under these circumstances: (1) when the guilt phase jury (a) voted to convict in accordance with the statutory requirements of capital murder, and (b) rejected any insanity claim, and (2) the prosecution (a) continued to seek the death penalty, (b) insisted on selecting a jury to decide the penalty, and (c) insisted that such a jury be fully questioned on its attitude on that penalty. 569 F Supp at 1319.

Judge Eisele faced the financial and judicial efficiency questions head on:

> [In such cases, which "comprise a miniscule percentage of all criminal trials"] the State would bear the cost of the additional jurors. There would be a second *voir dire*. It is likely that some portion of the evidence introduced during the guilt-determination trial would have to be re-introduced. Procedures could be developed so that the penalty-phase jury could be impaneled promptly after the conclusion of the guilt-determination trial so that witnesses would not become unavailable or other evidence lost. All of the actors in the drama would be the same except the jurors, so no significant additional preparation time would be required.

569 F Supp at 1320.

The judge noted that the present procedure can actually work to the detriment of the state if a court vacates only a death sentence but affirms a conviction. The state is precluded from retrying only the penalty phase of the trial to a new jury. It faces the choice of completely retrying the defendant through both the guilt and penalty phases or foregoing the attempt to again impose the death penalty. He pointed out that if the courts mandate separate juries, the state could also use that holding to its advantage in attempting more efficiently to reimpose a vacated death penalty.

Judge Eisele relied on *Ballew v Georgia* (1978) 435 US 223, at 244, in which the Supreme Court found that "a reduction in jury size from six to five or four or even three would save the states little," and concluded that cost savings alone could not justify the prejudicial effects on the rights of accused misdemeanants resulting from such a reduction. Furthermore, the judge averred: "When, as here, we are dealing literally with life and death, the cost-savings arguments of the state simply lose all force." 569 F Supp at 1321.

Judge Eisele also pointed out that the death-qualification process often takes up as much time as the trial itself, and that in a two-phase trial, the guilt-determination phase would be much shorter and more clearly focused on the true issue—the guilt or innocence of the accused.

Dr. Edward Bronson of California State University at Chico, one of the expert witnesses in the 1981 *Grigsby* hearing before Judge Eisele, has alternative proposals counsel may wish to consider by correspondence.

The bottom line for conscientious defense lawyers in capital and noncapital cases is to voir dire intensively and extensively on attitudes toward law and order, rights of the accused, "softness on crime," relationships with law enforcement officers, and all other subjects that indicate attitudes on capital punishment, without questioning directly on that subject. Studies cited in *Grigsby* show that jurors who "oppose" the death penalty (but not strongly), who "favor," and who "strongly favor" it, are much more likely than those who "strongly oppose" it to, among other things:

1. Disregard the presumption of innocence.
2. Criticize the exercise of one's Fifth Amendment right to remain silent.
3. Believe courts are too concerned with protecting the rights of criminals.
4. Believe that the insanity defense is a loophole that allows the guilty to go free.

569 F Supp at 1293. Probing questions in these four areas should uncover guilt-prone jurors without contaminating all jurors by capital punishment questions that can lead to guilt-proneness.

### f. Requirement of a Cross-Section Jury §11.71

Separate from the issues of guilt-proneness (*Witherspoon*) and the impairment of proper jury functioning (*Ballew v Georgia*) is the issue of a fair cross-sectional jury. Alleging a Sixth Amendment violation on this ground differs from the others in that it is not necessary to prove the jury has been prejudiced after death-qualification. *Taylor v Louisiana* (1975) 419 US 522. *Taylor* and subsequent decisions hold that the neutrality and guilt-proneness determination under *Witherspoon* are not required under a pure cross-section approach. *Duren v Missouri* (1979) 439 US 357; *Grigsby v Mabrey* (ED Ark 1980) 483 F Supp 1372; (8th Cir 1980) 637 F2d 525. In *Hovey v Superior Court*, see §11.65, the opinion strongly suggests the court would have held for petitioner had the cross-sectional argument been raised.

In *Taylor v Louisiana*, the US Supreme Court reversed the state court criminal conviction of a male defendant who challenged the systematic exclusion of women from the jury pool. The Supreme Court held for the first time that the states are bound by a Sixth Amendment fair cross-section requirement.

*Duren v Missouri* (439 US at 364) set forth the requirements for a prima facie showing under *Taylor*:

> In order to establish a prima facie violation of the fair-cross-section requirement, the defendant must show (1) that the group alleged to be excluded is a *distinctive* group in the community; (2) that the representation of this group in venires from which juries are selected is not fair and reasonable in relation to the number of such persons in the community; and (3) that this underre-

presentation is due to systematic exclusion of the group in the jury-selection process.

In *Rubio v Superior Court* (1979) 154 Cal Rptr 734, the California Supreme Court held that the right to a trial by jury drawn from a representative cross-section of the community is violated when a "cognizable" group is systematically excluded from the jury. The two requirements to determine cognizability are that (1) the group's members must share a common perspective arising from their life experience in the group, and (2) no other members of the community are capable of adequately representing the perspective of the group being excluded. See §6.33. The defendant in *Rubio* challenged the exclusion of ex-felons and resident aliens from the jury. The state supreme court upheld the trial court's holding that the first element was satisfied as to both groups but that petitioner failed to make a showing that no other members of the community adequately represented the views of ex-felons and resident aliens.

The objective in challenging the nonrepresentativeness of the jury is thus to establish the cognizability of the group that is being excluded. The approach to this challenge can be made on three levels:

1. The argument that *Witherspoon*-excludables are a cognizable group.
2. The argument that a group with a commonly shared experience or value system is cognizable (*Rubio v Superior Court*).
3. The argument that the demographics of a particular group (i.e., blacks, women, etc.) establish its cognizability and hence nonexcludability.

The challenge to the exclusion of the group that would automatically oppose the death penalty in a capital punishment case is based on an analogy with the cases where the exclusion is due to the group's race (*California v Wheeler* (1978) 148 Cal Rptr 890), or, more recently, sex (*Taylor v Louisiana*). However, while in a race or sex exclusion case there is little doubt that the excluded group is "cognizable" (*Wheeler*) or "distinctive" (*Duren*), the defendant in the capital punishment case must prove that a group, determined by statistical data, meets these definitions. Judges are increasingly recognizing the *California v Wheeler* decision, a case in which the defendant challenged the prosecution's consistent exercise of peremptory challenges of black jurors. The court stated that when a party in a criminal action uses the peremptory challenge on the ground of group bias alone, the jury may fail to meet the cross-section representation requirement. The other party may, however, establish that peremptory challenges were exercised on grounds particularly relevant to the case. See discussion in chapter 20.

By analogy to *Wheeler*, death penalty defense counsel argue that the prosecution cannot exclude by peremptory challenge jurors who have strong views opposing the death penalty. They must prove that this is a cognizable group. The 1983 opinion in *Grigsby v Mabry* (ED Ark 1983) 569 F Supp 1273, goes through this analysis very convincingly:

> What is a "distinctive" group that may not systematically be excluded? First, it must be noted that if the exclusion of just any group were fatal, no practical jury system could survive. As a practical matter, one must first inquire whether the characteristic that defines the group is of any consequence to the proper functioning of the jury.

569 F Supp at 1281.

The opinion explains that, e.g., excluding the first 9 in every group of 10 names is not discriminatory, but rather aids in obtaining a random sample. One question in excluding strong opponents of capital punishment is whether this also has the indirect effect of lessening the representation of certain groups such as women and blacks.

The opinion then describes the unique feature of "Witherspoon Excludables" (WEs), both those who are so opposed to capital punishment that they would vote "not guilty" at the guilt phase as well as automatically voting against capital punishment at the punishment phase ("Nullifiers"), and those who will vote impartially on guilt and automatically against capital punishment at the punishment phase ("Guilt Phase Includables"). To exclude the second group

> has the effect of systematically excluding an entire group of fair and impartial jurors because of a particular attitude that they possess upon a matter that is irrelevant to their service as jurors in the trial of the issue of the guilt or innocence of the accused.
>
> . . .
>
> So this discussion brings us back to where we left off in this Court's first opinion in *Grigsby*. Do the "*Witherspoon*-excludables" constitute a "cognizable group," the systematic exclusion of which during the guilt determination phase would constitute a violation of the Sixth and Fourteenth Amendments?
>
> Since *Duncan*, the Sixth Amendment focus has been upon the interposition between the accused and his accuser of the common sense judgment of a jury chosen from a group which truly represents the full range of community attitudes and perspectives that are relevant to the jury functioning process.
>
> Empirical data [shows that views on capital punishment] are intimately tied to other attitudes and views which are directly implicated when jurors determine the guilt or innocence of a defendant in a criminal trial.

569 F Supp 1282, 1283.

The court concluded that the "Witherspoon excludable" "group is of substantial size both nationally and within the state of Arkansas, ranging between 11% and 17% of those eligible for jury service. So the group excluded is both distinctive and sizeable." 569 F Supp at 1285.

The court found that

> the petitioners have met the second test required by *Duren*: the representation of the excluded group after *voir dire* and the consequent challenges for cause, will not be fair and reasonable in relation to the number of such persons in the community. In fact, *no* representative of such group will remain after *voir dire*.
>
> . . .
>
> The only remaining question is: has the state justified its insistence upon the use of the challenged procedure?

569 F Supp at 1286. The court found that it had not.

The court then turned to another troubling aspect of excluding WEs.

> Taking the studies overall, the Court finds that the differences between the attitudes of blacks and whites with respect to the death penalty is highly statistically significant. For instance Dr. Bronson totalled the attitudes by race for his three studies and found that only 3.8% of blacks strongly favor the death penalty while 30.4% oppose it. This compares with 20.4% of the whites who strongly favor the death penalty while only 9.9% strongly oppose it.
>
> And the *Harris 1971* national demographic survey shows that, by virtue of their attitudes toward the death penalty, 46% of blacks would be excluded under the *Witherspoon* standard as compared with only 29% of the white subjects, a difference which is also highly statistically significant. And 37% of the women were WEs compared to only 24% of the male subjects.
>
> . . .
>
> So it is clear that the death qualification procedures which permit the removal of fair-minded prospective jurors from the guilt-innocence determination phase of capital trials solely because of their attitudes toward the death penalty will indirectly but inevitably result in the underrepresentation of blacks and women on such juries in Arkansas.

569 F Supp at 1293–94.

The court also noted that one of the studies "provides strong evidence for the opinion, so often expressed by petitioners' experts, that death penalty attitudes are a far better predictor of juror voting behavior than any other single characteristic." 569 F Supp at 1301.

Turning to jury deliberations:

> The Court finds that the systematic exclusion of WEs from capital juries will reduce the number of cases with an initial majority, or largest faction, in favor of acquittal or . . . a lesser included offense and will thereby substantially lessen the likelihood of acquittal and . . . of a vote of guilty to a lesser-included offense when the final unanimous jury verdict comes in.

569 F Supp at 1301.

Another finding made by Dr. Ellsworth which accords with intuitive common sense is that subjects who sat on "mixed" juries remembered the facts more accurately than subjects serving on juries composed of only death-qualified persons. This finding reinforces the legal requirement that juries reflect as nearly as possible a cross-section of the community and the variety of ideas, attitudes and opinions that exist therein. It is true that this will create a greater probability of argument and friction within such a jury, but, according to the evidence, logic and common sense, it also creates the likelihood of verdicts more accurately based upon the law and the evidence assuring as it does more vigorous and robust deliberations.

569 F Supp at 1302.

The court concluded that if WEs are excluded:

A jury so selected will not, therefore, be composed of a cross-section of the community. Rather, it will be composed of a group of persons who are uncommonly predisposed to favor the prosecution, a jury "organized to convict."

569 F Supp at 1304.

Another aspect of "death qualifying" voir dire was analyzed by the court, based on the *Haney* study:

. . .that regardless of the preconceptions which a juror might have before entering the courtroom, the questions and the answers and the dialogue pursued in the death qualification process have a clear tendency to suggest that the defendant is guilty. Death qualification, then, is comparable to saturating the jury pool with prejudicial pretrial publicity, which, as we know, is unconstitutional. See *Rideau v Louisiana* (1963) 373 US 723; *Irvin v Dowd* (1961) 366 US 717; and *Marshall v United States* (1959) 360 US 310. But the death qualification process is worse because the biasing information is transmitted to the prospective jurors *inside the courtroom* and is imparted, albeit unconsciously, not only by the attorneys *but also by the judge*. The reading of the *voir dire* transcripts in these cases makes this abundantly clear—so clear that the Court suggests that even without the strong empirical support of the *Haney* study, the Court could conclude on its own that a reasonable limitation on such *voir dire* procedures would be appropriate.

569 F Supp at 1304.

## B. Recent Developments §11.74

It is now possible to keep up with the law on jury selection in capital punishment cases the same way you keep up with the law in any other field—by reading the relevant advance sheets, subscribing to services on trial advocacy or criminal law, and reading daily newspapers and legal newspapers. In this field, Professor Anthony Amsterdam at New York University Law School is a constant source of information and ideas. Californians can contact the State Public Defender's Office, which does appellate work and publishes the *Death Penalty Update*, at 1390 Market Street, Suite 425, San Francisco, CA 94102.

The *Index to Legal Periodicals*, *Current Law Index*, and *Legal Resource Index* provide provocative (and sometimes descriptive) titles to law review articles, comments, and notes in this field, indicating what is happening at the cutting edge of the law. It is a good idea occasionally to ask your law librarian for an index to journals on psychology, applied psychology, and the social sciences, to pick up new ideas from these disciplines.

Increasingly, lawyers are learning to use *Lexis* and *Westlaw* in order to find the latest cases and interesting parallels in other fields of law. It is always necessary to Shepardize all citations.

The Annual Supplement to this volume will use this section to describe new cases, ideas, and articles that are worthy of note, and to warn of cases overruled and of rules and statutes amended or repealed.

## C. Jurors Affected by Pretrial Publicity §11.80

As media coverage of capital crimes is usually more extensive than for most other types of crimes, the factor of pretrial publicity becomes more prominent in a capital punishment case. Defense counsel should consider bringing a motion for change of venue whenever the pretrial publicity in a case has prejudiced the jury pool so much that there is a reasonable likelihood the defendant would be denied the right to a fair and impartial trial. Despite such a challenge, judges and prosecuting attorneys often face strong community pressure to try the case in the local community. See Mullen, "The Jury System in Death Penalty Cases: A Symbolic Gesture," 43 *Law Contemp Prob* 137 (1980).

In *Odle v Superior Court of Contra Costa County* (82 *Los Angeles Daily Journal* D.A.R. 3215 (Dec. 1982)) the court held that extensive media coverage itself, or in combination with other factors, does not establish a reasonable unlikelihood that a fair trial can be held in a county. In *Odle*, there was extensive media coverage of the crime—a police officer's murder—and the manhunt that followed. The trial judge ruled that if extensive media coverage were sufficient for establishing the unlikelihood of a fair and impartial trial in this case, courts would have to grant a change of venue in every case. A major factor in the judge's decision not to grant the change of venue was the amount of time—two years—that had passed between the time of the publicity and the scheduled trial date.

Along with evidence of the prejudicial pretrial publicity, in the form of newspaper articles and television broadcasts, a federal district court reviewing a state court's findings, must look at additional factors, at least in the Ninth Circuit. The court must review the voir dire transcript to determine the number of jurors interviewed at voir dire, the number excused for cause or peremptorily challenged, and the number who admitted to having preconceived notions about the defendant's guilt. *Harris v Pulley* (9th Cir 1982) 692 F2d 1189, at 1200.

See all other discussions of pretrial publicity throughout these volumes for ideas to adapt for capital cases.

## D. Sample Questions

### 1. Death Qualification §11.81

In the present unsettled state of the law on the effects of death qualification (see §§11.69–11.70), counsel should consult other experts in the jurisdiction, and the latest federal and state decisions in planning voir dire questions for the guilt and penalty phases of capital trials.

Dr. Craig Haney, of the Psychology Department, University of California at Santa Cruz, discussed death qualification and remedies to death qualification (prior to the opinion in *Grigsby v Mabry* (ED Ark 1983) 483 F Supp 1372), in his affidavit on voir dire procedures in *Maryland v Sails* (Prince Georges County Cir Ct No. 82–352).

38. If the Court does proceed with the death qualification of the jury prior to the guilt phase of the trial, I believe that it is imperative to allow attorneys to conduct the Witherspoon examination. From my in-court observations and interviews with veniremen from jury selections in over 30 capital cases, I have concluded that judge-conducted death qualification increases the likelihood that Witherspoon "errors" will occur and that persons will be improperly excluded from participation as jurors. Many prospective jurors are confused by the formal language that judges tend to employ in posing the relevant death-qualifying questions. Attorneys are invariably less committed to legalistic phrasing, more highly motivated to make the questions understood, and better able to rephrase the issue until the prospective jurors comprehend it. In addition, many prospective jurors have simply not seriously considered this issue until it is posed to them for the first time in the courtroom. The colloquy that occurs between them and opposing counsel is often essential to draw out the juror's true feelings, and to make the subtleties of the legal issue clearer to them.

For Haney's qualifications and general discussion of voir dire proceedures, see §8.80.

When the Southern Poverty Law Center handles capital cases, the defense team encourages articulate defendants to conduct part of the voir dire. In *Arkansas v Larry Wayne Jones*, a 20-year-old black prisoner was charged with killing his jailer during an attempted escape. The defendant, facing an all-white jury, began:

1. ___. Hello, my name is Larry Wayne Jones, and I'm on trial for my life. Do you think you could give me a fair trial?
2. ___. After hearing all the evidence, could you find it in your heart to show me mercy?

The defense felt it was conducting 50 mini-trials during the voir dire. After several weeks of defense questioning of jurors on their racial attitudes and capital punishment attitudes, the prosecutor decided not to try the case but instead to accept a plea leading to life imprisonment and foreclosing the death penalty. "Column 1," *Chicago Tribune*, May 27, 1977.

The Southern Poverty Law Center published *Voir Dire for Capital Cases* (1979), available from 1001 South Hull Street, Montgomery, Alabama 36101 for $3.75 plus postage.

### 2. Pretrial Publicity §11.82

1. N ___. Assuming you were on trial for [*your very sweet life*] as [*Mr./ Ms. Smith*] is on trial for [*his/her*] life, would you accept a juror who had had an opinion about your guilt for a long period of time, one who had the same frame of mind you have in this case?
2. N ___. As far as you are concerned, you have held this opinion that it was an open and shut case for the last [*nine*] months, and there has been nothing that you have read or seen that has changed your opinion except the fact that the Judge indicated that you should have an open mind?
3. N ___. In what way do you have an open mind? What has come into your own thinking that has eliminated the fixed opinion that you had that this was an open and shut case?
4. N ___. I am somewhat interested in how you can unwind. I don't

---

B=*Briggs*; C=questions traditionally asked by the trial judge; I=*Michigan v Hartwell*; J=*Michigan v Jeannette Smith*; N=*Huey Newton* case; O=*United States v Sherpix*; P=*Pentagon Papers* case; R=*United States v Satcher*; see §§14.1 and 14.3

mean unwinding in the sense of relaxing. I am talking about unwinding the previous subconscious mind to a point where you will undo in your own subconscious mind what has dwelled in there for the past [*nine or ten*] months: the fact this is an open and shut case, that [*Mr./Ms. Smith*] is guilty as charged—how are you going to unwind that?

5. N ___. And here you had for [*ten*] months a fixed opinion that this was an open and shut case and that [*Mr./Ms. Smith*] was guilty as charged, and there has been no evidence, no articles, nothing intervening that would change your mind, isn't that right?

6. N ___. In other words, as far as you are concerned, from [*the date of the incident*] until the present time, [*date of trial*], there has been nothing to change that so-called superficial opinion that you had that [*Mr./Ms. Smith*] [*killed Officer Clark*]?

### 3. Other Subjects §11.83

See §11.14.

---

B=*Briggs*; C=questions traditionally asked by the trial judge; I=*Michigan v Hartwell*; J=*Michigan v Jeannette Smith*; N=*Huey Newton* case; O=*United States v Sherpix*; P=*Pentagon Papers* case; R=*United States v Satcher*; see §§14.1 and 14.3